CW00485091

STREET ATLAS
Leicestershire
and Rutland

Hinckley, Leicester, Loughborough, Market Harborough, Melton Mowbray

www.philips-maps.co.uk

First published in 2000 by

Philip's, a division of
Octopus Publishing Group Ltd
www.octopusbooks.co.uk
2-4 Heron Quays, London E14 4JP
An Hachette Livre UK Company

Third edition 2007
First impression 2007
LEICA

ISBN-10   0-540-09173-1 (spiral)
ISBN-13   978-0-540-09173-7 (spiral)

© Philip's 2007

Ordnance Survey®

This product includes mapping data licensed
from Ordnance Survey® with the permission of
the Controller of Her Majesty's Stationery Office.
© Crown copyright 2007. All rights reserved.
Licence number 100011710.

No part of this publication may be reproduced,
stored in a retrieval system or transmitted in any
form or by any means, electronic, mechanical,
photocopying, recording or otherwise, without
the permission of the Publishers and the
copyright owner.

To the best of the Publishers' knowledge, the
information in this atlas was correct at the time
of going to press. No responsibility can be
accepted for any errors or their consequences.

The representation in this atlas of a road, track
or path is no evidence of the existence of a right
of way.

Data for the speed cameras provided by
PocketGPSWorld.com Ltd.

Ordnance Survey and the OS Symbol are
registered trademarks of Ordnance Survey, the
national mapping agency of Great Britain.

Printed by Toppan, China

Contents

II   **List of mobile speed cameras**

III   **Key to map symbols**

IV   **Key to map pages**

VI   **Route planning**

X   **Administrative and Postcode boundaries**

1   **Street maps** at 3½ inches to 1 mile

259   **Street map of Leicester city centre**
at 7 inches to 1 mile

260   **Index** of towns, villages, streets, hospitals, industrial
estates, railway stations, schools, shopping centres,
universities and places of interest

Digital Data

The exceptionally high-quality mapping found in this atlas is available as digital data in TIFF format, which is easily convertible to other bitmapped (raster) image formats.

The index is also available in digital form as a standard database table. It contains all the details found in the printed index together with the National Grid reference for the map square in which each entry is named.

For further information and to discuss your requirements, please contact james.mann@philips-maps.co.uk

Mobile speed cameras

The vast majority of speed cameras used on Britain's roads are operated by safety camera partnerships. These comprise local authorities, the police, Her Majesty's Court Service (HMCS) and the Highways Agency.

This table lists the sites where each safety camera partnership may enforce speed limits through the use of mobile cameras or detectors. These are usually set up on the roadside or a bridge spanning the road and operated by a police or civilian enforcement officer. The speed limit at each site (if available) is shown in red type, followed by the approximate location in black type.

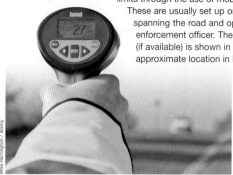

Mike Harrington / Alamy

Leicestershire and Rutland

A1
- 70 Empingham, Great North Rd
- 70 Stretton, Great North Rd

A5
- 60 Churchover, Watling Street (Clifton Fisheries)
- 60 Hinckley, Watling St (B578 to M69)
- 50 Hinckley, Watling St (M69 to A47)
- 70 Sharnford, Watling St (Highcross to B4114)

A6
- 40 Birstall, Loughborough Rd
- 40 Leicester, Abbey Lane
- 30 Leicester, London Rd (Knighton Drive)
- 30 Loughborough, Derby Rd
- 40 Oadby, Glen Rd/ Harborough Rd

A47
- 60 Barrowden, Peterborough Rd
- 60 Bisbrooke, Uppingham Rd
- 30 Earl Shilton, Hinckley Rd
- 40 Houghton on the Hill, Uppingham Rd
- 30 Leicester, Hinckley Rd
- 30 Leicester, Humberstone Rd
- 50 Morcott, Glaston Rd
- 50 Skeffington, Uppingham Rd
- 50 Tugby, Uppingham Rd

A50
- 40 Leicester/Glenfield, Groby Rd/Leicester Rd
- 30 Woodgate

A426
- 50 Dunton Bassett, Lutterworth Rd
- 40 Glen Parva, Leicester Rd
- 60 Lutterworth, Leicester Rd
- 60 Whetstone, Lutterworth Rd

A444
- 50 Fenny Drayton, Atherstone Rd
- 30 Twycross Village, Main St
- 50 Twycross, Norton Juxta

A447
- 60 Cadeby, Hinckley Rd
- 40 Ravenstone, Wash Lane

A512
- 30 Loughborough, Ashby Rd
- 40 Shepshed, Ashby Rd Central

A514
- 30 Harsthorne, Main St
- 40 Swadlincote to Hartshorne

A563
- 30 Leicester, Asquith Way
- 30 Leicester, Attlee Way
- 30 Leicester, Colchester Rd/Hungarton Boulevard
- 30 Leicester, Glenhills Way
- 40 Leicester, Krefield Way
- 30 Leicester, New Parks Way

A594
- 30 Leicester, St Georges Way

A606
- 60 Barnsdale, Stamford Rd
- 60 Leicester, Broughton/ Old Dalby
- 60 Tinwell, Stamford Rd

A607
- 30 Leicester, Melton Rd
- 50 Thurmaston, Newark Rd
- 60 Waltham on the Wolds, Melton Rd
- 60 Waltham/Croxton Kerrial, Melton Rd

A4304
- 40 Market Harborough, Lubbenham Hill

A5199
- 30 Leicester, Welford Rd
- 30 Wigston, Bull Head St
- 30 Wigston, Leicester Rd

A5460
- 40 Leicester, Narborough Rd

A6004
- 30 Loughborough, Alan Moss Rd

A6005
- 40 Breaston to Long Eaton

A6030
- 30 Leicester, Wakerley Rd/Broad Avenue

A6121
- 30 Ketton, Stamford Rd

B568
- 30 Leicester, Victoria Park Rd

B581
- 30 Broughton Astley, Broughton Way

B582
- 30 Blaby, Little Glen Rd

B590
- 30 Hinckley, Rugby Rd

B591
- 60 Charley, Loughborough Rd

B4114
- 40 Enderby/Narborough, Leicester Rd/King Edward Avenue
- 30 Leicester, Sharnford

B4616
- 30 Leicester, East Park Rd

B4666
- 30 Hinckley, Coventry Rd

B5003
- 40 Norris Hill, Ashby Rd

B5350
- 30 Loughborough, Foreset Rd
- 30 Loughborough, Nanpantan Rd

B5366
- 30 Leicester, Saffron Lane

UNCLASSIFIED
- 30 Barrow upon Soar, Sileby Rd
- 30 Blaby, Lutterworth Rd
- 30 Glenfield, Sation Rd
- 30 Ibstock, Leicester Rd
- 30 Leicester, Beaumont Leys Lane
- 30 Leicester, Fosse Rd South
- 30 Monks Kirby, Coalpit Lane
- 40 Norris Hill, Ashby Road
- 30 Shardlow, London Road
- 30 Shepshed, Leicester Rd

	Motorway with junction number
	Primary route – dual/single carriageway
	A road – dual/single carriageway
	B road – dual/single carriageway
	Minor road – dual/single carriageway
	Other minor road – dual/single carriageway
	Road under construction
	Tunnel, covered road
	Speed cameras - single, multiple
	Rural track, private road or narrow road in urban area
	Gate or obstruction to traffic (restrictions may not apply at all times or to all vehicles)
	Path, bridleway, byway open to all traffic, road used as a public path
	Pedestrianised area
DY7	**Postcode boundaries**
	County and unitary authority boundaries
	Railway, tunnel, railway under construction
	Tramway, tramway under construction
	Miniature railway
Walsall	**Railway station**
	Private railway station
South Shields	**Metro station**
	Tram stop, tram stop under construction
	Bus, coach station

	Ambulance station
	Coastguard station
	Fire station
	Police station
	Accident and Emergency entrance to hospital
H	**Hospital**
+	**Place of worship**
i	**Information Centre** (open all year)
	Shopping Centre
P P&R	**Parking, Park and Ride**
PO	**Post Office**
	Camping site, caravan site
	Golf course, picnic site
Prim Sch	**Important buildings, schools, colleges, universities and hospitals**
	Built up area
	Woods
River Medway	**Water name**
	River, weir, stream
	Canal, lock, tunnel
	Water
	Tidal water
Church	**Non-Roman antiquity**
ROMAN FORT	**Roman antiquity**
87	**Adjoining page indicators and overlap bands**
237	The colour of the arrow and the band indicates the scale of the adjoining or overlapping page (see scales below)

Enlarged mapping only

	Railway or bus station building
	Place of interest
	Parkland

Abbr	Full	Abbr	Full	Abbr	Full
Acad	**Academy**	Inst	**Institute**	Recn Gd	**Recreation Ground**
Allot Gdns	**Allotments**	Ct	**Law Court**		
Cemy	**Cemetery**	L Ctr	**Leisure Centre**	Resr	**Reservoir**
C Ctr	**Civic Centre**	LC	**Level Crossing**	Ret Pk	**Retail Park**
CH	**Club House**	Liby	**Library**	Sch	**School**
Coll	**College**	Mkt	**Market**	Sh Ctr	**Shopping Centre**
Crem	**Crematorium**	Meml	**Memorial**	TH	**Town Hall/House**
Ent	**Enterprise**	Mon	**Monument**	Trad Est	**Trading Estate**
Ex H	**Exhibition Hall**	Mus	**Museum**	Univ	**University**
Ind Est	**Industrial Estate**	Obsy	**Observatory**	W Twr	**Water Tower**
IRB Sta	**Inshore Rescue Boat Station**	Pal	**Royal Palace**	Wks	**Works**
		PH	**Public House**	YH	**Youth Hostel**

■ The small numbers around the edges of the maps identify the 1 kilometre National Grid lines

■ The dark grey border on the inside edge of some pages indicates that the mapping does not continue onto the adjacent page

The scale of the maps on the pages numbered in blue is 5.52 cm to 1 km • 3½ inches to 1 mile • 1: 18103

0	¼	½	¾	1 mile
0	250 m	500 m	750 m	1 kilometre

The scale of the maps on pages numbered in red is 11.04 cm to 1 km • 7 inches to 1 mile • 1: 9051

0	220 yards	440 yards	660 yards	½ mile
0	125 m	250 m	375 m	½ kilometre

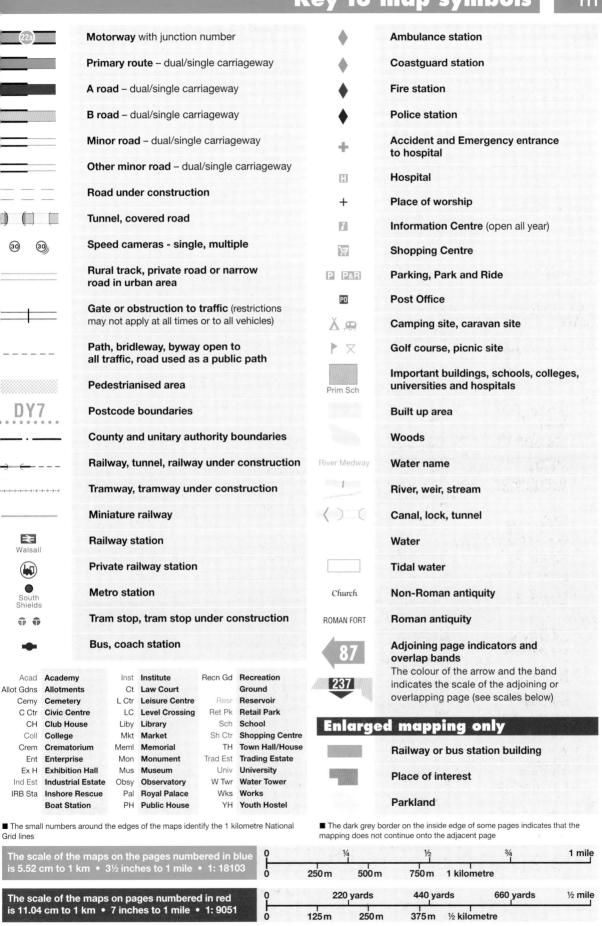

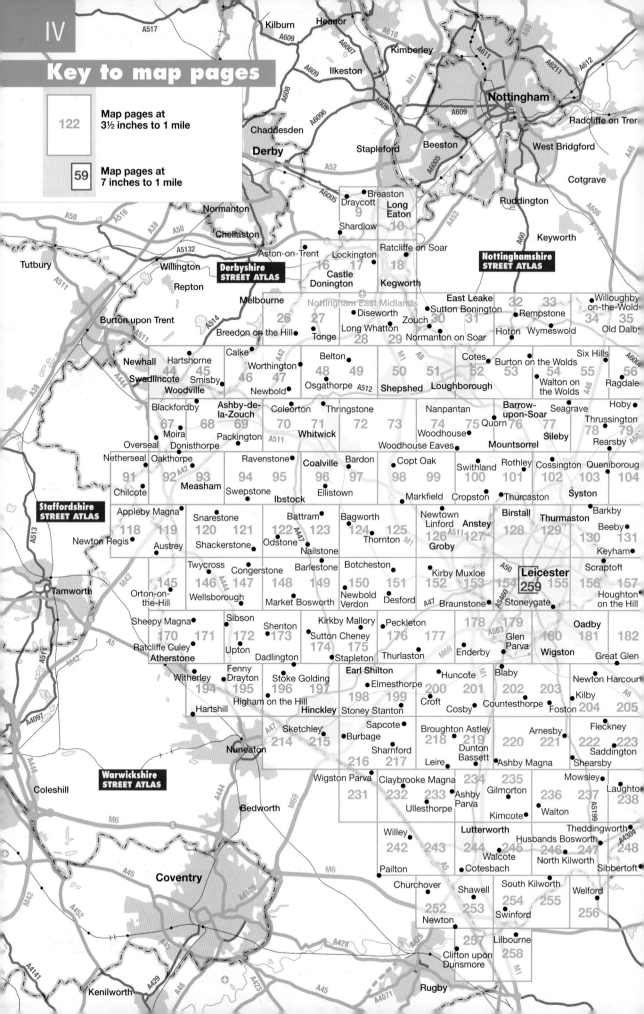

IV

Key to map pages

122	Map pages at 3½ inches to 1 mile
59	Map pages at 7 inches to 1 mile

Kilburn
Heanor
A517
A609
Kimberley
Ilkeston
A6007
A610
A6211
A612
A611
Nottingham
A609
Radcliffe on Trent
Chaddesden
A6096
A608
Stapleford
Beeston
West Bridgford
A46
Derby
A52
A6005
Cotgrave
A60
A6005
Ruddington
Keyworth
Normanton
A516
A50
A606
Chellaston
A38
A5132
Willington
Aston-on-Trent
Derbyshire STREET ATLAS
Breaston
Draycott
9
Long Eaton
10
Lockington
17
Shardlow
Ratcliffe on Soar
18
Nottinghamshire STREET ATLAS
Tutbury
Repton
16
Castle Donington
Kegworth
Melbourne
26
Nottingham East Midlands
East Leake
32 **33**
Willoughby on-the-Wolds
A511
Breedon on the Hill
27
Diseworth
Sutton Bonington
Rempstone
34 **35**
Burton upon Trent
Tonge
28
Long Whatton
29
Zouch
Normanton on Soar
30 **31**
Hoton
Wymeswold
Old Dalby
A514
Newhall
Hartshorne
Calke
Belton
Cotes
Six Hills
A46
44 **45**
Worthington
46 **47**
48 **49**
50 **51**
Burton on the Wolds
52 **53**
54 **55**
56
Swadlincote Smisby
Woodville
Newbold
Osgathorpe
A512
Shepshed
Loughborough
Walton on the Wolds
Ragdale
Blackfordby
Ashby-de-la-Zouch
Coleorton
Thringstone
Nanpantan
Barrow-upon-Soar
Seagrave
Hoby
67 **68** **69**
70 **71**
72 **73**
74 **75**
Quorn
76 **77**
78 **79**
Moira
Packington
A511
Whitwick
Woodhouse
Sileby
Thrussington
Overseal Donisthorpe
Woodhouse Eaves
Mountsorrel
Rearsby
Netherseal
Oakthorpe
Ravenstone
Coalville
Bardon
Copt Oak
Swithland
Rothley
Cossington
Queniborough
91 **92** **93**
94 **95**
96 **97**
98 **99**
100 **101**
102 **103** **104**
Staffordshire STREET ATLAS
Chilcote
Measham
Swepstone
Ellistown
Markfield
Cropston
Thurcaston
Syston
Ibstock
Appleby Magna
Snarestone
Battram
Bagworth
Newtown Linford
Anstey
Birstall
Thurmaston
Barkby
118 **119**
120 **121**
122 **123**
124 **125**
126 **127**
128 **129**
130 **131**
Newton Regis
Austrey
Shackerstone
Odstone
Nailstone
Thornton
M1
Groby
A511
Beeby
Keyham
Twycross
Congerstone
Barlestone
Botcheston
Kirby Muxloe
A50
Leicester 259
Scraptoft
145 **146** **147**
148 **149**
150 **151**
152 **153**
154 **155**
156 **157**
Orton-on-the-Hill
Wellsborough
Market Bosworth
Newbold Verdon
Desford
A47
Braunstone
Stoneygate
Houghton on the Hill
Tamworth
Sheepy Magna
Sibson
Shenton
Kirkby Mallory
Peckleton
178 **179**
Oadby
170 **171**
172 **173**
176 **177**
Glen Parva
180 **181** **182**
Ratcliffe Culey
Upton
Sutton Cheney
Enderby
Wigston
Atherstone
Dadlington
174 **175**
Thurlaston
M69
Great Glen
Stapleton
Witherley
Fenny Drayton
Stoke Golding
Earl Shilton
Huncote
Blaby
Newton Harcourt
194 **195**
196 **197**
198 **199**
200 **201**
202 **203**
Kilby
Hartshill
Higham on the Hill
Hinckley
Elmesthorpe
Croft
Cosby
Countesthorpe
Foston
204 **205**
Stoney Stanton
A6
Sketchley
Sapcote
Broughton Astley
Arnesby
Fleckney
214 **215**
Burbage
216 **217**
218 **219**
220 **221**
222 **223**
Nuneaton
Sharnford
Dunton Bassett
Saddington
Warwickshire STREET ATLAS
Leire
Ashby Magna
Shearsby
Wigston Parva
Claybrooke Magna
234 **235**
Mowsley
Laughton
Coleshill
231
232 **233**
Gilmorton
236 **237** **238**
Ullesthorpe
Ashby Parva
Walton
Kimcote
A5199
Bedworth
Willey
Lutterworth
Theddingworth
A4304
M69
242 **243**
244 **245**
Husbands Bosworth
246 **247** **248**
Pailton
Walcote
North Kilworth
Sibbertoft
Cotesbach
Coventry
Churchover
Shawell
South Kilworth
Welford
252 **253**
254 **255**
256
Newton
Swinford
A428
A45
Lilbourne
257 **258**
Clifton upon Dunsmore
Kenilworth
A429
Rugby
A4071

V

Sleaford

Bingham
Orston
Normanton
Staunton in the Vale
1
Allington
Barkston
Helpringham
2 **3** **4**
A52
Bottesford
Easthorpe
Sedgebrook
Grantham
A52
Horbling
Sutton
Muston
Billingborough
Granby
5 **6** **7** **8**
Redmile
Folkingham
Plungar
Barkestone-
le-vale
Woolsthorpe
Belvoir
Rippingale
11 **12** **13** **14** **15**
Stathern
Knipton
Harston
Harby
Harston
Croxton Kerrial
Hickling
Hose
Eastwell
Branston
Wyville
Bourne
19 **20** **21** **22** **23** **24** **25**
Upper
Broughton
Long Clawson
Goadby Marwood
Saltby
Lincolnshire
STREET ATLAS
Nether Broughton
Scalford
Chadwell
Waltham on
the Wolds
Sproxton
Skillington
Colsterworth
36 **37** **38** **39** **40** **41** **42** **43**
Ab Kettleby
Coston
Buckminster
Stainby
Saxelby
Sewstern
Gunby
North
Witham
Lobthorpe
58 **59** **60** **61** **62** **63** **64** **65** **66**
Melton Mowbray
Freeby
Garthorpe
57
Asfordby
Asfordby Hill
Saxby
Brentingby
Wymondham
South Witham
Castle Bytham
Frisby on
the Wreake
Kirby Bellars
Burton Lazars
Edmondthorpe
Market
Overton
Clipsham
80 **81** **82** **83** **84** **85** **86** **87** **88** **89** **90**
Great Dalby
Little
Dalby
Whissendine
Teigh
Barrow
Stretton
Greetham
Gaddesby
Thorpe Satchville
Pickwell
Ashwell
Cottesmore
Pickworth
Essendine
105 **106** **107** **108** **109** **110** **111** **112** **113** **114** **115** **116** **117**
Barsby
Burrough
on the Hill
Somerby
Cold
Overton
Burley
Exton
Ryhall
Belmesthorpe
Market Deeping
Langham
Deeping St James
Lowesby
Marefield
Knossington
Oakham
Whitwell
Empingham
Great Casterton
132 **133** **134** **135** **136** **137** **138** **139** **140** **141** **142** **143** **144**
Hungarton
Owston
Braunston-in-Rutland
Upper Hamleton
Normanton
Tinwell
Stamford
Uffington
Egleton
Old Ingarsby
Tilton on the Hill
Brooke
Manton
Lyndon
Edith Weston
Ketton
Easton on the Hill
158 **159** **160** **161** **162** **163** **164** **165** **166** **167** **168** **169**
Billesdon
Skeffington
Loddington
Ridlington
Preston
Wing
North Luffenham
Collyweston
Peterborough
Gaulby
Rolleston
Tugby
East Norton
Glaston
Morcott
Duddington
183 **184** **185** **186** **187** **188** **189** **190** **191** **192** **193**
Illston on
the Hill
Noseley
Goadby
Allexton
Uppingham
Bisbrooke
Wakerley
Seaton
Shangton
Hallaton
Stockerston
Lyddington
Harringworth
206 **207** **208** **209** **210** **211** **212** **213**
Kibworth
Beauchamp
Cranoe
Blaston
Gretton
Church Langton
Thorpe Langton
Great Easton
Caldecott
224 **225** **226** **227** **228** **229** **230**
Foxton
Ashley
Cottingham
Rockingham
Oundle
Great Bowden
239 **240** **241**
Lubenham
Market
Harborough
Marston
Trussell
East Farndon
Sawtry
249 **250** **251**
Braybrooke
Great Oxendon
Desborough
Rothwell

Scale

0 .... 5 .... 10 .... 15 km
0 .... 5 .... 10 miles

Kettering

Thrapston

Northamptonshire
STREET ATLAS

Burton Latimer

Raunds

Cambridgeshire
STREET ATLAS

Corby

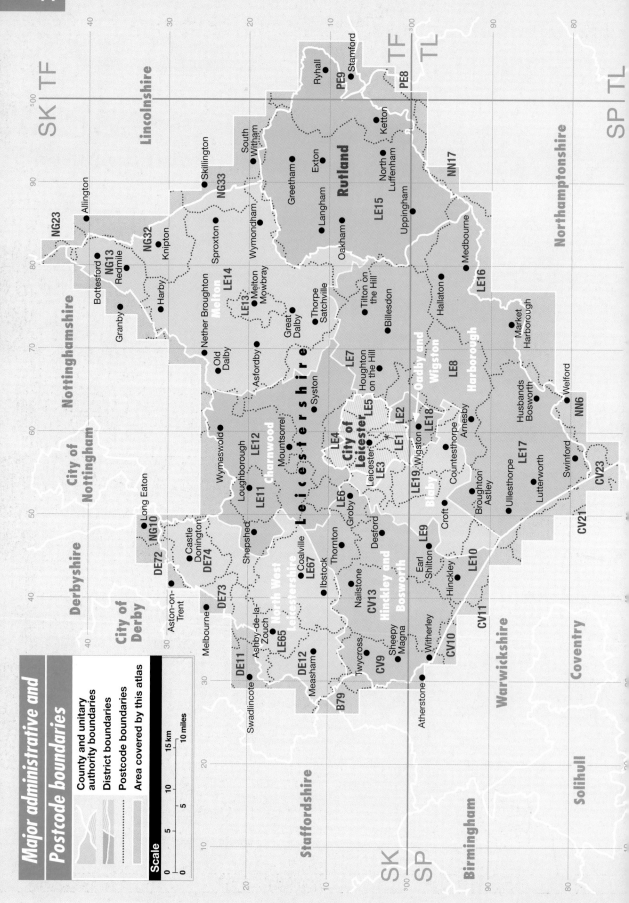

Major administrative and
Postcode boundaries

County and unitary
authority boundaries

District boundaries

Postcode boundaries

Area covered by this atlas

Scale

| 0 | 5 | 10 | 15 km |
| 0 | 5 | 10 miles |

Lincolnshire

Nottinghamshire

City of Nottingham

Derbyshire

City of Derby

Staffordshire

Birmingham

Solihull

Coventry

Warwickshire

Northamptonshire

Leicestershire

Charnwood

Melton

Rutland

Harborough

Oadby and Wigston

Hinckley and Bosworth

North West Leicestershire

City of Leicester

Blaby

NG23 · Allington
NG33 · Skillington
South Witham
NG32 · Knipton
Sproxton
Redmile
NG13 · Bottesford
Granby · Harby
Ryhall
PE9 · Stamford
Greetham · Exton
Langham
Ketton
PE8
North Luffenham
Oakham
LE15 · Uppingham
NN17
LE14 · Nether Broughton
Wymondham
Medbourne
LE13 · Melton Mowbray
Asfordby
Great Dalby
Thorpe Satchville
Old Dalby
Tilton on the Hill
Billesdon
Hallaton
LE16
LE7 · Houghton on the Hill
Syston
Market Harborough
Mountsorrel
Wymeswold
Charnwood
LE12
Loughborough
LE11
Long Eaton
NG10
Castle Donington
DE74
DE72
Aston-on-Trent
DE73
Melbourne
DE11 · Swadlincote
Ashby-de-la-Zouch
LE65
DE12 · Measham
B79
Coalville
LE67
Ibstock
Shepshed
Thornton
LE6 · Groby
Desford
Nailstone
CV13
Twycross
CV9 · Sheepy Magna
Witherley
CV10
Atherstone
CV11
Earl Shilton
Hinckley
LE10
LE9
Croft
Countesthorpe
Arnesby
Broughton Astley
Ullesthorpe
LE17 · Lutterworth
Swinford
CV23
CV21
Husbands Bosworth
NN6 · Welford
LE8
LE18 · Wigston
LE19
LE4 · LE5 · LE2 · LE1 · LE3
Leicester
CV18
LE15

TF · TL
SK · TF
SP · TL
SK · SP
SP

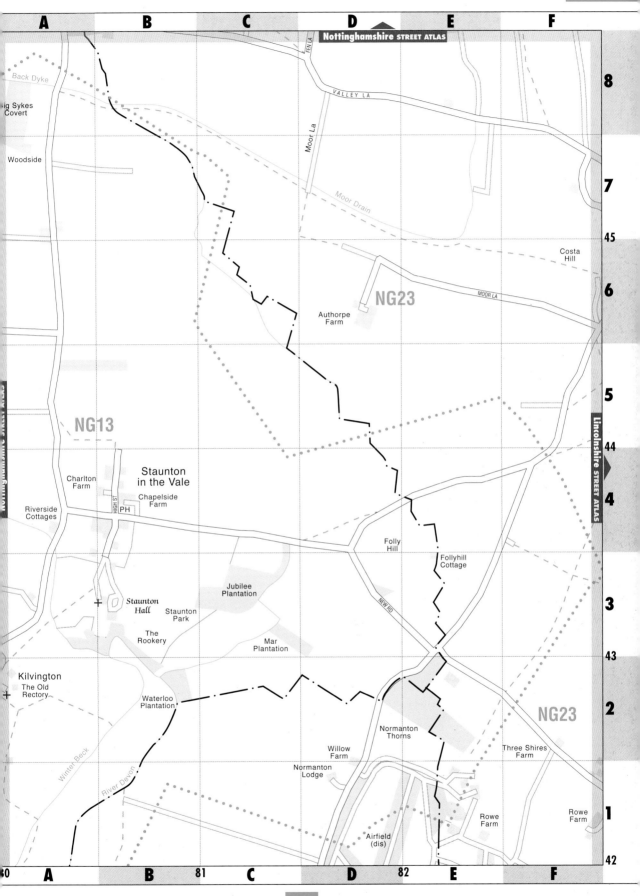

A B C D E F

Back Dyke

Big Sykes
Covert

Woodside

8

FEN LA

VALLEY LA

Moor La

Moor Drain

7

45

Costa
Hill

NG23

MOOR LA

6

Authorpe
Farm

NG13

5

44

Staunton
in the Vale

Charlton
Farm

HIGH ST

Riverside
Cottages

PH

Chapelside
Farm

Folly
Hill

Follyhill
Cottage

4

Jubilee
Plantation

NEW RD

3

Staunton
Hall

Staunton
Park

The
Rookery

Mar
Plantation

43

Kilvington

The Old
Rectory

Waterloo
Plantation

Normanton
Thorns

NG23

2

Willow
Farm

Three Shires
Farm

Winter Beck

River Devon

Normanton
Lodge

Rowe
Farm

Rowe
Farm

1

Airfield
(dis)

42

30 A B 81 C D 82 E F

Lodge Farm

Orston
Prim
Sch

CHURCH
ST

MILL LA

SPA LA

LOUGHBON

LOMBARD ST

Sports
Gd

Orston

HILL RD

HILLTOP

LORDSHIP LA

Manor
Farm

Mushroom
Farm

LONGHEDGE LA

Winter Beck

River Devon

BOTTESFORD LA

Elton & Orston

40

LC

NG13

Piggeries

ORSTON LA

Oldfield
Plantation

Winter Beck

Winterbeck
Ind Est

LONGHEDGE LA

BOWBRIDGE

COT

Longhedge Lane
Ind Est

LAUREL WAY

ROBERTS

A52 Nottingham

A52

Highfield
Farm

NOTTINGHAM RD

Nursery

Greenacres

Orston
Grange

A52

A   B   C   D   E   F

8

Piggery

Airfield
(disused)

7

Normanton
Hall

41

NG23

Normanton
House

6

Peacock
Farm

Little Covert
Farm

Normanton

Home
Farm

Elm
Farm

5

40

Beacon
Hill

Sewage
Works

4

NG13

Beckingthorpe

LC

Rectory
Farm

WIMBISHTHORPE CL

WINTERBECK CL

BECKINGTHORPE DR

The
Nook

PINFOLD CL

PINFOLD LA

RIVERSIDE CL

RIVERSIDE WLK

STREET
VIEW

BEACON VIEW
1
2

LC

Bottesford

3

1
2

1 MARSH CT
2 STROUD CT

Bottesford

FARMHOUSE BANK

CHURCH VIEW

THE
SQUARE

DEVON LA

CHURCH LA

RECTORY LA

ST MARY'S LA

BECKINGTHORPE DR

CHESTNUT CL

OLD STATION YD

FLEMING AVE

39

WEST END CL

SHEPPARDS
CT

ALBERT ST

CHAPEL ST

WALFORD
CL

QUEEN ST

MARKET ST

CHURCH
ST

WYGGESTON
AVE

DAY BELL CL

STATION RD

WALKERS CL

RUTLAND LA

EASTHORPE RD

VAUXHALL AVE

CASTLE

GRANTHAM RD

HIGH ST

HOOPERS
CL

PO
HAND'S
WLK

Liby

1 ST MARY'S LA
2 WYGGESTON TERR

2
WYGGESTON AVE

BEECH DR

South
View

2

WALNUT
RD

LINK

WARWICK
FLATS

GRANBY DR

NORTH
CRES

KEEL DR

HAND'S

SILVERWOOD RD

Manor
Farm

MANOR RD

River Devon

Bottesford
CE Prim
Sch

SCHOOL

SOUTH
CRES

VINE CL

BELVOIR AVE

JAY'S
CL

BELVOIR RD

The
Elms

GREEN LA

Easthorpe

CASTLE VIEW RD

MUSTON LA

SKERRY LA

BARKESTONE LA

Belvoir
High Sch

HOWITTS RD

Castleview
Farm

EASTHORPE LA

GRANTHAM RD

A52

Corner
Farm

MAIN ST

SKERRY

1

Winterbeck
Bridge

Hospital
Farm

A52

A52

38

A B C D E F

8

The Ashes

Camp (dis)

Thackson's Well Farm

Ease Drain

The Spinney

7

Moss' Plantation

NG23

41

Lowfield Farm

The Bungalow

LOWFIELDS LA

6

Stonepit Plantation

RED HOUSE GDNS 1
BURTON'S LA 2
MARSTON LA 3
GONERBY LA 4

Allington wit Sedgebrook CE Prim Sch

Hillside Plantation

PARK RD

Allington Hall

Allington

5

West Wong Plantation

Old Rectory

WEST MDWS

BERT'S WAY

PARK AVE

TRINITY CL

THE GREEN

PO

MAIN ST

PH

THE PADDOCK

SIDE ST

BOTTOM ST

LAMBERT P

Manor House

MANOR PADDOCK

DALESTORTH CT

BACK LA

40

Endcliffe Farm

BOTTESFORD RD

SEDGEBROOK RD

PEACH LA

ALLINGTON GDNS

THE CRESCEN

4

Glebe Farm

NG32

Salt Well (Chalybeate)

WEST WAY

Viking Way

SKERRY LA

Debdale Barn

3

39

The Debdale

Keeper's Plantation

Manor Farm

2

NG13

Barra-Don

ALLINGTON RD

Cox's Walk Farm

Station Farm

A52

GRANTHAM RD

PH

1

LC

Manor House

CHURCH LA

WHATT

CHURCH LA

38

6

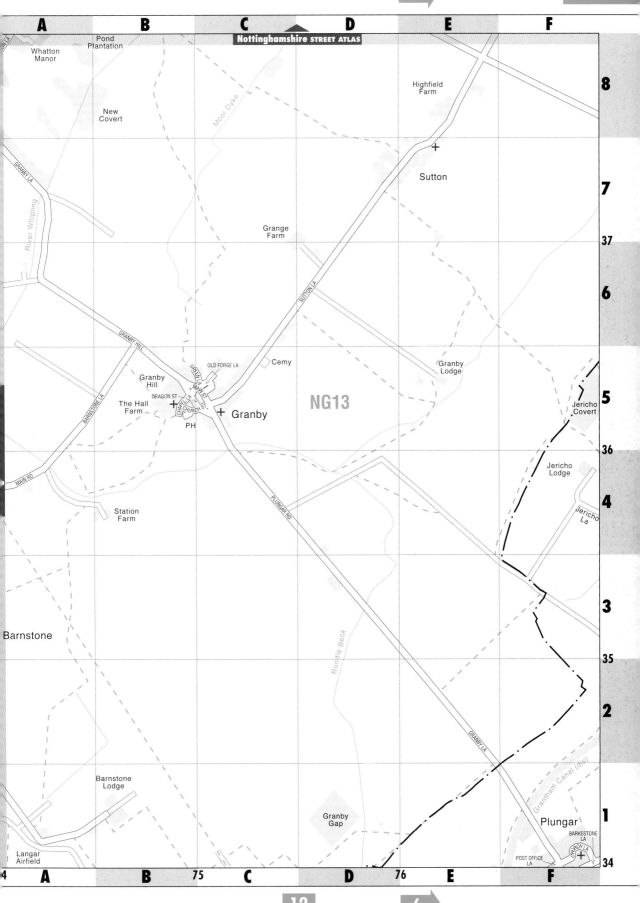

Nottinghamshire STREET ATLAS

Whatton Manor

Pond Plantation

New Covert

Moor Dyke

Highfield Farm

+ Sutton

Granby La

River Whipling

Grange Farm

Sutton La

Granby Hill

Barnstone La

Granby Hill

OLD FORGE LA

Cemy

Granby Lodge

NG13

GREEN LA

BRAGON ST

CHAPEL LA

CHURCH ST

MAIN ST

The Hall Farm

+ + Granby

PH

Jericho Covert

Jericho Lodge

Main Rd

Station Farm

Plungar Rd

Jericho La

Barnstone

Rundle Beck

Granby La

Barnstone Lodge

Granby Gap

Grantham Canal (dis)

Plungar

BARKESTONE LA

Langar Airfield

POST OFFICE LA

CHURCH LA

+

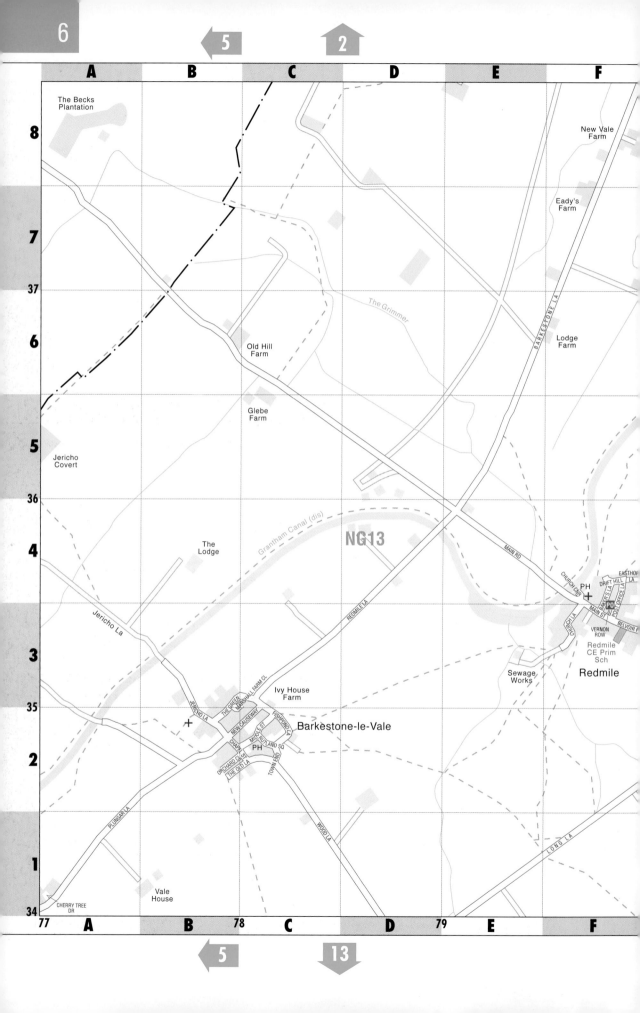

A B C D E F

8

7

37

6

5

36

4

3

35

2

1

34

77 A B 78 C D 79 E F

The Becks Plantation

New Vale Farm

Eady's Farm

The Grimmer

Old Hill Farm

Lodge Farm

Glebe Farm

Jericho Covert

Grantham Canal (dis)

NG13

The Lodge

MAIN RD

CHURCH CHR

PH

PO

DRIFT HILL

EASTHOF LA

BELVOIR I

BARKESTONE LA

Jericho La

REDMILE LA

CHURCH LA

MAIN ST

POST OFFICE LA

BAKER ST LA

VERNON ROW

Redmile CE Prim Sch

Redmile

Sewage Works

Ivy House Farm

THE GREEN

MARSHALL FARM CL

NEW CAUSEWAY

JERICHO LA

CHAPEL

MIDDLE ST

FISHPOND LA

RUTLAND SQ

PH

ORCHARD CLOSE

THE OLD LA

TOWN END

Barkestone-le-Vale

PLUNGAR LA

WOOD LA

LONG LA

Vale House

CHERRY TREE DR

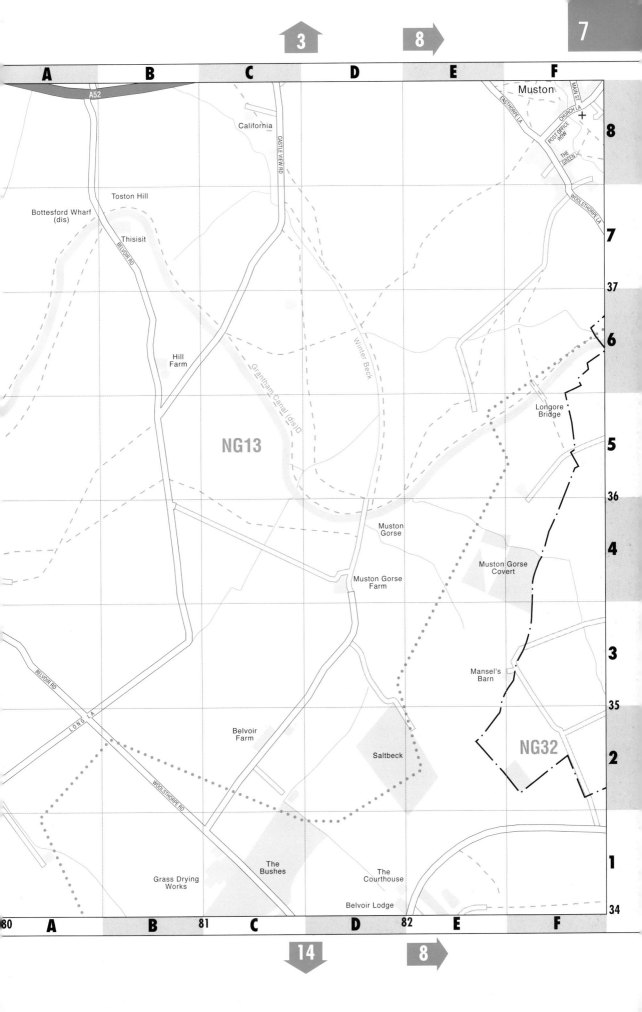

A   B   C   D   E   F

8

NG13

Mill Farm
Cottages

SEWSTERN LA

Mill Farm

A52

Sedgebrook

White House
Farm

VILLAGE ST

ROWAN'S WAY

THE
PADDOCKS

CHURCH LA

ABBEY LA

SCHOOL LA

7

Mill Farm

Shipman's
Plantation

Willow
Bridge

A52

37

DENTON LA

6

Muston
Bridge

Breeder Hills
Farm

Lock
House

New
Cottages

Casthorpe
Farm

Coe Farm

5

WOOLSTHORPE LA

Stenwith

Stenwith
Bridge

36

River Devon

Viking Way

Barlow's
Farm

NG32

4

Grantham Canal (dis)

Grange
Farm

SEDGEBROOK RD

PH
Woolsthorpe
Wharf
(dis)

Woolsthorpe
Bridge

Longmoor
Bridge

3

35

2

HUNT
COTTS

Cliff
Wood

Glebe
Farm

Sewage
Works

HILLSIDE RD

CLIFF RD

Belvoir Hunt
Stables

NEW ROW

VILLAGE ST

PH

Mickledales

Lanes Plantation

1

WORTHINGTON LA

BELVOIR LA

Woolsthorpe
by Belvoir

34

83   A   B   84   C   D   85   E   F

Lincolnshire Street Atlas

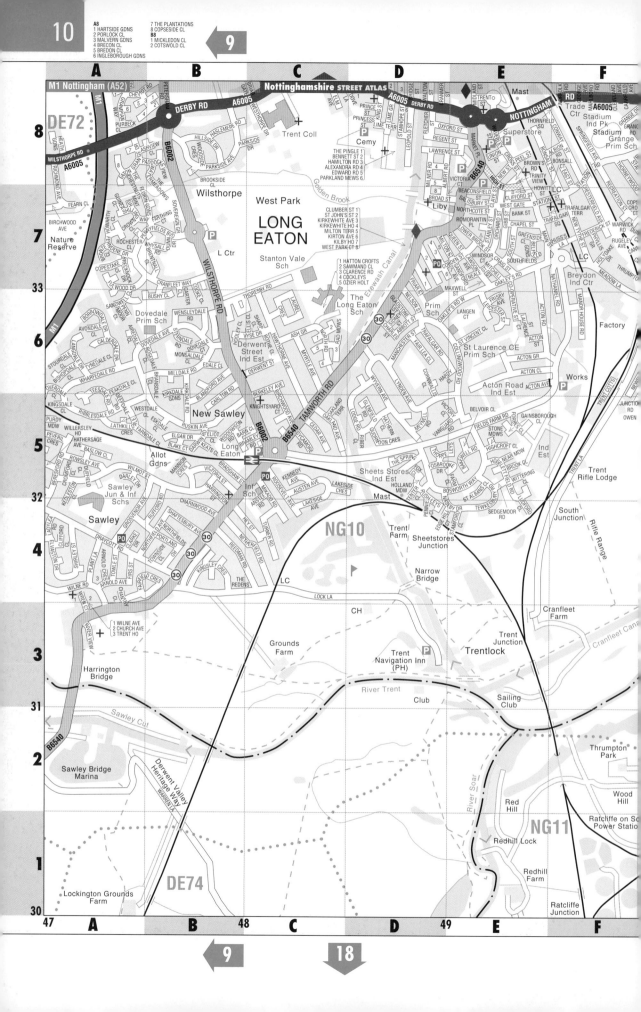

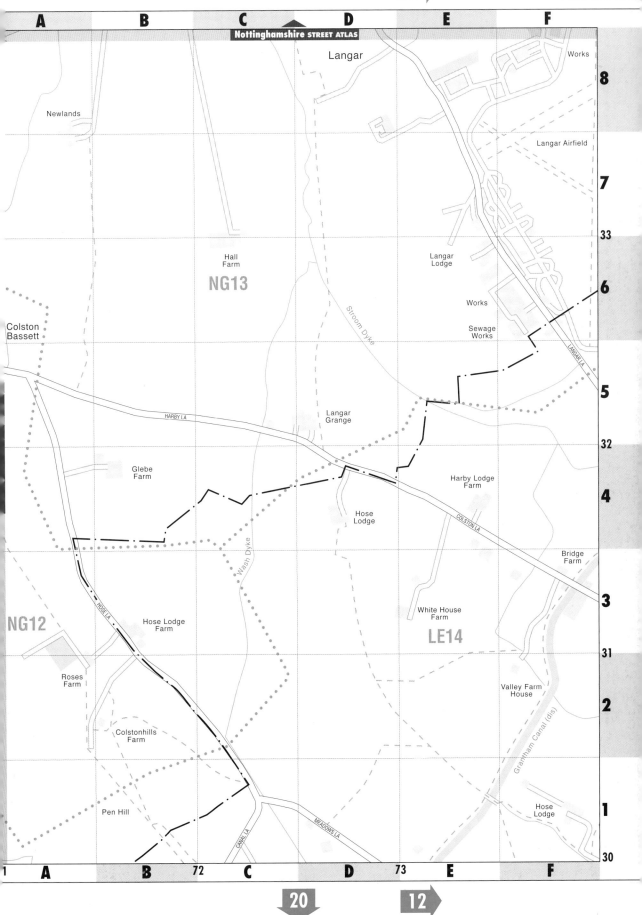

Nottinghamshire STREET ATLAS

Langar

Works

Newlands

Langar Airfield

Hall
Farm

NG13

Langar
Lodge

Colston
Bassett

Stroom Dyke

Works

Sewage
Works

LANGAR LA

HARBY LA

Langar
Grange

Glebe
Farm

Harby Lodge
Farm

COLSTON LA

Hose
Lodge

Wash Dyke

Bridge
Farm

NG12

HOSE LA

Hose Lodge
Farm

White House
Farm

LE14

Roses
Farm

Valley Farm
House

Colstonhills
Farm

Grantham Canal (dis)

Pen Hill

Hose
Lodge

CANAL LA

MEADOWS LA

8

7

33

6

5

32

4

3

31

2

1

30

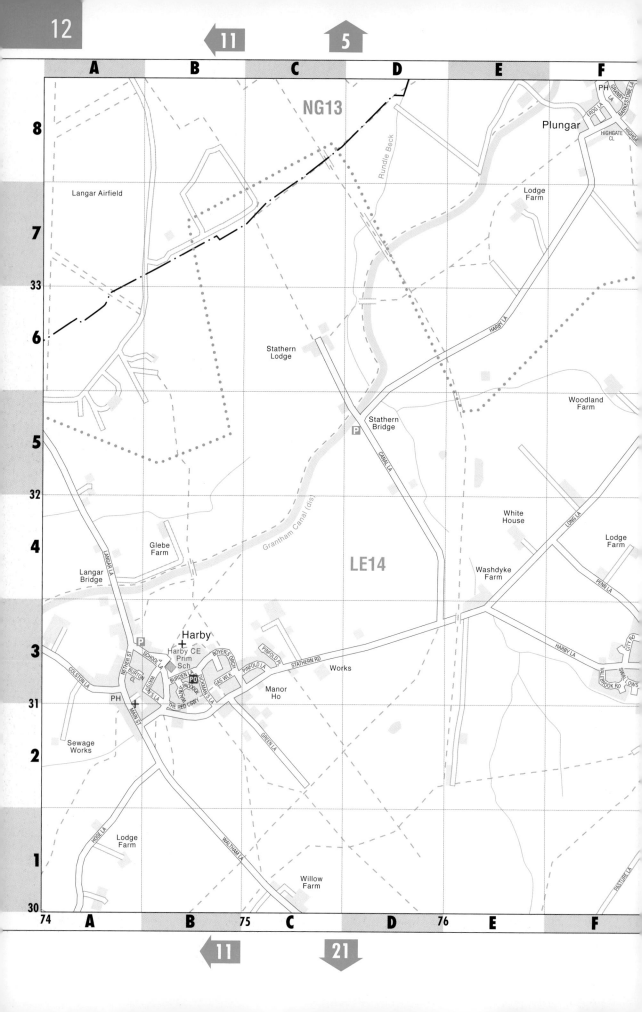

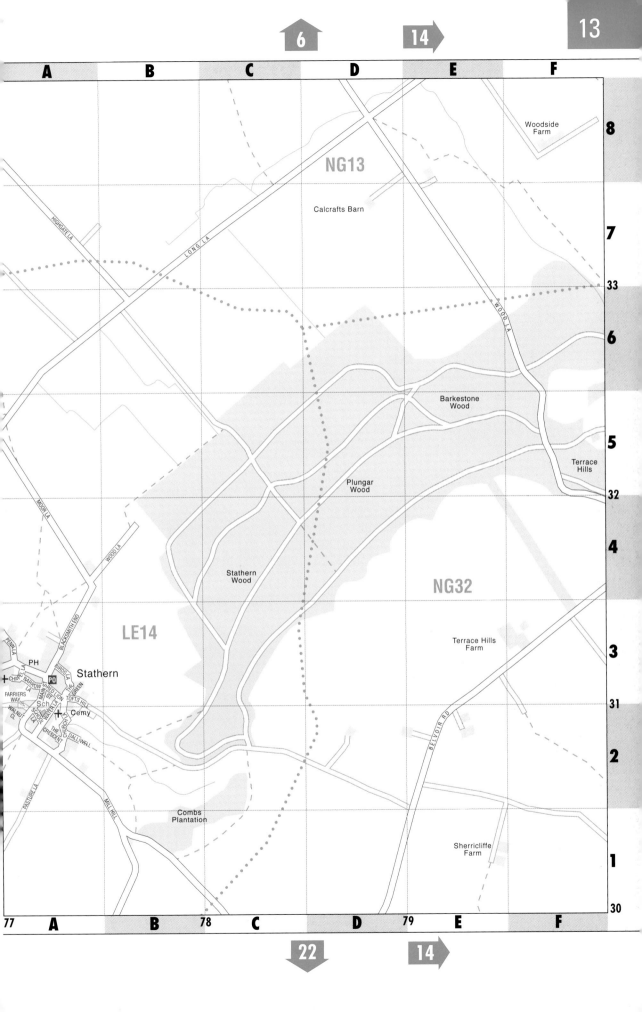

A   B   C   D   E   F

8
7
33
6
5
32
4
3
31
2
1
30

NG13

Woodside Farm

Calcrafts Barn

HIGHGATE LA

LONG LA

WOOD LA

Barkestone Wood

Terrace Hills

Plungar Wood

MOOR LA

WOOD LA

Stathern Wood

NG32

Terrace Hills Farm

BLACKSMITH END

LE14

PH

PENN LA

CHR

NARROW LA
MAIN ST
SPRED LON
THE GREEN
BIRDS LA
CHURCH
SCHOOL
WATER LA
TOFTS HILL

FARRIERS WAY

WALNUT CL

Sch

PO

Stathern

Cemy

DALLIWELL

THE CRESCENT

BELVOIR RD

PASTURE LA

MILL HILL

Combs Plantation

Sherricliffe Farm

13
7

| | A | B | C | D | E | F |

Belvoir

BREWERY ROW

Clayfield Cottage

8

NG13

The Ash Beds

West Wong

Belvoir Castle (restored)

Dairy Cottage

Fir Holt

Mausoleum

Middlesdale

Kennel Wood

7

Duchess Garden

33

Church Thorns

Briery Wood

Blackberry Hill

Briery Cottage

Kennels

6

Old Park Wood

Reeded Cottage

High Leys

Knipton Pasture

Sir John's Belt

Carlisle Wood

Windsor Hill

5

Frog Hollow

King's Wood

32

Granby Wood

WOOD LA

BELVOIR RD

High Leys Farm

NG32

Knipton Lodge

KNIPTON LA

4

Hart's Barn

The Priory

PASTURE LA

Glebe Farm

Granby Cottages

Middle Barn

Bunkers Wood

The Carrier

NURSERY LA

Knipton

3

Granby Farm

FINNS LA

PO

CHURCH HILL

THE OLD HILL

PH

Rectory

31

2

Reservoir Wood

Knipton Resr

Reservoir Cottage

Nursery Plantation

1

Keeper's Lodge

Cedar Hill

30

| 80 | A | B | 81 | C | D | 82 | E | F |

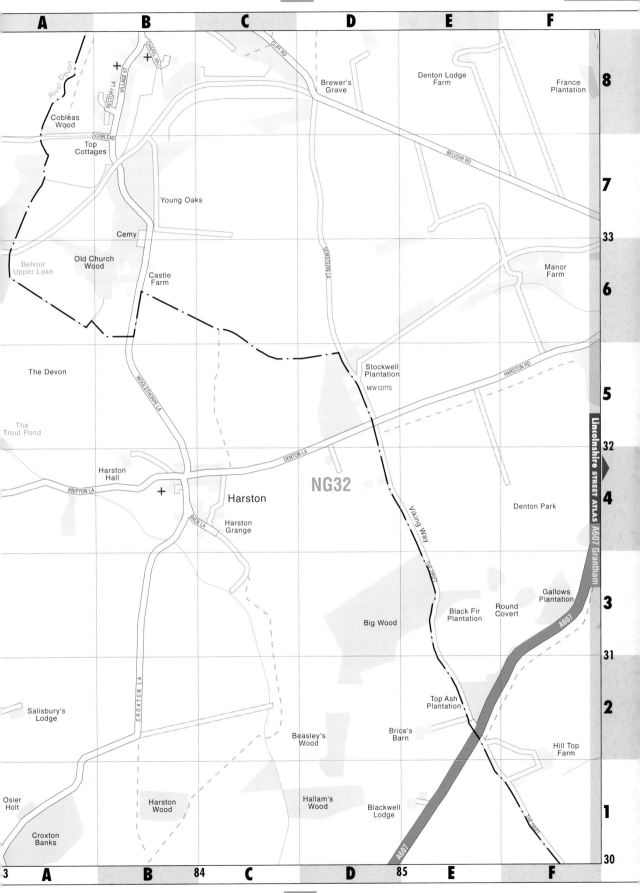

Lincolnshire STREET ATLAS A607 Grantham

NG32

A   **B**   **C**   **D**   **E**   **F**

8

7

33

6

5

32

4

3

31

2

1

30

River Devon

Cobleas Wood

Top Cottages

CHAPEL HILL

VILLAGE ST

RECTORY LA

COBLEAS

Young Oaks

Cemy

Old Church Wood

Belvoir Upper Lake

Castle Farm

CLIFF RD

Brewer's Grave

Denton Lodge Farm

France Plantation

BELVOIR RD

SEWSTERN LA

Manor Farm

The Devon

WOOLSTHORPE LA

The Trout Pond

Harston Hall

KNIPTON LA

Harston

BACK LA

Harston Grange

DENTON LA

Stockwell Plantation

NEW COTTS

HARSTON RD

Denton Park

Viking Way

THE DRIFT

Gallows Plantation

Black Fir Plantation

Round Covert

A607

Big Wood

CROXTON LA

Salisbury's Lodge

Beasley's Wood

Brice's Barn

Top Ash Plantation

Hill Top Farm

Osier Holt

Harston Wood

Hallam's Wood

Blackwell Lodge

Croxton Banks

A607

THE DRIFT

3   84   85

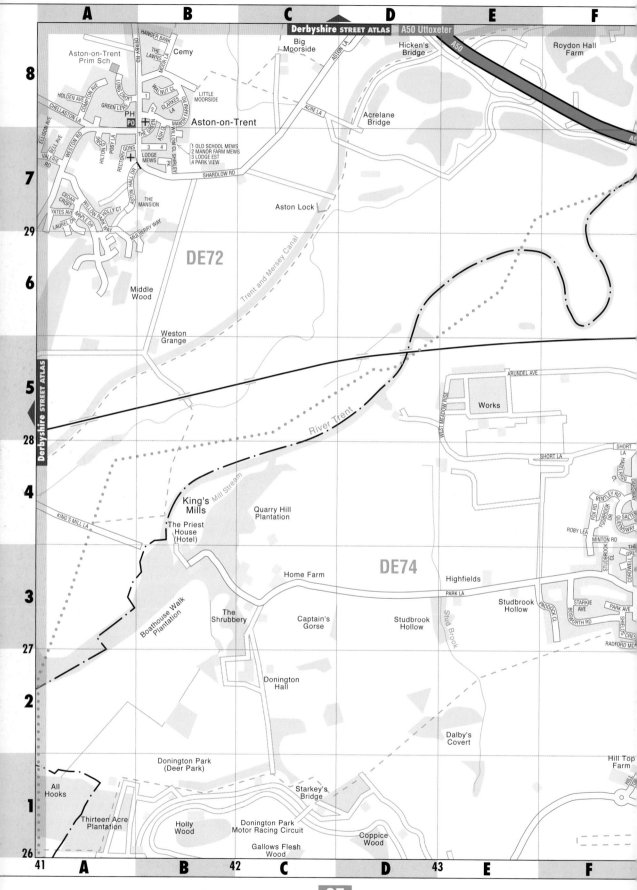

DE72

DE74

1 OLD SCHOOL MEWS
2 MANOR FARM MEWS
3 LODGE EST
4 PARK VIEW

Aston-on-Trent
Prim Sch

Cemy

Big
Moorside

Hicken's
Bridge

Roydon Hall
Farm

Little
Moorside

Aston-on-Trent

Acrelane
Bridge

Aston Lock

The
Mansion

Middle
Wood

Weston
Grange

Trent and Mersey Canal

River Trent

King's
Mills

Mill Stream

The Priest
House
(Hotel)

Quarry Hill
Plantation

Works

Home Farm

Highfields

Boathouse Walk
Plantation

The
Shrubbery

Captain's
Gorse

Studbrook
Hollow

Studbrook
Hollow

Studbrook
Hollow

Starkie
Ave

Donington
Hall

Dalby's
Covert

Donington Park
(Deer Park)

Starkey's
Bridge

Hill Top
Farm

All
Hooks

Thirteen Acre
Plantation

Holly
Wood

Donington Park
Motor Racing Circuit

Gallows Flesh
Wood

Coppice
Wood

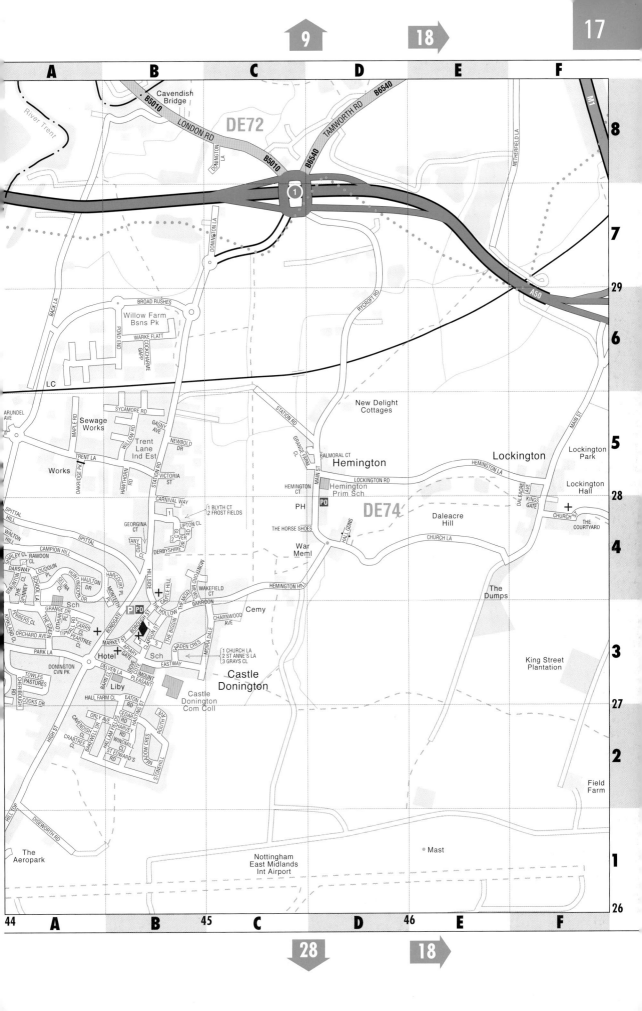

A B C D E F

8

7

29

6

5

28

4

3

27

2

26

1

Grounds Farm Cottages

WARREN LA

Warren Farm

M1

A50

24a

RATCLIFFE LA

RATCLIFFE LA

A453

A453 Nottingham

Power Sta

Mason's Barn

Ratcliffe on Soar

O D PARK CL

Barn Farm

Green Spot Wood

Manor Farm

NG11

The Bungalow

KEGWORTH RD

River Soar

Long Lane Farm

Willow Farm

Midshires Way

LONG LA

March Covert

Allot Gdns

DE74

Kingston Brook

Kingston on Soar

KEGWORTH RD

ST WINIFREDS CT

Park

CHURCH ST

Hotel

A50

24

A453

A6

Factory

Sewage Works

Works

Kegworth

Bridge Farm PH

KINGSTON LA

STATION RD

P

Computer Centre

CITRUS GR

JEFFARES CL

SIDELEY

LEATHERLANDS

GARDEN ROW

MOORE AVE

NEW ST

BRIDGE FIELDS

40

DERBY RD

VASSELLE

FREDERICK AVE

ROPEWALK

BOWELL

WALTON CT

HILLAMS WAY

HIGH ST

BORROUGH CT

WATTON ST

NOTTINGHAM RD

BRIDGWELL

KIRK AVE

MILL LA

THE OSIERS

PEPPERS DR

MUMMBRELL CL

PACKINGTON HILL

PLUMMER LA

SIBSON DR

STONEHILLS

SUTH.

NINE ACRES

MOUNT PLEASANT

Hotel

P

Kegworth Mus

PO

3

1 WINSER CT
2 TOMS CT
3 CHURCH GATE
4 MARKET PL

WINDMILL WAY

ASHBY RD

ASHBY RD

LANGLEY DR

SPRING.

BULLSTRODE PL

WEST BANK MEWS

OLDERSHAW AVE

BROADHILL RD

STAF.

Liby

ACRE

HIGH ST

PLEASANT PL

THE CROFT

MULBERRY

4

Old Cut

Sewage Works

LE12

FOXHILLS

WHATTON RD

SUTTON RD

Cemy

HILLSIDE

Kegworth Prim Sch

ST ANDREWS RISE

BEDFORD

BURLEY RISE

ROBERTS CL

BYARD

LONDON RD

CRES

NORMAN CT

SHEPERD WLK

KIRBY DR

THOMAS RD

Alton Lodge

30

A6

Molehill Farm

Broad Hill

NEW BRIXYARD LA

A453

M1

Nottinghamshire STREET ATLAS

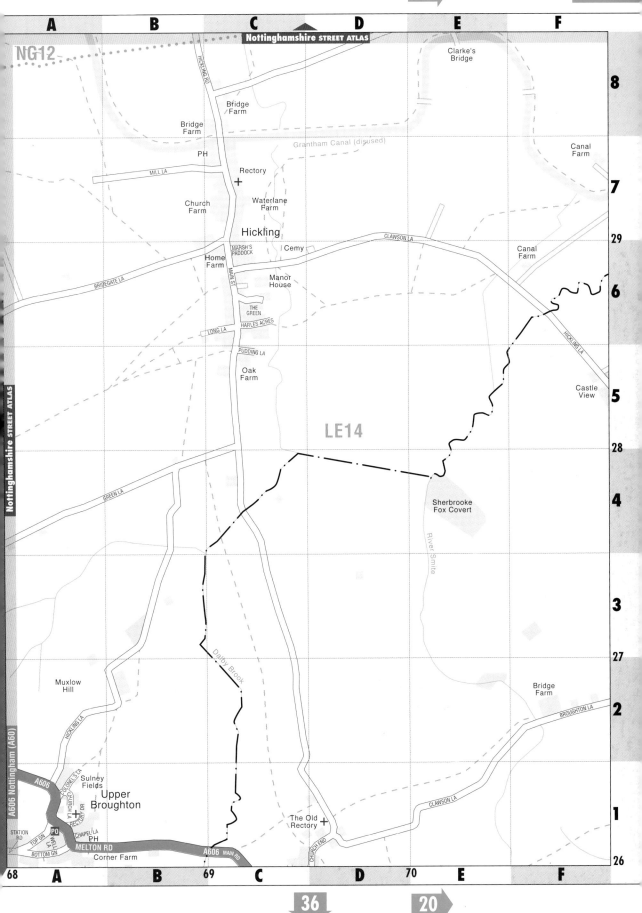

NG12

Nottinghamshire STREET ATLAS

Nottinghamshire STREET ATLAS

Clarke's Bridge

Canal Farm

Bridge Farm

Bridge Farm

HICKLING RD

Grantham Canal (disused)

PH

MILL LA

Rectory

Waterlane Farm

Church Farm

Canal Farm

Hickling

CLAWSON LA

MARSH'S PADDOCK

Cemy

Home Farm

BRIDEGATE LA

MAIN ST

Manor House

HICKLING LA

THE GREEN

Canal Farm

LONG LA

HARLES ACRES

PUDDING LA

Castle View

Oak Farm

LE14

Sherbrooke Fox Covert

GREEN LA

River Smite

Dalby Brook

Muxlow Hill

Bridge Farm

HICKLING LA

BROUGHTON LA

A606 Nottingham (A60)

A606

COLONEL'S LA

Sulney Fields

CHURCH LA

RECTORY DR

Upper Broughton

CLAWSON LA

The Old Rectory

STATION RD

PO

PH

CHAPEL LA

CHURCH END

TOP GN

WELL LA

MELTON RD

A606 MAIN RD

BOTTOM GN

Corner Farm

A B C D E F

8

The Grange

Grantham Canal (dis)

Long Clawson Bridge

Hose Thorns

Marriott's Bridge

Wash Dyke

MEADOWS LA

Bridge House

CANAL LA

Works

Hose

STROUD'S CL

Hose Lodge

CHAPEL LA

COAL LA

PH

THE GREEN

HOME PASTURES

DAIRY LA

MIDDLE CHURCH CL

HARBY LA

BOLTON LA

ST CHURCH WALK

7

River Smite

Hose CE Prim Sch

The Farm

PH

29

CANAL LA

Dam Dyke

6

Brook Farm

Glebe Farm

HOSE LA

5

Castle View

Highfield Farm

28

LE14

Hall Farm

4

HICKLING LA

WATER LA

PAGET'S END

EAST END

PH

Barkers Farm

BARKERS FIELD LA

SCHOOL LA

THE SANDS

PO

West End Farm

CHURCH LA

Long Clawson CE Prim Sch

BACK LA

MILL LA

3

Long Clawson

HOLLYTREE LA

STOKES PADDOCK

WEST END

OLD MANOR FARM

E CLIXTON RISE

27

BROUGHTON LA

Hill Farm

KINGS RD

Cemy

Mill Farm

WALTHAM LA

Brookhill Cottage

2

CORONATION AVE

MELTON RD

SAND PIT LA

Windmill (dis)

Slyborough Hill

Old Mill House

1

Sandpit Farm

26

71 A B 72 C D 73 E F

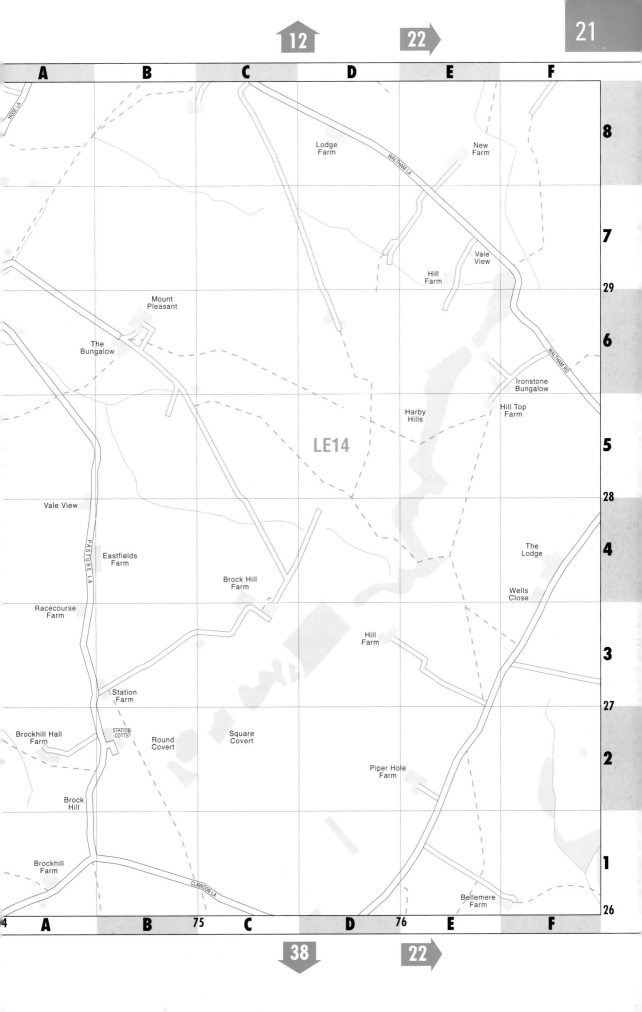

21 13

A　B　C　D　E　F

8

Lodge Farm

Sunnydene

High Leas Farm

Eaton Lodge

Thorn Hills

BELVOIR RD

7

NG32

Cemy

EATON CT

VICARAGE LA

LINGS CL

BLUE PITS LA

CHURCH

PO

MAIN ST

29

Home Farm

STATHERN RD

Eaton

ELM LA

CHAPEL ST

Castlehill Farm

6

Eastwell

MAIN ST

WATER LA

West End Farm

STANLEYS LA

PO

HALL LA

The Old Rectory

WALTHAM LA

SCALFORD RD

The Hall

5

Crossroads Farm Mus

Hall Farm

Glebe Farm

28

WALTHAM RD

4

LE14

White Lodge

Green Lodge

GREEN LA

STATION RD

3

27

2

Manor Farm

TOWNS LA

Goadby Marwood

The Hall

KEMP LA

MAIN ST

1

Goadby Hall Farm

WYCOMB LA

PO

26

21 39

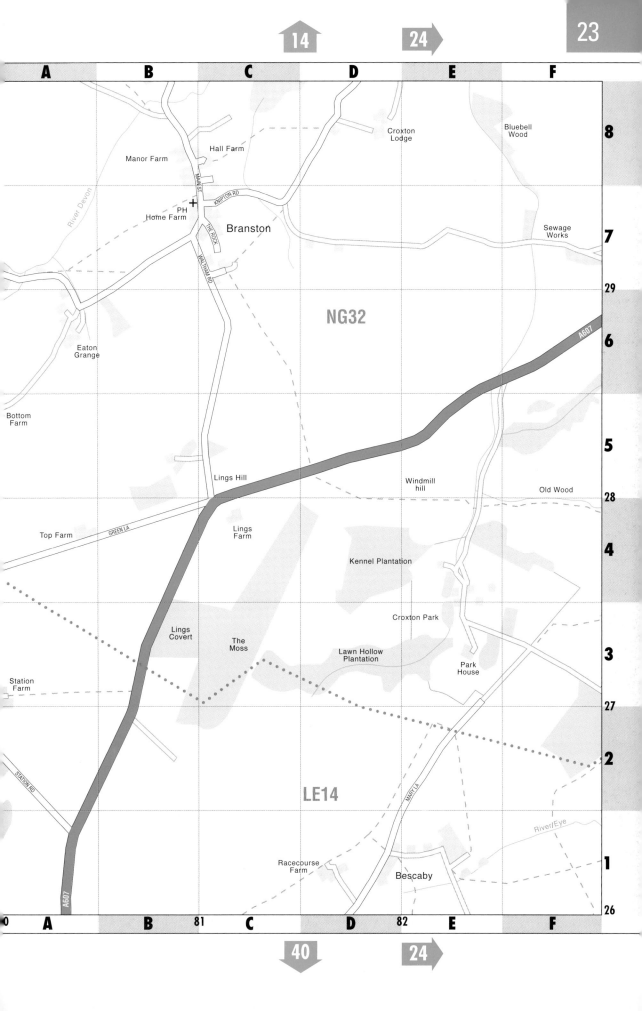

A **B** **C** **D** **E** **F**

8

Croxton
Lodge

Bluebell
Wood

Manor Farm

Hall Farm

MAIN ST

KNIPTON RD

PH
Home Farm

Branston

7

Sewage
Works

River Devon

THE ROCK

WALTHAM RD

29

NG32

A607

6

Eaton
Grange

Bottom
Farm

5

Lings Hill

Windmill
hill

Old Wood

28

Top Farm

GREEN LA

Lings
Farm

4

Kennel Plantation

Lings
Covert

The
Moss

Croxton Park

Lawn Hollow
Plantation

Park
House

3

Station
Farm

27

2

STATION RD

LE14

MARY LA

River Eye

A607

1

Racecourse
Farm

Bescaby

26

A B C D E F

8

Coneygear Wood

A607

+ Croxton Kerrial

CHURCH LA

CHAPEL LA

MIDDLE ST

THORPES LA

TOP RD

7

+

Croxton Kerrial CE Prim Sch

SCHOOL LA

MAIN ST

Inn

PO

SHIRES ORCH

MILL LA

SALTBY RD

HIGHFIELD CRES

THE NOOK

29

THE STACKYARD

A607

Highfields

Tipping Gorse

Tipping Lodge

6

NG32

Heath Farm

5

Barn Lodge Farm

Keeper's Cottage

28

4

Swallow Hole Covert

Swallow Hole Farm

CROXTON RD

3

Saltby Lodge

27

LE14

2

Bescaby Oaks

River Eye

Joey's Wood

Church Farm

Lower Farm

MAIN ST

THE BUTTS

+

Saltby

+

PH

THE CRESCENT

BACK ST

Hawthorn Farm

1

STONESBY RD

Dairy Farm

Chalybeate Spring

Cherry Tree Farm

26

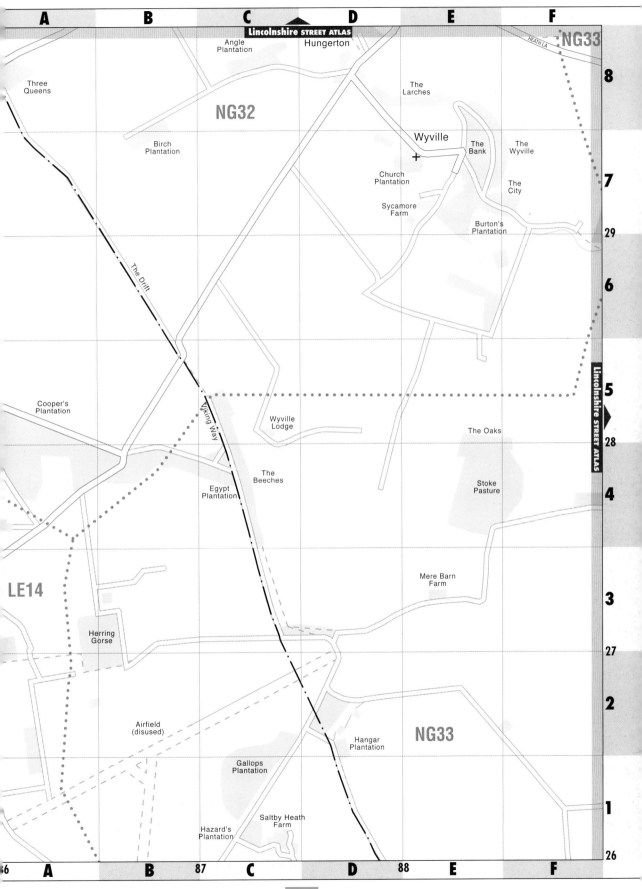

NG33

A   B   C   D   E   F

Angle
Plantation

Hungerton

HEATH LA

Three
Queens

NG32

The
Larches

8

Wyville

The
Bank

The
Wyville

Birch
Plantation

Church
Plantation

The
City

7

Sycamore
Farm

Burton's
Plantation

29

The Drift

6

Lincolnshire STREET ATLAS

5

Cooper's
Plantation

Viking Way

Wyville
Lodge

The Oaks

28

The
Beeches

Egypt
Plantation

Stoke
Pasture

4

LE14

Mere Barn
Farm

3

Herring
Gorse

27

2

Airfield
(disused)

NG33

Hangar
Plantation

Gallops
Plantation

1

Hazard's
Plantation

Saltby Heath
Farm

26

A   B   87   C   D   88   E   F

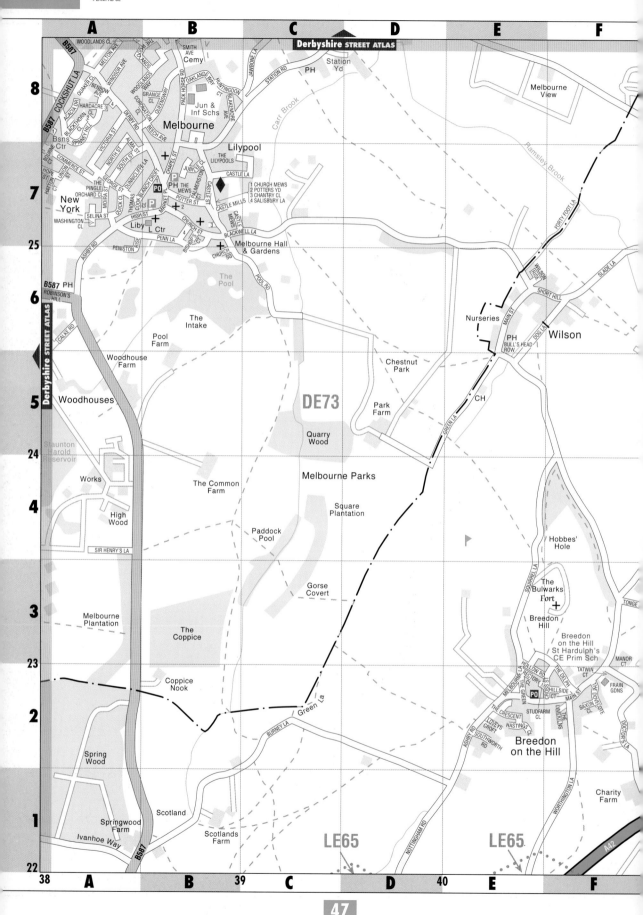

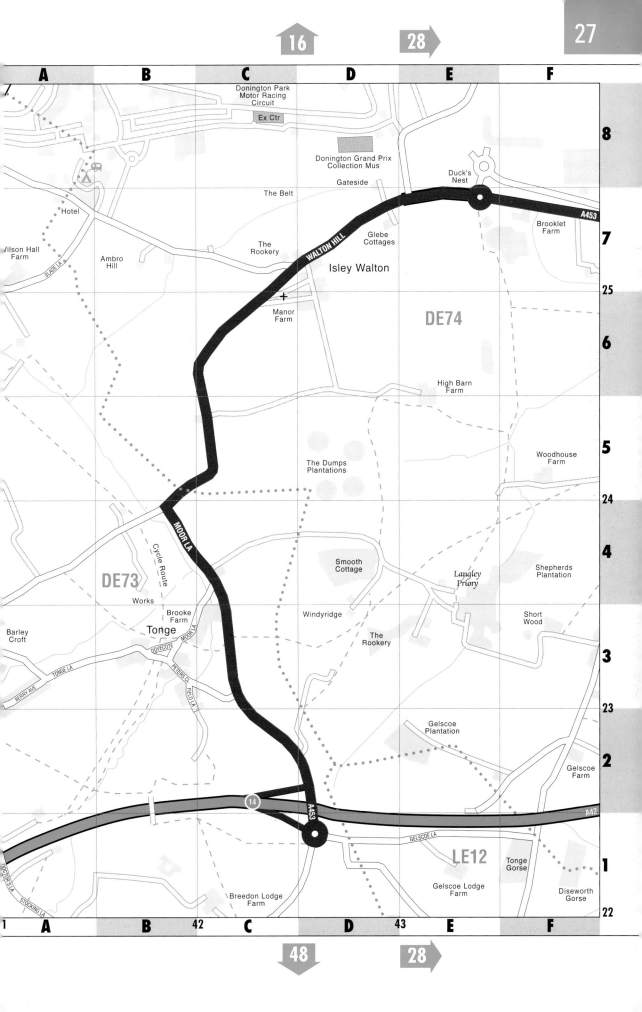

A   B   C   D   E   F

8
7
25
6
5
24
4
23
2
1
22

1   A   B   42   C   D   43   E   F

Donington Park
Motor Racing
Circuit
Ex Ctr
Donington Grand Prix
Collection Mus
Gateside
Duck's
Nest
The Belt
Hotel
Brooklet
Farm
A453
Wilson Hall
Farm
The Rookery
Glebe
Cottages
WALTON HILL
Ambro
Hill
SLADE LA
Isley Walton
DE74
Manor
Farm
High Barn
Farm
Woodhouse
Farm
The Dumps
Plantations
MOOR LA
Cycle Route
DE73
Smooth
Cottage
Langley
Priory
Shepherds
Plantation
Works
Windyridge
Short
Wood
Barley
Croft
Brooke
Farm
Tonge
MOOR LA
The
Rookery
DOVECOTE
TONGE LA
BERRY AVE
PETERS CL
FIELD LA
Gelscoe
Plantation
Gelscoe
Farm
14
A453
A42
GELSCOE LA
LE12
Tonge
Gorse
DOCTORS LA
STOCKING LA
Breedon Lodge
Farm
Gelscoe Lodge
Farm
Diseworth
Gorse

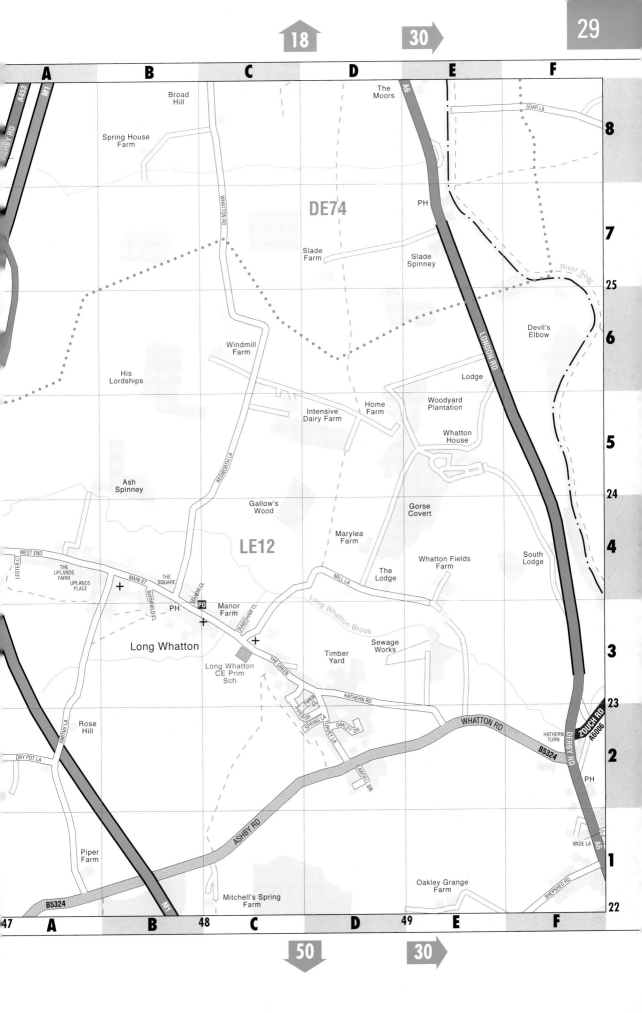

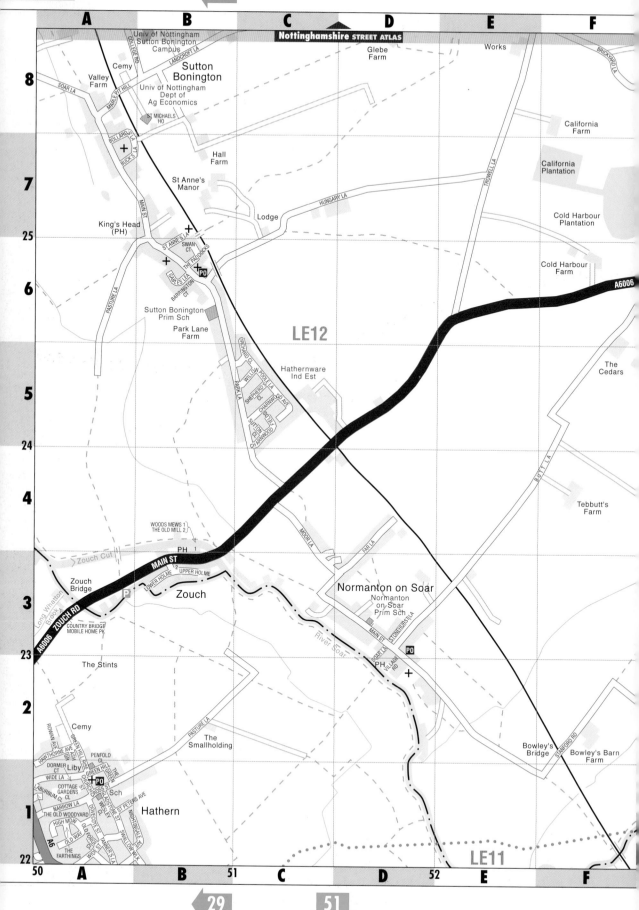

Nottinghamshire STREET ATLAS

Univ of Nottingham
Sutton Bonington Campus
COLLEGE RD
LANDCROFT LA
Glebe
Farm
Works
BRICKYARD LA

Cemy
Valley
Farm
SOAR LA
Sutton
Bonington
California
Farm

Univ of Nottingham
Dept of
Ag Economics
ST MICHAELS HO
BOLLARD LA
BUCK'S LA
MAPLE PIT HILL
MAIN ST

Hall
Farm
California
Plantation
TROWELL LA

St Anne's
Manor
HUNGARY LA
Cold Harbour
Plantation

King's Head
(PH)
ST ANNE'S LA
SWAN CT
THE PADDOCKS
GABLE'S LEA
BARRINGTON CT
PO
Lodge

Cold Harbour
Farm
A6006

Sutton Bonington
Prim Sch
Park Lane
Farm
PASTURE LA
ORCHARD CL
WILLOW POOLE LA
SHEPHERD CL
PARK LA
CHARNWOOD AVE
SUTTON CL
CHARNWOOD

LE12

Hathernware
Ind Est
The
Cedars

BUTT LA

Tebbutt's
Farm

WOODS MEWS 1
THE OLD MILL 2
PH
MAIN ST
LOWER HOLME
UPPER HOLME
MOOR LA
FAR LA

Zouch
Bridge
P
Zouch
COUNTRY BRIDGE
MOBILE HOME PK
LONG WHATTON BROOK
A6006 ZOUCH RD
Normanton on Soar
Normanton
on Soar
Prim Sch
MAIN ST
STONEHURST LA
PO

River Soar
SOAR LA
VILLAGE RD
PH

The Stints

STANFORD RD
Bowley's
Bridge
Bowley's Barn
Farm

Cemy
PASTURE LA
The
Smallholding

ROWAN AVE
HANTHORNE AVE
ASH GR
GREEN HILL RISE
PENFOLD CL
DORMER CT
THE GREEN
WIDE LA
LABURNUM CL
Liby
PO
Sch
COTTAGE GARDENS
GREEN ST
ST AUSTINS DR
WESLEY ST
ST PETERS AVE

NARROW LA
THE OLD WOODYARD
HIGH MDW
OLD WAY
DOVECOTE ST
OLD FORGE LA
NIGHTINGALE AVE
SWALLOW WLK
TANNERS LA
A6
THE FARTHINGS
Hathern

LE11

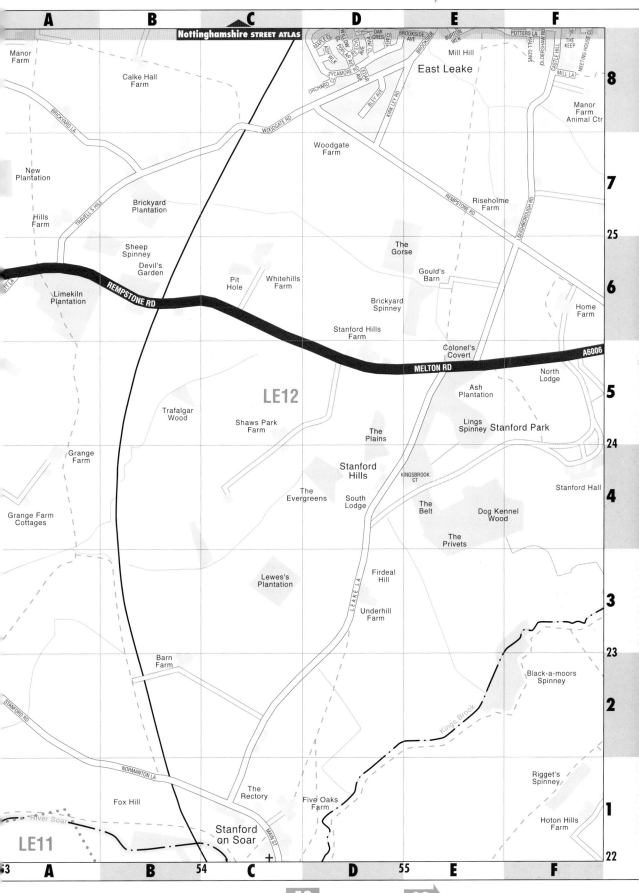

Nottinghamshire STREET ATLAS

A   B   C   D   E   F

East Leake

Manor Farm

Calke Hall Farm

Mill Hill

Manor Farm Animal Ctr

New Plantation

Woodgate Farm

Riseholme Farm

Hills Farm

Brickyard Plantation

Sheep Spinney

Devil's Garden

The Gorse

Gould's Barn

Pit Hole

Whitehills Farm

Brickyard Spinney

Home Farm

Limekiln Plantation

REMPSTONE RD

Stanford Hills Farm

Colonel's Covert

MELTON RD

A6006

North Lodge

LE12

Trafalgar Wood

Shaws Park Farm

Ash Plantation

Grange Farm

The Plains

Lings Spinney

Stanford Park

Stanford Hall

Stanford Hills

KINGSBROOK CT

Grange Farm Cottages

The Evergreens

South Lodge

The Belt

Dog Kennel Wood

The Privets

Lewes's Plantation

Firdeal Hill

LEAKE LA

Underhill Farm

Black-a-moors Spinney

Barn Farm

Kings Brook

STANFORD RD

Rigget's Spinney

NORMANTON LA

The Rectory

Fox Hill

MAIN ST

Five Oaks Farm

Hoton Hills Farm

River Soar

Stanford on Soar

LE11

8
7
25
6
5
24
4
3
23
2
1
22

53   54   55

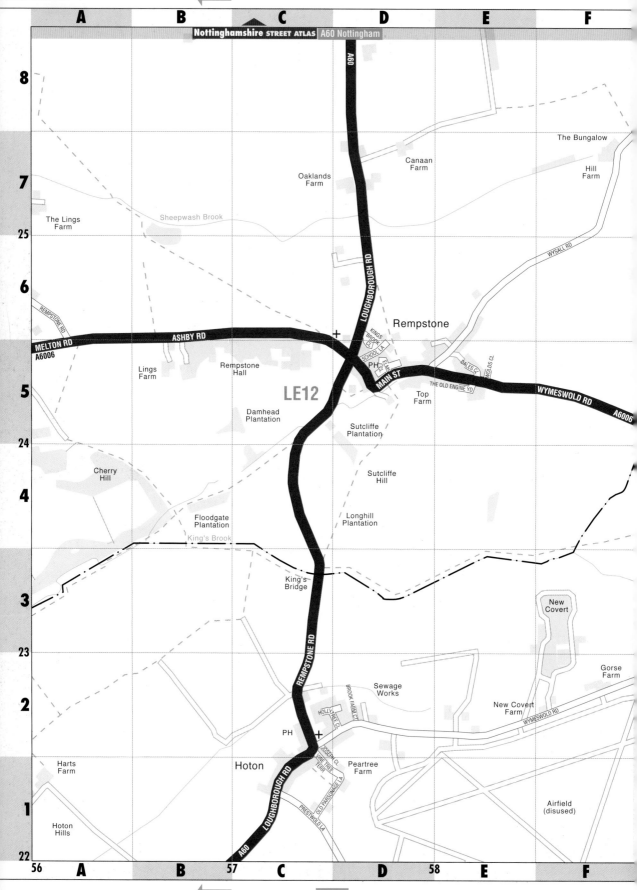

Nottinghamshire STREET ATLAS A60 Nottingham

A B C D E F

8
7
25
6

REMPSTONE RD
MELTON RD
A6006
ASHBY RD

LOUGHBOROUGH RD

Rempstone

KINGS
BROOK
CL
SCHOOL LA
PH
MAIN ST

DALES CL
COTSWOLDS CL
THE OLD ENGINE YD
WYMESWOLD RD
A6006

The Bungalow
Hill Farm
Canaan Farm
Oaklands Farm
Sheepwash Brook
The Lings Farm

WYSALL RD

Lings Farm
Rempstone Hall

LE12

Damhead Plantation
Sutcliffe Plantation
Top Farm

5
24
4

Cherry Hill

Floodgate Plantation
King's Brook
Sutcliffe Hill
Longhill Plantation

New Covert

3
23

King's Bridge

REMPSTONE RD

Gorse Farm

2

BROOK FARM CT
HOLLY TREE CL
PH
JOSEPH CL
LIME TREE TERR
OLD PARSONAGE LA
PRESTWOLD LA

Sewage Works
Peartree Farm
New Covert Farm
WYMESWOLD RD

1

Hoton

Harts Farm
Hoton Hills

LOUGHBOROUGH RD
A60

Airfield (disused)

22
56 A 57 B C 58 D E F

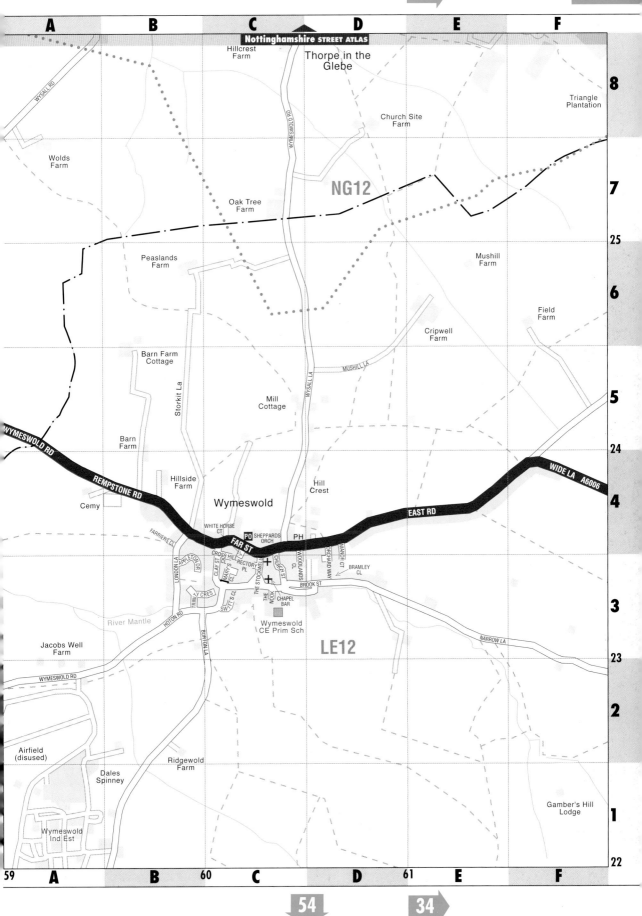

A B C D E F

Hillcrest Farm

Thorpe in the Glebe

8

Triangle Plantation

Church Site Farm

WYSALL RD

Wolds Farm

NG12

7

25

Oak Tree Farm

Mushill Farm

6

Peaslands Farm

Field Farm

Cripwell Farm

Barn Farm Cottage

Storkit La

WYSALL LA

MUSHILL LA

5

Mill Cottage

Barn Farm

24

WYMESWOLD RD

WIDE LA A6006

REMPSTONE RD

Hillside Farm

Hill Crest

EAST RD

4

Wymeswold

Cemy

FARRIERS CL

WHITE HORSE CT

PO SHEPPARDS ORCH

PH

FAR ST

LONDON LA

APPLETON DR

CROSS HILL

RECTORY PL

CLAY ST CL

MARY'S CL

THE STOCKWELL

CHURCH ST

WOODLANDS CL

ORCHARD WAY

MANOR CT

BRAMLEY CL

BROOK ST

TRINITY CRES

SW

ST'S CL

THE NOOK

CHAPEL BAR

3

HOTON RD

BURTON LA

River Mantle

Wymeswold CE Prim Sch

NARROW LA

23

Jacobs Well Farm

LE12

WYMESWOLD RD

2

Airfield (disused)

Ridgewold Farm

Dales Spinney

Gamber's Hill Lodge

1

Wymeswold Ind Est

22

59 A B 60 C D 61 E F

Nottinghamshire STREET ATLAS

NG12

Eelpool
Field

Willoughby-on-the-Wolds

WIDMERPOOL LA

MILL LA

FIELDS FARM
CL

CROSS HILL

MANOR CT

CHURCH LA

NEW
ROW

BAILEY'S
CROFT

HOLME
FARM
CL

PO

Old Hall
Farm

MAIN ST

Bryans La

Willoughby
Prim Sch

BROOK FARM
CT

Green La

CHAPEL LA

LONDON LA

Willoughby
Gorse

WEST THORPE

BACK LA

Midshires Way

Barrack
Cottages

OCCUPATION LA

Turnpost
Farm

A46

Kingston Brook

HARE'S LA

Dungehill
Farm

A6006

LE14

LE12

Lakeside

Eller's
Gorse

Hill
Farm

WIDE LA

Ella's Farm

Pasture
Lodge

Highthorn
Farm

Common
Farm

NARROW LA

Willoughby Fields
Farm

PADDY'S LA

A6006

Wymeswold
Lodge

A46

LE14

Wolds
Farm

The
Lodge

A   B   C   D   E   F

Manor Barn Farm

Manor Farm

STATION RD

Brookside Cottage

Top Cottage

Depot

Hotel

Fairham Brook

Dalby Brook

Longridge

Wad House Farm

Spruce Haven

NOTTINGHAM LA

Longcliff Hill

Midshires Way

North Lodge Farm

North Lodge

Old Dalby CE Prim Sch

STATION RD

Beazley's Farm

Dalby Lodges

LE14

LONGCLIFF HILL

HAWTHORN CL

LONGCLIFE CL

CROFT CLOS

Cemy

Vale View Farm

DERDALE HILL

PH

CHAPEL LA

PO

MAIN RD

PARADISE LA

Old Dalby

THE GREEN

CHURCH LA

Wood's Hill

WOOD HILL

Hall

Fishpond Plantation

Woodhill Farm

Woodhill Ind Est

Hall Plantation

Lawn Farm

Hill Top Farm

Old Dalby Wood

Upper Grange Farm

Old Dalby Lodge

Yard Farm

LAWN LA

Wavendon Grange

Grange Cottages

GIBSON'S LA

Old Dalby Grange

Bridgets Covert

PADDY'S LA

A6006

Lower Grange Farm

Lodge Farm

SIX HILLS LA

Dalby Wolds

8

7

25

6

5

24

4

3

23

2

1

22

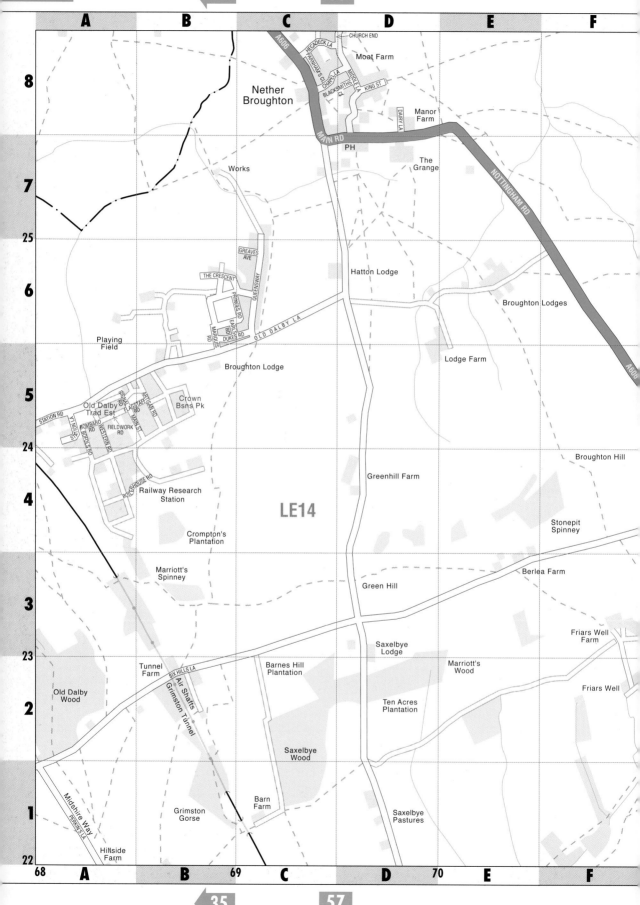

A B C D E F

8

Nether
Broughton

CHURCH END
Moat Farm
HECADECK LA
HARBURY'S CL
CHAPEL LA
MIDDLE LA
KING ST
BLACKSMITHS CL
DAIRY LA

Manor
Farm

MAIN RD
A606
PH
7

Works
The Grange

NOTTINGHAM RD
25

GREAVES AVE
Hatton Lodge

6
THE CRESCENT
QUEENSWAY
PRINCES RD
Broughton Lodges

Playing
Field
EARLS RD
MARQUIS RD
DUKES RD
OLD DALBY LA
Lodge Farm

A606

Broughton Lodge

5
SCHOOL RD
ARTISAN RD
FLAGSTAFF RD
MAIN ST
Old Dalby
Trad Est
Crown
Bsns Pk

STATION RD
BOMBARD RD
FIELDWORK RD
WESTERN RD
Broughton Hill

24
BOILS RD

Greenhill Farm

4
BOILSHOUSE RD
Railway Research
Station

LE14
Stonepit
Spinney

Crompton's
Plantation

Marriott's
Spinney
Green Hill
Berlea Farm

3
Friars Well
Farm

23
Tunnel
Farm
SIX HILLS LA
Barnes Hill
Plantation
Saxelbye
Lodge
Marriott's
Wood
Friars Well

Air Shafts
Grimston Tunnel
Old Dalby
Wood

2
Ten Acres
Plantation

Saxelbye
Wood

Barn
Farm
MIDSHIRE WAY
Grimston
Gorse

1
Saxelbye
Pastures

PERKINS LA
Hillside
Farm

22
68
A B 69 C D 70 E F

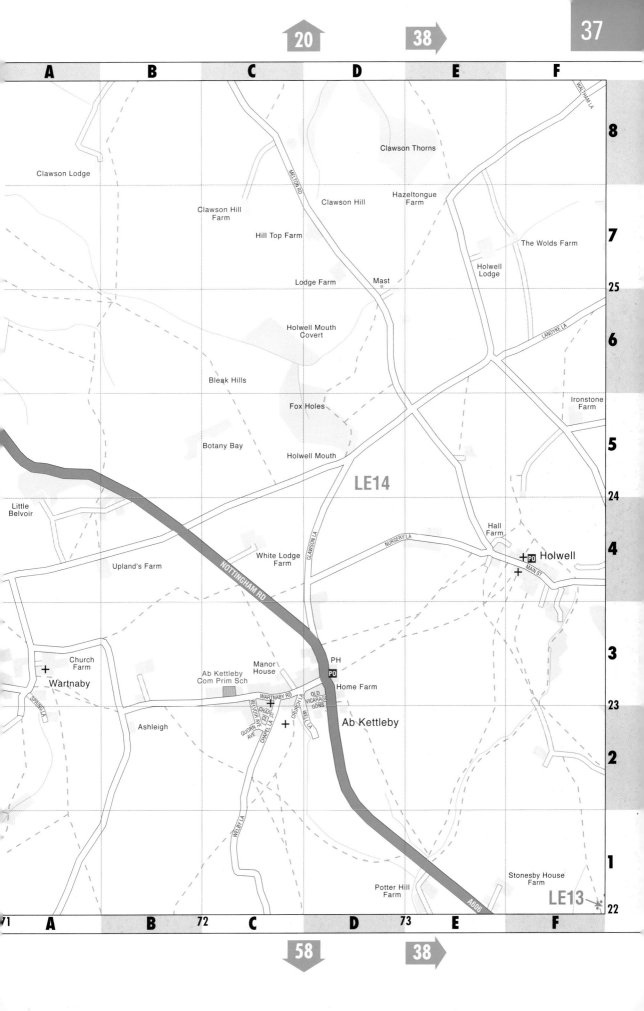

20
38

A B C D E F

8

Clawson Thorns

Clawson Lodge

Hazeltongue
Farm

Clawson Hill
Farm

Clawson Hill

7

Hill Top Farm

The Wolds Farm

Holwell
Lodge

Lodge Farm   Mast

25

WALTHAM LA

MELTON RD

LANDYKE LA

6

Holwell Mouth
Covert

Bleak Hills

Ironstone
Farm

Fox Holes

Botany Bay

5

Holwell Mouth

LE14

24

Little
Belvoir

Hall
Farm

Holwell

White Lodge
Farm

NURSERY LA

PO

4

Upland's Farm

NOTTINGHAM RD

CLAWSON LA

MAIN ST

3

Church
Farm

Manor
House

PH

Wartnaby

Ab Kettleby
Com Prim Sch

PO

Home Farm

23

SPRING LA

WARTNABY RD

OLD
VICARAGE
GDNS

Ashleigh

CHAPEL
CL

CHURCH LA

WELL LA

Ab Kettleby

BELVOIR AVE

QUORN
AVE

CHAPEL LA

2

WELBY LA

1

Stonesby House
Farm

Potter Hill
Farm

LE13

A606

22

58
38

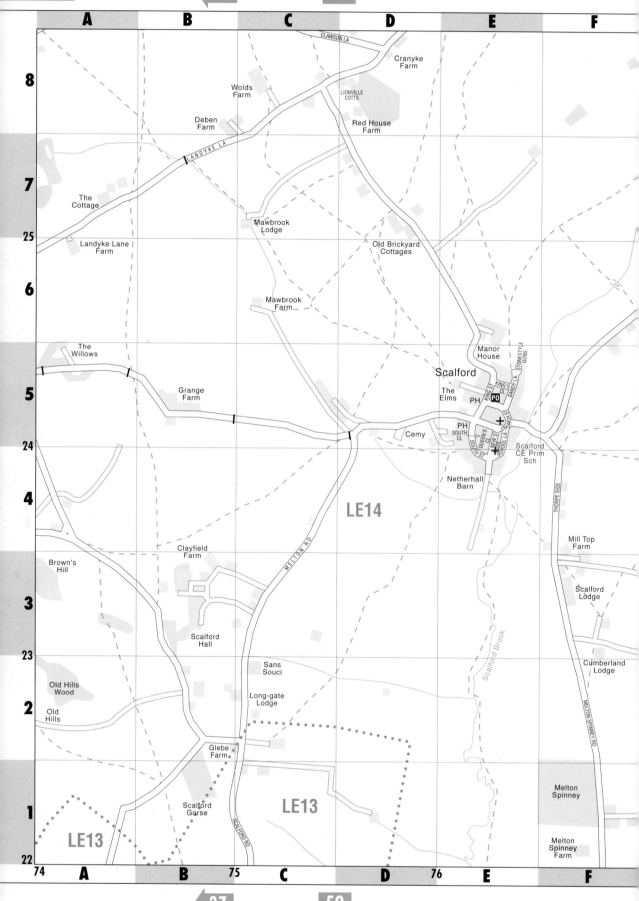

A B C D E F

8

CLAWSON LA

Cranyke
Farm

Wolds
Farm

LIONVILLE
COTTS

Deben
Farm

Red House
Farm

LANDYKE LA

7

The
Cottage

25

Mawbrook
Lodge

Landyke Lane
Farm

Old Brickyard
Cottages

6

Mawbrook
Farm

The
Willows

Manor
House

STONESTYLE
GDNS

Scalford

5

Grange
Farm

The
Elms

PH

KING'S CL

KING ST

SANDY LA

PO

Cemy

PH
SOUTH
CL

24

QUEEN'S
CL

NEW ST

SCHOOL LA

CHURCH ST

SOUTH ST

Scalford
CE Prim
Sch

THORPE SIDE

Netherhall
Barn

4

LE14

Mill Top
Farm

Brown's
Hill

Clayfield
Farm

Scalford
Lodge

3

Scalford
Brook

Scalford
Hall

23

Sans
Souci

Cumberland
Lodge

Old Hills
Wood

Long-gate
Lodge

MELTON SPINNEY RD

Old
Hills

2

Melton
Spinney

Glebe
Farm

1

Scalford
Gorse

LE13

SCALFORD RD

MELTON RD

LE13

59

Melton
Spinney
Farm

22

74 A B 75 C D 76 E F

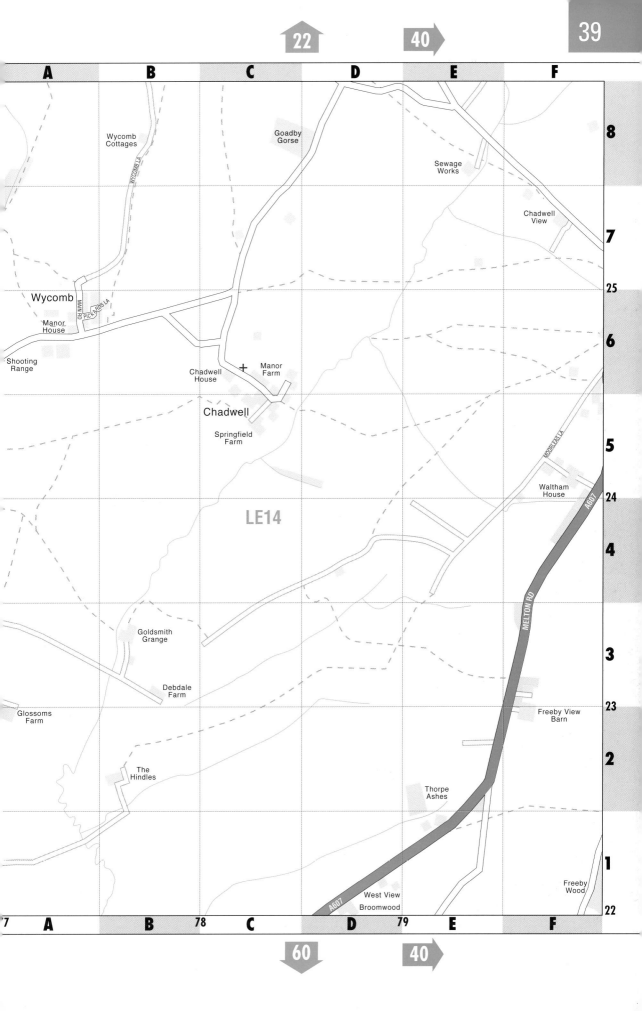

A   B   C   D   E   F

8

7

25

6

5

24

4

3

23

2

1

22

Wycomb
Cottages

Goadby
Gorse

Sewage
Works

Chadwell
View

Wycomb

Manor
House

Shooting
Range

Chadwell
House

Manor
Farm

Chadwell

Springfield
Farm

LE14

Waltham
House

Goldsmith
Grange

Debdale
Farm

Glossoms
Farm

Freeby View
Barn

The
Hindles

Thorpe
Ashes

West View
Broomwood

Freeby
Wood

MAIN RD

WYCOMB LA

PICKARDS LA

MOORLEAS LA

A607

MELTON RD

A607

7   A   B   78   C   D   79   E   F

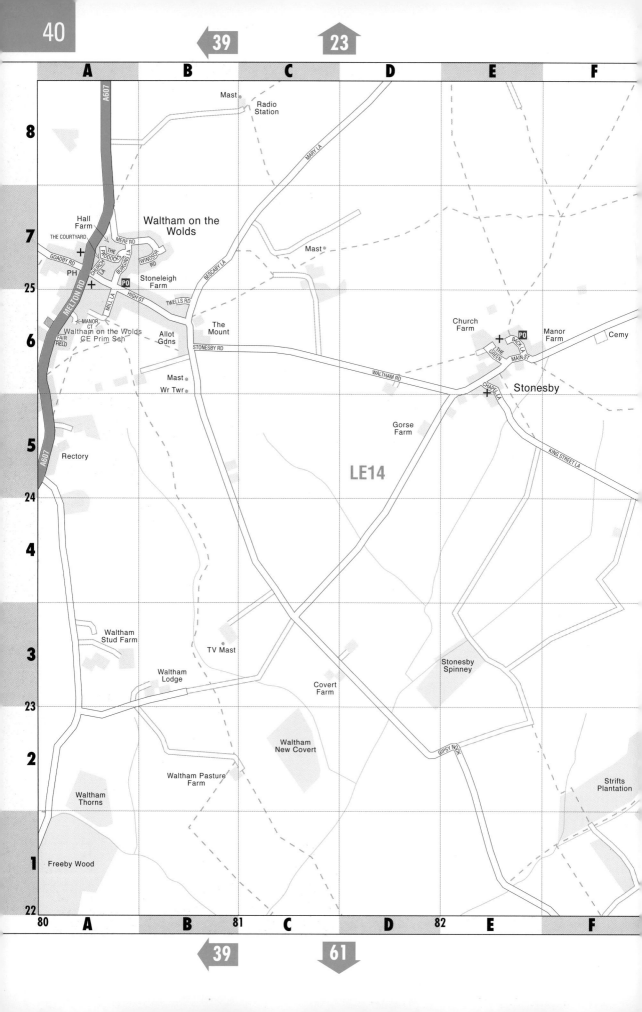

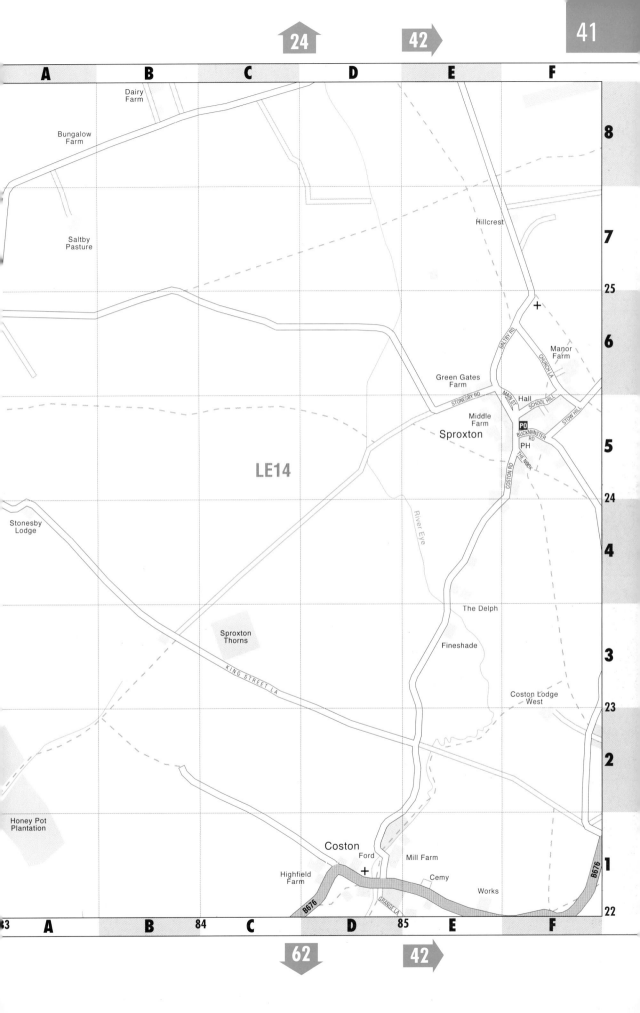

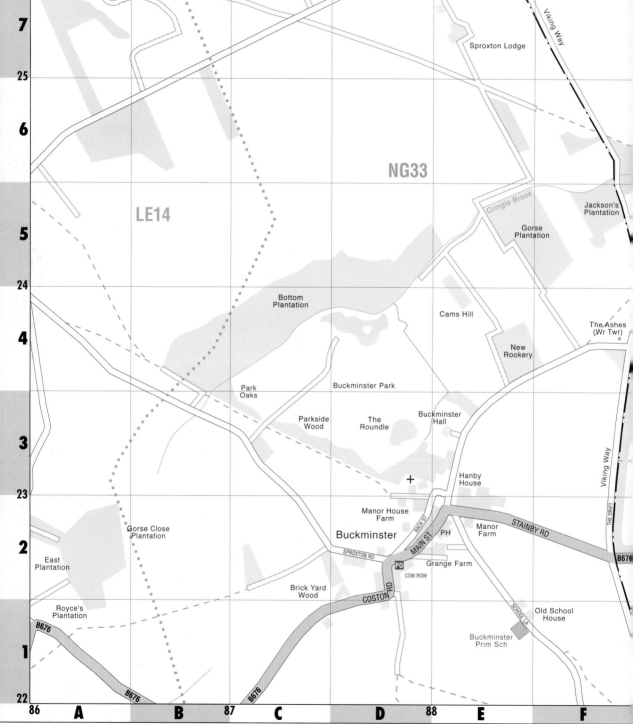

	A	B	C	D	E	F

8

Annises Plantation

7

25

Sproxton Lodge

Viking Way

6

NG33

LE14

Cringle Brook

Jackson's Plantation

5

Gorse Plantation

24

Bottom Plantation

Cams Hill

4

New Rookery

The Ashes (Wr Twr)

Park Oaks

Buckminster Park

Parkside Wood

The Roundle

Buckminster Hall

3

Hanby House

23

Manor House Farm

Buckminster

BACK ST

MAIN ST

PH

Manor Farm

STAINBY RD

Viking Way

THE DRIFT

2

East Plantation

Gorse Close Plantation

SPROXTON RD

PO

COW ROW

Grange Farm

B676

Brick Yard Wood

COSTON RD

SCHOOL LA

Old School House

Royce's Plantation

B676

Buckminster Prim Sch

1

B676

B676

22

86	A	B	87	C	D	88	E	F

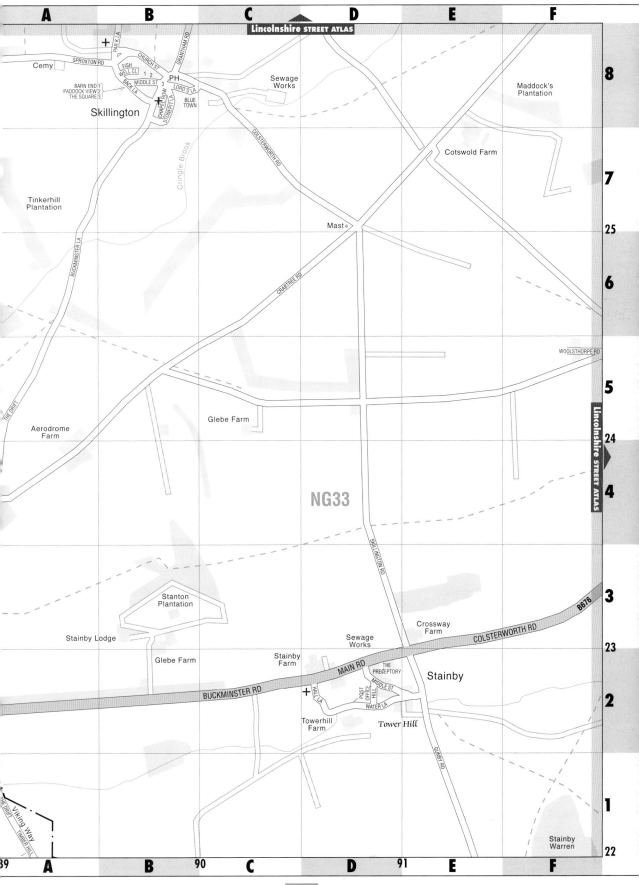

Cemy

SPROXTON RD

PAR K LA

CHURCH ST

GRANTHAM RD

FISH WELL CL

1 2

MIDDLE ST

BACK LA

PH

LORD S LA

CHAPEL ROW

STONEPIT LA

BLUE TOWN

BARN END 1
PADDOCK VIEW 2
THE SQUARE 3

3

Skillington

Sewage Works

Maddock's Plantation

COLSTERWORTH RD

Cotswold Farm

Tinkerhill Plantation

Cringle Brook

BUCKMINSTER LA

Mast

CRABTREE RD

WOOLSTHORPE RD

THE DRIFT

Aerodrome Farm

Glebe Farm

NG33

SKILLINGTON RD

Stanton Plantation

B676

Stainby Lodge

Crossway Farm

COLSTERWORTH RD

Glebe Farm

Stainby Farm

Sewage Works

MAIN RD

THE PRECEPTORY

Stainby

HALL LA

POST OFFICE

MIDDLE ST

HILL

BUCKMINSTER RD

WATER LA

Towerhill Farm

Tower Hill

GUNBY RD

THE DRIFT

Viking Way

TIMBER HILL

Stainby Warren

64

39   A   B   90   C   D   91   E   F

A   B   C   D   E   F

8   7   25   6   5   24   4   3   23   2   1   22

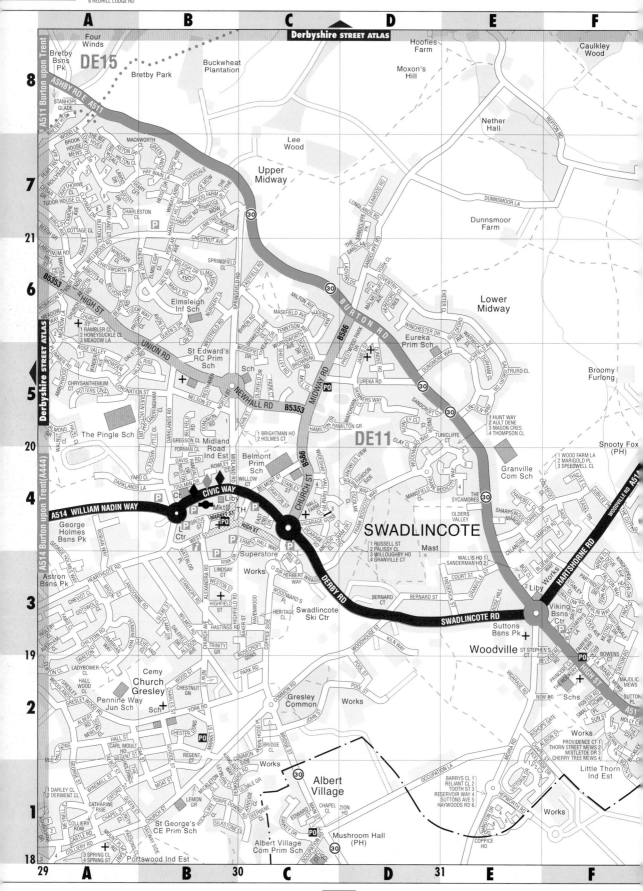

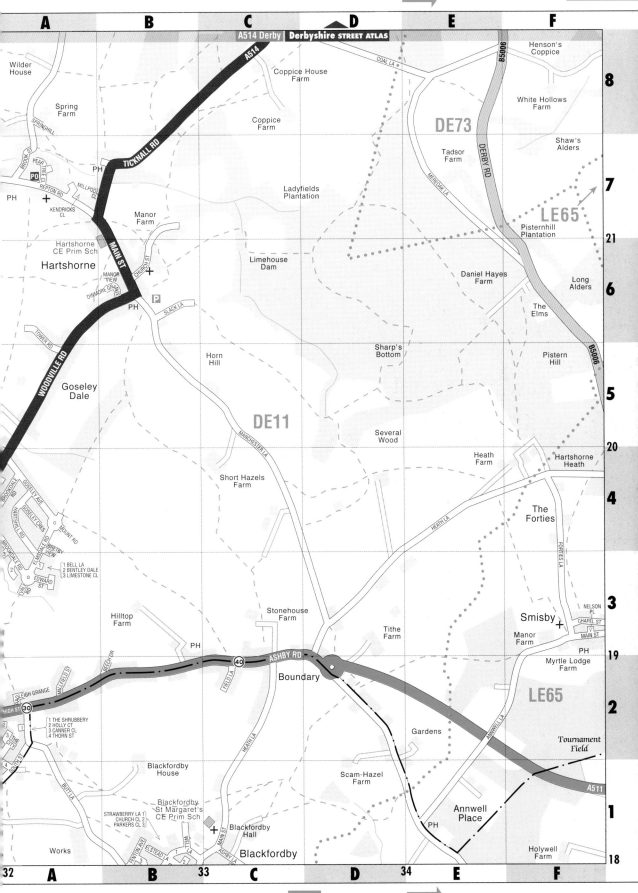

A   B   C   D   E   F

8
7
21
6
5
20
4
3
19
2
1
18

DE73

LE65

DE11

LE65

Wilder House
Spring Farm
SPRINGHILL
BROOK ST
PEAR TREE CL
PO
REPTON RD
MILLPOOL CL
PH
KENDRICKS CL
Hartshorne CE Prim Sch
Hartshorne
MANOR VIEW
DINMORE GRANGE
MAIN ST
CHURCH ST
PH
P
SLACK LA
TICKNALL RD
A514

Coppice House Farm
Coppice Farm
Ladyfields Plantation
Manor Farm
Limehouse Dam
Horn Hill

COAL LA
B5006
DERBY RD
Henson's Coppice
White Hollows Farm
Tadsor Farm
MEROAK LA
Shaw's Alders
Pisternhill Plantation
Daniel Hayes Farm
Long Alders
The Elms
Pistern Hill
B5006

WOODVILLE RD
TOWER RD
Goseley Dale
MANCHESTER LA
Short Hazels Farm

Sharp's Bottom
Several Wood
Heath Farm
Hartshorne Heath

GOSELEY AVE
GOSELEY CRES
HARTSHILL RD
MOUNT RD
BROOKDALE RD
VALE RD
ELMSDALE RD
LIBRETBY VIEW
EDWARD ST
1 BELL LA
2 BENTLEY DALE
3 LIMESTONE CL

HEATH LA
The Forties
FORTIES LA

Hilltop Farm
BEECH DR
MILLFIELD ST
PH
FIELD LA
ASHBY RD
40
Boundary

Stonehouse Farm
Tithe Farm
Manor Farm
Smisby
NELSON PL
CHAPEL ST
MAIN ST
PH
Myrtle Lodge Farm

HIGH ST
30
PAX LEIGH GRANGE
1 THE SHRUBBERY
2 HOLLY CT
3 CANNER CL
4 THORN ST
3
2
1 THE CITY
SOUTH ST
BUTT LA
Blackfordby House
PENTON AVE
ELSTEAD LA
STRAWBERRY LA 1
CHURCH CL 2
PARKERS CL 3
Blackfordby St Margaret's CE Prim Sch
WELL LA
MAIN ST
ASHBY LA
Blackfordby Hall
Blackfordby
Works

HEATH LA
Gardens
ANNWELL LA
Scam-Hazel Farm
PH
Annwell Place
Tournament Field
A511
Holywell Farm

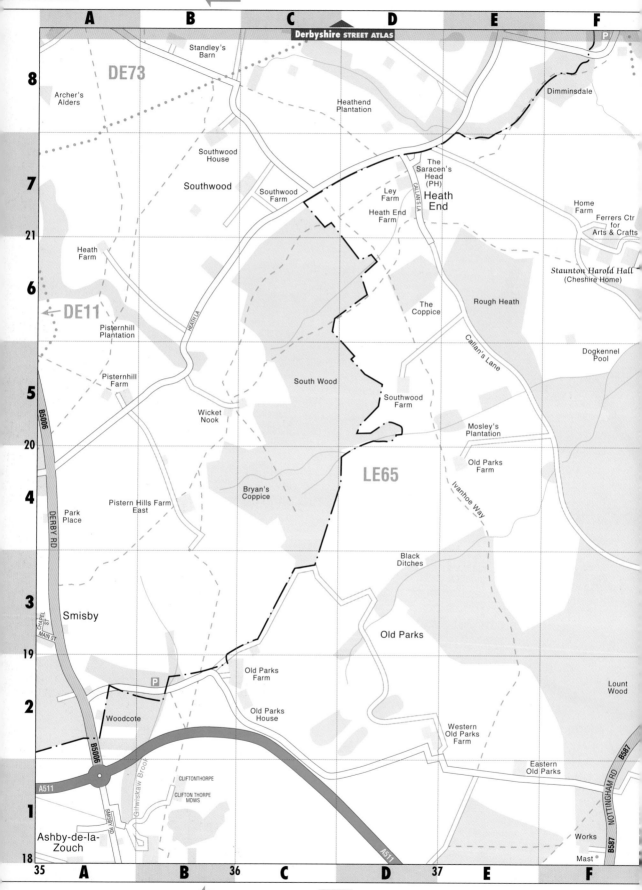

A   B   C   D   E   F

P

8

DE73

Standley's Barn

Archer's Alders

Heathend Plantation

Dimminsdale

Southwood House

7

Southwood

The Saracen's Head (PH)

Heath End

Southwood Farm

Ley Farm

Home Farm

Ferrers Ctr for Arts & Crafts

21

Heath End Farm

CALLAN'S LA

Heath Farm

Staunton Harold Hall (Cheshire Home)

6

DE11 ←

The Coppice

Rough Heath

Pisternhill Plantation

HEATH LA

Callan's Lane

Dogkennel Pool

Pisternhill Farm

South Wood

Southwood Farm

5

Wicket Nook

Mosley's Plantation

20

Old Parks Farm

LE65

Ivanhoe Way

4

Pistern Hills Farm East

Bryan's Coppice

Park Place

Black Ditches

B5006

3

Smisby

Old Parks

CHAPEL ST

MAIN ST

19

DERBY RD

Old Parks Farm

P

2

Woodcote

Old Parks House

Western Old Parks Farm

Lount Wood

NOTTINGHAM RD

B5006

SMISBY RD

Chwiskaw Brook

Eastern Old Parks

B587

A511

1

CLIFTONTHORPE

CLIFTON THORPE MDWS

A511

Works

Mast

B587

18

Ashby-de-la-Zouch

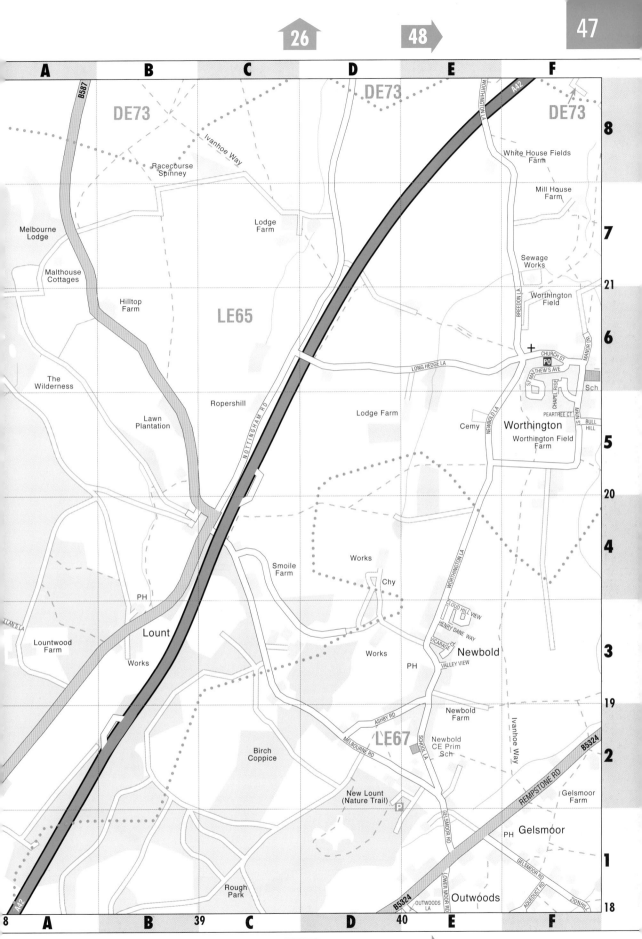

A B C D E F

8

DE73

Racecourse Spinney

Ivanhoe Way

DE73

White House Fields Farm

Mill House Farm

7

Melbourne Lodge

Lodge Farm

Sewage Works

21

Malthouse Cottages

Worthington Field

6

Hilltop Farm

LE65

BREEDON LA

WORTHINGTON LA

A42

LONG HEDGE LA

CHURCH ST
PO

ST MATTHEW'S AVE

MANOR DR

Sch

The Wilderness

Ropershill

Lodge Farm

CHAPEL RISE

NEWBOLD LA

PEARTREE CT

MAIN ST

BULL HILL

Worthington

Lawn Plantation

NOTTINGHAM RD

Cemy

Worthington Field Farm

5

20

Smoile Farm

Works

Chy

WORTHINGTON LA

4

ALLAN'S LA

PH

Lount

Works

CLOUD HILL VIEW

HENRY DANE WAY

VICARAGE CT

VALLEY VIEW

Newbold

PH

3

19

Lountwood Farm

Works

ASHBY RD

MELBOURNE RD

LE67

SCHOOL LA

Newbold Farm

Newbold CE Prim Sch

Ivanhoe Way

B5324

REMPSTONE RD

Gelsmoor Farm

2

Birch Coppice

New Lount (Nature Trail)
P

GELSMOOR RD

GELSMOOR RD

PH Gelsmoor

A42

LOWER MOOR RD

AQUEDUCT RD

ZION HILL

1

18

Rough Park

B5324 OUTWOODS LA

Outwoods

8 A B 39 C D 40 E F

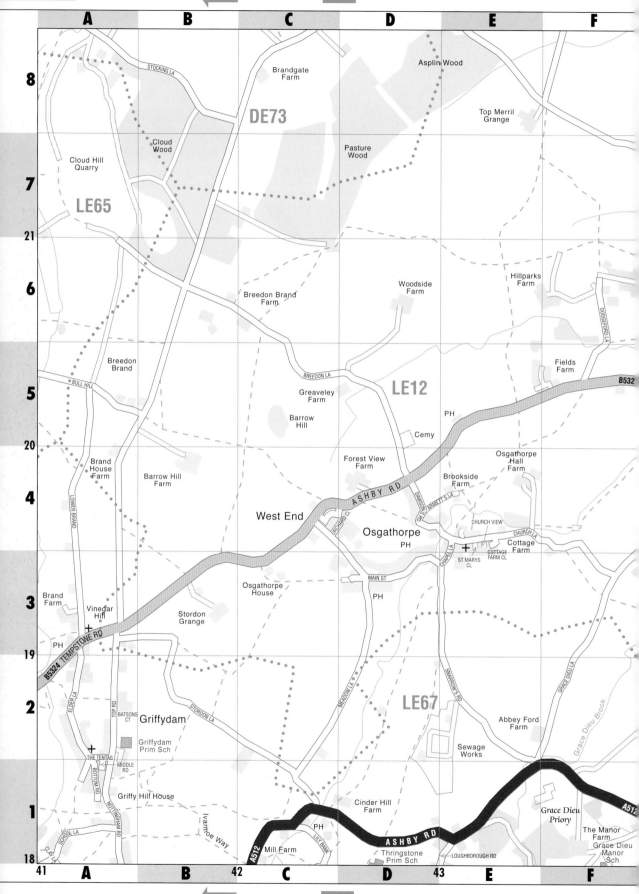

A B C D E F

8

DE73

Brandgate Farm

Asplin Wood

Top Merril Grange

Cloud Wood

7

Cloud Hill Quarry

LE65

Pasture Wood

STOCKING LA

21

Hillparks Farm

6

Breedon Brand Farm

Woodside Farm

DODEFORD LA

Fields Farm

B532

5

Breedon Brand

BULL HILL

BREEDON LA

LE12

Greaveley Farm

Barrow Hill

PH

Cemy

20

Brand House Farm

Barrow Hill Farm

Forest View Farm

Osgathorpe Hall Farm

Brookside Farm

4

LOWER BRAND

West End

ASHBY RD

DAWSONS RD

ARMETT'S LA

CHURCH VIEW

CHURCH LA

Cottage Farm

Osgathorpe

PH

CHAPEL LA

St Marys Cl

Cottage Farm Cl

3

Brand Farm

Vinegar Hill

Osgathorpe House

Stordon Grange

MAIN ST

PH

PH

TEMPSTONE RD

19

B5324

PH

ELDER LA

TOP RD

STORDON LA

MEADOW LA

SNARROW'S RD

LE67

Abbey Ford Farm

GRACE DIEU LA

2

BATSONS CT

Griffydam

Griffydam Prim Sch

Sewage Works

Grace Dieu Brook

THE TENTAS

MIDDLE RD

NOTTINGHAM RD

BOTTOM RD

Griffy Hill House

Cinder Hill Farm

Grace Dieu Priory

A512

1

Ivanhoe Way

LILY BANK

PH

ASHBY RD

The Manor Farm

CLAY LA

SCHOOL LA

Mill Farm

A512

Thringstone Prim Sch

LOUGHBOROUGH RD

Grace Dieu Manor Sch

18

41 A 42 B C 43 D E F

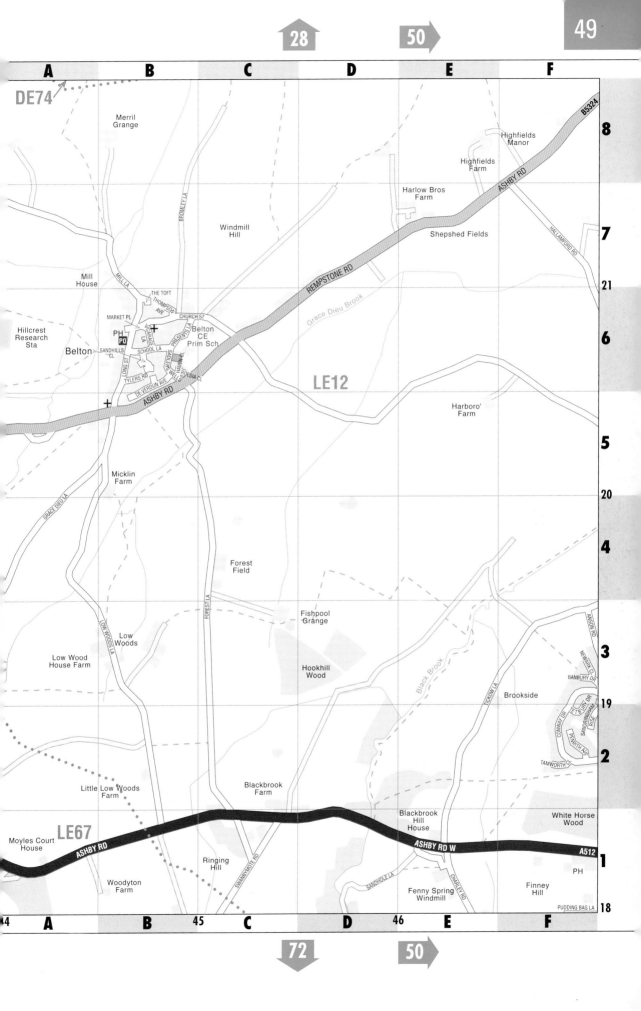

A B C D E F

8

B5324

Piper Wood

Oakley Wood

Hathern Hill

7

Woodlands Farm

Shepshed Fields

Lounds Farm

Bedlam Barn Farm

21

LE12

Shepshed Mill Farm

PEAR-TREE

6

Black Brook

Sewage Works

HALLAMFORD RD

OAKLEY RD

HATHERN RD

HATHERN DR

GOLDEN

5

Tyler-Brigg Farm

1 WOODMANS WAY
2 SHEPHERDS CL
3 PLOUGHMANS DR
4 BLACKSMITHS AVE
5 COACHMANS CT
6 WOODLANDS DR
7 LANSDOWNE AVE

BUTTHOLE LA

Carr Bridge

20

Carr Hill

St Botolph's CE Prim Sch

Hind Leys Com Coll

The Hermitage

SHEPSHED

Bunker Hill

Shepshed High Sch

Liby

4

St Winefride's RC Prim Sch

Bull Ring

Oxley Prim Sch

3

Newcroft Prim Sch

White Lodge

LE11

Home Covert

Temple of Venus

19

THE PARADE

Shepshed Nook

Shortcliff Brook

Oxley Gutter

2

Cemy

Gelders Hall Ind Est

Cow Hill

Ind Est

GELDERS HALL RD

HOLT RISE

BRENDON CL

23

A512

1

A512 ASHBY RD W

ASHBY ROAD CENTRAL

ASHBY RD E

A512

PH

B591

M1

Hurst Farm

18

47 A 48 B C 48 D 49 E F

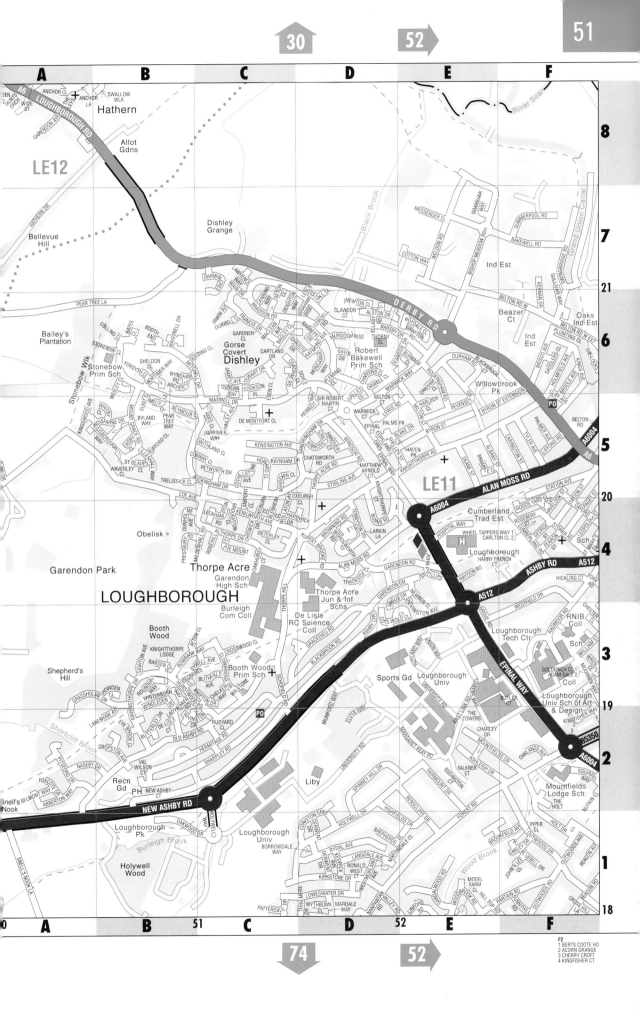

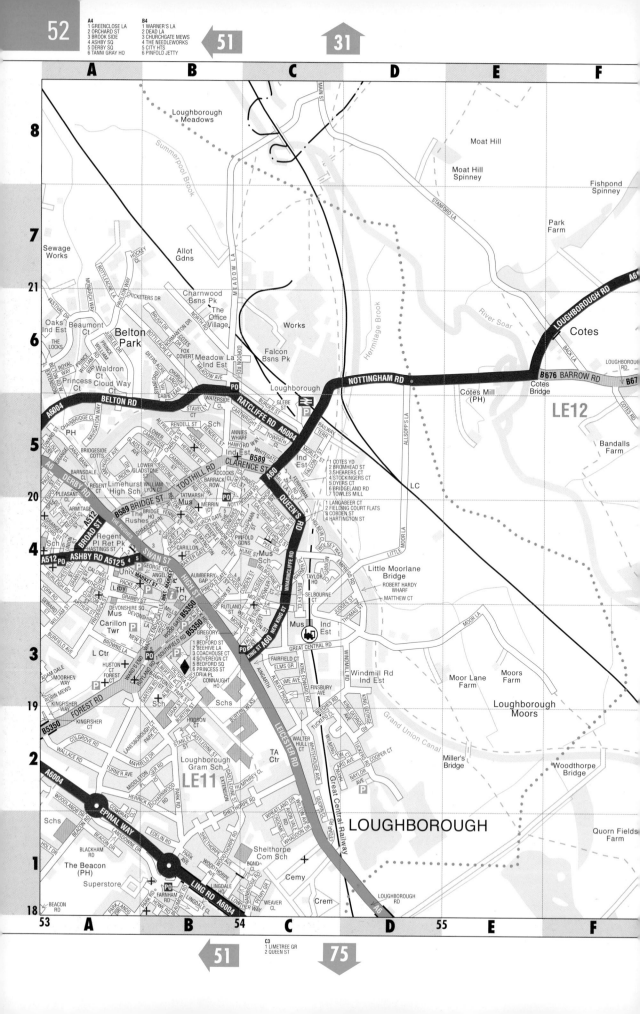

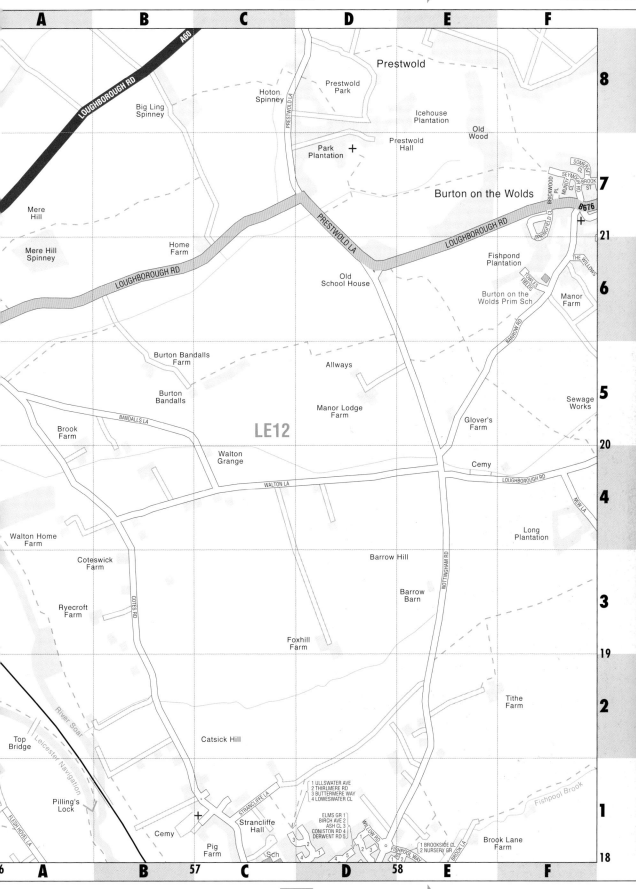

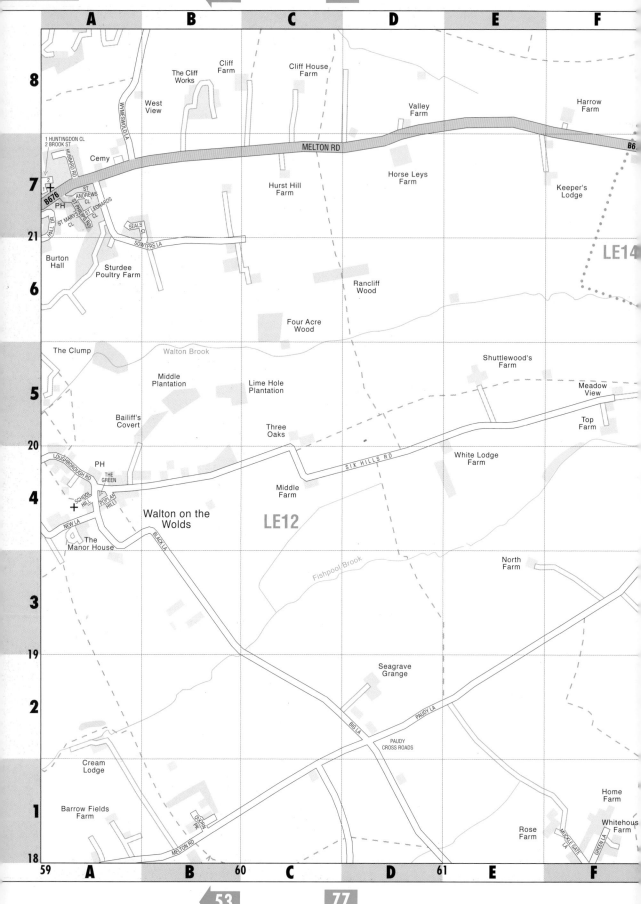

A   B   C   D   E   F

8

The Cliff
Works

Cliff
Farm

Cliff House
Farm

Valley
Farm

Harrow
Farm

West
View

WYMESWOLD LA

MELTON RD

B6

HUBBARD RD

Cemy

1 HUNTINGDON CL
2 BROOK ST

2
1

7

ST
ANDREWS
CL

Hurst Hill
Farm

Horse Leys
Farm

Keeper's
Lodge

B676

PH

ST PHILIPS CL
ST LEONARDS
CL

ST MARYS CL

21

PALL DR

SEALS

SOWTERS LA

LE14

Burton
Hall

Sturdee
Poultry Farm

6

Rancliff
Wood

Four Acre
Wood

The Clump

Walton Brook

5

Middle
Plantation

Lime Hole
Plantation

Shuttlewood's
Farm

Meadow
View

Bailiff's
Covert

Three
Oaks

Top
Farm

20

LOUGHBOROUGH RD

PH

THE GREEN

SIX HILLS RD

White Lodge
Farm

4

SCHOOL
HILL

POPLAR
HILL

Middle
Farm

LE12

NEW LA

Walton on the
Wolds

The
Manor House

BLACK LA

North
Farm

Fishpool Brook

3

19

Seagrave
Grange

2

BIG LA

PAUDY LA

PAUDY
CROSS ROADS

Cream
Lodge

Home
Farm

1

Barrow Fields
Farm

MELTON RD

OXPEN PK

Rose
Farm

MUCKLE GATE

GREEN LA

Whitehous
Farm

18

59   A   B   60   C   D   61   E   F

A   B   C   D   E   F

LE12

Burton Wolds

Lodge
Farm

Willoughby
Lodge

LE14

8

Ashbrook
Farm

Egmont
Farm

LE12

NARROW LA

Holly Lodge
Farm

MELTON RD

7

Seldom Seen
Farm

Park
Farm

Twenty
Acre

Six Hills
Farm

21

Hotel

B676

SIX HILLS LA

Old Park
Farm

Egypt Lodge
Farm

LE14

Six Hills

6

Mast

Cradock's
Ashes

The Oaks
Farm

Walton
Thorns

5

Walton
Thorns

Mount Pleasant
Farm

Wolds
Farm

Ragdale
Wood

PAUDY LA

20

Lodge
Farm

4

Seagrave
Wolds

Thrusington Wolds
Gorse

New York
Farm

LE12

3

The
Lodge

Bunker Hill
Farm

Charlton Gorse
Farm

BERRYCOTT LA

19

LE7

2

Thrussington
Grange

OLD GATE RD

Ox Brook

1

North Hill
Farm

A46

18

62   A   B   63   C   D   64   E   F

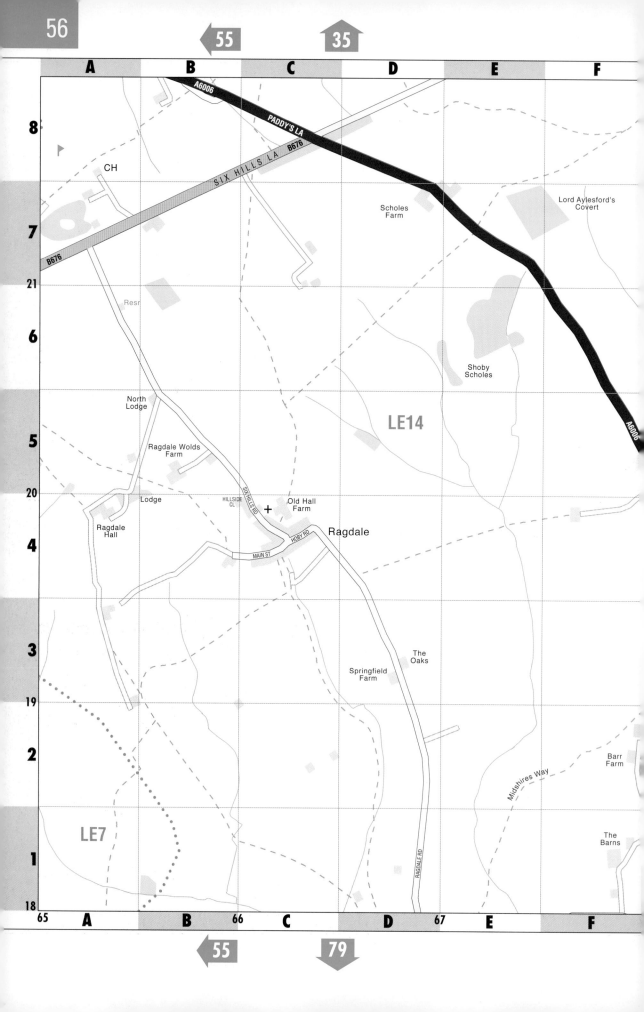

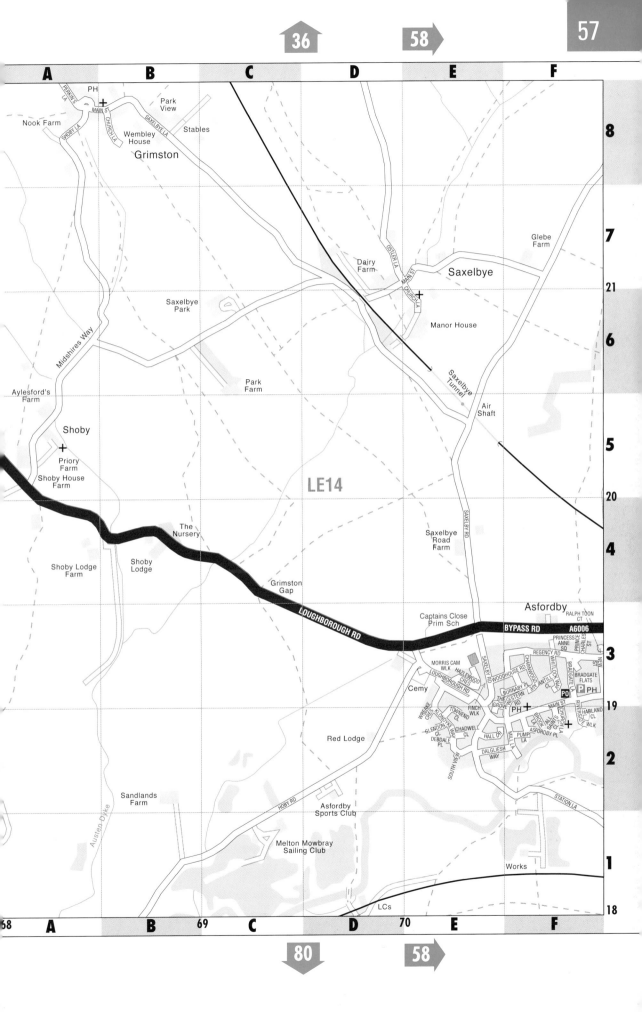

A   B   C   D   E   F

8

Nook Farm

Grimston

PERKIN'S LA
PH
MAIN ST
SHOBY LA
CHURCH LA
SAXELBYE LA
Park View
Stables
Wembley House

7

Saxelbye Park

Dairy Farm

OSTLER LA
MAIN ST
CHURCH LA
Saxelbye

Glebe Farm

21

6

Park Farm

Manor House

Midshires Way

Saxelbye Tunnel

Air Shaft

5

Aylesford's Farm

Shoby

Priory Farm

Shoby House Farm

LE14

SAXELBY RD

Saxelbye Road Farm

20

4

Shoby Lodge Farm

The Nursery

Shoby Lodge

Grimston Gap

LOUGHBOROUGH RD

Captains Close Prim Sch

Asfordby

RALPH TOON CT

BYPASS RD   A6006

PRINCESS ANNE SQ
PRINCE CHARLES ST
REGENCY RD
CHANNWOOD
WHITLOCK WAY
BRADGATE
BRADGATE FLATS

3

Morris Cam Wlk
Hazlewood Cres
Loughborough Rd
Burnaby Pl
Woodhouse Rd
Antill
The Grove
Eastern Rd

Cemy

PH
PO
P
PH

FINCH Wlk
Townend Cl

Wreake Cres
Klondyke Way
Glendon Cl
Debdale Pl
Chadwell Cl
Hall Dr
South View
Dalgliesh Way
Pump La
Main St
Church La
Brook Cl
All Saints
Asfordby Pl
Harland Cl
Riverside Wlk

19

Red Lodge

2

Sandlands Farm

Austen Dyke
HOBY RD

Asfordby Sports Club

Melton Mowbray Sailing Club

STATION LA

1

Works

LCs

18

57
37

A **B** **C** **D** **E** **F**

8

Cant's
Thorns

Ash
Plantation

Oak
Plantation

Potter
Hill

A606 NOTTINGHAM RD

Sysonby Lodge
Farm

WELBY LA

7

Welby
Grange

Hilltop
Farm

21

Welby

St Bartholomews Way

WELBY LA

6

JAMES LAMBERT

Asfordby
Farm

5

LE14

Works

LE13

20

WELBY RD

Remount
Depot

4

A6006 BYPASS RD

MAIN RD

NORTH
VIEW
ROSEBERY
AVE
NORTH
ST
BROOK
CRES

Asfordby
Tunnel

WEST SIDE
ST JOHNS
RD
SOUTH
ST
WELBY RD

Asfordby
Hill

A6006

QUORN DI
COLLINGWOOD

CHETWYND DR
RIVERSIDE RD

3

THE CRESCENT
COWMAN CL
MARRIOTT CL
JUBILEE AVE
RIDINGS CL
MAIN ST

Playing
Field

Asfordby
Valley

MELTON RD

PO

Home
Farm

GLEBE RD
CRAMPTON RD
STANION RD

Asfordby Hill
Prim Sch

PO

ASFORDBY RD

Halfway
House

CH

Sysonby

Butt
Close

19

DWYERS CL
MAIN ST
SARSON CL

The
Grange House

SYSONBY GRANGE LA

2

Sysonby Grange
Farm

1

STATION LA

The
Hollies

Old Lock
Water

MAIN ST

River Wreake

Sewage
Works

A607 LEICESTER RD

Mill

18

White Lodge

LC

PO

WASHDYKE LA

A **B** **C** **D** **E** **F**

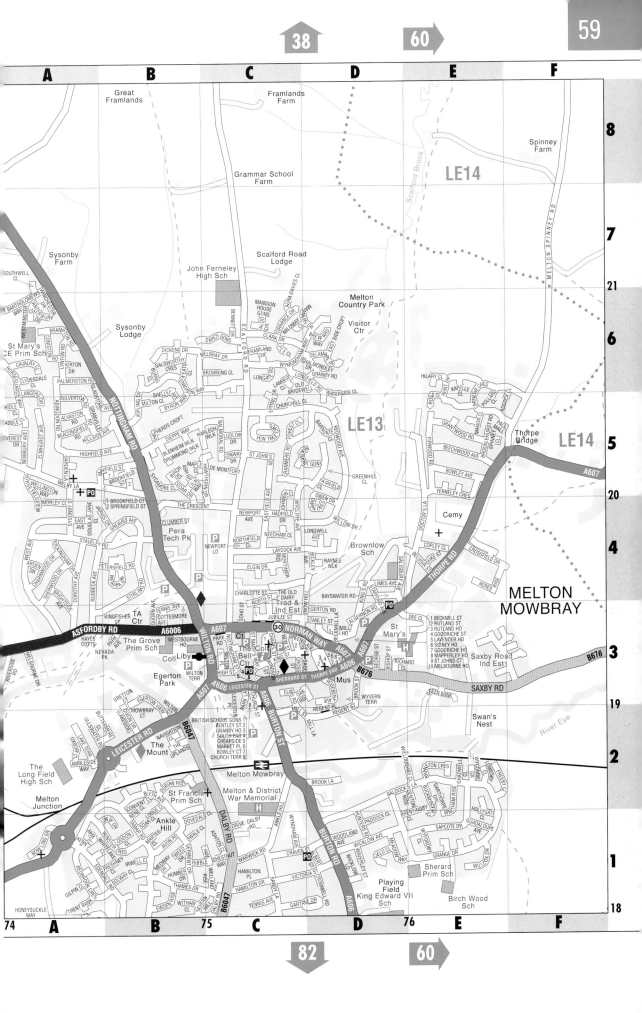

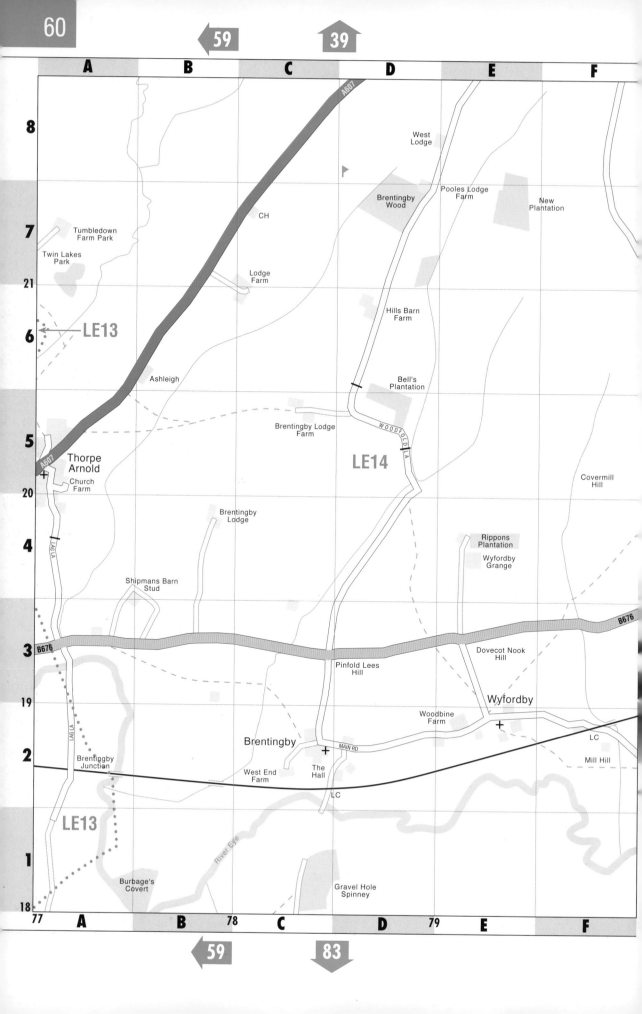

A B C D E F

8

West Lodge

CH

Brentingby Wood

Pooles Lodge Farm

New Plantation

7

Tumbledown Farm Park

Twin Lakes Park

21

Lodge Farm

Hills Barn Farm

6

LE13

Ashleigh

Bell's Plantation

WOODFOLD LA

Covermill Hill

5

Brentingby Lodge Farm

LE14

Thorpe Arnold

A607

Church Farm

20

Brentingby Lodge

Rippons Plantation

Wyfordby Grange

4

LAG LA

Shipmans Barn Stud

3

B676

Pinfold Lees Hill

Dovecot Nook Hill

B676

19

Wyfordby

Woodbine Farm

LC

2

Brentingby Junction

LAG LA

Brentingby

West End Farm

MAIN RD

The Hall

Mill Hill

LC

LE13

LC

1

Burbage's Covert

River Eye

Gravel Hole Spinney

18

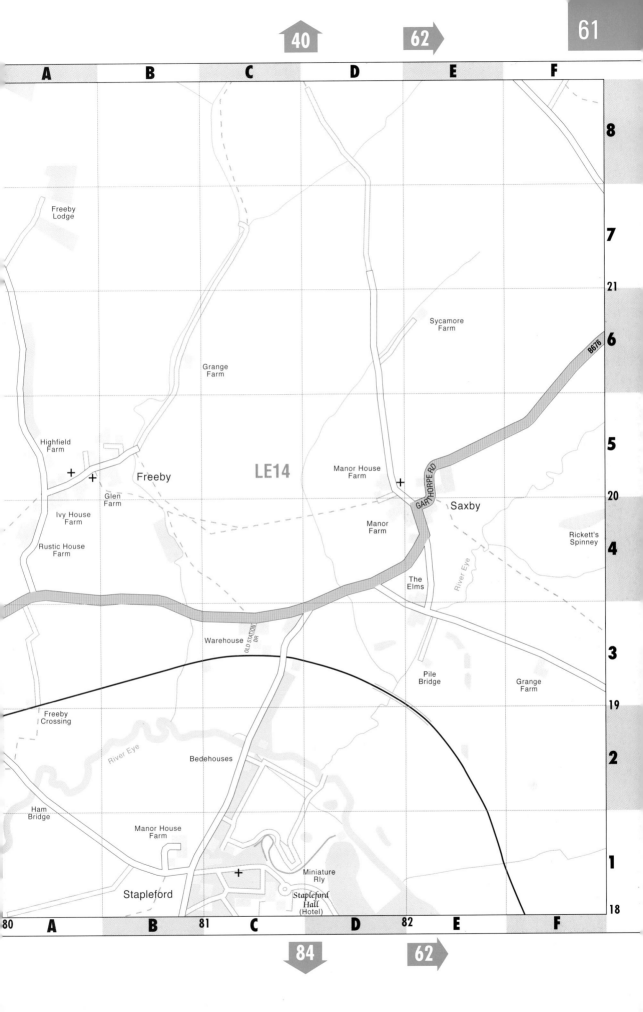

A   B   C   D   E   F

8

7

21

6   B676

Freeby
Lodge

Grange
Farm

Sycamore
Farm

5

Highfield
Farm

Freeby

LE14

Manor House
Farm

GARTHORPE RD

Saxby

20

Glen
Farm

Ivy House
Farm

Manor
Farm

River Eye

Rickett's
Spinney

4

Rustic House
Farm

The
Elms

Warehouse

OLD STATION DR

Pile
Bridge

Grange
Farm

3

19

Freeby
Crossing

River Eye

Bedehouses

2

Ham
Bridge

Manor House
Farm

Miniature
Rly

1

Stapleford

Stapleford
Hall
(Hotel)

18

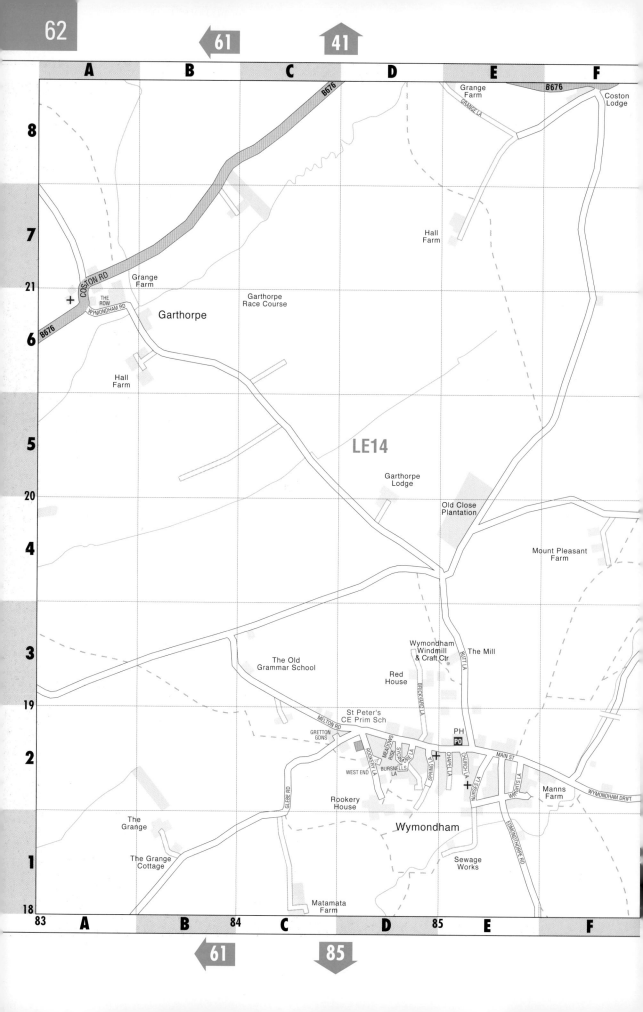

A   B   C   D   E   F

8

7

21   Coston Rd   Grange Farm   Garthorpe Race Course   Hall Farm   Grange Farm   Coston Lodge   B676

The Row   Wymondham Rd

6   B676   Garthorpe

Hall Farm

5   LE14

Garthorpe Lodge

20   Old Close Plantation   Mount Pleasant Farm

4

3   The Old Grammar School   Wymondham Windmill & Craft Ctr   The Mill   Butt La

Red House   Brickyard La

19   Melton Rd   St Peter's CE Prim Sch   PH   PO

Gretton Gdns

2   Rookery La   Meadows Rise   Sycas   Sycamore La   Spring La   Chapel La   Church La   Main St   Manns Farm   Wymondham Drift

West End   Bursnells La

Glebe Rd   Rookery House   Nursery La   Wrights La   Edmondthorpe Rd

The Grange   Wymondham

The Grange Cottage   Sewage Works

1

18   Matamata Farm

83   A   84   B   C   D   85   E   F

A B C D E F

Old
Manor Farm

Sewstern

PH

8

B676

B676

Manor
Farm

7

Coston
Covert

21

Buckminster
Lodge

Mast

Viking Way

6

Sewstern
Grange

NG33

5

20

4

Marriott's
Spinney

LE14

3

19

Highfield
Farm

2

The
Pastures

DRIFT HILL

Wr Twr

EDMONDTHORPE DRIFT

Rutland Round

LE15

1

Prince's
Hovel

18

A B 87 C D 88 E F

SCHOOL LA
MAIN ST
CHURCH LA
BACK LA

63
43

A **B** **C** **D** **E** **F**

8

Main St
Timber Hill
PO
Allot Gdns
Stamford Rd
Manor Farm
Back La
Gunby Rd
Saw Mill
Mast
Factory
Sewstern Rd
Brook House
Main St
Gunby
Mill Farm
Stainby Rd
Stainby Warren
Gunby Dale
Witham Rd
Glebe Farm

7

21

6

The Drift

NG33

5

Gunby Gorse

The Forty Acre

20

Moor La

4

Blue Point Farm

LE14

3

Viking Way

River Witham

19

Mill La

Melton Mowbray Quarry

2

Cribb's Lodge

Fosse La

Thistleton Gap

LE15

1

LE15

School La

Main St

Witham Rd

18
89 **A** **B** 90 **C** **D** 91 **E** **F**

A B C D E F

A1 Grantham

8

GUNBY RD

OLD POST LA

CL

NORTHERN'S LA

RECTORY LA

CHURCH ST

North Witham

HONEY POT LA

A1

7

Mast

Black Bull
Farm

South Lodge
Farm Cottages

WOOLLEY'S LA

Hillview

BULL LA

Mickley
Cottage

21

Mickley
Wood

6

Temple
Hill

River Witham

NG33

Witham
Common

5

Battlebourn
Head

20

Cemy

MOOR LA

UNWIN GN

TROUGHTON WLK

LAUNDS
GN

GREAT CL

NORTH WITHAM RD

THE
PARKSIDE

Sewage
Works

1 HALFORD CL
2 COVERLEY RD
3 HARRINGTON RD

Fox Hill
(PH)

Woodbine
Farm

4

WIMBERLEY
WAY

TEMPLARS WAY

WELLFIELD CL

2

1

3

South Witham

TOLLEMACHE FIELDS

PRIORY
CT

CHURCH LA

WALTER LA

Motel

MORKERY LA

3

South Witham
Com Prim Sch

RUTLAND

HILL
VIEW
RD

CHURCH LA

Manor
Farm

BROADGATE RD

South Witham
Nature Reserve

MILL LA

PH

HIGH ST

MARKET
CT

STATION AVE

19

THISTLETON LA

PENDLETON CL

RAILWAY CL

2

Green La

Morkery Wood

LE15

WITHAM RD

NEW RD

Stanton
Plantation

1

A1

LE15

18

Lincolnshire STREET ATLAS

A   B   C   D   E   F

8   Wr Twr

Beaumont
Wood

Hall
Farm

7   WOOLLEY'S LA

21

Chapel
Hill

Lobthorpe

6

South
Lodge

Park House
Farm

Park
Grounds

NG33

5

Rec
Barn

20

Tortoiseshell
Wood

4

Porter's Lodge
Farm

MORKERY LA

3

Angel Wells
Farm

Morkery Wood
Nature Trail

19

STONE DR

Leach
Farm

Potter's
Hill

2   Morkery Wood

Potter's Hill
Farm

LE15

1   STOCKEN HALL MEWS

STOCKEN HALL
FARM COTTS

Stocken Hall
Farm

18

95   A   B   96   C   D   97   E   F

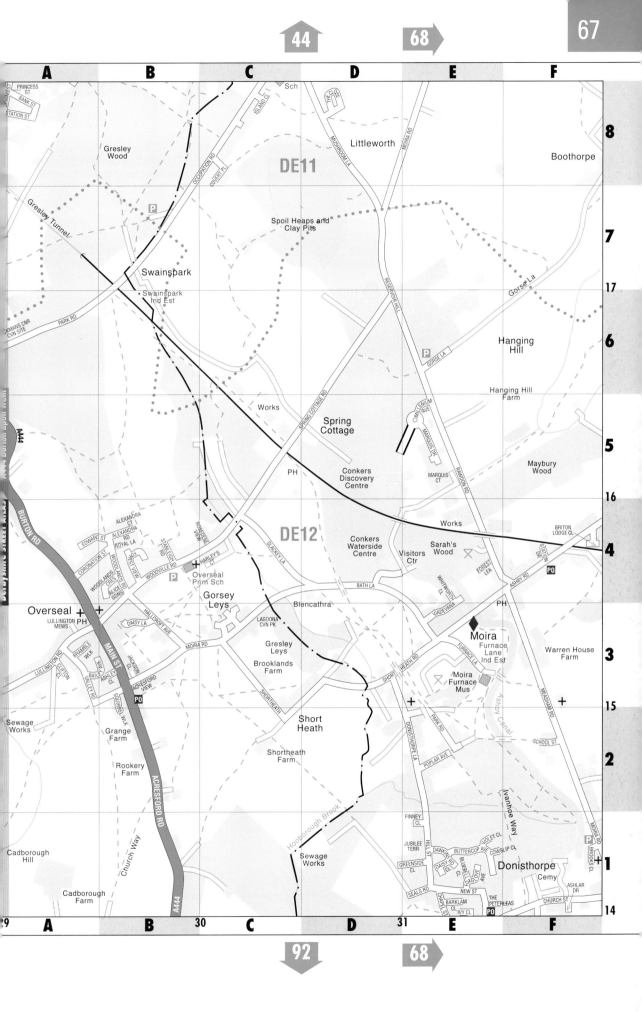

A   B   C   D   E   F

8

PH

VICARAGE CL

BOOTHORPE LA

BUTT LA

STRANBERRY LA

NORTH CL

ELSTEAD

SOUTH CL

MAIN ST

HALL CL

ASHBY LA

SANDTOP LA

PO

DRIFT CL

THORNTOP CL

SANDTOP CL

BROWN

DE11

Lynwood

Blackfordby Fields

Prestop Park Farm

BURTON RD

Ingles Hill Farm

Ingle Bank

INGLE HILL

Thorntop

Prestop Park

Holywell Spring Farm

7

Norrishill Farm

DRIFT SIDE

Drift Farm

Moira Inf Sch

BLACKFORDBY LA

HAZEL GR

ELM GR

Shell Brook

BROWN CT

ATKINSON RD

WESTFIELDS TERR

BURTON RD

PH

17

CORONATION AVE

CEDAR GR

WOODLANDS WAY

ASHFIELD DR

HOLLY

DEVON DR

1 ROWAN CL
2 FIRTREE WLK
3 CHERRY TREE CT
4 WILLOW CL
5 WOULDS CT
6 PINE CT

Cheatle's Barn

White House Farm

Shellbrook

MATTHEW

INGLE DR

PRESTOP DR

IVANHOE DR

WESTFIELDS DR

CHURCH

6

Norris Hill

PH

SYCAMORE

KOPPE

DORSET DR

MOIRA RD

SHELLBROOK CL

ABBEY CL

ABBEY DR

HIGHFIELDS CL

Ashby Hilltop Prim Sch

BEAUMONT RD

FERRERS CL

LOUDON AVE

PAUL

HUNTINGDON

WOODSIDE

Shellbrook Farm

Woodside Farm

NORRIS HILL

TANDY AVE

Chestnut Farm

Ivanhoe Way

5

CHESTNUT CL

ASHBY RD

DE12

MARSTON CL

SWEETHILL

YATES CL

Sweethill

Dilworth New Clumps

LE65

BOWKER CRES 1
GRIFFITH GDNS 2
MORETON WLK 3

RIDGWAY RD

SMEDLEY CL

BAKER AVE

STALEY AVE

16

HARVEST CL

BRAMLEY AVE

BEEHIVE AVE

PRENTICE CL

KEEPERS CL

BETAYLOR

ALBION CL

PARSONS RD

DAYBELL RD

REGAN CL

NAYLYN CL

WELLS RD

WILLESLEY GDNS

4

NEW ROW

Newfields

WILLESLEY LA

P

WILLESLEY CL

CH

Spoil Heap

Valley Farm

3

Bramborough Farm

Wood Farm

WILLESLEY LA

Works

White Lodge

15

Wood Farm Cottages

2

Hill Farm

WILLESLEY WOODSIDE

Willesley

Willesley Park

The Spinney

MEASHAM RD

Mon

A42

12

1

MOIRA RD

PO

ASHBY RD

Donisthorpe Prim Sch

MEASHAM RD

MEASHAM RD

B4116

14

Redholme Farm

P

A42

32   A   B   33   C   D   34   E   F

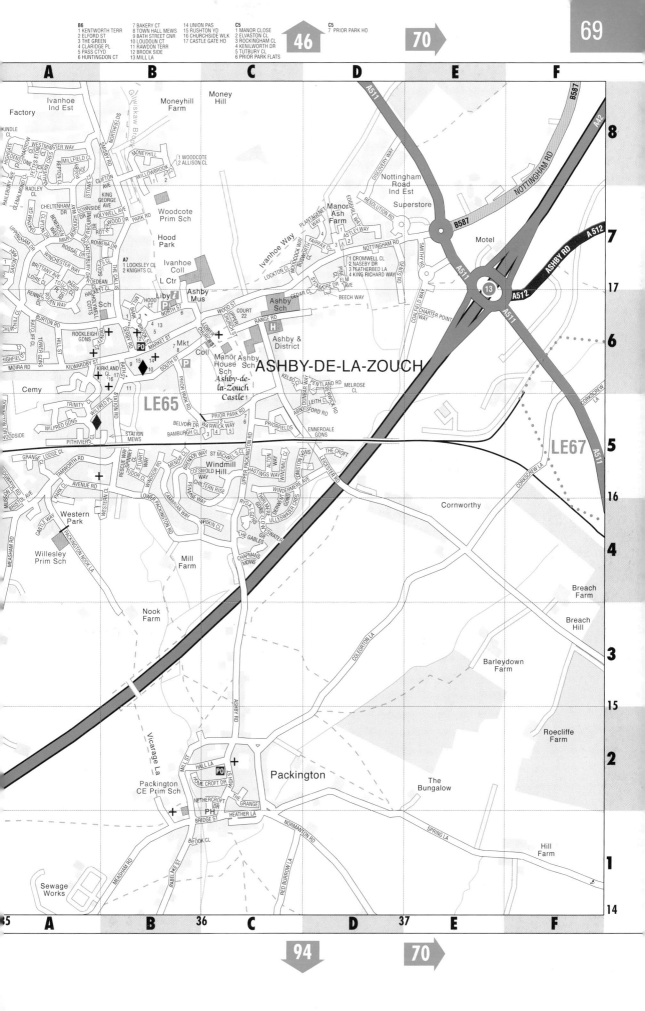

69
47

A B C D E F

8

Bishops Cottage

B5324

Keepers Cottage

Ginn Stables Farm

OUTWOODS LA

AQUEDUCT RD

THE WOOLROOMS

SCHOOL LA

Hall Farm

CHAPEL LA

Coleorton

STONEY LA

LOWER MOOR RD

BACKWELL'S LA

LAVENDER WLK

THE STABLE YD

REMPSTONE RD

WORDSWORTH CL

PO

PH

7

A512

The Cottage

COLEORTON HALL

B5324

BRADFORD'S

OVERTON CL

LOUGHBOROUGH RD

A512

ASHBY RD

Flagstaff Farm

Church Town

PRESTON'S LA

Windmill (dis)

17

LE65

Viscount Beaumont's CE Prim Sch

ASHBY RD

THE MOOR

MOOR LA

6

Rectory

Bottom Farm

West Farm

Pastures Farm

THE ROWLANDS

CORKSCREW LA

Farm Town

P

PITT LA

Coleorton Moor

LIMBY HALL LA

5

Gamekeepers Cottage

Moor Farm

PH

Limb Hall

16

A511

LE67

Broomy Husk

THE MOORLANDS

4

FORRESTER CL

Botany Bay

BIRCHWOOD CL

THE SPINNEY MOBILE HOME PK

Sinope

ASHBY RD

3

LE65

Little Alton Farm

THE MOORLANDS MOBILE HOME PK

A511

Hoo Ash Farm

Demonaic Plantation

ALTON HILL

15

GLEBE VIEW

SWANNINGTON RD

A447

Alton House

Alton Grange

Glebe Farm

THORNTREE CL

ORCHARD CL

Ravenstone

2

CLAREMONT

PH

CHAPEL

COALVILL

1

SPRING LA

PH

BEAMANS

WASH LA

A447

Church La

Piper La

The Altons

14

38 A B 39 C D 40 E F

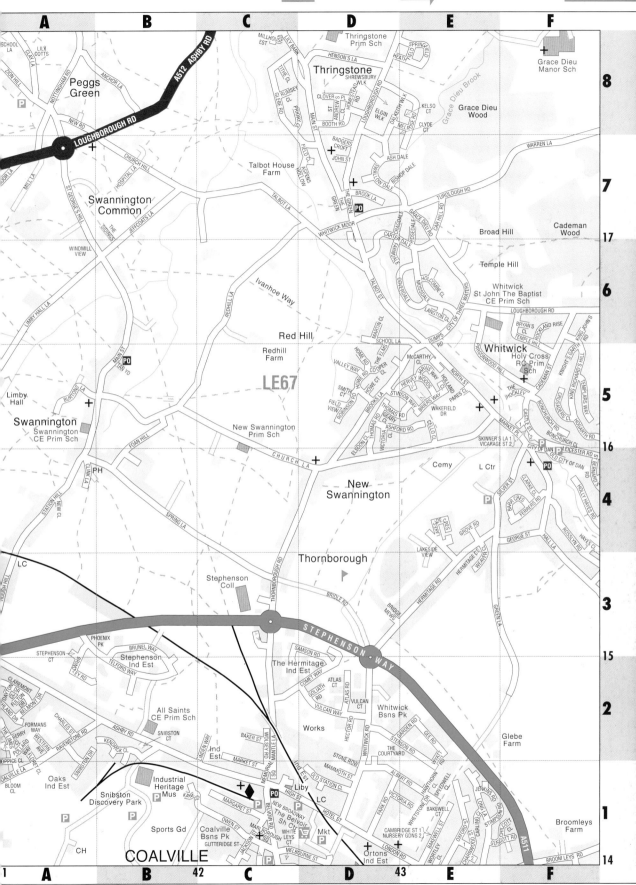

71
49

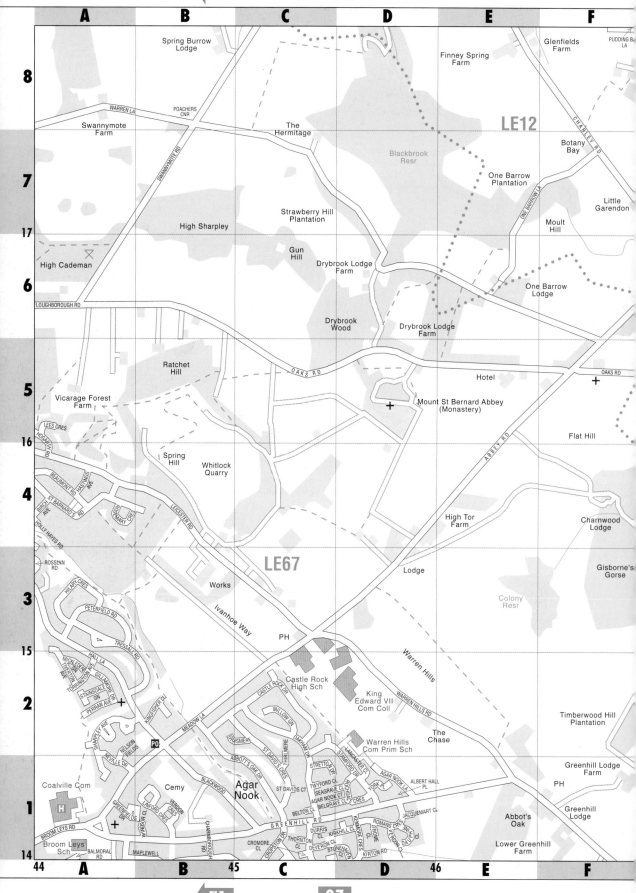

71
97

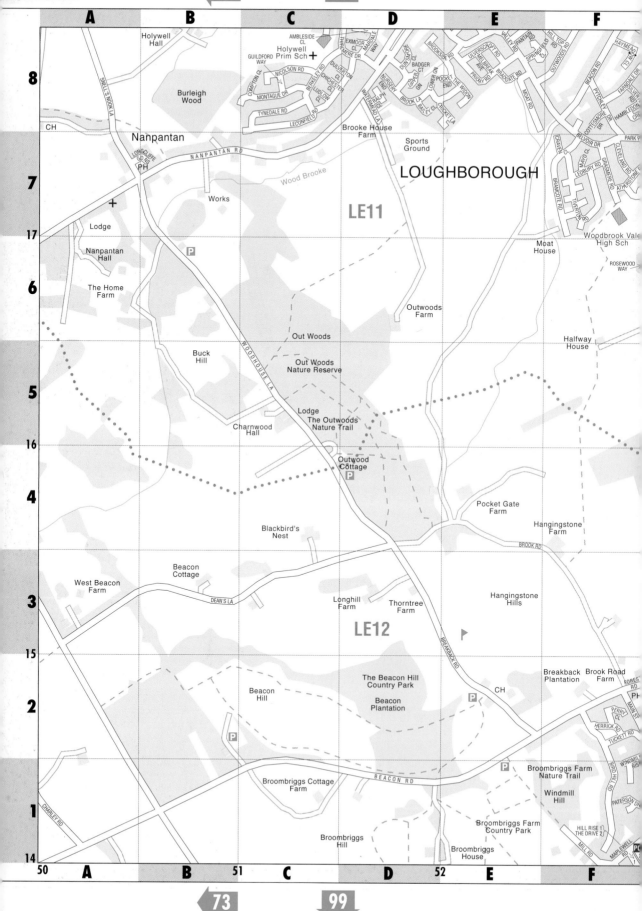

A   B   C   D   E   F

8

Holywell
Hall

AMBLESIDE
CL

Holywell
Prim Sch

GUILDFORD
WAY

Burleigh
Wood

EXMOOR
CL

MARTDALE
WAY

MARDALE

THIRLMERE DR

COMPTON CL

NICOLSON RD

MONTAGUE DR

BERKELEY RD

CHICHESTER
RD

DULVERTON
CL

CHICHESTER
CL

LUDLOW
RD

LECONFIELD RD

LOWER GRN

NURSERY
END

WATERMEAD LA

BROOK LA

BALEY CL

UPPER RD

POCKET
GN

THE WOOD

CRICKET LA

BROOK LA

BADGER
CT

BROOKSIDE RD

ULVERSCROFT RD

NETHER BREAK

BRADGATE RD

VALE RD

PRIORY

HILL TOP RD

OUTWOODS RD

BEACON RD

FANDDALE CT

PYCHLEY RD

HAMBLEDON RD

CRAVEN CL

COTTESMORE RD

BELVOIR DR

MAJO CL

LEDBURY RD

GRASMERE RD

CLEVELAND RD

ATHERSTONE

PARK P

BRAMCOTE RD

TIVERTON
RD

TYNEDALE RD

Brooke House
Farm

Sports
Ground

LOUGHBOROUGH

CH

Nanpantan

NANPANTAN RD

LONGCLIFFE
RD

PH

Works

Wood Brooke

LE11

Woodbrook Vale
High Sch

17

Lodge

Nanpantan
Hall

Moat
House

ROSEWOOD
WAY

6

The Home
Farm

Outwoods
Farm

Halfway
House

WOODHOUSE LA

Out Woods

Buck
Hill

Out Woods
Nature Reserve

5

Charnwood
Hall

Lodge
The Outwoods
Nature Trail

16

Outwood
Cottage

4

Pocket Gate
Farm

Hangingstone
Farm

Blackbird's
Nest

BROOK RD

Beacon
Cottage

West Beacon
Farm

DEAN'S LA

Longhill
Farm

Thorntree
Farm

Hangingstone
Hills

3

LE12

BREAKBACK RD

15

Beacon
Hill

The Beacon Hill
Country Park

Beacon
Plantation

CH

Breakback
Plantation

Brook Road
Farm

FOREST
PH

PERRY
CL

MAIN ST

2

HERRICK RD

TUCKETT RD

Broombriggs Farm
Nature Trail

Windmill
Hill

BIRCH HILL RD

WINDMILL

PATERSON DR

BEACON RD

Broombriggs Cottage
Farm

1

CHARLEY RD

Broombriggs
Hill

Broombriggs Farm
Country Park

Broombriggs
House

HILL RISE 1
THE DRIVE 2

MILL RD

MAPLEWELL
RD

PC

14

50   A   B   51   C   D   52   E   F

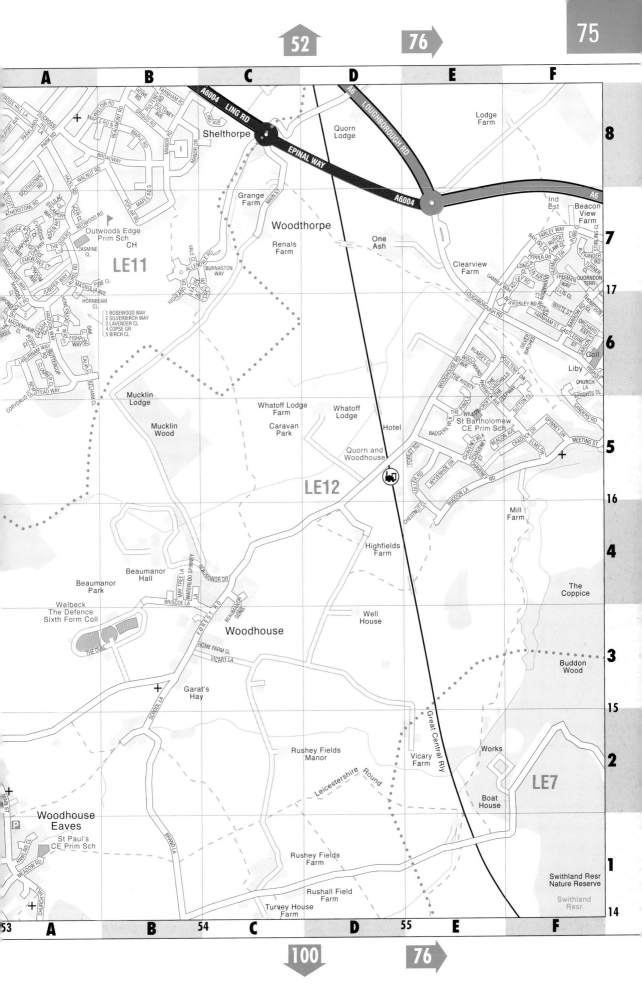

A   B   C   D   E   F

8
7
17
6
5
16
4
3
15
2
1
14

A6004 LING RD
LING AVE

Shelt025

Woodthorpe

EPINAL WAY

A6

LOUGHBOROUGH RD

Lodge Farm

Quorn Lodge

One Ash

A6004

A6

Ind Est

Beacon View Farm

Clearview Farm

Grange Farm

Renals Farm

LE11

Outwoods Edge Prim Sch   CH

1 ROSEWOOD WAY
2 SILVERBIRCH WAY
3 LAVENDER CL
4 COPSE GR
5 BIRCH CL

Mucklin Lodge

Mucklin Wood

Whatoff Lodge Farm

Whatoff Lodge

Caravan Park

Hotel

LE12

Quorn and Woodhouse

St Bartholomew CE Prim Sch

Coll

Liby

Beaumanor Park

Beaumanor Hall

Welbeck The Defence Sixth Form Coll

THE OVAL

Woodhouse

Home Farm Cl

Vicary La

Garat's Hay

Highfields Farm

Well House

Mill Farm

The Coppice

Buddon Wood

Rushey Fields Manor

Leicestershire   Round

Vicary Farm

Great Central Rly

Works

LE7

Boat House

Woodhouse Eaves

St Paul's CE Prim Sch

Rushey Fields Farm

Rushall Field Farm

Turvey House Farm

Swithland Resr Nature Reserve

Swithland Resr

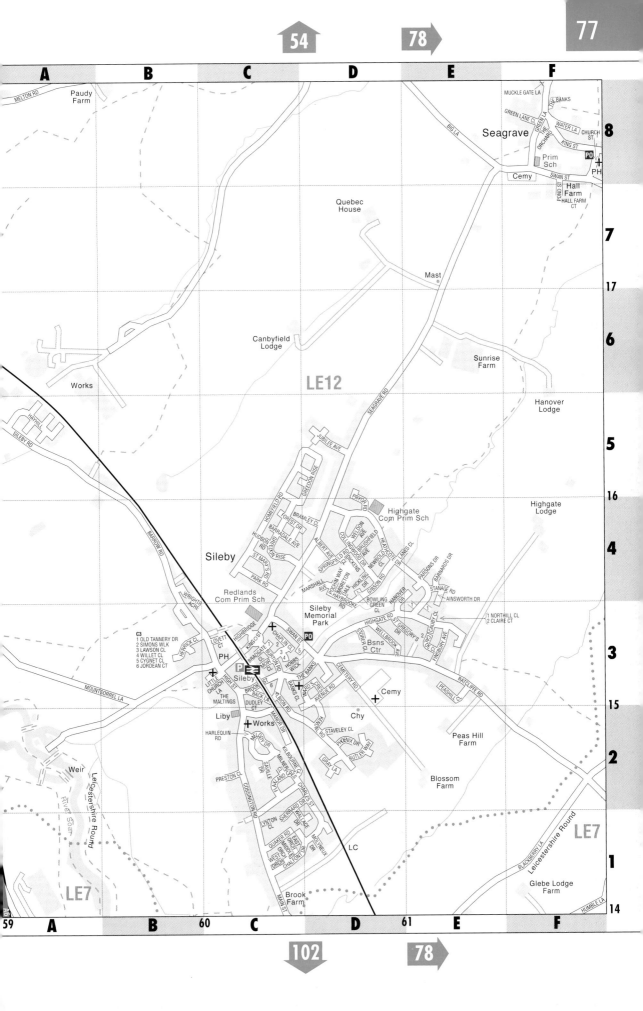

A B C D E F

8
7
17
6
5
16
4
3
15
2
1
14

59 A 60 B C 61 D E F

MELTON RD
Paudy Farm

Seagrave
MUCKLE GATE LA
THE BANKS
GREEN LANE CL
GREEN LA
ORCHARD
WATER LA
CHURCH ST
KING ST
BIG LA
PO
Prim Sch
PH
Cemy
SWAN ST
Hall Farm
POND ST
Hall Farm CT

Quebec House

Mast

Canbyfield Lodge

LE12

Sunrise Farm

Hanover Lodge

Works

HAYHILL
SILEBY RD

JUBILEE AVE
SEAGRAVE RD
Highgate Lodge

BARROW RD

GREEDON RISE
HOMEFIELD RD
FOREST DR
BRAMLEY CL
GREEN RISE
BARRADALE AVE
HUDSON RD
ST MARY'S RD
Sileby
PARK RD
WRIGHT'S ACRE
Redlands Com Prim Sch
ALBERT AVE
SPRINGFIELD RD
COL LINGWOOD DR
DICKENS CL
MORTON CL
PYCHYN WAY
HICKLING RD
HAYBROOKE
GIBSON RD
MARSHALL AVE
PRYOR CL
WELTON AVE
BRUSHFIELD CL
HERITAGE DR
OAKS CL
NORTHILL CL
Highgate Com Prim Sch
16
PARSONS DR
STANAGE RD
BARNARDS DR
AINSWORTH DR
Bowling Green CL
HANOVER DR
1 NORTHILL CL
2 CLAIRE CT
HIGHGATE RD
WELLBROOK AVE
ST GREGORY'S
SILVER CL
CK CL
CALLEY CL
FINSBURY AVE
Bsns Ctr
C3
1 OLD TANNERY DR
2 SIMONS WLK
3 LAWSON CL
4 WILLET CL
5 CYGNET CL
6 JORDEAN CT
HERRICK CL
LOVETT CT
PH
HIGHBRIDGE
KING ST
BRANDGATE
BURTON RD
MUIR RD
SWAN ST
CHAPLIN CT
HOBBS WICK
PO
THE BANKS
SILEBY
P
Sileby
BROOK ST
BACK LA
DUDLEY CT
Liby
CROSS ST
BYRON RD
CEMETERY RD
Cemy
Chy
MOUNTSORREL LA
LITTLE CHURCH LA
HIGH ST
THE MALTINGS
HARLEQUIN RD
Works
MELODY DR
KILBOURNE CT
SAVILLE DR
MILNERS CRES
WEST DR
PRESTON CL
CROSSINGTON RD
CLAND CL
CHARLES ST
STAVELEY CL
PHOENIX DR
GRAY CL
BUTLER WAY
RATCLIFFE RD
PEASHILL CL
Peas Hill Farm
Blossom Farm
Weir
River Soar
Leicestershire Round
LE7
LYNTON RD
QUAKER RD
SHERRARD DR
EAST ORCH
WEST ORCH
CHALTON CT
VILLAGE
MALTINEUX DR
LC
BLACKBERRY LA
Leicestershire Round
LE7
Brook Farm
MAIN ST
Glebe Lodge Farm
HUMBLE LA
LE7

77
55

	A	B	C	D	E	F

8

BERRYCOTT LA

IVY HOUSE CL

KING ST

BUTCHERS LA

Jericho Farm

The Lodge Farm

OX LANE

7

Park Hill

LE12

Park Hill House

Motel

OLD GATE RD

17

Hilltop

6

PARK HILL LA

CH

SEAGRAVE RD

5

Thrussington CE Prim Sch

GLEBELAND CL

16

Padge Hall

REGENT ST

BLACKSMITHS CT

THE GREEN

FERNELEY RISE

HOBY RD

BACK LA

CHURCH LA

REARSBY RD

4

Ratcliffe Farm

Mast

LE7

PH

Thrussington

RATCLIFFE RD

Manor Farm

Longlands

Leicestershire Round

Spinney Farm

3

Ratcliffe Coll

The Elms Farm

ROSMINIAN WAY

Ratcliffe Barn

River Wreake

15

Ratcliffe on the Wreake

THRUSSINGTON RD

North's Lodge

Rearsby Mill (disused)

2

MAIN ST

LC

Rearsby House Farm

1

HUMBLE LA

RATCLIFFE RD

Ratcliffe Hall

CHURCH LA

Priory Farm

HASSELL MEWS

ORTON RD

MILL HILL

A-46

Ratcliffe Mill (disused)

BROOME LA

LC

KAYES GARDEN NURSERY

PH

NEW AVE

WESTON CL

MELTON RD

14

62	A		B	63	C		D	64	E		F

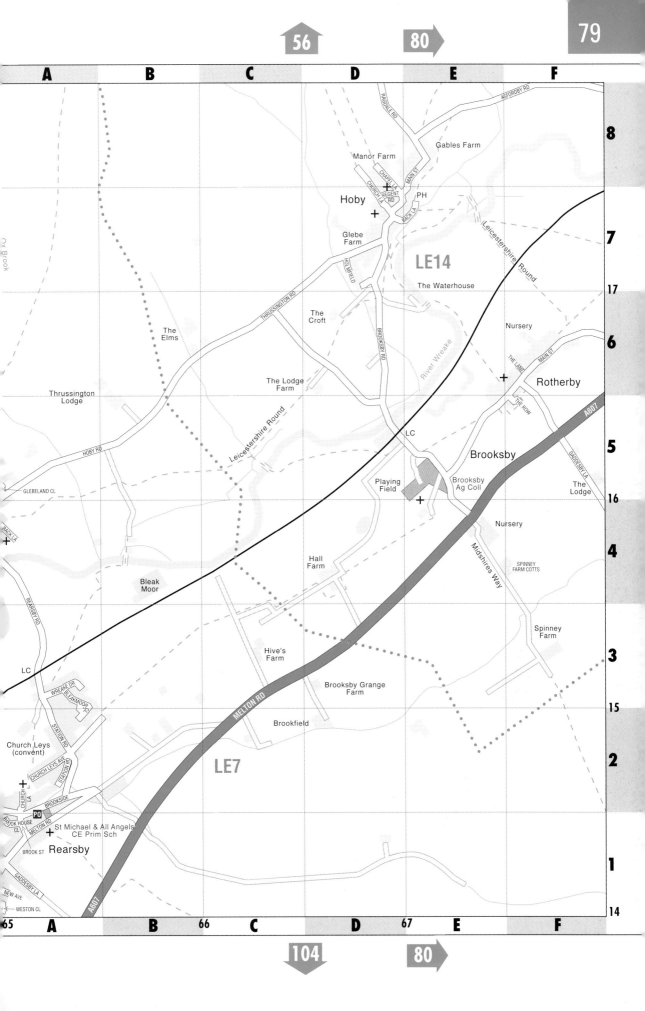

56
80

A   B   C   D   E   F

8

7

17

Gables Farm

Manor Farm

Hoby

Glebe
Farm

LE14

The Waterhouse

Leicestershire Round

PH

Nursery

6

The Elms

The Croft

BROOKSBY RD

HOLMFIELD

River Wreake

THE LANE

MAIN ST

Rotherby

Thrussington
Lodge

The Lodge
Farm

Leicestershire Round

THE ROW

A607

Brooksby

GADDESBY LA

5

16

HOBY RD

LC

Playing
Field

Brooksby
Ag Coll

The
Lodge

GLEBELAND CL

Nursery

4

BACK LA

Bleak
Moor

Hall
Farm

Midshires Way

SPINNEY
FARM COTTS

Spinney
Farm

3

15

REARSBY RD

Hive's
Farm

MELTON RD

Brooksby Grange
Farm

WREAKE DR

BLEAKMOOR RD

Brookfield

LC

Church Leys
(convent)

STATION RD

CHURCH LEYS AVE

STATION RD

LE7

2

BROOKSIDE

CHURCH LA

PO

BROOK HOUSE CL

MELTON RD

St Michael & All Angels
CE Prim Sch

Brook St

Rearsby

1

NEW AVE

GADDESBY LA

WESTON CL

A607

14

65   A   B   66   C   D   67   E   F

80

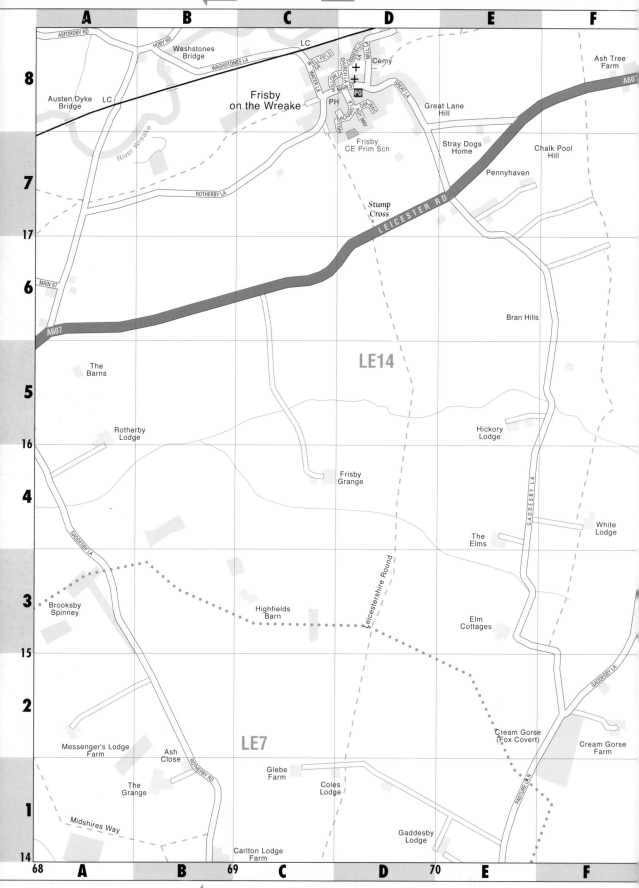

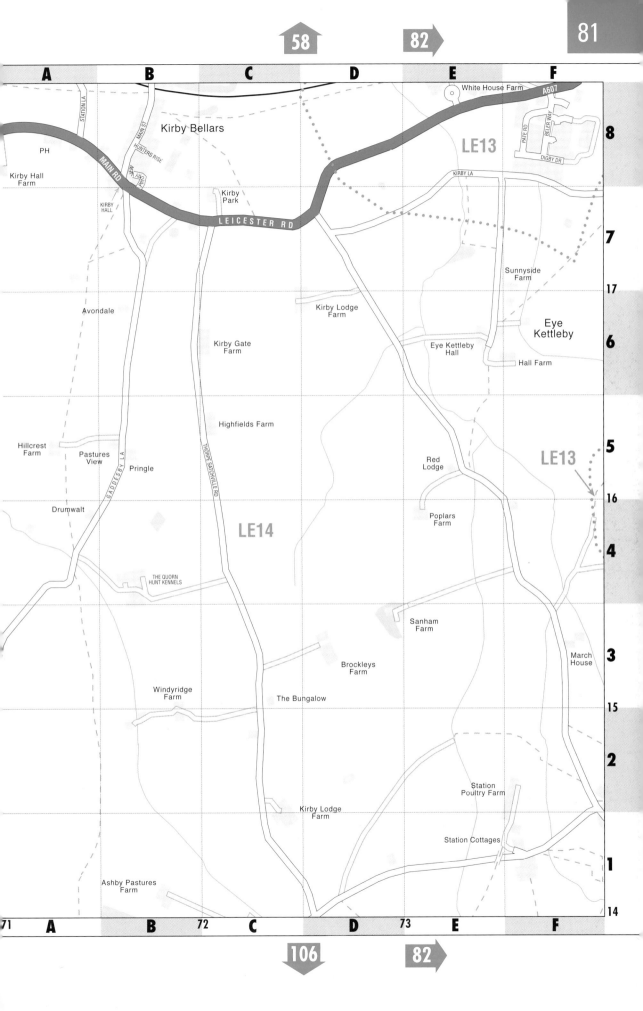

A B C D E F

White House Farm
A607

Kirby Bellars

LE13

PATE RD
BELER WAY
DIGBY DR

STATION LA
PH
MAIN ST
HUNTERS RISE
MAIN RD
ARMY WAY
8

Kirby Hall
Farm

KIRBY
HALL

Kirby
Park

KIRBY LA

LEICESTER RD

7

17

Avondale

Kirby Lodge
Farm

Sunnyside
Farm

Eye
Kettleby

6

Kirby Gate
Farm

Eye Kettleby
Hall

Hall Farm

Highfields Farm

Hillcrest
Farm

Pastures
View

Pringle

GADDESBY LA

THORPE SATCHVILLE RD

Red
Lodge

LE13

5

16

Drumwalt

LE14

Poplars
Farm

4

THE QUORN
HUNT KENNELS

Sanham
Farm

March
House

Brockleys
Farm

3

Windyridge
Farm

The Bungalow

15

2

Station
Poultry Farm

Kirby Lodge
Farm

Station Cottages

1

Ashby Pastures
Farm

14

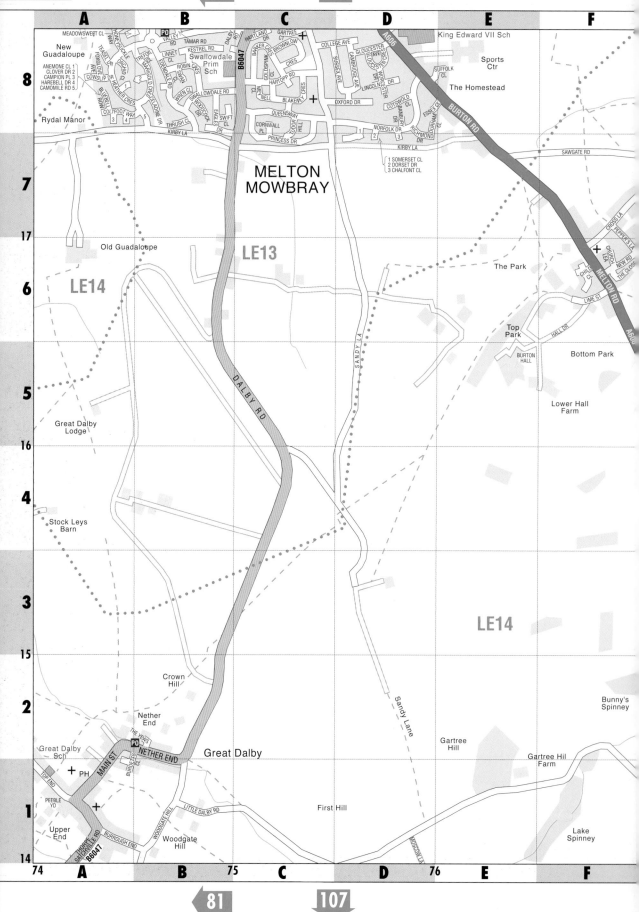

MELTON MOWBRAY

LE13

LE14

LE14

A B C D E F

8

The Kiln
Close

Burton Lodge
Cottage

Burton Lodge
Farm

Sawgate Lodge
Farm

Stapleford
Lodge

Sewage Works

SAWGATE RD

7

East
Farm

Felstead's
Spinney

Stapleford
Barn

The Drift

17

Burton Lazars

Highfields
Spinney

Brickyard
Plantation

Decoy
Cottage

6

LE14

5

Burton Bridge

Sapcoat's
Spinney

Hose Hill

16

Burton Brook

MELTON RD

4

Ellaby's
Spinney

Berry Covert
(Fox Covert)

Great Close
Plantation

WHISSENDINE RD

Jericho
Farm

3

Wild's Lodge

Brickfield
Farm

15

OAKHAM RD

2

Lower
Leesthorpe

Ash Pole
Spinney

LE15

1

LITTLE DALBY RD

Manor
Farm

Leesthorpe
Hill

Little Dalby

CHURCH WLK

Hollies
Farm

Lodge
Spinney

A606

14

Village Farm

A   B   C   D   E   F

8

Cottage
Plantation

Stapleford Park

Crossing
Covert

LC

7

Bryans Lodge

SAWGATE RD

Laxtons
Cottage

The Lodge

17

Paget's
Spinney

Holygate
Farm

6

Cuckoo Hill

Laxton's
Covert

LE14

5

The Grange

16

Waterloo Lodge

4

STAPLEFORD RD

Whissendine Brook

3

15

Browne's Lodge

LE15

WILLOW CL

SHERRARD
CL

2

MELTON RD

HARBROUGH CL

Whissendine
CE Prim Sch

STANILANDS

WALTON
CL

ST ANDREWS CL

PH

1

Whissenthorpe

THORPE GDNS

OAKHAM RD

BOUVERIE
CT

MAIN ST

PO

COW LA

TRENOOK

Whissendine
Windmill

MILL GR

LAMMAS
COTTS

Whissendine
Lodge

14

80   A   B   81   C   D   82   E   F

Whissendine

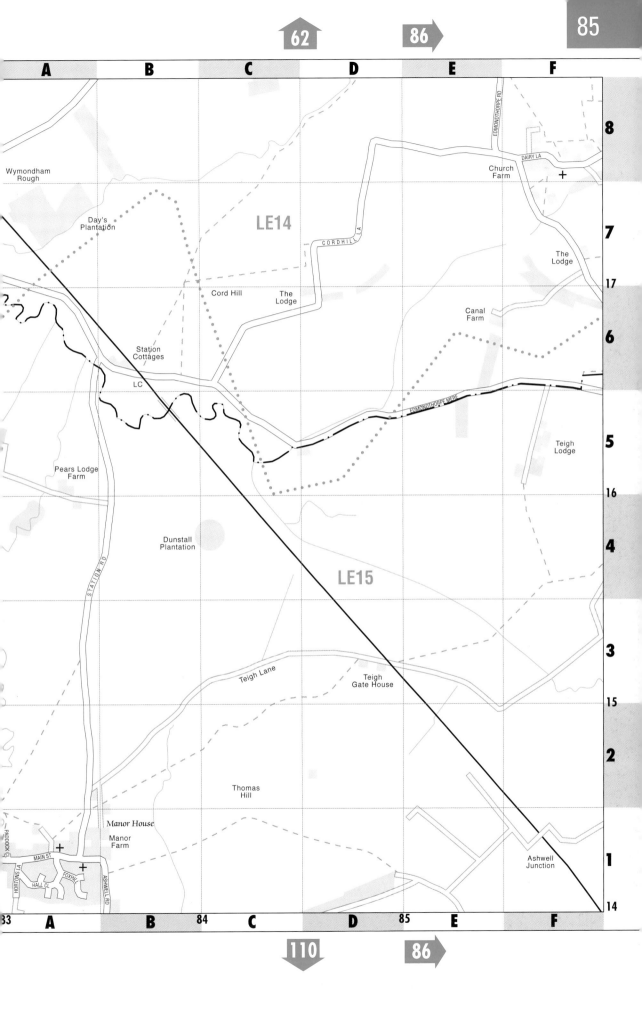

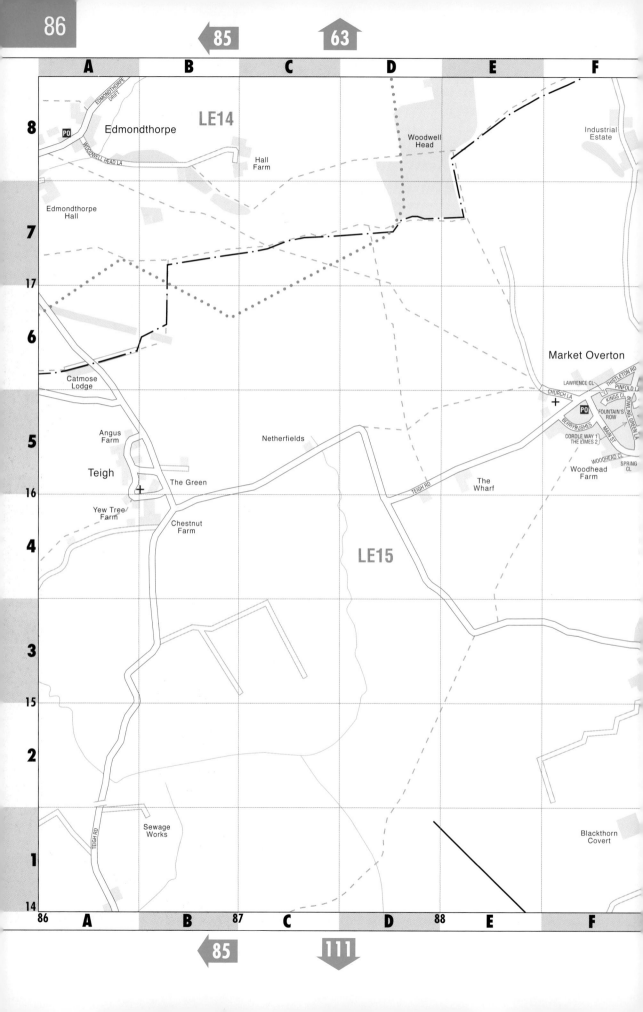

LE14

Edmondthorpe

PO

EDMONDTHORPE DRIFT

WOODWELL HEAD LA

Hall Farm

Woodwell Head

Industrial Estate

Edmondthorpe Hall

Market Overton

Catmose Lodge

LAWRENCE CL.

THISTLETON RD

PINFOLD LA

CHURCH LA

PO

KINGS CL

ROWLING GREEN LA

Angus Farm

Netherfields

FOUNTAIN'S ROW

BERRYBUSHES

CORDLE WAY 1

THE LIMES 2

MAIN ST

Teigh

The Green

TEIGH RD

The Wharf

WOODHEAD CL

SPRING CL

Woodhead Farm

Yew Tree Farm

Chestnut Farm

LE15

TEIGH RD

Sewage Works

Blackthorn Covert

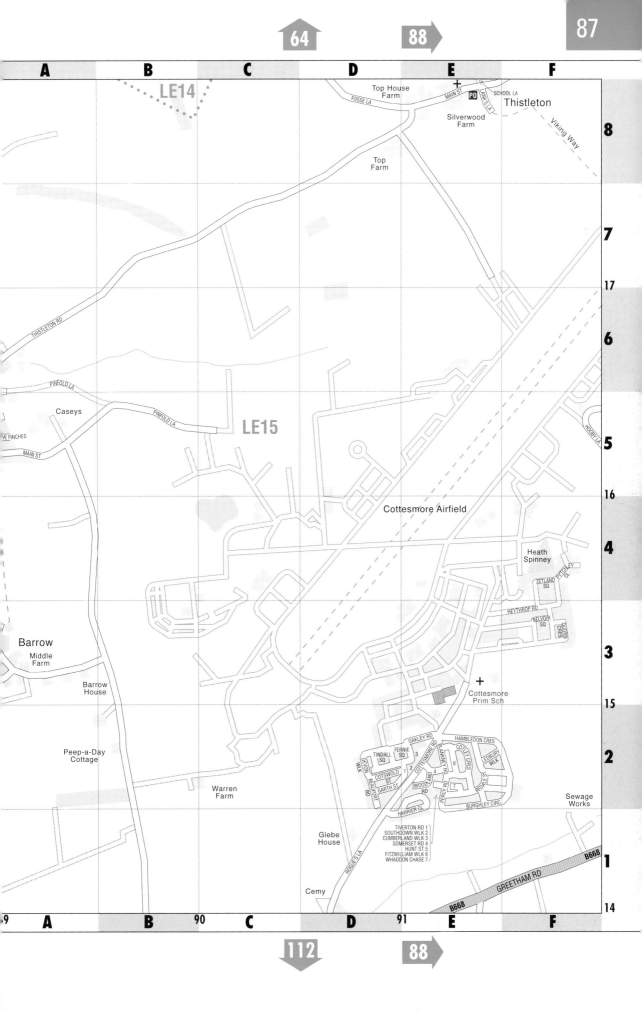

A B C D E F

LE14

Top House Farm

FOSSE LA

Top House Farm

MAIN ST

PO

LAMB'S LA

SCHOOL LA

Thistleton

Silverwood Farm

Viking Way

8

Top Farm

7

17

THISTLETON RD

6

PINFOLD LA

Caseys

PINFOLD LA

LE15

YE FINCHES

MAIN ST

HOOBY LA

5

16

Cottesmore Airfield

Heath Spinney

ZETLAND SQ

PYTCHLEY CL

4

HEYTHROP RD

BELVOIR SQ

QUEEN CRES

Barrow

Middle Farm

Barrow House

Cottesmore Prim Sch

3

15

Peep-a-Day Cottage

OAKLEY RD

HAMBLEDON CRES

TINDALL SQ

FERNIE SQ

3

COTTESMORE RD

BLANKNEY RD

COTLEY CRES

LEDBURY WLK

DEVON WLK

2

1

COTSWOLD ST

GARTH ST

BEAUFORT

WOODLAND RD

PERCY RD

6

7

BELLES ST

Sewage Works

Warren Farm

HARRIER CL

BURGHLEY CIRC

TIVERTON RD 1
SOUTHDOWN WLK 2
CUMBERLAND WLK 3
SOMERSET RD 4
HUNT ST 5
FITZWILLIAM WLK 6
WHADDON CHASE 7

Glebe House

ROGUE'S LA

Cemy

B668

GREETHAM RD

B668

1

14

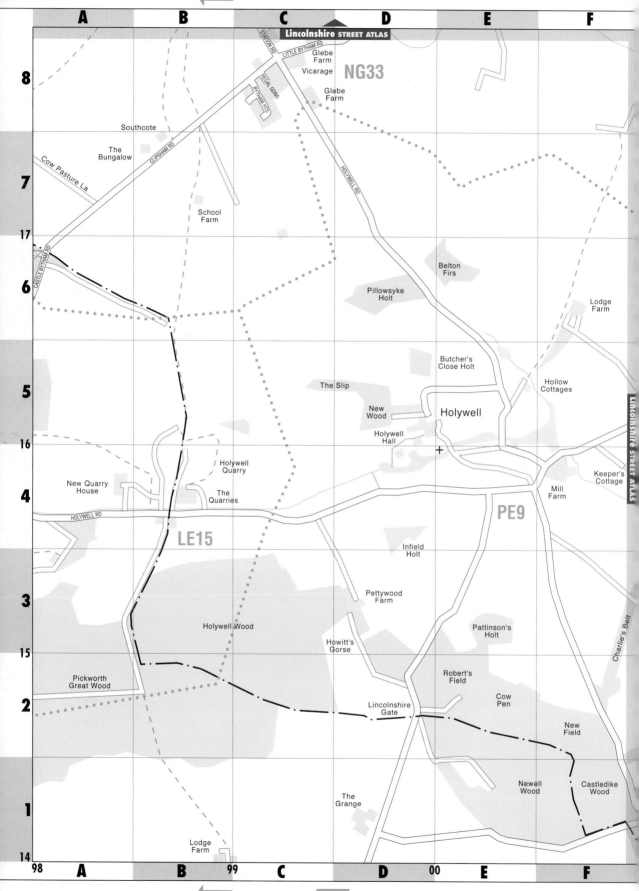

NG33

8

Glebe Farm
Vicarage
Glebe Farm

STATION RD
LITTLE BYTHAM RD

Southcote

The Bungalow

REGAL GDNS
BYTHAM HTS
CLIPSHAM RD

Cow Pasture La

7

School Farm

HOLYWELL RD

17

6

CASTLE BYTHAM RD

Belton Firs

Pillowsyke Holt

Lodge Farm

Butcher's Close Holt

Hollow Cottages

5

The Slip

New Wood

Holywell

Holywell Hall

16

Keeper's Cottage

New Quarry House

Holywell Quarry

The Quarries

Mill Farm

PE9

4

HOLYWELL RD

LE15

Infield Holt

Pettywood Farm

3

Holywell Wood

Pattinson's Holt

Howitt's Gorse

Charlie's Belt

15

Pickworth Great Wood

Robert's Field

Cow Pen

Lincolnshire Gate

New Field

2

Newell Wood

Castledike Wood

The Grange

1

Lodge Farm

14

Lincolnshire STREET ATLAS

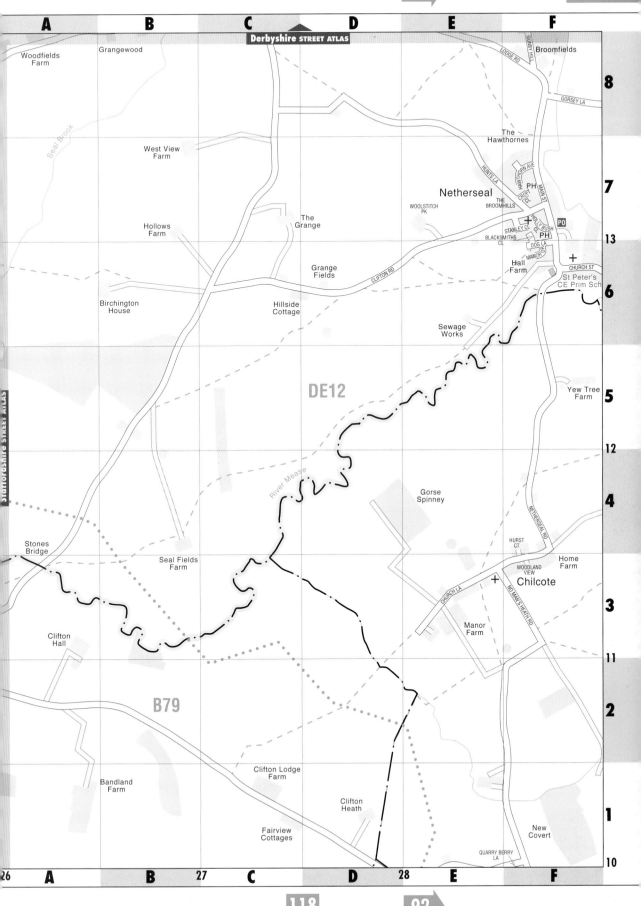

A   B   C   D   E   F

Staffordshire STREET ATLAS

Woodfields Farm

Grangewood

Seal Brook

West View Farm

Hollows Farm

The Grange

Birchington House

Grange Fields

Hillside Cottage

Clifton Rd

Stones Bridge

Seal Fields Farm

River Mease

DE12

Gorse Spinney

Sewage Works

Yew Tree Farm

Clifton Hall

B79

Clifton Lodge Farm

Bandland Farm

Clifton Heath

Fairview Cottages

LODGE RD

GUNBY HILL

Broomfields

GORSEY LA

The Hawthornes

HUNTS LA

Netherseal

WOOLSTITCH PK

THE BROOMHILLS

HAWTHORN AVE

CROFT CL

MAIN ST

PH

STANLEY CL

HOLT BUSH CL

PH

PO

BLACKSMITHS CL

DOG LA

MANOR

Hall Farm

CHURCH ST

St Peter's CE Prim Sch

NETHERSEAL RD

HURST CT

WOODLAND VIEW

Home Farm

Chilcote

CHURCH LA

NO MAN'S HEATH RD

Manor Farm

New Covert

QUARRY BERRY LA

8

7

13

6

5

12

4

3

11

2

1

10

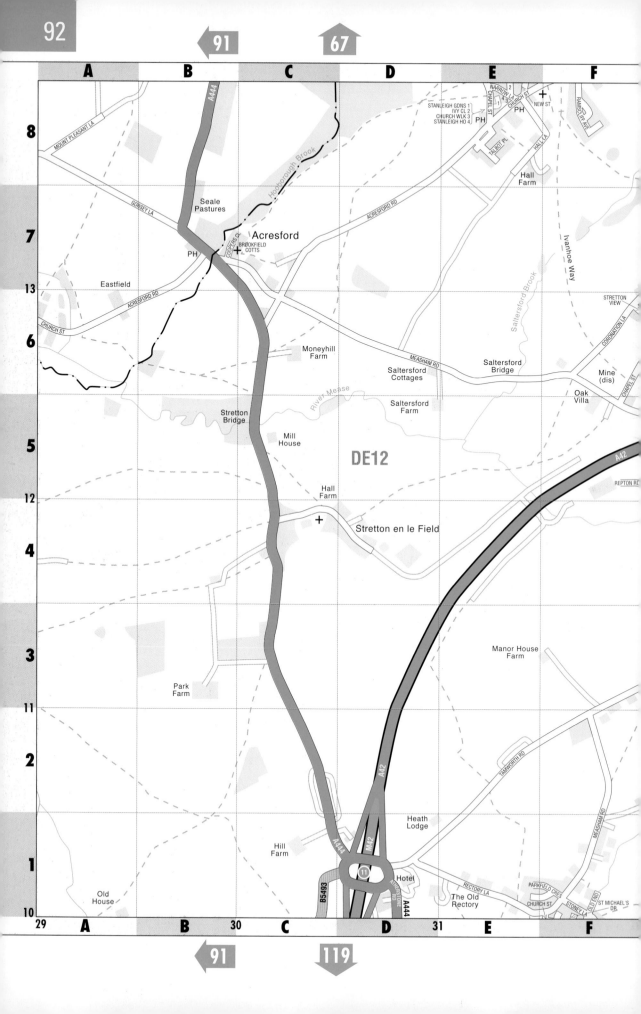

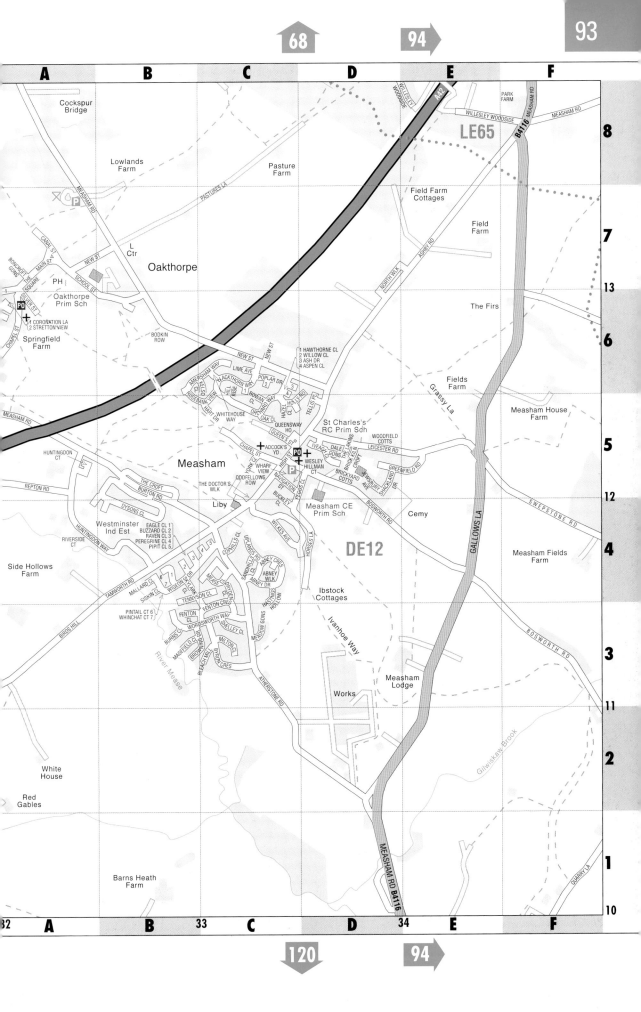

Cockspur Bridge

Lowlands Farm

Pasture Farm

PASTURES LA

WILLESLEY WOODSIDE

A42

LE65

PARK FARM

WILLESLEY WOODSIDE

MEASHAM RD

B4116

MEASHAM RD

Field Farm Cottages

Field Farm

The Firs

8

7

13

6

MEASHAM RD

CANAL ST

MAIN ST

THE SQUARE

BONCROFT GDNS

SILVER ST

CHAPEL ST

THE

PH

PO

NEW ST

SCHOOL ST

L Ctr

Oakthorpe

Oakthorpe Prim Sch

1 CORONATION LA
2 STRETTON VIEW

Springfield Farm

BODKIN ROW

NEW ST

LIME AVE

NEW ST

POPLAR DR

AMPSHAM WAY

BLACKTHORN WY

KILSBY

HILL RISE

ROSEBANK

HART DR

ROWAN CL

ORCHARD WAY

OAK CL

HAZEL CL

HOLLY RD

LILY RD

TELLIS PL

WHITEHOUSE WAY

QUEENSWAY

QUEENSWAY HO

1 HAWTHORNE CL
2 WILLOW CL
3 ASH DR
4 ASPEN CL

NORTH WLK

ASH BT RD

St Charles's RC Prim Sch

Fields Farm

Grassy La

Measham House Farm

5

12

MEASHAM RD

Measham

HUNTINGDON CT

REPTON RD

THE CROFT

BURTON RD

DYSONS CL

Westminster Ind Est

RIVERSIDE CT

HUNTINGDON WAY

CHAPEL ST

ADCOCK'S YD

QUEEN'S ST

YORK CL

WHARF VIEW

THE DOCTOR'S WLK

ODDFELLOWS ROW

Liby

HIGH ST

NAVIGATION ST

PEGGS CL

PO

WESLEY HILLMAN CT

IVEAGH CL

DALE

DALE GDNS

THE LAWNS

BRICK KILN

CROFT

NEWBURY AVE

BRICKYARD COTTS

SHACKLAND DR

GREENFIELD RD

WOODFIELD COTTS

LEICESTER RD

BOSWORTH RD

Measham CE Prim Sch

Cemy

SWEPSTONE RD

Measham House Farm

DE12

Side Hollows Farm

EAGLE CL 1
BUZZARD CL 2
RAVEN CL 3
PEREGRINE CL 4
PIPIT CL 5

TAMWORTH RD

MALLARD CL

SISKIN CL

WIGEON CL

SKYLARK

COPPHILLS CL

UPLANDS RD

SANDHILLS CL

MEASE CL

ABNEY CRES

ABNEY WLK

ABNEY DR

WILKES AVE

HORSES LA

Ibstock Cottages

Ivanhoe Way

GALLOWS LA

Measham Fields Farm

Measham Lodge

BOSWORTH RD

4

3

11

PINTAIL CT 6
WHINCHAT CT 7

FENTON CL

TENNYSON CL

BURNS CL

MASEFIELD CL

BROWNING

WORDSWORTH WAY

GENTON CRES

SHELLEY CL

MILTON CL

BLEACH MILL

BYRON CRES

MEADOW GDNS

HASTINGS HOLLOW

ATHERSTONE RD

River Mease

Works

Gilwiskaw Brook

QUARRY LA

2

1

10

White House

Red Gables

Barns Heath Farm

A   B   C   D   E   F

32   33   34

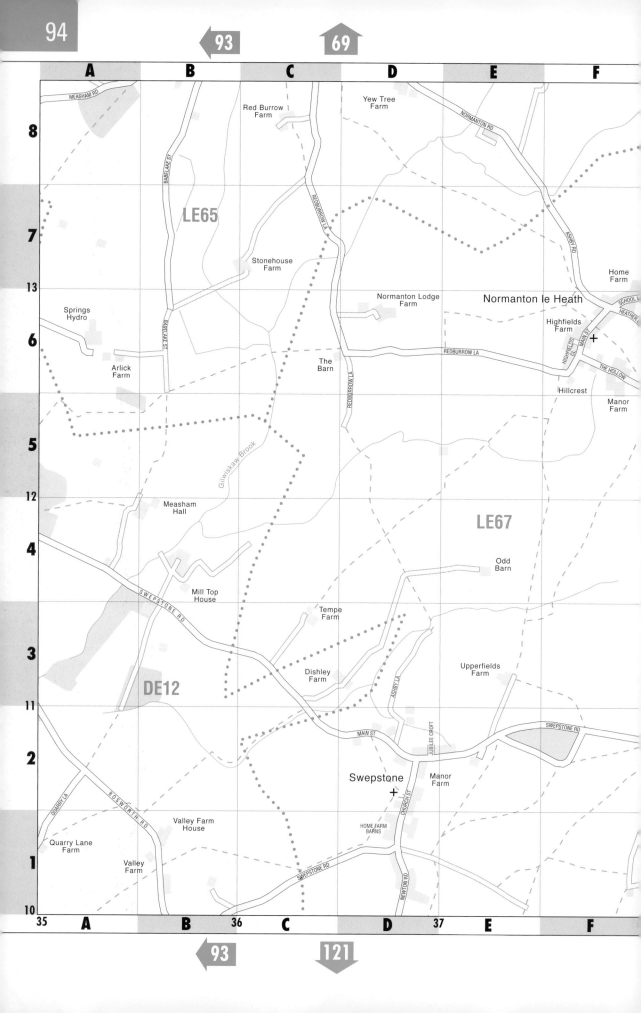

LE65

LE67

Ravenstone

Ravenstone
CT

THE LEACROFTS

PH

Woodstone
Com Prim Sch

Sewage
Works

Long Moor
Farm

Blowers Brook

HEATHER LA

HEATHER LA

RAVENSTONE RD

Kelham Bridge
Farm

MELBOURNE RD

IBSTOCK RD
A447 WASH LA

THE CROFT

LEICESTER RD

ST MARY'S LA

Sewage
Works

BLACKBERRY LA

Cattows
Farm

NORMANTON LA

Sence Valley
Forest Park

RAVENSTONE RD

Ibstock

VICTORIA RD

CHRISTOPHER
CL

Ind
Est

MARSTON
WAY

BELCHER CL

THE ROOKERY

BLACKETT DR

SPARKENHOE
EST

MANOR DR

MAIN ST

HEATHER
HO

ST JOHN'S CL

PO
P

HOLYOAKE CRES

HOLYOAKE
DR

Heather
PHPrim Sch

PISCA LA

Heather

Beresford
CT

COTSMORE CL

MILL LA

SWEPSTONE RD

Heather
Hall

Ind
Est

NEWTON RD

STATION TERR

Works

STATION RD

Springbank
Farm

Clare
Farm

ASHBY RD

ASHDALE

LAUD CL

VALLEY RD

ST DENYS CRES

Schs

Ibstock
Com Coll

Liby

BERNARD
CL

HIGH ST

ORCHARD ST

GRANGE RD

ENFIELD ST

CURZON ST

SPRINGFIELD CL

BROOKSIDE

DEEPDALE CL

MEADOW
WLK

Ind
Est

PAGET RD

LEICESTER RD

GAMBLE CL

FLATTS CL

COSTELLO CL

ALBERT ST

PENISTONE

WINCHESTER
CL

CHARTERS
CL

JACQUES ST

ELIZABETH AVE

ARGYLE ST

HASTINGS ST

CHAPEL ST

SPRY
WLK

WEST WLK

WIDGOOSE
WAY

SWIFTS
CL

THE
STRAND

COSTPAN AVE

CENTRAL AVE

WOODGATE

MAPLE
DR

SYCAMORE
CL

ROWAN
DR

CHESTNUT
CL

FERNDALE

HEATHERDALE

THORNDALE

WILLOW
CL

OAK DR

CEDAR DR

ELM CL

PARKDALE

BEECH
WAY

LINDEN
CL

MELBOURNE RD

A447

GLADSTONE

HARRATTS CL

Ravenstone Rd to Ibstock area map

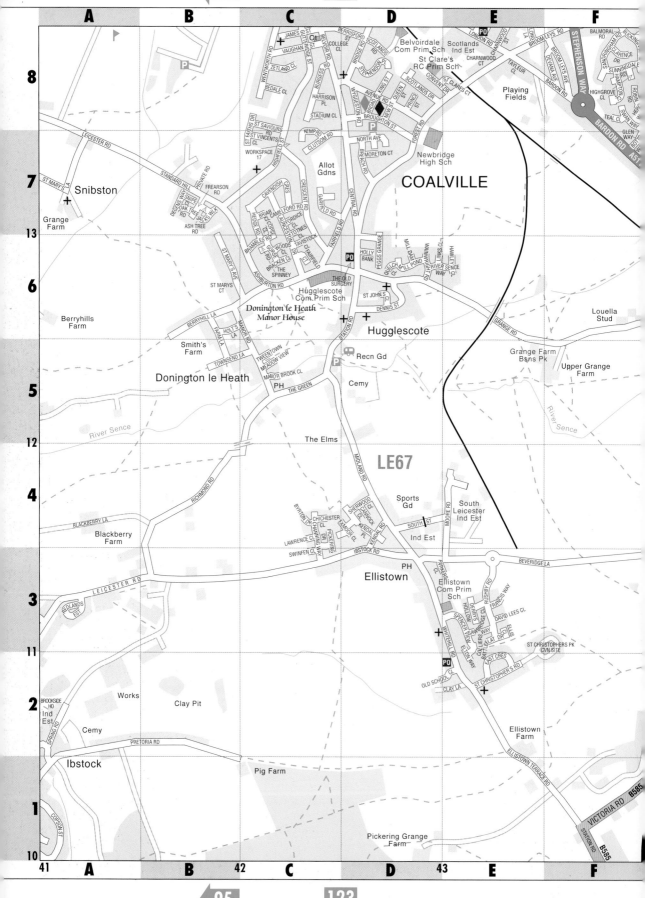

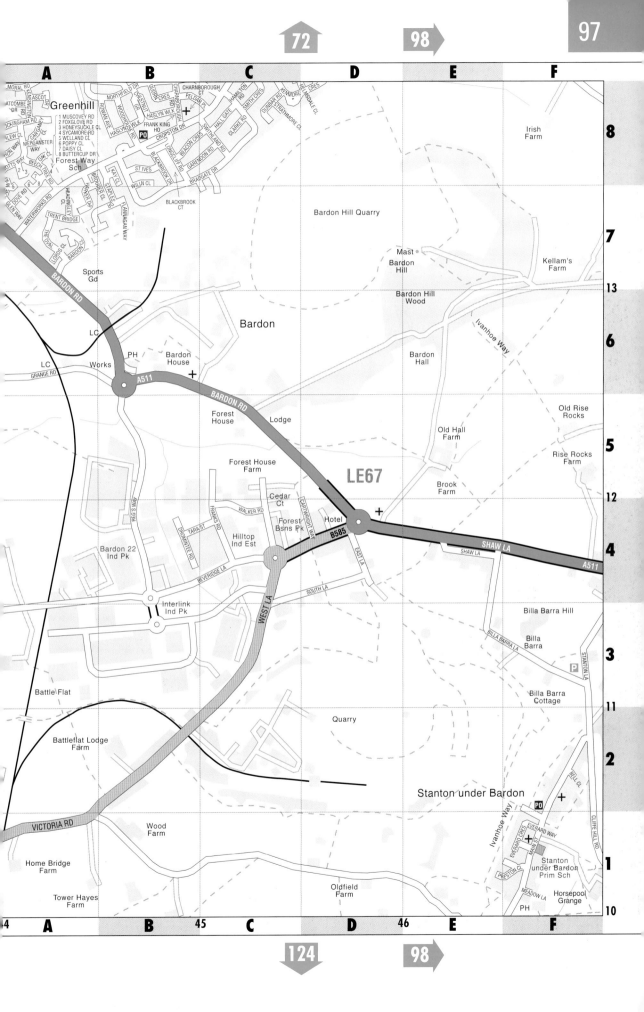

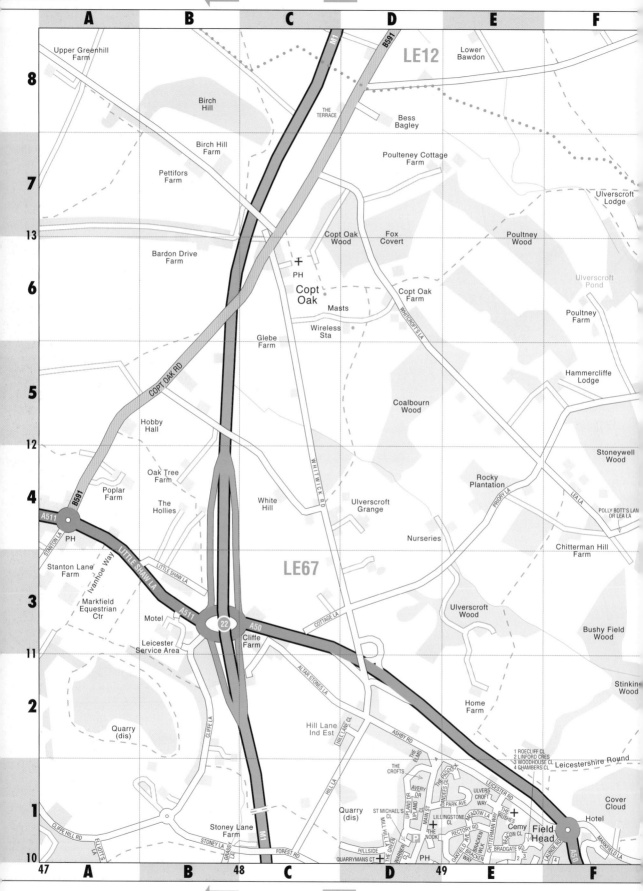

LE12

Upper Greenhill Farm

Birch Hill

Birch Hill Farm

Pettifors Farm

Bardon Drive Farm

Lower Bawdon

Bess Bagley

THE TERRACE

Poulteney Cottage Farm

Copt Oak Wood

Fox Covert

Ulverscroft Lodge

Poultney Wood

COPT OAK RD

Hobby Hall

Oak Tree Farm

The Hollies

Poplar Farm

PH

Copt Oak

Masts

Wireless Sta

Glebe Farm

Copt Oak Farm

WHITCROFT'S LA

Coalbourn Wood

Ulverscroft Pond

Poultney Farm

Hammercliffe Lodge

Stoneywell Wood

Rocky Plantation

PRIORY LA

LEA LA

White Hill

Ulverscroft Grange

WHITWICK RD

Nurseries

POLLY BOTT'S LAN OR LEA LA

Chitterman Hill Farm

STANTON LA

PH

A511

B591

LITTLE SHAW LA

Ivanhoe Way

LITTLE SHAW LA

LE67

Stanton Lane Farm

Markfield Equestrian Ctr

Motel

Leicester Service Area

A511

22

A50

Cliffe Farm

COTTAGE LA

Ulverscroft Wood

Bushy Field Wood

Quarry (dis)

CLIFFE LA

ALTAR STONES LA

Stinkin Wood

Home Farm

Hill Lane Ind Est

HILL LANE CL

ASHBY RD

1 ROECLIFF CL
2 LINFORD CRES
3 WOODHOUSE CL
4 CHAMBERS CL

Leicestershire Round

HILL LA

Quarry (dis)

THE CROFTS

THE ELMS

THE PADDOCK

DANDOES CL

Cover Cloud

Hotel

Field Head

Cliffe Hill Rd

ELLIOTTS LA

Stoney Lane Farm

STONEY LA

GRASSY LA

M1

FOREST RD

HILLSIDE

QUARRYMANS CT

MILL HILL LA

THE GREEN

WARNER CL

ST MICHAEL'S CL

UPLAND DR

UPLAND

AVERY DR

MAIN ST

THE NOOK

PH

RECTORY RD

LILLINGSTONE CL

PARK AVE

OAKFIELD AV

BRACKEN WALK

ULVERS CROFT WAY

MEADOW WAY

CHITTERMAN WAY

BRACKEN WAY

LEICESTER RD

THE RUSHES

THE PULLINS

Cemy

CON CL

BRADGATE RD

LALINGE RD

A50

MARKFIELD LA

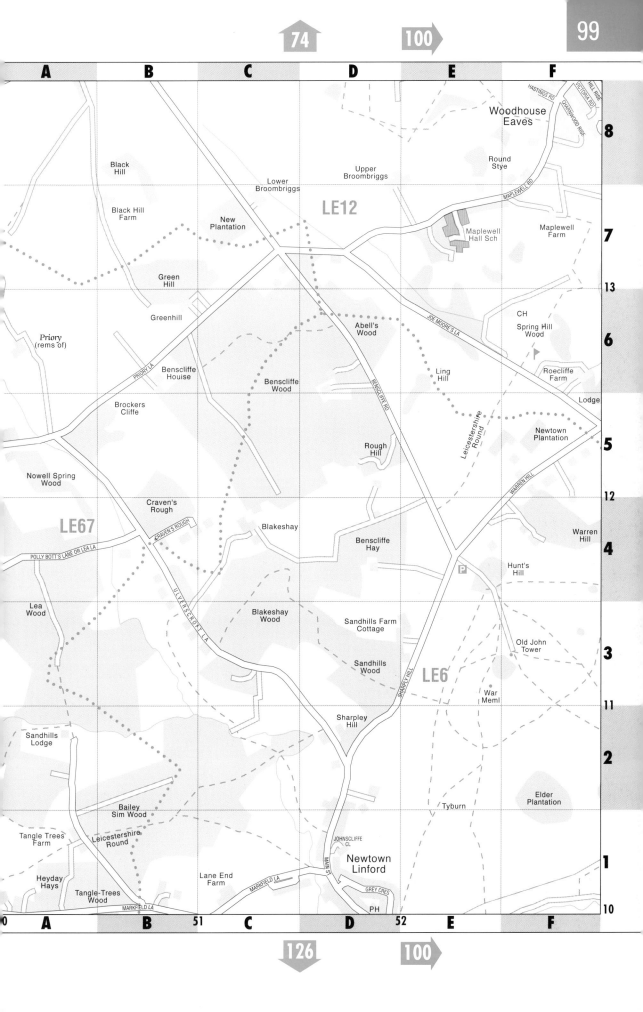

A B C D E F

8

Woodhouse
Eaves

Black
Hill

Round
Stye

HASTINGS RD
HILL RISE
VICTORIA RD
CHARNWOOD RISE

Lower
Broombriggs

Upper
Broombriggs

Black Hill
Farm

LE12

New
Plantation

Maplewell
Hall Sch

Maplewell
Farm

MAPLEWELL RD

7

Green
Hill

13

Greenhill

Abell's
Wood

JOE MOORE'S LA

CH
Spring Hill
Wood

Priory
(rems of)

Benscliffe
House

Benscliffe
Wood

Ling
Hill

6

Roecliffe
Farm

PRIORY LA

Brockers
Cliffe

BENSCLIFFE RD

Lodge

Rough
Hill

Leicestershire
Round

Newtown
Plantation

5

Nowell Spring
Wood

12

LE67

Craven's
Rough

Blakeshay

Benscliffe
Hay

WARREN HILL

Warren
Hill

4

CRAVEN'S ROUGH

POLLY BOTT'S LANE OR LEA LA

P

Hunt's
Hill

ULVERSCROFT LA

Lea
Wood

Blakeshay
Wood

Sandhills Farm
Cottage

Old John
Tower

3

Sandhills
Wood

SHARPLEY HILL

LE6

11

War
Meml

Sandhills
Lodge

Sharpley
Hill

2

Bailey
Sim Wood

Tyburn

Elder
Plantation

Tangle Trees
Farm

Leicestershire
Round

MAIN ST

JOHNSCLIFFE
CL

Lane End
Farm

Newtown
Linford

1

Heyday
Hays

Tangle-Trees
Wood

MARKFIELD LA

GREY CRES

MARKFIELD LA

PH

10

99 75

A B C D E F

8

LE7

THE DRIVE
HILL RISE
NANHILL DR
Hunger Hill
CHARNWOOD HO
BRAND HILL
SWITHLAND CT
THE GRANGE
PH
BRAND LA

Swithland Resr
Nature Reserve

Swithland Resr

7

Barn Farm
The Brand
Brand Hills

Swithland

The Rectory
Swithland
St Leonard's
CE Prim Sch

13

The White House

LE12

PH
KEEPERS CL
CHASNA GR

Hall Farm

6

Roecliffe Hill

MAIN ST

Swithland Hall

Roecliffe Manor

Swithland Camp
Swithland Wood Farm
Swithland Wood

Moore Spinney

LEICESTER LA

The Rough

5

Swithland Woods
Nature Reserve

Cropston Leys

Bybrooke Lodge Farm

12

SWITHLAND RD

4

Filter Sta
ROECLIFFE RD

BRADGATE RD

Hallgate Hill Spinney
Hallgates

LODGE LA

Water Works

LE7

Cropston

STATION RD
SANDHAM BRIDGE RD
GUILD CL
CAUDLE CL
LATIMER

3

Sliding Stone Enclosure

Coppice Plantation

Bradgate Country Park

RESERVOIR RD

Cropston Resr
Nature Reserve

PH
PO
PH
FOX HOLLOW
STAMFORD
THISTLE CL
OUTFIELDS DR
WATERFIELD RD
PAISLEY CL

11

Dale Spinney

Cropston Resr

JOSEPH CL
LYCHGATE CL

2

Bradgate Park
(Deer Park)

LE6

Deer Park Spinney

Boat House

Cvn Site
CAUSEWAY LA
Cropston House Farm

LEICESTERSHIRE ROUND

Bowling Green Spinney

CROPSTON RD

1

Bradgate
(rems of)

10

Sewage Works

53 A B 54 C D 55 E F

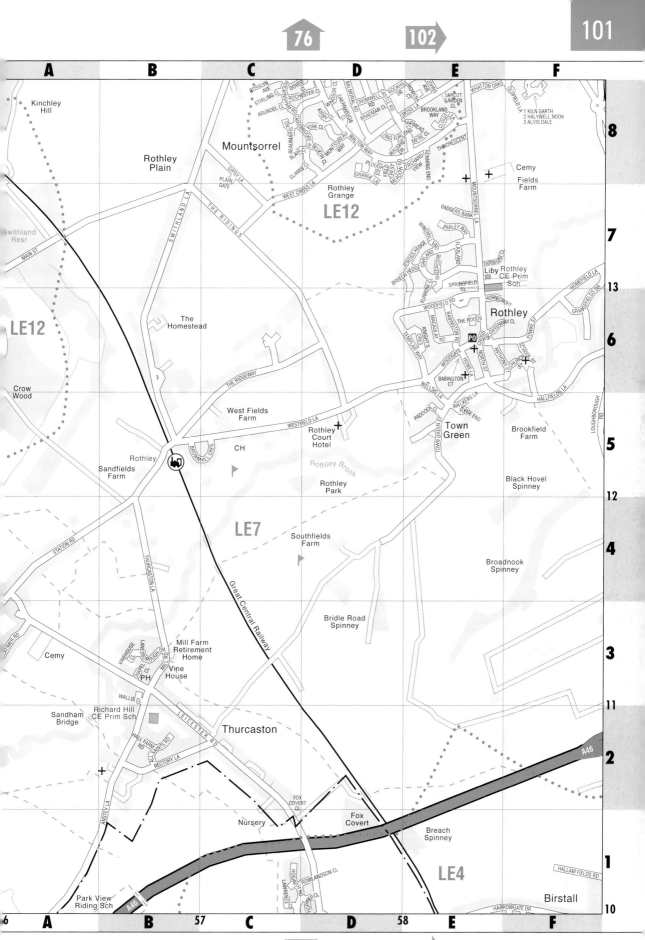

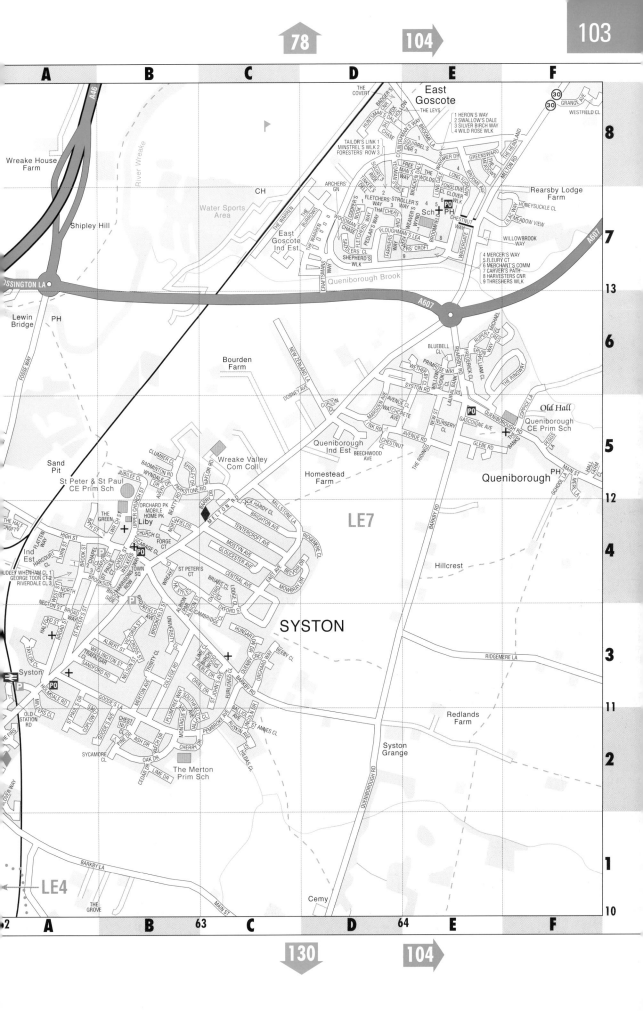

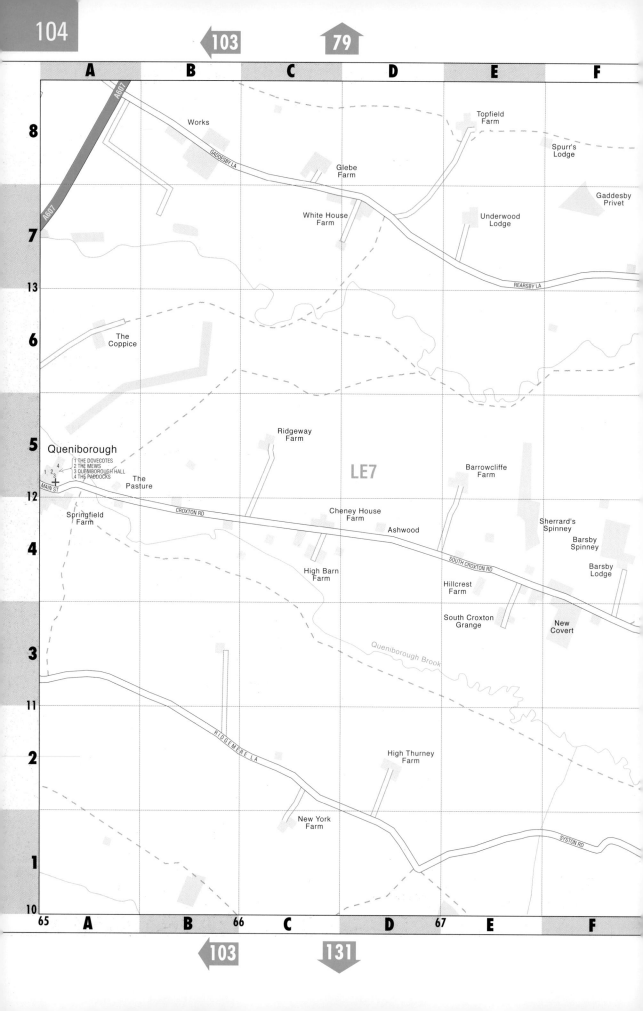

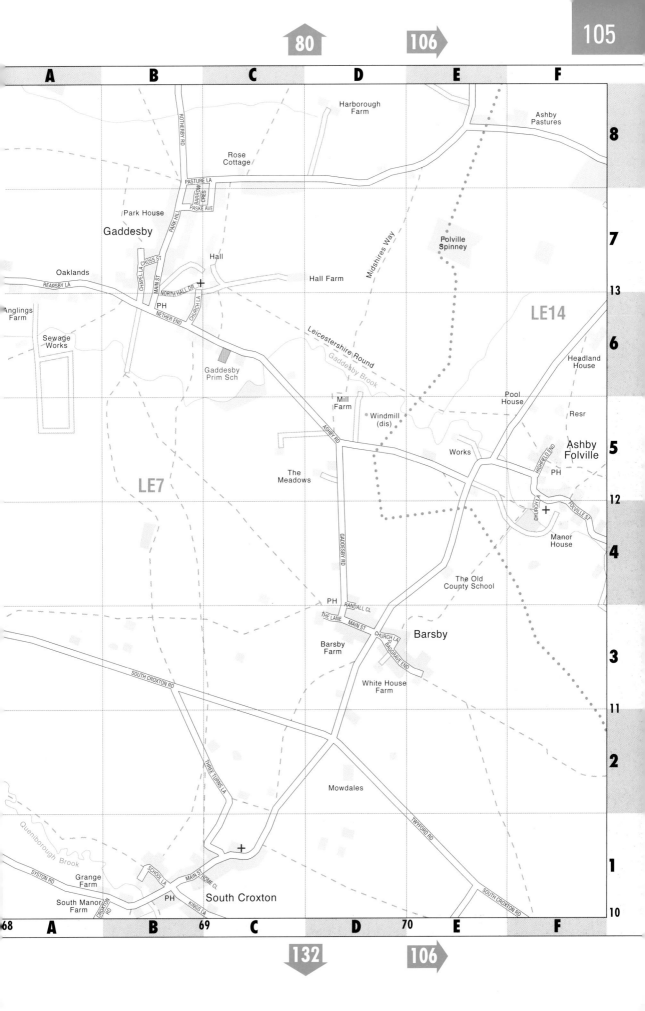

A   B   C   D   E   F

8

Harborough
Farm

Ashby
Pastures

Rose
Cottage

PASTURE LA

BARROW
CRES

Park House

PASKE AVE

Gaddesby

7

ROTHERBY RD

PARK HILL

Midshires Way

Polville
Spinney

Hall

CHAPEL LA

CROSS ST

MAIN ST

Hall Farm

13

Oaklands

REARSBY LA

NORTH HALL DR

CHURCH LA

+

LE14

PH

NETHER END

Anglings
Farm

Leicestershire Round

Gaddesby Brook

Headland
House

6

Sewage
Works

Gaddesby
Prim Sch

Mill
Farm

Windmill
(dis)

Pool
House

Resr

LE7

The
Meadows

ASHBY RD

Works

HIGHFIELD END

Ashby
Folville

5

PH

CHURCH LA

FOLVILLE ST

12

GADDESBY RD

Manor
House

4

The Old
County School

PH

RANDALL CL

THE LANE

MAIN ST

CHURCH LA

Barsby

3

Barsby
Farm

SAXBY END

11

White House
Farm

SOUTH CROXTON RD

2

THREE TURNS LA

Mowdales

TWYFORD RD

+

Quenborough Brook

1

SYSTON RO

Grange
Farm

SCHOOL LA

MAIN ST

HOME CL

South Croxton

CROXTON RD

PH

KINGS LA

SOUTH CROXTON RD

South Manor
Farm

10

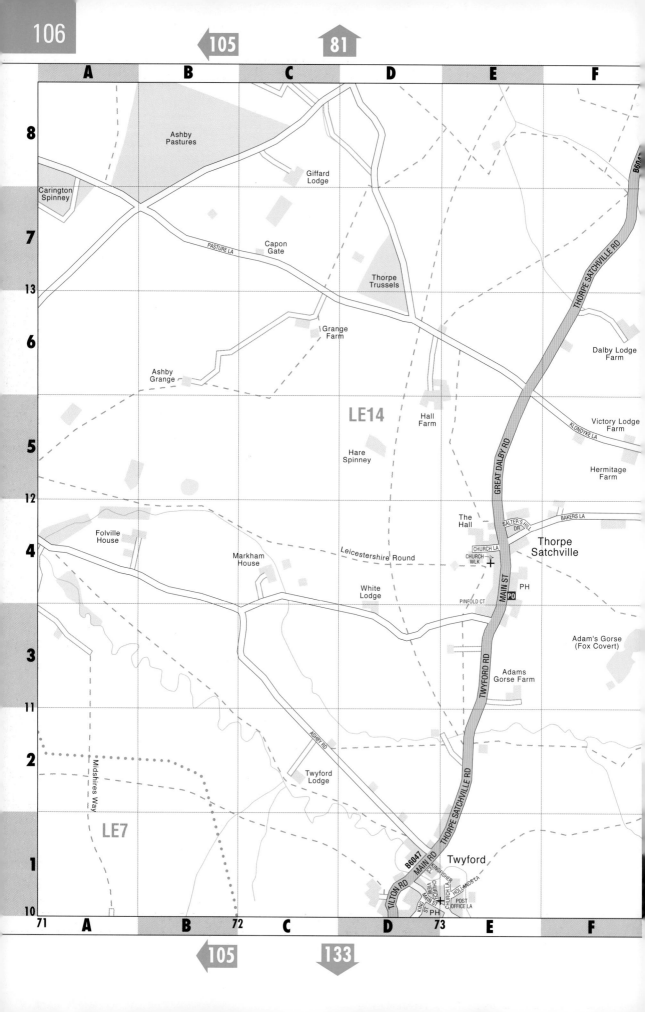

A   B   C   D   E   F

8

Ashby Pastures

Giffard Lodge

Carington Spinney

7

PASTURE LA   Capon Gate

Thorpe Satchville Rd

13

Thorpe Trussels

6

Grange Farm

Dalby Lodge Farm

Ashby Grange

LE14

Hall Farm

Victory Lodge Farm

Klondyke La

5

Hare Spinney

Hermitage Farm

12

Folville House

The Hall

Salter's Hill Dr   Bakers La

4

Markham House

Leicestershire Round

Church Wlk   Church La

Thorpe Satchville

Great Dalby Rd

White Lodge

Main St   PH   PO

Pinfold Ct

Adam's Gorse (Fox Covert)

3

Twyford Rd

Adams Gorse Farm

11

2

Ashby Rd

Twyford Lodge

Midshires Way

LE7

1

B6047   Main Rd   Twyford

Tilton Rd   Kingfisher View   Church La Horbu   Holl Mids La

Church St   Main St   King...   Post Office La   PH

10

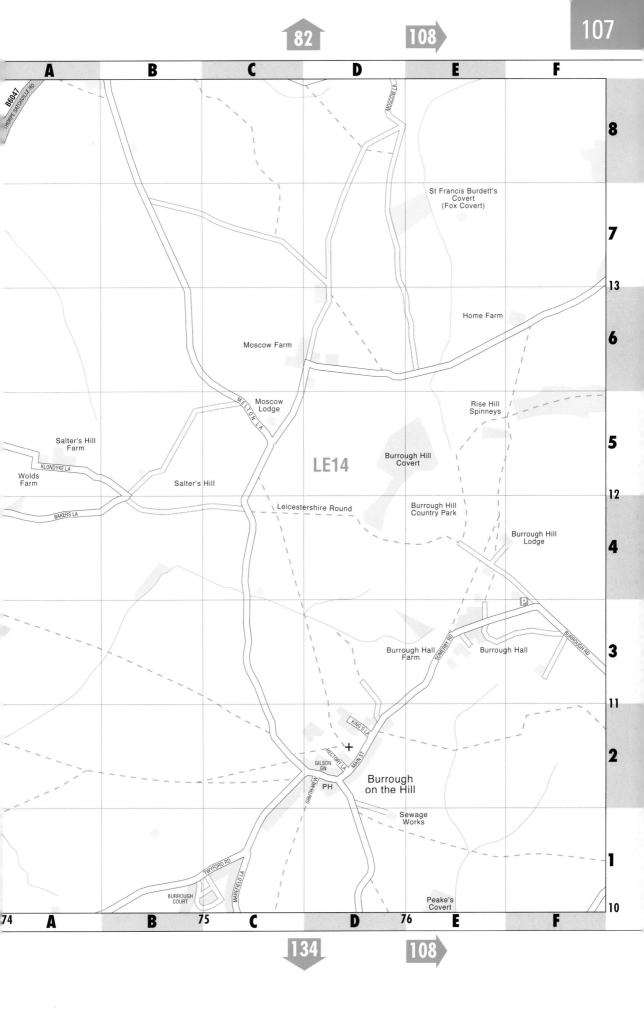

| | A | B | C | D | E | F |

BENSKIN CL
CHURCH LA
Wheat Hill Spinney
Grange Cottages
OAKHAM RD
A606

8

Mill Hill Spinney
Little Dalby Hall
The Hall
The Grange
A606

BURROUGH RD
Leesthorpe

7

Landfield Spinney
Hall Farm
Leesthorpe House Farm
Alpine Cottages

The Breeches

13

Green Spinney
Debdale Lodge

6

Buttermilk Hill Spinney
Debdale Spinney
Brocker Farm

LE15
LEESTHORPE RD

Kyte Hill

Punch Bowl Covert

STYGATE LA

5

12

LE14

4

Leicestershire Round

THE CRESCENT
SAXONS LEA
STONEPIT TERR

Pickwell
WEST END COTTS
MAIN ST
STRAWBERRY CT

3

Pickwell Manor

11

The Grange
SOMERBY RD

BURROUGH RD

2

Somerby Hall Farm
PICKWELL RD

GROVE COTTS
SCHOOL COTTS
Somerby Prim Sch
GROVE STUD
THE FIELD
MILL LA
HIGH ST
P.H. PO
CHURCH LA
MANOR LA
CHAPEL LA
Firdale Farm
Cemy
Oaklands
The Grove
WEST VIEW
TOWN END
EAST ACRE
FIRDALE

1

Somerby
Somerby Lodge

KNOSSINGTON RD
OAKHAM RD
Dinghills Farm

10

| 77 | A | | B | 78 | C | | D | 79 | E | | F |

A   B   C   D   E   F

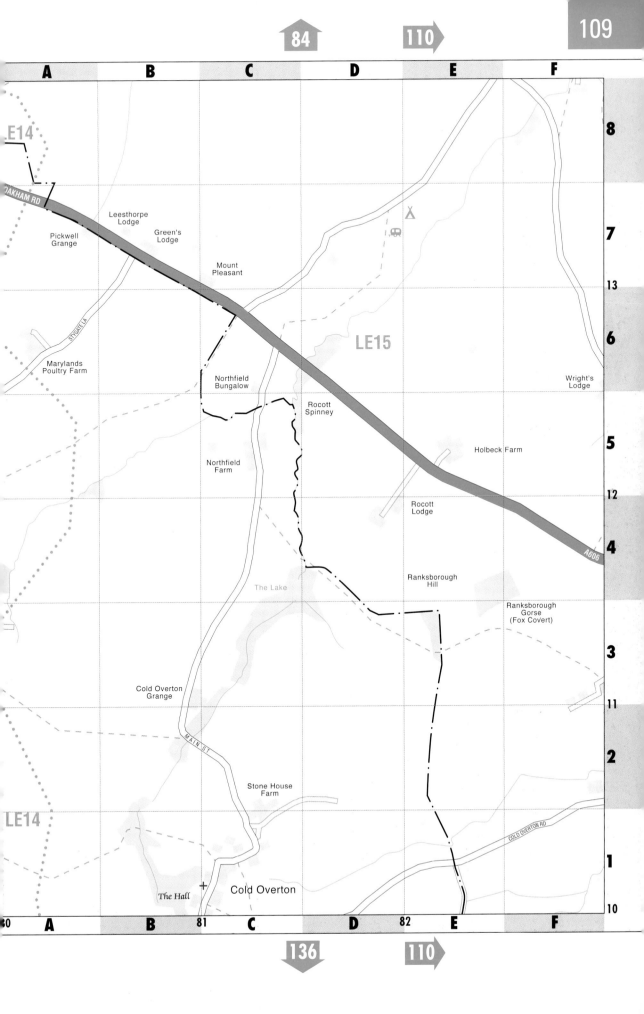

LE14

8

OAKHAM RD

Leesthorpe
Lodge

Green's
Lodge

Pickwell
Grange

7

Mount
Pleasant

13

LE15

6

STYGATE LA

Marylands
Poultry Farm

Wright's
Lodge

Northfield
Bungalow

Rocott
Spinney

Northfield
Farm

Holbeck Farm

5

Rocott
Lodge

12

A606

4

Ranksborough
Hill

The Lake

Ranksborough
Gorse
(Fox Covert)

3

Cold Overton
Grange

11

MAIN ST

2

Stone House
Farm

LE14

COLD OVERTON RD

1

The Hall

Cold Overton

10

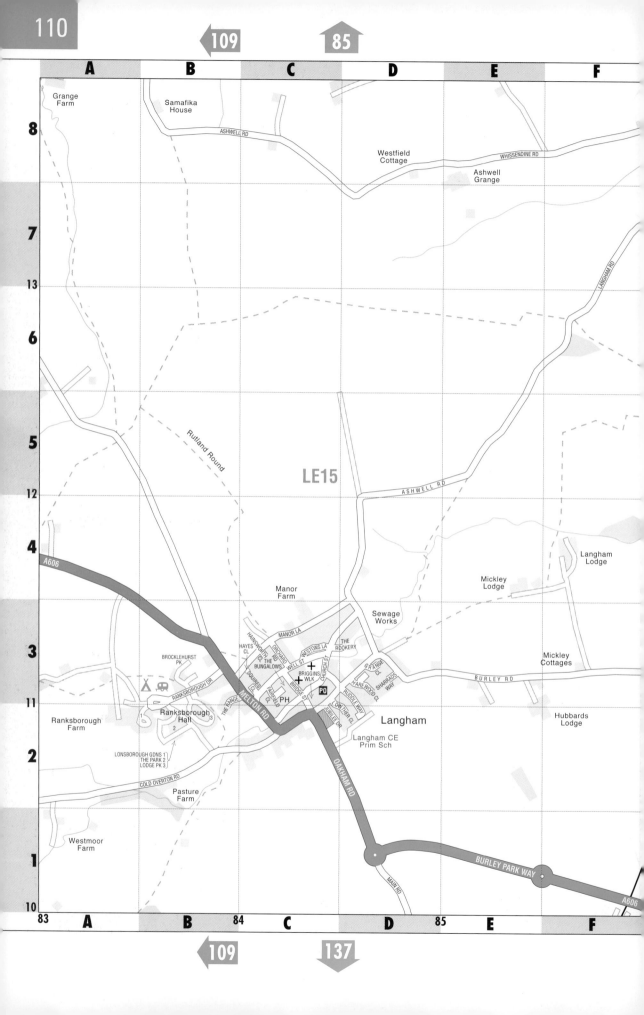

109
85

A   B   C   D   E   F

8

Grange
Farm

Samafika
House

ASHWELL RD

Westfield
Cottage

WHISSENDINE RD

Ashwell
Grange

7

LANGHAM RD

13

6

Rutland Round

5

LE15

ASHWELL RD

12

4

A606

Langham
Lodge

Manor
Farm

Mickley
Lodge

3

MANOR LA

THE
ROOKERY

HAINSWORTH RD
HAYES CL
THE
BUNGALOWS
ORCHARD RD
NESTONS LA
WELL ST

Sewage
Works

Mickley
Cottages

BROCKLEHURST
PK

GRANGE CL

SHARRADS WAY

BURLEY RD

BRIGGINS WLK

SQUIRES CL
FAIRFIELD CL
CHURCH ST
BRIDGE ST

HAREWOOD CL
RUDDLE WAY

PO

11

RANKSBOROUGH DR
THE RANGE
MELTON RD
PH

LOWTHER CL

Ranksborough
Hall

3

JUBILEE DR

Langham

Hubbards
Lodge

Ranksborough
Farm

2

LONSBOROUGH GDNS 1
THE PARK 2
LODGE PK 3

COLD OVERTON RD

Pasture
Farm

Langham CE
Prim Sch

OAKHAM RD

1

Westmoor
Farm

MAIN RD

BURLEY PARK WAY

A606

10

83   A   B   84   C   D   85   E   F

109
137

A   B   C   D   E   F

8

7

13

6

5

12

4

3

11

2

1

10

Manor Farm

LC

WHISSENDINE RD

TEIGH RD

CROFT LA

BRAESIDE

PO

CHURCH CL

Ashwell

BROOK DENE

WATER LA

Cottesmore Bridge

Cottesmore Rd

Rutland Railway Line

Rutland Railway Mus

LANGHAM RD

LC

Home Farm

Eastfield Farm

OAKHAM RD

Ashwell Hall

Flint's Covert

Langham Place

LE15

Brownswell's Covert

Hollow Close Covert

Poor Close Covert

KIMBALL CL

Bottom Mill Covert

HM Prison Ashwell

Brick Kiln Covert

LC

BURLEY RD

BURLEY CRES

Millfield Spinney (Fox Covert)

B668

COTTESMORE RD

HOME FARM CL

Langham La

Cemy

Home Farm

Egg Spinney

ASHWELL RD

Hillside Farm

CHURCH RD

Burley

THE STABLES

Burley on the Hill

Burley Park

Purveyor's Covert

OAKHAM RD

Springfield House

Oakham Veterinary Hospl

A606

B668

111
87

A   B   C   D   E   F

8

St Nicholas CE Prim Sch

SHEEPDYKE
MILL LA
DEBDALE
CLATTERPOT LA
CRESWELL
HALL CL
ROGUE'S LA
LONG MEADOW WAY
WESTLAND RD
HEATH DR
NETHER CL
GREETHAM RD
B668

Cottesmore Lodge

ST NICHOLAS CT
PO
MAIN ST
THE SPINNEY
THE LEAS
TOLL BAR
THE BECK
Cottesmore

7

ASHWELL RD
WYXTON CL
BURLEY RD
ALSTHORP GR
PH
Manor Farm

Cottesmore House

EXTON RD

Cottesmore Wood

13

6

Watkin's Gorse

Rattling Jack Spinney

5

Chapel Farm

Hall Farm

12

LE15

COTTESMORE RD

Nursery

4

Alstoe Farm

Cow Close Farm

Ry Gate Lake

3

B668
COTTESMORE RD
Wr Twr

Brick Kiln Spinney

Brook Farm

Exton Park

11

Glebe Farm

The Grange

Ry Gate Plantation

OAKHAM RD

2

Egg Spinney
Crow Spinney

EXTON LA

Barnsdale Gardens

BARNSDALE AVE

Lodge

Springfield Barn

1

Burley Park

Rutland Falconry & Owl Ctr
Burley Bushes

10

89   A   B   90   C   D   91   E   F

111
139

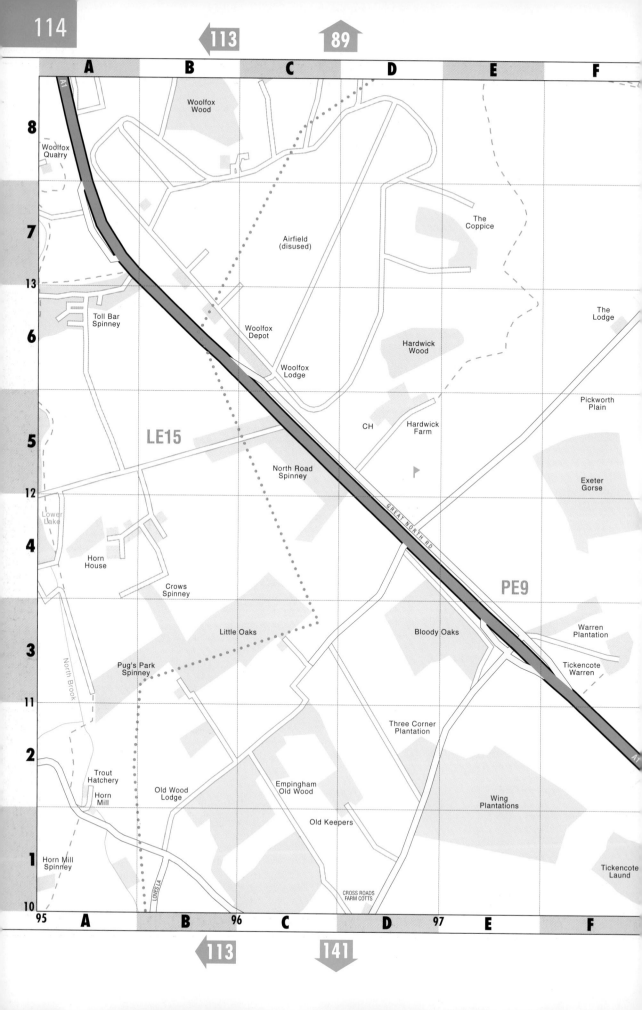

A **B** **C** **D** **E** **F**

The Limekiln

Manor Farm

Pickworth

Turnpole Wood

Christian's Lodge

Taylor's Farm

PE9

Eayres Lodge

Woodhead

East Wood

PICKWORTH RD

Mounts Lodge

A1

Tickencote Laund

RYHALL RD

Lincolnshire STREET ATLAS

A   B   C   D   E   F

8

7

13

6

5

12

4

11

3

2

1

10

Little
Warren

Barbers Hill
Farm

Heath
Farm

Crossroads
Spinney

Vale
Farm

Ryhall Heath
Farm

Clay
Hill

THE DRIFT

Tolethorpe
Oaks

PE9

Ryhall Farm
Cottage

Grange
Farm

Ryhall Farm
Cottage

Walk
Farm

Top
Farm

Frith
Farm

Gwash Valley
Farm

River Gwash

Rob Hall
Farm

Rutland
Open Air
Theatre

Tolethorpe
Mill

Tolethorpe
Hall

The
Rookery

Home
Farm

B1176

TURNPIKE RD

ESSENDINE RD

A6121

A6121

MILL ST

CROWN ST

FOUNDRY RD

MANOR CT

GWASH CL

WATERSIDE

BRIDGE ST

POST
OFFICE LA

THE SQUARE

PO

PH

HIGHLANDS

LEA VIEW

NEW RD

The
Hall

Cemy

Liby

St John's Cl

BALK RD

CHURCH ST

SPINNEY LA

SPINNEY CL

COPPICE RD

FRANCIS
CT

Ryhall
CE Prim
Sch

ST TIBBA WAY

BURLEY RD

RUTLAND WAY

PARKFIELD RD

MEADOW LA

BEECH DR

Ryhall

Ryhall RD

01   A   B   02   C   D   03   E   F

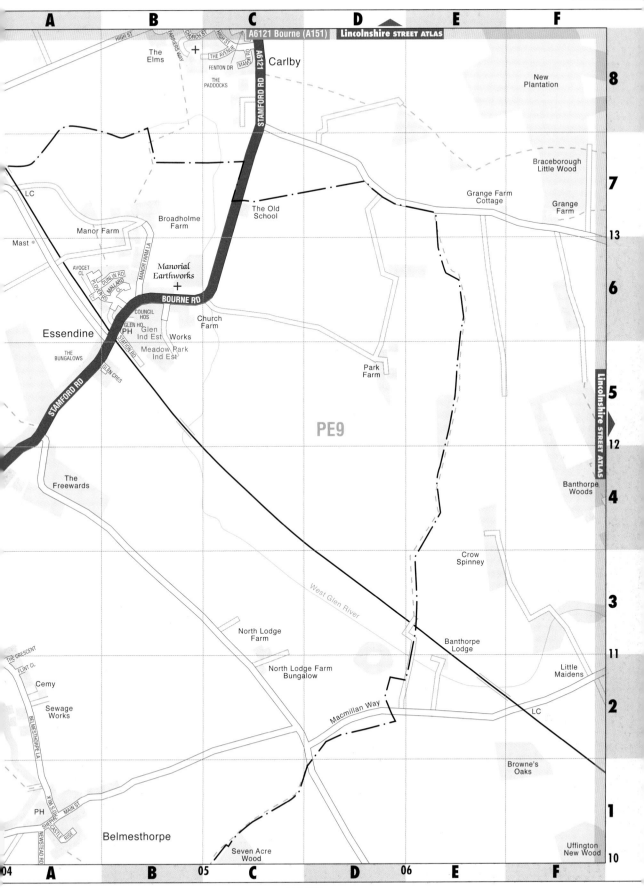

A6121 Bourne (A151)

Carlby

High St
CHURCH ST
The Elms
FARRIERS WAY
THE AVENUE
FENTON DR
MAIN RD
THE PADDOCKS
High St
STAMFORD RD A6121

New Plantation

Braceborough Little Wood

The Old School

Grange Farm Cottage

Grange Farm

Broadholme Farm

Manor Farm

LC

Mast

Manorial Earthworks

AVOCET CL
DUNLIN RD
PLOVER RD
MALLARD CL
MANOR FARM LA
BOURNE RD

COUNCIL HOS
GLEN HO
Glen Ind Est
PH
Essendine
STATION RD
The Bungalows
GLEN CRES

Church Farm
Works
Meadow Park Ind Est

Park Farm

PE9

STAMFORD RD

Banthorpe Woods

The Freewards

Crow Spinney

West Glen River

Banthorpe Lodge

North Lodge Farm

North Lodge Farm Bungalow

Little Maidens

THE CRESCENT
FLINT CL
Cemy
Sewage Works
BELMESTHORPE LA

Macmillan Way

LC

Browne's Oaks

PH
KNM S DRIVE
CASTLE RISE
MAIN ST
SHEPPERTON CL
NEWSTEAD RD
Belmesthorpe

Seven Acre Wood

Uffington New Wood

8
7
13
6
5
12
4
3
11
2
1
10

A   B   05   C   D   06   E   F
04

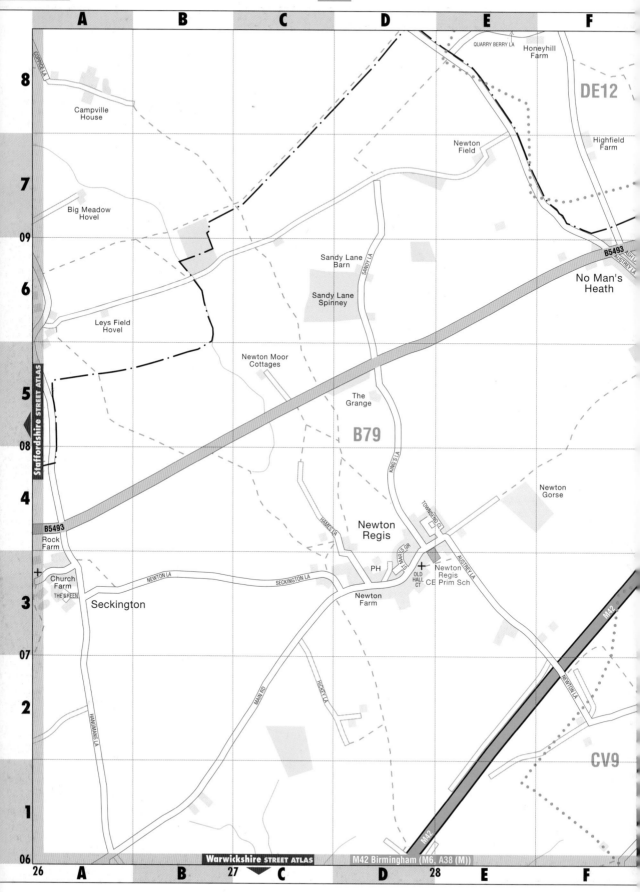

A B C D E F

8

7

09

6

5

08

4

B5493

3

07

2

1

06

26 A 27 B C 28 D E F

DE12

Quarry Berry La

Honeyhill Farm

Newton Field

Highfield Farm

B5493 · Astl La · Austrey La

No Man's Heath

Campville House

Big Meadow Hovel

Sandy Lane Barn

Sandy La

Sandy Lane Spinney

Leys Field Hovel

Newton Moor Cottages

The Grange

B79

King S La

Newton Gorse

Townsend Cl

Staffordshire STREET ATLAS

Rock Farm

Hames La

Newton Regis

Mares Gr

PH

Austrey La

Old Hall Ct

CE

Newton Regis Prim Sch

M42

Church Farm

THE GREEN

Newton La

Seckington La

Seckington

Newton Farm

Hangmans La

Main Rd

Hickey La

Newton La

CV9

M42

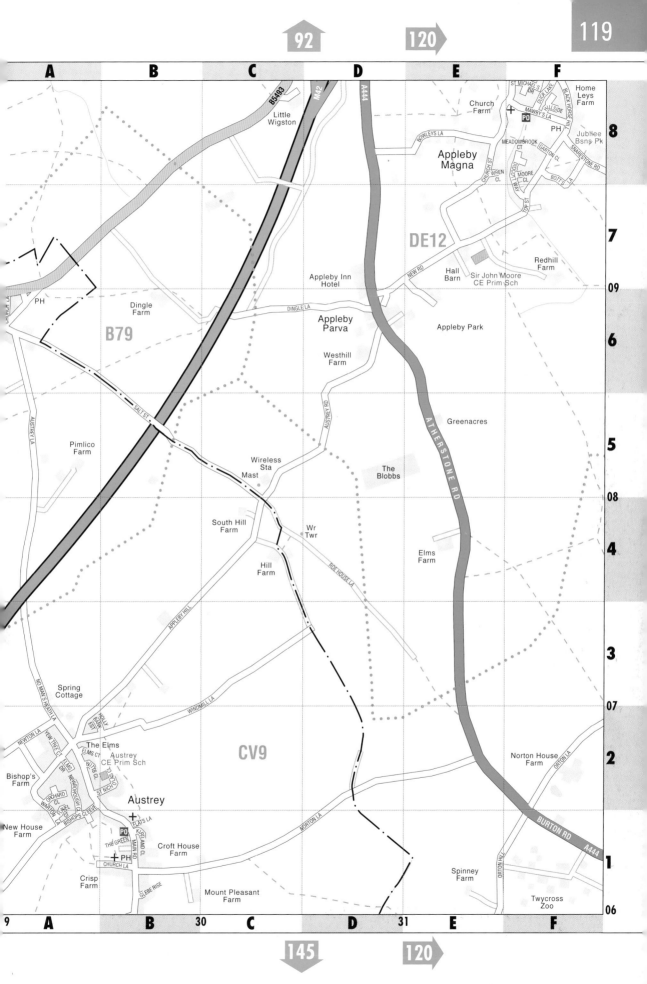

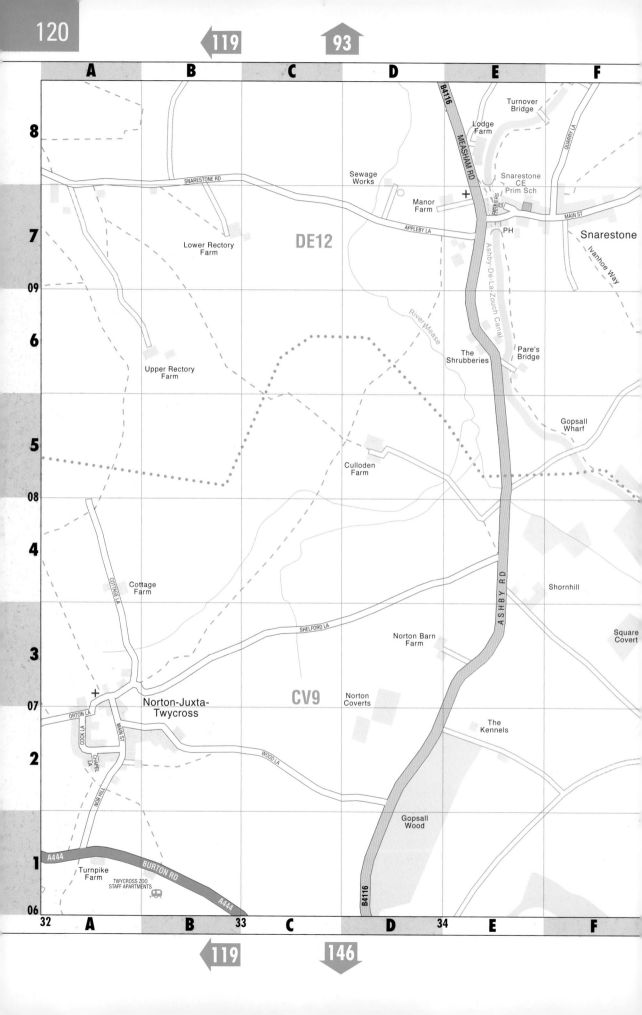

A   B   C   D   E   F

8

SNARESTONE RD

DE12

B4116

MEASHAM RD

Turnover
Bridge

Lodge
Farm

Sewage
Works

Snarestone
CE
Prim Sch

Manor
Farm

Main St

Snarestone

PERRERS CL

PH

Quarry La

Ivanhoe Way

7

APPLEBY LA

09

River Mease

Ashby-De-La-Zouch Canal

The
Shrubberies

Pare's
Bridge

6

Upper Rectory
Farm

Lower Rectory
Farm

Gopsall
Wharf

5

Culloden
Farm

08

4

Cottage
Farm

COTTAGE LA

ASHBY RD

Shornhill

Square
Covert

3

SHELFORD LA

CV9

Norton Barn
Farm

07

Norton-Juxta-
Twycross

ORTON LA

COCK LA

MAIN ST

CHAPEL LA

Norton
Coverts

The
Kennels

2

WOOD LA

HILL TOP RD

1

A444

BURTON RD

Turnpike
Farm

TWYCROSS ZOO
STAFF APARTMENTS

A444

Gopsall
Wood

B4116

06

32   A   33   B   C   33   D   34   E   F

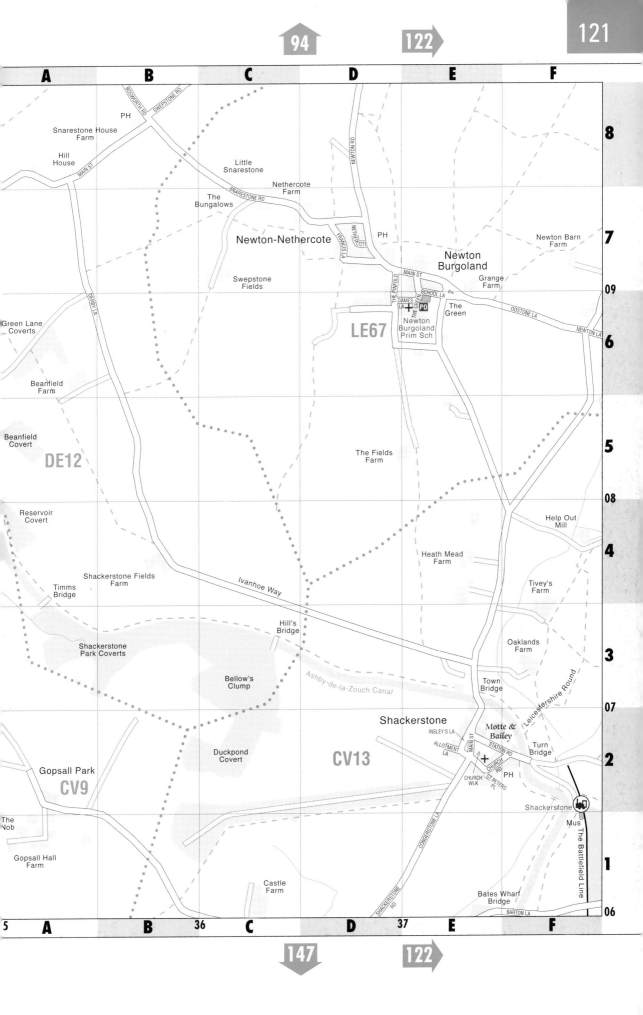

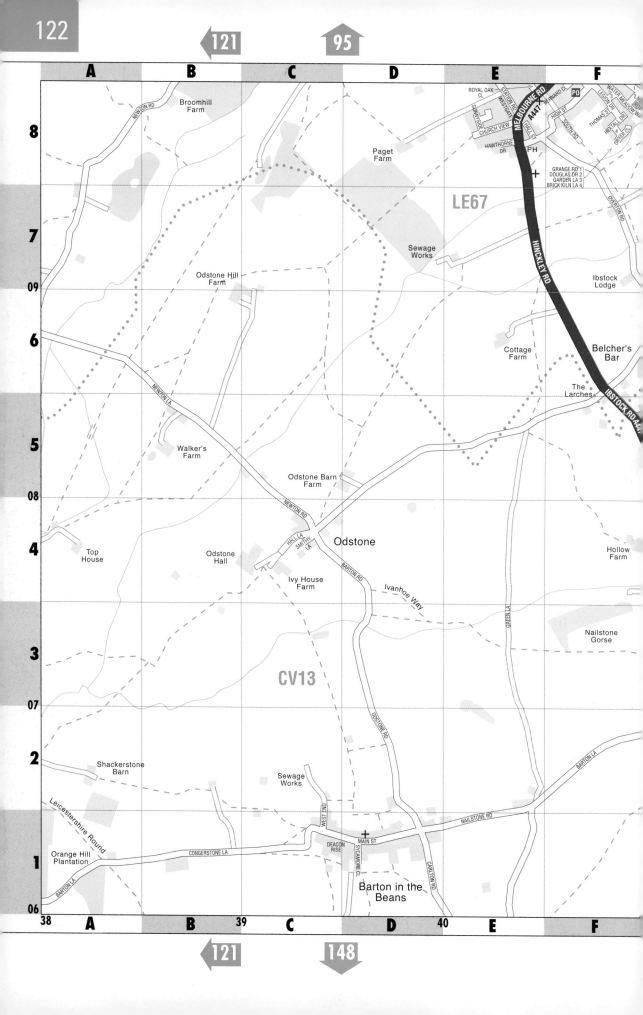

121
95

A B C D E F

8
7
09
6
5
08
4
3
07
2
1
06

38 A B 39 C D 40 E F

LE67

CV13

Broomhill Farm

Newton Rd

Paget Farm

Royal Oak Cl
Station Rd
West Gate
Sunnyside
Church View
Hawthorne Dr
Hill St
Hall St
Melbourne Rd
A447
PH
Bernard Cl
High St
South Rd
PO
Water Meadow W
Legion Dr
Thomas St
Hextall Dr
Hextall Cl
Orter Cl

Grange Rd 1
Douglas Dr 2
Garden La 3
Brick Kiln La 4

Hinckley Rd

Overton Rd

Ibstock Lodge

Sewage Works

Odstone Hill Farm

Cottage Farm

Belcher's Bar

The Larches

Ibstock Rd A447

Newton La

Walker's Farm

Odstone Barn Farm

Hollow Farm

Top House

Hall La
Smithy La
Newton Rd

Odstone Hall

Ivy House Farm

Odstone

Barton Rd

Ivanhoe Way

Green La

Nailstone Gorse

Shackerstone Barn

Sewage Works

West End

Odstone Rd

Barton La

Leicestershire Round

Orange Hill Plantation

Barton La

Congerstone La

Deacon Rise
Main St
Sycamore Cl

Nailstone Rd

Carlton Rd

Barton in the Beans

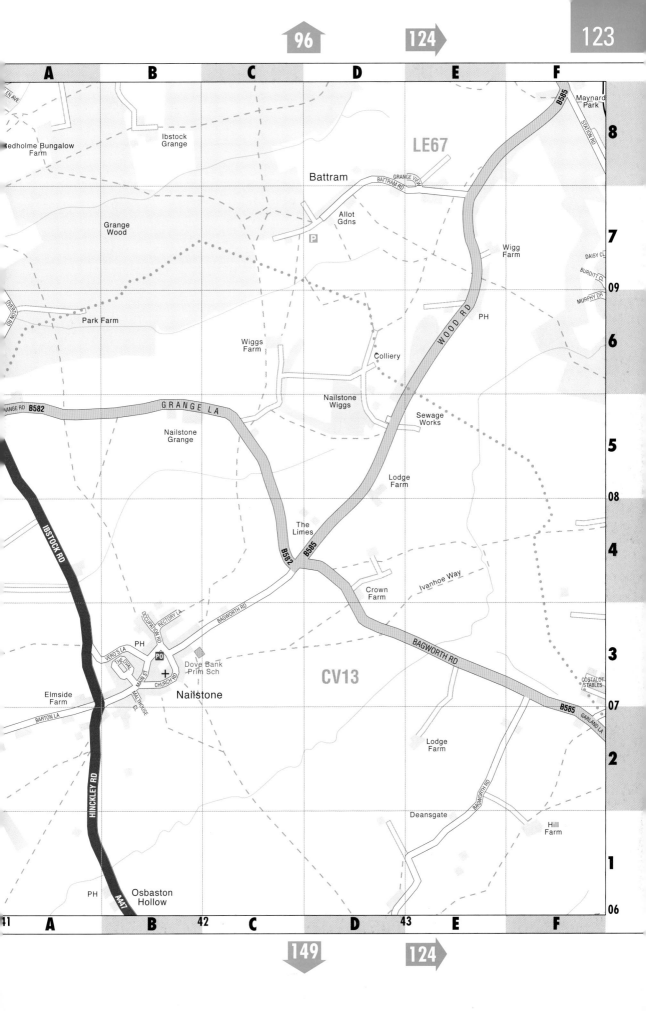

← 123   97 ↑

A   B   C   D   E   F

8

Bagworth Wood

Manor
Farm

NORTHFIELD
STATION
TERR
PH
P0

Spring
Farm

Sewage
Works

7

DAISY CL
BLOSSOM
CL
BEACON
VIEW
MURPHY JACKSON
DR
STATION RD
PARK LA

Willow
Farm

09

CHESTNUT
DR
HAWTHORN
RD
ALMOND WAY

Bagworth
Park

LE67

THORNTON LA

DURHAM CL

Factories

6

DURHAM WLK
MAYNARD WLK
MAYNARD CL
WARWICK CL

Ivanhoe Way

STANTON LA

MARKFIELD LA

Sports
Ground

5

Bagworth

Leicestershire Round

BAGWORTH LA

THE SQUARE
LIME GR
MEADOW
CL

Thornton Com
Prim Sch

Thornton
Resr

08

WHITE HOUSE CL 1
CHANTRELL CL 2
1 2
MAIN ST
THE HOLLOW
THORNTON LA
MILL LA

HAWTHORNE DR
BEECH DR
MAIN ST

PH
CHURCH HILL
OLD SCHOOL LA

4

Thornton

THE
ORCHARDS
SHARP'S CL
CHURCH LA
Visitor
Ctr
PH

BARLESTONE RD

GEARY'S
RESERVOIR
RD
HIGHFIELDS
WARWICK CL
MERRILESS RD
ST PETER OAKWOOD CL

3

COSTALOT
STABLES

HEATH RD

Bagworth Heath
Nature Reserve

07

Bagworth Heath

2

B585
GARLAND LA

CV13

P ✕

Sewage
Works

Oak
Farm

Fox Covert
Farm

BAGWORTH RD

Works

Heath
Farm

1

Garland Lane
Farm

HEATH RD

LE9

B585

Little Fox
Covert

LE9
LESIDE

06

44   A   B   45   C   D   46   E   F

← 125
↑ 99

A · B · C · D · E · F

MARKFIELD LA

8

Newtown Linford Prim Sch

PH / GREY CRES
MAIN ST
Leicestershire Round
Newtown Linford
P
PO
STAMFORD RISE
BRACKEN HILL
LADY JANE MOBILE HOME PK
BRADGATE RD

Lawn Wood

7

LE67

Cemy
Riding School
Cork Hall Farm

Old Wood
GROBY LA
Chaplain's Rough

New Plantation

09

Groby Park Farm

Bradgate House
BRADGATE HILL

6

Carter's Rough

Sheet Hedges Wood Country Pk

Little John

5

Lady Hay Wood
Groby Pool
Groby Quarries

Alder Spinney
Home Farm
ELSALENE DR
EL SALENE CL
LENA DR
WALLACE DR

Pool House
NEWTOWN LINFORD LA

08

Slate Brook
MARKFIELD RD

Groby Lodge Farm
SLATE PIT LA

Dowry Furlong Wildlife Area
P

4

LE6

1 THE ORCHARD
2 HOLMES CL
3 STEPHENSON CL
4 WINDMILL RISE
5 FIRTREE WLK

Martinshaw Prim Sch
MARKFIELD RD

Liby
GREYLAND PADDOCK
PARKSIDE
A50

M1

3

FERN CRES
WOODLANDS DR
PARKLANDS AVE
FOREST VIEW
WOOD CL
FIR TREE LA
FOREST RISE
FOREST RISE
STEPHENSON WAY
POPLARS CL
RATBY RD
CHAPEL HILL
ROCKERY LA
PO
LEICESTER RD
PYMM LEY GDNS
FIELD COURT RD
MARSTON RD

Martinshaw Wood

Groby
LANE WOOD CL
MARTINSHAW LA
HILARY CRES
CARADO
GLEBE RD
FERRERS CL
CHAPEL HILL
OLD HALL CL
PYMM LEY LA
MEADOW COURT RD
SYCAMORE CL
SLATE BROOK CL

Martinshaw Wood Nature Trail

07

WOODBANK RD
SPINNEY
OAKTREE CL
WHITE HOUSE CL
SPINNEY SIDE
HIGHFIELD RD
SPINNEY CL
BUCKINGHAM
TIMBERWOOD DR
Sch
BEACON CL
ELM CL
CEDAR
PINE TREE CL
CHESTNUT
SYCAMORE DR
BEAUMONT

Groby Com Coll
Brookvale High Sch

2

Cowpen Spinney
GREY'S DR
LANCASTER CT
QUEENSMEAD
GARRENDON WAY
OAKMEADOW RISE
ASH CL
CASTLE RISE
VICTORIA DR
WINDSOR RD
LOUISE AVE
WILLOW
BEECH AVE
TUDOR CL
LAUNDON WAY
LIME AVE
ULVERSCROFT RD
STAMFORD RD
BEDFORD
PINES AVE

Cemy
WARRINGTON DR
SACHEVERELL WAY

P
MARKFIELD RD

THE POPLARS
BEVINGTON CL
THORNWOOD
ASH CL
BRADGATE DR
WHITTINGTON DR
SAXONS RISE
WOLSEY

1 SOUTH WLK
2 EAST WLK
3 THE CLOSE
4 WHITTINGTON CT

GROBY RD

LE3
A46

1

BURROUGHS RD
Ford
STAMFORD CL
STAMFORD ST
MAIN ST
DANE HILL
COTTAGE CL
OVERFIELD WLK
M1

06

50 · A · B · 51 · C · D · 52 · E · F

← 125
↓ 152

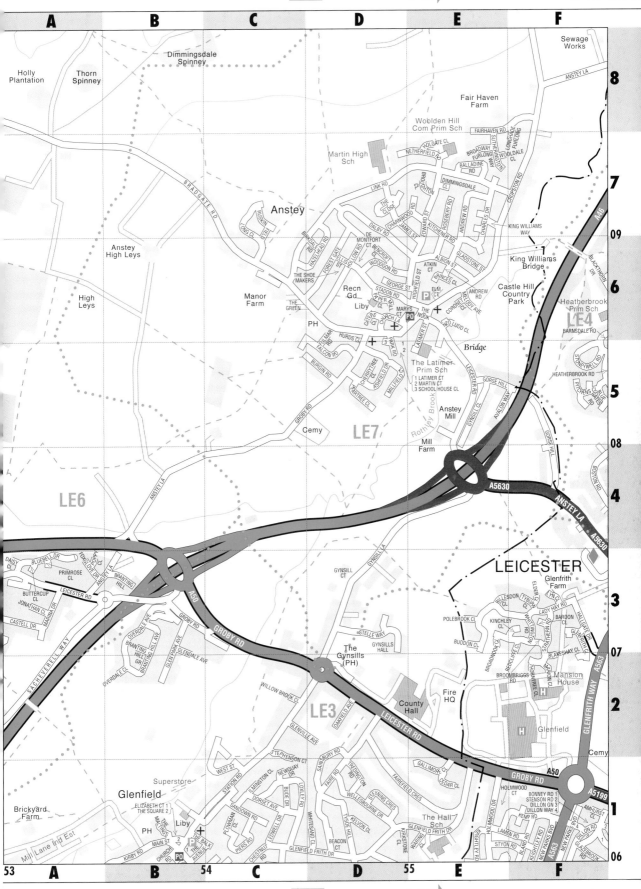

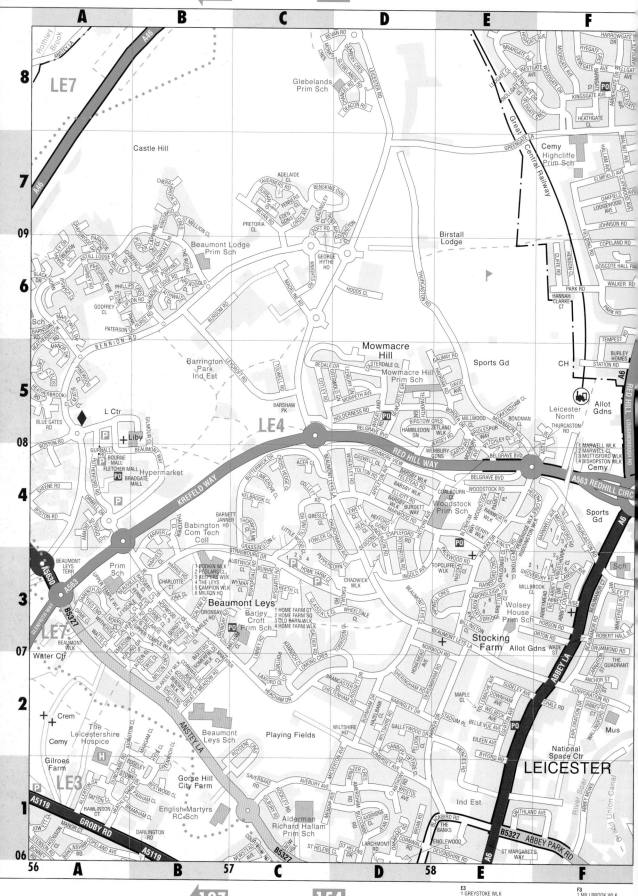

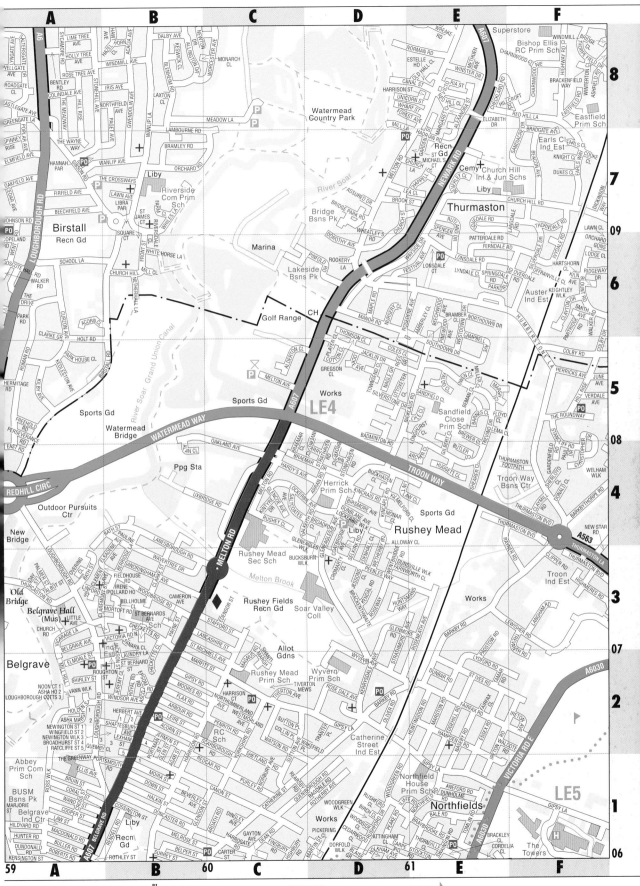

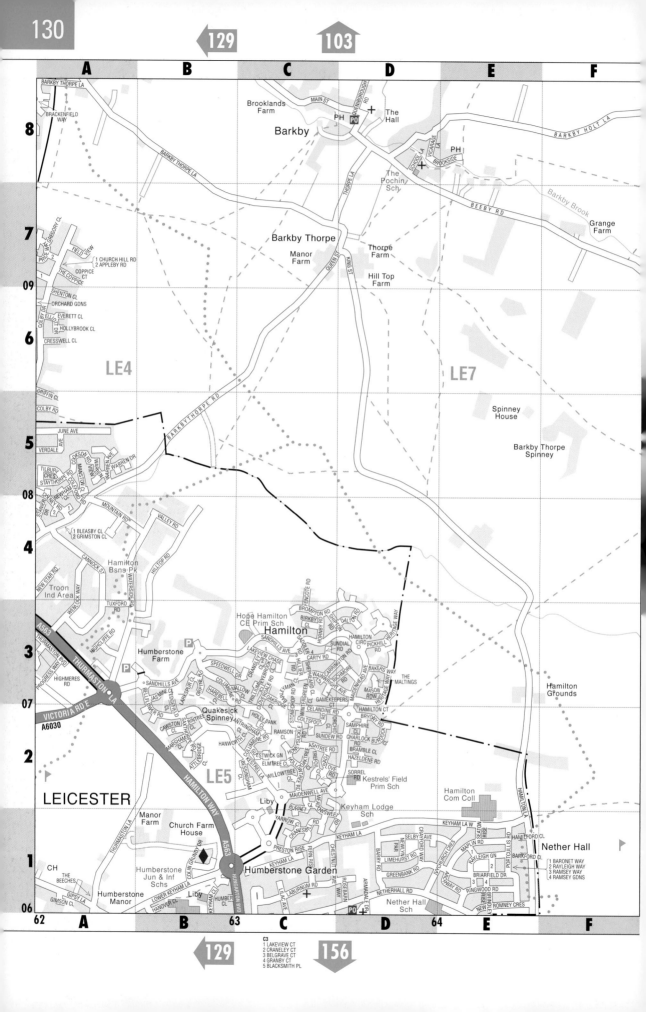

129
103

A B C D E F

8

BARKBY THORPE LA

BRACKENFIELD WAY

Brooklands Farm

MAIN ST

QUENIBOROUGH RD

PH PO

The Hall

Barkby

BARKBY HOLT LA

BARKBY THORPE LA

THORPE LA

VICARAGE LA

SCHOOL LA

PH

BROOKSIDE

The Pochin Sch

BEEBY RD

Barkby Brook

7

PYE WY

GREGORY CL

FIELD VIEW

Barkby Thorpe

Manor Farm

QUEEN ST

KING ST

Thorpe Farm

Grange Farm

1 CHURCH HILL RD
2 APPLEBY RD

COPPICE CT

THE COPPICE

Hill Top Farm

09

SHENTON CL

ORCHARD GDNS

EVERETT CL

COLBY DR

ELLIOT DR

HOLLYBROOK CL

CRESSWELL CL

LE4

LE7

6

Spinney House

GRIFFIN CL

COLBY RD

5

JUNE AVE

VERDALE AVE

BARKBYTHORPE RD

Barkby Thorpe Spinney

TILBURY CRES
STAYTHORPE CL

COOKSON RD

WARREN DR

WARREN VIEW

MANSTON CL

CULFORD RD

08

STAINER DR

CHENEY CL

NEWHAM CL

MOUNTAIN RD

VALLEY RD

1 BLEASBY CL
2 GRIMSTON CL

4

CANNOCK ST

Hamilton Bsns Pk

HILLTOP RD

WATERSIDE RD

New Star Rd

Troon Ind Area

WENLOCK WAY

TUXFORD RD

BENBOTE RD

BROMPTON RD

BIRKBY CL

DALTON RD

SHILTON CL

HERITAGE WAY

3

A563

THURMASTON LA

METCLIFFE RD

HIGHMERES RD

PROGRESS WAY

P

Humberstone Farm

P

SANDHILLS AVE

Hope Hamilton CE Prim Sch

Hamilton

LAKEVIEW CHASE

SPEEDWELL DR

GRANSTON CL

COLLARD

MALLOW

HILLER

SUNDIAL RD

HAMILTON CIRC

PICKHILL RD

HARRINGTON RD

BAKERS WAY

HAMILTON WAY

MASON ROW

THE MALTINGS

Hamilton Grounds

07

VICTORIA RD E

A6030

BELLFLOWER RD

JASMINE CL

SANDHILLS AVE

LARKSPIRIT CL

EDGEFIELD

ORPINE RD

OAKBRIDGE

PINETREE

CORNBRAKE

HAREBELL CL

STONECROP RD

WINTERGREEN RD

WAINWRIGHT AVE

GAMEKEEPERS CL

MAIDENHAIR RD

HAMILTON CT

BRYONY RD

2

LE5

CAWSTON CL

MARSHAM CL

SEATHORPE

ATTLEBRIDGE

BRESSINGHAM

HANWORTH CL

Quakesick Spinney

ANTRINGHAM

HOLLY BANK

COLUMBINE RD

KESTREL CL

CROSS HILL

ELMTREE CL

WILLOWTREE

RAMSON CL

CELANDINE RD

COLTSFOOT

HORSESUCKLE

SUNDEW RD

ORCHID

TREFOIL

CLOVE

ASHTREE RD

SAMPHIRE CL

CHARLOCK RD

BURDOCK

BRAMBLE CL

HAZELDENE RD

SORREL RD

Kestrels' Field Prim Sch

HAMILTON LA

Hamilton Com Coll

LEICESTER

Manor Farm

Church Farm House

Liby

MAIDENWELL AVE

BURNET CL

YARROW

MEADOWSWEET

Keyham Lodge Sch

KEYHAM LA W

1

THURMASTON LA

COLLIN GRUNDY DR

A563

HUMBERSTONE BVD

Humberstone Jun & Inf Schs

PRESTON RISE

KEYHAM LA

Humberstone Garden

FERN RISE

CHESTNUT AVE

KEYHAM LA

BARRY RD

ROSEBANK RD

SELBY RD

CRAYFORD WAY

NEW RD

LIMEHURST RD

LYCHGATE CL

MAPLIN RD

SEATON RISE

RAYLEIGH GN

PORTCULLIS RD

BARKFORD CL

HAMILFORD CL

Nether Hall

1 BARONET WAY
2 RAYLEIGH WAY
3 RAMSEY WAY
4 RAMSEY GDNS

CH

THE BEECHES

GIPSY LA

GIMSON CL

Humberstone Manor

LOWER KEYHAM LA

HANOVER CL

Liby

KEYHAM CL

LILAC AVE

LABURNUM AVE

GREENBANK RD

NETHERHALL RD

Nether Hall Sch

RINGWOOD RD

ARMADALE DR

BRINSMEAD

ROMNEY CRES

PO

06

62 A B 63 C D 64 E F

129
156

C3
1 LAKEVIEW CT
2 CRANELEY CT
3 BELGRAVE CT
4 GRANBY CT
5 BLACKSMITH PL

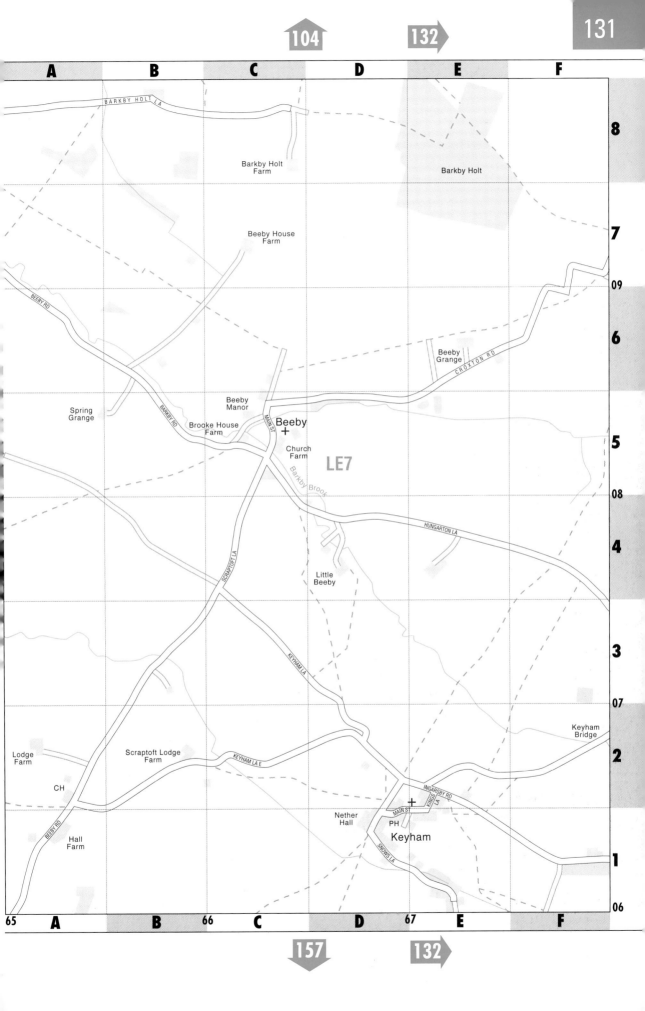

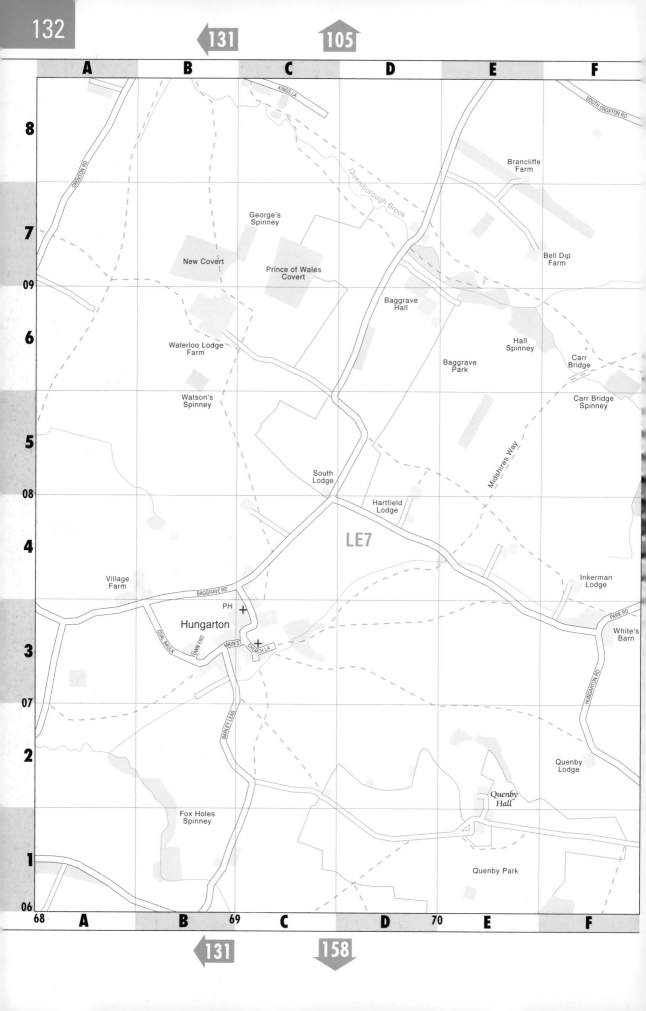

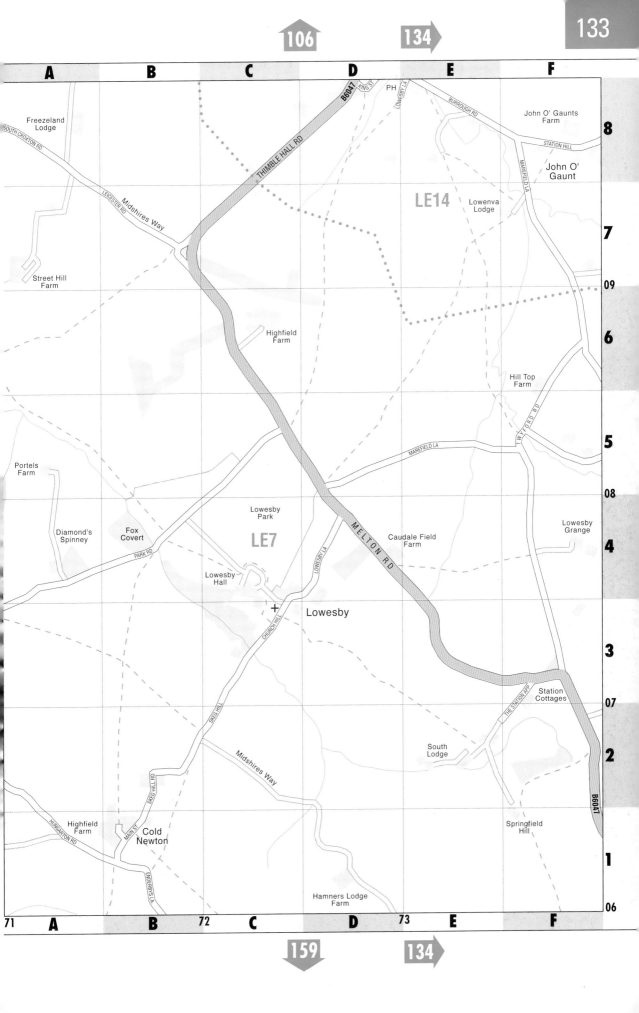

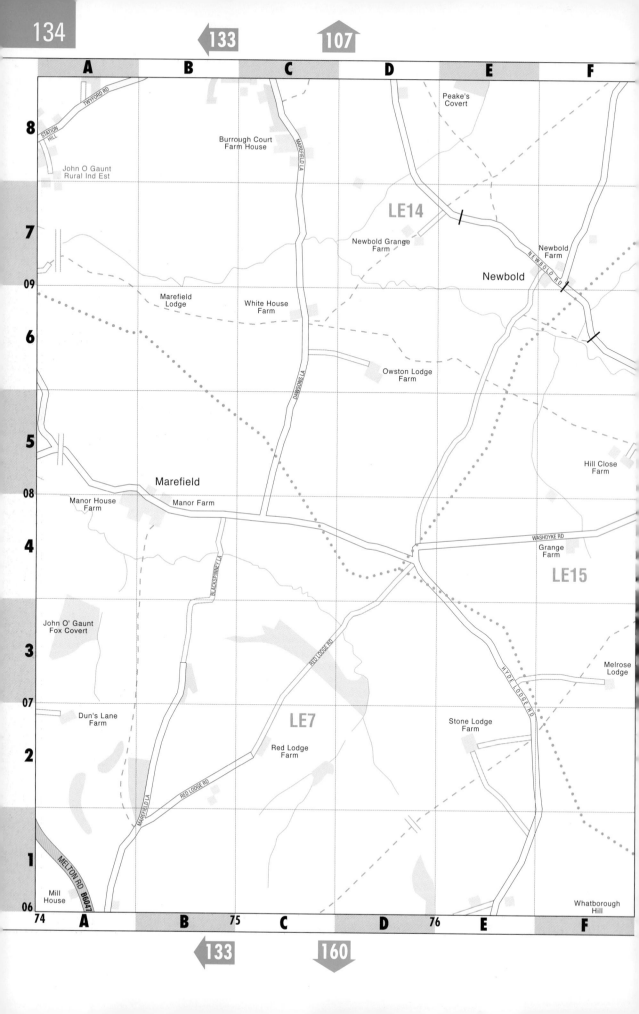

133
107

A B C D E F

8

7

09

6

5

08

4

3

07

2

1

06

74 A B 75 C D 76 E F

133
160

TWYFORD RD

STATION HILL

John O Gaunt
Rural Ind Est

Burrough Court
Farm House

MAREFIELD LA

Peake's
Covert

LE14

Newbold Grange
Farm

Newbold
Farm

NEWBOLD RD

Newbold

Marefield
Lodge

White House
Farm

Owston Lodge
Farm

OWSTON LA

Hill Close
Farm

Marefield

Manor House
Farm

Manor Farm

WASHDYKE RD

Grange
Farm

LE15

John O' Gaunt
Fox Covert

BLACKSPINNEY LA

RED LODGE RD

Melrose
Lodge

HYDE LODGE RD

Dun's Lane
Farm

LE7

Stone Lodge
Farm

Red Lodge
Farm

MAREFIELD LA

RED LODGE RD

MELTON RD
B6047

Mill
House

Whatborough
Hill

A B C D E F

8

7

09

6

LE14

Leicestershire Round

OWSTON RD

KNOSSINGTON RD

OAKHAM RD

SOMERBY RD

Sconsborough Hill Farm

SOMERBY RD

BRUCES LA

The Grange Therapeutic Sch

Brickyard Farm

Deane Bank Farm

SOMERBY RD

5

08

Cricket Gd

OWSTON RD

NEWBOLD RD

Oundle Farm

GREEN LA

Hill Close

WASHDYKE RD

+

Owston

MAIN ST

MIDDLE ST

COX'S LA

LONG LA

KNOSSINGTON RD

LE15

Furze Hill

Furze Hill Farm

4

Corn Close Farm

Hill Top Farm

WHATBOROUGH RD

OWSTON WOOD RD

Leicestershire Round

3

07

2

Owston Woods

LE7

OAKHAM RD

1

06

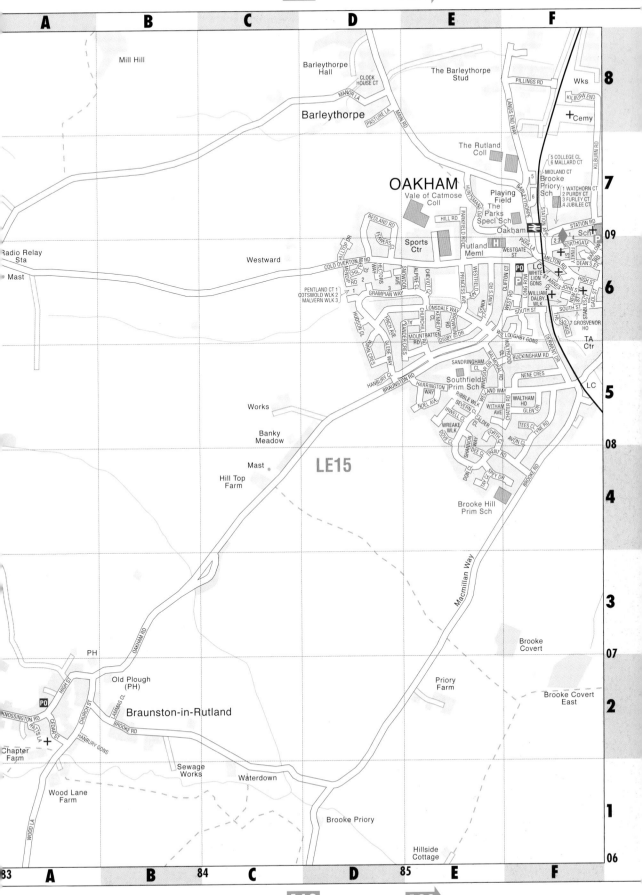

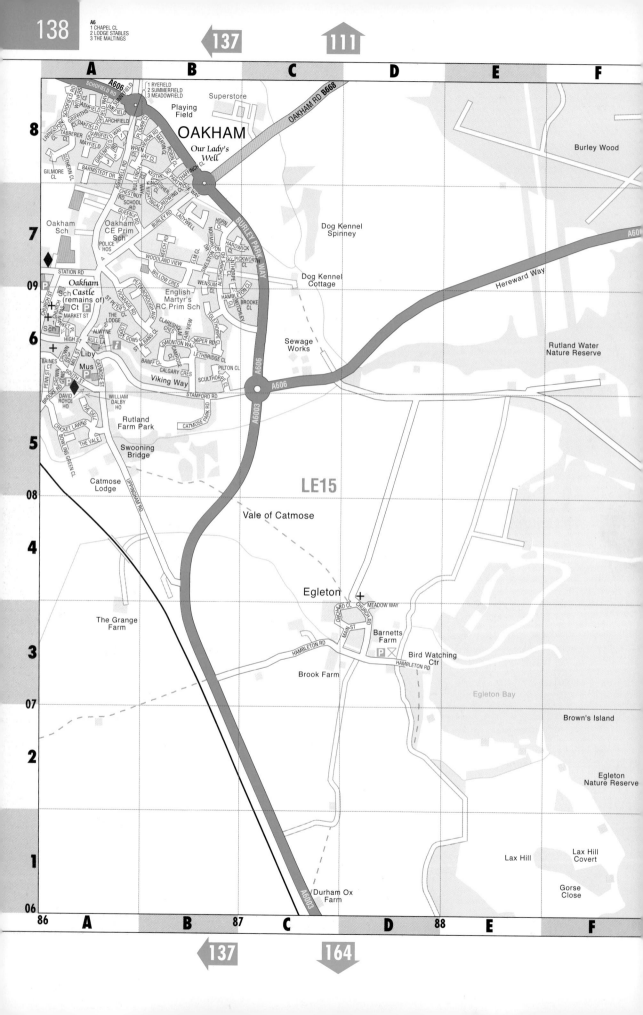

137
111
137
164

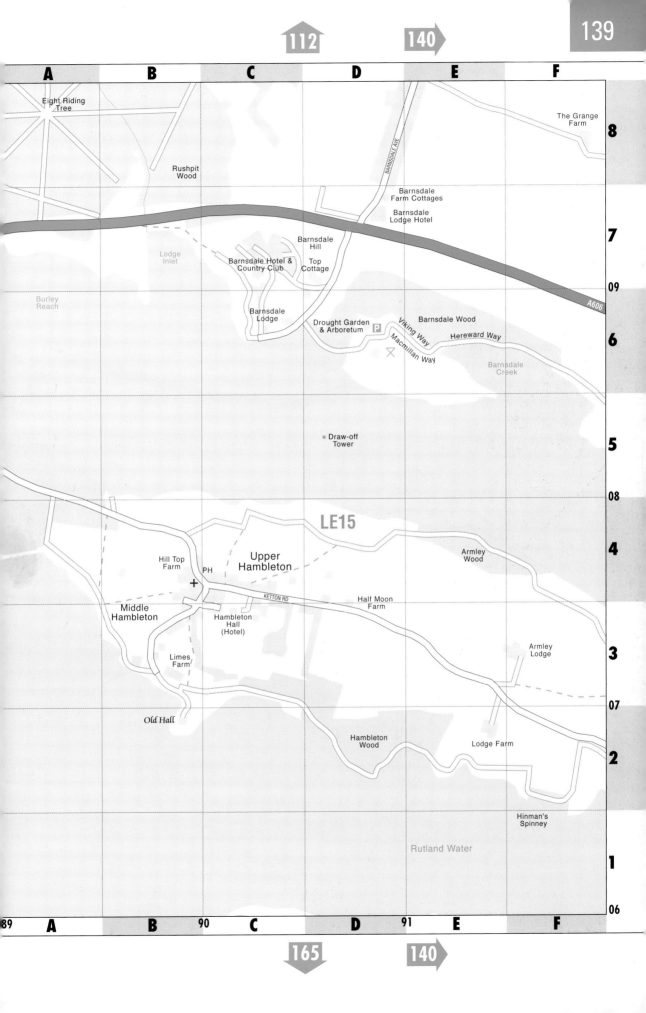

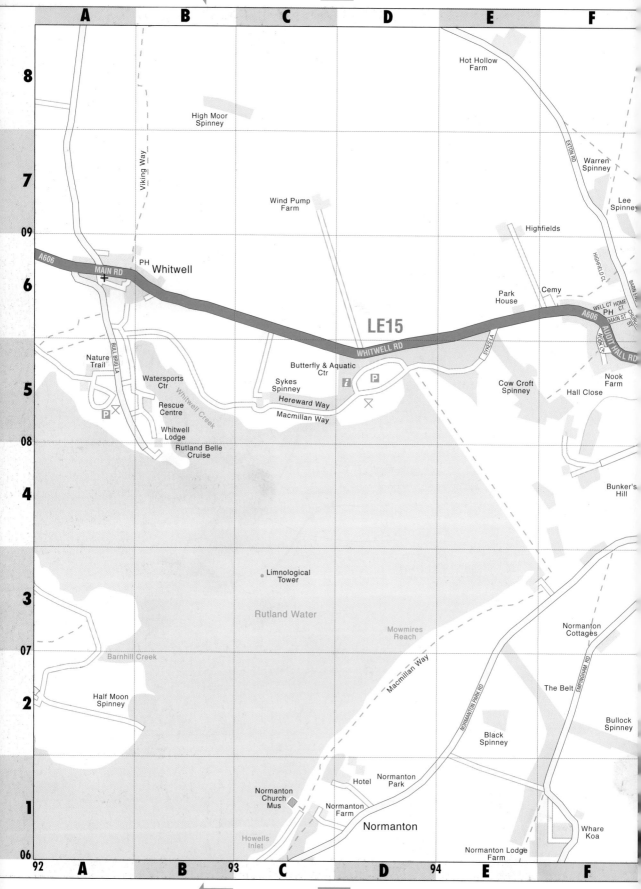

A   B   C   D   E   F

8

High Moor
Spinney

Hot Hollow
Farm

7

Viking Way

Warren
Spinney

EXTON RD

Lee
Spinney

Wind Pump
Farm

09

Highfields

HIGHFIELD CL

BARN LA

6

A606
MAIN RD   PH   Whitwell

Park
House

Cemy

WELL CT HOME
PH
CT

CHURCH ST

MAIN ST

LE15

A606

MOKLY

AUDIT HALL RD

Nature
Trail

BULL BRIG LA

Watersports
Ctr

Butterfly & Aquatic
Ctr

SYKES LA

Cow Croft
Spinney

Nook
Farm

5

Whitwell Creek

Sykes
Spinney

Hereward Way

Macmillan Way

Rescue
Centre

Hall Close

08

Whitwell
Lodge

Rutland Belle
Cruise

4

Bunker's
Hill

3

Limnological
Tower

Rutland Water

Normanton
Cottages

EMPINGHAM RD

Mowmires
Reach

07

Barnhill Creek

Macmillan Way

The Belt

2

Half Moon
Spinney

NORMANTON PARK RD

Black
Spinney

Bullock
Spinney

Hotel

Normanton
Park

1

Normanton
Church
Mus

Normanton
Farm

Normanton

Whare
Koa

Howells
Inlet

Normanton Lodge
Farm

06

92   A   B   93   C   D   94   E   F

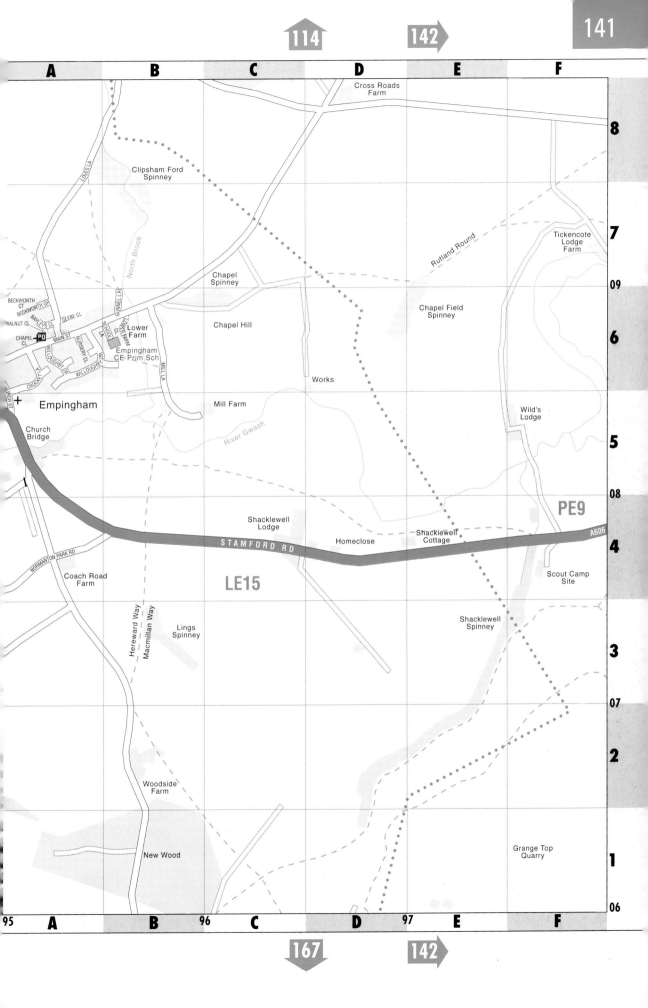

114
142
142

Cross Roads Farm

Clipsham Ford Spinney

North Brook

LOVES LA

Rutland Round

Tickencote Lodge Farm

Chapel Spinney

Chapel Field Spinney

BECKWORTH CT
BECKWORTH GR
BAYLEYS CL
WALNUT CL
GLEBE CL
CHAPEL CL
GUNNEL LA
LOWER FARM CL
SCHOOL LA
MAIN ST
WILLOUGHBY
NURSERY CL
WILLOUGHBY DR
CROCKET LA
HIGH ST

Chapel Hill

Lower Farm

Empingham CE Prim Sch

MILL LA

Works

Wild's Lodge

Empingham

Mill Farm

Church Bridge

River Gwash

PE9

08

STAMFORD RD

A606

Shacklewell Lodge

Homeclose

Shacklewell Cottage

NORMANTON PARK RD

Coach Road Farm

LE15

Shacklewell Spinney

Scout Camp Site

Hereward Way
Macmillan Way

Lings Spinney

07

Woodside Farm

Grange Top Quarry

New Wood

95   96   97

09
8
7
6
5
4
3
2
1
06

141
115

A B C D E F

8

Tickencote
Park

Tickencote

Mill
Pond

Tickencote
Hall

A1

B1081

B1081

PICKWORTH RD

RYHALL RD

Glebe
Barn

Casterton
Bsns & Ent
Coll

Sewage
Works

WEST
VIEW

WINDYRIDGE

ERMINE RISE

HIGH CRES

COLLEGE CL

PH

BURGHLEY CL

Great Casterton
CE Prim Sch

Great Casterton

7

09

Ingthorpe
Farm

Ingthorpe

HOME
FARM CL

OLD GREAT NORTH RD

PH
Church
Farm

6

Toll Bar

1 LAVENDER WAY
2 BUTTERCUP CL

PE9

MEADOWSWEET
FOXGLOVE RD

SWEETBRIAR

BLACKTHORN RD
PRIMROSE WAY

CAMPION GR

BLUEBELL RD

FOREST GDNS

TOBIAS GR

PH Quarry
Farm

B1081

5

08

Glebe
House

A606

STAMFORD RD

CLOVER GDNS 1
CORNFLOWER CL 2
MARIGOLD CL 3
SORREL CL 4
BRAMBLE GR 5

1

2

3

5

OAK RD

WILLOW RD

BIRCH GR

PINE CL

CEDAR RD

CHARLOCK DR

HAZEL GR

BEECH GR

ARRAN RD

ABERDEEN CL

MORAY CL

ANGUS CL

GARDEN
CL

A606

4

Tinwell Lodge
Farm Cottages

EMPINGHAM RD

Sidney
House

CHESTNUT
GDNS

GREAT NORTH RD

FIFE CL

3

07

Mast

STEADFOLD LA

The
Rookery

CASTERTON LA

A1

2

Grange Top
Quarry

Tinwell Lodge
Farm

Tinwell
House

1

Tinwell

TINWELL RD

PH

Cvn
Site

HOLME CL

A6121

MILL LA

WELLAND VIEW

THE
PADDOCKS

Mill
Farmhouse

Tinwell
Grange

The
Manor

River Welland

A6121

06

98 A B 99 C D 00 E F

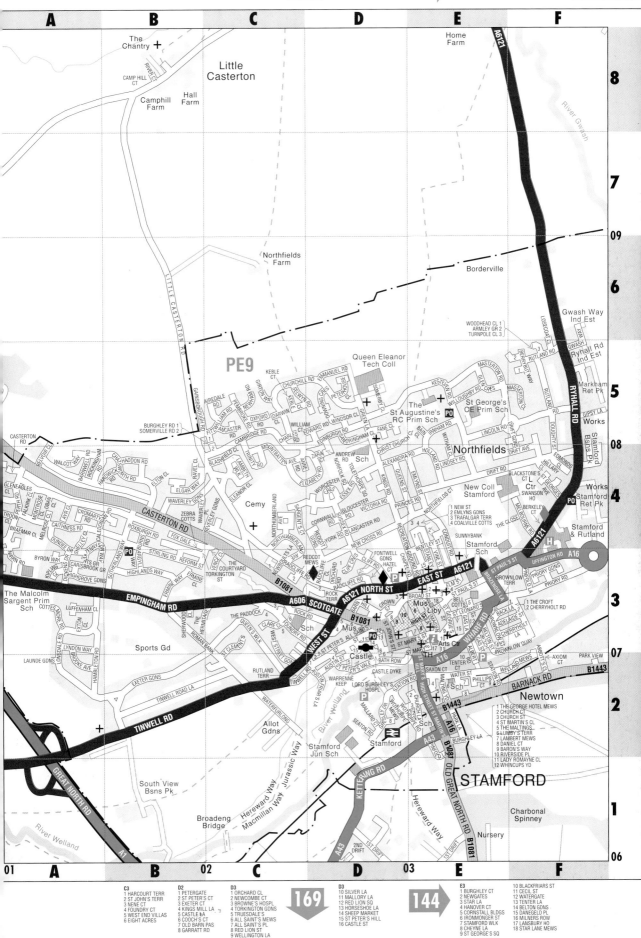

A B C D E F

8
7
09
6
5
08
4
3
07
2
1
06

The Chantry
Little Casterton
Camp Hill Ct
Camphill Farm
Hall Farm
Northfields Farm
Home Farm
Borderville
River Gwash

PE9
Queen Eleanor Tech Coll
Northfields
St Augustine's RC Prim Sch
St George's CE Prim Sch
Gwash Way Ind Est
Ryhall Rd Ind Est
Markham Ret Pk
Works
Stamford Bsns Pk

WOODHEAD CL 1
ARMLEY GR 2
TURNPOLE CL 3

New Coll Stamford
Stamford Sch
Sunnybank
Works
Stamford Ret Pk
Stamford & Rutland

1 NEW ST
2 EMLYNS GDNS
3 TRAFALGAR TERR
4 COALVILLE COTTS

BURGHLEY RD 1
SOMERVILLE RD 2
CASTERTON RD

The Malcolm Sargent Prim Sch
CASTERTON RD
EMPINGHAM RD
Cemy
Sports Gd

SCOTGATE
WEST ST
NORTH ST
EAST ST
Mus
Liby
Castle
Warrenne Keep
Lord Burghley's Hospl
Sch
Arts Ctr
TH
Brownlow Quay
Brownlow Mews
AXIOM LA
PARK VIEW
BARNACK RD
Newtown

1 THE CROFT
2 CHERRYHOLT RD

RUTLAND TERR
EXETER GDNS
TINWELL RD
TINWELL ROAD LA
LAUNDE GDNS
LONSDALE RD
Allot Gdns
River Welland
GREAT NORTH RD
South View Bsns Pk
Broadeng Bridge
Hereward Way
Macmillan Way
Jurassic Way
Stamford Jun Sch
Stamford
KETTERING RD
Hereward Way
A43
2ND DRIFT
1ST DRIFT
OLD GREAT NORTH RD
STAMFORD
Charbonal Spinney
Nursery

1 THE GEORGE HOTEL MEWS
2 CHURCH CT
3 CHURCH ST
4 ST MARTIN'S CL
5 THE MALTINGS
6 LUMBY S TERR
7 LAMBERT MEWS
8 DANIEL CT
9 BARON S WAY
10 RIVERSIDE PL
11 LADY ROMAYNE CL
12 WHINCUPS YD

C3
1 HARCOURT TERR
2 ST JOHN'S TERR
3 NENE CT
4 FOUNDRY CT
5 WEST END VILLAS
6 EIGHT ACRES

D2
1 PETERGATE
2 ST PETER'S CT
3 EXETER CT
4 KINGS MILL LA
5 CASTLE LA
6 COOCH'S CT
7 OLD BARN PAS
8 GARRATT RD

D3
1 ORCHARD CL
2 NEWCOMBE CT
3 BROWNE'S HOSPL
4 TORKINGTON GDNS
5 TRUESDALE'S
6 ALL SAINT'S MEWS
7 ALL SAINT'S PL
8 RED LION ST
9 WELLINGTON LA
10 SILVER LA
11 MALLORY LA
12 RED LION SQ
13 HORSESHOE LA
14 SHEEP MARKET
15 ST PETER'S HILL
16 CASTLE ST

D3

E3
1 BURGHLEY CT
2 NEWGATES
3 STAR LA
4 HANOVER CT
5 CORNSTALL BLDGS
6 IRONMONGER ST
7 STAMFORD WLK
8 CHEYNE LA
9 ST GEORGE'S SQ
10 BLACKFRIARS ST
11 CECIL ST
12 WATERGATE
13 TENTER LA
14 BELTON GDNS
15 DANEGELD PL
16 MILNERS ROW
17 LANSBURY HO
18 STAR LANE MEWS

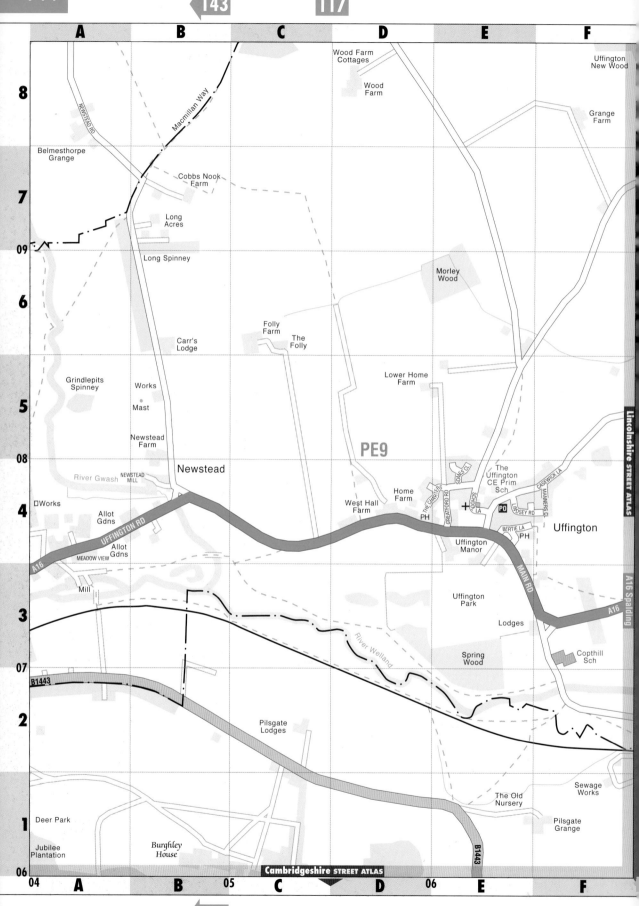

A B C D E F

8

Wood Farm
Cottages

Uffington
New Wood

Wood
Farm

Grange
Farm

Belmesthorpe
Grange

7

Cobbs Nook
Farm

Long
Acres

09

Long Spinney

Morley
Wood

6

Carr's
Lodge

Folly
Farm

The
Folly

Grindlepits
Spinney

Works

Lower Home
Farm

PE9

5

Mast

Newstead
Farm

08

River Gwash   NEWSTEAD
                MILL

Newstead

West Hall
Farm

Home
Farm

The
Uffington
CE Prim
Sch

4

□ Works

Allot
Gdns

UFFINGTON RD

Allot
Gdns

MEADOW VIEW

PH

Uffington
Manor

PH

PO

Uffington

A16

Mill

3

Uffington
Park

MAIN RD

A16

River Welland

Lodges

Copthill
Sch

07

B1443

Spring
Wood

2

Pilsgate
Lodges

The Old
Nursery

Sewage
Works

Pilsgate
Grange

1

Deer Park

Jubilee
Plantation

Burghley
House

B1443

06

04   A   B   05   C   D   06   E   F

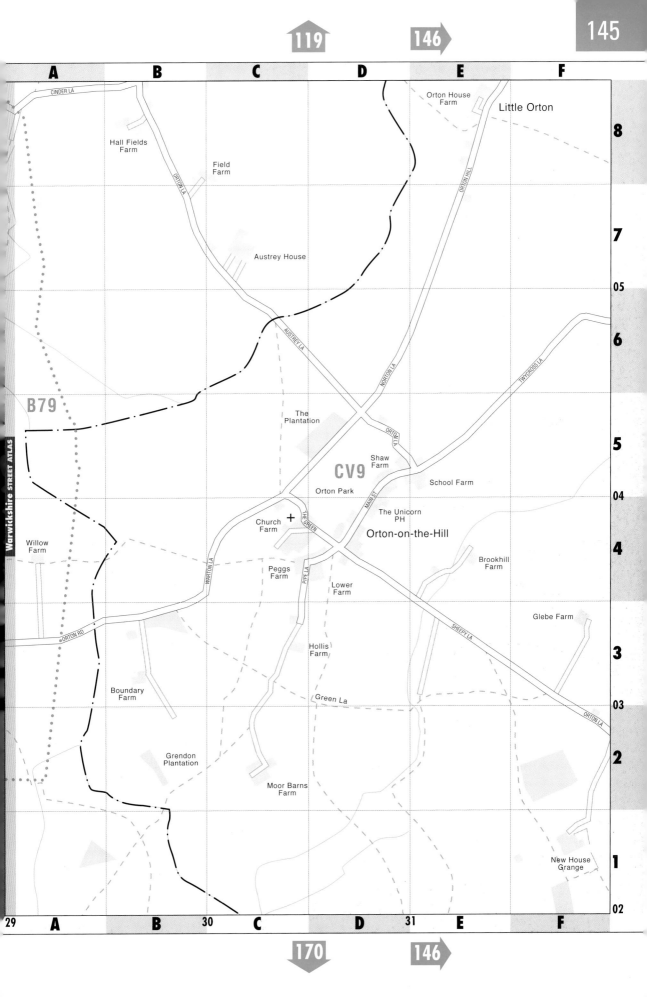

A   B   C   D   E   F

8

7

05

6

Little Orton

Orton House Farm

CINDER LA

Hall Fields Farm

ORTON LA

Field Farm

Austrey House

ORTON HILL

AUSTREY LA

NORTON LA

TWYCROSS LA

B79

The Plantation

CV9

Shaw Farm

ORTON LA

School Farm

5

04

Orton Park

MAIN ST

The Unicorn PH

Orton-on-the-Hill

4

Willow Farm

ORTON RD

WARTON LA

Church Farm

THE GREEN

Peggs Farm

PIPE LA

Lower Farm

Brookhill Farm

Glebe Farm

SHEEPY LA

03

Boundary Farm

Hollis Farm

Green La

ORTON LA

3

Grendon Plantation

Moor Barns Farm

2

New House Grange

1

02

Warwickshire STREET ATLAS

29   A   B   30   C   D   31   E   F

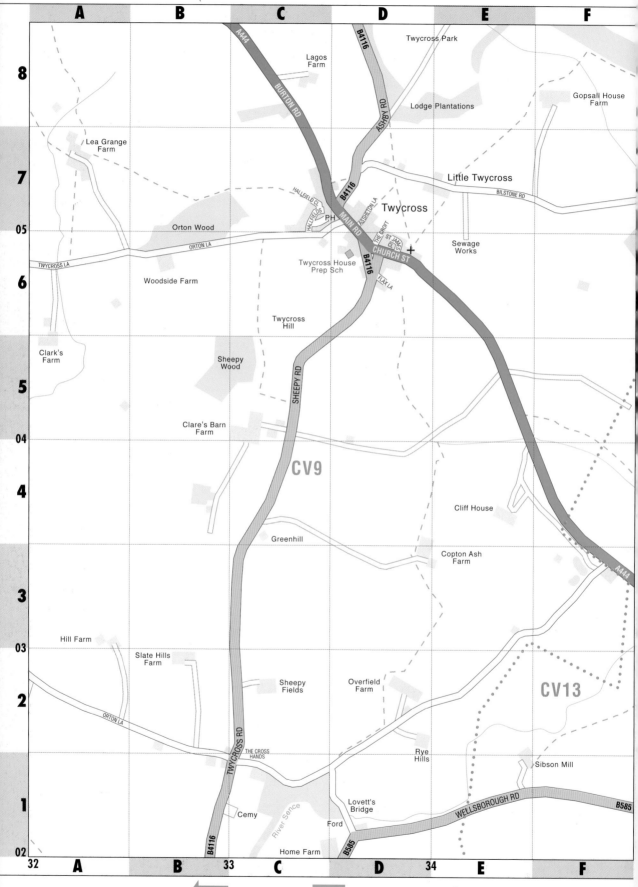

A B C D E F

8

7

05

6

5

04

4

3

03

2

1

02

32 A 33 B C 34 D E F

Twycross Park

Lagos Farm

Lodge Plantations

Gopsall House Farm

Lea Grange Farm

Little Twycross

BILSTONE RD

Orton Wood

HALLFIELD CL

HALLFIELDS

PH

Twycross

MAIN RD

ASSHETON LA

THE CROFT

ST JAMES CL

CHURCH ST

Sewage Works

TWYCROSS LA

ORTON LA

Woodside Farm

Twycross House Prep Sch

B4116

FLAX LA

Clark's Farm

Twycross Hill

Sheepy Wood

SHEEPY RD

Clare's Barn Farm

Cliff House

CV9

Greenhill

Copton Ash Farm

A444

Hill Farm

Slate Hills Farm

Sheepy Fields

Overfield Farm

CV13

ORTON LA

TWYCROSS RD

THE CROSS HANDS

Rye Hills

Sibson Mill

Cemy

River Sence

Lovett's Bridge

Ford

WELLSBOROUGH RD

B585

B4116

B585

Home Farm

BURTON RD

A444

ASHBY RD

B4116

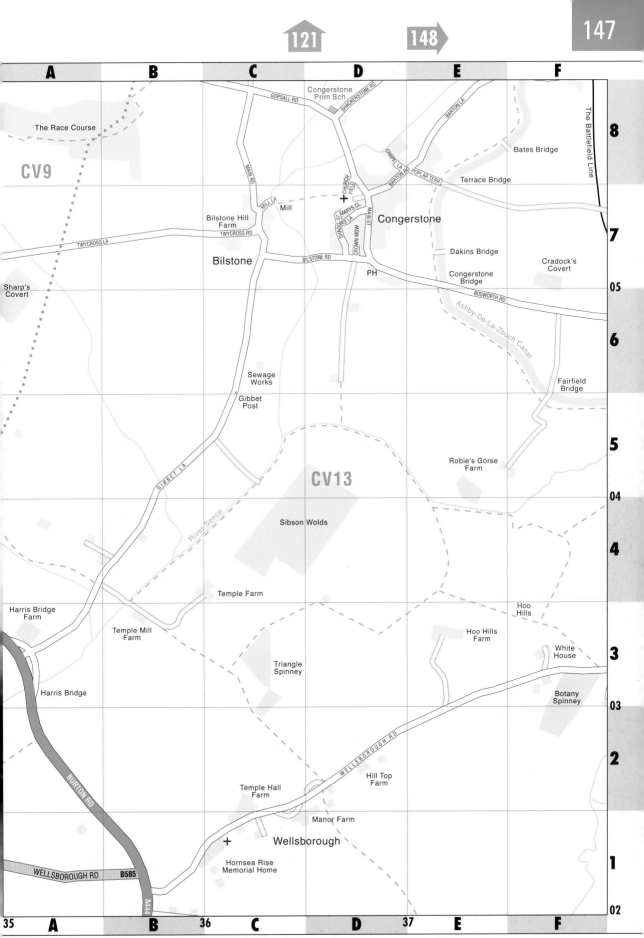

A B C D E F

8

The Race Course

CV9

7

Bilstone Hill Farm

TWYCROSS RD

TWYCROSS LA

Bilstone

Sharp's Covert

GOPSALL RD

Congerstone Prim Sch

SHACKERSTONE RD

Congerstone RD

MILL LA

Mill

MAIN RD

ST. MARYS CL

CHURCH FIELD

SHAWS LA

CROWN MDW

MAIN ST

BARTON RD

CHAPEL LA

POPLAR TERR

BARTON LA

The Battlefield Line

Bates Bridge

Terrace Bridge

Congerstone

Dakins Bridge

Congerstone Bridge

Cradock's Covert

BILSTONE RD

PH

BOSWORTH RD

05

Ashby-De-La-Zouch Canal

6

Sewage Works

Gibbet Post

Fairfield Bridge

GIBBET LA

CV13

Robie's Gorse Farm

5

04

River Sence

Sibson Wolds

4

Temple Farm

Harris Bridge Farm

Temple Mill Farm

Hoo Hills

Hoo Hills Farm

White House

Triangle Spinney

3

03

Botany Spinney

Harris Bridge

WELLSBOROUGH RD

2

BURTON RD

Temple Hall Farm

Hill Top Farm

Manor Farm

Wellsborough

1

WELLSBOROUGH RD

B585

A444

Hornsea Rise Memorial Home

02

35 A B 36 C D 37 E F

147
122

A B C D E F

8

Long Covert

Bufton

Bufton
Lodge

LOUNT RD

BUFTON LA

CARLTON RD

BARTON RD

NAILSTONE RD

7

Carlton
Gate

PH

05

Carlton

New House
Farm

MAIN ST

SHACKERSTONE WLK

BOSWORTH RD

6

Lineage
Farm

CONGERSTONE RD

CONGERSTONE LA

Bank
Farm

Bottle
Neck

Common
Farm

BOSWORTH RD

BARTON RD

Bosworth
Mill

5

Carlton
Bridge

The Battlefield Line

CV13

Mill
Covert

Westfield
Farm

04

Leicestershire Round

Old Park
Spinney

CARLTON RD

Ashby-de-la-Zouch Canal

King's
Bridge

Allotment
Covert

Jubilee
Spinney

4

Little
Friezeland

HARCOURT SPINNEY

Friezeland
Farm

Market
Bosworth

HOME FARM
MEWS

St Peters
CT

Hotel

3

1 PIPISTRELLE DR
2 HORSESHOE CL

St Peter's
CE Prim Sch

WARWICK

St PETERS
CT

CHURCH
ST

Bosworth Wharf
Bridge

WELLSBOROUGH RD

St PETER'S
CL

Market Bosworth
High Sch & Com Coll

MAIN ST

PO

PH

PARK ST

THE PARK

03

Market
Bosworth

Station Road
Ind Est

Station Road

GODSONS HILL

HILLSIDE

STATION RD

SPRINGFIELD
AVE

HEATH RD

PRIORY RD

MARLIN RISE

BREDMOOR
CL

SPINNEY
HILL

St CATHERINES
AVE

WESTON
RD

HAVEN
RD

AMBION
CT

WESTHAVEN
CT

SOUTHFIELD
WAY

BACK LA

WARWICK
CL

Sch

MARKET PL

MARKET
MEWS

RECTORY LA

WHEATSHEAF
CTYD

CEDAR DR

SYCAMORE
WAY

Bosworth Water
Trust

Sewage
Works

LANCASTER
AVE

YORK CL

STANLEY RD

NORTHUMBERLAND
AVE

BECKETT AVE

CHESTNUT CL

2

Coton
Bridge

Coton
Priory

SHENTON LA

SUTTON LA

Nursery
Barn

1

Fox
Bridge

Far Coton

02

38 A B 39 C D 40 E F

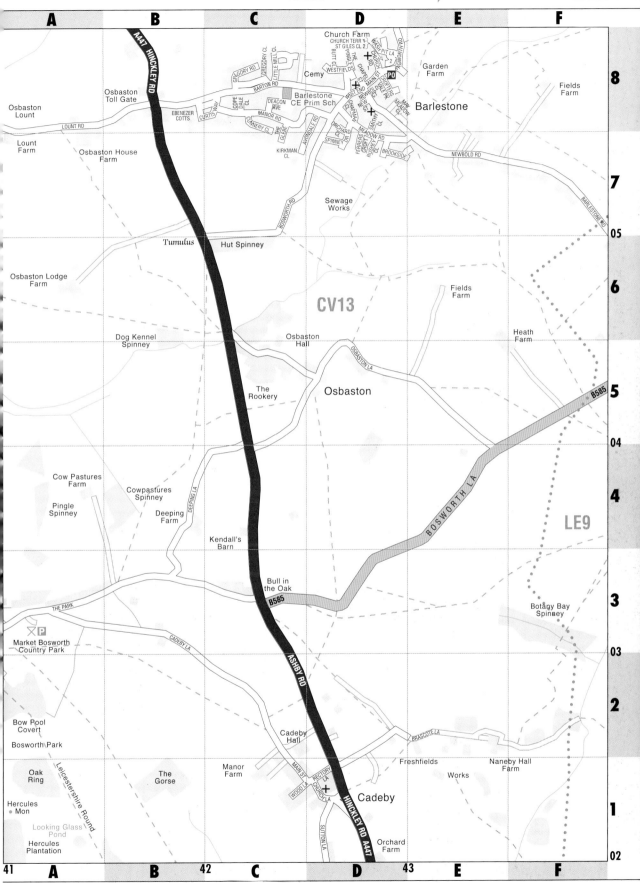

123
150
174
150

149
124

A B C D E F

LE67

CV13

LE67

Merry Lees
Ind Est

8

Heath Lodge
Farm

Great Fox
Covert

MERRYLEES RD

HEATH RD

LEESIDE

LINDRIDGE LA

CV13

Lindridge
Farm

7

Newbold
Heath

Pool House
Farm

05

Chater
Farm

Halifax
Farm

Hook
House

Lindridge Hall
Farm

6

BAGWORTH RD

B585

Lindridge
Wood

The Fields
Farm

St GEORGES
CL

5

BARLESTONE RD B582

BOSWORTH LA

B585

MONTAGUE
CL

LE9

Newbold
Verdon

Newbold Verdon
Prim Sch

GILLIVER ST

CADLE ST

STATHAM ST

HILL ST

DRAGON LA

PRESTON DR

MILL LA

ENSTON ST

HORNBEAM RD

Holly
Hedges

04

Hunt's Lane
Farm

4

CHURCH
VIEW

BELLS LA

GRANGE
CL

Liby

MAIN ST

SPARKENHOE

THE
BUNGALOWS

PINE TREE CL

PEDLON LA

DESFORD RD

HUNTS LA

B582

PH

PO

THE PADDOCK

SYCAMORE CL

ARNOLD'S AVE

JUBILEE RD

CHADWICK CL

JUBILEE CT

LORD CREWE CL

BRAMBLE DR

PASTURE LA

OAKS LA

PETERS AVE

Tumblin
Fields

Allot
Gdns

GILBERT'S DR

RUSH

MALLORY CL

WILLOW CL

BARBARA AVE

ALANS WAY

Newbold
Spinney

Cottage
Farm

3

Sewage
Works

KIRBY LA

03

PH
Allot
Gdns

BRASCOTE LA

Lockey
Farm

Shericles
Farm

2

Manor
Farm

Brascote

Kirby Old
Parks

Bullacre
Spinney

NEWBOLD RD

1

Brascote
House

Brascote
Covert

Beech
Spinney

Stocks
House

02

44 A B 45 C D 46 E F

149
175

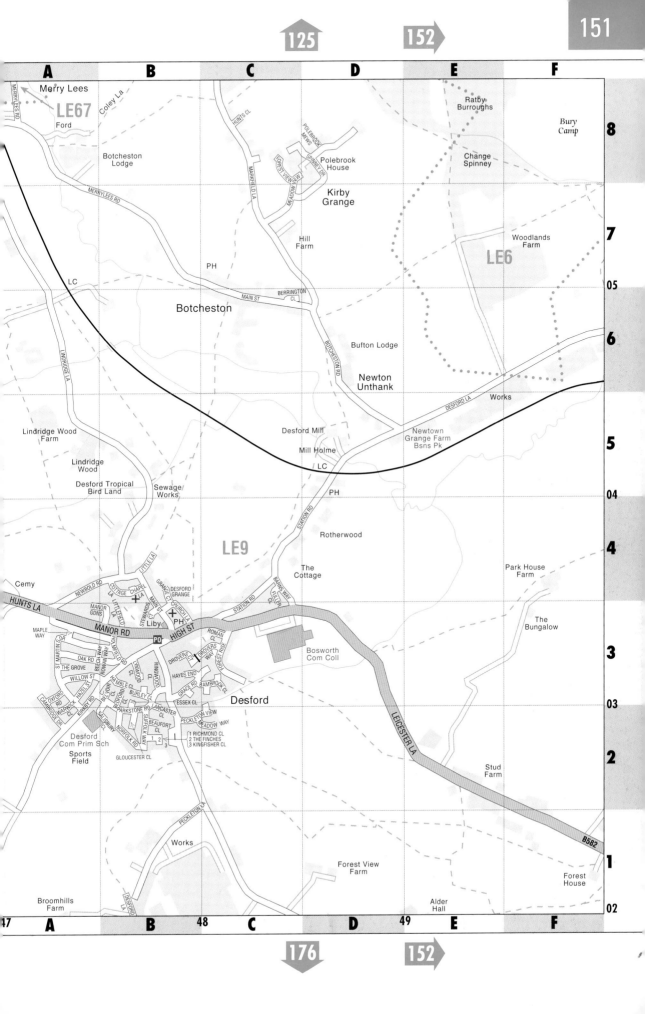

A B C D E F

8

BURROUGHS RD
Ratby Prim Sch
Liby
PH
PO
BERRY'S LA
Ratby
Hollywell Farm
LE6
Works

1 JOURNEYMAN'S GN
2 CALVERTON CL
3 CARDINAL CL
4 SPRING CL
5 PARKFIELD CL
6 WINDMILL CL
7 FREEMAN'S CT
8 ROBINS FIELD
9 JORDAN CT
10 MARTIN SQ

Mill Lane Ind Est
LE3

M1

Kirby Grange

7

Works
Rothley Brook
DESFORD LA
RATBY LA
B5380

05

Poultry Farm
Thorneyfields Farm
VICARAGE LA
PRIMROSE WAY
BLUEBELL CL

6

New Bridge
DESFORD LA
Newbridge Farm
Cemy
DESFORD RD
Liby
WOODLANDS LA
Blood's Hill
Kirby Muxloe Castle
21a

Barons Park Farm
THE HUNTINGS
BARNS CL
HEDGEROW LA
LADYSMITH RD
PRETORIA RD
FOX LA
MAIN ST
PO
ARNSON AVE
OAKCROFT AVE
GARFIT RD
Kirby Muxloe

LE9

THE KEEP
THE CROFT
CASTLE RD
P
Kirby Muxloe Prim Sch
COURT CL
LE3

5

GULLET LA
LINKS RD
WILSHERE DR
CAREY GDNS
BARWELL RD
CHURCH RD
Liby

04

The Homestead
PRINCESS DR
PORTLAND RD
HASTINGS RD
HOLLY WOOD DR
HOLMEWOOD DR
THE FAIRWAY
HOLT DR
ROSEDENE CL
Kirby Fields

4

Elms Farm
WENTWORTH RD
STATION RD
STATION CL
STATION DR
STAMFORD RD
WALTON CL
CH
LC
TOWERS DR
TOWERS CL
LINDEN LA
HEWITT DR

The Links
SOUTHVIEW CT
MARLBOROUGH HO
KIRBY RD
A47

3

Oaks Farm
BARRY CL
CHERRY TREE CT
MAYTREE CT
MAYTREE CL
BARRY DR
TREE AVE
CHERRY DR
MARTIN AVE
BARBARA AVE
FOREST RISE
ELLIS DR
HAMBLETON CL

03

SHEPHERD CL
HARENE CRES
HIGHLAND AVE
VALJEAN CRES
HAWTHORN CL
PINE TREE GR
ST DAVIDS CT
HENRY ST
SEYMOUR WAY
STAFFORD CL
BOYER ST

Forest Farm
BRICKMAN CL
BLUE POTS CL
MAGNOLIA CL
ALDER CL
JUNIPER CL
PLEASANT CL
BRACKEN CL
Jun & Inf Sch
SOMERFIELD WAY

2

The Hollows Farm
Leicester Forest East
WARREN LA
TALBOT CL
KESTREL CL
TEAL CL
ROSE CRES
RAVEN CL
KINGCUP CL
JUNIPER CL
ACACIA CL

Forest Hill Farm
KINGFISHER CL
MALLARD WAY
WOODPECKER CL
LARK CL
PETUNIA AVE
BEGONIA CL
HARVESTERS
FOREST TRUSSE LA
LE3

White House
HINCKLEY RD
SWALLOWS CL
COR CL
CARNATION CL
PLOUGH CL
HARROW CL
YEW CL

1

B582
PH
LEICESTER LA
B582
A47
Kingstand Farm
CH
BEGGARS LA
LE19
LE19

02

50 A B 51 C D 52 E F

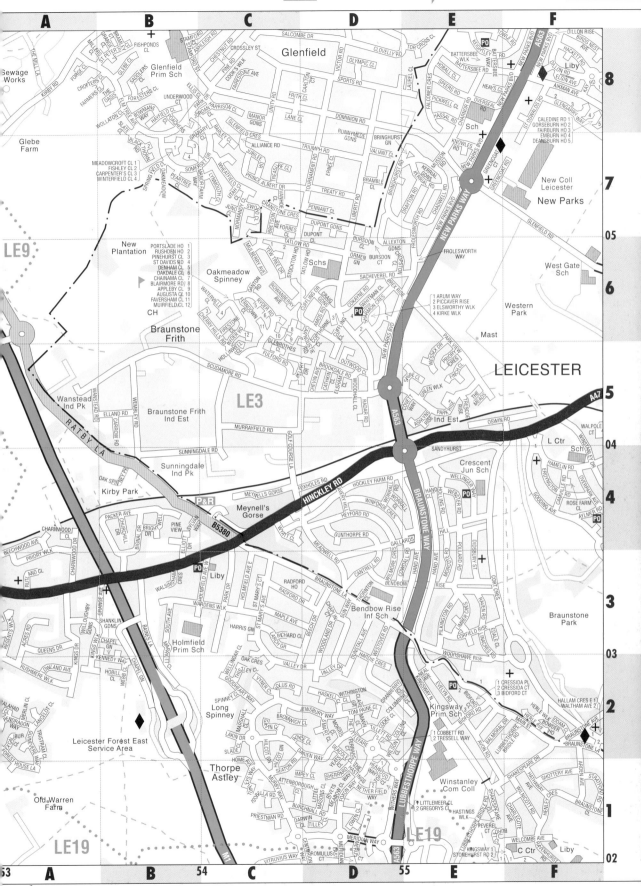

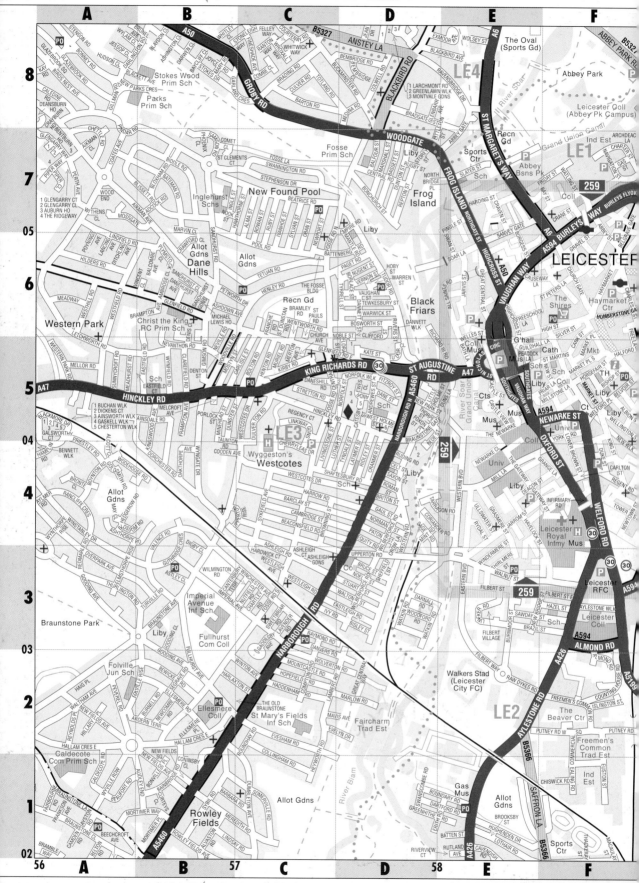

153
128
153
179

D4
1 WEST ST OPEN
2 THE RIVER BLDG
3 RIVER SOAR LIVING
D5
1 FREDERICK JACKSON HO
2 ARUNDEL ST

3 ANDREWES WLK
4 NORFOLK HO
5 MUSGROVE CL
6 COVENTRY ST
7 EARL HOWE TERR

For full street detail of the highlighted area see page 259.

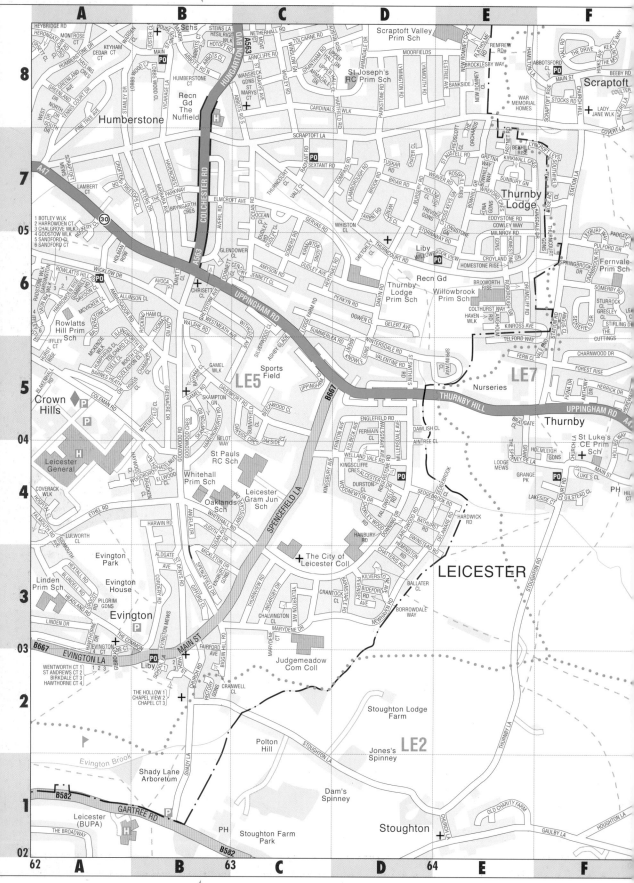

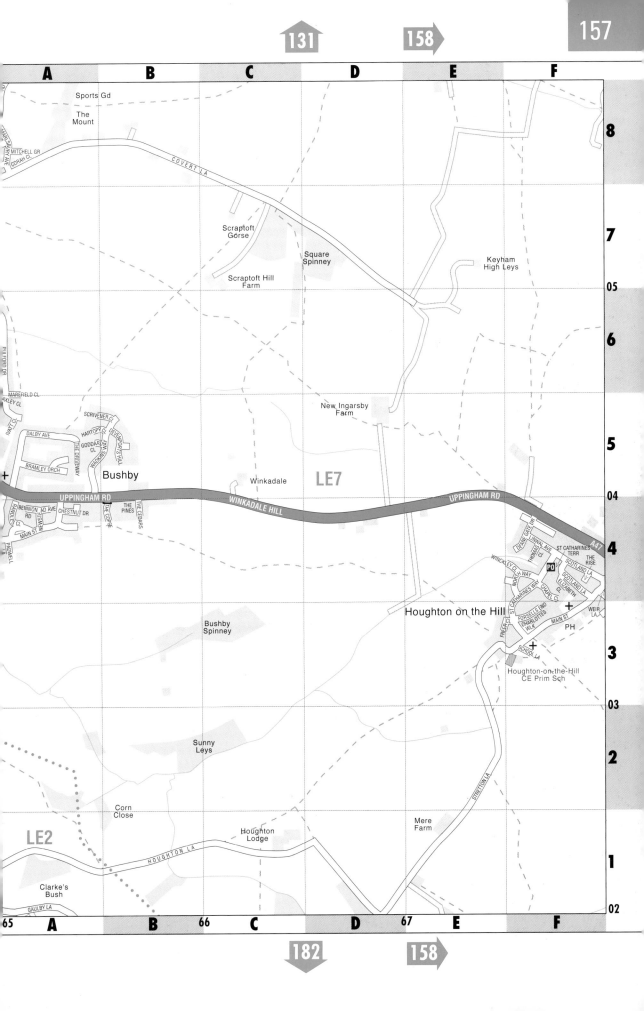

131
158

A   B   C   D   E   F

Sports Gd

The Mount

8

MITCHELL GR
CORAH CL

COVERT LA

MARLSM PIT AVE

Scraptoft
Gorse

7

Square
Spinney

Scraptoft Hill
Farm

05

6

PIT FORD DR
OXLEY CL

MAREFIELD CL

New Ingarsby
Farm

5

SCRIVENER CL
HARTOPP CL
GODDARDS CL
DEVONPORT'S HILL
WADKINS WAY
DALBY AVE
THE DRIVEWAY

Winkadale

LE7

04

BRAMLEY ORCH

Bushby

UPPINGHAM RD

WINKADALE HILL

UPPINGHAM RD

A47

BENNION RD
NEWSTEAD AVE
CHESTNUT DR
THE COPSE
THE PINES
THE CEDARS

DANE GATE DR
LINWAL AVE
THOMAS CL
ST CATHARINES TERR
SCOTLAND LA
ELIZABETH
THE RISE

FENTON CL
MAIN ST
PADWELL

PO

4

WINCKLEY CL
NORTH WAY
ST CATHARINES WAY
FORSELLS END
CHARLOTTES WLK
FREER CL
CHAPEL CL
MAIN ST
PH
WEIR LA

Houghton on the Hill

Bushby
Spinney

SCHOOL LA

3

Houghton-on-the-Hill
CE Prim Sch

03

Sunny
Leys

STRETTON LA

2

Corn
Close

Mere
Farm

LE2

Houghton
Lodge

HOUGHTON LA

1

Clarke's
Bush

GAULBY LA

02

65   A   B   66   C   D   67   E   F

182
158

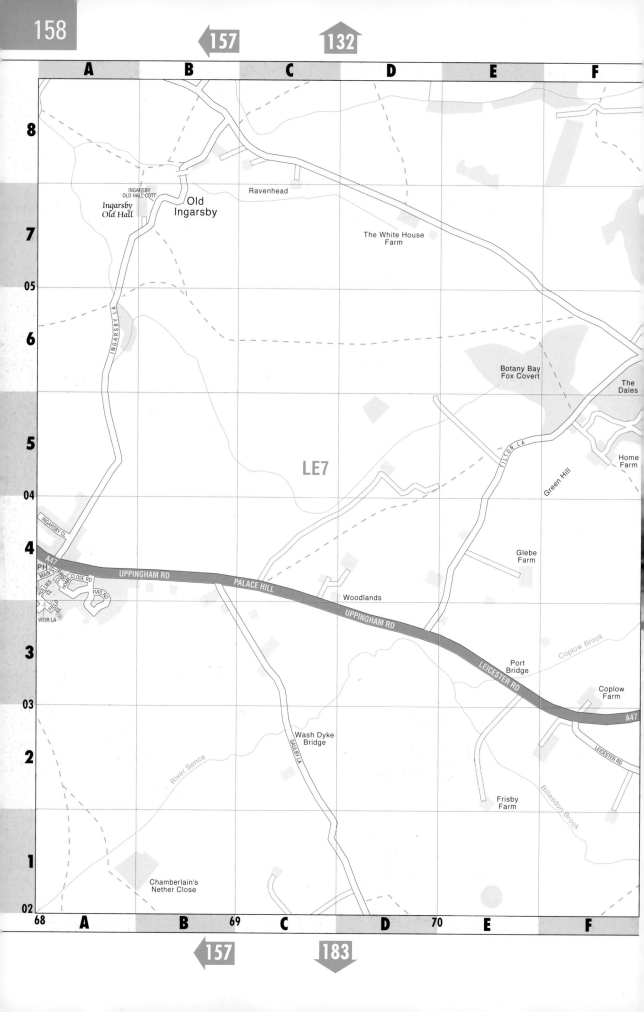

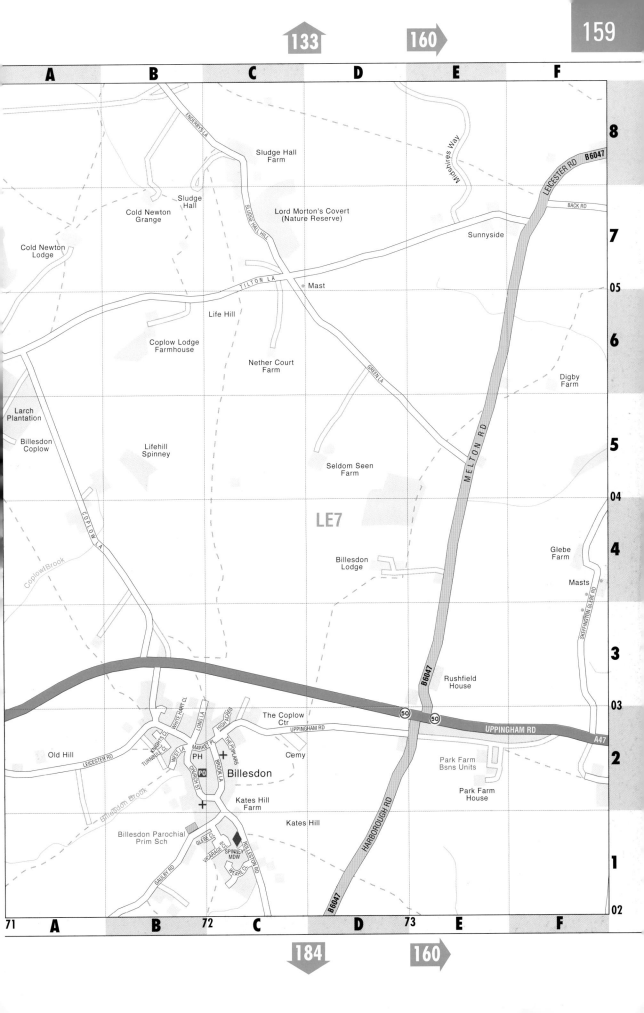

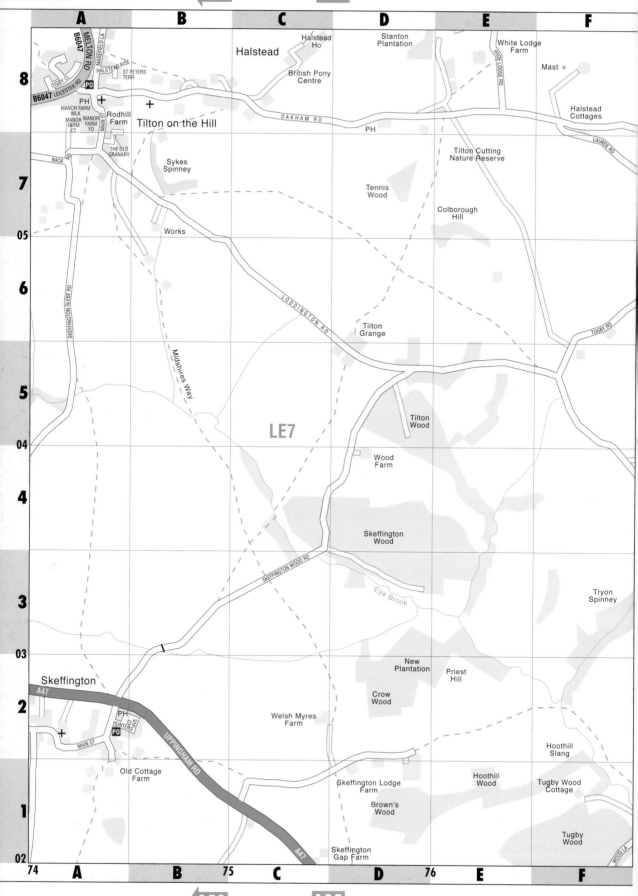

A	B	C	D	E	F

8

Whatborough Farm

Halstead Lodge

WHATBOROUGH RD

Brook Farm

OAKHAM RD

Castle Hill

Sauvey Plantation

LE15

Withcote Hall

7

River Chater

Leicestershire Round

Ash Hill Plantation

05

TUGBY RD

LAUNDE RD

Stone Lodge

LAUNDE CROSS RDS

Abbey Farm

6

Launde Abbey

Robin-a-Tiptoe Hill

Broom's Farm

Launde Park

5

Robin-a-Tiptoe Farm

LE7

Launde Big Wood

Hill Farm

04

4

LODDINGTON RD

Oxey Farm

Launde Wood Farm

OXEY CROSS RDS

Launde Cottage

Copthill Farm

3

Round Hill Spinney

WOOD LA

03

School Farm

2

Horspools Farm

MAIN ST

Loddington Reddish

Eye Brook

LODDINGTON LA

Loddington Hall

Hall Farm

BELTON RD

Loddington

1

02

A	B	C	D	E	F
77		78		79	

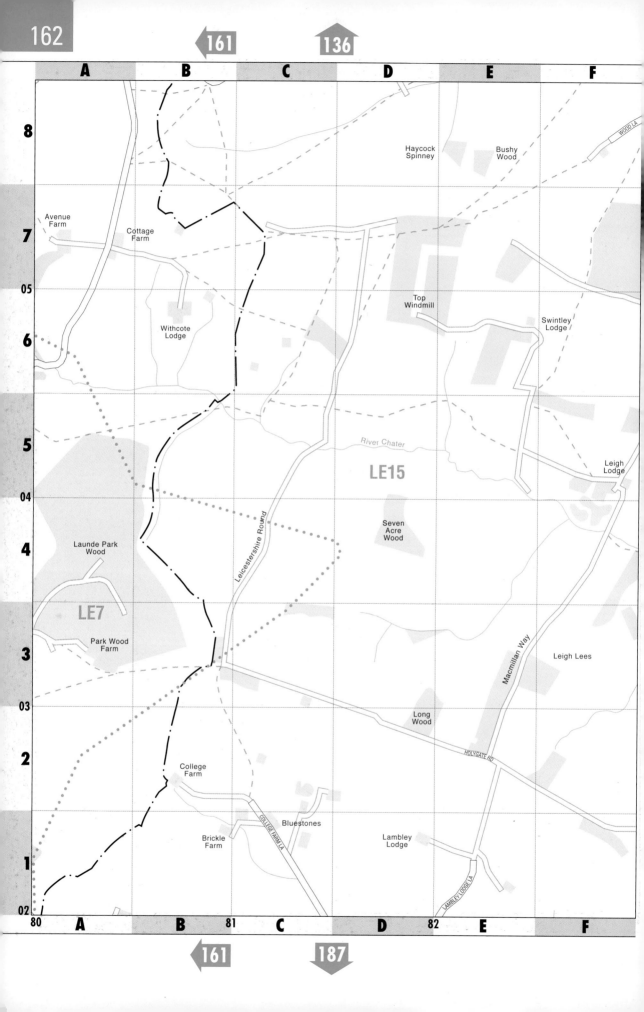

161
136

A   B   C   D   E   F

8

Haycock
Spinney

Bushy
Wood

WOOD LA

Avenue
Farm

Cottage
Farm

7

05

Top
Windmill

Swintley
Lodge

Withcote
Lodge

6

River Chater

5

LE15

Leigh
Lodge

04

Leicestershire Round

Launde Park
Wood

Seven
Acre
Wood

4

LE7

Park Wood
Farm

3

Macmillan Way

Leigh Lees

03

Long
Wood

2

HOLYGATE RD

College
Farm

Bluestones

Lambley
Lodge

Brickle
Farm

COLLEGE FARM LA

1

LAMBLEY LODGE LA

02

80   A   B   81   C   D   82   E   F

161
187

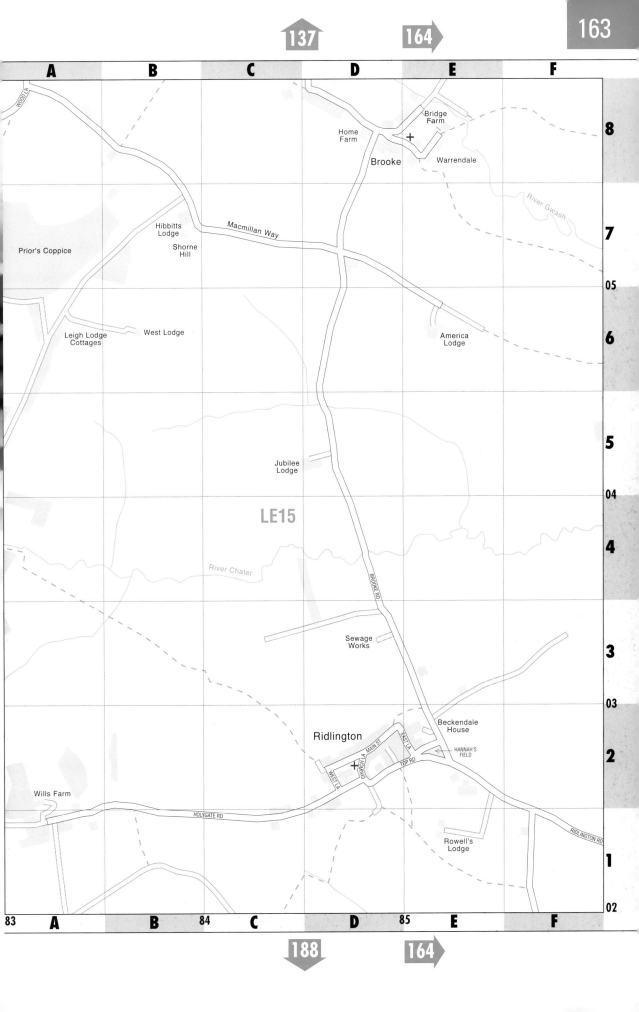

163
138

| A | B | C | D | E | F |

8 Gunthorpe

The Bungalows

Gunthorpe Bridge

A6003

Manton Bay

7

River Gwash

05

Sounding Bridge

6 Martinsthorpe

Cemy

PRIORY RD

THOMAS FRYER'S ALMSHOS

CEMETERY LA

ST MARY'S RD

Manton

PH

ST CHURCH LA

STOCKS HILL

LYNDON RD

Wellfield

Macmillan Way

CHATER CL

SOUTH VIEW CT

Mast

MANTON GRANGE

BADGERS CL

Fox Covert

5

Manton Lodge Farm

LE15

Manton Junction

WING RD

04

Works

4

River Chater

Crown Well Bridge

3

Cromwell Farm

STATION RD

03

2

Preston Hall

PRESTON RD

Wing Grange

OAKHAM RD

Preston

Holly Farm

MAIN ST

CROSS LA

BROOKLANDS

CHURCH LA

PRESTON CT

PH

1 RIDLINGTON RD

SOUTH VIEW

GLASTON RD

A6003 UPPINGHAM RD

02

| 86 | A | B | 87 | C | D | 88 | E | F |

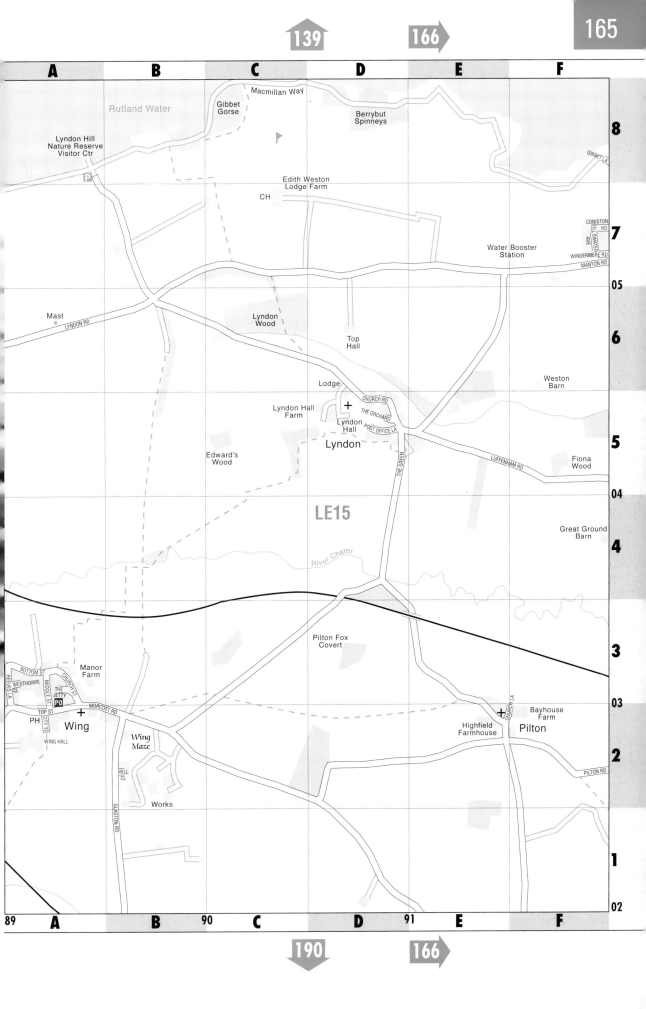

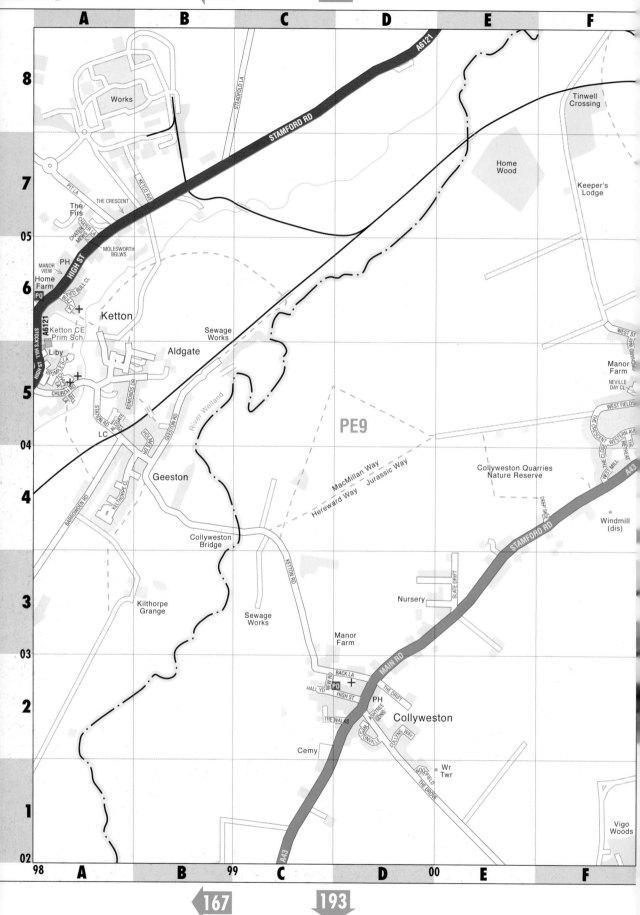

A6121

STAMFORD RD

Tinwell
Crossing

Home
Wood

Keeper's
Lodge

STADFOLD LA

PIT LA

KETCO AVE

THE CRESCENT

The
Firs

CHATER LA

MEWS

MOLESWORTH
BGLWS

MANOR
VIEW

PH

HIGH ST

Home
Farm

PO

A6121

PIED BULL CL

BULL

Ketton

Ketton CE
Prim Sch

STOCK'S HILL

HIGH ST

Liby

REDME'S LA

ALDGATE

CHATER RD

CHURCH HILL

Aldgate

EDMONDS DR

Sewage
Works

WEST ST

HOLYOAK RD

STATION RD

ALDGATE

GEESTON RD

Manor
Farm

NEVILLE
DAY CL

WEST FIELDS

THE CRESCENT

WESTERN AVE

THE RETREAT

WEST MILL

A43

River Welland

LC

PE9

Geeston

BARROWDEN RD

KILTHORPE CL

MacMillan Way

Hereward Way Jurassic Way

Collyweston Quarries
Nature Reserve

DEEP SIDE

STAMFORD RD

Windmill
(dis)

Collyweston
Bridge

KETTON RD

Kilthorpe
Grange

Sewage
Works

Nursery

SLATE DRIFT

Manor
Farm

MAIN RD

BACK LA

NEW RD

HALL YD

PO

HIGH ST

THE DRIFT

PH

ASHTREE
GDNS

THE WALKS

LYNDHURST
TERR

Collyweston

COLLYNS WAY

Cemy

WOODFIELD

THE DROVE

Wr
Twr

Vigo
Woods

A43

A B C D E F

8
05
7
6
05
5
04
4
03
3
2
02
1

Waterloo Plain
Burghley Park
Jacob's Ladder
CH Hereward Way
Wothorpe
Wothorpe House
WOTHORPE VILLAS
The Warren
GREAT NORTH RD
KETTERING RD
A43
SECOND DRV
1ST DRIFT
THE MALTINGS
B1081
LONDON RD
WARREN RD
George Farm
Macmillan Way
Jurassic Way
WOTHORPE HILL
Nursery
Wothorpe Farm
Wothorpe House
Wothorpe Groves
Dottrell Hill Plantation
Hereward Way
Pit Holes
A1
B1081
Carpenter's Lodge
A1
Sewage Works
PARK WLK
PE9
Mast
RACECOURSE RD
CHURCH ST
THE LANE
WEST ST
WESTHAVEN
HIGH ST
1 NEVILLE DAY CL
2 WEST FIELDS
NEW TOWN
Sch
NEW RD
GARFORD RD
PORTER'S LA
WESTERN'S LA
THE AVE
PH
Mast
Easton on the Hill
Works
Straight Mile
Racecourse Wood
CLIFFE RD
White Water Lake
Chalk Pit Hollow
Wittering Airfield
Masts
PE8
Easton Lodge

A1 Peterborough (A47)
Cambridgeshire STREET ATLAS

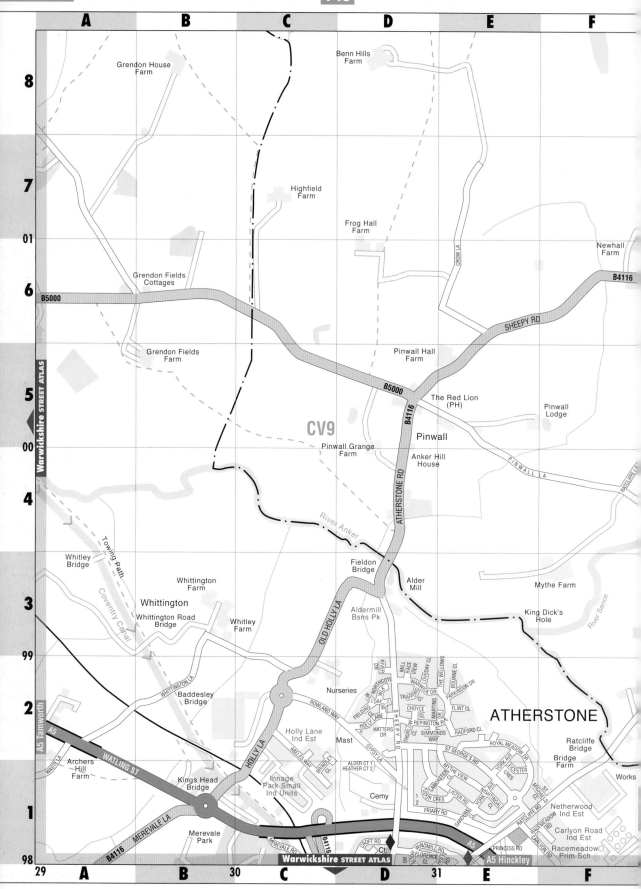

A B C D E F

8

01

7

6

5

00

4

3

99

2

1

98

B5000

Grendon House Farm

Benn Hills Farm

Highfield Farm

Frog Hall Farm

Grendon Fields Cottages

Grendon Fields Farm

Newhall Farm

B4116

SHEEPY RD

CROW LA

Pinwall Hall Farm

Pinwall Lodge

B5000

The Red Lion (PH)

Pinwall

PINWALL LA

CV9

Pinwall Grange Farm

Anker Hill House

ATHERSTONE RD

B4116

RATCLIFFE LA

River Anker

Whitley Bridge

Towing Path

Fieldon Bridge

Alder Mill

Mythe Farm

River Sence

Whittington Farm

Whitley Farm

Whittington

Whittington Road Bridge

Coventry Canal

Aldermill Bsns Pk

King Dick's Hole

WHITTINGTON LA

Baddesley Bridge

OLD HOLLY LA

Nurseries

RIVER DR

NORTHCOTE

MILL RACE VIEW

LOVEDAY CL

THE WILLOWS

BOURNE CL

PARKINSON DR

WARWICK DR

FIELDING

TRAFFS CL

DAY

HOLLY LANE

CHOYCE CL

MARTINS DR

THURLOW

FLINT CL

RADFORD CL

ATHERSTONE

Rowland Way

Holly Lane Ind Est

Mast

HATTERS DR

SHEEPY RD

REPINGTON AVE

SIMMONDS WAY

ROYAL MEADOW DR

Ratcliffe Bridge Farm

HOLLY LA

ABELES WAY

BRINDLE CL

GYPSY LA

ALDER CT 1
HEATHER CT 2

ST GEORGE'S RD

LANCASTER RD

MYTHE VIEW

YORK AVE

LEICESTER CRES

MITCHELS

NETHERWOOD

Works

A5

Archers Hill Farm

WATLING ST

WASTE LA

A5 Tamworth

A5

Kings Head Bridge

Innage Park Small Ind Units

LISTER RD

1

2

FLOOR CRES

YORK RD

Cemy

FRIARY RD

SANDERS

NIGHTINGALE CL

RATCLIFFE RD

Netherwood Ind Est

Carlyon Road Ind Est

Racemeadow Prim Sch

MEREVALE LA

B4116

Merevale Park

MEREVALE RD

B4116

Ct

CROFT RD

FLORENCE CL

WADMILL RD

HOLTE RD

PRINCESS RD

CARLYON RD

A5

A5 Hinckley

Warwickshire STREET ATLAS

29 A B 30 C D 31 E F

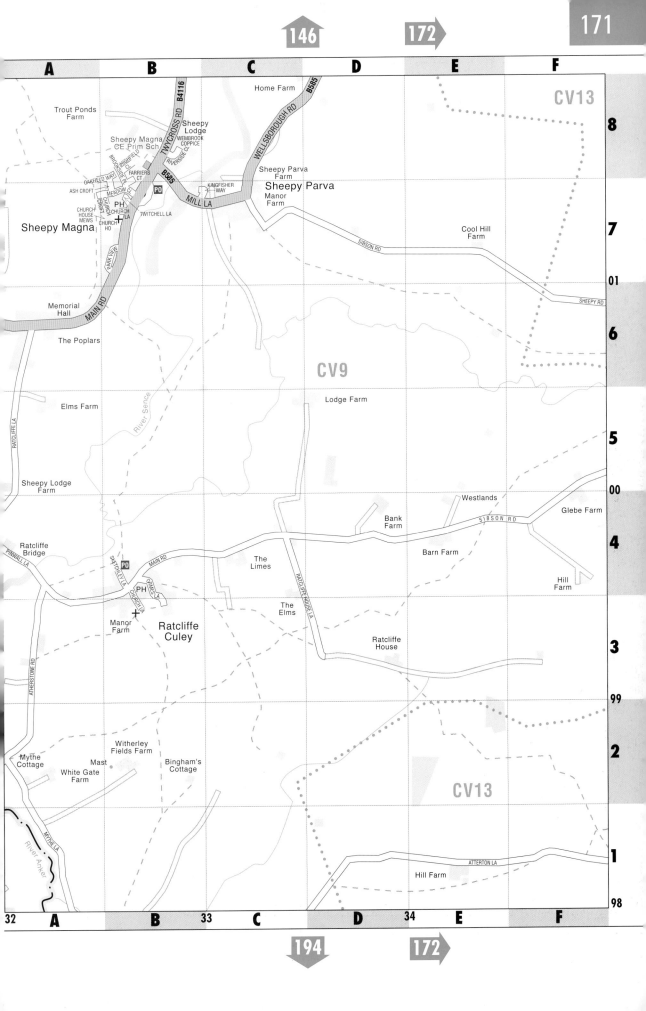

CV13

CV9

CV13

Trout Ponds Farm

Home Farm

Sheepy Magna CE Prim Sch

Sheepy Lodge

WEMBROOK COPPICE

Sheepy Parva Farm

Sheepy Parva

BROOKSIDE CL

HIGHFIELD

FARRIERS CT

KINGFISHER WAY

Manor Farm

OAKFIELD WAY

MEADOW CL

ASH CROFT

PO

MILL LA

TWITCHELL LA

CHURCH CROFT

PH

CHURCH LA

Cool Hill Farm

CHURCH HOUSE MEWS

CHURCH HO

Sheepy Magna

PARK VIEW

SIBSON RD

Sheepy Rd

Memorial Hall

MAIN RD

The Poplars

Lodge Farm

RATCLIFFE LA

Elms Farm

River Sence

Westlands

Bank Farm

SIBSON RD

Glebe Farm

Sheepy Lodge Farm

Ratcliffe Bridge

PINWALL LA

Barn Farm

Hill Farm

SKETCHLEY LA

PO

MAIN RD

The Limes

CHURCH LA

JAMES LA

PH

The Elms

RATCLIFFE HOUSE LA

Ratcliffe House

Manor Farm

Ratcliffe Culey

ATHERSTONE RD

Witherley Fields Farm

Bingham's Cottage

Mythe Cottage

Mast

White Gate Farm

MYTHE LA

River Anker

Hill Farm

ATTERTON LA

B4116

TWYCROSS RD

WELLSBOROUGH RD

B585

B585

RIVERSIDE CL

32   A   B   33   C   D   34   E   F

8

7

01

6

5

00

4

3

99

2

1

98

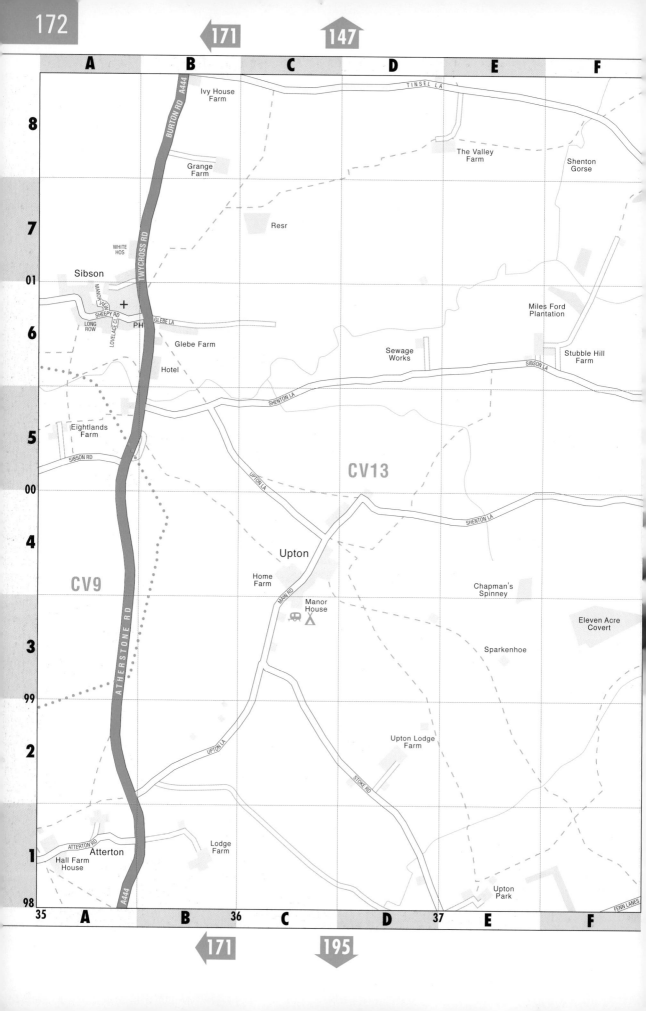

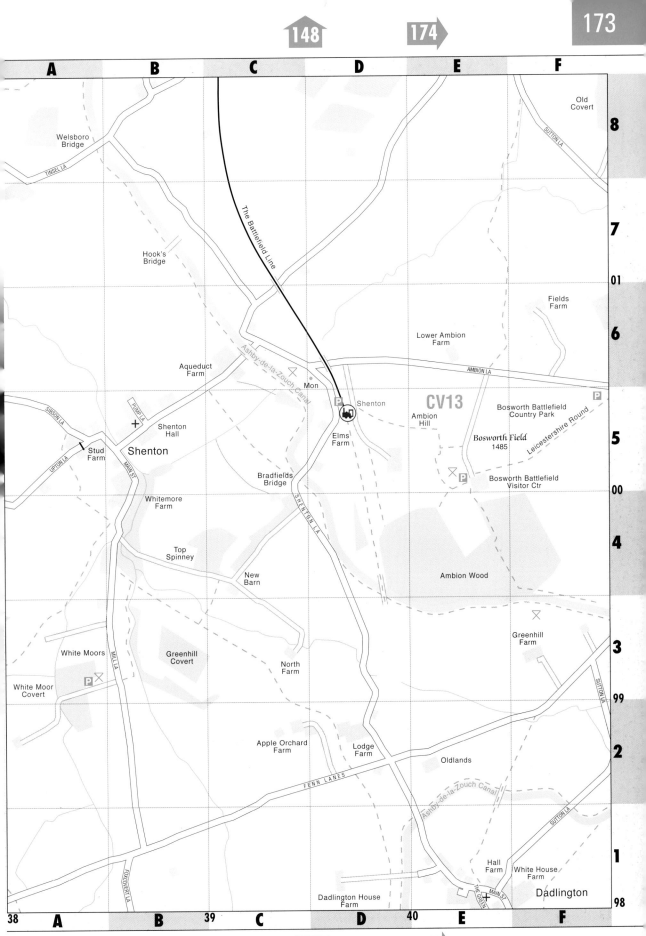

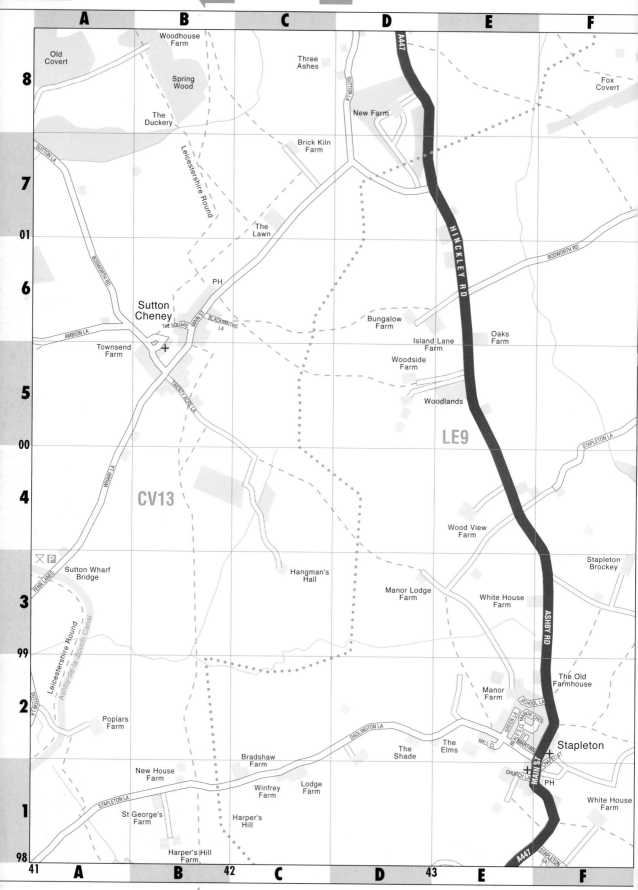

A B C D E F

8

7

01

6

5

00

4

3

99

2

1

98

41 A B 42 C D 43 E F

Old Covert

Woodhouse Farm

Spring Wood

The Duckery

Leicestershire Round

SUTTON LA

BOSWORTH RD

Three Ashes

SUTTON LA

New Farm

Brick Kiln Farm

The Lawn

A447

HINCKLEY RD

Fox Covert

BOSWORTH RD

PH

Sutton Cheney

THE SQUARE

MAIN ST

BLACKSMITHS LA

AMBION LA

Townsend Farm

TWENTY ACRE LA

Bungalow Farm

Island Lane Farm

Woodside Farm

Oaks Farm

Woodlands

LE9

WHARF LA

CV13

STAPLETON LA

Wood View Farm

Stapleton Brockey

Hangman's Hall

Manor Lodge Farm

White House Farm

ASHBY RD

Sutton Wharf Bridge

FENN LANES

Leicestershire Round

Ashby-de-la-Zouch Canal

SUTTON LA

The Old Farmhouse

Manor Farm

SCHOOL LA

GREEN LA

BEALES CL

MANOR CRES

ST MARTINS

Stapleton

Poplars Farm

DADLINGTON LA

The Shade

The Elms

MILL CL

MAIN ST

CHAPEL ST

CHURCH LA

PH

New House Farm

Bradshaw Farm

Winfrey Farm

Lodge Farm

White House Farm

STAPLETON LA

St George's Farm

Harper's Hill

Harper's Hill Farm

STAPLETON LA

A447

A   B   C   D   E   F

Kirkby
Moats

Becks
Farm

Fox
Covert

Peckleton
House

Kirkby
Lodge

Green
Spinney

Sandhole
Spinney

DESFORD LA

ARCHERS LA

Brook House
Farm

PH

BROOK LA

MAIN ST

NEWBOLD RD

BOSWORTH RD

MANOR LA

KIRKBY LA

CHURCH RD

THE CLOSE

MAIN ST

SUMMERS CL RD

PH

CHURCH RD

PECKLETON RD

Kirkby
Mallory

Manor
House

Peckleton
Hall

STAPLETON LA

Motor Racetrack

Mallory
Park

BARWELL RD

+

Glebe
Farm

New Park
Farm

LE9

Church
Spinney

BARWELL LA

Glebe
Farm

SHILTON RD

The Folly
Cottages

Folly
Farm

Brockey
Farm

Brockey
Farm

Brooklands
Farm

Glebe
Barn

Barwell Fields
Farm

KIRKBY RD

Brockey Farm
Cottages

Brockey
Farm

LEICESTER RD A47

CLEAR VIEW CRES

HIGH ST HILL TOP

The
Brockey

Earl
Shilton

PH

Westbury

The Brockey
Farm

THE BEECRES 1
Castle CL 2

CHURCH
ST 2

HIGH TOR W

HIGH TOR E

GREEN LA

KEATS CL

WEST ST

P

MAUGHAN'S ST

Barwell

ELWELL AVE

BARTON RD

BRADGATE RD

APPLE TREE CL

Brockey
Farm

Westfield
Farm

KEATS LA

PARK CL

PARK RD

WEST ST

HIGH ST A47

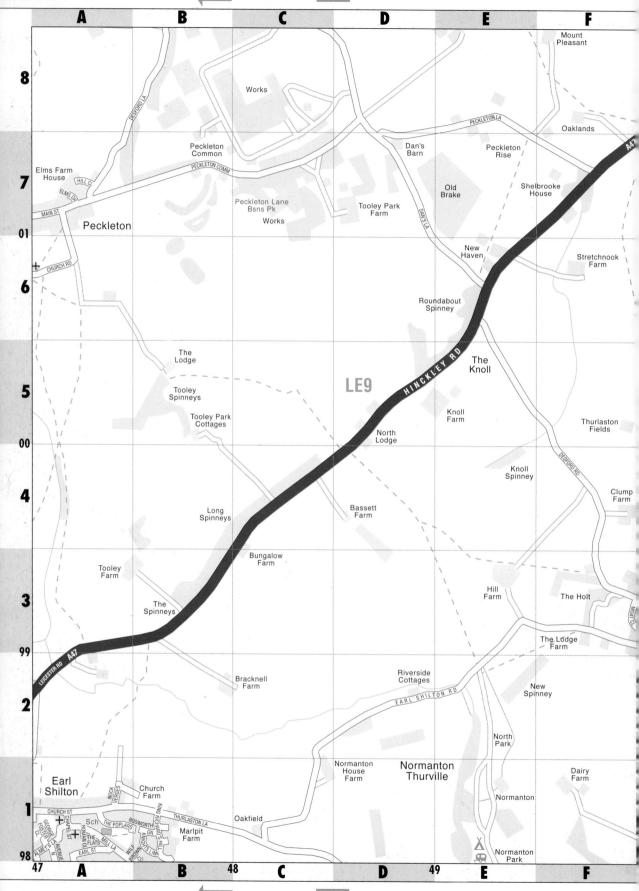

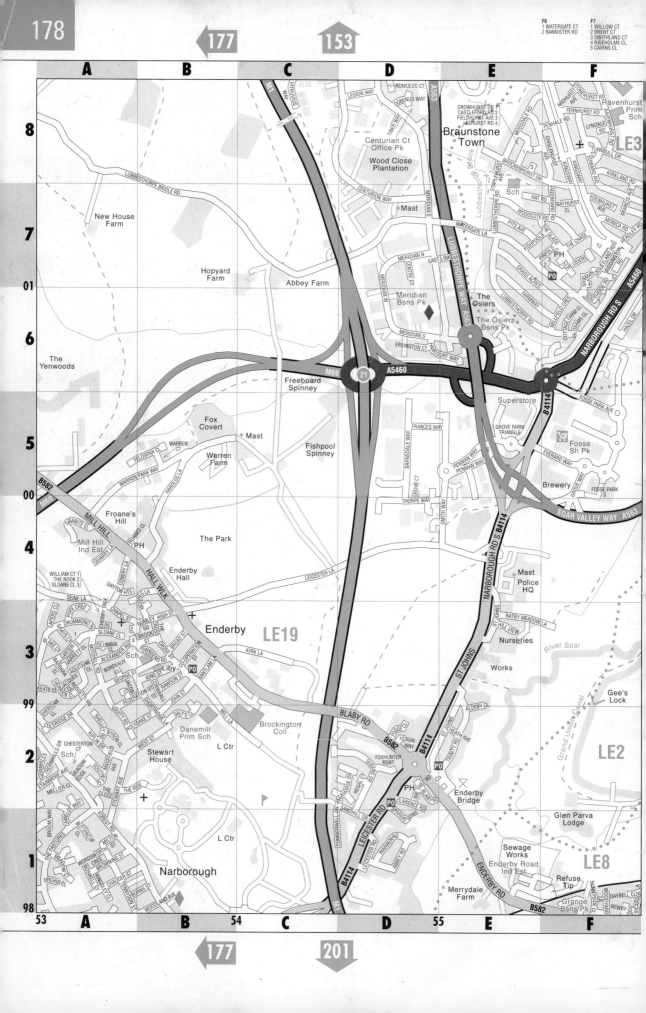

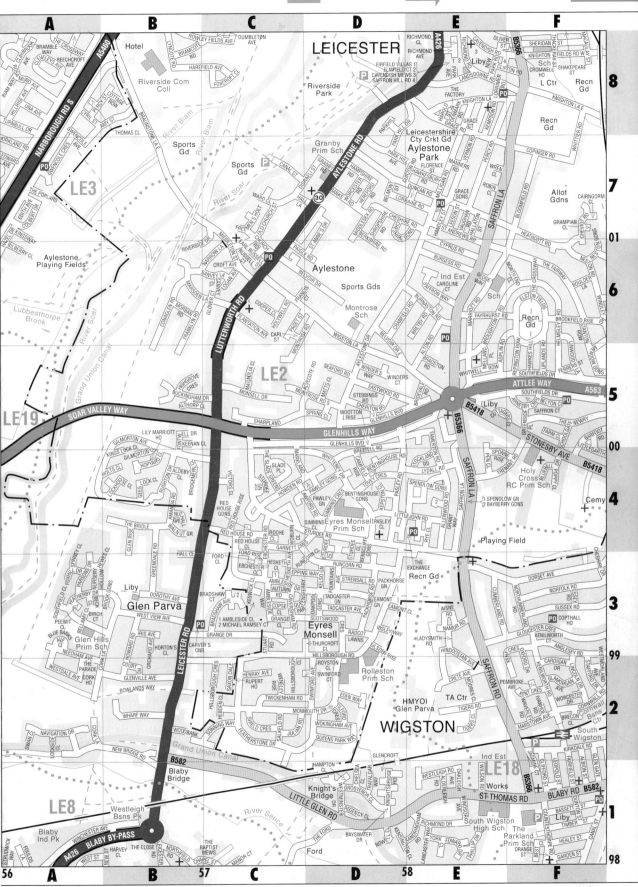

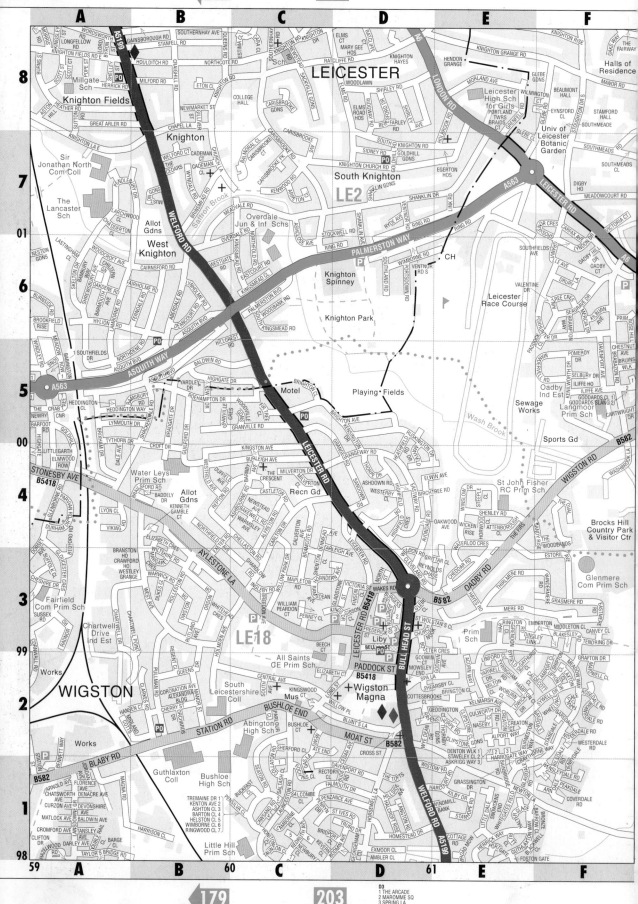

D3
1 THE ARCADE
2 MAROMME SQ
3 SPRING LA

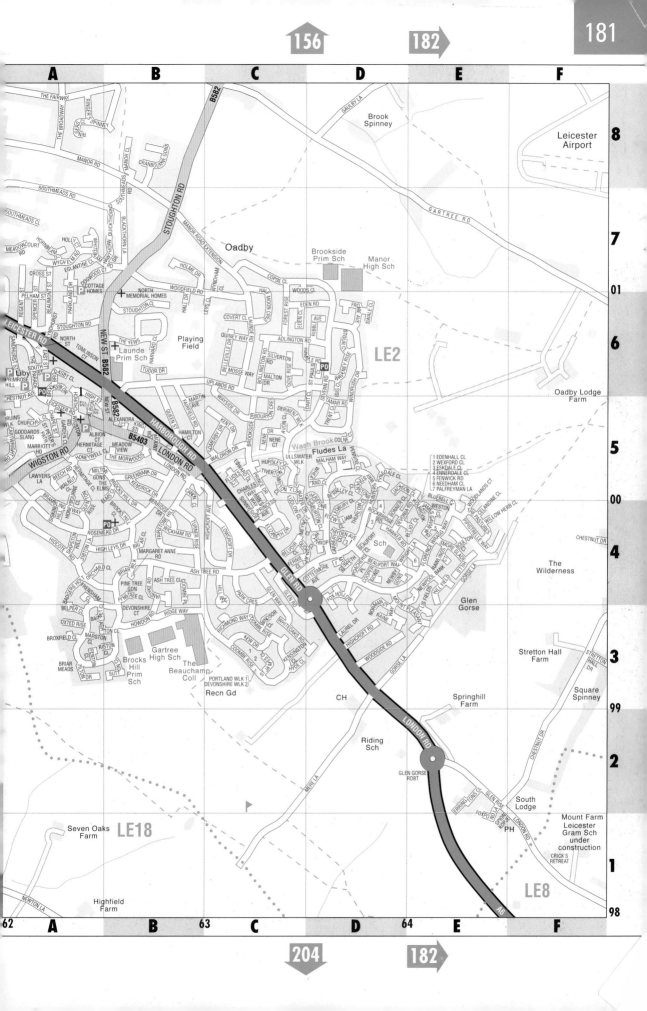

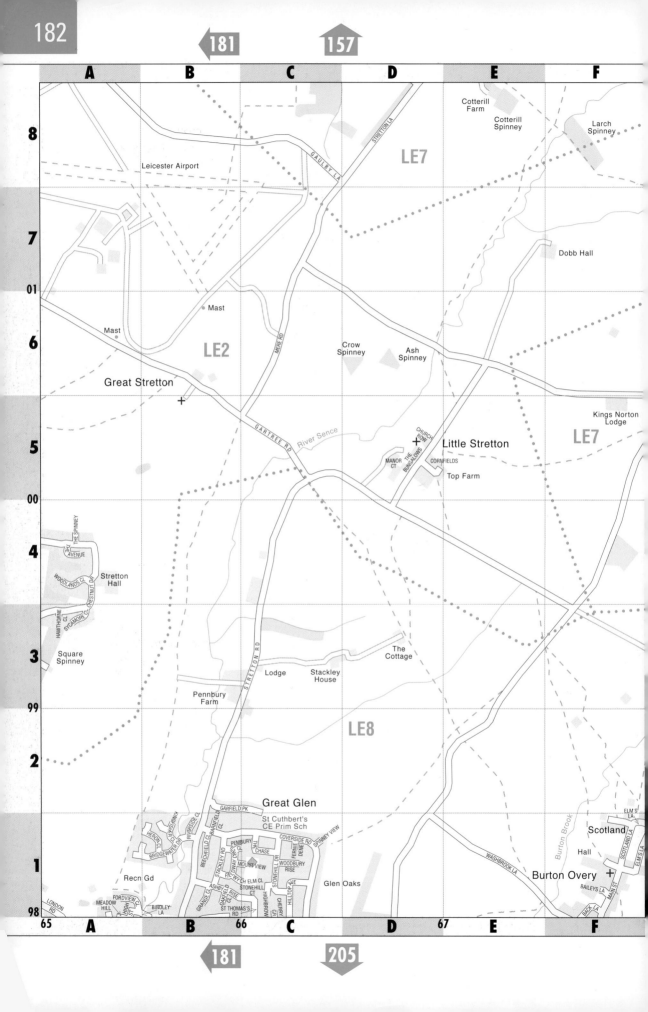

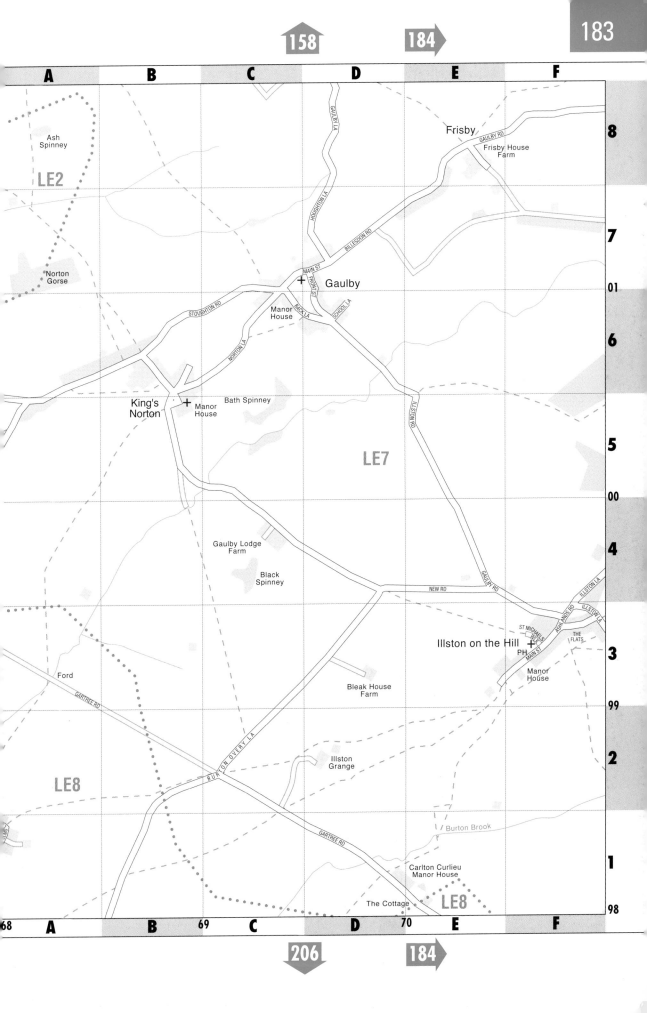

A   B   C   D   E   F

8

Ash
Spinney

LE2

01

Frisby

Frisby House
Farm

GAULBY RD

GAULBY LA

HOUGHTON LA

BILLESDON RD

7

Norton
Gorse

MAIN ST

FRONT ST

Gaulby

STOUGHTON RD

Manor
House

BACK LA

SCHOOL LA

6

NORTON LA

King's
Norton

Manor
House

Bath Spinney

LE7

ILSTON RD

5

00

Gaulby Lodge
Farm

Black
Spinney

4

NEW RD

GAULBY RD

ILLSTON LA

ILLSTON LA

ASH LANDS RD

St MICHAEL'S

THE
FLATS

Illston on the Hill

PH

MAIN ST

Manor
House

3

Ford

GARTREE RD

Bleak House
Farm

99

BURTON OVERY LA

Illston
Grange

2

LE8

GARTREE RD

Burton Brook

1

Carlton Curlieu
Manor House

The Cottage

LE8

98

183
159

A B C D E F

8

GAULBY RD

Rolleston Lodge
Farm

B6047

ROLLESTON RD

Vale
Cottage

Hubbard's
Spinney

7

01

Frisby
Lodge
Farm

HARBOROUGH RD

Blenheim
Plantation

BUSHY RD

Frisby
Lodge

6

SKEFFINGTON RD

Cranhill
Farm

Ashlands

Long Plantation

ILLSTON LA

LE7

Home
Farm

Rolleston

Rolleston
Hall

+

Pop's Spinney

Crow
Wood

5

00

New Inn

The Lodge

Old Pond
Wood

The
Farm

Whinney Pit
Spinney

Barn
Farm

4

Barn Close
Spinney

Rolleston
Wood

Millfield
Clump

3

NOSELEY RD

NEW INN LA

ILLSTON RD

Top
Lodge

THE AVENUE

99

ILLSTON LA

ILLSTON CROSS
ROADS

Lodge
Gates

2

Burton Brook

Southfield
Spinney

THREE GATES RD

Home
Plantation

Noseley

BACK RD

Foxhole
Spinney

Turner's Barn
Farm

Three
Gates

Coney Hill
Plantation

Noseley
Hall

+

Round
Spinney

1

MELTON RD

B6047

KIBWORTH RD

Long
Acre

Cottons Field
Farm

Old Park

New Park

Thistley
Cottages

Shangton
Holt

Noseley
Wood

98

71 A B 72 C D 73 E F

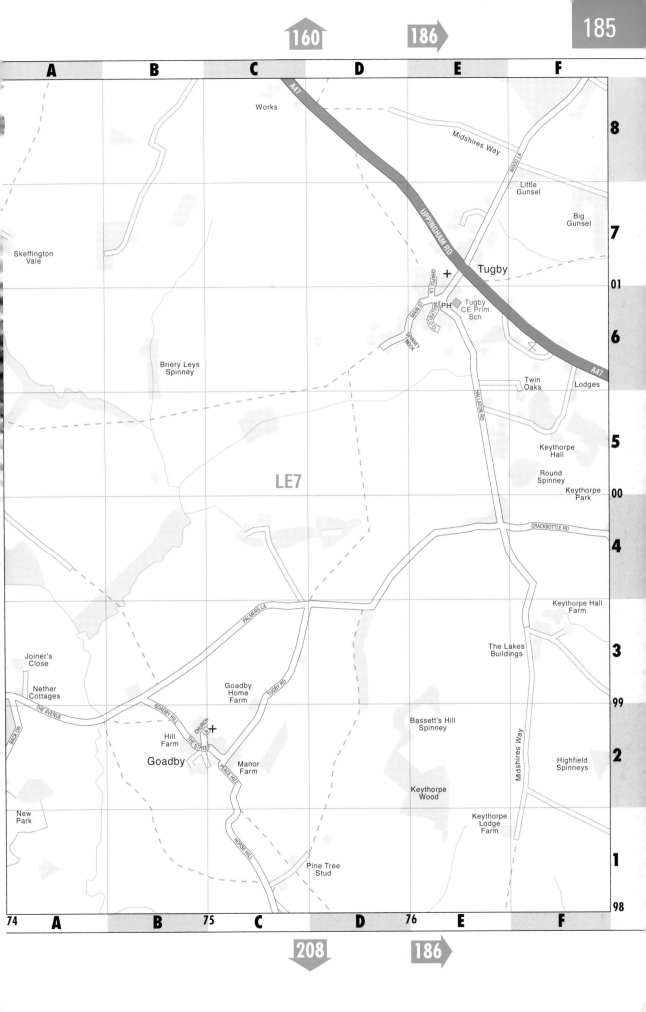

A   B   C   D   E   F

Works

Midshires Way

A47

UPPINGHAM RD

Little Gunsel

Big Gunsel

WOOD LA

8

7

Skeffington Vale

Tugby

CHAPEL LA

PH

MAIN ST

WELL RD

Tugby CE Prim Sch

01

6

SPINNEY BROOK

Briery Leys Spinney

HALLATON RD

Twin Oaks

Lodges

A47

5

Keythorpe Hall

Round Spinney

Keythorpe Park

00

LE7

CRACKBOTTLE RD

4

PALMERS LA

Keythorpe Hall Farm

The Lakes Buildings

3

Joiner's Close

TUGBY RD

Goadby Home Farm

Bassett's Hill Spinney

Midshires Way

99

Nether Cottages

THE AVENUE

GOADBY HILL

CHURCH LA

Highfield Spinneys

2

BACK DR

Hill Farm

THE STREET

Goadby

PEACE HILL

Manor Farm

Keythorpe Wood

New Park

HORSE HILL

Keythorpe Lodge Farm

1

Pine Tree Stud

98

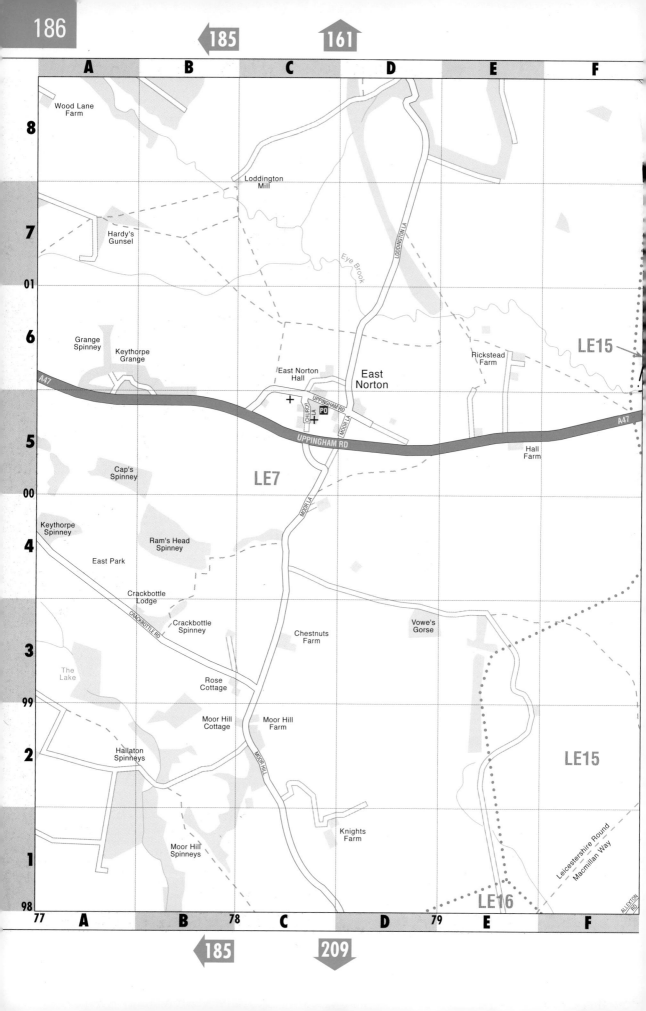

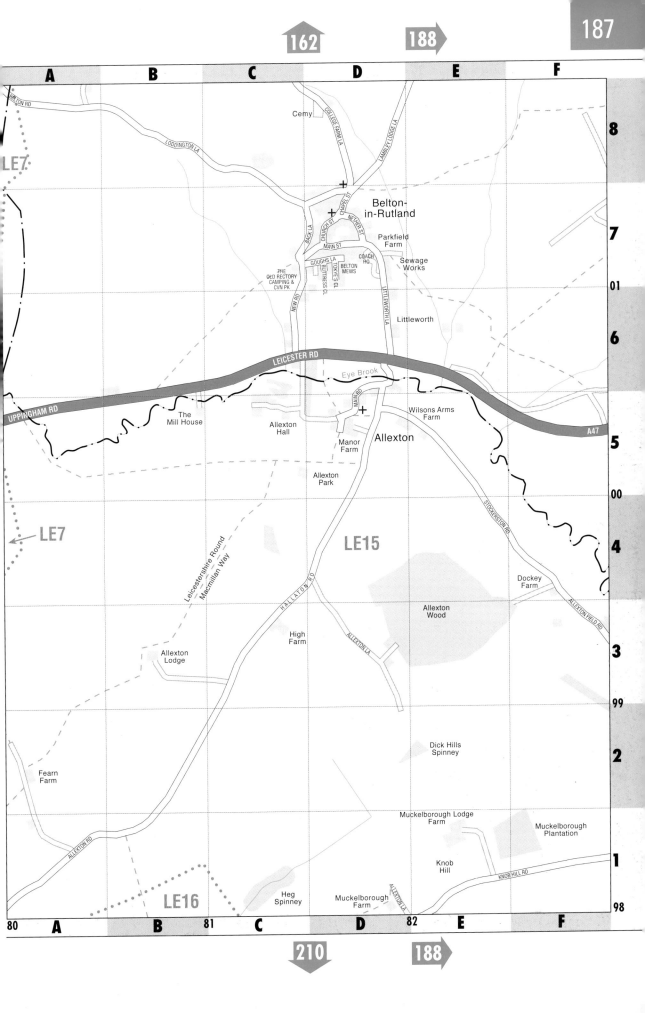

162
188
210
188

A B C D E F

8
7
01
6
00
4
3
99
2
1
98

LE7

LE7

LE15

LE16

BELTON RD
LODDINGTON LA
Cemy
COLLEGE FARM LA
LAMBLEY LODGE LA
CHAPEL ST
Belton-in-Rutland
BACK LA
CHURCH ST
NETHER ST
Parkfield Farm
MAIN ST
COACH HO.
Sewage Works
GOUGHS LA
TOKE'S CL
BELTON MEWS
THE OLD RECTORY CAMPING & CVN PK
BUTTRESS CL
NEW RD
LITTLEWORTH LA
Littleworth
LEICESTER RD
Eye Brook
UPPINGHAM RD
The Mill House
Allexton Hall
MAIN RD
Wilsons Arms Farm
Manor Farm
Allexton
A47
Allexton Park
STOCKERSTON RD
Leicestershire Round
Macmillan Way
HALLATON RD
Dockey Farm
Allexton Wood
ALLEXTON FIELD RD
High Farm
ALLEXTON LA
Allexton Lodge
Dick Hills Spinney
Fearn Farm
Muckelborough Lodge Farm
Muckelborough Plantation
ALLEXTON RD
Knob Hill
KNOB HILL RD
Heg Spinney
Muckelborough Farm
ALLEXTON LA

80 A B 81 C D 82 E F

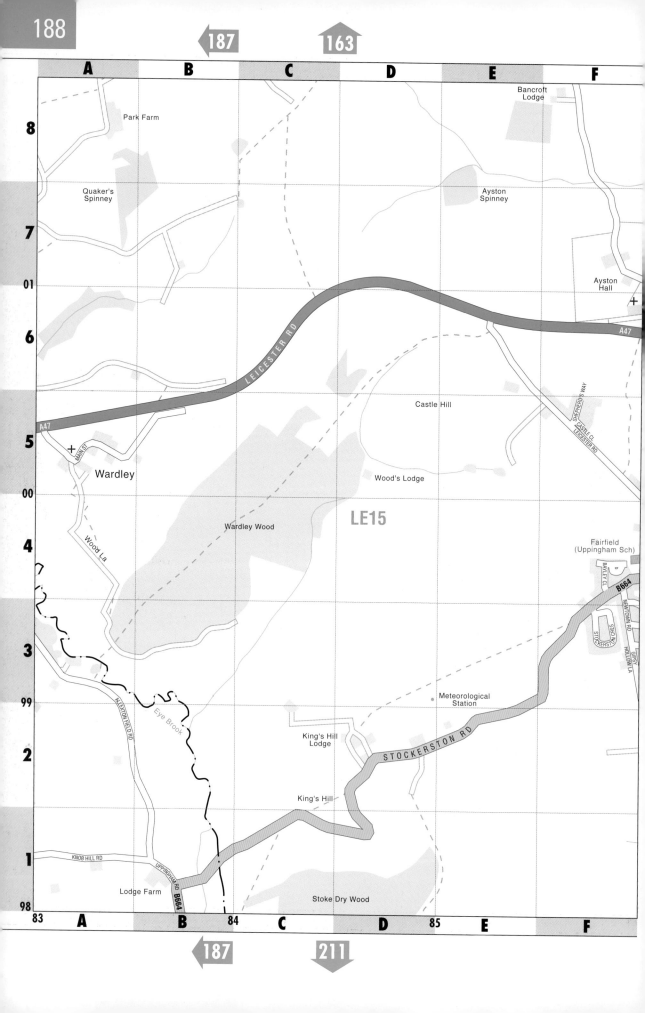

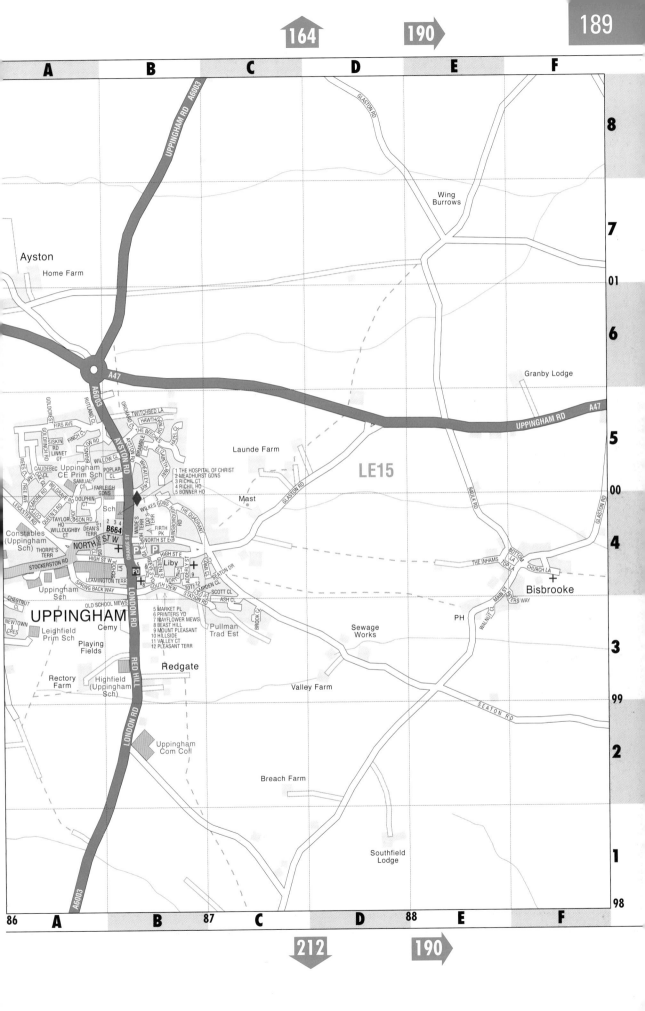

A B C D E F

8
7
01
6
5
00
4
Bisbrooke
3
99
2
1
98

Wing Burrows

Ayston
Home Farm

A47

A6003

UPPINGHAM RD

UPPINGHAM RD A47

Granby Lodge

LE15

Launde Farm

Mast

GLASTON RD

GLASTON RD

BAULK RD

BOTTOM LA
TOP LA
THE INHAMS
CHURCH LA

MAIN ST
PEERS WAY
WALNUT CL

PH

1 THE HOSPITAL OF CHRIST
2 MEADHURST GDNS
3 RICHIL CT
4 RICHIL HO
5 BONNER HO

Uppingham
CE Prim Sch

GOLDCREST CL
FIRS AVE
RUTLAND CL
TWITCHBED LA
HAWTH
ORCHARD CL
AYSTON RD
THE BEECHES
BRAMBLE CL
HAZEL CL
ELIZABETHAN WAY
WHEATLEY AVE

SISKIN RD
GOLDFINCH RD
LINNET CT
FINCH CL
WILLOW CL
POPLAR CL

REES CL
FREE AVE
OAK CL
CAUDEBEC CL
SAMUAL CT
FARLEIGH GDNS
DOLPHIN CT
AMORE RD
QUEEN'S RD
TAYLOR CT
SON RD
WILLOUGHBY CT
DEAN'S TERR
Sch
WILKES GDNS
THE QUADRANT
GAINSBROUGH RD
NORTH ST
TERR
FIRTH PK
STATION RD

LEICESTER RD
BELGRAVE RD
JOH
HO

THORPE'S TERR
SCHOOL LA

Constables
(Uppingham Sch)

B664
NORTH
ST W
NORTH ST
SHIELDS
HIGH ST W

STOCKERSTON RD
LEAMINGTON TERR

Uppingham
Sch

SPRING BACK WAY

OLD SCHOOL MEWS

CHESTNUT CL
NEWTOWN CRES

UPPINGHAM

Leighfield
Prim Sch

Cemy

RED HILL
LONDON RD

A6003

Playing
Fields

Rectory
Farm

Highfield
(Uppingham Sch)

Redgate

Uppingham
Com Coll

Breach Farm

Southfield
Lodge

P
P
P
PO
Liby
SOUTH VIEW
REEVE'S YD
ORANGE ST
WADE'S CH TERR
DODD'S CT
HIGH ST E
SEATON DR
CAMPDEN CL
SCOTT CL
ASH CL
BROOK CL

5 MARKET PL
6 PRINTERS YD
7 MAYFLOWER MEWS
8 BEAST HILL
9 MOUNT PLEASANT
10 HILLSIDE
11 VALLEY CT
12 PLEASANT TERR

Pullman
Trad Est

Sewage
Works

Valley Farm

SEATON RD

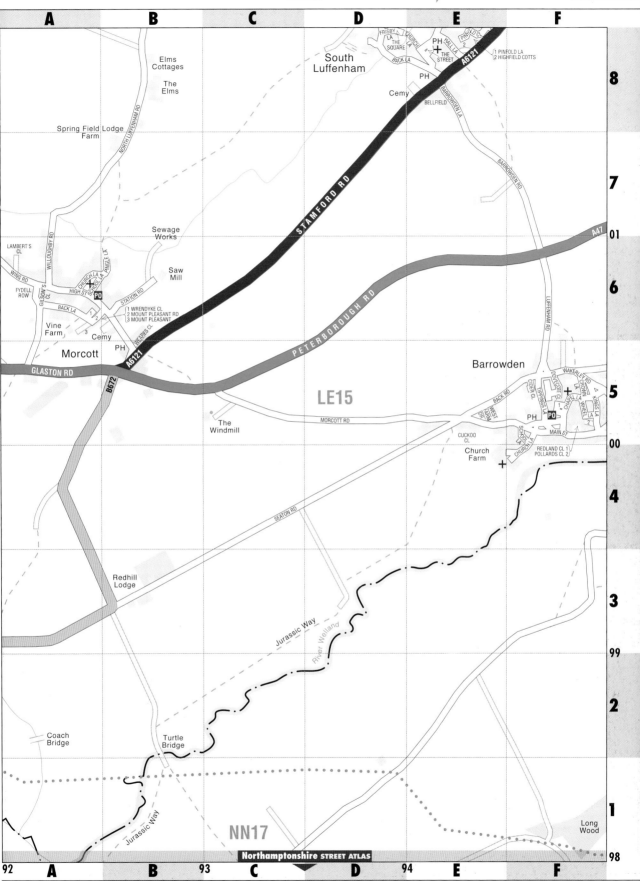

A B C D E F

8
7
01
6
5
00
4
3
99
2
1
98

South Luffenham

FRISBY LA
THE SQUARE
CHURCH
BACK LA
PH
HALL LA
THE STREET
PH
A6121
1 PINFOLD LA
2 HIGHFIELD COTTS
Cemy
BELLFIELD
BARROWDEN LA
BARROWDEN RD
A47
A47

Elms Cottages
The Elms

NORTH LUFFENHAM RD

Spring Field Lodge Farm

Sewage Works

LAMBERT'S CL
WILLOUGHBY RD
WING RD
FYDELL ROW
GILSON'S CL
BACK LA
CHURCH LA
SCHOOL LA
PINGLE LA
HIGH ST
PO
STATION RD
VICARS CL
Vine Farm
Cemy
PH
A6121
B672

Saw Mill

1 WRENDYKE CL
2 MOUNT PLEASANT RD
3 MOUNT PLEASANT

Morcott

GLASTON RD

STAMFORD RD

PETERBOROUGH RD

LUFFENHAM RD

Barrowden

BACK RD
WEST FARM
WAKERLEY RD
DOVECOTE CL
CUFFS CL
TIPPINGS LA
CHAPEL LA
CROWN LA
KINGS LA
WHEEL LA
PH
PO
MAIN ST
SCHOOL LA
CHURCH
CUCKOO CL
Church Farm
REDLAND CL 1
POLLARDS CL 2

LE15

The Windmill

MORCOTT RD

SEATON RD

Redhill Lodge

Jurassic Way

River Welland

Coach Bridge

Turtle Bridge

Jurassic Way

NN17

Long Wood

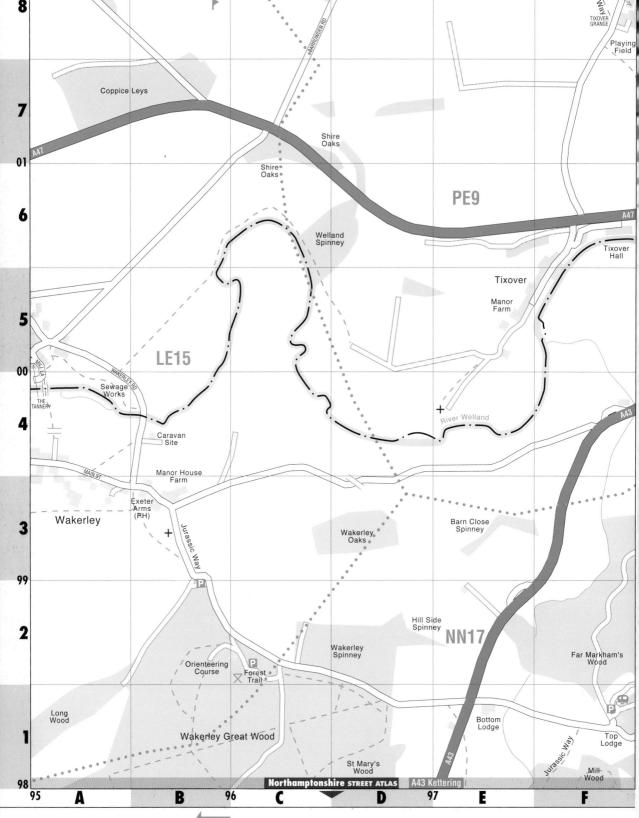

A B C D E F

Sewage Works

River Welland

A43

A47

Cuckoo Lodge

THE DROVE

Vigo Woods

A47 Peterborough

A47

8

Quarry

Little Wood

Collyweston Great Wood

01

HIGHFIELD
STAMFORD RD
GREEN LA
MILL ST
CHURCH LA
TODD'S HILL

PE9

7

6

Duddington

Manor House

PH

HIGH ST
GREEN LA

Gregory's Lodge

Cemy

The Assarts

5

00

Gore Piece

4

North Spinney

Long Spinney

Jurassic Way

Little Wood

PE8

Cambridgeshire STREET ATLAS

Noses Halt

Cunnington's Spinney

3

Dales Wood

Peter's Nook

99

Dumb Bob Spinney

Buxton Wood

The Gullet

Westhay Wood

2

NN17

Great Watkinson

Old Sale

TOP LODGE

Stockings

1

Jurassic Way

Hither Hazelwood

Northamptonshire STREET ATLAS

98

98 A 99 B C 99 D 00 E F

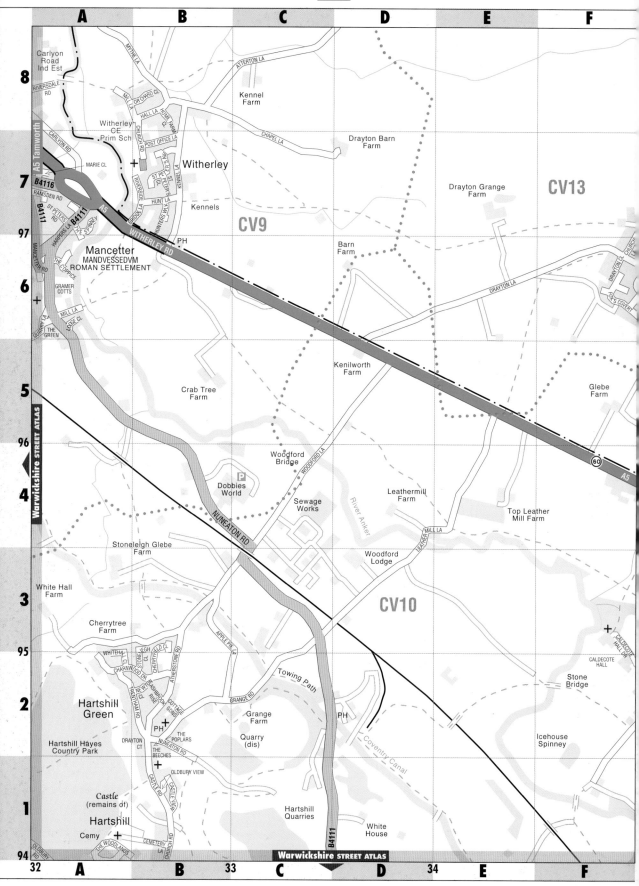

A B C D E F

8
7
97
6
5
96
4
95
2
1
94

White Gables
Farm
Meadowcroft
The White
Cottage

STONE RD

FENN LANES

Camp
(dis)
Ashpole
Spinney

CV13

Hill
Farm

ATHERSTONE RD

A444

Fenny
Drayton

CHURCH LA

OLD FORGE RD

QUAKER CL

ROOKERY CL

GEORGE FOX LA

FOX'S COVERT

HUNTERS LA

+

Rowden
Gorse

Lindley Hall
Farm

Lodge
Farm

Rowden House
Farm

Lindley
House

Proving Ground

Lindley
Park

PH

A444

70

Lindley
Grange

Works

MIRA DR

Hungry
Hill

Cherry Orchard
Court

HILARY BEVINS CL

STATION RD

MAIN ST

CHERRY ORCHARD EST

WOOD LA

95

The
Elms Farm

CV10

Caldecote

The Grange

CALDECOTE HALL DR

WEDDINGTON LA

Weddington
Wood Farm

The Kings
Lodge

Lindley
Lodge Farm

NUNEATON LA

A444

WEDDINGTON RD

Weddington Country Walk

Lower
Farm

Top
Farm

CV11

HIGHAM LA

Whitehouse Farm
Cottage

A5

195 173

A B C D E F

8

Foxcovert La
Grange Farm
Marina
Ivy House Farm
Stoke Golding
The Green
STAPLETON LA
STOKE LA
Lodge Farm

7

Fox Covert Farm
UPTON LA
Willow Park Ind Est
Crown Hill
CHURCH WLKS
PH
CHURCH CL
HIGH ST
ROSEWAY
GREENHILL
SHENTON
IVY CL
WHITEMOORS CL
SHERWOOD RD
GREENWOOD
HINCKLEY RD
St Martin's Convent
St Martin's RC Sch

Brook Farm
STATION RD
CROWN HILL CL
ANDREW CL
The Courtyard
The Stable Yd
St Margaret's CE Prim Sch
MARGARET RD
ST
HALL DR
PINE CL
THORNFIELD
Stokefields Farm
STOKE RD

97

HIGHAM FIELDS LA
MAIN ST
PO
BENN CL
ARNOLD RD
STONELEY RD
Cemy
AVE
TITHE CL
Willow Farm
Brook House
Brook Farm

6

HIGHAM FIELDS CT
HIGHAM LA
Millfield Farm
Highfield Farm
WYKIN LA
Oaklands

CV13

5

Oak Tree Farm
Cuckoo's Nest Farm
Basin Bridge Farm
Compass Fields Farm
Higham Fields

STOKE LA
Vale Farm
Basin Bridge
Ashby-De-La-Zouch Canal
BASIN BRIDGE LA

96

4

MILL GDNS
Higham on the Hill CE Prim Sch
Hall Farm
Wykin Fields
The Hollow
Wykin

3

PH
PO
NUNEATON LA
MAIN ST
Higham on the Hill
Higham Hall
HINCKLEY LA
Spring Hill Farm
Wykin-House Farm
WYKIN LA
WYKIN RD
Wykin Hall

95

BARR LA
NORMANDY WAY
A47

2

Grange Farm
Higham Thorns
LE10
MARCIAN CL
OUTLANDS DR
LIVIA

Harper's Hill
Jamia Islamia (Islamic Studies Ctr)
MARYWELL CL
FRESNICK CL
HADRIAN CL
CROSSKIRK RD
KINROSS WAY
LOSSIEMOUTH RD
CROMARTY DR
LEYSMILL CL
LAXFORD DR

1

OVERBROOK GRANGE
Hollow Farm
WATLING ST
A5
Change Brook
CV11
A47

94

38 A B 39 C D 40 E F

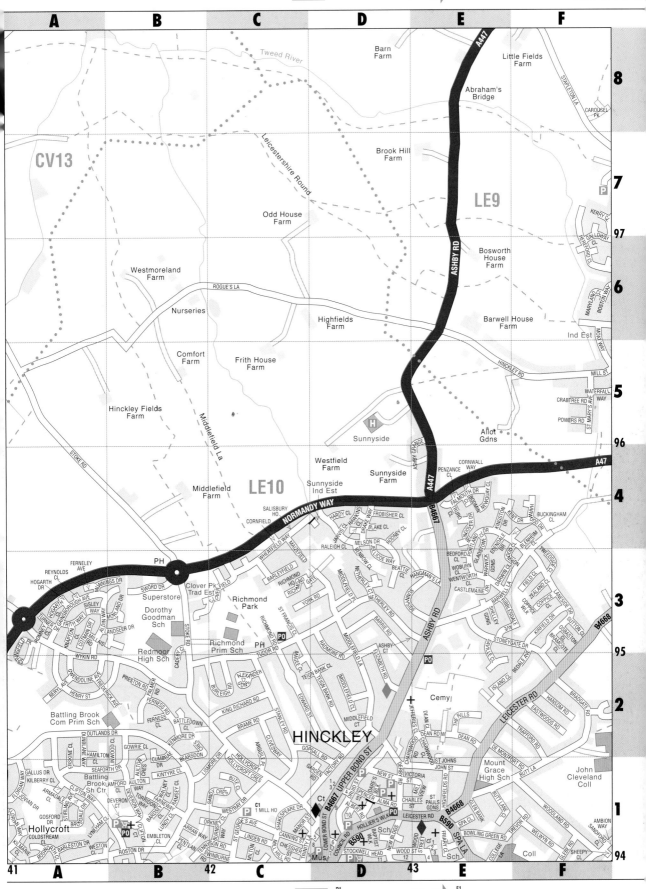

CV13

LE9

Tweed River

Barn Farm

Little Fields Farm

Abraham's Bridge

Brook Hill Farm

Leicestershire Round

Odd House Farm

CAROUSEL PK

Westmoreland Farm

ROGUE'S LA

Nurseries

Highfields Farm

Bosworth House Farm

ASHBY RD

KERRY CL

GALLOWAY

HEREFORD CL

MARYLAND CL

BOSTON WAY

Comfort Farm

Frith House Farm

Hinckley Fields Farm

Middlefield La

STOKE RD

Barwell House Farm

Ind Est

MILL ST

HINCKLEY RD

Sunnyside

WATERFALL WAY

CRABTREE RD

ST MARY'S AVE

POWERS RD

LE10

Middlefield Farm

Westfield Farm

Sunnyside Ind Est

Sunnyside Farm

ASHBY GRANGE

Allot Gdns

CORNWALL WAY

PENZANCE CL

FALMOUTH DR

A47

A47

SALISBURY HO

CORNFIELD

NORMANDY WAY

HARDY CL

HAWKINS

DRAKE WAY

FROBISHER CL

RODNEY CL

BLAKE CL

B4667

BUCKINGHAM CL

Superstore

Clover Pk Trad Est

Richmond Park

BARLEYFIELD

MAYFIELD

RICHMOND HO

RIGG'S GATE

RALEIGH CL

NELSON DR

BENBOW CL

NICOE WAY

BEATTIE

HANGMAN'S LA

BEDFORD CL

WOBURN CL

WENTWORTH

WARWICK

GLADSTONE

DARWIN DR

BLENHEIM CL

TWEEDS DR

FIELD CL

Reynolds

Ferneley Ave

Hogarth Dr

PH

Dorothy Goodman Sch

Redmoor High Sch

Richmond Prim Sch

ST FRANCIS CT

YORK RD

PO

PH

RICHMOND RD

MIDDLEFIELD PL

NETHERLEY RD

BARRIE RD

ASHBY CT

ELIZABETH RD

CASTLEMAINE

SHELLEY

BARWELL DR

STONEGATE DR

LAICESTER DR

SUTTON CL

OSBASTON CL

BRAMCOTE CL

B4668

SWORD DR

SISLEY WAY

ALAN WAY

MORELAND DR

LANDSEER DR

COTMAN DR

MILLAIS

WYKIN RD

Battling Brook Com Prim Sch

PO

A4667

UPPER BOND ST

Cemy

Mount Grace High Sch

John Cleveland Coll

HINCKLEY

TEIGN BANK CL

RADMORE RD

MIDDLEFIELD LA

Battling Brook Sh Ctr

GOWRIE CL

KENMORE DR

BEARSDON

CUMBRAE DR

HOLLYCROFT

HOLLYCROFT CRES

BUTT CL

THE RILLS

DEAN RD W

DE MONTFORT ST

LEICESTER RD

HANSOM RD

EASTWOODS RD

TRAFFORD RD

Hollycroft

COLDSTREAM

GOSFORD DR

C1 1 MILL HO

Ct

LOWER BOND ST

COUNCIL RD

Mus

STOCKWELL HEAD

B590

LEICESTER RD

B4668

B590

SPA LA

Coll

AMBION WAY

SANDFORD

SHEEPY RD

WELWYN RD

WOODLAND RD

BOWLING GREEN RD

FRIARY CL

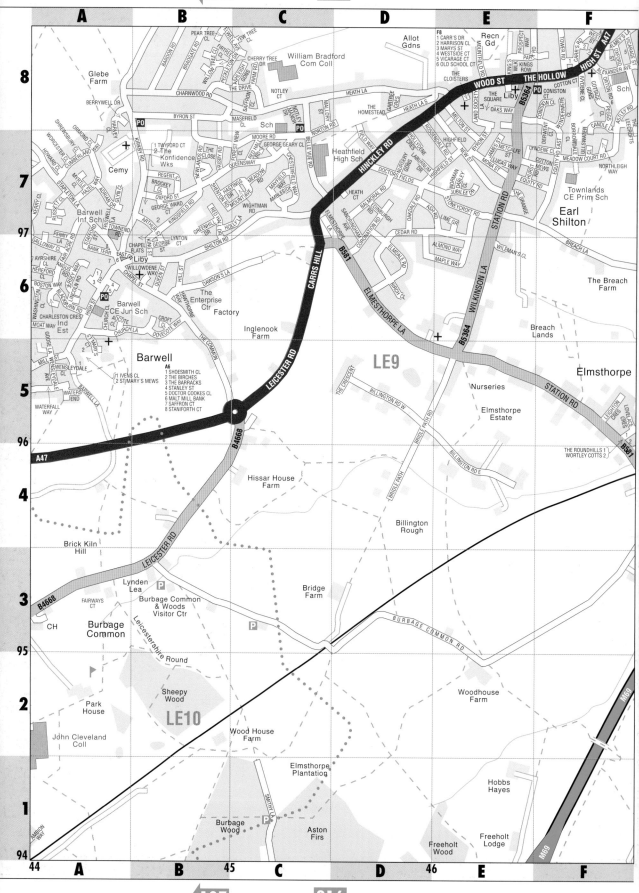

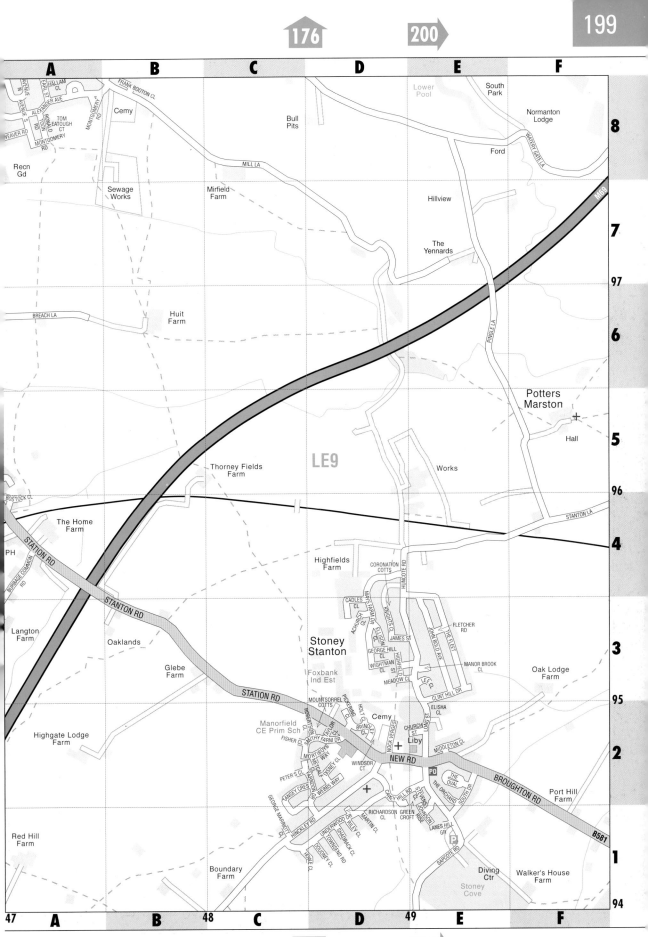

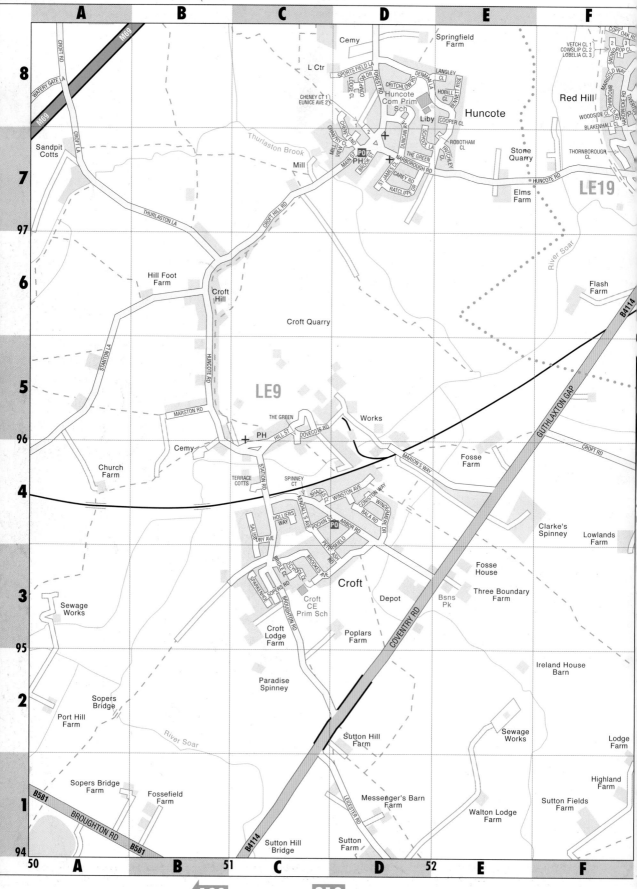

201 179

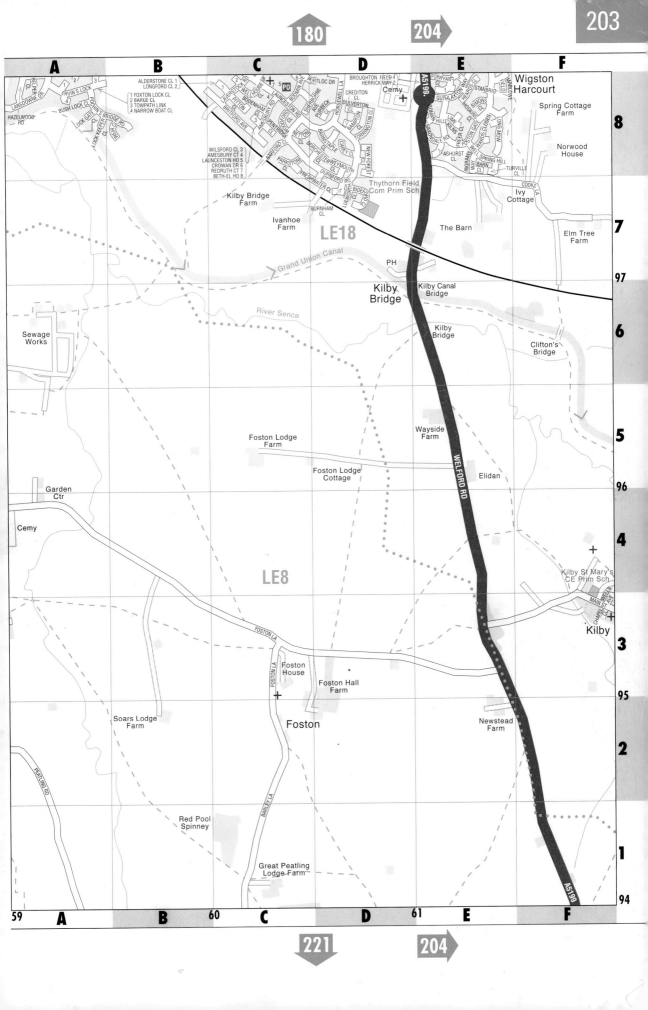

A B C D E F

Top labels (grid columns): A B C D E F

Grid rows (right side): 8 7 97 6 5 96 4 3 95 2 1 94

Map place names and labels:

BELPER GR
LANSDOWNE GR
HAZELWOOD RD
ERVIN'S LOCK
BUSH LOCK CL
LOCK GATE CL
LOCK KEEPER'S CL
POOH'S BRIDGE RD

ALDERSTONE CL 1
LONGFORD CL 2
1 FOXTON LOCK CL
2 BARGE CL
3 TOWPATH LINK
4 NARROW BOAT CL

WILSFORD CL 3
AMESBURY CT 4
LAUNCESTON HO 5
CROWAN DR 6
REDRUTH CT 7
BETH-EL HO 8

PORTLOC DR
BROUGHTON FIELD 1
HERRICK WAY 2
Cemy

Wigston Harcourt
Spring Cottage Farm
Norwood House

Thythorn Field Com Prim Sch

Kilby Bridge Farm
Ivanhoe Farm
BURNHAM CL

LE18

The Barn
Ivy Cottage
Elm Tree Farm
COOKS LA

PH
Kilby Canal Bridge
Kilby Bridge

Grand Union Canal

River Sence

Sewage Works

Kilby Bridge

Kilby Bridge
Clifton's Bridge

Foston Lodge Farm
Foston Lodge Cottage

Wayside Farm
Elidan

WELFORD RD

Garden Ctr
Cemy

LE8

Kilby St Mary's CE Prim Sch
MAIN ST
CHAPEL LA
Kilby

FOSTON LA
Foston House
Foston Hall Farm

Soars Lodge Farm

Foston

Newstead Farm

PEATLING RD
BARLEY LA

Red Pool Spinney

Great Peatling Lodge Farm

A5199
WELFORD RD

59 60 61

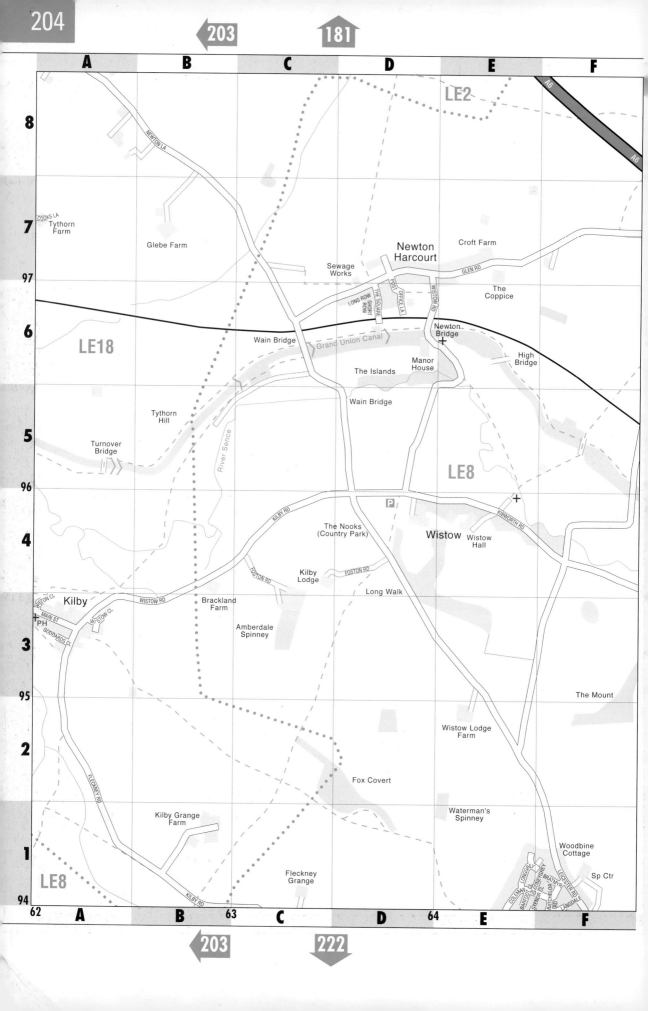

205
183

A B C D E F

8

CARLTON LA

Chestnut Farm

LE7

LE7

GARTREE RD

7

Manor Farm

Carlton Curlieu

GRANGE RD

Carlton Grange

Burton Brook

+

KIBWORTH RD

Carlton Curlieu Hall

97

The New House

Mark's Plantation

6

John's Belt

Clarrissa's Spinney

5

Home Farm Buildings

96

LE8

MERE RD

4

Carlton Clump

3

Kibworth Hall

CARLTON RD

Sheepthorns Spinney

95

2

BEECH TREE CL

THE CITY

Kibworth Harcourt

ALBERT ST

Sheepthorns Farm

KIBWORTH RD

The Manor

GAINSBOROUGH RD

WINDMILL GDNS

MARSH DR

LANGTON RD

MARSH AVE

Windmill

MAIN ST

SPINNEY DR

HARCOURT EST

A6 LEICESTER RD

PH

Windmill Farm

MERTON WAY

Kibworth Beauchamp

THE LEYS

HILL CRES AVE

1

WILFRID'S CL

THE TITHINGS

CHURCH RD

CHURCH CL

OAKTREE CL

Cemy

HARBOROUGH RD A6

Kibworth CE Prim Schl

THE VILLAS

RECTORY LA

SOUTH

THE LEA

+

94

68 A B 69 C D 70 E F

205
224

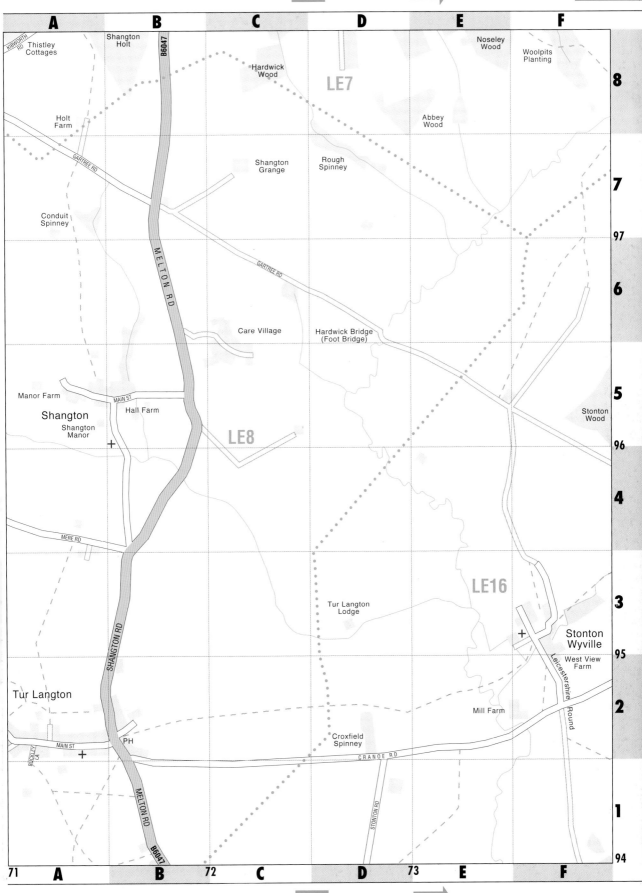

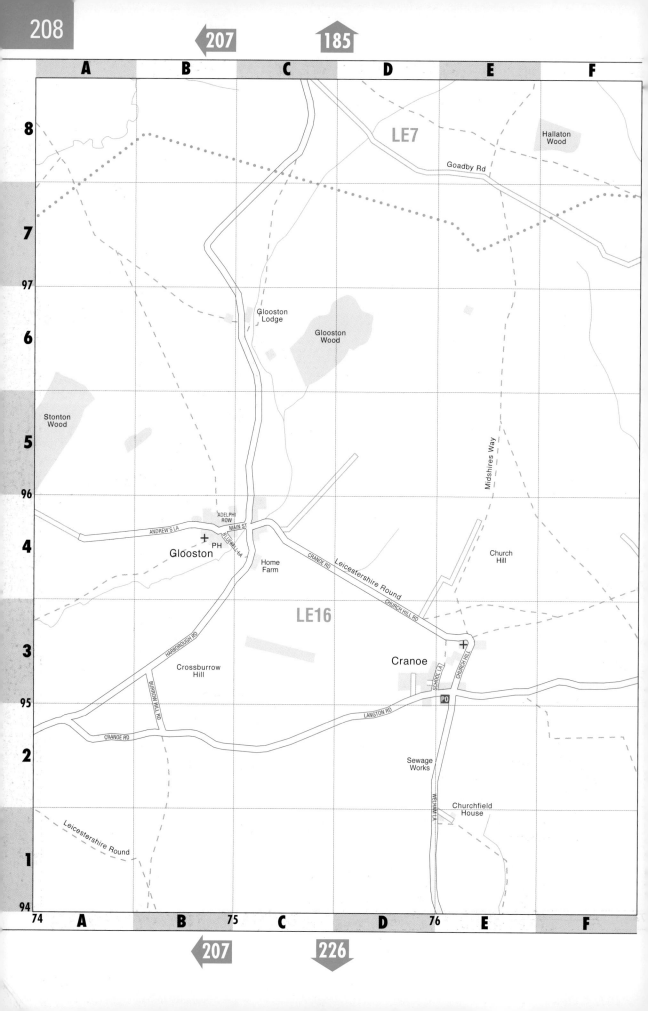

207
185

LE7

Hallaton
Wood

Goadby Rd

Glooston
Lodge

Glooston
Wood

Stonton
Wood

Midshires Way

ANDREW'S LA
ADELPHI
ROW
MAIN ST
BLUEBELL LA
PH
+
Glooston

Home
Farm

CRANOE RD
Leicestershire Round

CHURCH HILL RD

Church
Hill

LE16

HARBOROUGH RD

Crossburrow
Hill

BURROW HILL RD

+
Cranoe

SCHOOL LA
CHURCH HILL

PO

LANGTON RD

CRANOE RD

Sewage
Works

WELHAM LA

Churchfield
House

Leicestershire Round

207
226

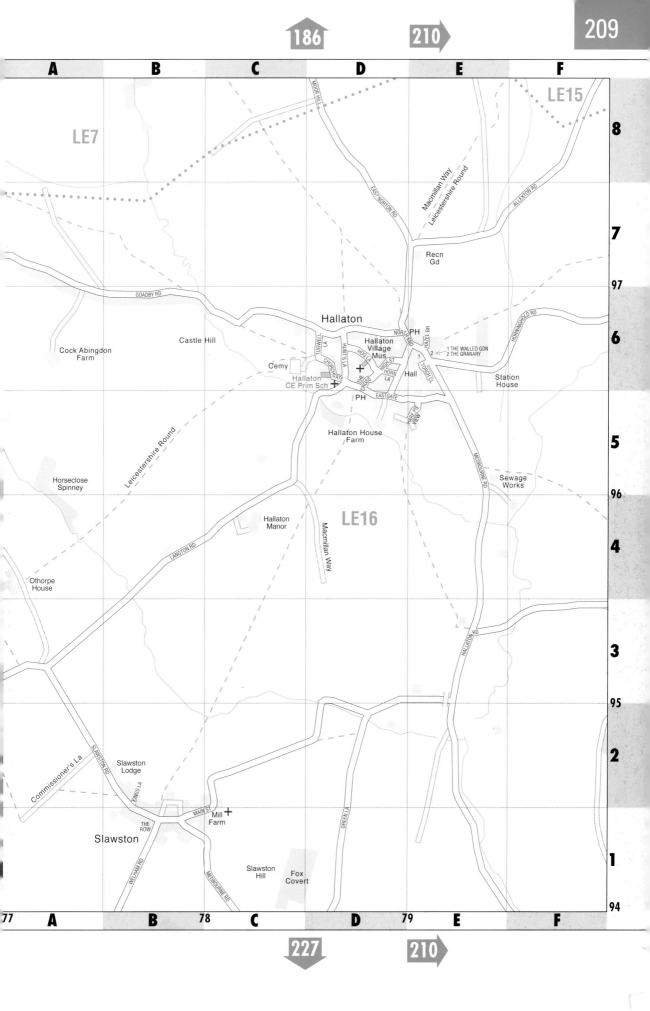

209
187

A · B · C · D · E · F

8

LE15

Knob Hill Farm

The Spinney

Frisby's Spinney

LE15

Park Wood

7

Horninghold Hall

Horninghold Wood

Burn Hill

Horninghold

KNOB HILL RD

Manor House Farm

97

HORNINGHOLD RD

HALLATON RD

Hoeback Spinney

BELCHER'S HILL

Belcher's Lodge

Bolt Wood

6

Red Hovel

HARBOROUGH HILL RD B664

Sturrad Spinney

Blaston Lodge

Stockerston Cross Rds

HORNINGHOLD LA

Overclose Spinney

Highland Spinney

STOCKERSTON LA

5

Pastures Farm

96

4

Blaston

Home Farm

BLASTON HILL

Blaston Hollows

LE16

Blaston Pastures

Manor Ho

HALLATON RD

Dent's Spinney

Priory Farm

3

UPPINGHAM RD

95

America Farm

2

Melbourne Grange

Grange Cottage

HOLT RD

Stone Lodge

1

B664

94

80 · A · B · 81 · C · D · 82 · E · F

188
212

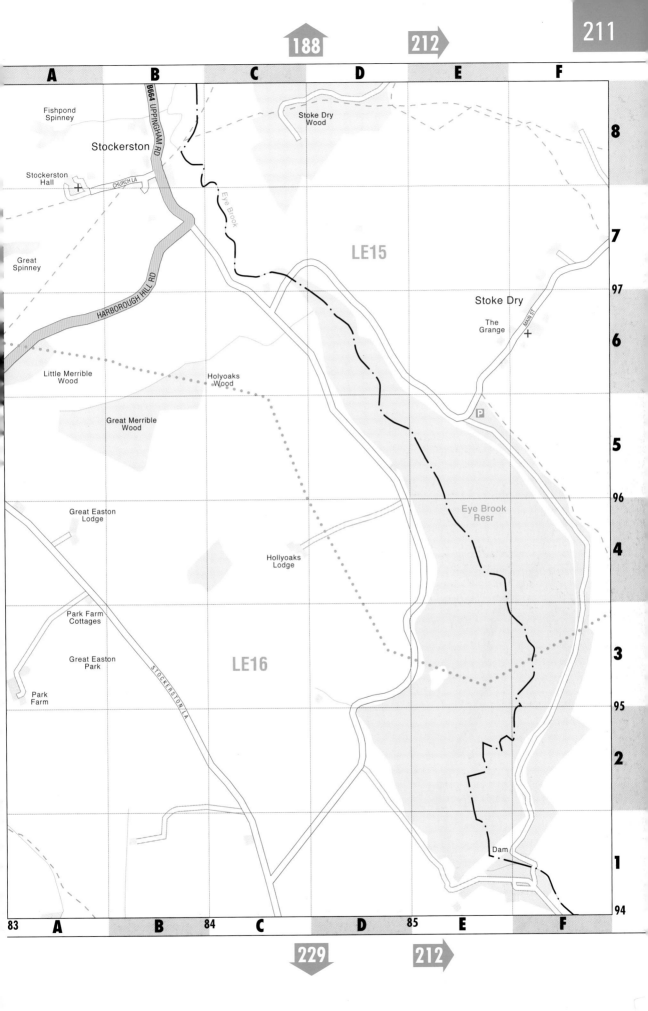

229
212

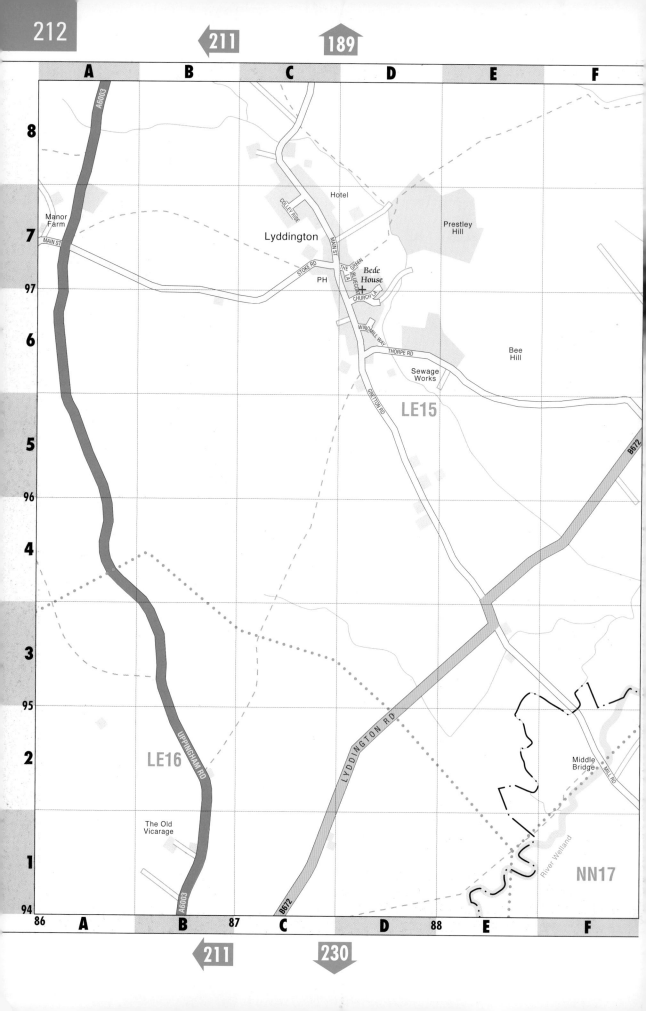

211
189

A   B   C   D   E   F

8

Manor
Farm

7   MAIN ST

Hotel

COLLEY RISE

Lyddington

Prestley
Hill

97   STOKE RD
PH   THE GREEN
BLUECOAT LA
MAIN ST
Bede
House
CHURCH LA

6   WINDMILL WAY
THORPE RD
Bee
Hill

Sewage
Works

GRETTON RD

LE15

A6003

5   B672

96

4

LE16   UPPINGHAM RD

3

LYDDINGTON RD

95

2   Middle
Bridge
MILL RD

The Old
Vicarage

1   River Welland   NN17

94   A6003   B672

86   A   B   87   C   D   88   E   F

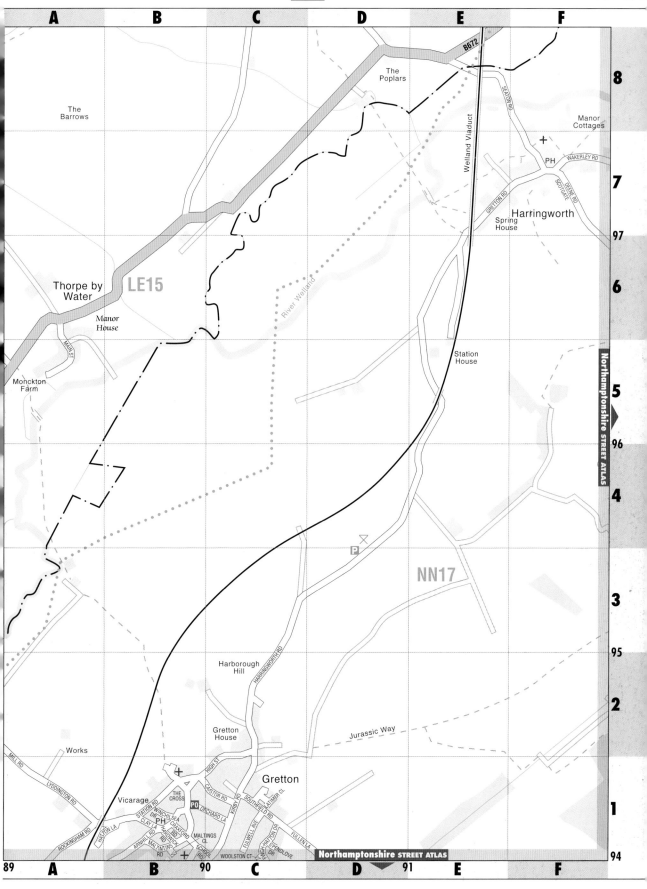

8

7

97

6

5

96

4

3

95

2

1

94

A   B   C   D   E   F

The Barrows

The Poplars

B672

Manor
Cottages

Welland Viaduct

PH   WAKERLEY RD

SEATON RD

GRETTON RD

Harringworth

Spring
House

DEENE RD

SCOTGATE

Thorpe by
Water

LE15

Manor
House

River Welland

Station
House

Monckton
Farm

NN17

P

Harborough
Hill

HARRINGWORTH RD

Jurassic Way

Gretton
House

Works

Gretton

MILL RD

LYDDINGTON RD

Vicarage

THE
CROSS

PH   PO

STATION RD

WINCHILSEA
DR

CRAXFORD RD

HARDWICK RD

HIGH ST

CAISTOR RD

KIRBY RD

SOUTHFIELD RD

SPENDLOVE DR

LATIMER CL

FULLEN LA

ROCKINGHAM RD

HATTON LA

ARNHILL RD

CLAY LA

MALTINGS RD

MALTINGS
CL

SCHOOL RD

FILWELL AVE

WOOLSTON CT

FINCH HATTON DR

89   A   B   90   C   D   91   E   F   94

196

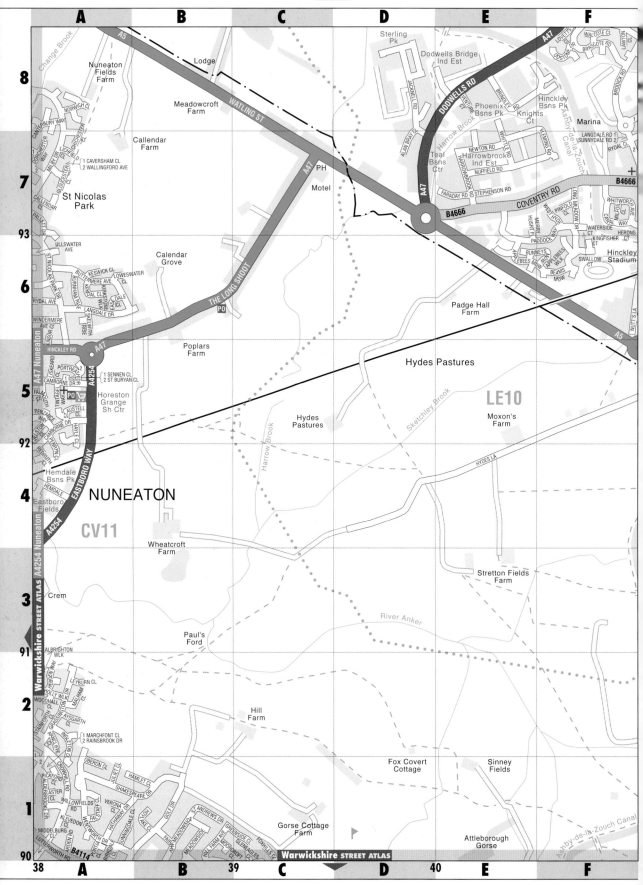

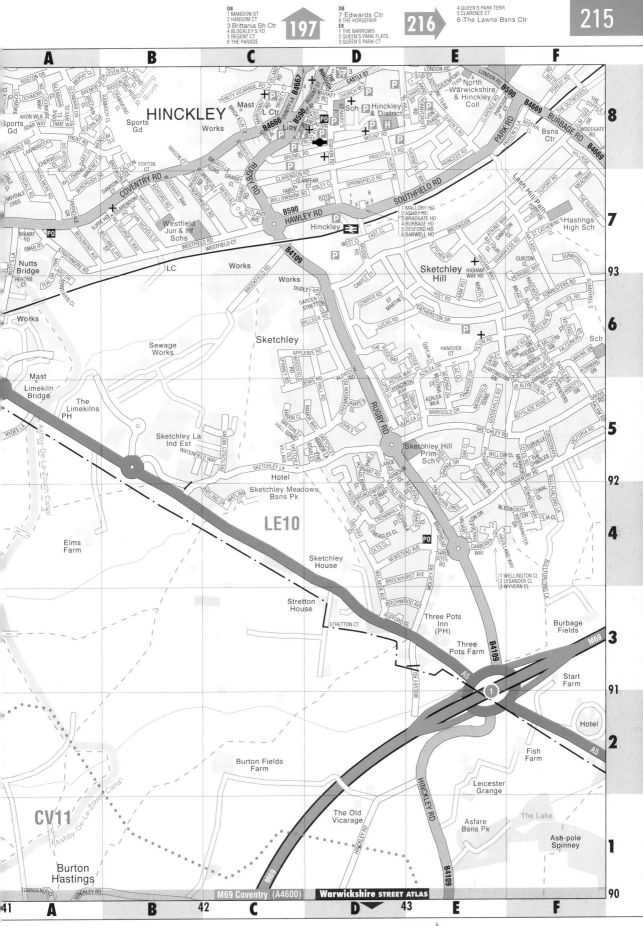

D8
1 MANSION ST
2 HANSOM CT
3 Brittania Sh Ctr
4 BLOCKLEY'S YD
5 REGENT CT
6 THE PARADE

197

D8
7 Edwards Ctr
8 THE HORSEFAIR
E8
1 THE NARROWS
2 QUEEN'S PARK FLATS
3 QUEEN'S PARK CT

216

4 QUEEN'S PARK TERR
5 CLARENCE CT
6 The Lawns Bsns Ctr

215
198

A　B　C　D　E　F

8

THE COPPICE

WOODGATE RD

BURBAGE RD

Threeways Farm

SMITHY LA

Aston Firs

CASTLEWOOD MOBILE HOME PK

SMITHY LA

ASTON FIRS CVN SITE

Averley House Farm

HINCKLEY RD

B4669

B466

2

HINCKLEY RD

LE9

The Homestead

B4669

B578

HILLRISE

THE FAIRWAY

7

SAPCOTE RD

ASTON FLAMVILLE RD

WOODBANK

MEADOW DR

WEST MARLBOROUGH CL

CHESTER DR

DORCHESTER RD

PRIOR RD

SHERB

ASTON LA

HINCKLEY RD

93

HINCKLEY RD

STOCKING LEYS

WOODLAND AVE

THE MEADOWS

LYNDHURST

REGENCY CT

SCHOOL CL

SAXON CL

SALISBURY RD

ILMINSTER CL

CAMBORNE RD

ASHBURTON CL

Pond Spinney

FORRESTERS RD

P

Leicestershire Round

Manor House

Manor Farm

6

THE LEYS

GRANGE HILL

LOVE LA

NEW RD

ASTON LA

CROSSLAND

1 GROSVENOR CRES
2 CEDAR CT
3 PILGRIMS GATE

Cottage Farm

MANOR HOUSE CL

SHARNFORD RD

Sch

GROVE RD

PURNE S CL

PO

F L BERE CRES

Burbage

Cemy

Aston Flamville

Sch

HORSEP

CHURCH CL

Liby

Oak Farm

LYCHGATE LA

CHURCH ST

5

WINDSOR ST

FREEMAN S LA

PURDEY CT

ORCHARD RD

LIBRARY CL

LYCHGATE CL

FLAMVILLE RD

FOSSE CL

Lychgate Farm

BRITANNIA RD

92

WORKHOUSE LA

LODGE CL

White House Farm

Deepdale Farm

LE10

Mickle Hill Spinney

Mickle Hill

4

M69

Fields Farm

WORKHOUSE LA

LUTTERWORTH RD

Orchard Farm

Mickle Hill Farm

3

M69

Burbage House

Soar Brook

91

Soar Brook Spinney

2

A5

Three Corner Spinney

Hogue Hall

B4114

1

Ash-pole Spinney

Crab-tree Spinney

B578

Lodge Farm

COVENTRY RD

B4114

90

B4114

CHURCH LA

44　A　B　45　C　D　46　E　F

A5

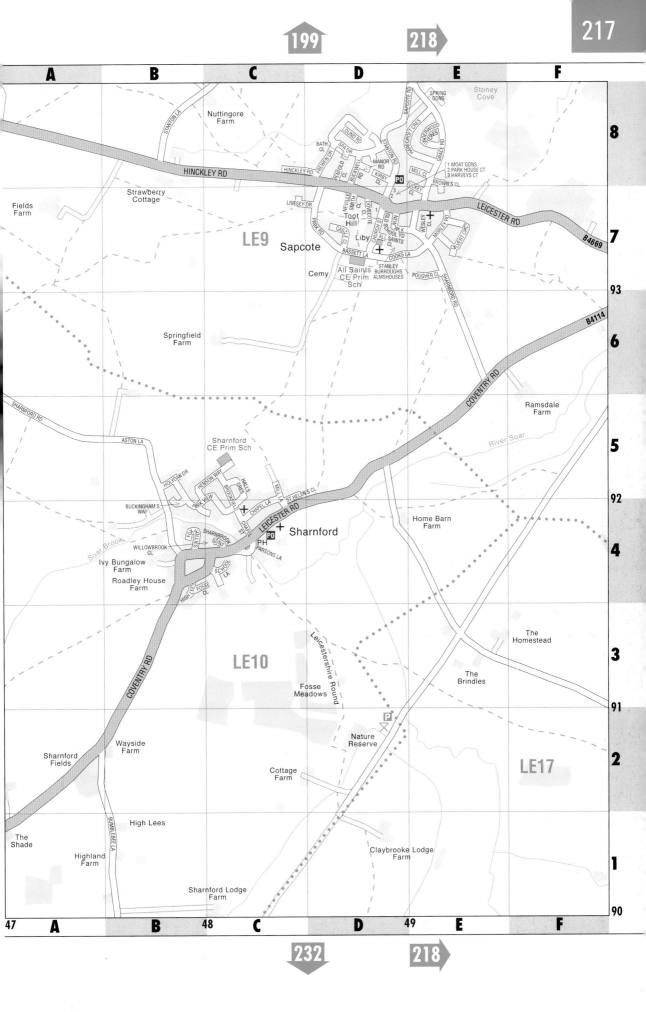

A   B   C   D   E   F

8

7

93

6

5

92

4

3

91

2

1

90

Stoney Cove

1 MOAT GDNS
2 PARK HOUSE CT
3 HARVEYS CT

SPRING GDNS

SAPCOTE RD

STANTON LA

Nuttingore Farm

LOUND RD

BATH CL

SPA DR

FREWEN DR

SINKERWOOD CRES

CAGEPOST CRES

GRACE RD

HINCKLEY RD

HINCKLEY RD

PENFOLD CL

BUCKWELL CL

STANTON RD

KIRBY CL

MANOR RD

MILL CL

PO

TUCKET CL

BROWN'S CL

LEICESTER RD

B4669

Strawberry Cottage

Fields Farm

LE9

Sapcote

LIVESEY DR

NEVILLE CL

SMITH CL

DOVECOTE RD

OLD SCHOOL YD

NEW WLK

WESLEY CL

MORLEY RD

CALVERT CRES

Toot Hill

Liby

PARK RD

CAS. CL

BASSETT LA

ALL SAINTS CL

CHURCH ST

COOKS LA

Cemy

All Saints CE Prim Sch

STANLEY BURROUGHS ALMSHOUSES

POUGHER CL

SHARNFORD RD

Springfield Farm

B4114

COVENTRY RD

Ramsdale Farm

River Soar

SHARNFORD RD

ASTON LA

Sharnford CE Prim Sch

HOLYOAK DR

HEDSON WAY

PARK VIEW

BROOKFIELD

HALLS CRES

CHAPEL LA

MILL LA

ST HELEN'S CL

LEICESTER RD

Home Barn Farm

BUCKINGHAM'S WAY

Soar Brook

SHARNBROOK GDNS

CHAPEL ST

PO

Sharnford

FIELDS CL

WILLOWBROOK CL

SCHOOL LA

PH

PARSONS LA

Ivy Bungalow Farm

Roadley House Farm

HIGH LEES CL

FOSSE CL

LE10

Leicestershire Round

Fosse Meadows

The Homestead

The Brindles

COVENTRY RD

P

Nature Reserve

91

Wayside Farm

Sharnford Fields

Cottage Farm

LE17

BUMBLEBEE LA

High Lees

The Shade

Highland Farm

Sharnford Lodge Farm

Claybrooke Lodge Farm

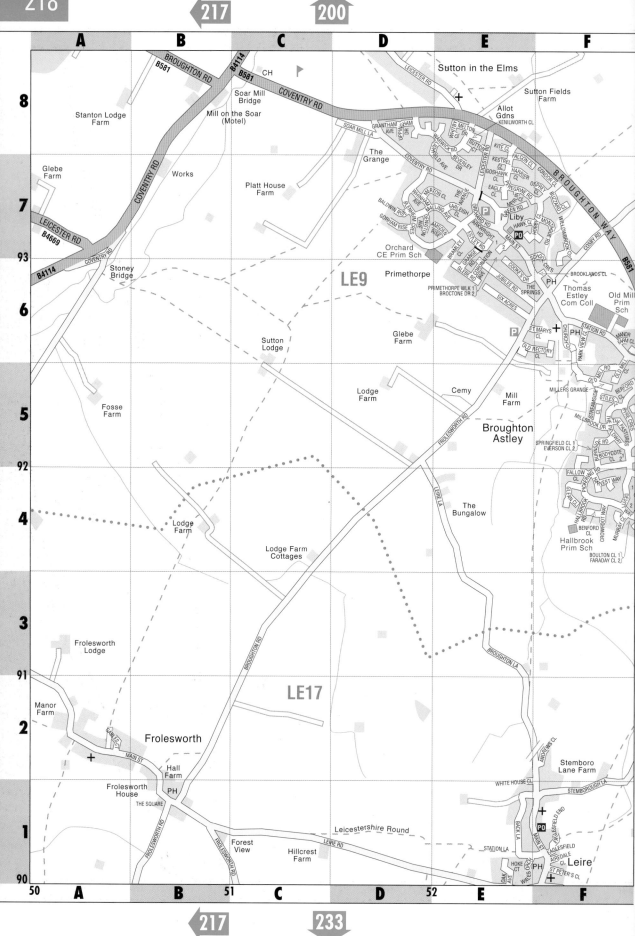

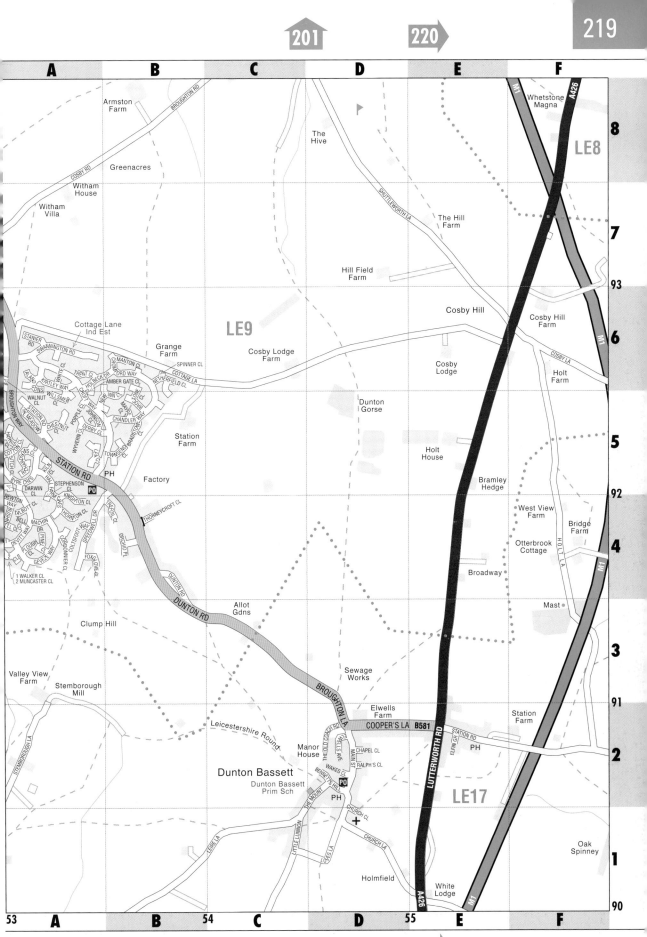

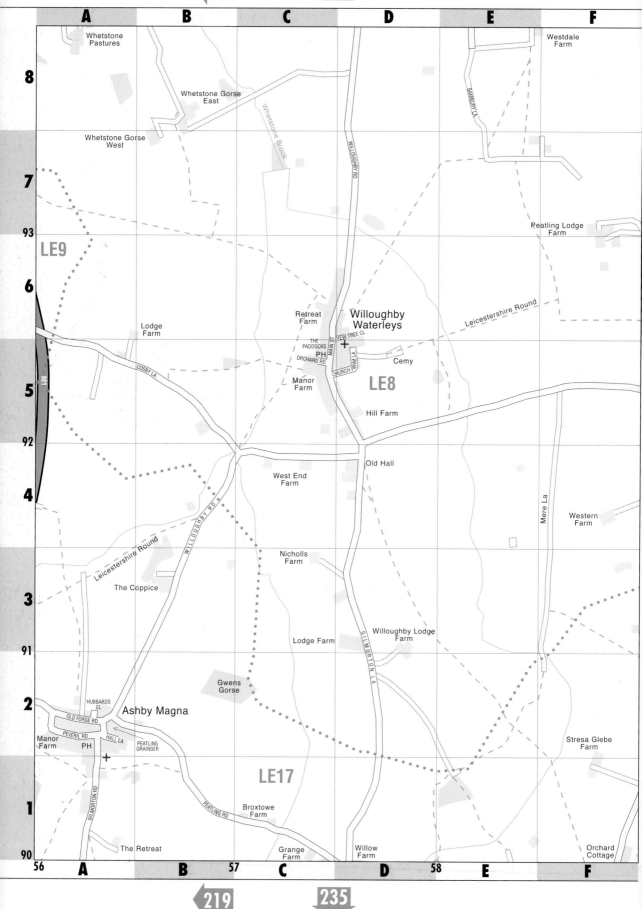

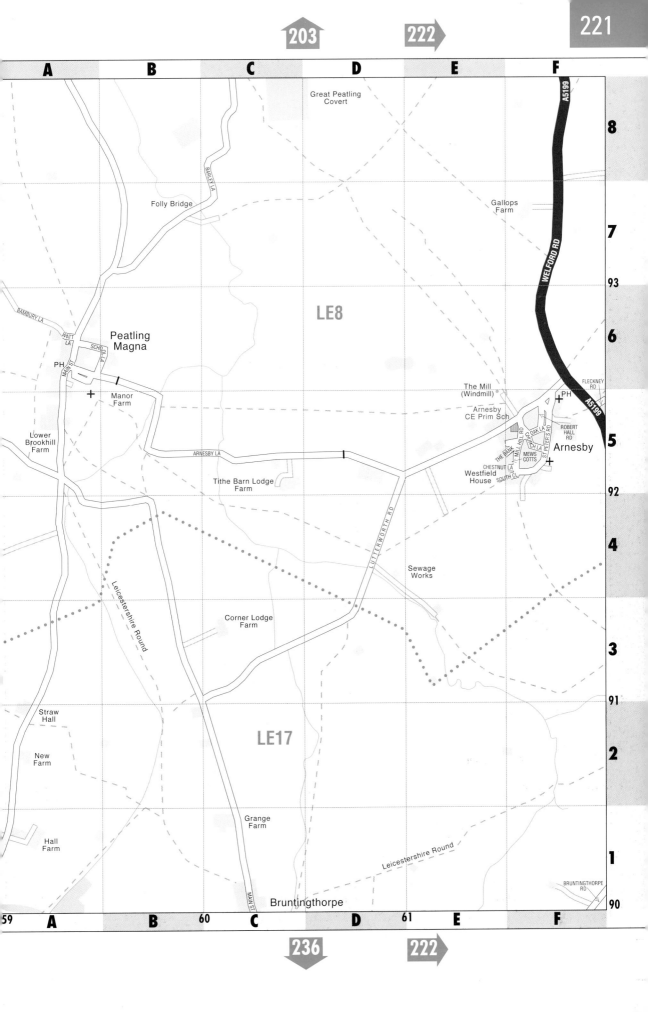

A **B** **C** **D** **E** **F**

LE18

8

Arnesby Lodge
Farm

Arnesby Lodge
Cottages

The Meadows
Riding Ctr

KILBY RD

Lyndon Lodge
Farm

PENCLOSE
RD

STENOR CL LANGDALE

PARK ST

KERTLEY
MIDDLETONS CL

LEICESTER RD

ALBERT ST

Fleckney
CE Prim Sch

SHOULBARD

HIGHFIELD ST

FURNIVAL

WOLSEY CL

Fleckney

STORES LA

FORGE

PELLS

CHURCH LA

PREST MDW

KIBWORTH
RD

PO

P

Liby

MAIN ST

LAMPLIGHTERS

PH

RICHMOND ST

ORCHARD ST

VICTORIA ST

SHORTH
CL

EDWARD RD

GLADSTONE ST

CROSSLEYS

ELIZABETH CL

WESTERN NCE

WESTERN AV

LODGE PL

7

93

The Grange

LE8

6

Fleckney
Lodge

Grange
Farm

Petit-Tor

FLECKNEY RD

The White
House

Glebe
Farm

5

The Elms

A5199

92

Brant Hill
Farm

Leicestershire Round

Rowley Fields
Farm

ARNESBY RD

Bloxham
Farm

SHEARSBY RD

4

Breach
Farm

3

New Inn
Farm

CHURCH LA

WELFORD RD

BACK LA

THE SQUARE

THE BANK

Saddington Lodge
Farm

Saddington Brook

91

SADDINGTON RD

2

MAIN ST

PENNY LA

PH

LE17

MILL LA

Shearsby

BRUNTINGTHORPE RD

John Ball
Hill

1

Jane Ball
Covert

John Ball
Farm

John Ball
Covert

A5199

Peashill
Farm

90

62   **A** 63   **B**   **C** 64   **D**   **E** 65   **F**

Bath Hotel
& Shearsby Spa

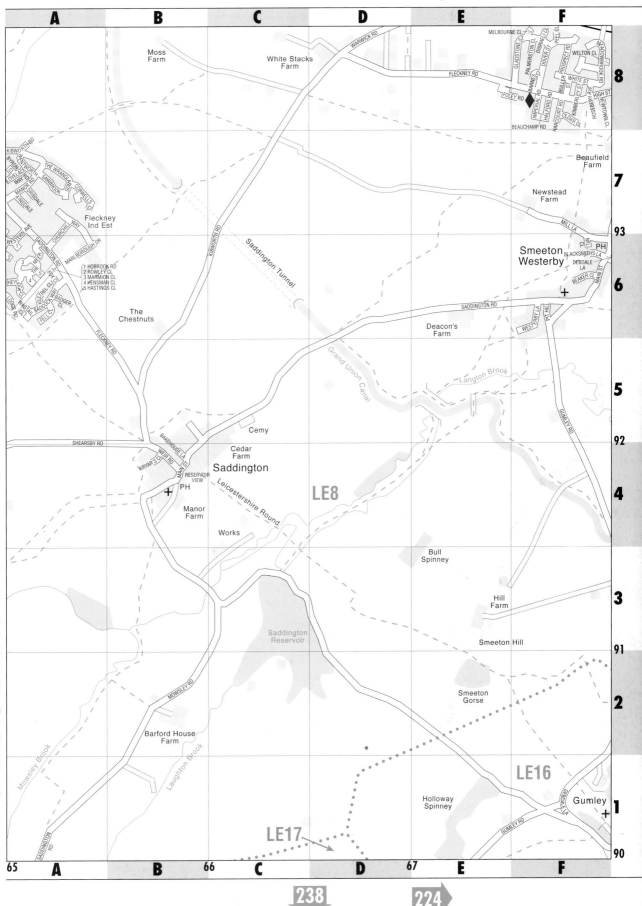

223
206

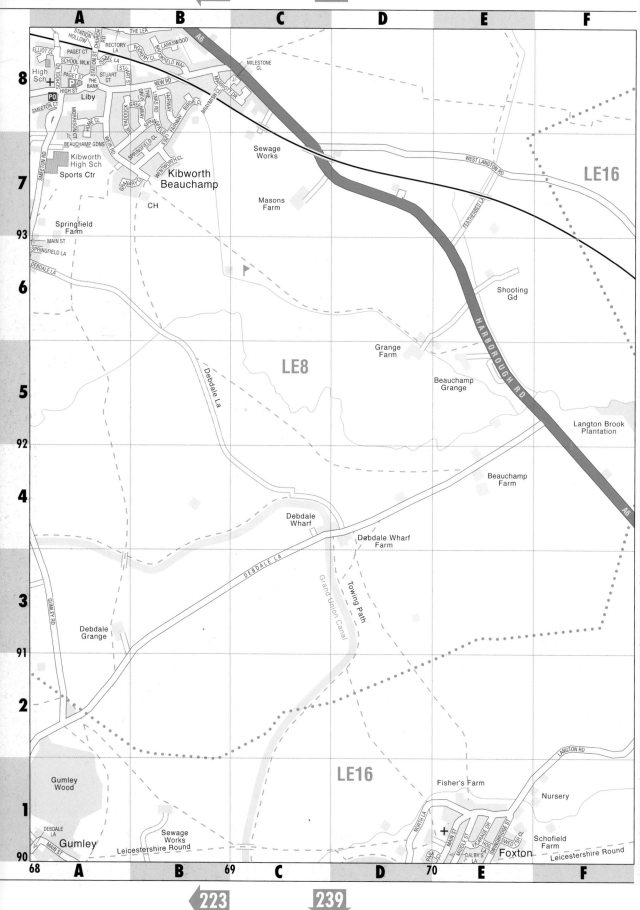

223
239

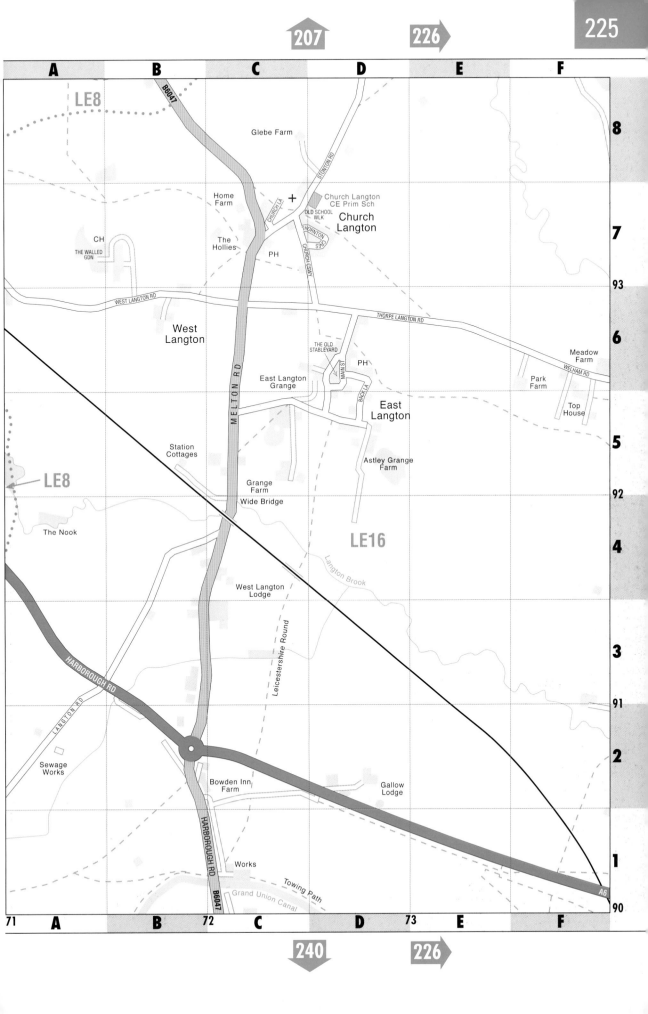

LE8

B6047

Glebe Farm

STONTON RD

Home Farm

Church Langton CE Prim Sch

CHURCH LA

OLD SCHOOL WLK

Church Langton

CH

THE WALLED GDN

The Hollies

PH

THORNTON CO S35

CHURCH GSWY

8

7

93

WEST LANGTON RD

West Langton

MELTON RD

THORPE LANGTON RD

6

Meadow Farm

WELHAM RD

THE OLD STABLEYARD

East Langton Grange

MAIN ST

PH

BACK LA

East Langton

Park Farm

Top House

LE8

Station Cottages

Astley Grange Farm

5

Grange Farm

Wide Bridge

92

The Nook

LE16

4

Langton Brook

West Langton Lodge

HARBOROUGH RD

Leicestershire Round

LANGTON RD

3

91

Sewage Works

2

Bowden Inn Farm

Gallow Lodge

HARBOROUGH RD

B6047

Works

1

Towing Path

Grand Union Canal

A6

90

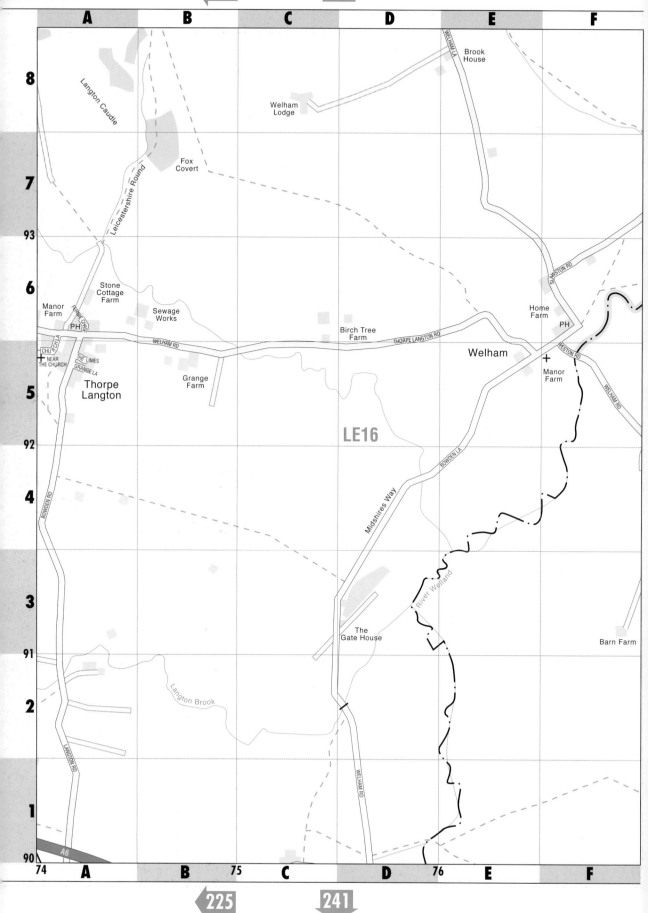

225
208

A B C D E F

8

7

93

6

Manor Farm
Stone Cottage Farm
Langton Caudle
Leicestershire Round
Fox Covert
Welham Lodge
Brook House
WELHAM LA
Sewage Works
PH
FERNIE CHASE
CHURCH LA
NEAR THE CHURCH
THE LIMES
GRANGE LA
Thorpe Langton
WELHAM RD
Birch Tree Farm
THORPE LANGTON RD
Welham
Home Farm
PH
Manor Farm
WESTON RD
SLAWSTON RD
WELHAM RD

5

Grange Farm

92

LE16

BOWDEN RD

4

Midshires Way
BOWDEN LA

3

The Gate House
River Welland
Barn Farm

91

Langton Brook

2

WELHAM RD

1

A6

90

74 A B 75 C D 76 E F

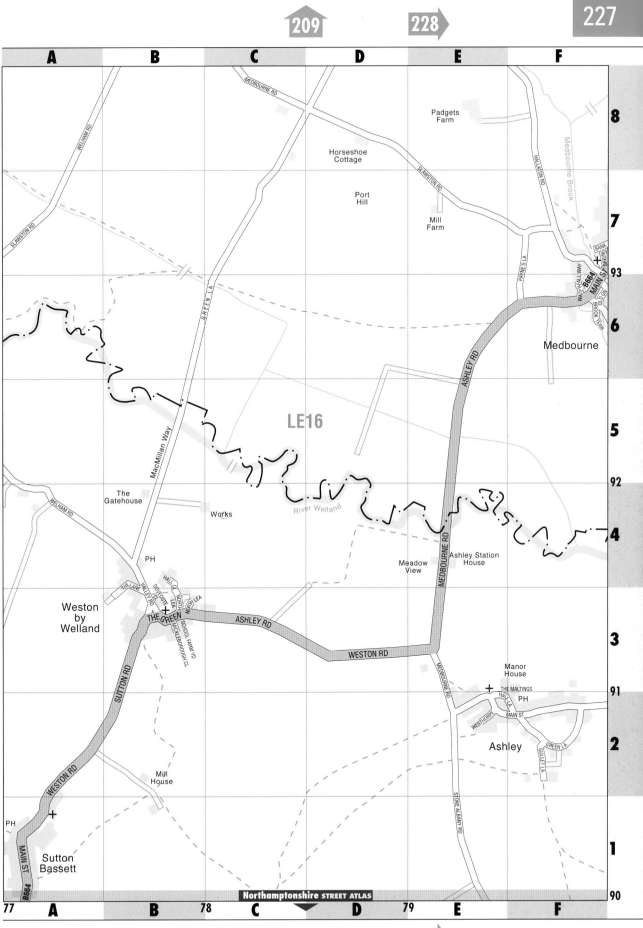

209

228

A B C D E F

8

Padgets
Farm

Horseshoe
Cottage

MEDBOURNE RD

Port
Hill

SLAWSTON RD

Mill
Farm

HALLATON RD

Medbourne Brook

7

WELHAM RD

SLAWSTON RD

GREEN LA

PAYNE'S LA

WATER FALL WAY

BANK

SHIRSH

BROOK TERR

MAIN ST

B664

93

Medbourne

6

ASHLEY RD

MacMillan Way

LE16

5

92

The
Gatehouse

Works

River Welland

MEDBOURNE RD

4

WELHAM RD

PH

Meadow
View

Ashley Station
House

Weston
by
Welland

THE LANE

VALLEY RD

HALL CL

DOVECOTE CL

NORTH LEA

NORTH LEA

IVY LEA

THE GREEN

SCHOOL FARM YD

MICKLEBOROUGH CL

ASHLEY RD

WESTON RD

MEDBOURNE RD

3

SUTTON RD

Manor
House

THE MALTINGS

HALL LA

PH

91

WESTHORPE

MAIN ST

Ashley

GREEN LA

GULLET LA

2

WESTON RD

Mill
House

STOKE ALBANY RD

PH

MAIN ST

B664

Sutton
Bassett

1

90

77 A B 78 C D 79 E F

228

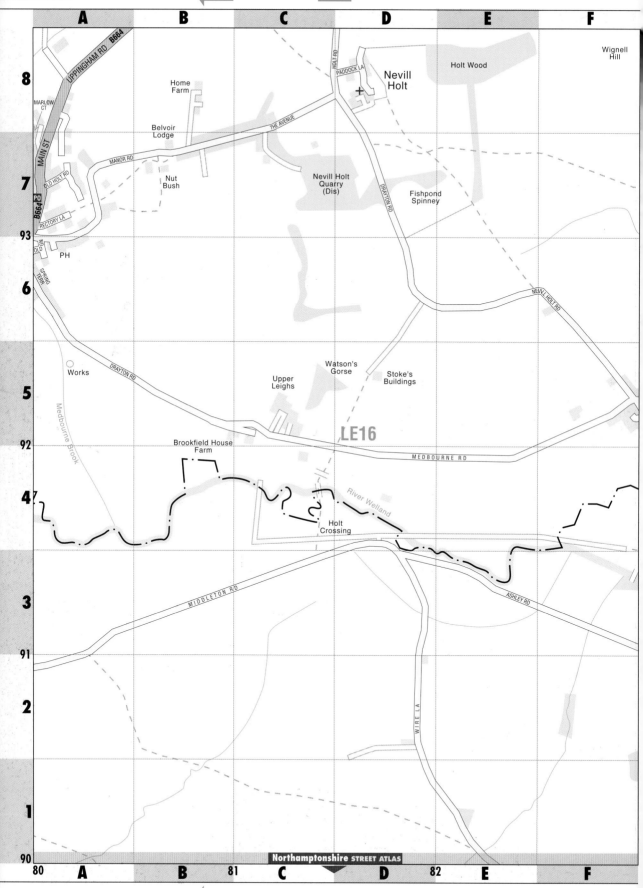

A B C D E F

Wignell
Hill

Holt Wood

Nevill
Holt

Home
Farm

PADDOCK LA

HOLT RD

Belvoir
Lodge

THE AVENUE

MANOR RD

Nut
Bush

Nevill Holt
Quarry
(Dis)

Fishpond
Spinney

DRAYTON RD

NEVILL HOLT RD

MARLOW
CT

UPPINGHAM RD B664

MAIN ST

OLD HOLT RD

RECTORY LA

B664

PO

OLD

PH

SPRING
TERR

Works

DRAYTON RD

Medbourne Brook

Watson's
Gorse

Stoke's
Buildings

Upper
Leighs

LE16

Brookfield House
Farm

MEDBOURNE RD

River Welland

Holt
Crossing

MIDDLETON RD

ASHLEY RD

WIRE LA

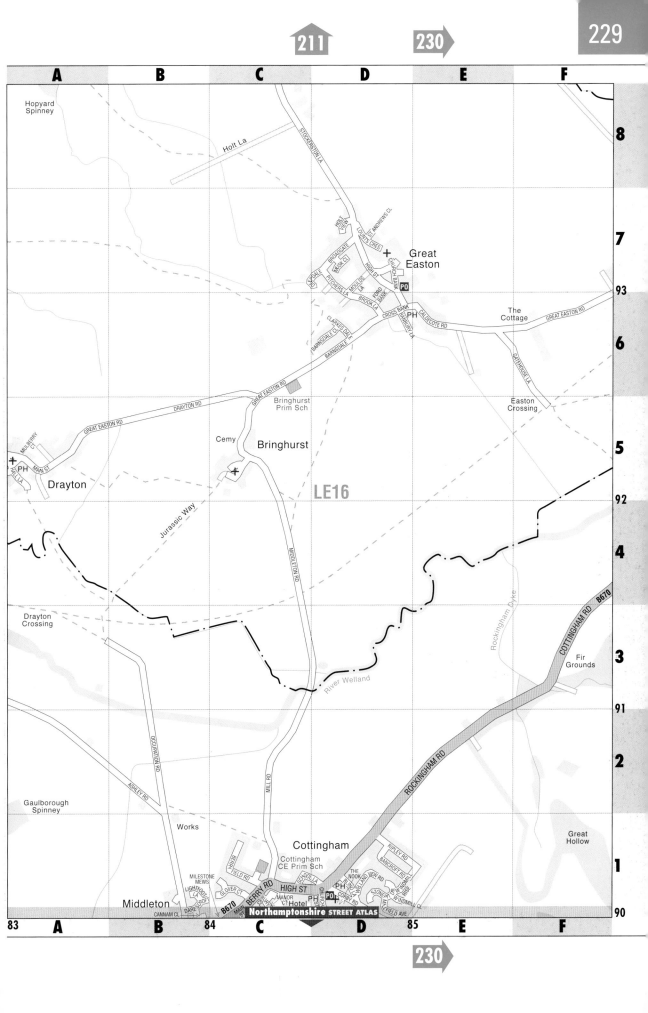

A | B | C | D | E | F

8

Hopyard
Spinney

Holt La

STOCKERSTON LA

7

HOLT VIEW
LOUNTS CRES
ST ANDREWS CL
BROADGATE
WASK CL
PITCHERS LA
MOULDS LA
HIGH ST
CHURCH BANK
Great
Easton
PO
UPDALE
BROOK LA
POND BANK
PH
CROSS BANK
BANBURY LA
CALTICOTE RD

93

CLARKES DALE
BARNSDALE CL
BARNSDALE
The
Cottage
GREAT EASTON RD

6

GREAT EASTON RD
DRAYTON RD
GREAT EASTON RD
Bringhurst
Prim Sch

GATEHOUSE LA

Easton
Crossing

MULBERRY CT
MAIN ST
HALL LA
PH
Cemy
Bringhurst

5

Drayton

LE16

92

Jurassic Way

MIDDLETON RD

4

Drayton
Crossing

Rockingham Dyke

COTTINGHAM RD
B670
Fir
Grounds

3

River Welland

91

OCCUPATION RD
ASHLEY RD

ROCKINGHAM RD

2

Gaulborough
Spinney

Works

Great
Hollow

Cottingham
CE Prim Sch
Cottingham
RIPLEY RD
BANCROFT RD

1

MILESTONE
MEWS
LIGHTFOOT
FERN FIELD RD
GLOVER CT
COLL LA
BERRY RD
HIGH ST
Hotel
PH
PH
CORBY RD
THE NOOK
PH
WELLAND VIEW RD
STONEYWINDMILL
WINDMILL CL
WINDMILL RISE

Middleton
MANOR CT
PO
FIELD AVE

CANNAM CL
DARESCROFT
MAIN ST
CHURCH
B670

90

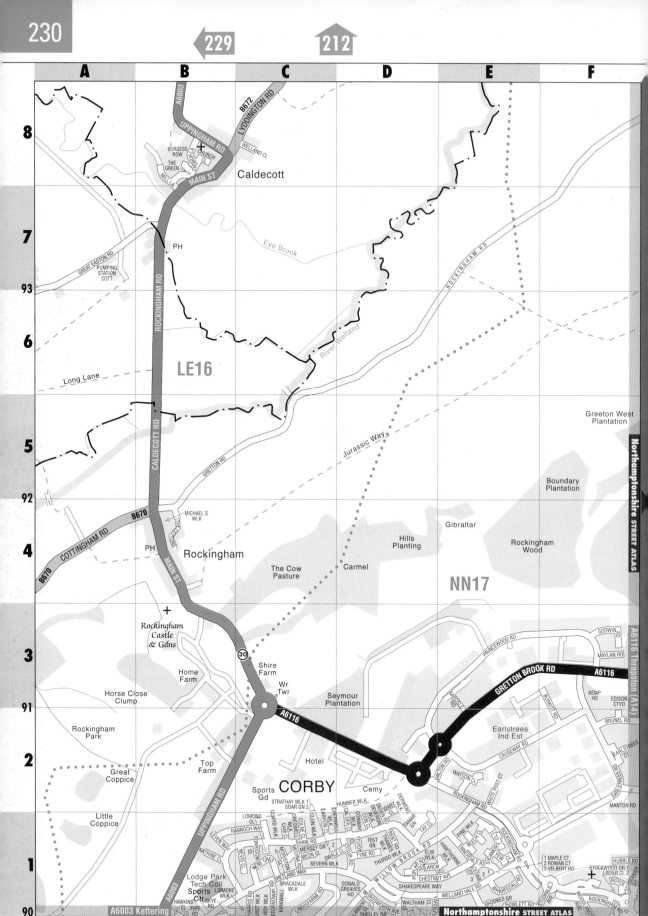

A   B   C   D   E   F

8

7

93

6

LE16

5

92

4

3

91

2

1

90

86   A   B   87   C   D   88   E   F

Caldecott

Rockingham

NN17

CORBY

Northamptonshire STREET ATLAS

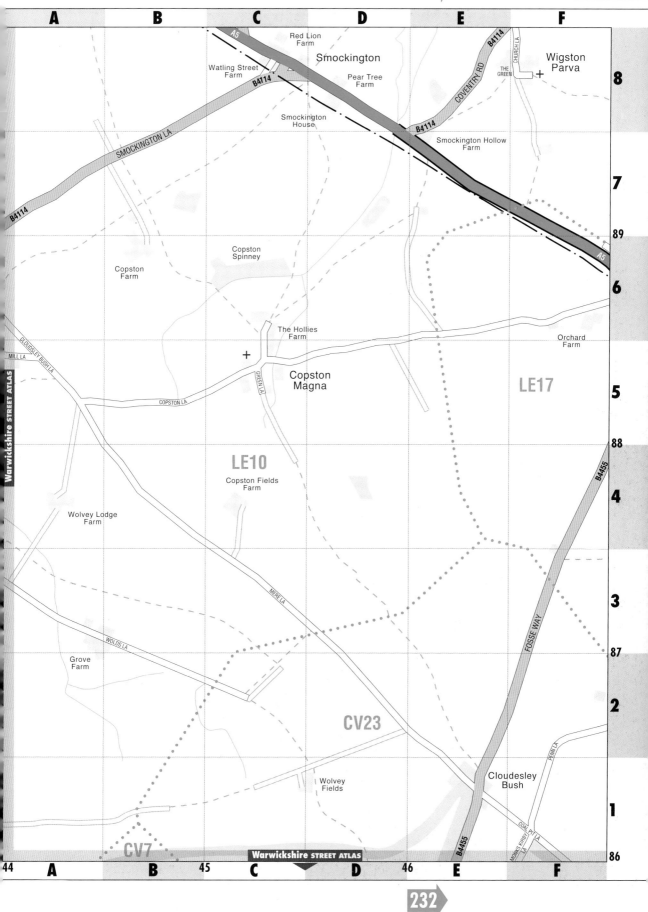

A B C D E F

Warwickshire STREET ATLAS

A5
Red Lion
Farm
Smockington
Watling Street
Farm
B4114
Pear Tree
Farm
B4114
COVENTRY RD
THE
GREEN
CHURCH LA
Wigston
Parva
8

SMOCKINGTON LA
Smockington
House
B4114
Smockington Hollow
Farm

B4114
7

B4114
A5
89

Copston
Spinney
Copston
Farm
Copston
Magna
Orchard
Farm
6

MILL LA
CLOUDSLEY BUSH LA
The Hollies
Farm
GREEN LA
COPSTON LA
Copston
Magna
LE17
5

88
B4455

LE10
Copston Fields
Farm
4

Wolvey Lodge
Farm
MERE LA
FOSSE WAY
3

87

WOLDS LA
2

Grove
Farm
CV23
PENN LA
1

Wolvey
Fields
Cloudesley
Bush
B4455
COAL PIT LA
MONKS KIRBY
LA
86

CV7

A B C D E F

8

The Bungalow

Hill Farm

LE10

Bumble-Bee Farm

7

Lodge Farm

Leicestershire Round

89

High Cross

Manor Farm

Gables Farm

Claybrooke Magna Mill

Frolesworth La

Victoria Farm

PH

Council Hos

Laurel Fields Gdns

The Paddock

Woodland Ave

Leicestershire Round

6

HIGH CROSS RD

Claybrooke Magna

Fosseway Gdns

The Vineyard

Sewage Works

High Cross Grange

Mount Pleasant Cottage

Back La

Roman Cl

Hotel

High-Cross Farm

Old Chapel Wlk

Bell St

Holly Tree Wlk

Claybrooke Farm

A5

B4455

Leicestershire Round

Greencock Cl

Main Rd

5

Fosse Way

B4455

Claybrooke Hall

Western Dr

88

LE17

Claybrooke Cl

Avenue Villas

Watling House

Claybrooke Prim Sch

Cemy

Claybrooke Parva

4

Alma House

Woodway La

Wibtoft

Woodway Cottage

Laurel Bank

Glebe Farm

Manor Farm

Green La

3

87

Lodge Farm

2

Penn La

White House Farm (Kennels)

1

CV23

Tithe Platts Farm

A5

86

47 A 48 B C 48 D 49 E F

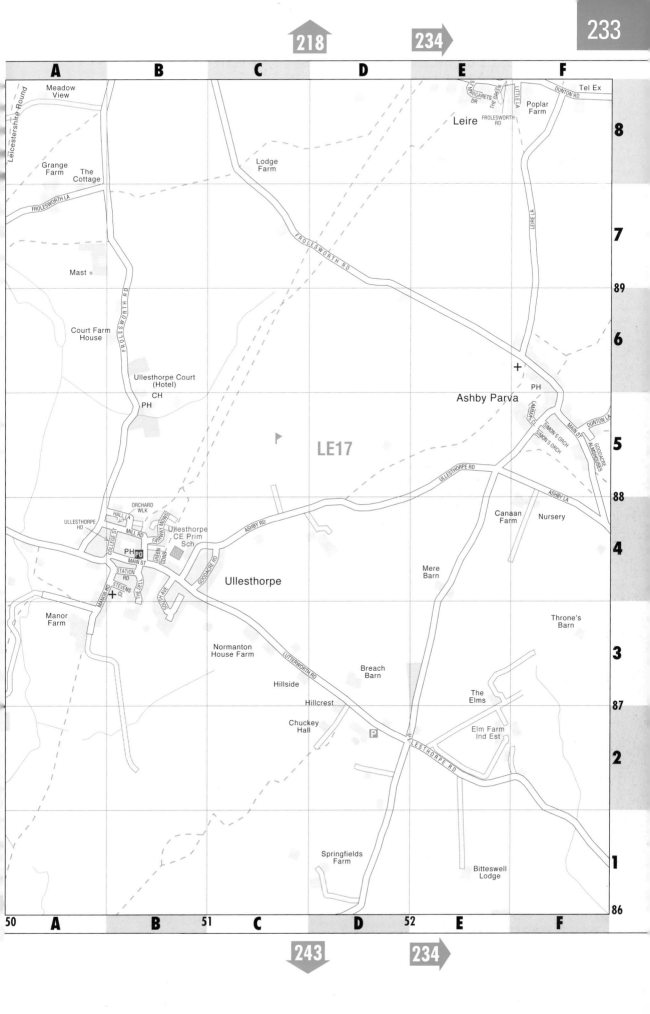

A B C D E F

8

7

89

6

5

88

4

3

87

2

1

86

Meadow View
Leire
Poplar Farm
Tel Ex
DUNTON RD
ST MARGARETS DR
THE GREEN
LITTLE LA
FROLESWORTH RD
LEIRE LA

Grange Farm
The Cottage
Lodge Farm
FROLESWORTH LA

FROLESWORTH RD

Mast

Court Farm House
FROLESWORTH RD

Ullesthorpe Court (Hotel)
CH
PH

Ashby Parva
PH
MAIN ST
SIMON'S ORCH
SIMON'S ORCH
SIMON'S CL
DUNTON LA
GOODACRE ALMSHOUSES

LE17

ULLESTHORPE RD
ASHBY LA

ORCHARD WLK
HALL LA
Ullesthorpe HO
COLLEGE ST
MILL RD
FAIRWAY MDWS
Ullesthorpe CE Prim Sch
GREEN GDNS
Canaan Farm
Nursery

ASHBY RD
GOODACRE RD

PH PO
MAIN ST
STATION RD
STEVENS CL
SOUTH AVE
THE DELL
Ullesthorpe
Mere Barn

Manor Farm
MANOR RD
Throne's Barn

Normanton House Farm
LUTTERWORTH RD
Breach Barn
The Elms

Hillside
Hillcrest
Chuckey Hall
P
Elm Farm Ind Est
ULLESTHORPE RD

Springfields Farm
Bitteswell Lodge

Leicestershire Round

50 A B 51 C D 52 E F

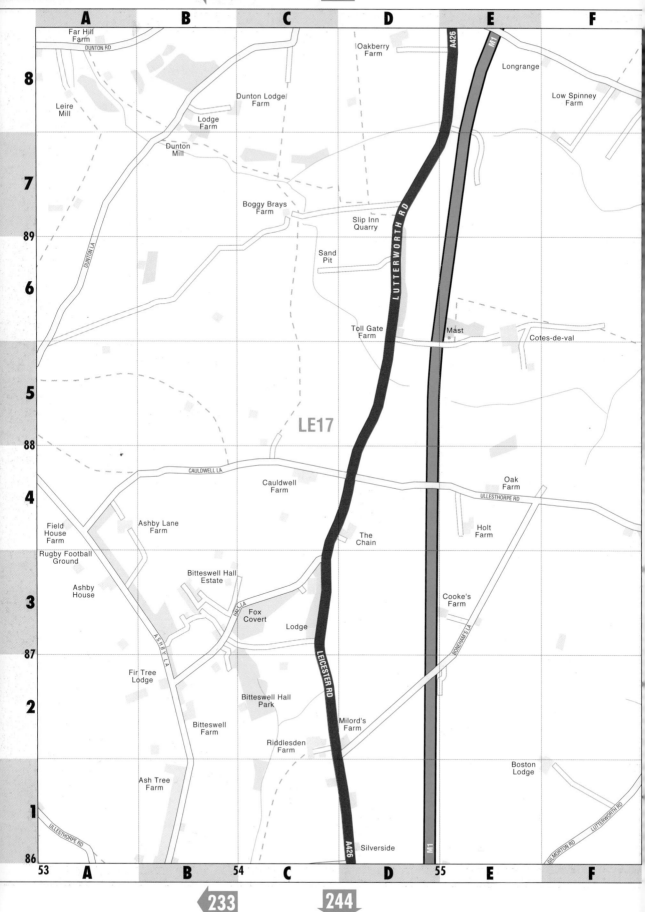

A B C D E F

8

7

89

6

5

88

4

3

87

2

1

86

53 A B 54 C D 55 E F

Far Hill Farm
DUNTON RD
Leire Mill
Dunton Lodge Farm
Lodge Farm
Dunton Mill
DUNTON LA
Oakberry Farm
A426
M1
Longrange
Low Spinney Farm
Boggy Brays Farm
Slip Inn Quarry
LUTTERWORTH RD
Sand Pit
Toll Gate Farm
Mast
Cotes-de-val
LE17
CAULDWELL LA
Cauldwell Farm
Oak Farm
ULLESTHORPE RD
Field House Farm
Ashby Lane Farm
The Chain
Holt Farm
Rugby Football Ground
Ashby House
Bitteswell Hall Estate
HALL LA
Fox Covert
Lodge
Cooke's Farm
BONEHAM'S LA
ASHBY LA
LEICESTER RD
Fir Tree Lodge
Bitteswell Hall Park
Bitteswell Farm
Milord's Farm
Boston Lodge
Riddlesden Farm
Ash Tree Farm
ULLESTHORPE RD
A426
Silverside
M1
GILMORTON RD
LUTTERWORTH RD

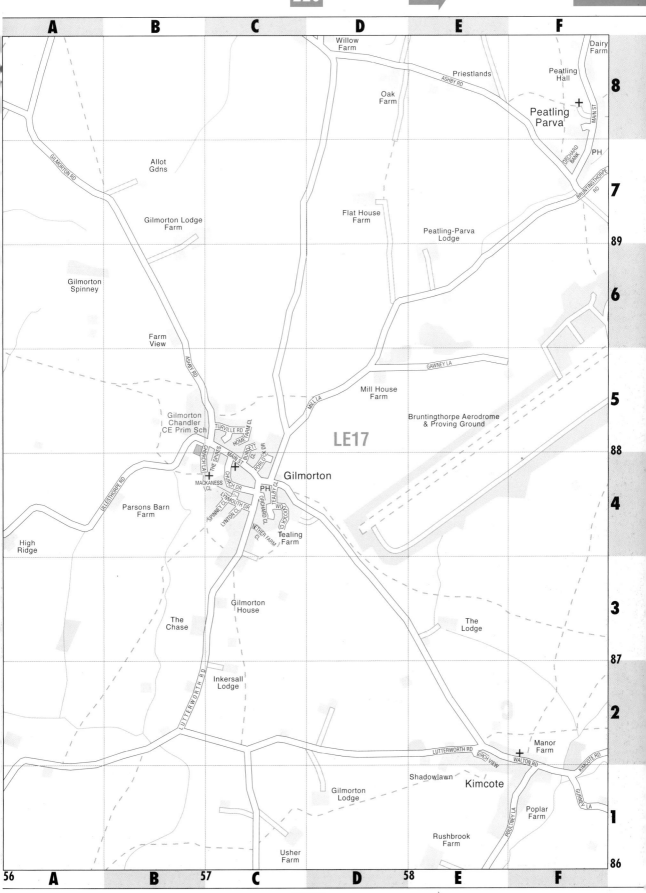

Dairy Farm

Willow Farm

Priestlands

ASHBY RD

Peatling Hall

Oak Farm

Peatling Parva

8

PH

ORCHARD BANK

MAIN ST

Allot Gdns

BRUNTINGTHORPE RD

7

Gilmorton Lodge Farm

Flat House Farm

Peatling-Parva Lodge

89

Gilmorton Spinney

6

Farm View

ASHBY RD

GAWNEY LA

5

MILL LA

Mill House Farm

Bruntingthorpe Aerodrome & Proving Ground

Gilmorton Chandler CE Prim Sch

TURVILLE RD

HOME FARM CL

BURKETT CL

LE17

88

THE SPIRS

MAIN ST

POPLOCK DR

CHURCH LA

Gilmorton

MACKANESS CL

CHURCH DR

PH

TEALBY CL

4

ULLESTHORPE RD

LYNMOUTH DR

ORCHARD CL

WO

SPINNEY CL

NETHER FARM CL

LYNTON CL

Parsons Barn Farm

Tealing Farm

High Ridge

Gilmorton House

The Lodge

3

The Chase

87

LUTTERWORTH RD

Inkersall Lodge

2

LUTTERWORTH RD

Manor Farm

BIRCH VIEW

WALTON RD

KIMCOTE RD

Gilmorton Lodge

Shadowlawn

Kimcote

GURNEY LA

POULTNEY LA

Poplar Farm

1

Rushbrook Farm

Usher Farm

86

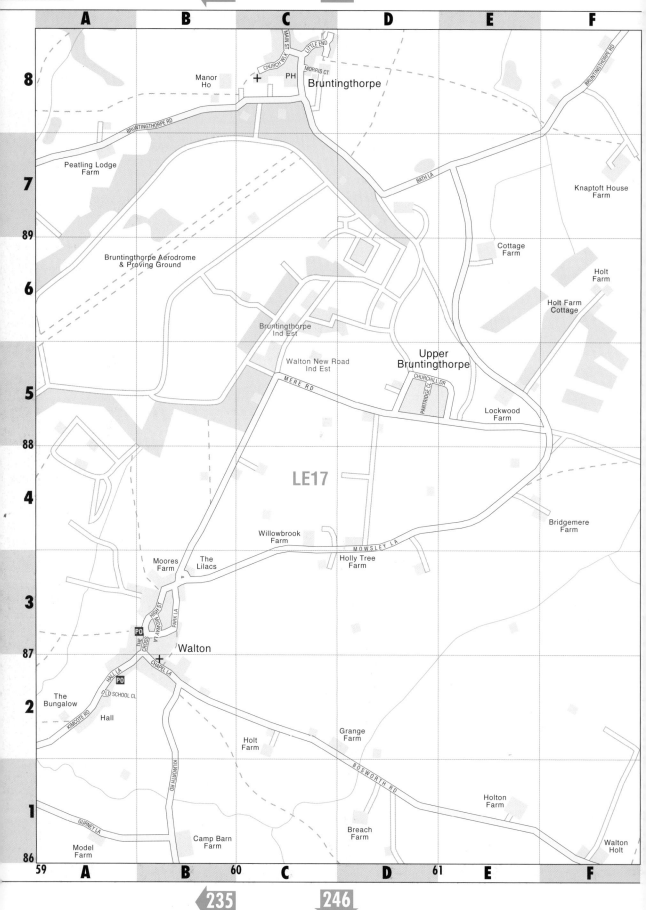

A **B** **C** **D** **E** **F**

8

Manor
Ho
+   PH
Morris Ct
MAIN ST
LITTLE END
CHURCH WLK
Bruntingthorpe
BRUNTINGTHORPE RD

7
Peatling Lodge
Farm
BATH LA
Knaptoft House
Farm

89
Bruntingthorpe Aerodrome
& Proving Ground
Cottage
Farm

6
Holt
Farm
Holt Farm
Cottage
Bruntingthorpe
Ind Est

Walton New Road
Ind Est
Upper
Bruntingthorpe
CHURCHILL DR
PARTRIDGE CL

5
MERE RD
Lockwood
Farm

88
LE17

4
Bridgemere
Farm

Willowbrook
Farm
MOWSLEY LA
Holly Tree
Farm

Moores
Farm
The
Lilacs

3
HIGH ST
PARK LA
THE CROSS
TAYLOUR LA
PO

87
+   Walton
CHAPEL LA
HALL LA
PO
OLD SCHOOL CL

The
Bungalow
KIMCOTE RD
Hall

2
Holt
Farm
Grange
Farm
Holton
Farm
KILWORTH RD
BOSWORTH RD

1
GURNEY LA
Breach
Farm
Walton
Holt
Model
Farm
Camp Barn
Farm

86
59 **A** **B** **60** **C** **D** **61** **E** **F**

237
223

| | A | B | C | D | E | F |

LE8

Wood Cottage

The Mot

Gumley Covert

8

LE16

Oak Spinney

7

GUMLEY RD

Laughton

Gumley Lodge

SADDINGTON RD

The Cottage

89

Laughton Brook

MAIN ST

LAUGHTON LA

Kingsmead

6

Laughton Rd

5

Bunker's Hill Farm

Lodge Farm

88

Laughton Manor Farm

The Lodge

MILL HILL

4

Kicklewell Spinney

Laughton Hills

BUNKERS HILL

Grand Union Canal

LE17

Ivy Lodge Farm

3

87

Lodge Farm

Theddingworth Lodge

2

MOWSLEY RD

SEATON RD

1

HARBOROUGH RD   A4304

Grand Union Canal

A4304

86

65   66   67

| | A | B | C | D | E | F |

237
248

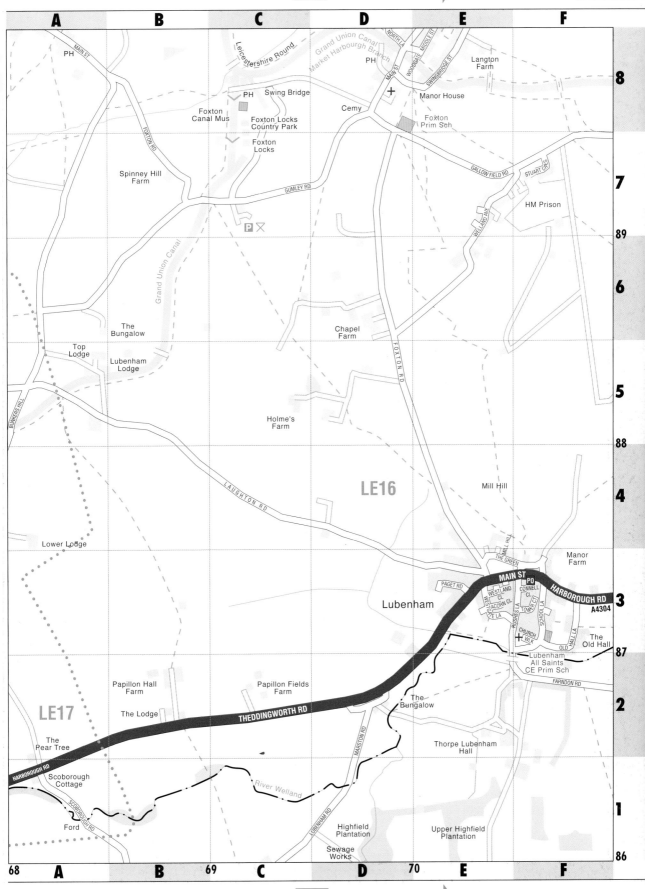

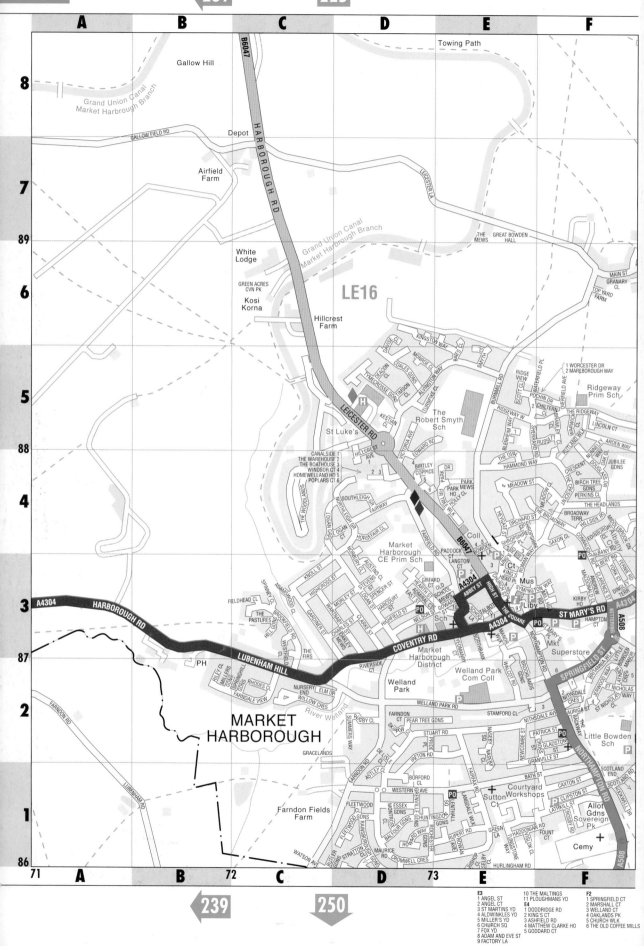

E3
1 ANGEL ST
2 ANGEL CT
3 ST MARTINS YD
4 ALDWINKLES YD
5 MILLER'S YD
6 CHURCH SQ
7 FOX YD
8 ADAM AND EVE ST
9 FACTORY LA

10 THE MALTINGS
11 PLOUGHMANS YD
E4
1 DODDRIDGE RD
2 KING'S CT
3 ASHFIELD RD
4 MATTHEW CLARKE HO
5 GODDARD CT

F2
1 SPRINGFIELD CT
2 MARSHALL CT
3 WELLAND CT
4 OAKLANDS PK
5 CHURCH WLK
6 THE OLD COFFEE MILLS

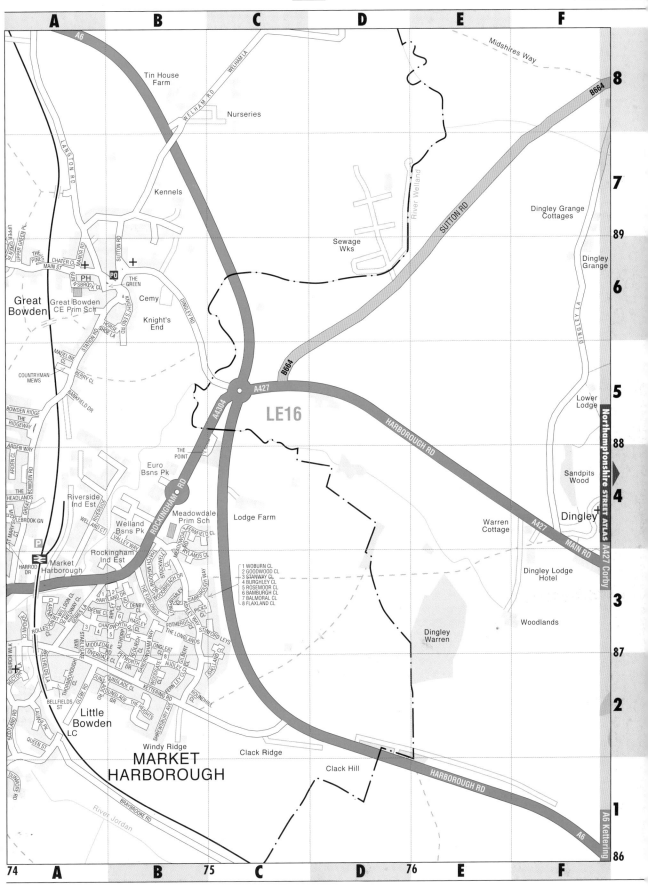

Midshires Way

A6

WELHAM LA

WELHAM RD

Tin House
Farm

Nurseries

B664

LANGTON RD

Kennels

River Welland

SUTTON RD

Dingley Grange
Cottages

Sewage
Wks

UPPER GREEN PL

THE
PINES

Great
Bowden

UPPER GREEN RD

MAIN ST

CHATER CL

MANOR RD

GUNN

PH

PO

NSBROOK CL

SUTTON CL

THE
GREEN

Cemy

Great Bowden
CE Prim Sch

HORSE SHOE LA

KNIGHT'S END RD

Knight's
End

DINGLEY RD

Dingley
Grange

Lower
Lodge

DINGLEY LA

STATION RD

MADELINE CL

BERRY CL

BANKFIELD DR

COUNTRYMAN
MEWS

BOWDEN RIDGE

THE
RIDGEWAY

ARDEN WAY

ARDEN CL

THE
HEADLANDS

GREAT BOWDEN RD

GLEBROOK GN

ST MARY'S CL

ST MARY'S CT

A504

A427

B664

LE16

Harborough RD

A427

MAIN RD

Northamptonshire STREET ATLAS A427 Corby

Dingley Grange

Sandpits
Wood

Dingley

THE
POINT

Euro
Bsns Pk

Riverside
Ind Est

WELLAND RISE

Welland
Bsns Pk

WELLAND CT

VALLEY WAY

Rockingham
Ind Est

ROCKINGHAM RD

Meadowdale
Prim Sch

MEADOWDALE RD

FERNFIELD CL

RYLANDS CL

Lodge Farm

Warren
Cottage

P

HARROD
DR

Market
Harborough

Hartland RD

DENBY
CL

STOCKWELL

WOODBEACH DR

SIMPORD RD

SIMFORD HIGH WAY

1 WOBURN CL
2 GOODWOOD CL
3 STANWAY CL
4 BURGHLEY CL
5 ROSEMOOR CL
6 BAMBURGH CL
7 BALMORAL CL
8 FLAXLAND CL

Dingley Lodge
Hotel

Dingley
Warren

Woodlands

CLARKSON DR

WILSON CL

ROLLESTON WAY

DEENE CL

GORSE CL

CHATSWORTH RD

MIDDLEDALE RD

OVERDALE CL

RIDLEY CL

HAGLEY

ALTHORP

FOTHERGILL WAY

PICKS

GRIMLEY

ASHLEY WAY

STIMFORD LEYS

THE LONGLANDS

GILBERT

HETHER WORTH

KENNETH

VOLGATE CL

FERN LEY CL

SCHELLAND CL

AUDLEY CL

CHURCH WLK

RECTORY

SCOTLAND RD

LAUNDE PK

QUEEN ST

DUNMORE RD

BELLFIELDS LA

THORBOROUGH RD

GLEBE RD

DUINS RD

DUNSLADE CL

DUNSLADE
GR

THE HEIGHTS

SANDRINGHAM WAY

SHREWSBURY AVE

KETTERING RD

ROUNDHILL

Little
Bowden
LC

Windy Ridge

Clack Ridge

Clack Hill

MARKET
HARBOROUGH

River Jordan

BRAYBROOKE RD

Harborough RD

A6

A6 Kettering

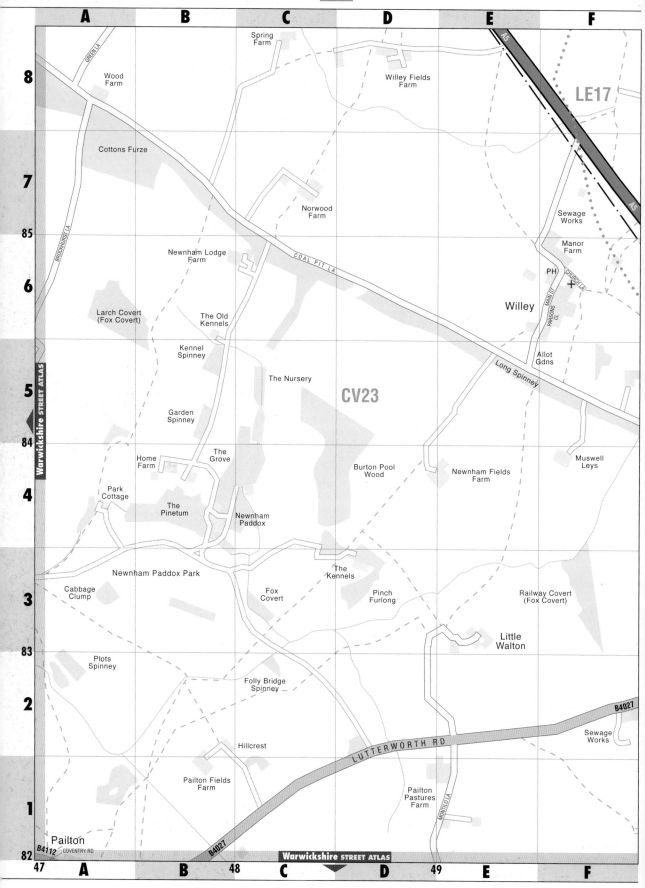

A · B · C · D · E · F

8

Spring Farm

Wood Farm

Willey Fields Farm

LE17

Cottons Furze

7

Norwood Farm

85

Newnham Lodge Farm

COAL PIT LA

Sewage Works

Manor Farm

PH

6

Larch Covert (Fox Covert)

The Old Kennels

Willey

CHURCH LA

Kennel Spinney

Allot Gdns

Long Spinney

The Nursery

CV23

5

MAIN ST

PARSONS CL

84

Garden Spinney

Home Farm

The Grove

Burton Pool Wood

Newnham Fields Farm

Muswell Leys

Park Cottage

4

The Pinetum

Newnham Paddox

Newnham Paddox Park

The Kennels

Cabbage Clump

Fox Covert

Pinch Furlong

Railway Covert (Fox Covert)

3

Plots Spinney

83

Little Walton

Folly Bridge Spinney

2

B4027

Sewage Works

Hillcrest

LUTTERWORTH RD

Pailton Fields Farm

Pailton Pastures Farm

MONTILO LA

1

Pailton

B4112

COVENTRY RD

B4027

82

Warwickshire STREET ATLAS

47 · A · B · 48 · C · D · 49 · E · F

BROCKHURST LA

GREEN LA

A5

Warwickshire STREET ATLAS

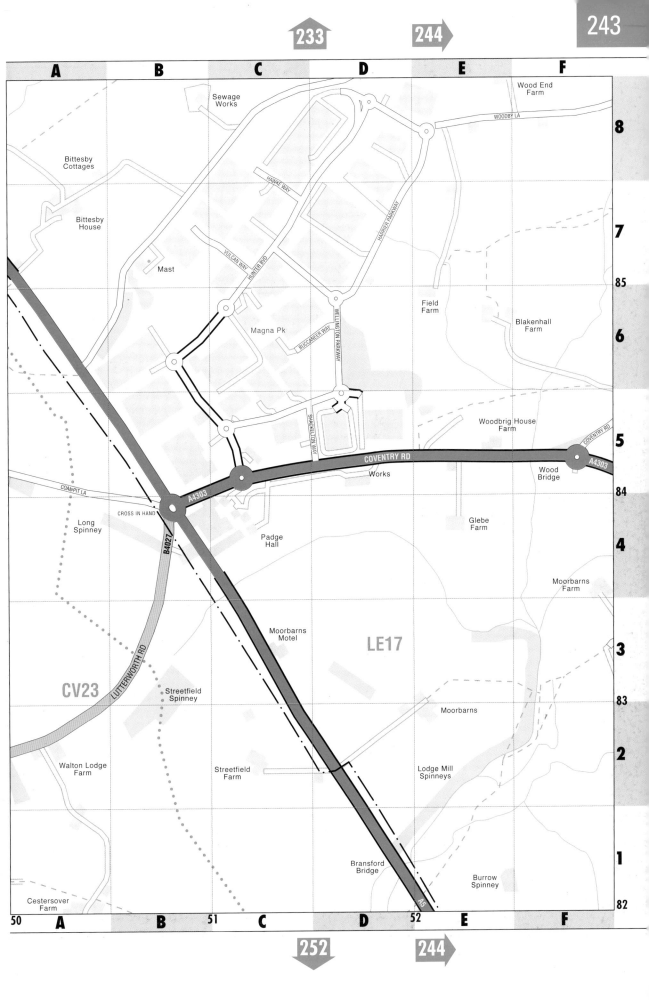

A B C D E F

8

7

85

6

5

84

4

3

83

2

1

82

Wood End Farm

WOODBY LA

Bittesby Cottages

Bittesby House

HAWKE WAY

HARRIER PARKWAY

Field Farm

Blakenhall Farm

Mast

VULCAN WAY

HUNTER BVD

Magna Pk

BUCCANEER WAY

WELLINGTON PARKWAY

Woodbrig House Farm

COVENTRY RD

SHACKLETON WAY

COVENTRY RD

A4303

Wood Bridge

A4303

Works

COALPIT LA

A4303

CROSS IN HAND

Glebe Farm

Long Spinney

B4027

Padge Hall

Moorbarns Farm

LE17

LUTTERWORTH RD

CV23

Streetfield Spinney

Moorbarns Motel

Moorbarns

Walton Lodge Farm

Streetfield Farm

Lodge Mill Spinneys

Bransford Bridge

A5

Burrow Spinney

Cestersover Farm

50 A B 51 C D 52 E F

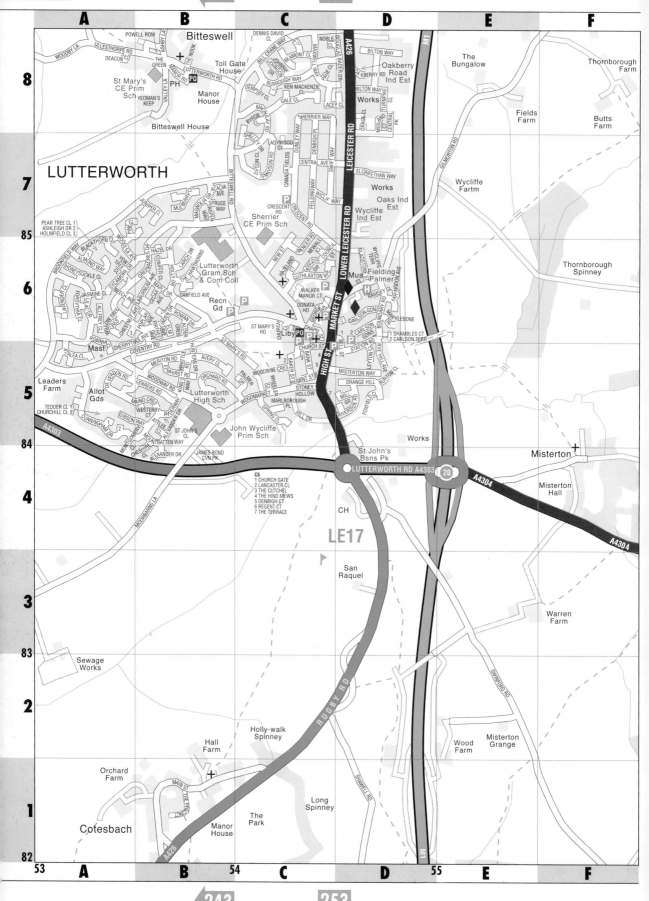

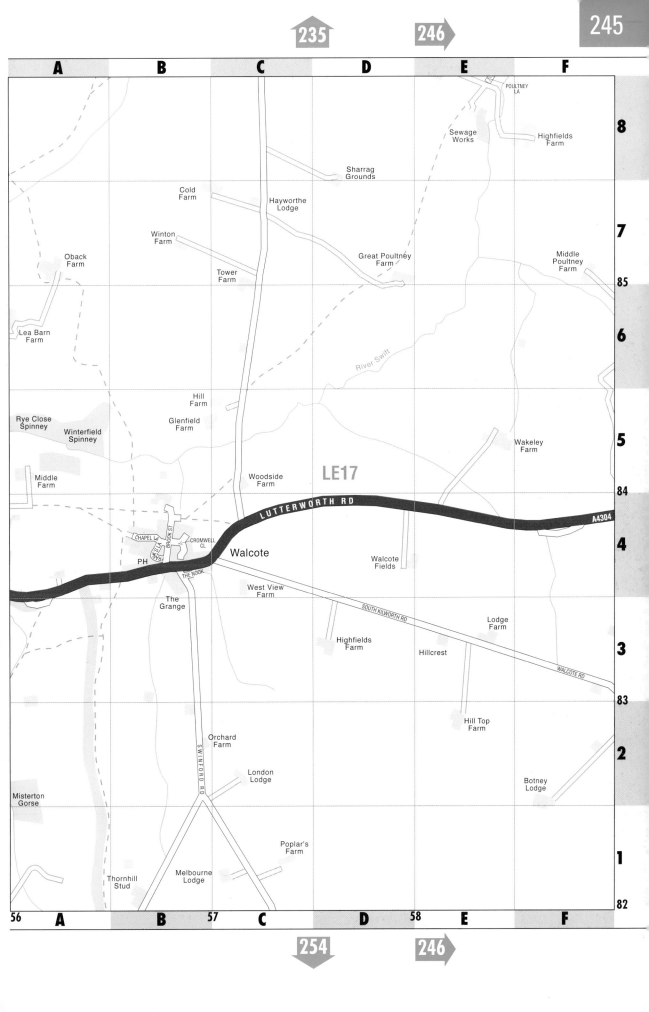

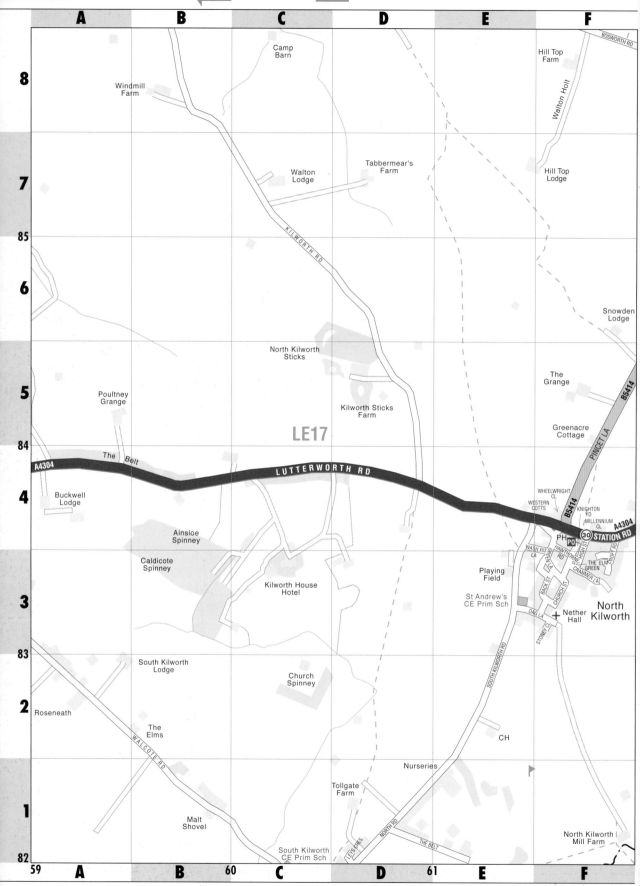

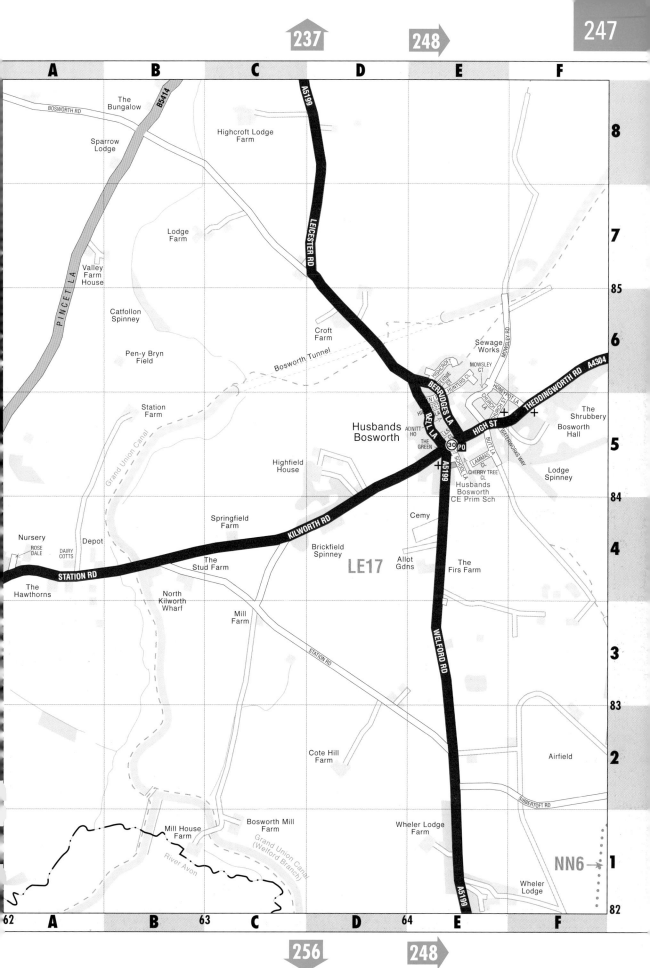

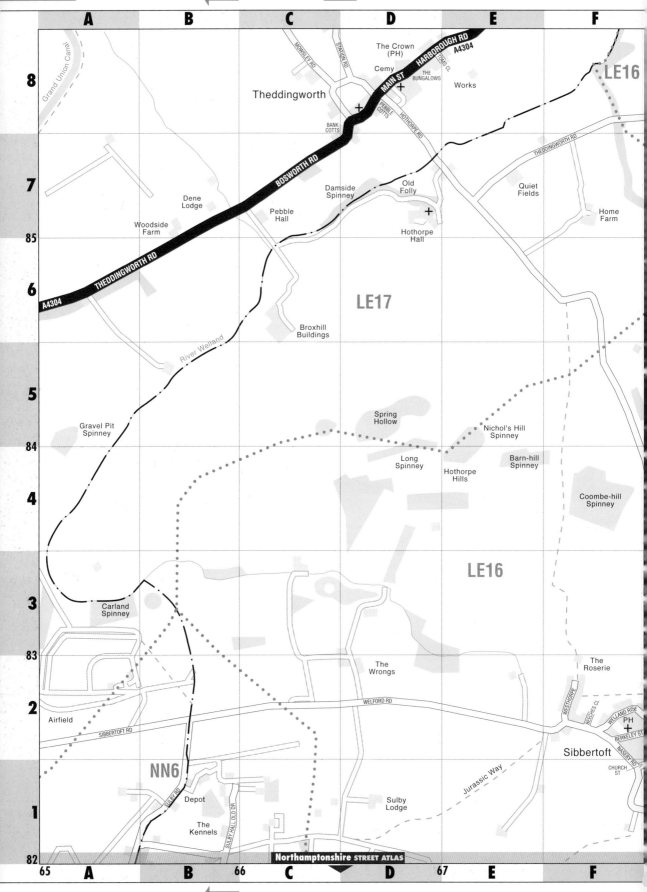

LE16

Grand Union Canal

8

Theddingworth

The Crown
(PH)

MOWSLEY RD

STATION RD

Cemy

MAIN ST

HARBOROUGH RD   A4304

The Crown
(PH)

TOM'S CL

THE
BUNGALOWS

Works

BANK
COTTS

PEBBLE
COTTS

HOTHORPE RD

BOSWORTH RD

7

Dene
Lodge

Damside
Spinney

Old
Folly

Theddingworth Rd

Quiet
Fields

Pebble
Hall

Home
Farm

Woodside
Farm

85

Hothorpe
Hall

LE17

A4304

6

THEDDINGWORTH RD

Broxhill
Buildings

River Welland

Spring
Hollow

Nichol's Hill
Spinney

5

Gravel Pit
Spinney

84

Long
Spinney

Hothorpe
Hills

Barn-hill
Spinney

Coombe-hill
Spinney

4

LE16

3

Carland
Spinney

83

The
Wrongs

The
Roserie

WESTHORPE

BEECHES CL

WELLAND RISE

2

Airfield

WELFORD RD

PH

BERKELEY ST

SIBBERTOFT RD

Sibbertoft

NASEBY RD

CHURCH
ST

NN6

Jurassic Way

1

SULBY RD

Depot

SULBY HALL OLD DR

Sulby
Lodge

The
Kennels

82

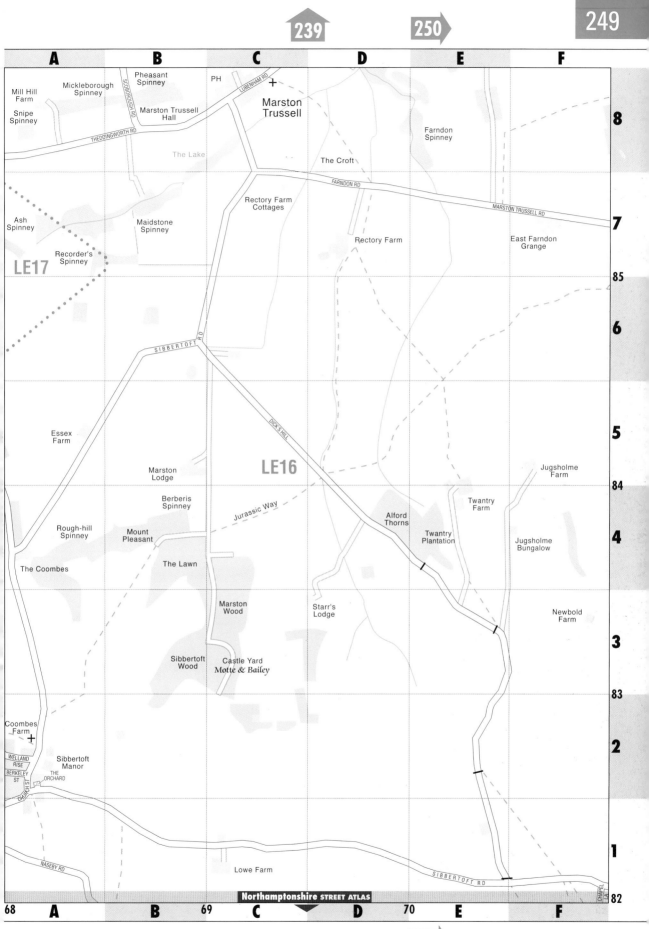

A B C D E F

Mill Hill Farm
Mickleborough Spinney
Pheasant Spinney
PH
Marston Trussell
Snipe Spinney
Marston Trussell Hall
The Lake
Farndon Spinney
The Croft
FARNDON RD
MARSTON TRUSSELL RD
Ash Spinney
Rectory Farm Cottages
Maidstone Spinney
Recorder's Spinney
Rectory Farm
East Farndon Grange
LE17
SIBBERTOFT RD
Essex Farm
DUCK'S HILL
LE16
Jugsholme Farm
Marston Lodge
Twantry Farm
Berberis Spinney
Jurassic Way
Alford Thorns
Twantry Plantation
Jugsholme Bungalow
Rough-hill Spinney
Mount Pleasant
The Lawn
Starr's Lodge
Newbold Farm
The Coombes
Marston Wood
Sibbertoft Wood
Castle Yard
Motte & Bailey
Coombes Farm
WELLAND RISE
BERKELEY ST
Sibbertoft Manor
THE ORCHARD
CHURCH ST
Lowe Farm
SIBBERTOFT RD
NASEBY RD
CHAPEL LA

A B C D E F

8

7

85

6

5

84

4

3

83

2

1

82

71 A B 72 C D 73 E F

Leisure
Ctr

TORCH
WAY

NORTHAMPTON RD · A508

WATSON
AVE
MAURICE RD
BARNARD GDNS
GERRARD
GDNS
HOPTON FIELDS
RAINSBOROUGH GDNS
LINDSEY
GDNS
RITCHIE PK
ARGYLE PK
JACKSON
BISHOP
SELBY CL
VAUGHAN CL
DALLISON CL

HARRISON
CL

Brierley
Farm

Farndon Fields
Prim Sch

New House
Farm

Oxendon Lodge
Farm

Oxendon Lodge
Cottages

JUSTIN PARK
CVN SITE

LUBENHAM RD

HARBOROUGH RD

THE EALAND

COUNCIL HO'S

HOME FARM CL

CH

MARSTON LA

The Dales

East Farndon
Hall

East Farndon

BACK LA

MAIN ST

Jurassic Way

+
RECTORY
CT

Farn Wood

OXENDON RD

Jurassic Way

Allot
Gdns

LE16

The
Lodge

Little Oxendon

CLIPSTON RD

FARNDON RD

Waterloo
House

HARBOROUGH RD

+

The
Spinney

MEWS
COTTS
OXENDON
HALL

West End

MAIN ST

PH

BRAYBROOKE RD

Oxendon
House

CLIPSTON LA

Great
Oxendon

Midshires Way

HARBOROUGH RD

Clipston

CLIPSTON RD

OXENDON RD

Sewage
Works

Station
Cottage

NORTHAMPTON RD

OXENDON RD

SIBBERTOFT RD

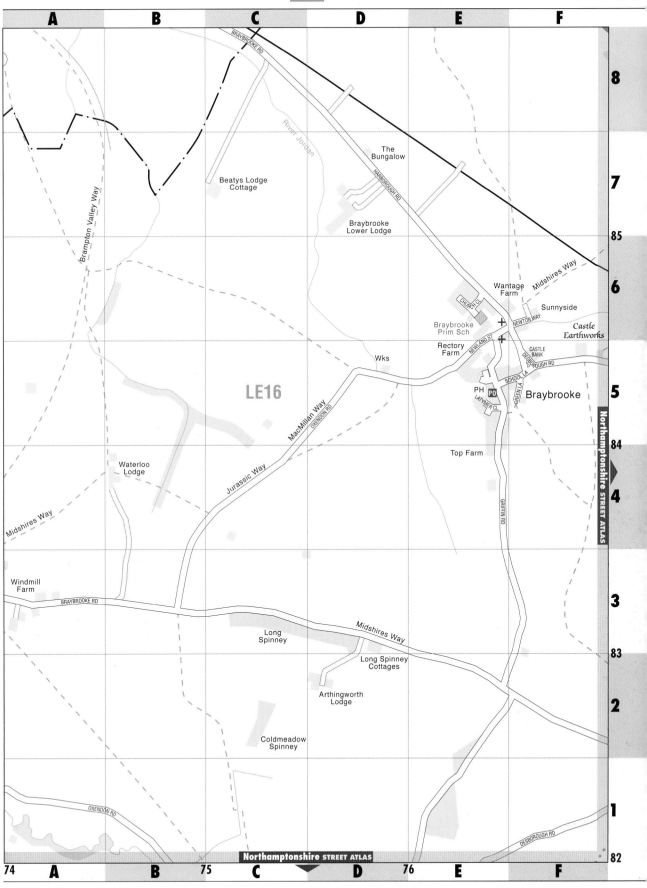

Braybrooke Rd

River Jordan

8

7

85

6

The Bungalow

Harborough Rd

Beatys Lodge Cottage

Brampton Valley Way

Braybrooke Lower Lodge

Wantage Farm

Midshires Way

Sunnyside

Church Cl

Newton Way

Braybrooke Prim Sch

Castle Earthworks

Rectory Farm

Newland St

Castle Bank

Wks

Desborough Rd

LE16

MacMillan Way

Oxendon Rd

School La

Green La

Braybrooke

5

84

PH

PO

Latymer Cl

Top Farm

Jurassic Way

Waterloo Lodge

Griffin Rd

4

Midshires Way

Windmill Farm

Braybrooke Rd

3

Long Spinney

Midshires Way

83

Long Spinney Cottages

Arthingworth Lodge

2

Coldmeadow Spinney

1

Oxendon Rd

Desborough Rd

82

Northamptonshire STREET ATLAS

Northamptonshire STREET ATLAS

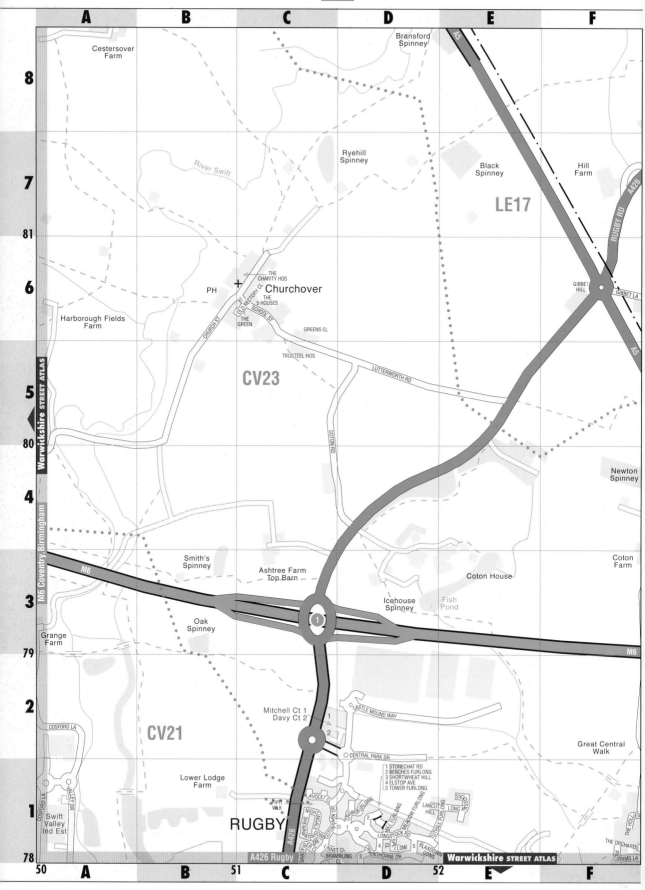

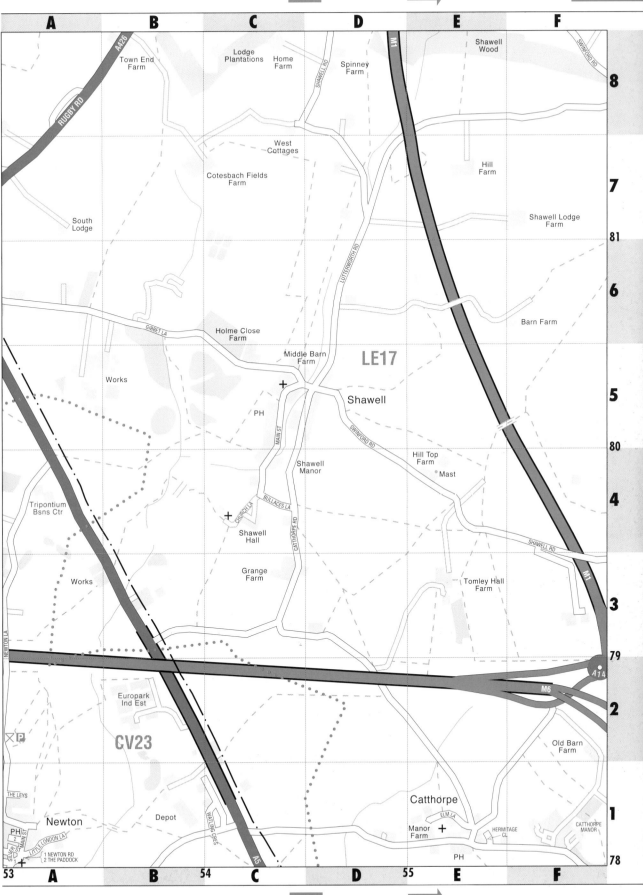

◄ 253
245 ►

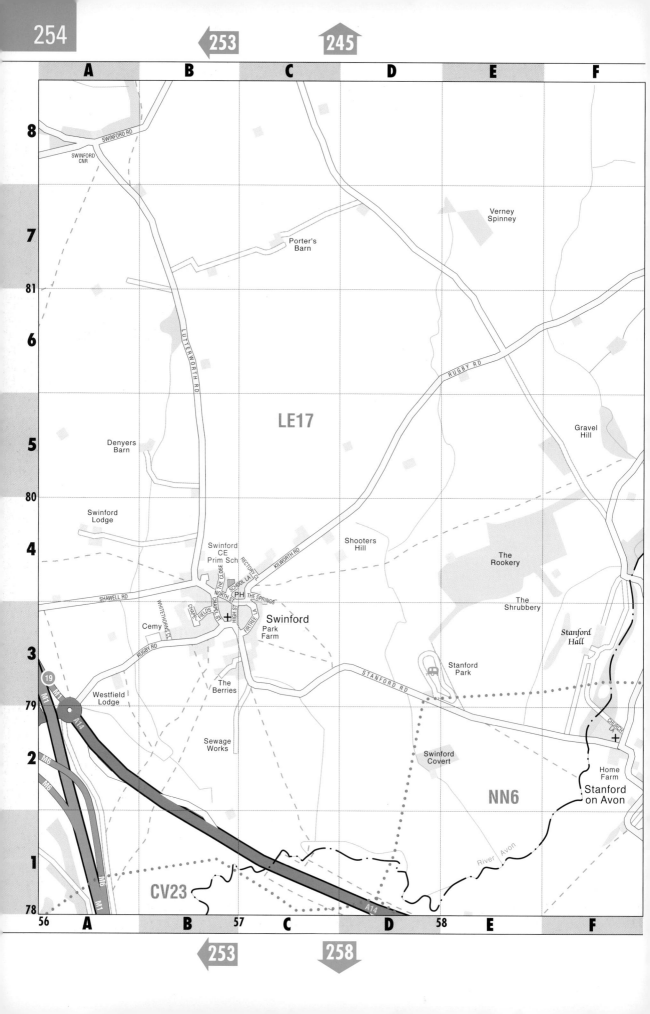

◄ 253
258 ►

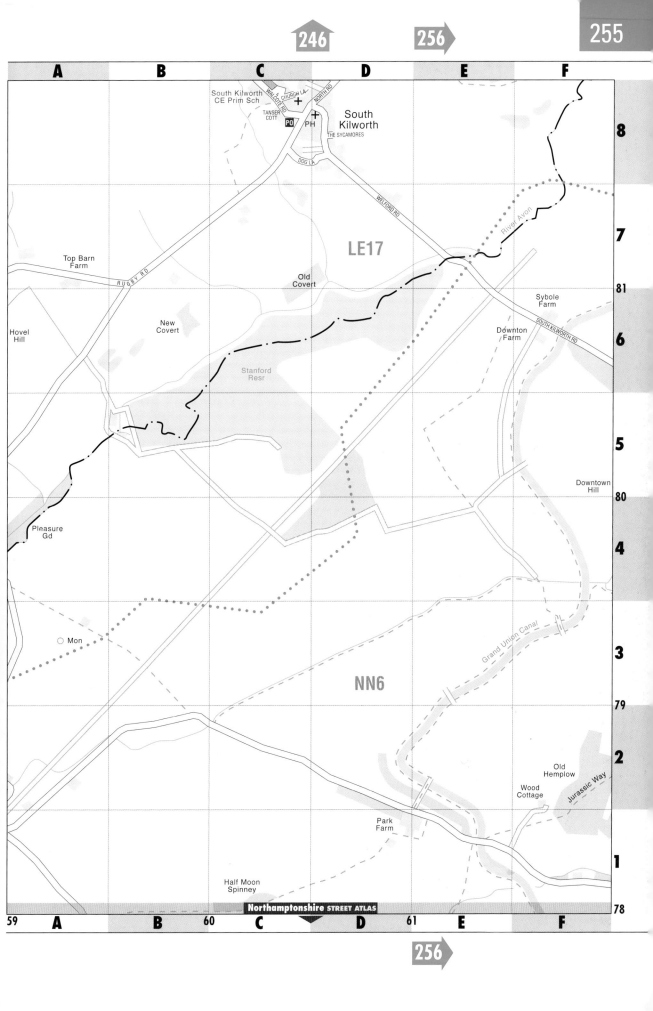

A B C D E F

8

South Kilworth
CE Prim Sch
TANSER
COTT
PO
PH
South Kilworth
THE SYCAMORES
DOG LA
WALCOTE RD
CHURCH LA
NORTH RD

WELFORD RD

LE17

7

River Avon

81

Top Barn
Farm
RUGBY RD

Old
Covert

Sybole
Farm
SOUTH KILWORTH RD

Downton
Farm

6

Hovel
Hill

New
Covert

Stanford
Resr

Downtown
Hill

5

80

Pleasure
Gd

4

Grand Union Canal

○ Mon

3

NN6

79

Old
Hemplow

2

Wood
Cottage

Jurassic Way

Park
Farm

1

Half Moon
Spinney

255

247

A B C D E F

8

Grand Union Canal

Glebe Farm

Grand Union Canal (Welford Branch)

LE17

A5199

WELFORD RD

SULBY RD

7

Sybolds Spinney

Lodge Farm

River Avon

Hill House

81

Marina

Welford Resr

Grange Lodge

Welford Grange Farm

Hotel

NASEBY RD

6

Sewage Works

Allot Gdns

Sulby Lodge Farm

FIELD CRES

WEST ST

SALFORD

1 CHAMBERS ROW
2 DOVEHOUSE CL
3 THE SQUARE

Welford Sibbertoft & Sulby Endowed Sch

ORCHARD TERR

HIGH ST

AVON FIELDS

PO

PH

Welford

Hallfield Cottage

5

WAKEFIELD DR

CHURCH LA

CHRISTOPHER CT

THE LEYS

WOODFORD GLEBE

SOUTH KILWORTH RD

HALL LA

80

WEST END

NEWLANDS RD

4

NORTHAMPTON RD

Jurassic Way

Court Lane Farm

COURT LA

NN6

3

Fish Pond Covert

Hemplow Hills

The Glebe

A5199

79

HEMPLOW DR

West Hill Farm

Hemploe Lodge Farm

2

Dark Spinney

Prince of Wales Spinney

Watts Lodge Farm

Welford Lodge Farm

1

78

255

Northamptonshire STREET ATLAS

A5199 Northampton

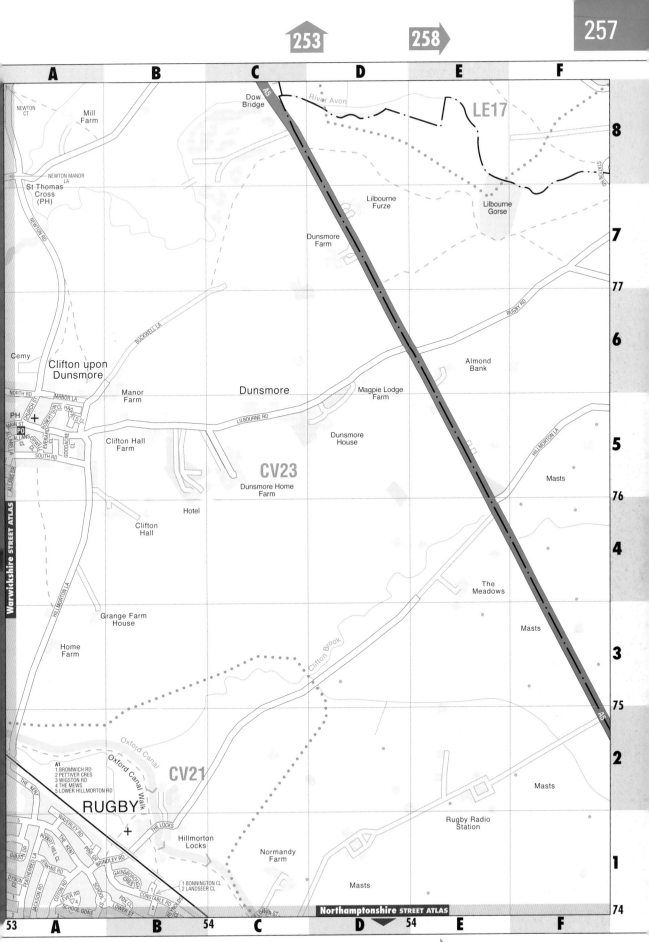

NEWTON CT
Mill Farm

LE17

Dow Bridge
A5
River Avon

8

NEWTON MANOR LA
St Thomas Cross (PH)

Lilbourne Furze
Lilbourne Gorse

NEWTON RD

7

Cemy
Clifton upon Dunsmore

BUCKWELL LA
Dunsmore Farm

RUGBY RD

77

6

Almond Bank

NORTH RD
Manor LA
Manor Farm

Dunsmore

Magpie Lodge Farm

HILLMORTON LA

PH
PO
CHURCH ST
ROBERTS CL
HAZEL CL
EVERARD CL
GOODACRE CL
ALLANS DR
MAIN ST
SOUTH RD

LILBOURNE RD

Dunsmore House

Masts

5

Clifton Hall Farm

CV23
Dunsmore Home Farm

76

Hotel

4

Clifton Hall

The Meadows

HILLMORTON LA

Masts

Grange Farm House

Clifton Brook

Masts

3

Home Farm

75

Oxford Canal

A5

Oxford Canal Walk

CV21

2

Masts

A1
1 BROMWICH RD
2 PETTIVER CRES
3 WIGSTON RD
4 THE MEWS
5 LOWER HILLMORTON RD

Rugby Radio Station

THE KENT

RUGBY

THE LOCKS

WAVERLEY RD
THE KENT
PINE GR
BRINDLEY RD

Hillmorton Locks

Normandy Farm

1

GIBSON DR
ROBERT HILL CL
JENKINS RD
DYSON DR
JACKSON RD
CLYON RD
LEVER RD
SCHOOL ST
LOWER ST
GAINSBOROUGH CRES
FOX CL
CONSTABLE RD
REYNOLDS CL

1 BONNINGTON CL
2 LANDSEER CL

Masts

FEATHERBED LA
SCHOOL GDNS

FLETCHER ST

Warwickshire STREET ATLAS

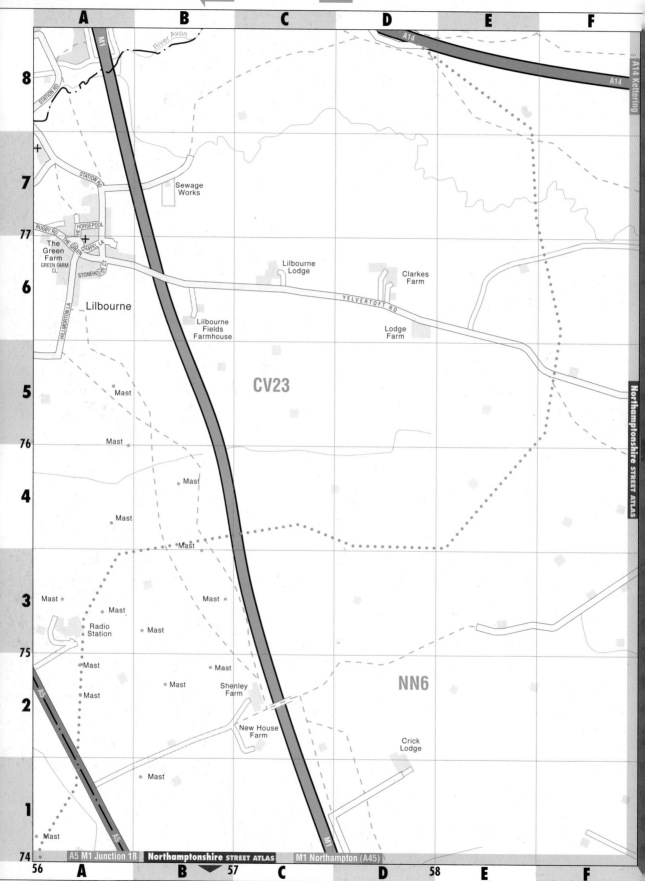

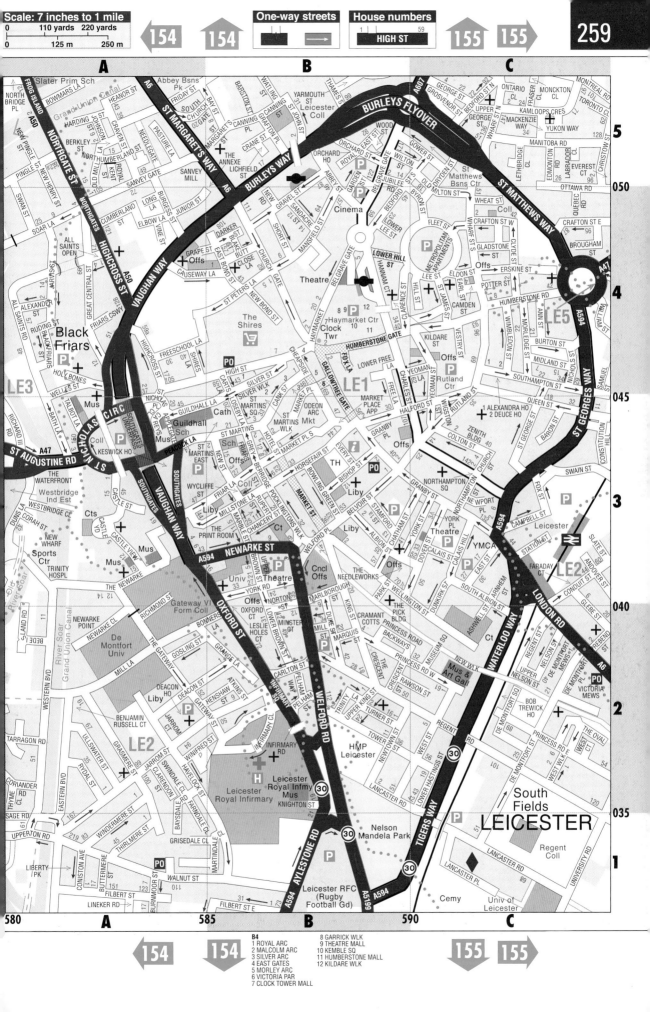

Index

Place name May be abbreviated on the map

Location number Present when a number indicates the place's position in a crowded area of mapping

Locality, town or village Shown when more than one place has the same name

Postcode district District for the indexed place

Page and grid square Page number and grid reference for the standard mapping

Church Rd 6 Beckenham BR2..........53 C6

Cities, towns and villages are listed in CAPITAL LETTERS

Public and commercial buildings are highlighted in magenta   **Places of interest** are highlighted in blue with a star*

Abbreviations used in the index

Acad	Academy	Comm	Common	Gd	Ground	L	Leisure	Prom	Promenade
App	Approach	Cott	Cottage	Gdn	Garden	La	Lane	Rd	Road
Arc	Arcade	Cres	Crescent	Gn	Green	Liby	Library	Recn	Recreation
Ave	Avenue	Cswy	Causeway	Gr	Grove	Mdw	Meadow	Ret	Retail
Bglw	Bungalow	Ct	Court	H	Hall	Meml	Memorial	Sh	Shopping
Bldg	Building	Ctr	Centre	Ho	House	Mkt	Market	Sq	Square
Bsns, Bus	Business	Ctry	Country	Hospl	Hospital	Mus	Museum	St	Street
Bvd	Boulevard	Cty	County	HQ	Headquarters	Orch	Orchard	Sta	Station
Cath	Cathedral	Dr	Drive	Hts	Heights	Pal	Palace	Terr	Terrace
Cir	Circus	Dro	Drove	Ind	Industrial	Par	Parade	TH	Town Hall
Cl	Close	Ed	Education	Inst	Institute	Pas	Passage	Univ	University
Cnr	Corner	Emb	Embankment	Int	International	Pk	Park	Wk, Wlk	Walk
Coll	College	Est	Estate	Intc	Interchange	Pl	Place	Wr	Water
Com	Community	Ex	Exhibition	Junc	Junction	Prec	Precinct	Yd	Yard

Index of towns, villages, streets, hospitals, industrial estates, railway stations, schools, shopping centres, universities and places of interest

260 1st–All

1st Drift PE9 . . . . .169 D8
5 Houses The CV23 . . . . .252 C6

A

Abberton Way LE11 . . . . . 51 A2
Abbey Bsns Pk LE4 . . . . .154 E7
Abbey Cl
  Ashby-de-la-Z LE65 . . . . 68 F6
  Shepshed LE12 . . . . 50 A1
Abbey Court Rd LE4. . . . .128 F3
Abbey Ct LE4 . . . . .128 F2
Abbey Dr
  Ashby-de-la-Z LE65 . . . . 68 F6
  Leicester LE4 . . . . .128 F3
  Shellbrook LE65 . . . . 68 F6
Abbey Gate LE4 . . . . .154 E7
Abbey La
  Leicester LE4 . . . . .128 F2
  Sedgebrook NG32 . . . . .8 F8
Abbey Lodge Cl **1**
  DE11 . . . . 44 A7
Abbey Mdws LE4 . . . . . . .128 F1
Abbeymead Rd LE4 . . . . .128 F3
ABBEY PARK 154 F8
Abbey Park Rd LE4. . . . . .154 F8
Abbey Park St LE4 . . . . . .155 A8
Abbey Prim Com Sch
  LE4 . . . . .129 A1
Abbey Rd
  Coalville LE67, LE12. . . . . 72 E4
  Narborough LE19. . . . . . .178 D1
Abbey Rise LE4 . . . . .128 F3
Abbey St
  Leicester LE1. . . . . .259 B5
  Market Harborough
  LE16. . . . . .240 E3
Abbots Cl LE5 . . . . .156 B8
Abbots Ct LE5 . . . . .156 B8
Abbotsford Cl LE7 . . . . . .156 F8
Abbotsford Rd
  Ashby-de-la-Z LE65 . . . . 69 C5
  Leicester LE5. . . . . .155 F7
Abbot's Rd N LE5 . . . . . .156 B8
Abbots Rd S LE5 . . . . . . .156 B8
Abbotts Cl
  Swadlincote DE11 . . . . . . 44 A6
  Syston LE7. . . . . .102 F3
Abbott's Cl PE9 . . . . .143 F2

Abbotts Gn LE10 . . . . . . .215 F5
Abbott's Oak Dr LE67 . . . 72 C1
Abbotts Rd DE11. . . . . 44 A6
Abbott St NG10 . . . . 10 D6
Abeles Way CV9 . . . . .170 C2
Aberdale Rd LE2. . . . . . . .180 B6
Aberdeen St PE9. . . . . . . .142 F4
Abingdon Rd
  Leicester LE2. . . . . .155 B4
  Melton Mowbray LE13. . . . 59 A5
Abington High Sch
  LE18 . . . . .180 C2
AB KETTLEBY 37 D2
Ab Kettleby Com Prim Sch
  LE14 . . . . 37 C3
Abney Cres DE12 . . . . 93 C4
Abney Dr DE12 . . . . 93 C4
Abney St LE5 . . . . .155 C4
Abney Wlk DE12 . . . . 93 C4
Acacia Ave
  Birstall LE4 . . . . .129 B8
  Lutterworth LE17 . . . . . . .244 B7
  Swadlincote DE11 . . . . . . 44 B7
Acacia Cl LE3. . . . . .152 F2
Acacia Dr DE73 . . . . 26 A8
Acan Way LE19 . . . . .201 A7
Acer Cl
  Leicester LE4. . . . . .128 C4
  Loughborough LE11. . . . . . 75 A7
  Narborough LE19. . . . . . .201 A7
Achurch Cl LE9 . . . . .199 D3
Acorn Cl
  Birstall LE4 . . . . .129 A6
  Lubenham LE16 . . . . .239 E3
Acorn Grange **2** LE11. . . 51 F2
Acorn St LE4 . . . . .129 B2
Acorn Way LE18 . . . . . . .180 E2
Acre La DE72 . . . . 16 C8
ACRESFORD 92 C7
Acresford Rd
  Donisthorpe DE12 . . . . . . 92 D7
  Netherseal DE12 . . . . 92 B6
  Overseal DE12. . . . . 67 B2
Acresford View DE12. . . . . 67 B3
Acres Rd LE3 . . . . .153 A3
Acres Rise LE15. . . . . 59 E4
Acton Ave NG10 . . . . 10 E6
Acton Cl NG10 . . . . 10 E6
Acton Gr NG10 . . . . 10 E6
Acton Rd NG10 . . . . 10 E6
Acton Road Ind Est
  NG10. . . . . 10 E6

Acton St NG10 . . . . 10 E6
Adam Dale LE11 . . . . 52 A3
Adam & Eve St **8**
  LE16. . . . . .240 E3
Adamswood Cl LE16 . . . .240 C3
Adcock Cl LE13 . . . . 59 F5
Adcock Rd LE3 . . . . .154 B7
Adcocks Cl LE11. . . . . 52 B5
Adcock's Yd DE12. . . . . . . 93 C5
Adcote Cl LE9 . . . . .198 A6
Adderley Rd LE2 . . . . . . .155 B1
Adderly St LE15. . . . . . . .189 B4
Adelaide Cl LE4. . . . . . . .128 C7
Adelaide St PE9 . . . . .143 E3
Adelphi Row LE16. . . . . . .208 B4
Adkins Ct LE2 . . . . 76 C8
Adlington Rd LE2 . . . . . . .181 C6
Admiral Ct LE16 . . . . .240 D3
Adnitt Ho LE17. . . . . .247 E5
Adrian Dr LE9 . . . . .198 A7
Aeropark The* DE74 . . . . 17 A1
Afton Cl LE11 . . . . 51 B3
AGAR NOOK 72 C1
Agar Nook Ct LE67. . . . . . 72 D1
Agar Nook La LE67. . . . . . 72 D1
Agar St LE4. . . . . .129 B2
Aikman Ave LE3 . . . . .154 B7
Aikman Cl LE3. . . . . .154 A7
Aingarth LE11 . . . . 52 C3
Ainsdale LE3 . . . . .154 A7
Ainsdale Rd LE3 . . . . . . .154 B5
Ainsworth Dr LE12. . . . . . 77 E4
Ainsworth Wlk LE3. . . . . .154 A5
Aintree Cl LE5 . . . . .156 D4
Aintree Cres LE2. . . . . . . .180 F6
Airedale Cl
  Leire LE17 . . . . .218 F1
  Long Eaton NG10. . . . . . . 10 A6
Airedale Rd PE9 . . . . .143 C5
Aisne Rd LE18 . . . . .179 E3
Alan Bray Cl LE10 . . . . . .214 D7
Alan Cl LE4. . . . . .129 B4
Aland Gdns LE9. . . . . . . .219 A6
Alan Moss Rd LE11. . . . . . 51 F5
Alans Way LE9. . . . . .150 B4
Albany Ct LE16 . . . . .240 F4
Albany Rd LE16 . . . . .240 F4
Albany St LE11. . . . . 51 E5
Albany The LE2 . . . . .155 C3
Alberta St LE5 . . . . .155 B5
Albert Ave LE12. . . . . 77 D4
Albert Ct
  Leicester LE2. . . . . .155 D2

Albert Ct *continued*
  Whetstone LE8 . . . . .201 F8
Albert Hall Pl LE67 . . . . . 72 D1
Albert Pl LE11 . . . . 52 B3
Albert Prom LE11. . . . . . . 52 C3
Albert Rd
  Breaston DE72. . . . . .9 B7
  Coalville LE67 . . . . 71 E1
  Hinckley LE10 . . . . .197 D1
  Leicester LE2. . . . . .155 C2
  Long Eaton NG10. . . . . . . 10 D8
  Market Harborough
  LE16 . . . . .240 F3
  Stamford PE9. . . . . .143 E3
  Swadlincote DE11 . . . . . . 44 A2
Albert St
  Bottesford NG13 . . . . .3 A3
  Fleckney LE8 . . . . .222 F8
  Heather LE67. . . . . 95 F3
  Kibworth Beauchamp
  LE8 . . . . .206 A2
  Loughborough LE11. . . . . . 52 B3
  Melton Mowbray LE13. . . . 59 D1
  Syston LE7. . . . . .103 B3
ALBERT VILLAGE 44 C1
Albert Village Com Prim
  Sch DE11. . . . . 44 C1
Albion Cl DE12. . . . . 68 A4
Albion Ct LE2 . . . . .181 A5
Albion Par LE7 . . . . .103 B3
Albion Rd
  Long Eaton NG10. . . . . . . 10 F8
  Sileby LE12 . . . . 77 C2
Albion St
  Anstey LE7. . . . . .127 E6
  Leicester LE1 . . . . .259 B3
  Leicester, Oadby LE2 . . . .181 A5
  Syston LE7. . . . . .103 B3
  Wigston LE18 . . . . .179 F1
  Woodville DE11 . . . . 44 F2
Albrighton Wlk CV11 . . . .214 A2
Alcester Dr LE5 . . . . .156 D4
Alcott Cl LE3 . . . . .154 A4
Aldeby Cl
  Leicester LE2. . . . . .179 B4
  Narborough LE19. . . . . . .178 E2
Alderbrooke Dr CV11 . . . .214 A1
Alder Cl LE3 . . . . .152 F2
Alder Cres LE17 . . . . .244 B6
Alder Ct CV9 . . . . .170 D1
Alderleigh Rd LE2 . . . . . .179 E1
Alderman Richard Hallam
  Prim Sch LE4. . . . . .128 C1

Aldermill Bsns Pk
  CV9. . . . . .170 D3
Alderstone Cl LE18. . . . . .203 C8
Alderton Cl LE4. . . . . . . .129 C5
ALDGATE 168 B5
Aldgate Ave LE5 . . . . . . .156 B3
Aldgate Ct PE9 . . . . .168 A5
Aldin Way LE10 . . . . .197 A3
Aldridge Rd LE10 . . . . . . .215 D6
Aldwinkles Yd **4**
  LE16. . . . . .240 E3
Alesworth Dr LE10 . . . . . .215 F4
Alexander Ave
  Earl Shilton LE9 . . . . .199 A8
  Enderby LE19. . . . . .178 A3
Alexander Cres LE15 . . . .137 E6
Alexander Dr LE17 . . . . . .244 B5
Alexander Gdns LE10. . . .197 C2
Alexander Rd LE12. . . . . . 75 F7
Alexander St LE3 . . . . . . .259 A4
Alexandra Bldg LE18. . . .180 B2
Alexandra Ct
  Leicester, Oadby LE2 . . . .181 B5
  Overseal DE12. . . . . 67 B4
Alexandra Ho LE1. . . . . . .259 C4
Alexandra Rd
  Leicester LE2. . . . . .155 D1
  Long Eaton NG10. . . . . . . 10 D8
  Overseal DE12. . . . . 67 B4
  Stamford PE9. . . . . .143 D4
  Swadlincote DE11 . . . . . . 44 B3
Alexandra St
  Narborough LE19. . . . . . .201 A8
  Thurmaston LE4. . . . . . . .129 E8
Alfred St LE11 . . . . 52 B5
Alfreton Cl LE10 . . . . . . .215 F5
Alfreton Rd LE18. . . . . . .180 C4
Algernon Rd LE13. . . . . . . 59 D3
Alice Gdns
  Overseal DE12. . . . . 67 B4
  Whetstone LE8 . . . . .201 F8
Allandale Rd LE2 . . . . . . .155 E1
Allans Cl CV23 . . . . .257 A5
Allans Dr CV23. . . . . .257 A5
Allans La CV23. . . . . .257 A5
Allen Ave LE12. . . . . 75 F7
Allendale Rd LE11 . . . . . . 75 B7
Allenwood Rd LE2 . . . . . .179 E4
Allerton Dr LE3 . . . . .128 A1
ALLEXTON 187 D5
Allexton Field Rd
  LE15. . . . . .188 D4
Allexton Gdns LE3 . . . . . .153 D6

Allexton La
  Allexton LE15.........187 D3
  Stockerston LE15......187 D1
Allexton Rd LE15......209 F7
Allfrey Cl LE17.......244 A6
Alliance Rd LE3.......153 C7
ALLINGTON...........4 E5
Allington Dr LE4......129 B8
Allington Gdns NG32....4 F4
Allington Rd NG32......4 E2
Allington St LE5......155 B8
Allington with Sedgebrook
  CE Prim Sch NG32.....4 F5
Allinson Cl LE5.......156 A6
Allison Ave DE11......44 B3
Allison Cl LE65.......69 B8
Allotment La CV13.....121 E2
Alloway Cl LE4........129 D4
All Saints CE Prim Sch
  Coalville LE67.......71 B2
  Sapcote LE9.........217 D7
  Wigston LE18........180 C2
All Saints Cl
  Asfordby LE14........57 F2
  Sapcote LE9.........217 D7
All Saint's Mews [6]
  PE9................143 D3
All Saints Open LE1...259 A4
All Saints' Pl [7] PE9..143 D3
All Saints Rd
  Leicester LE3.......259 A4
  Thurcaston LE7......101 B2
All Saints' St PE9....143 D2
Allsopp's La LE11.....52 D5
Alma Rd LE10..........197 D1
Alma St
  Leicester LE3.......154 C7
  Melbourne DE73......26 A7
Almey's La LE9........176 A1
Almond Cl
  Countesthorpe LE8...202 E4
  Loughborough LE11....75 A6
Almond Gr DE11.......44 A5
Almond Rd LE4........154 F3
Almond Way
  Bagworth LE67.......124 A6
  Earl Shilton LE9....198 E6
  Lutterworth LE17....244 A6
Alpine Cl LE15.......137 E6
Alport Way LE18......180 E2
Alsthorpe Rd LE15....138 B7
Alston Dr LE11.......51 D6
Altar Stones La LE67..98 C2
Althorp Cl
  Leicester LE2.......179 B5
  Market Harborough
  LE16...............241 B3
Althorpe Dr DE11.....51 C4
Alton Hill LE67......70 B3
Alton Rd LE2.........179 E6
Alton Way LE65.......69 C5
Alvaston Rd
  Leicester LE5.......154 B1
  Melton Mowbray LE13..59 A5
Alvecote Rd LE12.....179 D5
Alvington Way LE16...240 D5
Alvis Dale LE7.......101 F8
Alwyne Cl LE15.......138 A6
Alyssum Way LE19.....177 F1
Amadis Rd LE4........128 A4
Amanda Rd LE2........179 B4
Ambassador Rd
  Diseworth DE74......28 B7
  Leicester LE5.......156 A6
Amber Gate Cl LE9....219 A6
Ambergate Dr LE4.....128 F8
Amberley Cl LE4......129 E6
Amberwood DE11......44 A5
Ambion Cl CV13......148 E2
Ambion La CV13.......173 E6
Ambion Rise CV13.....148 D2
Ambion Way LE10......197 F1
Ambler Cl LE18......180 D1
Ambleside
  Barwell LE9.........198 C7
  Leicester LE2.......155 C2
Ambleside Cl
  Leicester LE2.......179 C3
  Loughborough LE11....74 C8
Ambleside Dr LE2.....179 C3
Ambleside Way
  Leicester LE2.......179 C3
  Melton Mowbray LE13..59 A2
Ambrose Cl LE3.......154 B6
Amersham Rd LE4......128 D1
Amersham Way DE12....93 C6
Amesbury Ct LE18.....203 C8
Amesbury Rd LE18.....203 C8
Amhurst Cl LE3.......127 F1
Amis Cl LE11.........51 C5
Amos Rd LE3..........153 D6
Amsden Rise LE9......218 E7
Amyson Rd LE5........156 C6
Amy St LE3...........179 B8
Ancaster Rd PE9......143 C5
Ancaster Way LE15....166 D3
Anchor Cl
  Hathern LE12........51 A8
  Swadlincote DE11....44 C4
Anchor La
  Hathern LE12........51 A8
  Peggs Green LE67....71 B8
Anchor St LE4........128 F2
Ancton Cl LE2........259 C3
Andrew Ave LE9.......201 D4
Andrew Ct CV13.......196 D7
Andrew Ct [3] LE2....155 B4
Andrewes Cl LE3......154 D5

Andrewes St LE3......154 D5
Andrewes Wlk [3] LE3..154 D5
Andrew Macdonald Cl
  LE16...............240 F3
Andrew Rd
  Anstey LE7..........127 E7
  Stamford PE9........143 D4
Andrews Cl LE17......218 F2
Andrew's La LE16.....208 B4
Aneford Rd LE4.......129 E1
Anemone Cl LE13......82 A8
Angela Dr LE5........156 B4
Angel Ct [2] LE16....240 E3
Angel St [1] LE16....240 E3
Angel Yd LE11........52 B4
Angle La LE15........166 D1
Anglesey Rd LE18.....179 F3
Anglian Water Bird
  Watching Ctr★
  LE15...............138 D3
Angus Cl
  Leicester LE7.......156 F6
  Stamford PE9........142 F4
Angus Dr LE11........51 E4
Angus Rd LE9.........198 A6
Ankle Hill LE13......59 C1
Anne Rd PE9..........143 C4
Annexe The LE1.......259 B5
Annies Wharf LE11....52 B5
Ann St LE1...........259 C4
Annwell La LE65......45 E2
Anson Rd
  Diseworth DE74......28 B8
  Shepshed LE12.......50 A3
Anstee Rd NG10.......10 C5
ANSTEY..............127 C7
Anstey La
  Groby LE6...........127 B3
  Groby LE6...........127 C4
  Leicester LE4.......128 B2
  Thurcaston LE7......101 B1
Anthony Cl LE7.......102 E2
Anthony Dr LE7.......156 F5
Anthony Rd LE4.......128 D1
Anthony St LE4.......101 F6
Antill Cl LE14.......57 F3
Antringham Cl LE5....130 C2
Apiary Gate DE74.....17 B3
Apollo Cl LE2........155 B5
Apollo Ct LE2........155 B5
Applebee Rd LE10.....215 D6
Applebees Mdw LE10...214 E6
Applebees Wlk LE10...214 E6
Appleby Cl LE3.......153 C6
Appleby Ho [1] LE10..197 E1
Appleby Hill CV9.....119 B3
Appleby La DE12......120 D7
APPLEBY MAGNA.......119 E8
APPLEBY PARVA.......119 D6
Appleby Rd LE4.......130 A7
Applegate LE1........259 A3
Appleton Ave LE4.....128 D4
Appleton Dr LE12.....33 B3
Apple Tree Cl LE5....175 B1
Approach The LE5.....155 F4
Aqueduct Rd LE67.....70 E8
Aquitaine Cl LE19....178 A3
Arbor Ct [11] LE2....155 B4
Arbor Rd LE9.........200 D4
Arbour Rd LE4........129 B2
Arbury Dale LE12.....50 C2
Arcade The [1] LE18..180 D3
Archdale Cl LE4......102 A1
Archdale St LE4......102 F3
Archer Cl
  Leicester LE4.......129 E4
  Loughborough LE11....51 B6
Archers' Gn LE7......103 D7
Archers La LE9.......175 F7
Archers Rdbt LE8.....205 A7
Archery Cl LE8.......202 F4
Archway Rd LE5.......130 E1
Ardath Rd LE4........129 C1
Arden Ave LE3........153 F1
Arden Cl LE16........241 A1
Arden Dr LE13........59 A4
Arden Rd CV11........214 A1
Arden Way LE16.......240 F5
Ardern Terr LE3......154 B2
Argosy Rd DE74.......28 E8
Arguile Pl LE10......197 C1
Argyle Pk LE16.......250 E6
Argyle St LE67.......95 F2
Argyll Way PE9.......143 B3
Arkwright Ho LE9.....218 E7
Armadale Cl LE10.....197 A1
Armadale Dr LE5......156 D8
Armadale Gn LE5......156 C8
Armett's La LE12.....48 C4
Armitage Cl LE11.....52 A4
Armley Gr PE9........143 F5
Armour Cl LE10.......215 D5
Armson Ave LE9.......152 E5
Armston Rd
  Cosby LE9...........201 D3
  Quorn (Quorndon) LE12..76 A5
Arncliffe Cl CV11....214 A4
Arncliffe Rd LE5.....156 C8
Arndale LE18.........180 F1
ARNESBY.............221 F5
Arnesby CE Prim Sch
  LE8................221 F5
Arnesby Cres LE2.....179 F5
Arnesby La LE8.......221 C5

Arnesby Rd LE8.......222 E6
Arnhem St LE1........259 C3
Arnhill Rd NN17......213 B1
Arnold Ave
  Long Eaton NG10.....10 A4
  Wigston LE18........180 A1
Arnold Cl LE9........201 D2
Arnold Cres NG10.....10 A4
Arnold Rd CV13.......196 D6
Arnold's Cres LE9....150 B3
Arnold Smith Ho LE12..50 B4
Arnold St LE1........155 B7
Arnside Cl LE2.......180 C7
Arran Rd
  Leicester LE4.......129 D4
  Stamford PE9........142 F4
Arran Way
  Countesthorpe LE8...202 F3
  Hinckley LE10.......197 B1
Arreton Cl LE2.......180 C7
Arthur St
  Barwell LE9.........198 B7
  Loughborough LE11....52 A3
Artisan Rd LE14......36 B5
Arum Way LE3.........153 D6
Arundel Ave DE74.....16 E5
Arundel Cl LE12......101 C8
Arundel Gr LE2.......50 A2
Arundel St [2] LE3...154 D5
Ascot Dr LE2.........155 D1
Ascot Rd LE4.........129 B2
Ascott Dr DE11.......44 A7
Asfare Bsns Pk LE10..215 E1
ASFORDBY............57 F3
Asfordby Hill Prim Sch
  LE14...............58 D3
Asfordby Hill LE14...58 D3
Asfordby Pl LE14.....57 F2
Asfordby Rd
  Hoby LE14...........79 F8
  Melton Mowbray LE13,
  LE14...............58 E3
Asfordby St LE5......155 D6
ASFORDBY VALLEY.....58 B3
Asha Ho LE4..........129 A4
Asha Margh LE4.......129 A2
Ashbourne Dr DE11....44 A1
Ashbourne Rd LE18....180 C4
Ashburton St LE3.....155 C5
Ashbrook Rise CV10...194 B2
Ashburton Cl LE10....216 A6
Ashburton Rd LE67....96 C6
Ashby Cres LE11......51 D3
Ashby Cl LE10........197 D3
ASHBY-DE-LA-ZOUCH
  ....69 C6
Ashby-de-la-Zouch
  Castle★ LE65.......69 C6
Ashby-de-la-Zouch CE
  Prim Sch LE65......69 B6
Ashby & District Hospl
  LE65...............69 C6
ASHBY FOLVILLE......105 F5
Ashby Glade LE5......156 C5
Ashby Grange LE10....197 E5
Ashby Hill Top Prim Sch
  LE65...............68 F6
Ashby Ho LE10........215 C7
Ashby La
  Bitteswell LE17.....234 B3
  Blackfordby DE11....68 C8
  Swepstone LE67......94 D3
ASHBY MAGNA.........220 A2
Ashby Mus★ LE65.....69 B6
ASHBY PARVA.........233 F5
Ashby Rd
  Ashby-de-la-Z LE65,
  LE67...............70 B7
  Barwell LE9.........197 E6
  Blackfordby DE11, LE65..45 D2
  Breedon on t H DE73..26 E2
  Cadeby CV13.........149 C2
  Coalville LE67......70 E3
  Coleorton LE67......70 D6
  Diseworth DE74......28 C7
  Donisthorpe DE12....68 A1
  Gaddesby LE7........105 D5
  Gilmorton LE17......235 B5
  Hinckley LE10.......197 E3
  Ibstock LE67........95 E2
  Kegworth DE74.......18 A2
  Kegworth DE74.......18 B2
  Loughborough LE11....51 F4
  Markfield LE67......98 D2
  Measham DE12........93 E7
  Melbourne DE73......26 A6
  Moira DE12..........67 F4
  Moira, Norris Hill DE12..68 B5
  Newbold LE67........47 D2
  Normanton Le H LE67..94 F7
  Osgathorpe LE67.....48 D4
  Packington LE65.....69 C2
  Peatling Parva LE17..235 E8
  Rempstone LE12......32 B6
  Ravenstone LE67.....95 E8
  Shepshed LE12.......49 F8
  Snarestone DE12.....120 E4
  Stapleton LE9.......174 F3
  Thringstone LE67....48 D1
  Twyford LE14........106 C2
  Ullesthorpe LE17....233 C4
Ashby Rd E LE12......50 D1
Ashby Rd W LE12......49 E1
Ashby Rise LE8.......182 B1
Ashby Road Central
  LE12...............50 B1
Ashby Sch LE65.......69 B1
Ashby Sq [4] LE11....52 A4

Ash Cl
  Aston-on-T DE72.....16 B7
  Barrow-u-S LE12.....53 D1
  Ratby LE6...........126 B1
  Uppingham LE15.....189 C3
Ashclose Ave LE2.....180 C6
Ash Croft CV9........171 B7
Ash Ct LE6...........126 E2
Ashdale LE67.........95 E1
Ashdale LE67.........71 D7
Ashdown Ave LE3......154 B6
Ashdown Cl LE11......51 C5
Ashdown Rd LE18.....180 D4
Ash Dr
  Measham DE12........93 C6
  Syston LE7..........103 B2
Ashfield LE15........138 A8
Ashfield Dr
  Anstey LE7..........127 D5
  Moira DE12..........68 B6
Ashfield Rd
  Leicester LE2.......155 D3
  [3] Market Harborough
  LE16...............240 E4
  Thurmaston LE4.....129 F8
Ash Field Sch LE5....155 F4
Ashford Ct LE2.......155 D1
Ashford Rd
  Hinckley LE10.......215 B7
  Leicester LE2.......155 A1
  Whitwick LE67......71 D5
Ash Gr
  Blaby LE8...........202 B8
  Bottesford NG13.....2 F3
  Hathern LE12........30 A2
  Long Eaton NG10.....10 C6
  Melton Mowbray LE13..59 B5
  Mountsorrel LE12....76 E1
Ashington Cl LE3.....154 B8
Ashland Dr LE67......71 A2
Ashlands Rd LE7......183 F3
Ashlands Way LE19....177 F1
Ashlar Dr LE2........67 F1
Ashleigh Ct LE3......154 C3
Ashleigh Dr
  Loughborough LE11....51 E2
  Lutterworth LE17....244 A6
Ashleigh Gdns
  Barwell LE9.........198 C8
  Leicester LE3.......154 C3
Ashleigh Rd
  Glenfield LE3.......153 C8
  Leicester LE3.......154 C3
ASHLEY..............227 F2
Ashley Cl LE12.......67 B3
Ashley Rd
  Medbourne LE16.....227 C6
  Middleton LE16.....229 B2
  Weston by W LE16....227 C3
Ashley Way LE16......241 B3
Ashlyns Rise LE3.....153 E5
Ashmead Cres LE4.....102 C1
Ashmount Sch LE11....52 A1
Ashover Cl LE9.......201 D4
Ashover Rd LE5.......155 D4
Ash Pl PE9...........142 F4
Ash Rd
  Croft LE9...........200 D3
  Earl Shilton LE9....198 D7
Ash St LE5...........155 C7
Ashthorpe Rd LE3.....154 A4
Ashton Cl
  Leicester, Oadby LE2..181 B3
  Melton Mowbray LE13..59 C1
  Wigston LE18........180 C1
Ash Tree Cl LE2......181 B4
Ashtree Gdns PE9.....168 D2
Ashtree Rd LE5.......130 C2
Ash Tree Rd LE67.....96 B7
Ash-Tree Rd LE9......201 D3
Ash Tree Rd LE2......181 C4
Ashurst Cl LE18......203 E8
Ashurst Rd LE3.......178 F8
Ashview Cl NG10......10 A8
Ashville Way LE8.....201 E4
Ash Way LE14.........80 D8
ASHWELL.............111 B8
Ashwell Rd
  Cottesmore LE15.....112 B7
  Langham LE15.......110 D5
  Oakham LE15........111 B2
  Whissendine LE15....110 B8
Ashwell St LE1.......259 C2
Ash Wlk LE12.........31 D8
Askrigg Way LE18.....180 E2
Aspen Ave LE11.......75 A7
Aspen Cl
  Measham DE12........93 C6
  Ravenstone LE67.....70 F2
Aspen Dr LE8.........202 E4
Aspens Hollow LE67...71 D7
Aspen Way LE17......244 B7
Asplin Rd LE2........179 E5
Asquith Bvd LE2, LE12..180 B5
Asquith Way LE2......180 B5
Assheton La CV9......146 D2
Assured Dr LE4.......129 D7
Aster Cl
  Hinckley LE10.......215 E6
  Nuneaton CV11......214 A1
Aster Way LE10.......215 D6
Astill Cl LE6........152 E8
Astill Dr LE4........128 C6
Astill Lodge Rd LE4..128 A6
Astley Cl
  Leicester LE3.......154 B3

Astley Cl continued
  Market Harborough
  LE16...............240 D1
Astley Rd LE16.......198 F8
Astley Way LE65......69 D7
Aston Dr DE11........44 A7
Aston Firs Cvn Site
  LE10...............216 E8
ASTON FLAMVILLE.....216 E6
Aston Flamville Rd
  LE10...............216 C7
Aston Hall Dr DE72...16 A7
Aston Hill LE2.......180 A8
Aston La
  Aston Flamville LE10..216 D7
  Aston-on-T DE72.....16 C8
  Hinckley LE10.......216 A6
  Sharnford LE10......217 B5
ASTON-ON-TRENT.....16 B8
Aston-on-Trent Prim Sch
  DE72...............16 A8
Astron Bsns Pk DE11..44 A3
ATHERSTONE..........170 E2
Atherstone Cl LE2....181 D4
Atherstone Rd
  Appleby Magna DE12..119 E5
  Atherstone CV9.....170 D4
  Fenny Drayton CV10,
  CV13...............195 A6
  Hartshill Green CV10..194 B2
  Loughborough LE11....75 A7
  Measham DE12........93 C3
  Ratcliffe Culey CV9..171 A3
  Sibson CV9, CV13....172 A3
Atkin Ct LE7.........127 E6
Atkinson Rd LE65.....68 F7
Atkinson St LE5......155 D6
Atkins St LE2........259 B2
Atkins Way LE10......215 E7
Atlas Cl LE2.........155 B5
Atlas Ct LE2.........71 D2
Atlas Rd LE67........71 D2
Attenborough Cl
  Braunstone Town LE3..153 C1
  Wigston LE18........180 E4
ATTERTON............172 A1
Atterton La CV9, CV13..171 E1
Atterbury Cl LE12....76 D7
Attewell Cl DE72.....9 B7
Attfield Dr LE3......201 F7
Attingham Cl LE4.....129 D1
Attlebridge Cl LE5...130 B2
Attlee Cl LE17.......244 B5
Attlee Way LE2.......179 E5
Auburn Ho
  Blaby LE8...........202 A8
  Leicester LE3.......154 A7
Auburn Rd LE8........202 B8
Auden Cl LE4.........128 B2
Audens Way DE11......44 C6
Audit Hall Rd LE15...140 F5
Audley Cl LE16.......241 B2
Audley End LE3.......154 B1
Augusta Cl LE3.......153 C6
Augustus Cl LE7......102 F4
Ault Dene DE11.......44 A4
Aulton Cres LE10.....197 B1
Aulton Way LE10......197 B1
Aumberry Gap LE11....52 B4
Auriga St LE3........240 F2
Austen Ave NG10......10 C5
Auster Ind Est LE4...129 F6
Austhorp Gr LE15.....112 B7
Austin Friar's La PE9..143 D2
Austin Rise LE5......156 D8
Austins Cl LE16......240 D3
Austin St PE9........143 D2
AUSTREY.............119 B2
Austrey CE Prim Sch
  CV9................119 B2
Austrey La
  Countesthorpe LE8...202 F3
  Newton Regis B79....118 E3
  No Man's Heath B79..119 A5
  Orton-on-t-H CV9....145 C6
Austrey Rd DE12......119 D5
Austwick Cl LE4......128 C3
Autumn Rd LE2........179 C3
Avalon Way LE7......127 E5
Avebury Ave LE4......128 C1
Aveland Rd PE9.......167 F5
Avenue Cl LE7........103 E5
Avenue Gdns LE2.....155 C1
Avenue N LE2.........199 A8
Avenue Prim Sch LE2..155 B1
Avenue Rd
  Ashby-de-la-Z LE65..69 A5
  Coalville LE67......96 D8
  Leicester LE2.......155 C1
  Queniborough LE7....103 E5
  Sileby LE12.........77 D3
Avenue Road Extension
  ....155 B1
Avenue S LE9.........199 A8
Avenue The
  Blaby LE8...........202 A8
  Broughton Astley LE9..218 E7
  Carlby PE9..........117 C8
  Glenfield LE3.......127 B1
  Leicester LE3.......155 C2
  Leicester, Oadby LE2..182 A4
  Medbourne LE16.....228 C8
  Noseley LE7.........184 F3
Averham Cl DE11......44 A3
Averil Rd LE5........156 B7

Avery Cl LE17 . . . . **244** B5
Avery Dr
  Markfield LE67 . . . . **98** D1
  Syston LE7 . . . . **103** B5
Avery Hill LE3 . . . . **153** D4
Avington Cl LE3 . . . . **128** A2
Avoca Cl LE5 . . . . **156** B6
Avocet Cl
  Essendine PE9 . . . . **117** A6
  Rugby CV23 . . . . **252** C1
Avon Cl
  Leicester, Oadby LE2 . . . . **181** C5
  Oakham LE15 . . . . **137** F5
  Swadlincote DE11 . . . . . . **44** B6
Avondale Cl NG10 . . . . **10** A6
Avondale Rd
  Barlestone CV13 . . . . . . **149** D8
  Wigston LE18 . . . . **180** D4
Avon Dr LE8 . . . . **201** F7
Avon Fields NN6 . . . . **256** E6
Avon Rd
  Barrow-u-S LE12 . . . . **76** D6
  Leicester LE3 . . . . **153** E2
  Melton Mowbray LE13 . . . **59** B1
Avonside Dr LE5 . . . . **155** F5
Avon St LE2 . . . . **155** B4
Avon Vale Rd LE11 . . . . . . **52** C1
Avon Wlk LE10 . . . . **215** A8
Axbridge Cl LE4 . . . . **128** D1
Axiom Ct PE9 . . . . **143** F2
AYLESTONE **179** D6
Aylestone Dr LE2 . . . . **179** D5
Aylestone La LE18 . . . . . . **180** B3
AYLESTONE PARK **179** E7
Aylestone Rd LE2 . . . . **179** D7
Aylestone Wlk LE2 . . . . . . **154** F3
Aylmer Rd LE3 . . . . **153** F4
Ayr Cl PE9 . . . . **143** A4
Ayrshire Cl LE9 . . . . **198** A6
Aysgarth Cl CV11 . . . . **214** A2
Aysgarth Rd LE8 . . . . **128** C3
AYSTON **189** A7
Ayston Rd
  Leicester LE3 . . . . **154** A1
  Uppingham LE15 . . . . . . **189** B5
Azad Ho **13** LE2 . . . . **155** B5
Azalea Cl
  Hinckley LE10 . . . . **215** E5
  Lutterworth LE17 . . . . . . **244** A5
Azalea Dr LE10 . . . . **215** E6
Azalea Wlk LE10 . . . . **215** E5

B

Babelake St LE65 . . . . **94** B8
Babingley Dr LE4 . . . . **128** D2
Babington Com Tech Coll
  LE4 . . . . **128** B3
Babington Ct LE7 . . . . **101** E6
Babington Rd
  Barrow-u-S LE12 . . . . **76** E8
  Rothley LE7 . . . . **101** E6
Babington Row LE2 . . . . . **180** A5
Back Dr LE7 . . . . **185** A2
Back La
  Allington NG32 . . . . **4** F5
  Belton-in-R LE15 . . . . . . **187** D7
  Burton Overy LE8 . . . . . . **182** F1
  Castle Donington DE74 . . . **17** A6
  Claybrooke Magna
    LE17 . . . . **232** E6
  Collyweston PE8 . . . . **168** D2
  Cossington LE7 . . . . **102** D7
  Cotes LE12 . . . . **52** F6
  East Farndon LE16 . . . . . **250** B7
  East Langton LE16 . . . . . **225** D6
  Gaulby LE7 . . . . **183** C6
  Harston NG32 . . . . **15** B4
  Hoby LE14 . . . . **79** E7
  Leire LE17 . . . . **218** E1
  Long Clawson LE14 . . . . . **20** C3
  Market Bosworth CV13 . . **148** E3
  Morcott LE15 . . . . **191** A6
  Sewstern NG33 . . . . **63** F8
  Shearsby LE17 . . . . **222** A2
  Sileby LE12 . . . . **77** C3
  Skillington NG33 . . . . **43** B8
  South Luffenham LE15 . . **191** D8
  Stamford PE9 . . . . **143** E3
  Stonesby LE14 . . . . **40** E6
  Thrussington LE7 . . . . . . **78** F4
  Willoughby-on-t-W LE12 . . **34** D7
Back Rd
  Barrowden LE15 . . . . **191** E5
  Tilton on t H LE7 . . . . . . **160** A7
Back St
  Buckminster NG33 . . . . . . **42** D2
  North Kilworth LE17 . . . . **246** F3
  Saltby LE14 . . . . **24** E1
Backway The LE16 . . . . . . **240** F2
Badcock Way LE8 . . . . . . **223** A6
Baddeley Dr LE18 . . . . . . **180** B4
Baden Rd LE5 . . . . **155** C8
Badgerbrook Prim Sch
  LE8 . . . . **201** F5
Badger Cl
  Fleckney LE8 . . . . **223** A6
  Narborough LE19 . . . . . . **201** A7
Badger Ct LE11 . . . . **74** D8
Badger Dr LE8 . . . . **201** F5
Badgers Bank LE7 . . . . . . **101** E7
Badgers Cl
  Leicester LE4 . . . . **128** B3
  Manton LE15 . . . . **164** D5

Badger's Cnr LE7 . . . . . . **103** D8
Badgers Croft LE67 . . . . . **71** D7
Badgers Holt LE2 . . . . . . **181** A4
Badgers Wlk LE12 . . . . . . **75** E5
Badmington Rd LE4 . . . . **129** D5
Badminton Rd
  Leicester LE4 . . . . **129** D5
  Syston LE7 . . . . **103** B5
Baggrave End LE7 . . . . . . **105** D3
Baggrave Rd LE7 . . . . **132** B4
Baggrave St LE5 . . . . **155** D6
Bagley Cl LE11 . . . . **51** C6
BAGWORTH **124** B5
Bagworth Heath Nature
Reserve ★ LE67 . . . . **124** D3
Bagworth La LE67 . . . . . . **124** D5
Bagworth Rd
  Barlestone CV13 . . . . . . **123** E2
  Barlestone CV13 . . . . . . **123** E3
  Nailstone CV13 . . . . **123** C3
  Newbold Verdon LE9 . . . **150** B7
Bailey Ave LE12 . . . . **67** A3
Bailey Cl LE11 . . . . **74** D8
Baileys Croft LE12 . . . . . **34** C7
Baileys La LE8 . . . . **182** F1
Bainbridge Rd
  Leicester LE3 . . . . **154** B1
  Loughborough LE11 . . . . **52** C1
  Wigston LE18 . . . . **180** E1
Bain Cl PE9 . . . . **143** E5
Baines La
  Braunstone Town LE3 . . **153** B3
  Seaton LE15 . . . . **190** C1
Baines' La **6** LE10 . . . . . **197** D1
Bakehouse La LE8 . . . . . . **223** B4
Baker Ave LE65 . . . . **68** F5
Bakers La LE14 . . . . **106** F4
Baker's La NG13 . . . . **6** F4
Baker St
  Coalville LE67 . . . . **71** C2
  Lutterworth LE17 . . . . . . **244** C5
  Swadlincote DE11 . . . . . . **44** C3
Bakers Way LE5 . . . . **130** D3
Bakery Cl LE9 . . . . **201** D2
Bakery Ct **7** LE65 . . . . . . **69** B6
Bakewell Rd
  Long Eaton NG10 . . . . . . **10** E5
  Loughborough LE11 . . . . **51** F7
  Wigston LE18 . . . . **180** C4
Bakewells La LE67 . . . . . . **70** F8
Bakewell St
  Coalville LE67 . . . . **71** E1
  Leicester LE2 . . . . **155** C6
Bala Rd LE9 . . . . **200** D4
Balcombe Ave LE3 . . . . . **154** B6
Balderstone Cl LE5 . . . . . **156** A6
Baldock's La LE13 . . . . . . **59** D2
Baldwin Ave LE18 . . . . . . **180** A1
Baldwin Rd LE2 . . . . **180** B5
Baldwin Rise LE9 . . . . . . **218** D7
Bale Rd LE4 . . . . **129** E1
Balfour Cl LE10 . . . . **215** E7
Balfour Gdns LE16 . . . . . **240** D1
Balfour St LE3 . . . . **154** D7
Balisfire Gr LE4 . . . . **128** B3
Balk Rd PE9 . . . . **116** E2
Balk The LE3 . . . . **127** B1
Balladine Rd LE7 . . . . . . **127** E7
Ballards Cl LE4 . . . . **128** B3
Ballater Cl LE5 . . . . **156** D3
Balliol Ave LE7 . . . . **103** C2
Balliol Rd LE10 . . . . **215** F6
Balmoral Ave
  Leicester LE2 . . . . **180** C7
  Market Harborough
    LE16 . . . . **241** B2
Balmoral Ct DE74 . . . . . . **17** D5
Balmoral Dr LE3 . . . . **153** E2
Balmoral Rd
  Coalville LE67 . . . . **97** A8
  Earl Shilton LE9 . . . . **198** D7
  Melton Mowbray LE13 . . . **59** C5
  Mountsorrel LE12 . . . . . . **101** D8
  Oakham LE15 . . . . **137** E5
Baltimore Cl **8** DE11 . . . . **44** A7
Bambrook Cl LE9 . . . . . . **151** C3
Bamburgh Cl
  Ashby-de-la-Z LE65 . . . . . **69** B5
  Market Harborough
    LE16 . . . . **241** B3
Bambury La
  Countesthorpe LE8 . . . . **202** D1
  Peatling Magna LE8 . . . . **221** A6
Bambury Way LE2 . . . . . . **180** A6
Bampton Cl LE18 . . . . . . **203** D8
Bampton St LE11 . . . . . . **52** B3
Banbury Dr
  Melton Mowbray LE13 . . . **82** D8
  Shepshed LE12 . . . . **49** F3
Banbury La LE16 . . . . **229** D6
Bancroft Rd LE9 . . . . **229** D1
Bandalls La LE12 . . . . **53** D5
Banff Cl LE15 . . . . **138** B6
Bankart Ave LE2 . . . . **155** E1
Bank Cotts LE16 . . . . **248** C8
Bankfield Dr LE16 . . . . . . **241** A5
Banks Cl LE12 . . . . **77** C3
Bankside LE5 . . . . **156** E8
Banks Rd LE2 . . . . **179** D7
Bank St
  Long Eaton NG10 . . . . . . **10** E7
  Lutterworth LE17 . . . . . . **244** C5
  Swadlincote DE11 . . . . . . **67** A8

Banks The
  Barrow-u-S LE12 . . . . **76** E8
  Cosby LE9 . . . . **201** D2
  Leicester LE4 . . . . **128** E1
  Queniborough LE7 . . . . . **103** F5
  Seagrave LE12 . . . . **77** F8
  Sileby LE12 . . . . **77** C3
Bank Terr LE9 . . . . **198** A6
Bank The
  Arnesby LE8 . . . . **221** F5
  Countesthorpe LE8 . . . . **202** F4
  Kibworth Beauchamp
    LE8 . . . . **224** A8
  Shearsby LE17 . . . . **222** A2
Banky Mdw LE10 . . . . . . **216** A7
Bannerman Rd LE5 . . . . . **155** E3
Bannister Rd **2** LE3 . . . . **178** F6
Bantlam La LE19 . . . . **178** B3
Baptist Mews The
  LE8 . . . . **179** C1
Baptist Wlk LE10 . . . . . . **197** D1
Barbara Ave
  Leicester Forest East
    LE9 . . . . **152** E3
  Leicester LE5 . . . . **156** B7
  Newbold Verdon LE9 . . . **150** B3
Barbara Cl LE19 . . . . **178** A3
Barbara Rd LE3 . . . . **154** B1
Barclay St LE3 . . . . **154** C4
Barden Cl LE11 . . . . **51** B3
Bardolph St E LE4 . . . . . **155** C8
Bardolph St LE4 . . . . **155** B8
BARDON **97** C6
Bardon 22 Ind Pk LE67 . . **97** B4
Bardon Cl
  Coalville LE67 . . . . **97** A7
  Leicester LE3 . . . . **127** F3
Bardon Rd
  Barwell LE9 . . . . **198** B8
  Coalville LE67 . . . . **97** A7
Bardsey Cl LE10 . . . . **197** B1
Bardsley Rd NN17 . . . . . . **230** E3
Barfoot Cl LE18 . . . . **204** E1
Barfoot Rd LE2 . . . . **179** F5
Barford Cl LE18 . . . . **203** C8
Barge Cl LE18 . . . . **180** A1
BARKBY **130** C6
Barkby Holt La LE7 . . . . . **130** F8
Barkby La LE7 . . . . **103** A1
Barkby Rd
  Beeby LE7 . . . . **131** B5
  Leicester LE4 . . . . **129** C3
  Queniborough LE7 . . . . . **103** E4
  Syston LE7 . . . . **103** C3
BARKBY THORPE **130** C7
Barkby Thorpe La
  LE4 . . . . **130** B8
Barkbythorpe Rd LE4,
  LE7 . . . . **130** B5
Barker Cres LE13 . . . . . . **82** C8
Barkers Field LE14 . . . . . **20** C3
Barker St LE5 . . . . **155** D7
Barkestone La NG13 . . . . . **6** E6
BARKESTONE-LE-VALE **6** C2
Barkford Cl LE7 . . . . **130** E1
Barklam Cl LE12 . . . . **67** E1
Barleston Dr LE10 . . . . . . **197** A1
BARLESTONE **149** E8
Barlestone CE Prim Sch
  CV13 . . . . **149** C8
Barlestone Rd
  Bagworth LE67, CV13 . . . **124** A4
  Newbold Verdon LE9 . . . **150** A6
Barley Cl LE3 . . . . **153** C7
Barley Croft Prim Sch
  LE4 . . . . **128** C3
Barleyfield LE10 . . . . **197** B1
Barley La LE8 . . . . **221** C8
Barley Leas LE7 . . . . **132** B2
Barleyman Cl LE5 . . . . . . **130** C3
BARLEYTHORPE **137** D8
Barleythorpe Rd LE15 . . **137** F7
Barley Way LE7 . . . . **101** E2
Barling Rd LE5 . . . . **155** F8
Barlow Rd LE15 . . . . **137** F6
Barmouth Ave LE2 . . . . . **180** A6
Barmstedt Dr LE15 . . . . . **138** A8
Barnabas Rd LE5 . . . . . . **155** E7
Barnack Rd PE9 . . . . **143** F2
Barnard Cl
  Burton Lazars LE14 . . . . . **83** A7
  Leicester LE2 . . . . **155** B5
Barnard Gdns LE16 . . . . **250** D8
Barnards Dr LE12 . . . . . . **77** E4
Barnard Way LE12 . . . . . . **76** D1
Barnby Ave LE18 . . . . . . **180** C4
Barn End
  Empingham LE15 . . . . . . **140** F6
  Skillington NG33 . . . . **43** B8
Barnes Cl
  Kibworth Beauchamp
    LE8 . . . . **223** F8
  Leicester LE4 . . . . **129** E5
Barnes Heath Rd LE5 . . . **156** A5
Barnet Cl LE2 . . . . **181** A3
Barnett Cl LE7 . . . . **102** D7
Barnett Janner Ho
  LE4 . . . . **128** C4
Barnfield Cl
  Great Glen LE8 . . . . **182** B1
  Long Whatton LE12 . . . . . **29** B4
Barngate Cl
  Birstall LE4 . . . . **128** F8

Barngate Cl continued
  Melton Mowbray LE13 . . . **59** D5
Barn Hill PE9 . . . . **143** D3
Barnley Cl LE8 . . . . **202** E4
Barns Cl LE15 . . . . **152** C5
Barnsdale
  Barnsdale LE16 . . . . **229** D6
  Barnsdale Ave LE15 . . . . **112** E1
Barnsdale Cl
  Great Easton LE16 . . . . . **229** D6
  Loughborough LE11 . . . . **52** A5
Barnsdale Gdns ★
  LE15 . . . . **112** E2
Barnsdale Rd LE4 . . . . . . **127** F5
Barnsdale Way LE19 . . . . **178** D5
Barnstaple Cl LE18 . . . . . **203** D8
Barnstaple Rd LE5 . . . . . **156** D3
Barnstone La NG13 . . . . . . **5** A5
Barns Way LE9 . . . . **151** C4
Barn Way LE67 . . . . **125** E8
Barnwell Ave LE4 . . . . . . **128** F4
Barnwell Rd PE9 . . . . **143** A4
Baronet Way LE5 . . . . . . **130** E1
Barons Cl LE3 . . . . **152** C5
Baron St LE1 . . . . **259** C3
Barons Way LE12 . . . . **76** E3
Baron's Way PE9 . . . . **143** E2
Barrack Row LE11 . . . . . . **52** B3
Barracks The **3** LE9 . . . . **198** A6
Barradale Ave LE12 . . . . . **77** C4
Barratt Cl LE2 . . . . **155** D2
Barr Cres LE67 . . . . **71** F4
Barrett Dr LE11 . . . . **51** D6
Barrie Rd LE10 . . . . **197** D3
Barrington Ct LE12 . . . . . **30** B6
Barrington Park Ind Est
  LE4 . . . . **128** B5
Barrington Rd LE2 . . . . . **155** E1
Barr La LE12 . . . . **196** B3
Barroon DE74 . . . . **17** B3
BARROW **87** A3
Barrowcliffe Cl LE12 . . . . **76** C8
Barrow Cres LE7 . . . . **105** B7
BARROWDEN **191** F5
Barrowden La LE15 . . . . . **191** E8
Barrowden Rd
  Ketton PE9 . . . . **167** E2
  South Luffenham LE15 . . **191** F7
Barrow-on-Soar Sta
  LE12 . . . . **76** D7
Barrow Rd
  Burton o t W LE12 . . . . . **53** F6
  Cotes LE12 . . . . **52** F6
  Quorn (Quorndon) LE12 . . **76** A7
  Sileby LE12 . . . . **77** B4
Barrow St LE11 . . . . **52** B3
BARROW-UPON-SOAR
  . . . . **76** E7
Barry Cl LE9 . . . . **152** E3
Barry Dr
  Leicester Forest East
    LE9 . . . . **152** E3
  Syston LE7 . . . . **103** C4
Barry Rd LE5 . . . . **130** D1
Barrys Cl DE11 . . . . **44** E1
BARSBY **105** E3
Barsby Dr LE11 . . . . **51** D6
Barsby Wlk LE4 . . . . **128** D4
Barshaw Pk LE4 . . . . **128** C5
Barston St LE1 . . . . **259** B5
Bartholomew St LE2 . . . . **155** C4
Bartles Hollow PE9 . . . . . **167** F5
Barton Cl
  Ratby LE6 . . . . **152** D7
  Wigston LE18 . . . . **180** C1
BARTON IN THE BEANS
  . . . . **122** D1
Barton La
  Congerstone CV13 . . . . . **121** F1
  Nailstone CV13 . . . . **122** F2
Barton Rd
  Barton in t B CV13 . . . . . **148** E8
  Carlton CV13 . . . . **148** E6
  Congerstone CV13 . . . . . **147** D8
  Leicester LE3 . . . . **154** C8
  Odstone CV13 . . . . **122** D4
  Osbaston CV13 . . . . **149** C8
BARWELL **175** B1
Barwell CE Jun Sch
  LE9 . . . . **198** A6
Barwell Ho LE10 . . . . **215** D7
Barwell Inf Sch LE9 . . . . **198** A7
Barwell La
  Barwell LE9 . . . . **198** A5
  Hinckley LE10 . . . . **197** E3
  Kirkby Mallory LE9 . . . . . **175** C4
Barwell Newlands Com
Prim Sch LE9 . . . . **198** C8
Barwell Rd
  Kirby Muxloe LE9 . . . . . **152** D2
  Kirkby Mallory LE9 . . . . . **175** D5
Basin Bridge La CV13 . . . **196** C4
Baslow Cl NG10 . . . . **10** A5
Baslow Rd LE5 . . . . **155** D4
Bassett Ave LE8 . . . . **202** E3
Bassett La LE9 . . . . **217** D7
Bassett St
  Leicester LE3 . . . . **154** D7
  Wigston LE18 . . . . **179** F1
Batchelor Rd LE8 . . . . . . **222** F8
Bateman Rd LE3 . . . . **154** B7
Bates Cl
  Loughborough LE11 . . . . **51** B6
  Market Harborough
    LE16 . . . . **240** E5
Bath Cl LE9 . . . . **217** D1
Bath La
  Bruntingthorpe LE17 . . . . **236** D7

Bath La continued
  Leicester LE3 . . . . **259** A3
  Moira DE12 . . . . **67** D4
Bath Row PE9 . . . . **143** D2
Bath St
  Ashby-de-la-Z LE65 . . . . . **69** B6
  Leicester LE4 . . . . **129** B4
  Market Harborough
    LE16 . . . . **240** E1
  Syston LE7 . . . . **103** A4
Bath Street Cnr 9
  LE65 . . . . **69** B6
Bathurst Rd LE5 . . . . **156** D4
Batsons Ct LE67 . . . . **48** A2
Battenberg Rd LE3 . . . . . **154** D6
Batten St LE2 . . . . **154** E1
Battersbee Way LE3 . . . . **153** E8
Battersbee Rd LE3 . . . . . **153** E8
Battersbee Wlk LE3 . . . . **153** E8
Battledown Cl LE10 . . . . **197** B2
Battlefield Line Mus The ★
  CV13 . . . . **121** F1
Battlefield Line The ★
  Market Bosworth
    CV13 . . . . **148** C5
  Shackerstone CV13 . . . . **121** F1
Battleflat Dr LE67 . . . . . . **96** E3
Battling Brook Com Prim
Sch LE10 . . . . **197** B2
Battling Brook Sh Ctr
  LE10 . . . . **197** B1
BATTRAM **123** D8
Battram Rd LE67 . . . . **123** D8
Baulk Rd LE15 . . . . **189** E4
Baxter Gate LE11 . . . . . . **52** B4
Baxters Cl LE4 . . . . **128** B3
Bayberry Gdns LE2 . . . . . **179** E4
Baycliff Cl LE3 . . . . **154** B8
Bayham Cl LE5 . . . . **156** B5
Bayley Cl LE15 . . . . **188** F4
Bayleys Cl LE15 . . . . **141** A6
Bayliss Cl LE12 . . . . **75** F7
Baysdale LE18 . . . . **180** F2
Baysdale Rd LE2 . . . . **259** A2
Bay St LE1 . . . . **259** B5
Bayswater Dr LE2 . . . . . . **179** D1
Bayswater Rd LE13 . . . . . **59** D4
Beacon Ave
  Loughborough LE11 . . . . **51** F1
  Quorn (Quorndon) LE12 . . **75** E5
  Thurmaston LE4 . . . . **129** F7
Beacon Cl
  Groby LE6 . . . . **126** F2
  Leicester LE4 . . . . **128** A4
  Markfield LE67 . . . . **98** E1
Beacon Cres LE67 . . . . . . **97** B8
Beacon Ct LE3 . . . . **127** D1
Beacon Dr LE11 . . . . **52** A1
Beacon Hill Ctry Pk The ★
  LE12 . . . . **74** D7
Beacon Rd
  Loughborough LE11 . . . . **52** A1
  Woodhouse Eaves LE12 . . **74** D1
Beaconsfield Rd
  Leicester LE3 . . . . **154** C4
  Melton Mowbray LE13 . . . **59** A5
Beaconsfield St NG10 . . . **10** E7
Beacon View
  Bagworth LE67 . . . . **124** A7
  Bottesford NG13 . . . . **3** B3
Beadmans Cnr LE67 . . . . **70** F1
Beadswell La LE8 . . . . . . **205** F8
Beaker Cl LE8 . . . . **223** F6
Beale's Cl LE9 . . . . **174** E2
Beal St LE2 . . . . **155** B6
Beamont Cl LE17 . . . . . . **244** C8
Beams Mdw LE10 . . . . . . **214** F6
Beardsley Rd LE12 . . . . . **75** F6
Beards Rd DE11 . . . . **44** A6
Bearsdon Cres LE10 . . . . **197** B3
Beast Hill LE15 . . . . **189** B4
Beatrice Rd LE3 . . . . **154** C7
Beattie Cl LE10 . . . . **197** D3
Beatty Ave LE5 . . . . **155** E7
Beatty Rd
  Leicester LE5 . . . . **155** E7
  Syston LE7 . . . . **103** B5
Beauchamp Coll The
  LE2 . . . . **181** B3
Beauchamp Gdns
  LE8 . . . . **224** A7
Beauchamp Rd LE8 . . . . . **223** F8
Beaufort Ave LE11 . . . . . . **75** A8
Beaufort Cl
  Desford LE9 . . . . **151** B2
  Hinckley LE10 . . . . **215** C4
  Leicester, Oadby LE2 . . . . **181** D4
Beaufort Rd
  Cottesmore LE15 . . . . . . **87** D2
  Leicester LE3 . . . . **154** A1
Beaufort Way LE2 . . . . . . **181** D4
Beaumanor Ct LE4 . . . . . **128** F3
Beaumanor Dr LE12 . . . . **75** C4
Beaumanor Gdns LE12 . . **75** C4
Beaumanor Rd LE4 . . . . . **128** F3
Beaumaris Cres LE12 . . . **50** A2
Beaumaris Rd LE12 . . . . **101** C8
Beaumont Ave
  Ashby-de-la-Z LE65 . . . . . **68** F5
  Hinckley LE10 . . . . **215** A7
Beaumont Ct LE11 . . . . . **52** A6
Beaumont Gdns LE13 . . . **59** D5
Beaumont Gn
  Coleorton LE67 . . . . **70** E8
  Groby LE6 . . . . **126** F2
Beaumont Hall LE2 . . . . . **180** F8
BEAUMONT LEYS **128** C3

Beaumont Leys Cl
LE4 . . . 128 D3
Beaumont Leys La
LE4 . . . 128 C4
Beaumont Leys Sch
LE4 . . . 128 B2
Beaumont Leys Terr
LE4 . . . 128 A3
Beaumont Lodge Prim Sch
LE4 . . . 128 B6
Beaumont Lodge Rd
LE4 . . . 128 B6
Beaumont Rd
Barrow-u-S LE12 . . . 76 C8
Leicester LE5 . . . 155 C6
Loughborough LE11 . . . 75 B8
Whitwick LE67 . . . 72 A4
Beaumont St LE2 . . . 181 A6
Beaumont Way LE4 . . . 128 B4
Beaumont Wlk LE4 . . . 128 A3
Beauville Dr LE4 . . . 128 A3
Beaver Cl LE8 . . . 201 F5
Beaver Ctr The LE2 . . . 154 F2
Beazer Ct LE11 . . . 51 F6
Beck Cl LE2 . . . 179 A3
Beckett Ave CV13 . . . 148 E2
Beckett Rd LE5 . . . 155 E8
Beckingham Rd LE2 . . . 155 C3
BECKINGTHORPE . . . 3 A3
Beckingthorpe Dr NG13 . . . 3 C3
Beckmill Ct LE13 . . . 59 D3
Beckmill La LE13 . . . 59 D3
Beckworth Ct LE15 . . . 141 A6
Beckworth Gr LE15 . . . 141 A6
Bedale Ave LE10 . . . 197 F2
Bedale Cl LE67 . . . 96 C8
Bedale Dr LE4 . . . 128 C5
Bedale St LE15 . . . 87 E2
Bede Ho* LE15 . . . 212 D7
Bede Island Rd LE2 . . . 259 A2
Bede St LE3 . . . 154 D5
Bedford Cl
Desford LE9 . . . 151 B3
Hinckley LE10 . . . 197 E3
Kegworth DE74 . . . 18 D1
Bedford Dr LE6 . . . 126 F2
Bedford Rd LE18 . . . 180 A3
Bedford St N LE1 . . . 259 C5
Bedford St S LE1 . . . 259 B4
Bedford Sq LE11 . . . 52 B3
Bedford St LE11 . . . 52 B3
BEEBY . . . 131 C5
Beeby Cl LE7 . . . 103 C3
Beeby Rd
Barkby LE7 . . . 130 E7
Leicester LE5 . . . 155 D6
Scraptoft LE7 . . . 131 A1
Beech Ave
Breaston DE72 . . . 9 F8
East Leake LE12 . . . 31 D8
Groby LE6 . . . 126 E1
Lutterworth LE17 . . . 244 A6
Melbourne DE73 . . . 26 B8
Ravenstone LE67 . . . 95 E8
Beech Cl
Corby NN17 . . . 230 E1
Markfield LE67 . . . 125 E8
Shepshed LE12 . . . 50 C4
Beechcroft Ave LE3 . . . 179 A8
Beechcroft Rd LE2 . . . 155 C1
Beech Ct LE18 . . . 180 C3
Beech Dr
Blackfordby DE11 . . . 45 B2
Bottesford NG13 . . . 3 C2
Braunstone Town LE3 . . . 153 D3
Ryhall PE9 . . . 116 E1
Syston LE7 . . . 103 B2
Thornton LE67 . . . 124 E4
Beeches Ave LE12 . . . 76 E2
Beeches Cl LE16 . . . 248 F2
Beeches Farm LE8 . . . 202 A4
Beeches Rd LE11 . . . 52 C3
Beeches The
Earl Shilton LE9 . . . 175 F1
Hartshill Green CV10 . . . 194 B2
Leicester, Clarendon Park
LE2 . . . 155 B2
Leicester, Humberstone
Garden LE5 . . . 130 A1
Uppingham LE15 . . . 189 B5
Beechfield Ave LE4 . . . 129 A7
Beechfield Cl LE8 . . . 182 B1
Beech Gr PE9 . . . 142 F4
Beechings Cl LE8 . . . 202 D3
Beech Rd
Blaby LE8 . . . 202 B7
Leicester, Oadby LE2 . . . 181 A5
Oakham LE15 . . . 138 B7
Beech St LE5 . . . 155 C7
Beech Tree Cl LE8 . . . 206 A2
Beech Tree Rd LE67 . . . 97 A8
Beech Way
Ashby-de-la-Z LE65 . . . 69 D6
Desford LE9 . . . 151 A3
Ibstock LE67 . . . 95 E2
Beech Wlk LE67 . . . 125 E8
Beechwood Ave
Hinckley LE10 . . . 215 D3
Leicester Forest East
LE3 . . . 153 A4
Melton Mowbray LE13 . . . 59 E5
Queniborough LE7 . . . 103 D5
Thurmaston LE4 . . . 129 E6
Beechwood Cl LE5 . . . 156 C5
Beechwood Rd LE19 . . . 201 B6
Beehive Ave DE12 . . . 68 A4
Beehive La LE11 . . . 52 B3
Bee Hives The DE11 . . . 44 A7
Beggar's La
Enderby LE19 . . . 177 F7
Leicester Forest East
LE3 . . . 152 E1
Beggars Roost LE8 . . . 205 B7
Begonia Cl
Hinckley LE10 . . . 215 E5
Leicester Forest East
LE3 . . . 152 F2
Begonia Dr LE10 . . . 215 E5
Belcher Cl LE67 . . . 95 B2
BELCHER'S BAR . . . 122 F6
Belcher's Hill LE16 . . . 210 D6
Beler Way LE13 . . . 81 F8
Belfield Gdns NG10 . . . 10 E7
Belfield Rd DE11 . . . 44 B5
Belfry Cl LE10 . . . 215 D4
Belfry Dr LE3 . . . 153 D5
BELGRAVE . . . 129 A2
Belgrave Ave LE4 . . . 129 A3
Belgrave Bvd
Leicester LE4 . . . 128 D5
Leicester LE4 . . . 128 E4
Belgrave Circ LE1 . . . 155 A8
Belgrave Cl LE67 . . . 72 D1
Belgrave Ct 3 LE5 . . . 130 C3
Belgrave Flyover LE1,
LE4 . . . 155 A8
Belgrave Gate
Leicester LE1 . . . 155 A7
Leicester LE1 . . . 259 B5
Belgrave Hall (Mus)*
LE4 . . . 129 A3
Belgrave Ind Ctr LE4 . . . 129 A1
Belgrave Rd
Leicester LE4 . . . 155 A8
Uppingham LE15 . . . 189 A5
Belgrave St Peter's CE
Prim Sch LE4 . . . 128 F3
Bellamy Cl LE2 . . . 179 A3
Bell Ave DE72 . . . 16 A7
Bell Cl
Broughton Astley LE9 . . . 219 A4
Ratby LE6 . . . 152 D8
Stanton u B LE67 . . . 97 F2
Bell Cotts PE9 . . . 143 E3
Bell Ctr The LE13 . . . 59 C3
Belleville Dr LE2 . . . 181 C6
Belle Vue Ave LE4 . . . 128 E2
Belle Vue Rd LE9 . . . 198 C7
Bellfield LE15 . . . 191 E8
Bellfields La LE16 . . . 241 A2
Bellfields St LE16 . . . 241 A2
Bellflower Rd LE5 . . . 130 B3
Bellholme Cl LE4 . . . 129 B3
Bell La
Burton Overy LE8 . . . 205 F8
Hartshorne DE11 . . . 45 A3
Husbands Bosworth
LE17 . . . 247 E5
Leicester LE1 . . . 155 B6
Narborough LE19 . . . 201 C7
Bells La LE9 . . . 150 A4
Bell St
Claybrooke Magna
LE17 . . . 232 E6
Lutterworth LE17 . . . 244 D5
Wigston LE18 . . . 180 D3
Bell View LE19 . . . 201 C8
BELMESTHORPE . . . 117 B1
Belmesthorpe La PE9 . . . 117 A2
Belmont Ave DE72 . . . 9 E8
Belmont Dr LE67 . . . 71 A2
Belmont Prim Sch
DE11 . . . 44 C4
Belmont St
Leicester LE2 . . . 179 D7
Swadlincote DE11 . . . 44 C4
Belmont Way LE11 . . . 51 A2
Belper Cl
Leicester, Oadby LE2 . . . 181 A3
Wigston LE18 . . . 203 A8
Belper St LE4 . . . 129 B1
BELTON . . . 49 A6
Belton CE Prim Sch
LE12 . . . 49 B6
Belton Cl
Coalville LE67 . . . 72 C1
Leicester LE2 . . . 179 F5
Belton Gdns 14 PE9 . . . 143 E3
BELTON-IN-RUTLAND
. . . 187 D7
Belton Mews LE15 . . . 187 D7
BELTON PARK . . . 52 A6
Belton Rd
Leicester LE3 . . . 154 A1
Loddington LE7 . . . 161 F1
Loughborough LE11 . . . 52 A5
Belton Rd W LE11 . . . 51 F6
Belton Rd W Extension
LE11 . . . 52 A6
Belton St
Shepshed LE12 . . . 50 B4
Stamford PE9 . . . 143 E3
Belt The LE17 . . . 246 D1
Belvedere Rd DE11 . . . 44 F2
BELVOIR . . . 14 E8
Belvoir Ave
Ab Kettleby LE14 . . . 37 C2
Bottesford NG13 . . . 3 A1
Belvoir Castle (restored)*
NG32 . . . 14 D8
Belvoir Cl
Breaston DE72 . . . 9 D7
Desford LE9 . . . 151 B3
Leicester, Oadby LE2 . . . 181 C4
Long Eaton NG10 . . . 10 E5
Mountsorrel LE12 . . . 101 D8
Belvoir Cl *continued*
Stamford PE9 . . . 143 A4
Belvoir Cres DE11 . . . 44 A6
Belvoirdale Com Prim Sch
LE67 . . . 96 D8
Belvoir Dr
Ashby-de-la-Z LE65 . . . 69 B5
Leicester LE2 . . . 179 D6
Loughborough LE11 . . . 74 F7
Syston LE7 . . . 103 C4
Belvoir Dr E LE2 . . . 179 D6
Belvoir High Sch NG13 . . . 3 A1
Belvoir La NG32 . . . 8 B1
Belvoir Rd
Bottesford NG13 . . . 7 B7
Coalville LE67 . . . 96 C8
Eaton NG32 . . . 13 E2
Redmile NG13 . . . 7 A3
Woolsthorpe by B NG32 . . . 15 E7
Belvoir Sh Ctr The
LE67 . . . 71 C1
Belvoir Sq LE15 . . . 87 F3
Belvoir St
Leicester LE1 . . . 259 B3
Melton Mowbray LE13 . . . 59 E4
Belvoir Way LE12 . . . 50 A2
Beman Cl LE4 . . . 129 E5
Bembridge Cl LE3 . . . 154 D8
Bembridge Rd LE3 . . . 154 D8
Benbow Ave DE73 . . . 26 A8
Benbow Cl LE10 . . . 197 D4
Benches Furlong
CV23 . . . 252 D1
Bencroft Cl LE7 . . . 127 D6
Bendbow Rise LE3 . . . 153 E3
Bendbow Rise Inf Sch
LE3 . . . 153 D3
Benenden Way LE65 . . . 69 A7
Benford Cl LE9 . . . 218 F4
Benjamin Russell Ct
LE2 . . . 259 A2
Bennet Cl CV13 . . . 196 D7
Bennett Dr LE13 . . . 59 C6
Bennett Rise LE9 . . . 200 E8
Bennetts Hill LE17 . . . 219 D2
Bennett's La LE7 . . . 102 D8
Bennett St NG10 . . . 10 D8
Bennett Way LE18 . . . 180 A1
Bennett Wlk LE3 . . . 154 A4
Bennion Rd
Bushby LE7 . . . 157 A4
Leicester LE4 . . . 128 A5
Benscliffe Dr LE11 . . . 51 E2
Benscliffe Gdns LE2 . . . 179 D3
Benscliffe Rd LE6 . . . 99 D5
Benskin Cl LE14 . . . 108 B8
Benskins Oval LE4 . . . 128 C7
Benskin Wlk LE4 . . . 128 B2
Benskyn Cl LE8 . . . 202 D4
Benson St LE5 . . . 155 E5
Bentburn Ho LE3 . . . 154 A7
Bentinghouse Gdns
LE2 . . . 179 D4
Bentinghouse Rd LE2 . . . 179 D4
Bentley Cl LE11 . . . 52 C4
Bentley Dale DE11 . . . 45 A3
Bentley Rd
Birstall LE4 . . . 129 A8
Castle Donington DE74 . . . 16 F4
Bentley St
Melton Mowbray LE13 . . . 59 C3
Stamford PE9 . . . 143 E4
Beresford Ct
Heather LE67 . . . 95 C2
Shepshed LE12 . . . 50 C4
Beresford Dr LE2 . . . 180 D8
Beresford Rd NG10 . . . 10 A5
Berford Cl LE9 . . . 218 F5
Berkeley Ave NG10 . . . 10 C6
Berkeley Cl
Leicester, Oadby LE2 . . . 181 D5
Mountsorrel LE12 . . . 76 F1
Berkeley Ct PE9 . . . 143 F4
Berkeley Rd LE11 . . . 74 C8
Berkeley St LE16 . . . 248 F2
Berkley St LE1 . . . 259 A5
Berkshire Rd LE2 . . . 179 D7
Bernard Cl LE67 . . . 95 F1
Bernard Ct DE11 . . . 44 D3
Bernard St DE11 . . . 44 D3
Berners St LE2 . . . 155 C5
Berridge Dr LE2 . . . 181 B4
Berridge La LE4 . . . 129 B3
Berridges La LE17 . . . 247 E5
Berridge St LE1 . . . 259 B3
Berrington Cl
Botcheston LE9 . . . 151 C6
Leicester LE5 . . . 155 E8
Berrisford St LE67 . . . 96 D8
Berry Ave DE73 . . . 27 A3
Berrybushes LE15 . . . 86 F5
Berrybut Way PE9 . . . 143 F5
Berry Cl
Great Bowden LE16 . . . 241 A5
Ravenstone LE67 . . . 71 A2
Berrycott La LE7, LE12 . . . 55 B3
Berry Field Rd LE16 . . . 229 C1
Berryhill La LE67 . . . 96 B6
Berry Rd LE16 . . . 229 C1
Berry's La LE6 . . . 152 C8
Berrywell Dr LE9 . . . 198 A8
Bertie La PE9 . . . 144 E4
Berts Coote Ho 1
LE11 . . . 51 F2
Bert's Way NG32 . . . 4 E5
Berwick Rd LE65 . . . 69 D5
Beryl Ave LE10 . . . 197 A2
BESCABY . . . 23 E1
Bescaby La LE14 . . . 40 B7
Bessingham Cl LE5 . . . 130 C2
Best Cl LE18 . . . 179 F1
Bestwood Cl LE3 . . . 128 B1
Beth-El Ho LE18 . . . 203 C8
Betty Henser's La LE12 . . . 76 D4
Bevan Rd
Leicester LE4 . . . 128 C7
Leicester LE4 . . . 128 D8
Beveridge La
Bardon LE67 . . . 97 C4
Ellistown LE67 . . . 96 E3
Beveridge St LE12 . . . 76 D7
Beverley Ave LE4 . . . 129 B1
Beverley Cl LE4 . . . 129 E7
Beverley Dr LE9 . . . 218 E7
Beverley Gdns PE9 . . . 143 C4
Beverley Rd DE74 . . . 28 D8
Bevington Cl LE6 . . . 126 B1
Bewcastle Gr LE4 . . . 128 D5
Bewicke Rd LE3 . . . 154 B2
Bexhill Rise LE5 . . . 156 E7
Biam Way LE3 . . . 179 A8
Bickley Ave LE13 . . . 59 D4
Biddle Rd
Leicester LE3 . . . 154 B7
Littlethorpe LE19 . . . 201 C6
Biddulph Ave LE2 . . . 155 C4
Biddulph St LE2 . . . 155 C4
Bideford Cl LE18 . . . 203 D7
Bideford Rd LE5 . . . 156 D3
Bidford Cl LE3 . . . 153 E2
Bidford Ct LE3 . . . 153 E2
Bidford Rd LE3 . . . 153 E2
Bidwell La LE15 . . . 89 D4
Biggin Hill Rd LE5 . . . 156 B3
Biggin St LE11 . . . 52 B4
Biggin The DE74 . . . 17 B3
Bigg's Cl LE8 . . . 202 A5
Big La
Barrow-u-S LE12 . . . 54 D2
Seagrave LE12 . . . 77 E8
Bignal Dr LE3 . . . 153 B4
Bilberry Cl LE3 . . . 179 A6
Billa Barra La LE67 . . . 97 E3
Bill Crane Way LE17 . . . 244 C8
BILLESDON . . . 159 C2
Billesdon Cl LE3 . . . 127 E3
Billesdon Parochial Prim
Sch LE7 . . . 159 B1
Billesdon Rd LE7 . . . 183 D7
Billington Cl LE4 . . . 128 E3
Billington Rd E LE9 . . . 198 E4
Billington Rd W LE9 . . . 198 D5
Bilsdale Rd LE18 . . . 180 F1
BILSTONE . . . 147 C7
Bilstone Rd
Congerstone CV13 . . . 147 D7
Twycross CV9 . . . 146 E7
Bilton Way LE17 . . . 244 D8
Bindley La LE8 . . . 182 B1
Bingley Rd LE19 . . . 201 C6
Bintree Cl LE5 . . . 130 B2
Birch Ave
Barrow-u-S LE12 . . . 53 D1
Swadlincote DE11 . . . 44 A7
Whitwick LE67 . . . 72 A4
Birch Cl
Earl Shilton LE9 . . . 198 D6
Leicester LE4 . . . 129 D1
Loughborough LE11 . . . 75 A6
Markfield LE67 . . . 125 E6
Melton Mowbray LE13 . . . 59 B5
Birch Ct LE2 . . . 179 A3
Birches The 2 LE9 . . . 198 A6
Birchfield Ave LE67 . . . 125 D8
Birch Rd PE9 . . . 142 F5
Birch Tree Ave LE4 . . . 102 A1
Birch Tree Gdns LE16 . . . 240 F4
Birchtree Rd LE18 . . . 180 D4
Birch View LE17 . . . 235 E2
Birchwood Ave
Long Eaton, Breaston
NG10 . . . 10 A7
Long Eaton, New Sawley
NG10 . . . 10 C5
Birchwood Cl
Coleorton LE67 . . . 70 D3
Leicester Forest East
LE3 . . . 152 F2
Syston LE7 . . . 103 C3
Birch Wood Sch LE13 . . . 59 E1
Bird Hill Rd LE12 . . . 74 F1
Birdie Cl LE8 . . . 224 B8
Birds La LE14 . . . 13 A3
Birds Nest Ave LE3 . . . 154 A8
Birkby Cl LE5 . . . 130 C3
Birkdale Ave LE2 . . . 155 D1
Birkdale Cl CV11 . . . 214 A1
Birkdale Ct LE5 . . . 156 A2
Birkdale Rd LE7 . . . 127 D6
Birkenshaw Rd LE3 . . . 128 A1
Birsmore Ave LE4 . . . 129 D4
BIRSTALL . . . 129 A7
Birstall Rd LE4 . . . 129 B5
Birstall St LE1 . . . 155 B7
Birstow Cres LE4 . . . 128 D5
Birtley Coppice LE16 . . . 240 D4
BISBROOKE . . . 189 F4
Bishop Cl LE16 . . . 250 E8
Bishop Dale LE67 . . . 71 D7
Bishopdale Cl NG10 . . . 10 A6
Bishopdale Rd LE4 . . . 128 C3
Bishop Ellis RC Prim Sch
LE4 . . . 129 F8
Bishop Meadow Rd
LE11 . . . 51 E7
Bishops Cleeve CV9 . . . 119 A1
Bishops Ct DE73 . . . 26 B7
Bishop's Ct DE73 . . . 26 A7
Bishops Gate DE11 . . . 44 E2
Bishop St
Leicester LE1 . . . 259 B3
Loughborough LE11 . . . 52 C5
Melton Mowbray LE13 . . . 59 D3
Bishopston Wlk LE4 . . . 128 F4
Bisley St LE3 . . . 154 D3
BITTESWELL . . . 244 B8
Bitteswell Rd LE17 . . . 244 B7
BLABY . . . 202 B8
Blaby By-Pass LE8 . . . 202 A7
Blaby Ind Pk LE8 . . . 179 A1
Blaby Rd
Narborough LE19 . . . 178 D2
Wigston LE18 . . . 180 A1
Blaby Stokes CE Prim Sch
LE8 . . . 202 A7
Blackberry La
Cossington LE7 . . . 77 F1
Ibstock LE67 . . . 96 A4
Blackbird Ave LE4 . . . 154 E8
Blackbird Rd LE4 . . . 154 D8
Blackbrook Cl LE12 . . . 50 A3
Blackbrook Ct
Coalville LE67 . . . 97 B8
Loughborough LE11 . . . 51 E6
Blackbrook Dr LE67 . . . 97 B8
Blackbrook Rd LE11 . . . 51 D3
Blackburn Rd LE9 . . . 198 A6
Blackett Ave LE3 . . . 154 A8
Blackett Dr LE67 . . . 95 B2
BLACKFORDBY . . . 45 C1
Blackfordby La DE12 . . . 68 B6
Blackfordby St Margaret's
CE Prim Sch DE11 . . . 45 C1
BLACK FRIARS . . . 259 A4
Blackfriars St
Leicester LE3 . . . 259 A4
10 Stamford PE9 . . . 143 E3
Blackham Rd LE11 . . . 52 A1
Black Horse Hill DE12 . . . 119 F8
Black La LE12 . . . 54 B4
Blackmore Dr LE3 . . . 154 A5
Blacksmith End LE14 . . . 13 A3
Blacksmith Pl 5 LE5 . . . 130 C3
Blacksmiths Ave LE12 . . . 50 C5
Blacksmiths Cl
Nether Broughton
LE14 . . . 36 D8
Netherseal DE12 . . . 91 F7
Thrussington LE7 . . . 78 F4
Blacksmiths La
Smeeton Westerby
LE8 . . . 223 F6
Sutton Cheney CV13 . . . 174 B6
Blacksmith's La
Exton LE15 . . . 113 B3
Woodville DE11 . . . 44 F3
Blackspinney La LE7 . . . 134 B4
Blackstone's Ct PE9 . . . 143 F4
Blackthorn PE9 . . . 142 E5
Blackthorn Cl
Lutterworth LE17 . . . 244 A6
Melbourne DE73 . . . 26 A8
Blackthorn Dr
Leicester LE4 . . . 128 A6
Syston LE7 . . . 102 F3
Blackthorn La LE2 . . . 181 B7
Black Thorn Rd LE3 . . . 153 B7
Blackthorn Way DE12 . . . 93 C6
Blackwell Cl LE18 . . . 180 E1
Blackwell La DE73 . . . 26 B7
Blackwood LE67 . . . 72 B1
Bladen Cl LE8 . . . 202 D4
Blair Cl LE12 . . . 101 C8
Blairmore Rd LE3 . . . 153 C6
Blaise Gr LE4 . . . 129 D1
Blake Cl LE10 . . . 197 D4
Blake Ct
Long Eaton NG10 . . . 10 B5
Narborough LE19 . . . 178 A3
Blake Dr LE11 . . . 51 E5
Blakemore Ave DE73 . . . 26 B8
Blakeney Cres LE13 . . . 82 C8
Blakenhall Cl LE19 . . . 200 F8
Blakenhall Rd LE5 . . . 156 A5
Blakeshay Cl LE3 . . . 127 F2
Blakesley Rd LE18 . . . 180 F3
Blakesley Wlk LE4 . . . 128 B2
Blake St LE1 . . . 259 B4
Blanch Croft DE73 . . . 26 B7
Blandford Ave NG10 . . . 10 B6
Bland Rd LE3 . . . 127 F1
Blankley Dr LE2 . . . 155 D1
Blanklyn Ave LE5 . . . 155 D5
Blankney Rd LE15 . . . 87 E2
Blashfield Cl PE9 . . . 143 C4
BLASTON . . . 210 B4
Blaston Hill LE16 . . . 210 C4
Blaston Rd LE16 . . . 209 C2
Blaydon Cl LE3 . . . 154 B8
Bleach Mill DE12 . . . 93 C3
Bleakmoor Cl LE7 . . . 79 A3
Bleasby Cl LE4 . . . 130 A4
Blenheim Cl
Hinckley LE10 . . . 197 F4
Loughborough LE11 . . . 51 C4
3 Swadlincote DE11 . . . 44 A7
Wigston LE18 . . . 202 F8
Blenheim Cres LE9 . . . 218 D7
Blenheim Rd LE4 . . . 129 B8
Blenheim Way
Leicester LE4 . . . 128 E4

Blenheim Way continued
Market Harborough
LE16 . . . . **240** E5
Blenheim Wlk LE13 . . . . . **59** B5
Bley Ave LE12 . . . . **31** D8
Blickling Wlk LE5 . . . . . . **155** E8
Blind La
Breaston DE72 . . . . **9** D8
Cottingham LE16 . . . . . . **229** D1
Blissett Rd LE3 . . . . **154** B7
Blithfield La LE11 . . . . . **51** C3
Blockley's Yd **4** LE10 . . **215** D8
Bloom Cl LE67 . . . . **71** A2
Bloomfield Rd LE2 . . . . . **179** F7
Blossom Rd LE3 . . . . **154** A4
Blossoms The LE67 . . . . . **125** E6
Blount Rd LE4 . . . . **129** F6
Bloxams Cl LE3 . . . . **178** F6
Bloxham Cl LE3 . . . . **154** B7
Bloxsom Cl LE67 . . . . . . **124** A7
Blue Banks Ave LE2 . . . . **179** A3
Bluebell Cl
Donisthorpe DE12 . . . . . **67** E1
Kirby Muxloe LE9 . . . . . **152** E6
Leicester, Oadby LE2 . . . **181** E4
Queniborough LE7 . . . . . **103** E6
Bluebell Dr
Groby LE6 . . . . **127** A3
Leicester LE2 . . . . **179** F4
Loughborough LE11 . . . . **51** F1
Bluebell La LE16 . . . . . . **208** B4
Bluebell Rd PE9 . . . . **142** F5
Bluebell Row LE13 . . . . . **82** A8
Blueberry Way DE11 . . . . **44** F3
Bluecoat La LE15 . . . . . . **212** D7
Bluecoat Sch The
PE9 . . . . **143** D4
Blue Gates Rd LE4 . . . . . **128** A5
Blue Pots Cl LE2 . . . . . . **152** F2
Blue Pots La NG32 . . . . . . **22** F7
Blue Town NG33 . . . . **43** B8
Blundell Rd LE5 . . . . **156** A3
Blunt's La LE18 . . . . **180** D2
Blyth Ave LE13 . . . . **59** B2
Blyth Ct DE74 . . . . **17** B4
Boathouse The LE16 . . . . **240** D4
Bob Trewick Ho LE1 . . . . **259** C2
Bodenham Cl LE18 . . . . . **203** C8
Bodicoat Cl LE8 . . . . **201** F5
Bodkin Row DE12 . . . . . . **93** B6
Bodkin Wlk LE4 . . . . **128** B3
Bodmin Ave LE18 . . . . . . **180** D1
Bodmin Cl LE10 . . . . **197** E4
Bodnant Ave LE5 . . . . . . **155** E3
Bodycote Cl LE9 . . . . **218** F5
Bofols Rd LE14 . . . . **36** A5
Boilerhouse Rd LE14 . . . . **36** A4
Bollard's La LE12 . . . . . . **30** A7
Bollington Rd LE2 . . . . . **181** C6
Bolsover St LE5 . . . . **155** E6
Bolton La LE14 . . . . **20** F7
Bolton Rd LE3 . . . . **154** C5
Bolus Rd LE3 . . . . **153** C2
Bombard Rd LE14 . . . . . . **36** A5
Bonchurch Cl LE67 . . . . . **71** F5
Bonchurch Rd LE67 . . . . . **71** F5
Bonchurch St LE3 . . . . . . **154** D7
Bond Cl LE11 . . . . **52** C1
Bondgate DE74 . . . . **17** B3
Bondman Cl LE4 . . . . **128** E5
Boneham's La LE17 . . . . . **234** E3
Bonner Cl LE2 . . . . **181** D4
Bonner Ho LE15 . . . . **189** A4
Bonners La LE2 . . . . **259** B2
Bonney Rd LE3 . . . . **154** A8
Bonnington Cl CV21 . . . . **257** B1
Bonnington Rd LE2 . . . . . **155** B1
Bonsall Ct NG10 . . . . **10** F8
Bonsall St
Leicester LE5 . . . . **155** C4
Long Eaton NG10 . . . . . . **10** E8
Bonville Pl LE3 . . . . **154** B1
Booth Cl LE5 . . . . **156** B5
Booth End LE11 . . . . **51** B6
BOOTHORPE **67** F8
Boothorpe La DE11 . . . . . **68** A8
Booth Rd LE67 . . . . **71** D8
Booth Wood Prim Sch
LE11 . . . . **51** C3
Bordeaux Cl LE19 . . . . . . **178** A3
Border Dr LE4 . . . . **128** E5
Borlace St LE3 . . . . **154** D6
Borough St
Castle Donington DE74 . . **17** B3
Kegworth DE74 . . . . **18** D2
Borough The LE10 . . . . . **215** D8
Borrowcup Cl LE8 . . . . . . **202** C4
Borrowdale Cl LE9 . . . . . **198** F7
Borrowdale Dr NG10 . . . . **10** A6
Borrowdale Way
Leicester LE5 . . . . **156** D3
Loughborough LE11 . . . . **51** D1
Borrowell DE74 . . . . **18** D3
Bostock Cl LE9 . . . . **199** A4
Boston Rd LE4 . . . . **128** A4
Boston Way LE9 . . . . **198** A6
Boswell St LE19 . . . . **178** A1
Bosworth Battlefield Ctry
Pk★ CV13 . . . . **173** F5
Bosworth Battlefield
Visitor Ctr★ CV13 . . . . . **173** E5
Bosworth Cl
Ashby-de-la-Z LE65 . . . . . **69** D7

Bosworth Cl continued
Hinckley LE10 . . . . **197** A1
Bosworth Com Coll
LE9 . . . . **151** C3
Bosworth Field★
CV13 . . . . **173** E5
Bosworth Gn LE9 . . . . . . **176** B1
Bosworth Ho **3** LE10 . . **197** E1
Bosworth La CV13 . . . . . **149** E4
Bosworth Rd
Barlestone CV13 . . . . . . **149** C7
Carlton CV13 . . . . **148** E7
Castle Donington DE74 . . . **16** F3
Congerstone CV13 . . . . . **147** E6
Kirkby Mallory LE9 . . . . . **175** B7
Measham DE12 . . . . **93** D4
Sutton Cheney CV13 . . . . **174** A6
Theddingworth LE17 . . . . **248** C7
Walton LE17 . . . . **236** D1
Bosworth St LE3 . . . . **154** D6
Bosworth Water Trust★
CV13 . . . . **148** A2
Bosworth Way NG10 . . . . . **10** E5
BOTCHESTON **151** B6
Botcheston Rd LE9 . . . . . **151** D6
Bothe Cl NG10 . . . . **10** C6
Botley Wlk LE5 . . . . **156** A6
BOTTESFORD **3** C3
Bottesford CE Prim Sch
NG13 . . . . **3** A2
Bottesford La NG13 . . . . . **2** C5
Bottesford Rd NG32 . . . . . **4** D4
Bottesford Sta NG13 . . . . . **3** C3
Bottleacre La LE11 . . . . . . **52** B6
Bottom Gn LE14 . . . . **19** A1
Bottom La LE15 . . . . **189** F4
Bottom Rd LE67 . . . . **48** A1
Bottom St
Allington NG32 . . . . **4** F5
Wing LE15 . . . . **165** A3
Bott's La DE12 . . . . **119** F7
Botts Way LE67 . . . . **97** A8
Boulder La LE2 . . . . **179** F6
Boulter Cres LE18 . . . . . **180** D3
Boulton Cl LE9 . . . . **218** F4
Boulton Ct LE2 . . . . **181** E4
BOUNDARY **45** C2
Boundary Rd
Leicester LE2 . . . . **154** E1
Lutterworth LE17 . . . . . **244** D6
Mountsorrel LE12 . . . . . . **76** E1
Boundary Way LE12 . . . . . **50** C5
Bourne Cl CV9 . . . . **170** E2
Bourne Ct DE73 . . . . **26** A7
Bourne Mall LE4 . . . . . . **128** A4
Bourne Rd PE9 . . . . **117** B6
Bourne Sq DE72 . . . . **9** E7
Bourne Way DE11 . . . . . . **44** D4
Bourton Cres LE2 . . . . . . **181** C5
Bouverie Ct LE15 . . . . . . **84** F1
Bowbridge Gdns NG13 . . . . **3** A3
Bowbridge La NG13 . . . . . . **2** F3
Bowden La
Market Harborough
LE16 . . . . **240** E4
Welham LE16 . . . . **226** E4
Bowden Rd LE16 . . . . . . **226** A4
Bowden Ridge LE16 . . . . **241** A5
Bowder Ho LE3 . . . . **153** F2
Bowens Cl DE11 . . . . **44** F3
Bowhill Gr LE5 . . . . **156** E7
Bowhill Way LE5 . . . . . . **156** E7
Bowker Cres LE65 . . . . . . **68** F5
Bowler Ct LE11 . . . . **52** C4
Bowley Ave LE13 . . . . **59** E5
Bowley Ct LE13 . . . . **59** C3
Bowleys La DE12 . . . . . . **119** E8
Bowley The DE74 . . . . **28** B5
Bowling Gn LE13 . . . . **59** A1
Bowling Green Cl
Oakham LE15 . . . . **138** A5
Sileby LE12 . . . . **77** D4
Bowling Green La LE15 . . **86** F5
Bowling Green Rd
LE10 . . . . **197** E1
Bowling Green St
LE1 . . . . **259** B3
Bowman Gn LE10 . . . . . . **215** F6
Bowmans Way
Glenfield LE3 . . . . **153** B8
Sedgebrook NG32 . . . . **8** A4
Bowmars La LE3 . . . . **259** A5
Box Cl DE11 . . . . **44** E3
Boyer's Orch LE14 . . . . . . **12** B3
Boyer St LE11 . . . . **52** C4
Boyers Wlk LE3 . . . . **152** F3
Boynton Rd LE3 . . . . **154** A4
Boyslade Rd LE10 . . . . . . **215** F6
Boyslade Road E
LE10 . . . . **215** F5
Brabazon Rd LE2 . . . . . . **180** F5
Bracadale Wlk NN17 . . . . **230** C1
Bracken Cl
Coalville LE67 . . . . **96** C6
Leicester Forest East
LE3 . . . . **152** F2
Leicester LE5 . . . . **156** B4
Bracken Dale LE7 . . . . . . **103** E8
Brackenfield Way
LE4 . . . . **130** A8
Bracken Hill LE6 . . . . . . **126** B6
Brackenthwaite LE4 . . . . **129** D3
Bracken Way LE67 . . . . . . **98** L1
Bracken Wlk LE67 . . . . . . **125** E8
Brackley Cl LE4 . . . . **129** E1
Bradbourne Rd LE5 . . . . . **155** D5
Bradbury Cl LE67 . . . . . . **201** D2
Braddon Rd LE11 . . . . **51** C6

Bradfield Cl LE5 . . . . **155** E5
Bradford's La LE67 . . . . . **70** E7
Bradgate Ave LE4 . . . . . . **129** F7
Bradgate Cl
Leicester LE7 . . . . **156** E5
North End LE12 . . . . **76** D4
Sileby LE12 . . . . **77** C3
Bradgate Ctry Pk★ LE7,
LE6 . . . . **100** A2
Bradgate Dr
Coalville LE67 . . . . **97** C8
Ratby LE6 . . . . **126** C1
Wigston LE18 . . . . **180** B5
Bradgate Flats LE14 . . . . **57** F3
Bradgate Hill LE6 . . . . . **126** B6
Bradgate Ho LE10 . . . . . **215** D7
Bradgate La LE14 . . . . . . **57** F3
Bradgate Mall LE4 . . . . . **128** B4
Bradgate Rd
Barwell LE9 . . . . **198** B8
Cropston LE7 . . . . **100** E4
Hinckley LE10 . . . . **197** F2
Loughborough LE11 . . . . **74** E8
Markfield LE67 . . . . **98** L1
Newtown Linford LE6 . . . **127** B7
Bradgate St LE4 . . . . **154** D8
Brading Rd LE3 . . . . **154** C8
Bradley La LE15 . . . . **89** D5
Bradshaw Ave LE2 . . . . . **179** C3
Bradshaw Ct LE2 . . . . . . **179** C3
Bradshaw St NG10 . . . . . . **10** B5
Bradstone Cl LE9 . . . . . . **219** B5
Bradston Rd LE2 . . . . **179** E5
Braemar Cl
Leicester LE4 . . . . **129** C4
Mountsorrel LE12 . . . . . **101** D3
Stamford PE9 . . . . **143** A4
Braemar Dr LE4 . . . . **129** D4
Braeside LE15 . . . . **111** B8
Braids Ct LE2 . . . . **180** E8
Brailsford Rd LE18 . . . . . **180** B4
Braithewaite Cl PE9 . . . . **167** F5
Bramall Ct LE5 . . . . **155** E8
Bramall Rd LE5 . . . . **155** E7
Bramber Cl LE4 . . . . **129** E5
Bramble Cl
Hamilton LE5 . . . . **130** D2
Leicester LE3 . . . . **153** D7
Loughborough LE11 . . . . **51** E5
Uppingham LE15 . . . . . . **189** B5
Bramble Dr LE9 . . . . **150** B4
Bramble Gr PE9 . . . . **142** F4
Brambles Rd LE67 . . . . . . **96** C6
Bramble Way LE3 . . . . . . **179** A8
Brambling Cl CV23 . . . . . **252** C1
Brambling Rd LE5 . . . . . . **155** D7
Brambling Way LE2 . . . . **181** A4
Bramcote Cl LE10 . . . . . **197** F3
Bramcote Rd
Leicester LE3 . . . . **179** B8
Loughborough LE11 . . . . **74** F7
Wigston LE18 . . . . **180** C4
Brame Rd LE10 . . . . **197** C2
Bramham Cl LE3 . . . . . . **128** B1
Bramley Cl
Broughton Astley LE9 . . . **218** E7
Market Harborough
LE16 . . . . **240** F5
Moira DE12 . . . . **68** A4
Sileby LE12 . . . . **77** D4
Wymeswold LE12 . . . . . . **33** D3
Bramley Ct LE3 . . . . **153** B8
Bramley Orch LE7 . . . . . **157** A5
Bramley Rd
Birstall LE4 . . . . **129** B7
Leicester LE5 . . . . **154** C6
Long Eaton NG10 . . . . . . **10** C5
Brampton Ave LE3 . . . . . **154** B6
Brampton Rd LE13 . . . . . . **59** A6
Brampton Way LE2 . . . . . **180** F6
Brancaster Cl LE4 . . . . . **128** D2
Brand Hill LE12 . . . . **100** A8
Brand La LE12 . . . . **75** B1
Brandon Rd LE10 . . . . . . **215** B7
Brandon St LE4 . . . . **155** B8
Bransdale Cl NG10 . . . . . . **10** B6
Bransdale Rd LE18 . . . . . **180** F2
BRANSTON **23** C7
Branston Ave LE12 . . . . . . **76** E8
Branston Cres LE13 . . . . . **59** E2
Branston Ho LE18 . . . . . . **180** B3
Branston Rd LE15 . . . . . . **189** A5
Branting Hill LE6 . . . . . . **127** B3
Branting Hill Ave LE6 . . . **127** B3
Branting Hill Gr LE3 . . . . **127** B3
BRASCOTE **150** A2
Brascote La
Cadeby CV13 . . . . **149** E2
Newbold Verdon LE9 . . . . **150** A2
Brascote Rd LE10 . . . . . . **214** F8
Bratmyr LE8 . . . . **204** F1
Braunstone Ave LE3 . . . . **154** A1
BRAUNSTONE FRITH **153** B6
Braunstone Frith Ind Est
LE3 . . . . **153** B6
Braunstone Frith Inf Sch
LE3 . . . . **153** D6
Braunstone Frith Jun Sch
LE3 . . . . **153** D6
Braunstone Gate LE3 . . . **154** D5
Braunstone La
Braunstone Town
LE3 . . . . **153** D3
Leicester LE3 . . . . **154** A1

Braunstone Lane E LE2,
LE3 . . . . **179** B8
BRAUNSTONE TOWN
. . . . **178** E8
Braunstone Way LE3 . . . . **153** E4
BRAUNSTON-IN-RUTLAND
. . . . **137** B2
Braunston Rd
Knossington LE15 . . . . . **136** B5
Oakham LE15 . . . . **137** D5
BRAYBROOKE **251** F5
Braybrooke Prim Sch
LE16 . . . . **251** E6
Braybrooke Rd
Great Oxendon LE16 . . . . **251** A3
Leicester LE4 . . . . **129** E1
Market Harborough
LE16 . . . . **241** B1
Braymish Cl LE8 . . . . **224** B8
Brazenose La PE9 . . . . . . **143** E3
Brazil St LE2 . . . . **154** E3
Breachfield Rd LE12 . . . . **76** E7
Breach La LE9 . . . . **198** F6
Breach Rd LE67 . . . . **96** D7
Breadcroft La LE12 . . . . . **76** D8
Breadsall Cl DE11 . . . . . . **44** A7
Breakback Rd LE12 . . . . . **74** E3
BREASTON **9** C7
Breaston Ind Est DE72 . . . . **9** C7
Brechin Cl LE10 . . . . **215** A8
Brecknock Dr NG10 . . . . . **10** A7
Brecon Cl
4 Long Eaton NG10 . . **10** A8
Wigston LE18 . . . . **179** F2
Bredon Cl **5** NG10 . . . . **10** A8
Breech Hedge LE7 . . . . . **101** E7
Breedon Ave LE18 . . . . . **180** C3
Breedon La
Osgathorpe LE12 . . . . . . **48** C5
Worthington LE65 . . . . . . **47** F6
BREEDON ON THE HILL
. . . . **26** B2
Breedon on the Hill St
Hardulph's CE Prim Sch
DE73 . . . . **26** F2
Breedon St LE2 . . . . **155** C5
Brendon Cl LE12 . . . . **50** C1
Brendon Way LE65 . . . . . . **69** B5
Brenfield Dr LE10 . . . . . **215** A8
Brent Ct **2** LE3 . . . . . . **178** F7
BRENTINGBY **60** C2
Brentingby Cl LE13 . . . . . **59** E1
Brent Knowle Gdns
LE5 . . . . **156** D5
Brentnall Cl NG10 . . . . . . **10** B7
Brentwood Rd LE2 . . . . . **155** A1
Bretby Bsns Pk DE15 . . . . **44** A8
Bretby Hts DE11 . . . . **44** A8
Bretby Rd LE2 . . . . **179** E6
Bretby View DE11 . . . . . . **45** A4
Breton Cl LE18 . . . . **204** A3
Brettell Rd LE2 . . . . **179** D4
Bretton Cl LE4 . . . . **128** E3
Bretton Wlk **5** LE4 . . . . **128** E3
Breward Way LE13 . . . . . . **59** D6
Brewer Cl LE4 . . . . **129** E5
Brewery Row NG32 . . . . . **14** E8
Brex Rise LE3 . . . . **153** D6
Breydon Ind Ctr NG10 . . . **10** F7
Brian Rd LE4 . . . . **128** D1
Brians Cl LE7 . . . . **103** C4
Brianway The LE5 . . . . . . **155** F7
Briar Cl
Blackfordby DE11 . . . . . . **68** B8
Coalville LE67 . . . . **96** C7
Hinckley LE10 . . . . **215** F6
Leicester, Oadby LE2 . . . **181** B4
Briarfield Dr LE5 . . . . . . **130** E1
Briar Gdn NG10 . . . . **10** C8
Briargate Dr LE4 . . . . . . **128** E3
Briarmead LE10 . . . . **215** E4
Briar Meads LE2 . . . . . . **181** B3
Briar Rd LE5 . . . . **156** D7
Briar Wlk LE2 . . . . **181** B4
Brick Kiln Croft DE12 . . . **93** D5
Brick Kiln La
Ibstock LE67 . . . . **122** F8
Shepshed LE12 . . . . **50** A1
Brick Kiln St LE10 . . . . . **215** C8
Brickman Cl LE3 . . . . **152** F2
Brickwood Pl LE12 . . . . . **53** F7
Brickyard Cotts DE12 . . . **93** D5
Brickyard La
East Leake LE12 . . . . **31** A8
Wymondham LE14 . . . . . **62** D3
Bridegate La LE14 . . . . . . **19** B6
Bridevale Rd LE2 . . . . . . **179** E5
Bridge Bsns Pk LE4 . . . . **129** C7
Bridge Cl
Swadlincote DE11 . . . . . . **44** C2
Thurmaston LE4 . . . . . . **129** F8
Bridge Field DE72 . . . . **9** C7
Bridge Fields DE74 . . . . . **18** E3
Bridge Ho LE11 . . . . **52** B4
Bridge Jun Sch LE5 . . . . **155** C7
Bridge La
Greetham LE15 . . . . **88** B1
Witherley CV9 . . . . **194** B7
Bridgeland Rd LE11 . . . . . **52** C5
Bridgemere Cl LE2 . . . . . **179** B4
Bridge Mews LE67 . . . . . . **71** D3
Bridge Park Rd LE4 . . . . **129** D7
Bridge Rd
Coalville LE67 . . . . **96** D8
Hinckley LE10 . . . . **215** D7
Leicester LE5 . . . . **155** D7
Bridgeside Cotts LE11 . . . **52** A5

Bridge St
Barrow-u-S LE12 . . . . . . **76** C7
Langham LE15 . . . . **110** C3
Long Eaton NG10 . . . . . . **10** D8
Loughborough LE11 . . . . **52** A4
Packington LE65 . . . . . . **69** C1
Ryhall PE9 . . . . **116** F2
Shepshed LE12 . . . . **50** B4
Swadlincote DE11 . . . . . . **44** C2
Bridgewater Dr LE8 . . . . **182** B1
Bridge Way LE8 . . . . **201** F7
Bridle Cl
Croft LE9 . . . . **200** C3
Melton Mowbray LE13 . . . **59** A5
Bridle Path LE8 . . . . **198** D5
Bridle Rd LE67 . . . . **71** D3
Bridlespur Way LE4 . . . . **128** C5
Bridle The LE2 . . . . **179** B4
Bridport Cl LE18 . . . . . . **180** D1
Brierfield Rd LE9 . . . . . . **201** D2
Briers Cl LE19 . . . . **201** B7
Briers Way LE67 . . . . **71** E5
Briggins Wlk LE15 . . . . . **110** C3
Brightman Ho DE11 . . . . . **44** B5
Brighton Ave
Syston LE7 . . . . **103** C4
Wigston LE18 . . . . **180** D5
Brighton Cl LE18 . . . . . . **180** C5
Brighton Rd LE5 . . . . **155** E8
Brightside Ave LE13 . . . . **59** A4
Brightside Rd LE5 . . . . . **155** E4
Brightwell Dr LE3 . . . . . **153** B4
Brindle Path LE9 . . . . . . **198** D4
Brindley Cl
Atherstone CV9 . . . . **170** C1
Stoney Stanton LE9 . . . . **199** D2
Brindley Rd
Coalville LE67 . . . . **71** A2
Hinckley LE10 . . . . **214** E8
Rugby CV21 . . . . **257** B1
Brindley Rise LE5 . . . . . . **130** E1
BRINGHURST **229** C5
Bringhurst Gn LE3 . . . . . **153** E7
Bringhurst Prim Sch
LE16 . . . . **229** C6
Bringhurst Rd LE3 . . . . . **153** D7
Brington Cl LE18 . . . . . . **180** E2
Brinks The LE12 . . . . **76** B5
Brinsmead Rd LE2 . . . . . **180** B7
Brisco Ave LE11 . . . . **51** F6
Briscoe La LE12 . . . . **75** B4
Bristol Ave
Ashby-de-la-Z LE65 . . . . . **69** A7
Leicester LE4 . . . . **128** D1
Britannia Rd LE10 . . . . . **216** A5
Britannia St
Leicester LE1 . . . . **155** A7
Shepshed LE12 . . . . **50** B4
Britannia Way LE4 . . . . . **102** E1
Britannia Wlk LE16 . . . . . **240** F2
Britford Ave LE18 . . . . . . **203** C8
British Pony Ctr★
LE7 . . . . **160** C2
British School Gdns
LE13 . . . . **59** C3
Briton Lodge Cl DE12 . . . **67** F4
Briton St LE3 . . . . **154** D4
Brittania Sh Ctr **3**
. . . . **215** D8
Brittany Ave LE65 . . . . . . **69** A7
Brixham Dr LE2, LE18 . . . **180** A5
Brixworth Rise LE5 . . . . . **156** E6
Broad Ave LE5 . . . . **155** F5
Broadbent Cl LE8 . . . . . . **201** F7
Broadfield Way LE8 . . . . **202** C4
Broadford Cl LE4 . . . . . . **129** D4
Broadgate LE16 . . . . **229** D7
Broadgate Cl LE4 . . . . . . **129** A8
Broadgate Rd NG33 . . . . . **65** C3
Broadhill Rd DE74 . . . . . . **18** C2
Broadhurst St LE4 . . . . . **129** B2
Broad La LE67 . . . . **125** A7
Broadmead Rd LE8 . . . . . **202** A6
Broadnook Cl LE3 . . . . . . **127** C3
Broad Rushes DE74 . . . . . **17** B6
Broad St
Coalville LE67 . . . . **96** D8
Enderby LE19 . . . . **178** B3
Long Eaton NG10 . . . . . . **10** D7
Loughborough LE11 . . . . **52** A4
Stamford PE9 . . . . **143** E3
Syston LE7 . . . . **103** A3
Broadsword Way
LE10 . . . . **215** D4
Broadway
Loughborough LE11 . . . . **75** B8
Syston LE7 . . . . **103** A3
Broadway Furlong
LE7 . . . . **127** E7
Broadway Rd LE5 . . . . . . **155** D2
Broadway Terr LE16 . . . . **240** F4
Broadway The
Leicester LE2 . . . . **156** A1
Market Harborough
LE16 . . . . **240** F4
Brockenhurst Dr LE3 . . . . **178** E8
Brockey Cl LE9 . . . . **198** B7
Brockhurst Ave LE10 . . . . **215** D6
Brockhurst La CV23 . . . . **242** A6
Brockington Coll
LE19 . . . . **178** C2
Brocklehurst Dr LE3 . . . . **178** E8
Brocklehurst Rd LE13 . . . **59** E5
Brocklesby Way LE5 . . . . **156** E8
Brocks Hill Cl LE2 . . . . . **181** A2
Brocks Hill Country Pk &
Visitor Ctr★ LE2 . . . . . **180** F4

Bro–Cai 265

Brocks Hill Dr LE2 181 B5
Brocks Hill Prim Sch LE2 181 B3
Broctone Cl LE9 219 B5
Broctone Dr LE9 218 E7
Brodick Cl LE10 215 A8
Brodick Rd LE10 214 F8
Bromhead St LE11 52 C5
Bromley La LE12 49 B7
Brompton Rd LE5 130 C3
Bromwich Cl LE3 153 C2
Bromwich Rd 1 CV21 257 A1
Bronte Cl
  Leicester LE3 154 A4
  Long Eaton NG10 10 A7
Bronze Barrow Cl LE18 180 F1
Brook Bank LE5 155 F7
Brook Cl
  Long Eaton NG10 10 E5
  Packington LE65 69 B1
  Uppingham LE15 189 C3
Brook Cres LE14 58 B3
Brook Ct LE8 202 F4
Brookdale LE10 215 B7
Brookdale Rd
  Hartshorne DE11 45 A4
  Leicester LE3 153 D5
Brook Dene LE15 111 B8
Brook Dr LE6 152 C8
BROOKE 163 D8
Brooke Ave PE9 143 A2
Brooke Cl LE15 138 B7
Brooke Hill Prim Sch LE15 137 E4
Brooke House Coll LE16 240 E4
Brooke Priory Sch LE15 137 F7
Brooke Rd
  Braunston-in-R LE15 137 B2
  Oakham LE15 137 F4
  Ridlington LE15 163 D4
Brookes Ave LE9 200 C3
Brookes Gr NN17 230 E1
Brook Farm Ct
  Hoton LE12 32 D2
  Willoughby-on-t-W LE12 34 C7
Brookfield LE10 217 C5
Brookfield Ave
  Loughborough LE11 51 E1
  Syston LE7 103 B3
Brookfield Cotts DE12 92 C7
Brookfield Ct LE13 59 B5
Brookfield Rd
  Hinckley LE10 215 C6
  Market Harborough LE16 240 C3
Brookfield Rise LE2 179 F6
Brookfield St
  Melton Mowbray LE13 59 B5
  Syston LE7 103 B3
Brookfield Way
  Kibworth Beauchamp LE8 224 B8
  Lutterworth LE17 244 A6
Brook Gdns LE2 179 B3
Brookhouse Ave 2 LE2 155 B4
Brook House Cl LE7 79 A1
Brook House Mews DE11 44 A7
Brookhouse St 1 LE2 155 B4
Brook La
  Asfordby LE14 57 F2
  Barrow-u-S LE12 76 E8
  Billesdon LE7 159 C2
  Great Easton LE16 229 D6
  Loughborough LE11 74 D8
  Melton Mowbray LE13 59 D2
  Peckleton LE9 175 F7
  Thringstone LE67 71 D7
Brookland Rd LE2 155 A1
Brooklands LE15 164 C1
Brooklands Cl
  Broughton Astley LE9 218 F6
  Whetstone LE8 201 F7
Brooklands Gdns LE16 240 E2
Brooklands Prim Sch NG10 10 D6
Brooklands Rd LE9 201 D4
Brookland Way LE12 101 E8
Brook Rd
  Leicester LE5 156 D7
  Woodhouse Eaves LE12 74 E4
BROOKSBY 79 E5
Brooksby Ag Coll LE14 79 E5
Brooksby Cl LE2 181 A6
Brooksby Dr LE2 181 A6
Brooksby Melton Coll (King Street Annexe) LE13 59 C3
Brooksby Melton Coll (Melton Campus) LE13 59 B3
Brooksby Rd LE14 79 D6
Brooksby St LE2 154 E1
Brooks Cl DE12 67 F1
Brookside
  Barkby LE7 130 E8
  Barlestone CV13 149 D7
  Diseworth DE74 28 C5
  East Leake LE12 31 E8
  Hinckley LE10 215 E7
  Leicester LE5 155 D3
Brookside *continued*
  Rearsby LE7 79 A2
  Syston LE7 103 B4
  Whetstone LE8 201 F6
Brook Side
  12 Ashby-de-la-Z LE65 69 B6
  3 Loughborough LE11 52 A4
Brookside Ave LE12 31 E8
Brookside Cl
  Barrow-u-S LE12 53 D1
  Long Eaton NG10 10 B8
  Shepshed LE12 50 C2
Brookside Cres LE67 95 F1
Brookside Dr LE2 181 C5
Brookside Ho LE67 96 A2
Brookside Ind Est LE67 96 A2
Brookside Pl CV9 171 B8
Brookside Prim Sch LE2 181 D7
Brookside Rd LE11 74 D8
Brooks La LE67 71 D5
Brook St
  Ashby-de-la-Z LE65 69 B6
  Burton o t W LE12 53 F7
  Enderby LE19 178 B3
  Hartshorne DE11 45 A7
  Huncote LE9 200 D7
  Melton Mowbray LE13 59 D3
  Rearsby LE7 79 A1
  Shepshed LE12 50 C5
  Sileby LE12 77 C3
  Swadlincote DE11 44 A3
  Syston LE7 103 A4
  Thurmaston LE4 129 D7
  Walcote LE17 245 B4
  Whetstone LE8 201 F7
  Wymeswold LE12 33 D3
Brooks The LE15 113 B2
Brook Terr LE16 227 F6
Brookvale High Sch LE6 126 D2
Broom Ave LE11 75 A7
Broombriggs Farm Ctry Pk★ LE12 74 E1
Broombriggs Farm Nature Trail★ LE12 74 F1
Broombriggs Rd LE3 127 F3
Broome Ave LE7 103 E8
Broome La LE7 78 C1
Broomfield LE7 103 E7
Broomfield Com Prim Sch LE7 103 E7
Broomhills Rd LE19 200 F8
Broomhills The DE12 91 F7
Broomleys LE8 202 D4
Broom Leys Ave LE67 96 F8
Broom Leys Rd LE67 72 A1
Broom Leys Sch LE67 72 A1
Broom Way LE19 177 F1
Brosdale Dr LE10 197 A1
Brouder Cl LE67 97 A8
Brougham St LE1 259 C4
BROUGHTON ASTLEY 218 E5
Broughton Cl
  Anstey LE7 127 E7
  Loughborough LE11 51 C4
Broughton Field LE18 203 E8
Broughton La
  Dunton Bassett LE17 219 D2
  Leire LE17 218 E3
  Long Clawson LE14 20 A2
Broughton Rd
  Cosby LE9 201 C1
  Croft LE9 200 C3
  Frolesworth LE17 218 C3
  Leicester LE2 179 E6
  Stoney Stanton LE9 199 F2
Broughton St LE67 96 D8
Broughton Way LE9 218 F7
Brown Ave LE12 76 A6
Brown Ct LE65 68 F7
Browne's Hospl 3 PE9 143 D3
Brownhill Cres LE7 101 C5
Browning Cl LE13 59 C6
Browning Dr DE12 93 C3
Browning Rd
  Loughborough LE11 51 D4
  Oakham LE15 137 E6
  Swadlincote DE11 44 C5
Browning St
  Leicester LE3 154 C4
  Narborough LE19 178 A1
Brownlow Cres LE13 82 C8
Brownlow Quay PE9 143 E3
Brownlow Sch LE13 59 D4
Brownlow St PE9 143 E3
Brownlow Terr PE9 143 E3
Brown's Cl LE9 217 E8
Browns La LE11 52 A3
Brown's Rd NG10 10 E8
Brown's Way LE8 201 F5
Broxburn Cl LE4 129 D4
Broxfield Cl LE2 181 A3
Bruces La LE14, LE15 135 E6
Bruce St LE3 154 D3
Bruce Way LE8 201 E5
Bruin St LE4 129 A1
Bruins Wlk LE2 180 F5
Brunel Ave LE3 154 A8
Brunel Rd
  Corby NN17 230 F2
  Hinckley LE10 215 C8
Brunel Way LE67 71 B3
Brunswick St LE1 155 B6
BRUNTINGTHORPE 236 C8
Bruntingthorpe Aerodrome & Proving Ground LE17 236 B6
Bruntingthorpe Ind Est LE17 236 C6
Bruntingthorpe Rd
  Peatling Parva LE17 236 B8
  Shearsby LE17 222 A1
Brunt La DE11 44 F3
Brush Dr LE11 52 B6
Brushfield Ave LE12 77 D4
Bruxby St LE7 102 F3
Bryan Cl LE12 76 D8
Bryan's Cl LE67 71 F6
Bryar's Cl LE8 223 B4
Bryngarth Cres LE5 156 B7
Bryony Rd LE5 130 D2
Buccaneer Way LE17 243 D6
Buchan Wlk LE3 154 A5
Buckfast Cl
  Leicester LE5 155 F3
  Wigston LE18 180 C1
Buckhaven Cl LE4 129 D4
Buckingham Cl
  Groby LE6 126 E2
  Hinckley LE10 197 F4
Buckingham Dr
  Leicester LE2 179 B5
  Loughborough LE11 51 C5
Buckingham Rd
  Coalville LE67 96 F8
  Countesthorpe LE8 202 F4
  Oakham LE15 137 F5
Buckingham's Way LE9 217 B4
Buckland Rd LE5 155 D8
Buckley Cl
  Measham DE12 93 C4
  Woodville DE11 44 F2
Buckley La LE8 207 A2
BUCKMINSTER 42 D2
Buckminster Cl LE13 59 E2
Buckminster La NG33 43 A6
Buckminster Prim Sch NG33 42 E1
Buckminster Rd
  Leicester LE3 154 D8
  Sproxton LE14 41 F5
  Stainby NG33 43 C2
Bucksburn Wlk LE4 129 D4
Buck's La LE12 30 A7
Buckwell La CV23 257 B6
Buckwell Rd LE9 217 D8
Buddon Cl LE3 127 E3
Buddon Ct LE12 76 E1
Buddon La LE12 75 E5
Bude Dr LE3 127 C1
Bude Rd LE18 180 D1
BUFTON 148 E8
Bufton La CV13 148 E8
Bullaces La LE17 253 C4
Bull Brig La LE15 140 A5
Buller Rd LE4 129 A1
Buller St LE8 223 F8
Bullfield Cl LE15 88 B2
Bullfinch Cl LE15 138 A8
Bullfurlong La LE10 215 F4
Bull Head St LE18 180 D3
Bull Hill LE12, LE65 48 A5
Bull La
  Ketton PE9 168 A6
  North Witham NG33 65 C7
  Oakham LE15 138 A6
Bull Ring LE12 50 B4
Bull's Head Row DE73 26 E6
Bulrush Cl LE12 76 F1
Bulstrode Pl DE74 18 C2
Bulwer Rd LE2 155 B1
Bumblebee La LE9 217 B1
Bungalows The
  Essendine PE9 117 A5
  Langham LE15 110 C3
  Little Stretton LE2 182 D5
  Newbold Verdon LE9 150 B4
  Theddingworth LE17 248 D8
Bunkers Hill LE17 238 F4
Bunneys Mdw LE10 214 E6
BURBAGE 216 B6
Burbage CE Inf Sch LE10 216 A5
Burbage Cl LE11 51 E6
Burbage Comm★ LE10 198 A3
BURBAGE COMMON 198 A3
Burbage Common Rd LE9 198 D3
Burbage Common & Woods Visitor Ctr★ LE10 198 B3
Burbage Ho LE10 215 D7
Burbage Jun Sch LE10 215 F6
Burbage Rd LE10 216 A7
Burchnall Rd LE3 153 D1
Burden La LE14 12 B3
Burder St LE11 52 C5
Burdet Cl LE3 153 E1
Burdett Cl LE17 235 C4
Burdetts Cl LE14 82 A1
Burdett Way LE4 128 D4
Burditt Cl LE67 123 F7
Burdock Cl LE5 130 D2
Burfield Ave LE11 52 A3
Burfield St LE4 155 B8
Burford Cl LE16 240 D1
Burgess Rd
  Coalville LE67 96 C8
  Leicester LE2 179 E6
Burgess Row LE16 230 B8
Burgess St
  Leicester LE1 259 A4
  Wigston LE18 180 D3
Burghley Circ LE15 87 E2
Burghley Cl
  Great Casterton PE9 142 E7
  Market Harborough LE16 241 A3
Burghley Ct 1 PE9 143 E3
Burghley Ho★ PE9 144 B1
Burghley La PE9 143 E2
Burghley Rd PE9 143 C5
Burgin Rd LE7 127 D5
Burgins La LE14 40 A7
Burkitt Rd NN17 230 F3
Burleigh Ave LE18 180 C4
Burleigh Com Coll LE11 51 C3
Burleigh Rd
  Hinckley LE10 197 C2
  Loughborough LE11 52 A4
BURLEY 111 E1
Burley Cl
  Cosby LE9 201 D3
  Desford LE9 151 B3
Burley Cres LE15 111 B3
Burley Homes LE4 128 F5
Burley Park Way LE15 138 C7
Burley Rd
  Cottesmore LE15 112 B7
  Langham LE15 110 E3
  Oakham LE15 138 B7
  Ryhall PE9 116 E1
Burley Rise DE74 18 D1
Burleys Flyover LE1 259 B5
Burleys Way LE1 259 B5
Burlington Cl DE72 9 D8
Burlington Rd LE2 155 C1
Burnaby Ave LE5 155 D6
Burnaby Pl LE14 57 F3
Burnaston Rd LE2 179 E6
Burnaston Way LE12 75 C7
Burnell Rd LE3 154 B2
Burneston Way LE18 180 E2
Burnet Cl LE5 130 C2
Burney La DE73 26 C2
Burnham Cl LE18 203 D7
Burnham Dr
  Leicester LE4 128 D2
  Whetstone LE8 201 F6
Burnham Rise CV11 214 A6
Burnhams Rd PE9 167 F5
Burnmill Rd LE16 240 E5
Burnmoor St LE2 154 E3
Burns Cl
  Measham DE12 93 B3
  Melton Mowbray LE13 59 B6
Burnside Rd
  Broughton Astley LE9 218 F5
  Leicester LE2 180 A6
Burns Rd
  Loughborough LE11 51 D4
  Stamford PE9 143 B4
Burns St
  Leicester LE2 180 A8
  Narborough LE19 178 B1
Burnsway LE10 197 C1
Burrough Ct LE14 107 B1
Burrough End LE14 82 A1
Burrough Hill Ctry Pk★ LE14 107 E4
BURROUGH ON THE HILL 107 D2
Burrough Rd
  Little Dalby LE14 108 A7
  Somerby LE14 108 A2
  Twyford LE14 133 E8
Burroughs Rd LE6 126 A1
Burrough Way LE17 244 C8
Burrough Wood Nature Trail★ LE6 125 F1
Burrow Hill Rd LE16 208 B3
Burrows Cl LE19 201 B7
Burrows The
  East Goscote LE7 103 D7
  Narborough LE19 201 A8
Bursdon Cl LE3 153 D6
Bursdon Ct LE3 153 D6
Bursnells La LE14 62 D2
Bursom Rd LE4 128 B6
Burton Cl
  Harby LE14 12 A3
  Leicester, Oadby LE2 181 D4
  Lutterworth LE17 244 D5
Burton Hall LE14 82 E5
BURTON HASTINGS 215 A1
Burton La LE12 33 B3
BURTON LAZARS 83 A6
BURTON ON THE WOLDS 53 F7
Burton on the Wolds Prim Sch LE12 53 F6
BURTON OVERY 182 F1
Burton Overy La LE7, LE8 183 C2
Burton Rd
  Ashby-de-la-Z LE65 69 A6
  Measham DE12 93 B5
  Melton Mowbray LE13 59 D1
  Orton-on-t-H CV9 119 F1
  Overseal DE12 67 A4
  Sileby LE12 77 C3
  Swadlincote DE11 44 D6
  Twycross CV9 146 C8
  Wellsborough CV13 147 A2
Burtons La LE67 71 A5
Burton's La NG32 4 F5
Burton St
  Leicester LE1 259 C4
  Loughborough LE11 52 B2
  Melton Mowbray LE13 59 C2
Burton Wlk LE12 31 E8
Burton Wlks LE11 52 B2
BURTON WOLDS 55 A8
Bury Cl LE16 229 C1
Buscot Cl LE4 155 D8
BUSHBY 157 B5
Bushby Rd LE5 155 D7
Bushey Cl LE19 201 B8
Bush Lock Cl LE18 203 A8
Bushloe Ct LE18 180 C2
Bushloe End LE18 180 C2
Bushloe High Sch LE18 180 B1
Bushnell Cl LE9 219 A4
Bushy Cl NG10 10 B6
Bushy Rd LE7 184 D7
BUSM Bsns Pk LE4 129 A1
Buswells Lodge Prim Sch LE4 128 A3
Butchers La LE12 78 A7
Butcombe Rd LE4 128 D1
Bute Cl LE10 197 C1
Bute Way LE8 202 F3
Butler Cl
  Leicester LE4 129 E4
  Ratby LE6 152 D8
Butler Ct LE11 51 F3
Butler Gdns LE16 240 C1
Butler Way LE12 77 D2
Butt Cl
  Barlestone CV13 149 D8
  Wigston LE18 180 E1
Butt Close La LE1 259 B4
Buttercup Ave DE12 67 E1
Buttercup Cl
  Groby LE6 127 A3
  Mountsorrel LE12 76 F2
  Narborough LE19 178 A1
  Stamford PE9 142 F5
Buttercup Dr LE67 97 A8
Buttercup Rd LE11 75 A6
Butterley Dr LE11 51 B2
Buttermere Ave CV11 214 A6
Buttermere Cl LE13 59 B2
Buttermere St LE2 259 A1
Buttermere Way LE12 53 C1
Butterwick Dr LE4 128 C4
Butthole La LE12 50 D5
Butt La
  Blackfordby DE11 45 A1
  Hinckley LE10 197 F1
  Husbands Bosworth LE17 247 E5
  Normanton on S LE12 30 F4
  North Luffenham LE15 166 D3
  Wymondham LE14 62 E3
Butt Lane Cl LE10 197 E1
Buttress Cl LE15 187 D7
Butts Cl CV9 119 A2
Butts The LE14 24 E1
Buxton Cl
  Swadlincote DE11 44 A7
  Whetstone LE8 201 F7
Buxton St LE2 155 C6
Buzzard Cl
  Broughton Astley LE9 218 F7
  Measham DE12 93 B4
Byfield Dr LE18 180 E2
Byford Rd LE4 128 E2
Byland Way LE11 51 B5
Bypass Rd LE14 57 F3
Byre Cres LE9 218 F5
Byron Cl
  Fleckney LE8 223 A7
  Lutterworth LE17 244 C8
  Narborough LE19 178 A2
Byron Cres DE12 93 C3
Byron Ct LE8 222 F7
Byron Rd DE11 44 C6
Byron St Extension LE11 51 F5
Byron St
  Barwell LE9 198 B8
  Earl Shilton LE9 198 E7
  Leicester LE1 259 C4
  Loughborough LE11 51 E5
Byron Way
  Melton Mowbray LE13 59 B5
  Stamford PE9 143 A3
Byrton Dr LE67 96 C4
Bytham Hts NG33 90 C8
Byway Rd LE5 155 E2

C

Cabin Leas LE11 52 B5
CADEBY 149 D1
Cadeby Cl LE10 197 B3
Cadeby La CV13 149 B3
Cademan Cl LE2 180 B7
Cademan Ct LE2 180 B7
Cademan St LE67 71 F5
Cadles Cl LE9 199 D3
Cadle St LE9 150 B5
Caernarvon Cl
  Mountsorrel LE12 101 D8
  Shepshed LE12 50 A2
Cairngorm Cl LE2 179 F7
Cairns Cl 5 LE3 178 F7

Cairnsford Rd LE2 . . . . . 180 B6
Caistor Rd NN17 . . . . . . 213 C1
Caithness Rd PE9 . . . . . . 143 A4
Calais Hill LE1 . . . . 259 C3
Calais St LE1 . . . . 259 C3
CALDECOTE 195 A2
Caldecote Com Prim Sch
LE3 . . . . 154 A1
Caldecote Hall CV10 . . . . 194 F2
Caldecote Hall Dr
CV10 . . . . 194 F3
Caldecote Rd
Great Easton LE16 . . . . . 229 E6
Leicester LE3 . . . . 154 A1
CALDECOTT 230 C8
Caldecott Cl LE18 . . . . . . 180 F2
Caldecott Rd LE16 . . . . . 230 B5
Calder Cl
Corby NN17 . . . . 230 D1
Oakham LE15 . . . . 137 E5
Calderdale Dr NG10 . . . . . 10 A4
Calder Rd LE4 . . . . 128 C3
Caldon Cl LE10 . . . . 215 B8
Caldwell St LE11 . . . . 52 A4
Caledine Rd LE4 . . . . 154 A8
Caledonian Rd PE9 . . . . . 143 B6
Calgary Cres LE15 . . . . . . 138 B6
Calgary Rd LE1 . . . . 155 A7
Calke Cl LE11 . . . . 75 A6
Calke Rd DE73 . . . . 26 A6
Callan Cl LE19 . . . . 201 A8
Callan's La LE65 . . . . 46 D7
Callendar Cl CV11 . . . . . . 214 A2
Callis Pk LE65 . . . . 69 B7
Caloe Cl LE12 . . . . 77 E3
Calver Hey Rd LE4 . . . . . 128 B3
Calvert Cres LE19 . . . . . . 180 C4
Calverton Ave LE18 . . . . . 180 C4
Calverton Cl LE6 . . . . 152 D8
Camborne Cl LE18 . . . . . 180 C1
Camborne Dr CV11 . . . . . 214 A5
Cambourne Rd LE10 . . . . 216 A6
Cambrian Cl LE9 . . . . 201 D2
Cambrian Way
Ashby-de-la-Z LE65 . . . . . 69 B4
Swadlincote DE11 . . . . . . 44 A3
Cambridge Ave LE13 . . . . . 82 D8
Cambridge Cl LE7 . . . . . 103 C3
Cambridge Dr LE9 . . . . . 151 A2
Cambridge Rd
Cosby LE8, LE9 . . . . 201 E5
Stamford PE9 . . . . 143 C5
Cambridge St
Coalville LE67 . . . . 71 E1
Leicester LE3 . . . . 154 C4
Loughborough LE11 . . . . . 52 B5
Shepshed LE12 . . . . 50 B2
Cam Cl NN17 . . . . 230 C1
Camden Rd LE3 . . . . 154 A1
Camden St LE1 . . . . 259 C4
Camelford Rd LE67 . . . . . . 96 C7
Camellia Cl LE17 . . . . . . 177 F1
Camelot Way LE19 . . . . . 178 A1
Cameron Ave LE4 . . . . . . 129 E5
Camfield Rise LE2 . . . . . . 179 D4
Camomile Rd LE13 . . . . . . 82 B8
Campbell Ave LE4 . . . . . . 129 E5
Campbell St LE1 . . . . . . 259 C2
Campden Cl
Exton LE15 . . . . 113 B2
Uppingham LE15 . . . . . . 189 B4
Camp Hill Ct PE9 . . . . . . 143 B8
Campion Cl LE19 . . . . . . 201 A8
Campion Gr PE9 . . . . . . 142 F5
Campion Hill DE74 . . . . . . 17 A4
Campion Pl LE13 . . . . 82 A8
Campion Rd DE11 . . . . . . 44 F4
Campion Wlk LE4 . . . . . . 128 B3
Campton Cl LE10 . . . . . . 215 E2
Camrose Cl LE15 . . . . . . 138 B6
Camville Rd LE3 . . . . 153 F4
Canada Fields LE17 . . . . 244 C6
Canal Bank
Loughborough LE11 . . . . . 52 A5
Shardlow DE72 . . . . 9 A1
Canal La
Harby LE14 . . . . 12 D5
Hose LE14 . . . . 20 E8
Long Clawson LE14 . . . . . 20 C6
Canalside LE16 . . . . 240 D4
Canal St
Leicester LE2 . . . . 179 C7
Oakthorpe DE12 . . . . 93 A7
Thurmaston LE4 . . . . . . 129 E8
Wigston LE18 . . . . 179 F1
Canal Way LE10 . . . . 214 F7
Canberra Way LE10 . . . . 215 E4
Candle La LE9 . . . . 198 F8
Cank St LE1 . . . . 259 B4
Cannam Cl
Middleton LE16 . . . . 229 B1
Whetstone LE8 . . . . 202 A5
Canner Cl DE11 . . . . 45 A2
Canning Pl LE1 . . . . 259 B5
Canning St
Hinckley LE10 . . . . 197 C1
Leicester LE1 . . . . 259 B5
Canning Way LE11 . . . . . . 51 C6
Cannock Cl LE67 . . . . 96 D4
Cannock St LE4 . . . . 130 A4
Cannock Way NG10 . . . . . 10 F7
Canon Cl LE2 . . . . 181 B5
Canons Cl LE19 . . . . 201 B8
Canonsleigh Rd LE4 . . . . 128 E3

Canonsleigh Wlk ⑥
LE4 . . . . 128 E3
Canon St LE4 . . . . 129 C1
Canterbury Dr
Ashby-de-la-Z LE65 . . . . . 69 A7
Melton Mowbray LE13 . . . . 59 A6
Canterbury Ho ① LE4 . . . 129 B1
Canterbury Terr LE3 . . . . 154 B3
Canterbury Way CV11 . . . 214 A8
Cantrell Rd LE3 . . . . 153 D3
Canvey Cl LE18 . . . . 180 F3
Capendale Cl PE9 . . . . . . 167 F5
Capers Cl LE19 . . . . 178 A3
Capesthorne Cl LE5 . . . . 155 D8
Captains Close Prim Sch
LE14 . . . . 57 E3
Cara Cl LE2 . . . . 180 C8
Carbery Cl LE2 . . . . 181 D4
Cardigan Dr LE18 . . . . . . 179 F2
Cardinal Cl LE6 . . . . 152 B8
Cardinals Wlk LE5 . . . . . 156 C8
Carey Cl LE18 . . . . 203 D8
Carey Gdns LE9 . . . . 152 D5
Carey Hill Rd LE9 . . . . . . 199 D2
Carey Rd LE9 . . . . 200 D7
Careys Cl LE1 . . . . 259 A3
Carfax Ave LE2 . . . . 180 F7
Car Hill Rd LE67 . . . . 71 E7
Carillon Ct LE11 . . . . 52 B4
Carillon Tower & War
Meml★ LE11 . . . . 52 A3
Carington St LE11 . . . . . . 51 F5
Carisbrooke Ave LE2 . . . . 180 C7
Carisbrooke Ct LE2 . . . . . 180 C7
Carisbrooke Gdns
LE2 . . . . 180 C8
Carisbrooke Pk LE2 . . . . . 180 C8
Carisbrooke Rd
Leicester LE2 . . . . 180 C7
Mountsorrel LE12 . . . . . . 101 D8
Carisbrook Gr PE9 . . . . . 143 A4
CARLBY 117 C8
Carlin Cl DE72 . . . . 9 E8
Carling Cl LE67 . . . . 71 E1
Carlisle St LE3 . . . . 154 C5
Carl Moult Ho DE11 . . . . . 44 A2
Carlson Gdns LE14 . . . . . 244 D6
Carlson Terr LE17 . . . . . . 244 D6
Carl St LE2 . . . . 179 C6
CARLTON 148 D7
Carlton Ave LE19 . . . . . . 201 C8
Carlton Cl LE11 . . . . 51 F4
Carlton Ct
Glenfield LE3 . . . . 153 D8
Leicester LE2 . . . . 155 D1
CARLTON CURLIEU 206 D7
Carlton Dr LE18 . . . . 180 C4
Carlton Gdns LE8 . . . . . . 205 B7
Carlton La LE8 . . . . 205 F8
Carlton Rd
Barton in B CV13 . . . . . . 122 D1
Carlton CV13 . . . . 148 B4
Kibworth Beauchamp
LE8 . . . . 206 B3
Long Eaton NG10 . . . . 10 B5
Carlton St LE1 . . . . 259 B2
Carlyon Ct LE9 . . . . 152 E5
Carlyon Rd
Atherstone CV9 . . . . 170 F1
Atherstone, Mancetter
CV9 . . . . 194 A7
Carlyon Road Ind Est
Atherstone CV9 . . . . 170 F1
Atherstone CV9 . . . . 194 A8
Carmen Gr LE6 . . . . 126 E3
Carnation Cl LE3 . . . . . . 152 F2
Carnation St LE4 . . . . . . 128 F2
Carnegie Cres LE13 . . . . . 59 E6
Carnival Way DE74 . . . . . . 17 B4
Carnoustie Rd LE3 . . . . . 153 D6
Caroline Ct LE2 . . . . 179 E6
Carousel Pk LE9 . . . . 197 F8
Carpenters Cl LE10 . . . . . 215 F5
Carpenter's Cl LE3 . . . . . 153 B7
Carpe Rd LE4 . . . . 129 D1
Carrfield Ave NG10 . . . . . 10 F8
Carrfields La LE14 . . . . . . 80 D8
Carriageway The
LE15 . . . . 136 A6
Carrick Point LE5 . . . . . . 155 F4
Carrington Rd LE5 . . . . . 130 C3
Carron Cl NN17 . . . . 230 C1
Carrow Rd LE3 . . . . 153 B5
Carrs Cl DE74 . . . . 17 A3
Carr's Dr ① LE9 . . . . 198 F8
Carrs Hill LE9 . . . . 198 C6
Carr's Rd LE9 . . . . 198 F8
Carter Cl
Enderby LE19 . . . . 178 A3
Long Eaton NG10 . . . . 10 B6
Carter Dale LE67 . . . . 71 D7
Carter St LE4 . . . . 155 C8
Cartland Dr LE11 . . . . 51 C6
Carts La LE1 . . . . 259 B4
Cartwright Dr LE2 . . . . . . 181 A5
Cartwright St LE11 . . . . . . 52 C5
Cartwright Way LE67 . . . . . 97 D4
Carty Rd LE5 . . . . 130 C3
Carver Ct PE9 . . . . 167 F5
Carver's Cnr LE2 . . . . . . 179 B3
Carver's Path LE7 . . . . . 103 C3
Casewick La LE9 . . . . . . 144 F4
Cashmore View LE4 . . . . 128 D4
Castell Dr LE4 . . . . 155 A8
Casterton Bsns & Ent Coll
PE9 . . . . 142 E7
Casterton La PE9 . . . . . . 142 E2
Casterton Rd PE9 . . . . . . 143 B4

Castle Bank LE16 . . . . . . 251 F5
Castle Bytham Rd LE15 . . . 89 F5
Castle Cl
Bottesford NG13 . . . . 3 D2
Earl Shilton LE9 . . . . 175 F1
Sapcote LE9 . . . . 217 D7
Uppingham LE15 . . . . . . 188 F5
Castle Ct LE10 . . . . 215 D6
Castledine Ave LE12 . . . . . 76 A6
Castledine St Extension
LE11 . . . . 52 B2
Castledine St
Loughborough LE11 . . . . . 52 B2
Quorn (Quorndon) LE12 . . . 75 F6
CASTLE DONINGTON 17 C3
Castle Donington Com
Coll DE74 . . . . 17 B3
Castle Dyke PE9 . . . . . . 143 D2
Castle Fields LE4 . . . . . . 128 A5
Castleford Rd LE3 . . . . . . 178 E8
Castlegate Ave LE4 . . . . . 128 F8
Castle Gate Ho ⑰ LE65 . . . 69 B7
Castle Hill
Castle Donington DE74 . . . 17 B2
East Leake LE12 . . . . 31 F8
Leicester LE2 . . . . 155 C4
Loughborough LE11 . . . . . 52 C1
Stamford PE9 . . . . 142 F4
Castle La
Melbourne DE73 . . . . 26 B7
⑤ Stamford PE9 . . . . . . 143 D2
Castlemaine Dr LE10 . . . . 197 E3
Castle Mews DE73 . . . . . . 26 B7
Castle Mews The ⑤
DE11 . . . . 44 A7
Castle Mills DE73 . . . . 26 B7
Castle Mound Way
CV23 . . . . 252 D2
Castle Rd
Hartshill CV10 . . . . 194 B1
Kirby Muxloe LE9 . . . . . . 152 D5
Mountsorrel LE12 . . . . . . 101 D8
Castle Rise
Belmesthorpe PE9 . . . . . 117 A1
Groby LE6 . . . . 126 F2
Castle Rock Dr LE67 . . . . . 72 C2
Castle Rock High Sch
LE67 . . . . 72 C2
Castle St
Hinckley LE10 . . . . 215 D8
Leicester LE1 . . . . 259 A3
Melbourne DE73 . . . . 26 B7
⑯ Stamford PE9 . . . . . . 143 D3
Whitwick LE67 . . . . 71 F5
Castleton Rd LE18 . . . . . 180 C4
Castle View
Hartshill CV10 . . . . 194 B1
Leicester LE1 . . . . 259 A3
Castle View Rd NG13 . . . . . 7 C3
Castle Way LE65 . . . . 69 A4
Castlewood Mobile Home
Pk LE9 . . . . 216 D8
Castle Yd LE1 . . . . 259 A3
Caswell Cl LE4 . . . . 128 D4
Caters Cl LE67 . . . . 127 D6
Catesby St LE3 . . . . 154 D5
Catharine Rise DE11 . . . . . 44 A1
Catherine Inf Sch LE4 . . . 155 B8
Catherine Jun Sch
LE4 . . . . 155 B8
Catherines Cl LE12 . . . . . . 76 B6
Catherine St LE4 . . . . . . 129 C1
Catherine Street Ind Est
LE4 . . . . 129 D2
Cathkin Cl LE3 . . . . 153 D5
Catmose Park Rd
LE15 . . . . 138 B5
Catmose St LE15 . . . . . . 138 A6
CATTHORPE 253 E1
Catthorpe Manor
LE17 . . . . 253 F1
Catthorpe Rd LE17 . . . . . 253 C4
Cattle Market LE11 . . . . . . 52 B3
Cauby St LE9 . . . . 77 E3
Caudebec Cl LE15 . . . . . 189 A5
Caudle Cl LE17 . . . . 100 F3
Cauldwell La LE17 . . . . . 234 B4
Causeway La
Cropston LE7 . . . . 100 E2
Leicester LE1 . . . . 259 A4
Causeway Rd NN17 . . . . 230 E2
Cavalry Cl LE13 . . . . 59 A6
Cavendish Cl
Castle Donington DE74 . . . 17 A2
Shardlow DE72 . . . . 9 A2
⑨ Swadlincote DE11 . . . . 44 A7
Cavendish Cres LE67 . . . . 96 C7
Cavendish Ct DE72 . . . . . . 9 A1
Cavendish Mews LE2 . . . . 179 E8
Cavendish Rd LE2 . . . . . 179 E8
Cave Rd LE12 . . . . 76 E8
Caversham Cl CV11 . . . . 214 A7
Caversham Rd LE2 . . . . . 179 C3
Cawdell Dr LE12 . . . . 29 D2
Cawsand Rd LE18 . . . . . . 180 C1
Cawston Cl LE5 . . . . 130 B2
Caxton Pl LE12 . . . . 76 D7
Caxton St LE16 . . . . 240 F1
Cecil Ct ⑪ PE9 . . . . 143 E3
Cecilia Rd LE2 . . . . 155 B2
Cecil Rd LE2 . . . . 155 B6
Cedar Ave
Birstall LE4 . . . . 129 A7
East Leake LE12 . . . . 31 D8
Long Eaton NG10 . . . . 10 C5
Lutterworth LE17 . . . . . . 244 B6
Wigston LE18 . . . . 180 D2
Cedar Cl
Ashby-de-la-Z LE65 . . . . . 69 C6
Glenfield LE3 . . . . 127 E1

Cedar Cl continued
Kibworth Beauchamp
LE8 . . . . 223 F8
Uppingham LE15 . . . . . . 189 C4
Cedar Cres LE19 . . . . . . 201 B7
Cedar Croft DE72 . . . . 16 A7
Cedar Ct LE67 . . . . 97 C5
Cedar Ct
Corby NN17 . . . . 230 E1
Groby LE6 . . . . 126 F2
Hinckley LE10 . . . . 216 A6
Leicester LE5 . . . . 156 A8
Cedar Dr
Ibstock LE67 . . . . 95 E2
Market Bosworth CV13 . . . 148 F2
Melton Mowbray LE13 . . . . 59 B5
Syston LE7 . . . . 103 B2
Cedar Gr
Moira DE12 . . . . 68 B6
Mountsorrel LE12 . . . . . . 76 E1
Cedar Rd
Blaby LE8 . . . . 202 B6
Castle Donington DE74 . . . 17 B2
Earl Shilton LE9 . . . . 198 D7
Leicester LE2 . . . . 155 C4
Loughborough LE11 . . . . . 52 C1
Stamford PE9 . . . . 142 F4
Cedars Ct LE2 . . . . 155 C3
Cedar St LE15 . . . . 137 A2
Cedars The
Bushby LE7 . . . . 157 B4
Leicester LE2 . . . . 180 B7
Cedarwood Cl LE4 . . . . . 129 D1
Celandine Cl
Leicester, Oadby LE2 . . . . 181 E4
Mountsorrel LE12 . . . . . . 76 F2
Celandine Pl DE11 . . . . . . 44 E4
Celandine Rd LE5 . . . . . . 130 C2
Cello Cl LE67 . . . . 71 E5
Celt St LE3 . . . . 154 D4
Cemetery La
Hartshill CV10 . . . . 194 B1
Manton LE15 . . . . 164 D6
Cemetery Rd
Sileby LE12 . . . . 77 D3
Whetstone LE8 . . . . 201 F7
Central Ave
Ibstock LE67 . . . . 95 F1
Leicester LE2 . . . . 155 C2
Lutterworth LE17 . . . . . . 244 C7
Shepshed LE12 . . . . 50 B3
Syston LE7 . . . . 103 C4
Wigston LE18 . . . . 180 C2
Central Cl LE8 . . . . 201 F8
Central Park Dr CV23 . . . 252 D2
Central Pk LE17 . . . . 244 D8
Central Rd
Coalville LE67 . . . . 96 D7
Leicester LE3 . . . . 154 D7
Central St LE8 . . . . 202 F4
Centre Ct LE17 . . . . 178 D7
Centurian Ct Office Pk
LE19 . . . . 178 D8
Centurion Ct LE6 . . . . . . 152 D8
Centurion Way LE19 . . . . 178 D7
Century Ct LE5 . . . . 156 C6
Chadderton Cl LE2 . . . . . 180 A7
CHADWELL 39 C5
Chadwell Cl
Asfordby LE14 . . . . 57 E2
Melton Mowbray LE13 . . . . 59 E2
Chadwell Rd LE3 . . . . . . 153 E7
Chadwick Cl LE5 . . . . . . 130 B4
Chadwick Wlk LE4 . . . . . 128 D3
Chaffinch Cl
Leicester LE4 . . . . 128 B6
Oakham LE15 . . . . 138 B8
Chainama Cl LE3 . . . . . . 153 C6
Chainbridge Cl LE11 . . . . . 52 A5
Chale Rd LE4 . . . . 128 F2
Chalfont Cl LE13 . . . . 82 D7
Chalfont Dr LE11 . . . . 77 C1
Chalgrove Wlk LE5 . . . . . 156 A6
Challottee LE12 . . . . 50 C3
Chalmondley Dr LE13 . . . . 59 D6
Chalvington Cl LE5 . . . . . 156 C3
Chambers Cl LE67 . . . . . 125 F8
Chambers Row NN6 . . . . 256 E6
Champion Cl LE5 . . . . . . 156 B5
Chancel Rd LE4 . . . . 128 D8
Chancery St LE1 . . . . . . 259 B3
Chandlers Croft LE67 . . . . 95 F3
Chandler Way LE9 . . . . . 219 B5
Chandos St LE2 . . . . 155 C4
Channing Way LE67 . . . . . 96 C4
Chantrell Cl LE67 . . . . . . 124 B5
Chantry Cl
Huncote LE9 . . . . 200 D7
Long Eaton NG10 . . . . 10 A4
Melbourne DE73 . . . . 26 B7
Chapel Bar LE12 . . . . 33 C3
Chapel Cl
Ab Kettleby LE14 . . . . 37 C2
Dunton Bassett LE17 . . . . 219 D2
Empingham LE15 . . . . . . 141 A6
Houghton on t H LE7 . . . . 157 F4
Kilby LE18 . . . . 203 F3
Moira DE12 . . . . 44 C1
① Oakham LE15 . . . . . . 138 A6
Ravenstone LE67 . . . . . . 70 F1
Syston LE7 . . . . 103 A4
Thurcaston LE7 . . . . 101 B3
Chapel Ct
Leicester LE5 . . . . 156 B2
Littlethorpe LE19 . . . . . . 201 C7
Chapel Fields LE17 . . . . . 254 B3

Chapel Flats LE9 . . . . . . 198 B6
Chapel Gn LE3 . . . . 153 B3
Chapel Hill
Groby LE6 . . . . 126 E3
Woolsthorpe by B NG32 . . . 15 B8
Chapel La
Ab Kettleby LE14 . . . . 37 C2
Barrowden LE15 . . . . . . 191 F5
Clipston LE16 . . . . 249 F1
Coleorton LE67 . . . . 70 E8
Congerstone CV13 . . . . . 147 D8
Cosby LE9 . . . . 201 D2
Croxton Kerrial NG32 . . . . 24 A7
Desford LE9 . . . . 151 B4
Gaddesby LE7 . . . . 105 B7
Granby NG13 . . . . 5 B5
Hoby LE14 . . . . 79 D8
Hose LE14 . . . . 20 F8
Ketton PE9 . . . . 168 A5
Leicester LE2 . . . . 180 B8
Lilbourne CV23 . . . . 258 A6
Mowsley LE17 . . . . 237 F7
Nether Broughton LE14 . . . 36 C8
North Luffenham LE15 . . . 166 D3
Norton-J-T CV9 . . . . 120 A2
Old Dalby LE14 . . . . 35 E4
Osgathorpe LE12 . . . . . . 48 E3
Ratby LE6 . . . . 152 C8
Sharnford LE10 . . . . 217 C4
Somerby LE14 . . . . 108 B2
Stathern LE14 . . . . 13 A3
Tugby LE7 . . . . 185 E6
Upper Broughton LE14 . . . 19 A1
Walcote LE17 . . . . 245 C6
Walton LE17 . . . . 236 B2
Willoughby-on-t-W LE12 . . . 34 D7
Witherley CV9 . . . . 194 C7
Wymondham LE14 . . . . . . 62 C2
Chapel Rise LE65 . . . . . . 47 F5
Chapel Row NG33 . . . . . . 43 B8
Chapel St
Barkestone-le-V NG13 . . . . 6 B2
Barlestone CV13 . . . . . . 149 D8
Barwell LE9 . . . . 198 B6
Belton-in-R LE15 . . . . . . 187 D7
Blaby LE8 . . . . 179 C1
Bottesford NG13 . . . . 3 B3
Donisthorpe DE12 . . . . . . 92 E8
Earl Shilton LE9 . . . . 176 A1
Eaton NG32 . . . . 22 F6
Enderby LE19 . . . . 178 A3
Ibstock LE67 . . . . 95 F1
Leicester, Oadby LE2 . . . . 181 A5
Long Eaton NG10 . . . . 10 E7
Lutterworth LE17 . . . . . . 244 C6
Measham DE12 . . . . 93 C5
Melbourne DE73 . . . . 26 B7
Melton Mowbray LE13 . . . . 59 C3
Oakthorpe DE12 . . . . 93 A6
Sharnford LE10 . . . . 217 C4
Shepshed LE12 . . . . 50 B5
Smisby LE65 . . . . 45 F3
Stapleton LE9 . . . . 174 F1
Swadlincote, Church Gresley
DE11 . . . . 44 A1
Swinford LE17 . . . . 254 B3
Syston LE7 . . . . 103 B4
Woodville DE11 . . . . 44 F2
Chapel View LE5 . . . . . . 156 B2
Chapel Yd PE9 . . . . 143 E3
Chaplin Cl LE12 . . . . 77 C3
Chaplin Ct LE3 . . . . 153 D3
Chapman Cl CV13 . . . . . 149 D8
Chapmans Mdws LE65 . . . 69 C4
Chapman St LE11 . . . . . . 52 C4
Chappell Cl LE4 . . . . 129 E7
Charity Hos The CV23 . . . 252 C6
Charlecote Ave LE3 . . . . . 153 F1
Charles Dr LE7 . . . . 127 F7
Charles Hall Cl LE12 . . . . . 50 C4
Charles Rd PE9 . . . . 143 C5
Charles St
Hinckley LE10 . . . . 197 E1
Leicester LE1 . . . . 259 B4
Long Eaton NG10 . . . . 10 D6
Loughborough LE11 . . . . . 52 B5
Market Harborough
LE16 . . . . 240 D3
Ravenstone LE67 . . . . . . 71 A2
Sileby LE12 . . . . 77 C2
Swadlincote DE11 . . . . . . 44 B2
Charleston Cl DE11 . . . . . 44 A7
Charleston Cres LE9 . . . . 198 A6
Charles Way
Leicester, Oadby LE2 . . . . 181 A5
Whetstone LE8 . . . . 202 A5
Charley Dr LE11 . . . . 51 E2
Charley Rd
Shepshed LE12 . . . . 72 F7
Woodhouse Eaves LE12 . . . 73 F2
Charlock Dr PE9 . . . . . . 142 F4
Charlock Rd LE5 . . . . . . 130 D2
Charlotte Ct
Blaby LE8 . . . . 202 A8
Leicester LE4 . . . . 128 B3
Charlotte St LE13 . . . . . . 59 C3
Charlottes Wlk LE7 . . . . . 157 F3
Charlton Cl LE18 . . . . . . 202 A6
Charnborough Ct LE67 . . . 97 B8
Charnborough Rd LE67 . . . 97 B8
Charnia Gr LE12 . . . . . . 100 F6
Charnor Rd LE3 . . . . 153 E8
Charnwood LE6 . . . . 126 D5
Charnwood Ave
Asfordby LE14 . . . . 57 F3
Castle Donington DE74 . . . 17 C3
Long Eaton NG10 . . . . 10 B4
Sutton Bonington LE12 . . . 30 C5

Charnwood Ave *continued*
Thurmaston LE4.......... **129** F8
Whetstone LE8.......... **201** F8
Charnwood Bsns Pk
LE11 .... **52** B6
Charnwood Cl
Hinckley LE10 .... **197** E2
Leicester Forest East
LE3 .... **153** A4
Thurmaston LE4......... **129** F8
Charnwood Ct LE67 ..... **96** E8
Charnwood Dr
Hartshill Green CV10..... **194** B2
Leicester Forest East
LE3 .... **153** A3
Markfield LE67.......... **125** F8
Melton Mowbray LE13..... **59** A4
Thurnby LE7........... **156** F5
Charnwood Fields
LE12................. **30** C5
Charnwood Ho LE12 .... **100** A8
Charnwood Ind Units LE2,
LE5................. **155** B6
Charnwood Manor
LE19................ **201** C8
Charnwood Mus*
LE11................. **52** A4
Charnwood Prim Sch
LE2................. **155** B6
Charnwood Rd
Anstey LE7............ **127** D7
Barwell LE9 .... **198** B8
Hinckley LE10 .... **197** D2
Loughborough LE11...... **52** B2
Shepshed LE12 .... **50** B2
Charnwood Rise LE12.... **99** F8
Charnwood St
Coalville LE67 .... **71** E1
Leicester LE5.......... **155** C6
Charteris Cl LE11 ...... **51** D6
Charter Point Way
LE65................ **69** E6
Charter St LE1........ **154** F7
Charters The PE9 ...... **144** E4
Chartley Rd LE3 .... **154** C3
Chartwell Dr LE18 ...... **180** A3
Chartwell Drive Ind Est
LE18................ **180** A3
Chartwell Point LE18.... **180** B3
Chase The
Braunstone Town LE3 .... **178** F7
East Goscote LE7....... **103** D8
Great Glen LE8 .... **182** C1
Markfield LE67......... **125** E8
Chater Cl
Great Bowden LE16...... **241** A4
Leicester LE5.......... **156** D7
Manton LE15 .... **164** E6
Chater La PE9 .... **168** A7
Chater Mews PE9...... **168** A7
Chater Rd LE15 .... **137** F5
Chatham St LE1....... **259** B3
Chatsworth Ave LE18... **180** A1
Chatsworth Cl
Hinckley LE10 .... **215** F6
Shepshed LE12 .... **50** A3
Chatsworth Dr
Market Harborough
LE16................ **241** B3
Syston LE7............ **102** F3
Chatsworth Rd
Loughborough LE11...... **51** D5
Stamford PE9.......... **143** B4
Swadlincote DE11 ...... **44** A6
Chatsworth St LE2 ..... **155** C6
Chatteris Ave LE5...... **156** D3
Chaucer St
Leicester LE2.......... **155** C3
Narborough LE19....... **178** A1
Chaveney Ct LE12...... **75** E5
Chaveney Rd LE12...... **75** E5
Chaveney Wlk LE12..... **75** E5
Cheapside
Leicester LE1.......... **259** B4
Melton Mowbray LE13.... **59** C3
Shepshed LE12 .... **50** C4
Checketts Cl LE4....... **129** B2
Checketts Rd LE4...... **129** B3
Checkland Rd LE4...... **129** E8
Cheddar Rd LE18...... **180** E3
Cheer Cl LE8......... **201** F4
Chelker Way LE11...... **51** F2
Chellaston La DE72..... **16** A8
Chellaston Rd LE18..... **180** C4
Chelsea Cl LE2........ **179** D1
Cheltenham Dr LE65 .... **69** A7
Cheltenham Rd LE4..... **128** D2
Cheney Ct LE9........ **200** D8
Cheney Rd LE4........ **130** A4
Chepstow Rd LE2...... **155** C3
Cheribough Rd DE74.... **17** A3
Cheriton Rd LE2....... **179** D5
Cherrybrook Cl LE4..... **128** B7
Cherry Cl
Breaston DE72.......... **9** E8
Loughborough LE11...... **75** A7
Cherry Croft ❸ LE11.... **51** F2
Cherry Dr LE7........ **103** B2
Cherryfield Cl CV10..... **194** B2
Cherry Gr LE8........ **182** C1
Cherry Hills Rd LE3..... **153** C6
Cherryholt La PE9...... **143** F3
Cherryholt Rd PE9...... **143** F3
Cherryleas Dr LE3...... **154** C4
Cherry Orchard Est
CV13................ **195** F3
Cherry Rd LE8........ **202** B7

Cherry St LE18........ **180** B2
Cherrytree Ave LE17.... **244** A6
Cherry Tree Ave LE9.... **152** E3
Cherrytree Cl
Anstey LE7............ **127** D5
Countesthorpe LE8...... **202** E4
Cherry Tree Cl LE17.... **247** E5
Cherry Tree Ct
Leicester Forest East
LE9................. **152** E3
Moira DE12 .... **68** B6
Cherry Tree Dr
Barwell LE9 .... **198** B8
Plungar NG13 .... **6** A1
Cherry Tree Gr LE19.... **178** A3
Cherry Tree Mews
DE11................ **44** F2
Cherwell Cl LE10....... **215** A8
Cherwell Rd LE12...... **76** D7
Cherwell Wlk NN17..... **230** C1
Cheshire Cl LE17....... **244** B4
Cheshire Dr LE18...... **180** A3
Cheshire Gdns LE2..... **179** D7
Cheshire Rd LE2....... **179** D7
Chessher St LE10...... **197** C1
Chester Cl
Blaby LE8............. **202** C7
Leicester LE1.......... **155** B7
Loughborough LE11..... **51** F3
Chesterfield Ave NG10 .. **10** F7
Chesterfield Rd LE5.... **155** D4
Chesterfield Way LE9 ... **198** C7
Chester Gdns DE11 .... **44** B2
Chester Rd LE8....... **202** C7
Chesterton Ct LE19.... **178** A2
Chesterton Wlk LE3.... **154** A5
Chestnut Ave
Corby NN17 .... **230** D1
Leicester LE5.......... **130** D1
Leicester, Oadby LE2.... **181** A5
Lutterworth LE17....... **244** A6
Swadlincote DE11 ...... **44** B6
Chestnut Cl
Bottesford NG13 .... **3** C3
Broughton Astley LE9 ... **219** A5
Ibstock LE67 .... **95** E1
Littlethorpe LE19....... **201** B6
Market Bosworth CV13 .. **148** F2
Moira DE12 .... **68** B5
Queniborough LE7...... **103** D5
Quorn (Quorndon) LE12... **75** E4
Shepshed LE12 .... **50** C3
Syston LE7............ **103** B2
Uppingham LE15 .... **189** A3
Chestnut Ct LE12...... **76** E2
Chestnut Dr
Bagworth LE67 .... **124** A6
Bushby LE7 .... **157** A4
Leicester, Oadby LE2.... **182** A4
Chestnut Gdns PE9..... **142** F3
Chestnut Gn DE11 ..... **44** B2
Chestnut Gr LE67 ..... **97** B8
Chestnut La LE8...... **221** F5
Chestnut Pl LE12...... **76** D7
Chestnut Rd
Glenfield LE3 .... **153** C8
Oakham LE15.......... **138** A7
Chestnut St LE11 ..... **52** A4
Chestnuts The
Countesthorpe LE8...... **202** E4
Long Eaton NG10....... **10** A8
Chestnut Way
East Goscote LE7....... **103** E7
Melton Mowbray LE13.... **59** C1
Chestnut Wlk
Groby LE6 .... **126** F2
Markfield LE67......... **125** E6
Chettle Rd LE3........ **154** A7
Chetwynd Dr LE13..... **58** F3
Chevin Ave LE3....... **153** D5
Cheviot Cl
Oakham LE15.......... **137** E6
Swadlincote DE11 ...... **44** A3
Cheviot Dr LE12...... **50** C3
Cheviot Rd
Leicester LE2.......... **179** F7
Long Eaton NG10....... **10** A8
Cheyne La ❽ PE9..... **143** E3
Chichester Cl
Ellistown LE67 .... **96** C4
Loughborough LE11..... **74** C8
Nuneaton CV11 .... **214** A7
Chilcombe Cl LE4...... **128** E3
Chilcombe Wlk ❹
LE4................. **128** E3
CHILCOTE **91** F3
Chilcot Cl LE67........ **71** F1
Child Cl LE14......... **82** F6
Chiltern Ave
Cosby LE9 .... **201** D2
Shepshed LE12 .... **50** D3
Chiltern Cl
Market Harborough
LE16................ **240** F5
Oakham LE15.......... **137** D6
Chiltern Dr LE15...... **166** C7
Chiltern Gn LE2....... **180** A6
Chiltern Rd DE11...... **44** A3
Chiltern Rise LE65..... **69** C5
Chislehurst Ave LE3.... **178** F8
Chiswick Dr LE11...... **51** C4
Chiswick Rd LE2....... **154** F1
Chitterman Way LE67... **125** E8
Chorley Wood Rd
LE5................. **156** D4
Choyce Cl CV9........ **170** D2
Chrisett Cl LE5....... **156** B6
Christ Church Cl PE9.... **143** D4

Christ Church & St Peter's
CE Prim Sch LE2....... **76** E2
Christie Dr LE11....... **51** D6
Christopher Cl
Countesthorpe LE8...... **202** E3
Heather LE67........... **95** F3
Christopher Ct NN6..... **256** D5
Christopher Dr LE4..... **129** F4
Christow St LE1....... **155** B7
Christ the King RC Prim
Sch LE3.............. **154** B6
Chrysanthemum Ct
DE11................ **44** A5
Church Ave
Leicester LE3.......... **154** C5
Long Eaton NG10....... **10** A4
Swadlincote DE11 ...... **44** B3
Church Bank LE16...... **229** D7
Church Cl
Ashwell LE15 .... **111** B8
Barwell LE9 .... **198** A6
Blackfordby DE11 ...... **45** B1
Braybrooke LE16 ...... **251** E6
Broughton Astley LE9 ... **218** F6
Caldecott LE16......... **230** B8
Dunton Bassett LE17.... **219** D1
Hinckley LE10 .... **216** A5
Hose LE14 .... **20** F7
Kibworth Beauchamp
LE8................ **206** A1
Lutterworth LE17....... **244** C6
Stoke Golding CV13..... **196** D7
Syston LE7............ **103** B4
Church Cnr NG13........ **6** A7
Church Croft CV9....... **171** B7
Church Cswy LE16...... **225** C7
Church Ct PE9........ **143** E2
Church Dr
Gilmorton LE17........ **235** C4
Markfield LE67......... **125** D8
Church End LE14....... **19** D1
Church Farm La LE8 .... **220** D5
Church Field CV13...... **147** D8
Churchgate LE16....... **209** D6
Church Gate
Kegworth DE74 .... **18** D2
Leicester LE1.......... **259** B4
Loughborough LE11..... **52** B4
❶ Lutterworth LE17..... **244** C5
Shepshed LE12 .... **50** C4
Churchgate Mews ❸
LE11................ **52** B4
CHURCH GRESLEY **44** B2
Church Gresley Inf Sch
DE11................ **44** B2
Church Hill
Bagworth LE67 .... **124** B4
Birstall LE4 .... **129** B6
Cranoe LE16 .... **208** E3
Knipton NG32 .... **14** E3
Scraptoft LE7.......... **156** F8
Swannington LE67...... **71** B7
Tilton on t H LE7 ...... **133** C3
Woodhouse Eaves LE12... **75** A1
Church Hill CE Jun Sch
LE4................. **129** F7
Church Hill Inf Sch
LE4................. **129** F7
Church Hill Rd
Cranoe LE16 .... **208** D3
Mountsorrel LE12 ...... **76** D1
Thurmaston LE4........ **129** F7
Church Ho CV9........ **171** B7
Church House Mews
CV9................. **171** B7
Churchill Dr
Leicester Forest East
LE3 .... **153** B4
Upper Bruntingthorpe
LE17................ **236** D5
Churchill Rd
Oakham LE15.......... **137** E6
Stamford PE9.......... **143** C5
Churchill St LE2....... **155** B4
Churchill Way LE8...... **223** A7
Church La
Ab Kettleby LE14....... **37** C3
Anstey LE7............ **127** D4
Arnesby LE8........... **221** F5
Asfordby LE14 .... **57** F2
Ashby Folville LE14..... **105** F4
Austrey CV9........... **119** B1
Barrowden LE15 .... **191** E4
Barrow-u-S LE12....... **76** D8
Barsby LE7............ **105** B3
Barwell LE9 .... **198** A6
Bisbrooke LE15 .... **189** F4
Bottesford NG13 .... **3** B3
Cadeby CV13 .... **149** D1
Caldecott LE16......... **230** B8
Castle Donington DE74 .. **17** B3
Chilcote DE12 .... **91** E3
Church Langton LE16.... **225** C7
Clipsham LE15 .... **89** D5
Croxton Kerrial NG32 ... **24** B7
Desford LE9........... **151** B3
Duddington PE9........ **193** B6
Dunton Bassett LE17.... **219** D1
East Norton LE7....... **186** C5
Eaton NG32 .... **22** F7
Edith Weston LE15...... **166** B7
Fenny Drayton CV13 ... **194** F6

Church La *continued*
Fleckney LE8.......... **222** F7
Frisby on t W LE14 ..... **80** D8
Gaddesby LE7......... **105** B6
Gilmorton LE17........ **235** B4
Glaston LE15 .... **190** B6
Goadby LE7........... **185** B2
Greetham LE15 .... **88** A2
Grimston LE14 .... **57** B8
Hemington DE74 .... **17** E4
Hoby LE14 .... **79** D7
Hungarton LE7......... **132** C3
Husbands Bosworth
LE17................ **247** E5
Leicester LE2.......... **180** B7
Leicester, Stoughton
LE2................ **156** E1
Little Dalby LE14 ...... **108** B8
Long Clawson LE14 .... **20** C3
Lyddington LE15 ...... **212** D6
Manton LE15 .... **164** E6
Market Overton LE15.... **86** F5
Morcott LE15.......... **191** A6
Muston NG13........... **7** F8
Narborough LE19....... **201** C8
No Man's Heath B79 .... **119** A6
Old Dalby LE14 .... **35** E4
Osgathorpe LE12....... **48** E4
Pilton LE15........... **165** E2
Plungar NG13 .... **5** F1
Preston LE15.......... **164** C1
Quorn (Quorndon) LE12... **76** A6
Ratby LE6 .... **152** C8
Ratcliffe Culey CV9 .... **171** B3
Ratcliffe on t W LE7.... **78** C2
Ravenstone LE67....... **70** E1
Rearsby LE7........... **79** A2
Redmile NG13........... **6** F3
Ridlington LE15 .... **163** D2
Saxelbye LE14 .... **57** E6
Seaton LE15........... **190** C1
Sedgebrook NG32....... **4** F1
Sewstern NG33 .... **63** F8
Shawell LE17 .... **253** C4
Shearsby LE17......... **222** A3
Sheepy Magna CV9..... **171** B7
Somerby LE14 .... **108** B1
South Kilworth LE17 .... **255** C8
South Luffenham LE15... **191** E8
South Witham NG33 .... **65** B3
Sproxton LE14 .... **41** F6
Stamford PE9.......... **143** E2
Stanford on A NN6 ..... **254** F2
Stapleton LE9 .... **174** E1
Stathern LE14 .... **13** A2
Stockerston LE15....... **211** B8
Stretton LE15.......... **88** F4
Swannington LE67...... **71** C4
Thornton LE67......... **124** F4
Thorpe Langton LE16.... **226** A5
Thorpe Satchville LE14 .. **106** E4
Thrussington LE7....... **78** F4
Thurlaston LE9........ **177** A3
Thurmaston LE4........ **129** E7
Thurnby LE7........... **156** F4
Twyford LE14 .... **106** E1
Upper Broughton LE14... **19** A1
Waltham on t W LE14 ... **40** A7
Welford NN6 .... **256** E5
Whetstone LE8 .... **201** F8
Wigston Parva LE10 .... **231** F8
Willey CV23 .... **242** F6
Willoughby-on-t-W LE12.. **34** C7
Wymondham LE14...... **62** E2
Church Lands LE11 ..... **52** B6
CHURCH LANGTON **225** D7
Church Langton CE Prim
Sch LE16............ **225** D7
Church Lea LE14....... **82** F6
Church Leys Ave LE7.... **79** A2
Church Mews DE73 .... **26** B7
Church Nook LE18...... **180** D3
CHURCHOVER **252** C6
Church Pas LE15....... **138** A6
Church Ponds Cl LE6.... **152** D8
Church Rd
Barlestone CV13 .... **149** D8
Burley LE15 .... **111** E2
Egleton LE15.......... **138** D3
Glenfield LE3 .... **127** B1
Great Glen LE8 .... **205** A8
Hartshill CV10 .... **194** B1
Ketton PE9............ **168** A5
Kibworth Beauchamp
LE8................ **206** A1
Kirby Muxloe LE9...... **152** D5
Kirkby Mallory LE9..... **175** C6
Leicester, Aylestone
LE2................ **179** C6
Leicester, Evington LE5.. **156** B2
Leicester LE4.......... **129** A3
Lyndon LE15.......... **165** D5
Nailstone CV13 .... **123** B3
Peckleton LE9 .... **176** A6
Shackerstone CV13 .... **121** E2
Swadlincote DE11 ..... **44** A6
Wanlip LE7............ **102** C2
Witherley CV9 .... **194** B7
Church Row LE2....... **182** D5
Church Side LE12...... **50** C4
Churchside Wlk ❶❻
LE65................ **69** B6
Church Sq
❻ Market Harborough
LE16................ **240** E3
Melbourne DE73........ **26** B6
Church St
Appleby Magna DE12.... **119** E8
Barrow-u-S LE12....... **76** D8

Church St *continued*
Belton-in-R LE15 .... **187** D7
Belton LE12 .... **49** B6
Billesdon LE7.......... **159** B2
Blaby LE8............ **202** C8
Bottesford NG13 .... **3** B3
Braunston-in-R LE15 ... **137** A2
Carlby PE9 .... **117** B8
Churchover CV23 ...... **252** B6
Clifton u D CV23 ...... **257** A5
Cottingham LE16 ...... **229** D1
Countesthorpe LE8..... **202** F3
Donisthorpe DE12 ..... **67** F1
Earl Shilton LE9 ...... **176** A1
Easton o t H PE9 ...... **169** A6
Empingham LE15 ...... **141** A6
Granby NG13 .... **5** B5
Hartshorne DE11....... **45** B6
Hathern LE12.......... **30** A1
Hinckley LE10 .... **216** A5
Husbands Bosworth
LE17................ **247** E5
Langham LE15......... **110** C3
Leicester LE1.......... **259** C3
Leicester, Oadby LE2.... **181** A5
Lockington DE74....... **17** F4
Lutterworth LE17....... **244** C5
Market Bosworth CV13 .. **148** F3
Market Harborough
LE16................ **240** E3
Melbourne DE73........ **26** B7
Melton Mowbray LE13.... **59** C3
Netherseal DE12 ...... **91** F6
North Kilworth LE17 .... **246** F3
North Luffenham LE15... **166** D3
Oakham LE15.......... **138** A6
Orston NG13.......... **2** A7
Rothley LE7........... **101** F6
Ryhall PE9 .... **116** F2
Sapcote LE9........... **217** D7
Scalford LE14 .... **38** E5
Seagrave LE12......... **77** F8
Shepshed LE12 .... **50** C4
Sibbertoft LE16........ **249** A2
Skillington NG33 ...... **43** B8
South Witham NG33 ... **65** B3
Stamford PE9.......... **143** E2
Stoney Stanton LE9 .... **199** E2
Swadlincote DE11 ..... **44** B1
Swadlincote, Lower Midway
DE11................ **44** C4
Swadlincote, Newhall
DE11................ **44** A6
Swepstone LE67 ...... **94** D2
Thurlaston LE9........ **177** A3
Twycross CV9 .... **146** D6
Wing LE15............ **165** A3
Worthington LE65 ..... **47** F6
Wymeswold LE12....... **33** C3
Church Terr
Barlestone CV13 ...... **149** D8
Melton Mowbray LE13... **59** C3
CHURCH TOWN **70** C7
Church View
Bottesford NG13 .... **3** A3
Breaston DE72........... **9** D7
Ibstock LE67 .... **122** E8
Narborough LE19....... **201** C8
Newbold Verdon LE9 ... **150** A4
Osgathorpe LE12....... **48** E4
Twyford LE14 .... **106** D1
Churchward Ave LE4.... **128** D4
CHURCH WILNE **9** B4
Church Wlk
Blaby LE8............ **202** B8
Bruntingthorpe LE17.... **236** C8
Donisthorpe DE12 ..... **92** E8
Hinckley LE10 .... **215** D8
Hose LE14 .... **20** F7
Little Dalby LE14 ...... **83** B1
Lubenham LE16 .... **239** F3
Market Harborough
LE16................ **241** A2
Shackerstone CV13 .... **121** E2
Thorpe Satchville LE14 .. **106** E4
Church Wlks CV13...... **196** D7
Cider Cl LE15......... **191** E5
Cinder La CV9........ **145** A8
Circle The LE5........ **155** F5
Citrus Gr DE74........ **18** C3
City Of Dan LE67....... **71** F4
City of Leicester Coll The
LE5................. **156** C3
City Of Three Waters
LE67................ **71** E6
City Rd LE14......... **12** F3
City The
Blackfordby DE11 ...... **45** A2
Kibworth Beauchamp
LE8................ **206** A2
Woodville DE11........ **44** F2
City Yd LE15......... **165** A2
Civic Way DE11....... **44** B4
Claire Ct LE12........ **77** E3
Clamp Dr DE11....... **44** B3
Clapgun St DE74...... **17** B3
Clare Cl PE9......... **143** C3
Clarefield Rd LE3...... **154** B5
Clare Gr LE3......... **153** D2
Claremont Dr
Market Harborough
LE16................ **241** A3

Claremont Dr continued
Ravenstone LE67 . . . . **70** F2
Claremont St LE4 . . . . **129** A3
Clarence Ct 5 LE10 . . **215** E8
Clarence Dr LE67 . . . . . **96** F8
Clarence Rd
Hinckley LE10 . . . . **215** C8
Long Eaton NG10 . . . . . . **10** C6
Narborough LE19 . . . . . . **178** D2
Clarence St
Leicester LE1 . . . . **259** B4
Loughborough LE11 . . . . . **52** C5
Market Harborough
LE16 . . . . **240** F3
Clarendon Bsns Pk
LE2 . . . . **155** A1
Clarendon Ct LE2 . . . . . **155** B2
Clarendon Ho LE10 . . **215** B7
CLARENDON PARK . **155** B1
Clarendon Park Rd
LE2 . . . . **155** B1
Clarendon Rd LE10 . . . **215** C7
Clarendon St LE2 . . . . . **259** A2
Claresholm Cres
LE15 . . . . **138** B6
Claridge Pl 4 LE65 . . . **69** B6
Clark Dr LE13 . . . . **59** C6
Clarke Cl LE67 . . . . **71** F4
Clarke Dr NG10 . . . . **10** A4
Clarke Gr LE4 . . . . **129** A6
Clarke Rd LE67 . . . . **97** C8
Clarkes Dale LE16 . . . . **229** D6
Clarkes La DE72 . . . . . . **16** B8
Clarkes Rd LE18 . . . . . . **180** B2
Clarke St
Leicester LE4 . . . . **129** B3
Market Harborough
LE16 . . . . **240** D3
Clark Gdns LE8 . . . . **202** A8
Clatterpot La LE15 . . . **112** C8
Clawson Cl LE11 . . . . . . **51** D6
Clawson La
Ab Kettleby LE14 . . . . **37** D4
Hickling LE14 . . . . **19** D7
Long Clawson LE14 . . . . . **21** C1
Upper Broughton LE14 . . **19** E1
Claxton Rise LE14 . . . . . **20** C2
Claybrook Ave LE3 . . . **179** A8
Claybrooke Ct LE17 . . **232** F5
CLAYBROOKE MAGNA
. . . . **232** D6
CLAYBROOKE PARVA
. . . . **232** F4
Claybrooke Prim Sch
LE17 . . . . **232** E4
Clay Cl DE11 . . . . **44** D5
Claydon Rd LE5 . . . . . . **155** E8
Claye St NG10 . . . . **10** E7
Clay La
Ellistown LE67 . . . . **96** E2
Gretton NN17 . . . . **213** D1
Peggs Green LE67 . . . . . . **71** A8
Claymar Dr DE11 . . . . . . **44** A7
Claymill Rd LE4 . . . . . . **129** F4
Clay St
Draycott DE72 . . . . **9** A7
Wymeswold LE12 . . . . **33** C3
Clayton Dr LE4 . . . . **129** F6
Clear View Cres LE9 . . **175** F1
Cleeve Mount LE11 . . . . **51** C4
Clematis Cl LE4 . . . . . . **128** A5
Clement Ave LE4 . . . . . **129** A3
Clements Gate DE74 . . **28** D6
Clevedon Cres LE4 . . . **155** E8
Cleveland Ave
Draycott DE72 . . . . **9** A7
Long Eaton NG10 . . . . . . **10** F8
Cleveland Cl DE11 . . . . . **44** B3
Cleveland Rd
Hinckley LE10 . . . . **215** C8
Loughborough LE11 . . . . . **74** F7
Wigston LE18 . . . . **180** D3
Cleveleys Ave LE3 . . . . **179** A8
Cliff Ave LE11 . . . . **51** F5
Cliff Cres PE9 . . . . **143** D3
Cliffe Hill Rd LE67 . . . . **98** A1
Cliffe House Mews
LE8 . . . . **201** F8
Cliffe La LE67 . . . . **98** B2
Cliffe Rd
Birstall LE4 . . . . **128** F6
Easton o t H PE9 . . . . . . **169** A3
Clifford Cl NG10 . . . . . . **10** A4
Clifford Rd LE11 . . . . . . **51** F5
Clifford St
Leicester LE3 . . . . **154** D6
Long Eaton NG10 . . . . . . **10** E7
Wigston LE18 . . . . **179** F1
Cliff Rd
Stamford PE9 . . . . **143** D3
Woolsthorpe by B NG32 . . . **8** C1
Cliffwood Ave LE4 . . . **128** F7
Clifton Ave
Ashby-de-la-Z LE65 . . . . . **69** B8
Long Eaton NG10 . . . . . . **10** F7
Clifton Cl
Overseal DE12 . . . . **67** A3
Swadlincote DE11 . . . . . . **44** A2
Clifton Ct
Hinckley LE10 . . . . **197** B1
Oakham LE15 . . . . **137** F6
Clifton Dr
Ashby-de-la-Z LE65 . . . . . **69** A7
Wigston LE18 . . . . **180** A1

Clifton Rd
Leicester LE2 . . . . **179** F8
Netherseal DE12 . . . . **91** D6
Cliftonthorpe LE65 . . . . **46** B1
Clifton Thorpe Mdws
LE65 . . . . **46** B1
**CLIFTON UPON
DUNSMORE** **257** A6
Clifton Way LE10 . . . . . **197** A1
Clink La LE67 . . . . **71** A4
Clipper Rd LE4 . . . . **129** F3
CLIPSHAM **89** E5
Clipsham Rd
Castle Bytham NG33 . . . . . **90** B7
Stretton LE15 . . . . **89** A4
*Clipsham Woods Nature
Trail* ★ LE15 . . . . **89** E7
CLIPSTON **250** A1
Clipstone Cl LE18 . . . . **180** A2
Clipstone Gdns LE18 . . **180** E2
Clipstone Ho 2 LE2 . . . **155** B5
Clipston La LE16 . . . . . **250** A1
Clipston Rd
East Farndon LE16 . . . . . **250** B4
Great Oxendon LE16 . . . . **250** D2
Clipston St LE16 . . . . . . **240** F1
Clivesway LE10 . . . . **197** C2
Clock House Ct LE15 . . **137** D8
Clock Tower Mall 7
LE1 . . . . **259** B4
Cloisters The LE9 . . . . **198** E8
Close The
Anstey LE7 . . . . **127** D7
Barwell LE9 . . . . **198** B7
Blaby LE8 . . . . **179** B1
Burton Lazars LE14 . . . . . **82** F6
Easton o t H PE9 . . . . . . **168** F4
Kirkby Mallory LE9 . . . . . **175** D6
Narborough LE19 . . . . . . **178** A2
Ratby LE6 . . . . **126** C1
Stamford PE9 . . . . **143** F4
Swadlincote DE11 . . . . . . **67** D8
Swinford LE17 . . . . **254** B4
CLOUDESLEY BUSH . . **231** E1
Cloud Hill View LE67 . . **47** E3
Cloud Lea LE12 . . . . **101** E8
Cloudsley Bush La
LE10 . . . . **231** A5
Cloud Way Ct LE11 . . . . **52** A6
Clovelly Rd
Glenfield LE3 . . . . **153** D8
Leicester LE5 . . . . **155** F4
Clover Cl LE9 . . . . **201** A8
Cloverdale DE11 . . . . . . **44** B7
Cloverdale Rd LE5 . . . . **130** C3
Clover Dr LE13 . . . . **82** B8
Clover Gdns PE9 . . . . . **142** E4
Clover La LE12 . . . . **76** F1
Clover Pk Trad Est
LE10 . . . . **197** B3
Clover Pl LE67 . . . . **71** D8
Clover Way LE7 . . . . . . **103** A2
Clover Wlk LE7 . . . . **103** E7
Clowbridge Dr LE11 . . . **51** C3
Clumber Cl
Loughborough LE11 . . . . . **75** A6
Syston LE7 . . . . **103** B5
Clumber Ct LE6 . . . . . . **152** D7
Clumber Rd LE5 . . . . . . **155** E6
Clumber St
Long Eaton NG10 . . . . . . **10** D7
Melton Mowbray LE13 . . . **59** B4
Clun Wlk NN17 . . . . **230** C1
Clutsom Rd LE67 . . . . . . **96** C7
Clwyd Wlk NN17 . . . . . **230** C1
Clyde Cl LE67 . . . . **71** E8
Clydesdale Cl LE13 . . . . **59** A6
Clyde St LE1 . . . . **259** C4
Coach Ho LE15 . . . . **187** D7
Coachhouse Mews 4
DE11 . . . . **44** A7
Coachmans Ct LE12 . . . **50** C5
Coachouse Ct LE11 . . . . **52** B3
Coach Rd LE12 . . . . **50** D3
Coal Baulk LE7 . . . . **132** B3
Coalbourn Cl LE4 . . . . . **128** E4
Coales Ave LE8 . . . . **202** A5
Coales Gdns LE16 . . . . **240** D5
Coalfield Way LE65 . . . . **69** E6
Coal La
Hartshorne DE11,
DE73 . . . . **45** D8
Hose LE14 . . . . **20** F8
Coal Pit La
Cloudesley Bush
CV23 . . . . **231** F1
Willey CV23 . . . . **242** C6
COALVILLE **96** D7
Coalville Bsns Pk LE67 **71** C1
Coalville Com Hospl
LE67 . . . . **72** A1
Coalville Cotts PE9 . . . **143** E4
Coalville La LE67 . . . . . . **71** A1
Coatbridge Ave LE4 . . **129** D4
Coates Ave LE3 . . . . . . **154** A7
Cobbett Rd LE3 . . . . . . **153** D2
Cobden Ho LE1 . . . . **155** B7
Cobden Prim Sch LE11 . **52** C4
Cobden St
Leicester LE1 . . . . **155** B7
Long Eaton NG10 . . . . . . **10** E7
Loughborough LE11 . . . . . **52** C4
Cobden Street Ind Est
LE1 . . . . **155** B7
Cobleas NG32 . . . . **15** B7
Cobwells Cl LE8 . . . . . . **223** A7

Cockcharme Gapp
DE74 . . . . **17** B6
Cock La CV9 . . . . **120** A2
Cockleys NG10 . . . . **10** C6
Cockshut La DE73 . . . . . **26** A8
Cockshut Lane Bsns Ctr
DE73 . . . . **26** A7
Coe Ave LE11 . . . . **51** B5
Cokayne Rd LE3 . . . . . . **153** D6
Colbert Dr LE3 . . . . **179** A7
Colby Dr LE4 . . . . **130** A4
Colby Rd LE4 . . . . **129** F5
Colchester Rd LE5 . . . . **156** B7
COLD NEWTON **133** B1
COLD OVERTON **109** C1
Cold Overton Rd
Knossington LE15 . . . . . . **136** B7
Langham LE15 . . . . **110** B2
Oakham LE15 . . . . **137** D6
Coldstream Cl LE10 . . . **197** A1
Colebrook Cl LE5 . . . . . **155** E3
Coleford Cl LE4 . . . . **130** A5
Coleman Cl LE5 . . . . . . **155** F7
Coleman Ct LE5 . . . . . . **155** F7
Coleman Prim Sch
LE5 . . . . **155** E4
Coleman Rd
Fleckney LE8 . . . . **204** E1
Leicester LE5 . . . . **156** A5
COLEORTON **70** E8
Coleorton Hall LE67 . . . **70** C7
Coleorton La LE65 . . . . **69** D3
COLEORTON MOOR . . . **70** E5
Coleridge Dr LE19 . . . . **178** A2
Coles Cl LE4 . . . . **129** D5
Coley Cl LE10 . . . . **215** D7
Colgrove Rd LE11 . . . . . . **52** A2
Colindale Ave LE4 . . . . **129** A8
Colin Grundy Dr LE5 . . **130** B1
Collaton Rd LE18 . . . . . **180** C1
College Ave
Leicester LE2 . . . . **155** B4
Melton Mowbray LE13 . . . **82** C8
College Cl
Coalville LE67 . . . . **96** C8
Great Casterton PE9 . . . . **142** E7
Oakham LE15 . . . . **137** F7
College Farm La
LE15 . . . . **187** D8
College Hall LE2 . . . . . . **180** C8
College Ho LE8 . . . . **202** A8
College La LE10 . . . . . . **197** E1
College Rd
Sutton Bonington LE12 . . **30** A8
Syston LE8 . . . . **103** B3
Whetstone LE8 . . . . **202** A8
College St
Leicester LE2 . . . . **155** B4
Ullesthorpe LE17 . . . . . . **233** B4
Collett Rd LE4 . . . . **128** C4
Colley Rise LE15 . . . . . . **212** C7
Colliers Way LE67 . . . . . **96** B3
Colliery Rd LE11 . . . . . . **44** A1
Colliery Row DE11 . . . . **44** A1
Colling Cl LE11 . . . . **51** B6
Collingham Rd LE3 . . . **154** C1
Collingwood Cl LE13 . . . **58** F3
Collingwood Cres LE13 **58** F3
Collingwood Dr LE12 . . **77** D4
Collingwood Rd NG10 . . **10** E6
Collin Pl LE4 . . . . **129** C2
Collins Cl LE3 . . . . **153** D2
Collyns Way PE9 . . . . . . **168** D2
COLLYWESTON **168** D2
Colne Cl
Corby NN17 . . . . **230** C1
Leicester, Oadby LE2 . . . **181** D5
Colonel's La LE14 . . . . . **19** A1
Colsterdale Cl LE4 . . . . **128** D5
Colsterworth Rd
Skillington NG33 . . . . **43** C7
Stainby NG33 . . . . **43** F3
COLSTON BASSETT . . . **11** A6
Colston La LE14 . . . . **11** E4
Coltbeck Ave LE19 . . . . **201** A4
Coltfoot Way LE13 . . . . **82** A8
Colthurst Way LE5 . . . . **156** E6
Colton St LE1 . . . . **259** C3
Colts Cl LE10 . . . . **215** D4
Coltsfoot Cl DE11 . . . . . **44** F4
Coltsfoot Rd LE5 . . . . . **130** C2
Coltsfoot Way LE9 . . . . **219** A4
Columbia Cl LE19 . . . . . **178** A3
Columbine Cl LE3 . . . . . **153** E2
Columbine Rd LE5 . . . . **130** B3
Colwell Rd LE3 . . . . **154** D8
Combe Cl LE3 . . . . **154** C8
Comet Cl LE3 . . . . **154** B7
Comet Way LE67 . . . . . . **71** D2
Commerce St DE73 . . . . **26** A7
Commercial Sq LE2 . . . **154** F1
Common Rd DE11 . . . . . **44** C2
Common Side DE11 . . . . **44** C2
Common The
Barwell LE9 . . . . **198** B5
Leicester LE5 . . . . **156** A3
Compass Rd LE5 . . . . . **156** D7
Compton Ave DE72 . . . . **16** A8
Compton Cl LE11 . . . . . . **74** C8
Compton Dr LE9 . . . . . . **200** D8
Compton Rd LE3 . . . . . **154** C2
Conaglen Rd LE9 . . . . . **179** B6
Condon Rd LE12 . . . . . . **76** E7
Condor Cl LE9 . . . . **218** F7
Conduit Rd PE9 . . . . . . **143** E4
Conduit St LE2 . . . . **259** C3
Cone La LE2 . . . . **155** C3
Coneries The LE11 . . . . **52** B4

Conery La LE19 . . . . . . **178** A4
Coneygrey LE8 . . . . **204** F1
CONGERSTONE **147** D7
Congerstone La
Barton in B CV13 . . . . . . **122** B1
Carlton CV13 . . . . **148** C6
Shackerstone CV13 . . . . **121** E1
Congerstone Prim Sch
CV13 . . . . **147** D8
Congerstone Rd
CV13 . . . . **148** A6
Conifer Cl
4 Leicester LE2 . . . . . . **155** C4
Lutterworth LE17 . . . . . . **244** B6
Coninsby Cl LE3 . . . . . . **154** B1
Coniston Ave LE2 . . . . . **259** A1
Coniston Cl LE9 . . . . . . **198** F8
Coniston Cres LE11 . . . . **51** D1
Coniston Gdns LE65 . . . **69** C5
Coniston Rd
Barrow-u-S LE12 . . . . **76** D8
Edith Weston LE15 . . . . . **166** A7
Melton Mowbray LE13 . . . **59** A6
Coniston Way LE9 . . . . **200** D4
Conkers Discovery Ctr ★
DE12 . . . . **67** D5
Conkers Waterside Ctr ★
. . . . DE12 . . . **67** D4
Connaught Ho LE11 . . . . **52** B3
Connaught Rd LE16 . . . **240** F4
Connaught St LE2 . . . . **155** B4
Connell Cl LE16 . . . . . . **239** F3
Constable Ave LE4 . . . . **155** B8
Constable Rd CV21 . . . **257** B1
**Constables (Uppingham
Sch)** LE15 . . . . **189** A4
Constance Rd LE5 . . . . **155** D5
Constitution Hill LE1 . . **259** C3
Convent Cl LE13 . . . . **59** B2
Convent Dr LE67 . . . . . . **96** D8
Conway Cl LE11 . . . . **51** C5
Conway Dr
Melton Mowbray LE13 . . . **59** C5
Shepshed LE12 . . . . **49** F2
Conway Rd
Leicester LE2 . . . . **155** D3
Long Eaton NG10 . . . . . . **10** F8
Mountsorrel LE12 . . . . . . **76** D1
Conway St NG10 . . . . . . **10** F8
Conway Wlk NN17 . . . . **230** D1
Cooch's Ct 6 PE9 . . . . **143** D2
Cooden Ave LE3 . . . . . . **154** B4
Cooke Cl
Braunstone Town
LE3 . . . . **153** D2
Long Eaton NG10 . . . . . . **10** B7
Thurmaston LE4 . . . . **129** F7
Cooke's Dr LE9 . . . . **218** E6
Cooks Dr DE74 . . . . **17** A3
Cooks La
Sapcote LE9 . . . . **217** D7
Wigston LE18 . . . . **203** F7
Cookson Pl LE11 . . . . . . **51** C6
Cookson Rd LE4 . . . . . . **130** A5
Cook's Wlk LE3 . . . . . . **153** C8
Coombe Cl LE12 . . . . **50** C2
Coombe Pl LE2 . . . . **181** B4
Coombe Rise LE2 . . . . . **181** C3
Co-operation St LE19 . . **178** B3
Co-operative St NG10 . . **10** E6
Cooper Cl
Huncote LE9 . . . . **200** E8
Leicester LE2 . . . . **179** C6
Whitwick LE67 . . . . **71** D5
Cooper Ct LE11 . . . . **52** D2
Cooper Gdns LE2 . . . . . **181** D4
Cooper La LE6 . . . . **152** D8
Coopers Cl DE12 . . . . . . **92** B7
Cooper's La LE17 . . . . . **219** D2
Cooper's Nook LE7 . . . **103** D7
Copdale Rd LE5 . . . . . . **155** E5
Cope Dale CV13 . . . . . . **149** C8
Copeland Ave LE3 . . . . **128** A1
Copeland Cres LE11 . . . **51** D5
Copeland Rd LE4 . . . . . **128** F6
Cophills Cl DE12 . . . . . . **93** C4
Copinger Rd LE2 . . . . . **179** F7
Copley Cl LE13 . . . . **59** E4
Coplow Ave LE5 . . . . . . **155** E2
Coplow Cres LE7 . . . . . **103** A2
Coplow La LE7 . . . . **159** A4
Coppice Cl
Hinckley LE10 . . . . **197** F3
Ravenstone LE67 . . . . **71** A2
Coppice Ct LE4 . . . . **130** A7
Coppice Ho DE11 . . . . . . **44** E1
Coppice La
Newton Regis B79 . . . . . **118** A8
Queniborough LE7 . . . . . **103** F5
Coppice Rd PE9 . . . . . . **116** E2
Coppice Side DE11 . . . . . **44** C3
Coppice The
Atherstone CV9 . . . . **194** A6
Countesthorpe LE8 . . . . **202** E4
Hinckley LE10 . . . . **215** F8
Markfield LE67 . . . . **125** E8
Narborough LE19 . . . . . . **201** A8
Quorn (Quorndon) LE12 . . **76** B4
Thurmaston LE4 . . . . **130** A7
Coppice Wlk LE10 . . . . **197** F3
Copse Cl
Coalville LE67 . . . . **96** C7
Leicester Forest East
LE3 . . . . **152** A1
Leicester LE2 . . . . **179** C3

Copse Cl continued
Leicester, Oadby LE2 . . . **181** C7
Copse Gr LE11 . . . . **75** A6
Copse Rise DE11 . . . . . . **44** B7
Copseside Cl 8 NG10 . . **10** A8
Copse The LE7 . . . . **157** B4
Copsey Croft Ct NG10 . . **10** F7
Copson St LE67 . . . . **96** A1
Copston La LE18 . . . . . **231** B5
COPSTON MAGNA **231** C5
Copthall Ho LE18 . . . . . **179** F3
Copthill Sch PE9 . . . . . **144** F3
Copthorne Cl LE3 . . . . . **153** D6
COPT OAK **98** C6
Copt Oak Rd
Copt Oak LE67 . . . . **98** B5
Narborough LE19 . . . . . . **200** F8
Narborough LE19 . . . . . . **201** A8
Corah Cl LE7 . . . . **157** A8
Corah St LE3 . . . . **259** A3
Coral Cl LE10 . . . . **215** F4
Coral St LE4 . . . . **129** A1
Corbet Cl LE3 . . . . **128** B3
CORBY **230** C2
Corby Rd LE16 . . . . **229** D1
Cordelia Cl LE5 . . . . **155** E8
Cordell Rd LE11 . . . . **51** D6
Cordery Rd LE5 . . . . . . **156** B3
Cordhill La LE14 . . . . **85** D7
Cordle Way LE15 . . . . . . **86** F5
Cordonnier Cl LE9 . . . . **219** A4
Cordwell Cl DE74 . . . . . . **16** F3
Corfield Rise LE3 . . . . . **153** E3
Coriander Rd LE2 . . . . . **154** D4
Cork Ho LE2 . . . . **179** A2
Cork La LE2 . . . . **179** A2
Corkscrew La
Ashby-de-la-Z LE65 . . . . . **69** F5
Coleorton LE67 . . . . **70** A6
Cork St LE5 . . . . **155** C5
Cornfield LE10 . . . . **197** C4
Cornfield Cl LE19 . . . . . **201** C7
Cornfields LE2 . . . . **182** D5
Cornflower Cl PE9 . . . . **142** E4
Cornstall Bldgs 5
PE9 . . . . **143** E3
Cornwall Bsns Ctr
LE18 . . . . **179** F2
Cornwallis Ave LE4 . . . **128** B2
Cornwallis Cl NG10 . . . . **10** D6
Cornwall Pl LE13 . . . . . . **82** C8
Cornwall Rd
Leicester LE4 . . . . **128** D1
Stamford PE9 . . . . **143** D4
Wigston LE18 . . . . **179** F2
Cornwall St LE19 . . . . . **178** B3
Cornwall Way LE10 . . . **197** E4
Coronation Ave
Broughton Astley LE9 . . . **218** E6
Long Clawson LE14 . . . . . **20** B2
Moira DE12 . . . . **68** B6
Wigston LE18 . . . . **180** B2
Coronation Cl DE73 . . . . **26** B8
Coronation Cotts LE9 . . **199** D3
Coronation La DE12 . . . . **92** F6
Coronation Rd LE9 . . . . **198** D7
Coronation St
Overseal DE11 . . . . **67** A4
Swadlincote DE11 . . . . . . **44** A5
Coronet Cl LE67 . . . . . . **127** E6
Corporation Rd LE4 . . . **128** F2
Corshaw Wlk LE5 . . . . . **155** D8
Cort Cres LE3 . . . . **153** C3
Corydalis Cl LE11 . . . . . . **75** A6
COSBY **201** C3
Cosby La LE8, LE9 . . . . **220** B5
Cosby Prim Sch LE9 . . **201** D4
Cosby Rd
Broughton Astley LE9 . . . **219** A8
Countesthorpe LE8 . . . . **202** B3
Littlethorpe LE19 . . . . . . **201** C6
Cosford La
Rugby CV21 . . . . **252** A1
Rugby CV21 . . . . **252** A2
COSSINGTON **102** D8
Cossington CE Prim Sch
LE7 . . . . **102** C8
Cossington La
Rothley LE7 . . . . **102** A6
Syston LE7 . . . . **103** A7
Cossington Rd LE12 . . . **77** C2
Cossington St LE4 . . . . **129** B1
Costalot Stables LE67 . . **124** A3
Costello Cl LE67 . . . . . . **95** F3
COSTON **41** D1
Coston Rd
Buckminster NG33 . . . . . . **42** D2
Garthorpe LE14 . . . . **62** A7
Sproxton LE14 . . . . **41** F5
COTES **52** F6
COTESBACH **244** A1
Cotes Dr LE11 . . . . **52** B6
Cotes Rd
Barrow-u-S LE12 . . . . **53** B3
Hinckley LE10 . . . . **215** F5
Cotes Yd LE11 . . . . **52** C5
Cothelstone Ave LE11 . . **51** C5
Cotley Cres LE15 . . . . . . **87** E2
Cotley Rd LE4 . . . . **128** C5
Cotman Dr LE10 . . . . . . **197** A3
Coton Park Dr CV23 . . . **252** C1
Coton Rd
Churchover CV23 . . . . . . **252** C5
Rugby CV23 . . . . **257** A1
Cotsmore Cl LE67 . . . . . **95** B2
Cotswold Ave LE9 . . . . **201** A4
Cotswold Cl
2 Long Eaton NG10 . . . **10** B8

Cotswold Cl *continued*
Loughborough LE11 . . . . 51 D3
Melton Mowbray LE13 . . . . . 82 D8
Swadlincote DE11 . . . . 44 A3
Cotswold Gn LE4 . . . . 128 D5
Cotswold St LE15 . . . . 87 D2
Cotswold Way LE65 . . . . . . 69 B5
Cotswold Wlk LE15 . . . . . 137 D6
Cottage Cl
Ratby LE6 . . . . 126 D1
Swadlincote DE11 . . . . 44 A7
Cottage Farm Cl
Braunstone Town LE3 . . . 178 F6
Osgathorpe LE12 . . . . 48 E4
Cottage Gardens Cl
LE12 . . . . 30 A1
Cottage Gdns
Earl Shilton LE9 . . . . 198 F8
Hartshill Green CV10 . . . . 194 B2
Cottage Homes LE2 . . . . 181 A7
Cottage La
Broughton Astley LE9 . . . 219 B6
Desford LE9 . . . . 151 B4
Markfield LE67 . . . . 98 C3
Norton-J-T CV9 . . . . 120 A4
Cottage Lane Ind Est
LE9 . . . . 219 A6
Cottage Rd LE18 . . . . 180 E1
Cottage Row LE3 . . . . . . 179 B8
Cottagers Cl LE2 . . . . 179 F5
Cottesbrooke Cl LE18 . . . 180 D2
COTTESMORE 112 D8
Cottesmore Ave
Leicester, Oadby LE2 . . . 181 D4
Melton Mowbray LE13 . . . . 59 B3
Cottesmore Dr LE11 . . . . 74 F8
Cottesmore Prim Sch
LE15 . . . . 87 E3
Cottesmore Rd
Ashwell LE15 . . . . 111 C8
Burley LE15 . . . . 111 F2
Cottesmore LE15 . . . . 87 E2
Exton LE15 . . . . 112 E4
Leicester LE5 . . . . 155 D7
Stamford PE9 . . . . 143 A3
Uppingham LE15 . . . . . . 189 A4
COTTINGHAM 229 C1
Cottingham CE Prim Sch
LE16 . . . . 229 C1
Cottingham Rd LE16 . . . . 230 A4
Cotton Cl
Broughton Astley LE9 . . . 219 A5
Leicester LE4 . . . . 129 D5
Cotton Croft LE12 . . . . . . 50 B2
Cotton Ct LE9 . . . . 198 F8
Cotton Mews LE9 . . . . . . 198 F7
Cottons The LE16 . . . . . . 230 B4
Cotton Way LE11 . . . . 51 E7
Coulson Cl LE8 . . . . 202 A6
Coulter Cl LE7 . . . . 156 F8
Council Hos
Claybrooke Magna
LE17 . . . . 232 E6
Essendine PE9 . . . . 117 B6
Council Ho's LE16 . . . . . . 250 B8
Council Rd LE10 . . . . 197 D1
Council St LE17 . . . . 244 C6
COUNTESTHORPE 202 D3
Countesthorpe Com Coll
LE8 . . . . 202 C3
Countesthorpe Rd
Countesthorpe LE8,
LE18 . . . . 202 F7
Whetstone LE8, LE9 . . . . 201 E2
Wigston LE18 . . . . 179 F1
Counting House Rd
LE2 . . . . 154 F2
Country Bridge Mobile
Home Pk LE12 . . . . 30 A3
Countrymans Mews
LE16 . . . . 241 A5
Countrymans Way
LE12 . . . . 50 C5
Countryman's Way
LE7 . . . . 103 E8
Countryman Way
LE67 . . . . 125 E8
Court 22 LE65 . . . . 69 C6
Court Cl LE9 . . . . 152 E5
Courtenay Rd LE3 . . . . . . 154 C5
Court La NN6 . . . . 256 D3
Court Rd
Glen Parva LE2 . . . . 179 B2
Thurnby LE7 . . . . 156 F4
Court St DE11 . . . . 44 E3
Courtyard The
Coalville LE67 . . . . 71 D2
Lockington DE74 . . . . 17 F4
Stamford PE9 . . . . 143 C3
Stoke Golding CV13 . . . . 196 C7
Waltham on t W LE14 . . . 40 A7
Courtyard Workshops
LE16 . . . . 240 E1
Coventry Cl DE11 . . . . 44 D6
Coventry Rd
Broughton Astley LE9 . . . 218 D7
Croft LE9 . . . . 200 D3
Hinckley LE10 . . . . 215 D7
Hinckley, Sketchley Hill
LE10 . . . . 215 F5
Lutterworth LE17 . . . . . 244 B5
Market Harborough
LE16 . . . . 240 D3
Narborough LE19 . . . . . 201 B7
Pailton CV23 . . . . 242 A1
Sapcote LE9 . . . . 218 B7
Sharnford LE10 . . . . 217 B3
Willey LE17 . . . . 243 D5

Coventry St 6 LE3 . . . . . 154 D5
Coverack Wlk LE5 . . . . . . 156 A4
Coverdale LE67 . . . . 71 E6
Coverdale Rd LE18 . . . . . 180 F1
Coverley Rd NG33 . . . . . . 65 B4
Coverside Rd LE8 . . . . . . 182 C1
Covert Cl
Leicester, Oadby LE2 . . . 181 C6
Syston LE7 . . . . 102 E3
Covert La LE7 . . . . 157 B8
Covert Pl DE11 . . . . 67 C8
Covert The LE7 . . . . 103 D8
Covett Way LE3 . . . . 153 E5
Cowdall Rd LE3 . . . . 153 E3
Cowdray Cl LE11 . . . . 52 A1
Cow La
Ratby LE6 . . . . 125 F2
Whissendine LE15 . . . . . . 84 F1
Cowley Way LE5 . . . . 156 E7
Cowman Cl LE14 . . . . 58 A3
Cowper Rd LE10 . . . . 215 D6
Cow Row NG33 . . . . 42 D2
Cowslip Cl
Donisthorpe LE12 . . . . . . 67 E1
Narborough LE19 . . . . . 200 F8
Cowslip Dr LE13 . . . . 82 A8
Cowslip Mdw DE72 . . . . . . 9 A7
Cox Dr NG13 . . . . 2 F3
Cox's La LE15 . . . . 135 B4
Crabtree Cl DE74 . . . . 17 A2
Crabtree Cnr LE2 . . . . . . 180 A5
Crabtree Rd
Barwell LE9 . . . . 197 F5
Skillington NG33 . . . . 43 C6
Crackbottle Rd LE7 . . . . 186 B3
Crackthorne Dr CV23 . . . 252 D1
Cradock Dr LE12 . . . . 75 F5
Cradock Rd LE2 . . . . 155 B2
Cradock St
Leicester LE1 . . . . 155 B6
Loughborough LE11 . . . . . 52 B4
Crafton St E LE1 . . . . 259 C4
Crafton St W LE1 . . . . . . 259 C4
Craftsmans Way LE7 . . . 103 D7
Cragdale LE67 . . . . 71 D7
Craig Gdns LE3 . . . . 153 D6
Craighill Rd LE2 . . . . . . 180 B8
Craig St NG10 . . . . 10 E7
Cramant Cotts LE1 . . . . . 259 B2
Crammond Rd LE10 . . . . 215 B8
Cramps Cl LE12 . . . . 76 D7
Cranberry Cl LE3 . . . . . . 153 D2
Cranbourne Gdns
LE2 . . . . 181 B8
Cranbrook Rd LE7 . . . . . 156 F6
Craneley Ct 2 LE5 . . . . . 130 C3
Crane-Ley Rd LE7 . . . . . 126 E3
Cranesbill Rd LE5 . . . . . 130 C1
Crane St LE1 . . . . 259 B5
Cranfield Rd LE2 . . . . . . 179 D6
Cranfleet Way NG10 . . . . 10 B7
Cranmer Cl LE8 . . . . 202 A6
Cranmer Dr LE7 . . . . 102 F3
Cranmere Rd LE13 . . . . . 59 C5
Cranmer La LE17 . . . . . . 246 F3
Cranmer St
Leicester LE3 . . . . 154 D4
Long Eaton NG10 . . . . . . 10 D8
CRANOE 208 D3
Cranoe Rd
Glooston LE16 . . . . 208 C4
Stonton Wyville LE16,
LE8 . . . . 207 D2
Cransley Cl LE5 . . . . 130 C3
Cranstone Cres LE3 . . . . 153 C7
Crantock Cl LE15 . . . . . . 156 D3
Cranwell Cl LE5 . . . . 156 B2
Craven Cl LE11 . . . . 74 F7
Craven's Rough LE67 . . . . 99 B4
Craven St
Leicester LE1 . . . . 259 A5
Melton Mowbray LE13 . . . 59 C1
Crawford Cl LE3 . . . . 154 B6
Crawford Ho LE18 . . . . . 180 B3
Crawshaw Cl LE12 . . . . . . 29 C3
Craxford Rd NN17 . . . . . 213 B1
Crayburn Ho LE3 . . . . . . 154 A8
Crayford Way LE5 . . . . . 130 D1
Craythorne Cl DE11 . . . . . 44 A7
Craythorne Way LE18 . . 180 E2
Creaton Cl LE18 . . . . 180 E2
Creaton Rd LE18 . . . . . . 180 E2
Crediton Cl LE18 . . . . . . 203 D8
Crescent Cl LE16 . . . . . . 240 F4
Crescent Ho LE17 . . . . . 244 C8
Crescent Jun Sch
LE3 . . . . 153 E4
Crescent Rd
Coalville LE67 . . . . 96 C7
Lutterworth LE17 . . . . . 244 C7
Crescent St LE1 . . . . 259 B2
Crescent The
Allington NG32 . . . . 4 F4
Asfordby LE14 . . . . 58 A3
Blaby LE8 . . . . 202 B7
Breaston DE72 . . . . 9 C7
Breedon on t H DE73 . . . . 26 E2
Easton o t H PE9 . . . . . . 168 F5
Elmesthorpe LE9 . . . . . . 198 D5
Great Glen LE8 . . . . 205 B8
Ketton PE9 . . . . 168 A7
Leicester LE1 . . . . 259 B4
Market Harborough
LE16 . . . . 240 F4
Melton Mowbray LE13 . . . 59 B4
Mountsorrel LE7 . . . . . . 101 E8
Old Dalby LE14 . . . . 36 B6
Pickwell LE14 . . . . 108 C3

Crescent The *continued*
Ryhall PE9 . . . . 117 A2
Saltby LE14 . . . . 24 E1
Stathern LE14 . . . . 13 A2
Wigston LE18 . . . . 180 C4
Cressida Ct LE3 . . . . 153 E2
Cressida Rd LE3 . . . . 153 E2
Cresswell Cl LE4 . . . . 130 A6
Cresswell Dr LE15 . . . . . 112 C8
Crestway The LE8 . . . . . . 201 F8
Creswell Dr LE67 . . . . 95 E8
Creswell Wlk NN17 . . . . . 230 C1
Crete Ave LE18 . . . . 179 E2
Cricketers Dr LE11 . . . . . 52 A6
Cricket La LE11 . . . . 74 E8
Cricket Lawns LE15 . . . . 138 A5
Crick's Retreat LE2 . . . . 181 F1
Critchlow Rd LE9 . . . . . . 200 D8
Crocket La LE15 . . . . 141 A6
CROFT 200 D3
Croft Ave LE2 . . . . 179 C6
Croft CE Prim Sch
LE9 . . . . 200 C3
Croft Cl
Barwell LE9 . . . . 198 B6
Netherseal DE12 . . . . 91 F7
Croft Dr LE18 . . . . 180 B4
Crofters Cl LE3 . . . . 153 B8
Crofters Dr LE5 . . . . 156 A7
Crofters Vale Pk
CV13 . . . . 149 D8
Croft Gdns LE14 . . . . 35 E4
Croft Hill Rd LE9 . . . . . . 200 C7
Croft La
Ashwell LE15 . . . . 111 B8
Huncote LE9 . . . . 200 A4
Croft Rd
Atherstone CV9 . . . . 170 D1
Cosby LE9 . . . . 201 B3
Leicester LE4 . . . . 128 C7
Thurlaston LE9 . . . . 177 A1
Crofts The LE67 . . . . 98 D1
Croft The
Ashby-de-la-Z LE65 . . . . . 69 D5
Draycott DE72 . . . . 9 A6
Kegworth DE74 . . . . 18 D2
Kirby Muxloe LE9 . . . . . 152 E5
Measham DE12 . . . . 93 B5
2 Melbourne DE73 . . . . . 26 A8
Ravenstone LE67 . . . . . . 95 F8
Stamford PE9 . . . . 143 F3
Twycross CV9 . . . . 146 D6
Croftway LE67 . . . . 125 D8
Croft Way LE9 . . . . 219 A5
Cromarty Cl LE4 . . . . 129 D3
Cromarty Dr LE10 . . . . . 196 F1
Cromarty Rd PE9 . . . . . . 143 A4
Cromer St LE2 . . . . 155 C3
Cromford Ave LE18 . . . . 180 A1
Cromford Cl NG10 . . . . . 10 A5
Cromford Rd LE9 . . . . . . 201 D4
Cromford St LE2 . . . . . . 155 C6
Cromford Way LE9 . . . . . 219 B6
Cromore Cl LE67 . . . . 72 C1
Crompton Rd LE14 . . . . . 58 C3
Cromwell Cl
Ashby-de-la-Z LE65 . . . . . 69 D7
Walcote LE17 . . . . 245 B4
Cromwell Cres LE16 . . . . 240 D1
Cromwell Ho LE2 . . . . . . 179 F8
Cromwell Rd
Great Glen LE8 . . . . 205 B8
Melton Mowbray LE13 . . . 59 D1
Mountsorrel LE12 . . . . . 101 D8
Croome Cl LE11 . . . . 52 C1
CROPSTON 100 E3
Cropston Ave LE11 . . . . . 51 B2
Cropston Cl LE3 . . . . 153 D6
Cropston Dr LE67 . . . . . . 97 B8
Cropston Rd
Anstey LE7 . . . . 127 F7
Cropston LE7 . . . . 100 F1
Cropston Resr Nature
Reserve ★ LE7 . . . . . . 100 D3
Cropthorne Ave LE5 . . . 155 F5
Crosby Rd LE16 . . . . 240 F1
Cross Bank LE16 . . . . . . 229 D6
Crossfield Dr LE13 . . . . . 59 E4
Cross Gn LE7 . . . . 101 E6
Cross Hands The CV9 . . . 146 C1
Cross Hedge LE7 . . . . . . 101 E7
Cross Hedge Cl LE4 . . . . 128 C7
Cross Hill LE2 . . . . 34 D7
Cross Hill Cl LE12 . . . . . . 33 C3
Cross Hill La LE11 . . . . . 75 A8
Cross In Hand LE17 . . . . 243 B4
Cross Keys Gn LE5 . . . . . 156 E7
Crosskirk Rd LE10 . . . . . 196 F1
Cross La
Burton Lazars LE14 . . . . 82 F7
Mountsorrel LE12 . . . . . 101 D8
Preston LE15 . . . . 164 C1
Crossland Row LE10 . . . 216 A6
Crossley Cl LE12 . . . . 76 C7
Crossleys LE8 . . . . 222 F7
Crossley St LE3 . . . . 153 C8
Cross Rd LE2 . . . . 155 C1
Cross Roads Farm Cotts
PE9 . . . . 114 D1
Crossroads Farm Mus ★
LE14 . . . . 22 A5
Cross St
Blaby LE8 . . . . 202 B8
Breedon on t H DE73 . . . . 26 F2
Enderby LE19 . . . . 178 B3
Gaddesby LE7 . . . . 105 B7
Hathern LE12 . . . . 30 A1
Leicester LE4 . . . . 129 A1

Cross St *continued*
Leicester, Oadby LE2 . . . 181 A7
Long Eaton NG10 . . . . . . 10 E8
Loughborough LE11 . . . . . 52 C5
Market Harborough
LE16 . . . . 240 F2
Syston LE7 . . . . 103 B3
Wigston LE18 . . . . 180 D2
Cross The
Enderby LE19 . . . . 178 B3
Gretton NN17 . . . . 213 B1
Hallaton LE16 . . . . 209 D6
Walton LE17 . . . . 236 B3
Crossways LE15 . . . . 215 F5
Crossways Ho LE8 . . . . . 202 B8
Crossways The LE4 . . . . 129 B7
Crossway The
Braunstone Town LE3 . . . 179 A8
Leicester LE1 . . . . 259 F6
Crosswood Cl LE11 . . . . . 51 C3
Crowan Dr LE18 . . . . 203 C8
Crowfoot Way LE9 . . . . . 218 F4
Crowhill Rd CV11 . . . . . . 214 A1
Crowhurst Dr LE3 . . . . . 178 E8
Crow La
Atherstone CV9 . . . . 170 E6
Leicester LE3 . . . . 154 D4
Crown Bsns Pk LE14 . . . . 36 B5
Crown Cl NG10 . . . . 10 A7
Crown Ct 11 LE10 . . . . . . 197 D1
Crown Gdns LE15 . . . . . . 138 A6
Crown Hill Cl CV13 . . . . . 196 D7
Crownhill Rd LE10 . . . . . 215 D6
CROWN HILLS 156 A5
Crown Hills Ave LE5 . . . . 155 E5
Crown Hills Com Coll
LE5 . . . . 155 F4
Crown Hills Rise LE5 . . . 155 E5
Crown La
Barrowden LE15 . . . . . . 191 F5
Mountsorrel LE12 . . . . . . 76 D3
Crown Mdw CV13 . . . . . . 147 D7
Crown St
Oakham LE15 . . . . 138 A6
Ryhall PE9 . . . . 116 F3
Stamford PE9 . . . . 143 D3
Crowsfurlong CV23 . . . . 252 D1
Crowson Cl LE12 . . . . 50 B1
CROXTON KERRIAL 24 A7
Croxton Kerrial CE Prim
Sch NG32 . . . . 24 A7
Croxton La NG32 . . . . . . 15 B2
Croxton Rd
Queniborough LE7 . . . . . 104 B4
Saltby LE14 . . . . 24 D3
South Croxton LE7 . . . . . 132 A8
Croyde Cl LE5 . . . . 155 F4
Croyland Gn LE5 . . . . . . 156 E6
Crummock Ave LE15 . . . 166 A7
Crusaders Cl LE67 . . . . . . 71 F5
Cuckoo Cl LE15 . . . . 191 E5
Cufflin Cl LE6 . . . . 152 D8
Cuffling Cl LE3 . . . . 153 D6
Cuffling Dr LE3 . . . . 153 D6
Culham Ave LE5 . . . . . . 155 D8
Culver Rd LE3 . . . . 154 C8
Culworth Dr LE18 . . . . . 180 E2
Cumberland Rd
Loughborough LE11 . . . . . 51 F4
Wigston LE18 . . . . 179 E3
Cumberland St LE1 . . . . 259 A4
Cumberland Trad Est
LE11 . . . . 51 F4
Cumberland Wlk LE4 . . . 198 A7
Cumberland Wlk LE15 . . 87 E2
Cumberwell Dr LE19 . . . 178 C1
Cumbrae Dr LE10 . . . . . 197 B2
Cumbrian Way LE12 . . . . 50 D3
Cunery Cl CV13 . . . . 149 C8
Cunningham Dr LE17 . . . 244 A5
Curlew Cl
Coalville LE67 . . . . 97 A8
North End LE12 . . . . 76 C4
Syston LE7 . . . . 102 E4
Curlew Wlk LE5 . . . . 155 C7
Curteys Cl LE3 . . . . 154 B1
Curtis Cl LE8 . . . . 201 F7
Curtis Way CV13 . . . . . . 149 C8
Curzon Ave
Birstall LE4 . . . . 129 A6
Wigston LE18 . . . . 180 A1
Curzon Cl
Hinckley LE10 . . . . 215 F7
Queniborough LE7 . . . . . 103 D5
Curzon Rd LE2 . . . . 179 E7
Curzon St
Ibstock LE67 . . . . 95 F1
Leicester LE1 . . . . 155 B7
Loughborough LE11 . . . . . 52 A4
Cutchel The 3 LE17 . . . . 244 C5
Cutters Cl LE8 . . . . 201 B7
Cutting La LE15 . . . . 166 C1
Cuttings The LE7 . . . . . . 156 F6
Cutting The DE11 . . . . . . 44 F4
Cygnet Cl
5 Sileby LE12 . . . . 77 C3
Syston LE7 . . . . 102 F4
Cypress Cl LE11 . . . . 75 A7
Cyprus Rd LE2 . . . . 179 E6
Cyril St LE3 . . . . 179 A8

D

Dabey Cl LE67 . . . . 125 D8
DADLINGTON 173 F1
Dadlington La LE9 . . . . . 174 D2
Dag La
Mowsley LE17 . . . . 237 F7
North Kilworth LE17 . . . . 246 F3
Dahlia Cl LE10 . . . . 215 E6
Dairy Cotts LE17 . . . . . . 247 A4
Dairy La
Edmondthorpe LE14 . . . . 85 F8
Hose LE14 . . . . 20 F7
Daisy Cl
Bagworth LE67 . . . . 124 A7
Coalville LE67 . . . . 97 A8
Donisthorpe DE12 . . . . . . 67 E1
Groby LE6 . . . . 127 A3
Daisy La DE12 . . . . 67 E3
Dakota Rd DE74 . . . . 28 B8
Dakyn Rd LE5 . . . . 156 D6
Dalby Ave
Birstall LE4 . . . . 129 B8
Bushby LE7 . . . . 157 A5
Dalby Dr LE6 . . . . 126 F3
DALBY LODGES 35 C4
Dalby Rd
Anstey LE7 . . . . 127 D7
Melton Mowbray LE13,
LE14 . . . . 82 B5
Dalby's La LE16 . . . . 224 E1
DALBY WOLDS 35 A1
Dale Acre LE18 . . . . 202 F4
Daleacre Ave DE74 . . . . . 17 F5
Dale Ave LE18 . . . . 180 A4
Dale Cl DE72 . . . . 9 D8
Dale End LE10 . . . . 215 A7
Dalefield Dr DE11 . . . . . . 44 B3
Dale Gdns DE12 . . . . 93 D5
Dales Cl LE12 . . . . 32 E5
Dale St LE2 . . . . 155 C5
Dales The LE2 . . . . 202 C4
Dalestorth Ct NG32 . . . . . . 4 F5
Dalgliesh Way LE14 . . . . 57 E2
Dalkeith Rd LE4 . . . . 129 D4
Dalkeith Wlk LE67 . . . . . 71 D8
Dalley Cl LE7 . . . . 103 B2
Dallison Cl LE16 . . . . 250 E8
Dalley Cl LE7 . . . . 103 B2
Dalliwell LE14 . . . . 13 A2
Dalston Rd DE11 . . . . 44 A5
Dalton Rd
Corby NN17 . . . . 230 E2
Hamilton LE5 . . . . 130 D3
Dames La LE67 . . . . 121 E6
Damson Cl LE10 . . . . 215 B7
Danbury Dr LE4 . . . . 128 D2
Dandees Cl LE67 . . . . 98 E1
Danegeld Pl 15 PE9 . . . . 143 E3
Danehill LE6 . . . . 152 C8
DANE HILLS 154 B6
Danehurst Ave LE3 . . . . 154 B6
Danemill Prim Sch
Enderby LE19 . . . . 178 B2
Enderby LE19 . . . . 178 B3
Daneshill Rd LE3 . . . . . . 154 C5
Dane St LE3 . . . . 154 D5
Daniel Ct PE9 . . . . 143 E2
Dannett St LE3 . . . . 154 D6
Dannett Wlk LE3 . . . . . . 154 D6
Dan's La LE7 . . . . 176 D7
Danvers Rd
Leicester LE3 . . . . 154 C3
Mountsorrel LE12 . . . . . . 76 E1
Darby Way LE19 . . . . . . 201 A7
Darcy Gdns LE13 . . . . . . 59 C6
Darenth Dr LE4 . . . . 128 A3
Dare's Wlk LE10 . . . . 197 D1
Darien Way LE3 . . . . 153 D2
Darker St LE1 . . . . 259 B4
Darklands La DE11 . . . . . 44 A4
Darklands Rd DE11 . . . . . 44 B5
Darley Ave LE18 . . . . . . 180 A4
Darley Cl DE11 . . . . 44 A1
Darley Dr NG10 . . . . 10 A5
Darley Rd
Blaby LE8 . . . . 202 A7
Hinckley LE10 . . . . 215 E6
Darley St LE2 . . . . 155 C5
Darlington Rd LE3 . . . . . 154 A8
Darnall Rd LE2 . . . . 154 D3
Darswang DE74 . . . . 16 F4
Dart Cl
Corby NN17 . . . . 230 D2
Hinckley LE10 . . . . 215 A8
Leicester, Oadby LE2 . . . 181 C5
Dartford Rd LE2 . . . . 154 E1
Darwen Cl LE3 . . . . 154 B8
Darwin Cl
Braunstone Town LE3 . . . 153 C1
Broughton Astley LE9 . . . 219 A5
Hinckley LE10 . . . . 197 E3
Stamford PE9 . . . . 143 C5
Darwin Cres LE11 . . . . . . 51 C7
Darwin Rd NG10 . . . . . . 10 B5
Dashwood Rd LE2 . . . . . 155 C3
Dauphine Cl LE67 . . . . . . 72 D1
Davenport Ave LE2 . . . . 180 F5
Davenport Rd
Leicester LE5 . . . . 156 C5
Wigston LE18 . . . . 180 D1
Davenport Terr LE10 . . . 215 E8

Davett Cl LE5 156 B6
David Ave LE4 128 E5
David Lees Cl LE67 96 E3
David Royce Ho LE15 138 A6
Davies Cl LE16 240 D5
Davison Cl LE5 156 A6
Davis Rd DE11 44 B4
Davy Ct CV23 252 C2
Dawkins Rd DE12 67 E1
Dawlish Cl LE5 156 D5
Dawsons La LE7, LE14 134 C6
Dawson's La LE9 198 B6
Dawson's Rd LE12 48 D4
Daybell Cl
Bottesford NG13 3 B3
Whetstone LE8 178 F1
Daybell Rd DE12 68 A4
Day St LE4 129 A3
Dayton Cl LE67 71 A2
Deacon Ave CV13 149 C8
Deacon Cl
Bitteswell LE17 244 A8
Market Harborough LE16 240 D5
Shepshed LE12 50 C3
Deacon Ho LE2 259 A2
Deacon Rd LE4 128 D8
Deacon Rise CV13 122 C1
Deacon St LE2 259 A2
Deacon's Workshop (Mus)★ LE1 259 A3
Dead La 2 LE11 52 B4
Dean Cl LE10 197 E2
Deancourt Rd LE2 180 B6
Deane Gate Dr LE7 157 F4
Deanery Cres LE4 128 D8
Deane St LE11 51 E5
Dean Rd
Hinckley LE10 197 E2
Leicester LE4 129 C1
Dean Rd W LE10 197 E2
Deansburn Ho LE3 153 F8
Deanside Dr LE11 51 E6
Dean's La LE12 74 B3
Dean's St LE15 137 F6
Dean's Terr LE15 189 A4
Debdale LE15 112 C8
Debdale Hill LE14 35 E4
Debdale La
Gumley LE16 224 C3
Smeeton Westerby LE8 224 A6
Debdale Pl LE14 57 E2
Deben Rd NN17 230 D1
Dee Cl
Melton Mowbray LE13 59 E3
Oakham LE15 137 E4
Deeming Dr LE12 75 F7
Deene Cl LE16 241 A3
Deene Rd NN17 213 F7
Deepdale
Great Easton LE16 229 D7
Leicester LE5 155 F6
Deepdale Cl LE67 95 F2
Deepdale Rd NG10 10 A5
Deepdene Cl DE11 44 C1
Deeping La CV13 149 B4
Deep Side PE9 168 F4
Deepway The LE12 75 E5
Deers Acre LE11 52 B6
Degens Way LE67 96 B7
De Havilland Way LE10 215 E4
Deighton Way LE11 51 C6
De-La-Bere Cres LE10 216 A6
Delamare Rd LE13 59 D6
Delamere Cl DE72 9 D8
Delaware Rd LE5 156 E4
De Lisle Cl LE16 240 D2
De Lisle Ct LE11 51 B2
De Lisle RC Science Coll LE11 51 D3
Dell The
Oakham LE15 138 A5
Ullesthorpe LE17 233 B4
Delph The DE73 26 F2
Delven La DE74 17 B3
De Montford University (Charles Frears Campus) LE2 155 C2
De Montfort LE13 59 C5
De Montfort Cl LE11 51 C5
De Montfort Ct
Anstey LE7 127 D6
Leicester LE2 155 C2
De Montfort Mews LE1 259 C2
De Montfort Pl LE1 259 C2
De Montfort Rd LE10 197 E1
De Montfort Sq LE1 259 C2
De Montfort St LE1 259 C2
De Montfort Univ
Leicester LE1 259 B3
Leicester LE2 259 A2
Dempsey Cl LE17 244 C8
Denacre Ave LE18 180 A1
Denbigh Ct 5 LE17 244 C5
Denbigh Pl LE17 244 C7
Denbydale LE18 180 F1
Denegate Ave LE4 128 F8
Denfield Cl LE15 190 B5
Denham Cl LE3 153 C6
Denis Cl LE3 154 B5
Denis Rd LE10 215 D5
Deniston Ave LE9 218 D7
Denman La LE9 200 D8
Denmark Rd LE2 179 E8
Denmead Ave LE18 180 C4
Dennis David Cl LE17 244 C8
Dennis St LE67 96 D6
Denstone Cl LE65 69 A8
Denton La
Harston NG32 15 C4
Sedgebrook NG32 8 F6
Denton Rise LE13 59 E2
Denton St LE3 154 B5
Denton Wlk LE18 180 E2
Dents Rd LE65 69 D7
Derby Cl LE9 219 A5
Derby La DE12 121 A6
Derby Rd
Ashby-de-la-Z LE65 69 B6
Aston-on-T DE72 16 A8
Draycott DE72 9 A7
Hathern LE12 29 F2
Hinckley LE10 197 D1
Kegworth DE74 18 C2
Long Eaton NG10 10 D8
Long Eaton, Wilsthorpe NG10 10 B8
Loughborough LE11 51 E6
Melbourne DE73 26 A8
Smisby LE65 46 A4
Swadlincote DE11 44 C3
Ticknall DE11, DE73 45 F7
Derbyshire Dr DE74 17 B4
Derby Sq 5 LE11 52 A4
Derrys Hollow LE67 96 E3
Derry Wlk LE4 128 E4
Dersingham Rd LE4 128 E2
De Ruthyn Cl DE12 68 A4
Derwent Ave LE15 166 A7
Derwent Cl
Earl Shilton LE9 198 F8
Swadlincote DE11 44 A1
Derwent Dr
Loughborough LE11 51 D1
Melton Mowbray LE13 59 B1
Oakham LE15 137 F5
Derwent Gdns LE65 69 C5
Derwent Rd LE12 76 D8
Derwent St
Draycott DE72 9 A7
Leicester LE2 155 C5
Long Eaton NG10 10 C6
Derwent Street Ind Est NG10 10 C6
Derwent Wlk
Corby NN17 230 D2
Leicester, Oadby LE2 181 C5
Desborough Rd
Braybrooke LE16 251 F5
Great Oxendon LE16 251 F1
DESFORD 151 C3
Desford Com Prim Sch LE9 151 A2
Desford Cross Roads LE9 177 B8
Desford Grange LE9 151 B4
Desford Ho LE10 215 D7
Desford La
Kirkby Mallory LE9 175 D7
Peckleton LE9 176 B8
Ratby LE6, LE9 152 B7
Desford Rd
Enderby LE9, LE19 177 D6
Kirby Muxloe LE9 152 D6
Narborough LE19 201 B8
Newbold Verdon LE9 150 D4
Thurlaston LE9 176 F4
Desford Tropical Bird Land★ LE9 151 B5
Deuce Ho LE1 259 C4
Devana Ave LE67 96 F8
Devana Rd LE2 155 C3
Devenports Hill LE7 157 B5
De Verdon Rd LE17 244 A5
De Verdun Ave LE12 49 B6
Deveron Cl LE67 72 C1
Deveron Ct LE10 197 B1
Deveron Way LE10 197 B1
Deveron Wlk NN17 230 D1
Devitt Way LE9 218 F4
Devon Cl DE12 68 C6
Devonia Rd LE2 181 D4
Devon La NG13 3 B3
Devonshire Ave LE18 180 A1
Devonshire Ct LE2 181 B3
Devonshire La LE11 52 B3
Devonshire Rd LE4 128 E1
Devonshire Sq LE11 52 B3
Devonshire Wlk LE2 181 C3
Devon Way LE5 155 F5
Devon Wlk LE15 87 D2
Deweys Cl LE15 166 D3
Dexters Cl LE12 76 A7
Dickens Cl LE12 77 D4
Dickens Ct LE3 154 A5
Dickens Dr
Melton Mowbray LE13 59 B6
Stamford PE9 143 A3
Swadlincote DE11 44 C5
Dicken The LE8 201 F7
Dickinson Way LE4 129 F7
Dickman's La LE14 12 B3
Dick's Hill LE16 249 C5
Didcott Way DE12 119 F8
Didsbury St LE3 153 E3
Dieppe Way LE13 59 B5
Digby Cl
Leicester LE3 154 B3
Tilton on t H LE7 160 A8
Digby Dr
Melton Mowbray LE13 81 F8
North Luffenham LE15 166 D3
Oakham LE15 137 E6
Digby Ho LE2 180 F7
Dillon Gn LE3 127 F1
Dillon Rd LE3 153 F8
Dillon Rise LE3 153 F8
Dillon Way LE3 127 F1
Dimmingsdale Cl LE7 127 E7
Dingle La B79, DE12 119 C6
DINGLEY 241 F4
Dingley Ave LE4 129 C1
Dingley La LE16 241 F6
Dingley Link LE18 180 E3
Dingley Rd LE16 241 B6
Dingley Terr LE16 240 F3
Dinmore Grange DE11 45 B6
Discovery Way LE65 69 D8
DISEWORTH 28 C5
Diseworth CE Prim Sch DE74 28 C6
Diseworth Rd DE74 17 A1
Diseworth St LE2 155 C5
DISHLEY 51 C6
Disney Cl LE9 199 D2
Disraeli Cl LE8 223 F8
Disraeli St
Leicester LE2 179 D7
Quorn (Quorndon) LE12 76 A6
Ditchling Ave LE3 154 A6
Dixie Gram Sch The CV13 148 F3
Dixon Dr LE2 155 C3
Dixon Dr (Lakeside) LE13 59 B2
Dobbies World★ CV9 194 B4
Dobney Ave LE7 103 C6
Doctor Cookes Cl 5 LE9 198 A6
Doctors Fields LE9 198 D7
Doctor's La
Breedon on t H DE73 26 F2
Melton Mowbray LE13 59 E4
Doctor's Wlk The DE12 93 C5
Doddridge Rd 1 LE16 240 E4
Dodgeford La LE12 48 F6
Dodwells Bridge Ind Est LE10 214 E8
Dodwells Rd LE10 214 E8
Dog & Gun La LE8 201 F5
Dog La
Burton Lazars LE14 83 A7
Netherseal DE12 91 F6
South Kilworth LE17 255 C8
Wilson DE73 26 E6
Dogwood Ct LE2 181 A7
Dolphin Ct LE15 189 A4
Dominion Rd
Glenfield LE3 153 D8
Swadlincote DE11 44 B5
Dominus Way LE19 178 D8
Domont Cl LE12 50 B3
Donald Cl LE4 129 F4
Donald Greaves Ho NN17 230 D1
Donaldson Rd LE4 155 A8
Donata Ho LE17 244 C6
Doncaster Rd LE4 129 B1
Don Cl
Corby NN17 230 D1
Oakham LE15 137 E4
Donington Cvn Pk DE74 17 A3
Donington Dr
Ashby-de-la-Z LE65 68 F5
Woodville DE11 44 E1
Donington Grand Prix Collection Mus★ DE74 27 D8
Donington La
Castle Donington DE72, DE74 17 C7
Castle Donington DE72, DE74 17 C8
DONINGTON LE HEATH 96 B5
Donington le Heath Manor Ho★ LE67 96 C6
Donington Park Motor Racing Circuit★ DE74 16 C1
DONISTHORPE 67 F1
Donisthorpe La DE12 67 E2
Donisthorpe Prim Sch DE12 68 A1
Donnett Cl LE5 156 B6
Donnington Park Motor Racing Circuit★ DE74 27 C8
Donnington St LE2 155 C5
Dorchester Cl
Blaby LE8 202 B6
Wigston LE18 203 D8
Dorchester Rd
Hinckley LE10 216 B7
Leicester LE3 154 B4
Dorchester Way CV11 214 A7
Dore Rd LE5 155 C4
Dorfold Wlk LE4 129 D1
Dorian Rise LE13 59 B2
Dormer Ct LE12 30 A1
Dorothy Ave
Glen Parva LE2 179 B3
Melton Mowbray LE13 59 A4
Thurmaston LE4 129 D6
Dorothy Goodman Sch LE10 197 B3
Dorothy Rd LE5 155 D5
Dorset Ave
Glenfield LE3 127 C1
Wigston LE18 179 F3
Dorset Dr
Melton Mowbray LE13 82 D7
Moira DE12 68 C6
Dorset St LE4 155 A8
Double Rail Cl LE18 180 A1
Doudney Cl LE9 199 D1
Doughty St PE9 143 F5
Douglas Bader Dr LE17 244 D8
Douglas Dr LE67 122 F8
Douglas Jane Cl LE13 59 A4
Douglass Dr LE16 240 F4
Dove Bank Prim Sch CV13 123 B3
Dove Cl
Hinckley LE10 215 A8
Oakham LE15 137 E5
Woodville DE11 44 F3
Dovecote
Castle Donington DE74 17 B3
Shepshed LE12 50 C4
Tonge DE73 27 B3
Dovecote Cl
Barrowden LE15 191 F5
Sapcote LE9 217 D7
Weston by W LE16 227 B3
Dovecote Rd LE9 200 C5
Dovecote St LE12 30 A1
Dovecotes The LE7 104 A5
Dovecote The DE73 26 F2
Dovecote Way LE9 198 B6
Dovedale Ave
Blaby LE8 202 B7
Long Eaton NG10 10 B6
Dovedale Cl LE13 59 B1
Dovedale Ct NG10 10 B6
Dovedale Prim Sch NG10 10 B6
Dovedale Rd
Leicester LE2 155 E1
Thurmaston LE4 129 E7
Dovehouse Cl NN6 256 E6
Dove La NG10 10 C8
Dovelands Prim Sch LE3 154 B5
Dover Cl LE12 101 D8
Dove Rd
Coalville LE67 97 A7
Diseworth DE74 28 C8
Dove Rise LE2 181 C6
Dover St
Kibworth Beauchamp LE8 223 F8
Leicester LE1 259 C3
Dower House Gdns LE12 76 A6
Downham Ave LE4 128 E2
Downing Cres PE9 143 D5
Downing Dr LE5 156 D4
Downside Dr LE65 69 A7
Down St LE4 129 B1
Dowry Furlong Wildlife Area★ LE6 126 E4
Doyle Cl LE11 51 D6
Drage Cl LE17 244 D8
Dragon La LE9 150 A5
Dragon St NG13 5 B5
Dragwell DE74 18 D2
Drake Way LE10 197 D4
Draper St LE2 155 C3
DRAYCOTT 9 B6
Draycott Com Prim Sch DE72 9 A7
Draycott Mills DE72 9 A7
Draycott Rd
Breaston DE72 9 C7
Long Eaton NG10 10 A4
DRAYTON 229 A5
Drayton Cl CV13 194 F6
Drayton Ct CV10 194 B2
Drayton Ho LE2 155 B2
Drayton La CV13 194 E6
Drayton Rd
Bringhurst LE16 229 B5
Drayton LE16 228 D7
Leicester LE3 153 E7
Medbourne LE16 228 A5
Drayton St DE11 44 C4
Dribdale LE8 223 A7
Drift Ave PE9 143 F4
Drift Cl DE11 68 B8
Drift Gdns PE9 143 F5
Drift Hill
Redmile NG13 6 F4
Wymondham LE14 63 A2
Drift Rd PE9 143 E4
Drift Side DE11 68 B7
Drift The
Collyweston PE9 168 D2
Denton NG32 15 E3
Essendine PE9 116 D6
Sewstern NG33 42 F2
Thistleton NG33 64 B5
Drinkstone Rd LE5 155 E5
Drive, Dalby Rd LE13 59 C1
Drive The
Barwell LE9 198 C8
Birstall LE4 129 A6
Countesthorpe LE8 202 C4
Kibworth Beauchamp LE8 224 B8
Scraptoft LE7 156 F8
Drive The *continued*
Woodhouse Eaves LE12 100 A8
Driveway The LE7 157 A5
Drome Cl LE67 72 D1
Dromintee Rd LE67 97 B4
Dronfield St LE5 155 C5
Drought Gdn & Arboretum★ LE15 139 D6
Drovers Ct LE9 151 B3
Drovers Way
Desford LE9 151 C3
Narborough LE19 201 B7
Drove The PE9 168 D1
Druid St LE10 197 D1
Drumcliff Rd LE5 156 E6
Drummond Rd
Enderby LE19 178 A3
Leicester LE4 128 F3
Drummond Wlk LE13 59 B5
Drury La LE2 180 F6
Drurys La LE15 190 C1
Dryden Cl DE12 93 C4
Dryden St LE1 259 C5
Dryer Cl LE67 122 F8
Dry Pot La LE12 28 F2
Du Cane Cl LE12 50 A1
Duck Lake DE12 119 F8
DUDDINGTON 193 B6
Dudleston Cl LE5 156 A5
Dudley Ave LE5 156 C6
Dudley Cl LE5 156 C6
Dudley Ct LE12 77 C3
Dudley Ho LE5 156 C6
Dudley Rise LE10 215 D6
Dudley Whenham Cl LE7 103 A4
Duffield Ave LE18 180 B4
Duffield Cl NG10 10 A5
Duffield St LE2 155 C5
Dukes Cl
Thurmaston LE4 129 F7
Wigston LE18 180 B3
Dukes Dr LE2 155 C2
Dukes Dr Flats LE2 155 C2
Dukes Rd LE14 36 B6
Duke St
Leicester LE1 259 B2
Loughborough LE11 52 B5
Melton Mowbray LE13 59 E4
Dulverton Cl
Loughborough LE11 74 D8
Wigston LE18 203 D8
Dulverton Rd
Leicester LE3 154 C5
Melton Mowbray LE13 59 A5
Dumbleton Ave LE3 154 C1
Dumps Rd LE67 71 E6
Dunbar Rd
Coalville LE67 97 C8
Leicester LE4 129 E2
Dunbar Way LE65 69 D6
Dunblane Ave LE4 129 D4
Dunblane Way LE10 197 A2
Duncan Ave LE9 200 D7
Duncan Rd LE2 179 E7
Duncan Way LE11 51 C6
Duncombe Rd LE3 128 A1
Dundee Dr PE9 143 A4
Dundee Rd
Blaby LE8 202 B6
Swadlincote DE11 44 D5
Dundonald Rd LE4 129 A1
Dunholme Ave LE11 51 B4
Dunholme Rd LE4 129 E1
Dunire Cl LE4 128 C3
Dunkirk St LE1 259 C3
Dunley Way LE17 244 C7
Dunlin Rd
Essendine PE9 117 B6
Leicester LE5 155 C7
Dunmore Rd LE16 241 A1
Dunn Dr NG10 10 B7
Dunnicliffe La DE73 26 A7
Dunnsmoor La DE11 44 E7
Duns La LE3 259 A3
Dunslade Cl LE16 241 B2
Dunslade Gr LE16 241 B2
Dunslade Rd LE16 241 A2
DUNSMORE 257 C6
Dunsmore Cl LE11 74 D8
Dunsmore Way DE11 44 D5
Dunstall Ave LE3 153 D3
Dunster Rd LE12 76 D1
Dunster St LE3 154 B5
Dunston Cl NG10 10 F7
Dunsville Wlk LE4 129 D3
DUNTON BASSETT 219 C2
Dunton Bassett Prim Sch LE17 219 D2
Dunton La LE17 234 A6
Dunton Rd
Broughton Astley LE17, LE9 219 B3
Leire LE17 234 A8
Dunton St
Leicester LE3 154 D7
Wigston LE18 179 F1
Dupont Cl LE3 153 D7
Dupont Gdns LE3 153 D7
Duport Rd LE10 215 F7
Durban Rd LE4 128 C7
Durham Cl
Bagworth LE67 124 A6
Melton Mowbray LE13 82 D8
Swadlincote DE11 44 E5
Durham Dr LE18 180 A4

Durham Rd LE11 . . . . 51 E6
Durham Wlk LE67 . . . . . . 124 A6
Durnford Rd LE18 . . . . . . 203 D7
Durrell Cl LE11 . . . . 51 C6
Durris Cl LE67 . . . . 72 C1
Durston Cl LE5 . . . . 156 D4
Duxbury Rd LE5 . . . . 155 E7
Dwyer Cl LE7 . . . . 102 F2
Dwyers Cl LE14 . . . . 58 A3
Dyers Ct LE11 . . . . 52 C5
Dysart Way LE1 . . . . 155 B7
Dyson Cl
  Lutterworth LE17 . . . . 244 C7
  Rugby CV21 . . . . 257 A1
Dysons Cl DE12 . . . . 93 B4

E

Eagle Cl
  Broughton Astley LE9 . . . 218 E7
  Measham DE12 . . . . 93 B4
Eagles Dr LE13 . . . . 82 B8
Eaglesfield LE17 . . . . . . 218 E1
Eaglesfield End LE17 . . . 218 E1
Ealing Rd LE2 . . . . 154 F1
Eamont Cl LE2 . . . . 179 D3
Eamont Gn LE2 . . . . 179 D3
Earle Smith Cl LE8 . . . . . 202 A7
Earl Howe St LE2 . . . . . . 155 C4
Earl Howe Terr **7**
  LE3 . . . . 154 D5
Earl Russell St LE2 . . . . . 179 C6
Earls Cl LE4 . . . . 129 F7
Earls Cl Ind Est LE4 . . . . 129 F7
EARL SHILTON 198 F7
Earl Shilton Rd LE9 . . . . 176 D2
Earls Rd LE14 . . . . 36 B6
Earl St
  Earl Shilton LE9 . . . . . 176 A1
  Leicester LE1 . . . . 259 C4
Earlstrees Ct NN17 . . . . 230 E2
Earlstrees Ind Est
  NN17 . . . . 230 E2
Earlstrees Rd NN17 . . . . 230 E2
Earls Way LE4 . . . . 129 F7
Earlswood Cl DE72 . . . . . . 9 D8
Earlswood Rd LE5 . . . . . 156 D4
Easby Cl LE11 . . . . 51 B5
Easedale Cl CV11 . . . . . . 214 A6
East Acre LE14 . . . . 108 C1
East Ave
  Leicester LE2 . . . . 155 C2
  Melton Mowbray LE13 . . . 59 A4
  Syston LE7 . . . . 103 C4
  Whetstone LE8 . . . . 201 F8
East Bond St LE1 . . . . . . 259 B4
Eastboro Fields CV11 . . . 214 A4
Eastboro Way CV11 . . . . 214 A4
East Cl LE10 . . . . 215 D7
Eastcourt Rd LE2 . . . . . . 180 C6
East Cres LE67 . . . . 96 E2
East End LE14 . . . . 20 D4
East End Dr DE11 . . . . . . 44 C4
Eastern Bvd LE2 . . . . . . 259 A2
EAST FARNDON 250 B7
Eastfield Ave LE13 . . . . . 59 C4
Eastfield Ct LE3 . . . . 154 B5
Eastfield Prim Sch
  LE4 . . . . 129 F8
Eastfield Rd
  Leicester LE3 . . . . 154 B5
  Swadlincote DE11 . . . . . 44 C6
  Thurmaston LE4 . . . . . 129 F8
Eastgate LE16 . . . . 209 D5
East Gates **4** LE1 . . . . . 259 B4
East Gn LE9 . . . . 198 A6
EAST GOSCOTE 103 E8
East Goscote Ind Est
  LE7 . . . . 103 C7
EASTHORPE 3 B1
Easthorpe La
  Muston NG13 . . . . 3 E1
  Redmile NG13 . . . . 3 B3
Easthorpe Rd NG13 . . . . . 3 C2
Easthorpe View NG13 . . . . 3 C2
East La
  Bardon LE67 . . . . 97 D4
  Ridlington LE15 . . . . . 163 E2
EAST LANGTON 225 D5
EAST LEAKE 31 E8
Eastleigh Rd LE3 . . . . . . 154 D3
East Link LE19 . . . . 178 E7
East Link Rd LE11 . . . . . . 51 E2
Eastmere Rd LE18 . . . . . 180 F3
EAST NORTON 186 D6
East Norton Rd LE16 . . . 209 D7
Easton Garford CE Sch
  PE9 . . . . 169 A5
EASTON ON THE HILL
  . . . . 169 A4
East Orch LE12 . . . . 77 C1
East Park Rd LE5 . . . . . . 155 D5
East Rd
  Birstall LE4 . . . . 129 A3
  Wymeswold LE12 . . . . . 33 E4
East Side Croft LE13 . . . . 59 D6
East St
  Leicester LE1 . . . . 259 C3
  Leicester, Oadby LE2 . . . 181 A6
  Long Eaton NG10 . . . . . 10 F8
  Market Harborough
    LE16 . . . . 240 D3
Eastway DE74 . . . . 17 B3
Eastway Rd LE18 . . . . . . 180 D4
EASTWELL 22 B6

East Wlk
  Ibstock LE67 . . . . 95 F1
  Ratby LE6 . . . . 126 C1
Eastwood Rd LE2 . . . . . . 179 D5
Eastwoods Rd LE10 . . . . 197 F2
EATON 22 E6
Eaton Ct NG32 . . . . 22 F7
Eaton Grange Dr NG10 . . . 10 A8
Eaton Rd DE74 . . . . 17 B3
Ebchester Cl LE2 . . . . . . 179 C3
Ebchester Rd LE2 . . . . . . 179 C4
Ebenezer Cotts CV13 . . . 149 B8
Edale Cl
  Leicester LE3 . . . . 153 E3
  Long Eaton NG10 . . . . . 10 B6
Edale Gn LE10 . . . . 215 F6
Eddystone Rd LE5 . . . . . 156 E7
Edelin Rd LE11 . . . . 52 B1
Eden Cl
  Leicester, Oadby LE2 . . . 181 C6
  Loughborough LE11 . . . . 51 C5
Edendale Dr LE10 . . . . . . 197 E4
Edendale Rd LE13 . . . . . . 82 B8
Eden Gdns LE4 . . . . 128 C7
Edenhall Cl
  Leicester LE4 . . . . 129 D3
  Leicester, Oadby LE2 . . . 181 D4
Edenhurst Ave LE3 . . . . . 178 F7
Eden Rd LE2 . . . . 181 D6
Edensor St LE4 . . . . 129 C3
Eden Way LE2 . . . . 179 D2
Edgbaston Cl LE4 . . . . . . 128 D7
Edgcote Ct LE5 . . . . 155 E8
Edgecote Dr DE11 . . . . . . 44 A7
Edgefield Cl LE5 . . . . . . 130 B2
Edgehill Cl LE8 . . . . 205 B8
Edge Hill Rd NG10 . . . . . . 10 C4
Edgehill Rd LE4 . . . . 129 C2
Edgehill Way LE65 . . . . . . 69 D7
Edgeley Cl LE3 . . . . 128 E1
Edgeley Rd LE8 . . . . 202 F4
Edinburgh Cl LE16 . . . . . 240 F4
Edinburgh Rd
  Earl Shilton LE9 . . . . . 198 D7
  Stamford PE9 . . . . 143 D5
Edinburgh Way LE12 . . . . 76 C1
Edison Ctyd NN17 . . . . . 230 F3
Edith Ave LE3 . . . . 179 A7
EDITH WESTON 166 B7
Edith Weston Prim Sch
  LE15 . . . . 166 A4
Edith Weston Rd
  LE15 . . . . 166 D4
Edmonds Cl LE2 . . . . . . 143 F4
Edmonds Dr PE9 . . . . . . 168 A5
EDMONDTHORPE 86 A8
Edmondthorpe Drift
  LE14 . . . . 63 B1
Edmondthorpe Mere
  LE15 . . . . 85 E5
Edmondthorpe Rd
  LE14 . . . . 62 E1
Edmonton Rd LE1 . . . . . 259 C5
Edmonton Way LE15 . . . 138 B6
Edward Ave LE3 . . . . 178 F8
Edward Cl LE2 . . . . 181 C5
Edward Dr LE2 . . . . 179 C1
Edward Rd
  Fleckney LE8 . . . . 222 F7
  Leicester LE2 . . . . 155 B2
  Long Eaton NG10 . . . . . 10 D8
  Market Harborough
    LE16 . . . . 240 D5
  Stamford PE9 . . . . 143 D5
Edwards Ctr **7** LE10 . . . 215 D8
Edward St
  Anstey LE7 . . . . 127 C7
  Hartshorne DE11 . . . . . 45 A3
  Hinckley LE10 . . . . . . 197 C2
  Leicester LE5 . . . . 155 C7
  Loughborough LE11 . . . . 52 A5
  Moira DE11 . . . . 44 C1
  Overseal DE12 . . . . 67 A4
Egerton Ave LE4 . . . . . . 128 E2
Egerton Hos LE2 . . . . . . 180 E7
Egerton Rd LE13 . . . . 59 D3
Egerton View LE13 . . . . . 59 B3
Eggington St LE11 . . . . . 51 E2
Egginton St LE5 . . . . . . 155 C5
Eglantine Cl LE2 . . . . . . 181 A7
Egleton LE15 . . . . 138 C4
Egleton Nature Reserve ★
  LE15 . . . . 138 F2
Eider Cl LE8 . . . . 201 F4
Eight Acres **6** PE9 . . . . 143 C3
Eileen Ave LE4 . . . . 128 E2
Elbow La LE1 . . . . 259 A4
Elder Cl LE3, LE7 . . . . . . 127 F3
Elder La LE67 . . . . 48 A2
Eldon St LE1 . . . . 259 C4
Eleanor Cl PE9 . . . . 143 C4
Elfin Gr LE7 . . . . 219 E2
Elford St **2** LE65 . . . . . . 69 B6
Elgar Dr NG10 . . . . 10 B5
Elgar Way PE9 . . . . 143 B4
Elgin Ave LE3 . . . . 153 F8
Elgin Dr LE3 . . . . 59 C4
Elgin Wlk LE67 . . . . 71 D8
Eliot Cl
  Long Eaton NG10 . . . . . 10 B5
  Loughborough LE11 . . . . 51 B6
Elisha Cl LE9 . . . . 199 E2
Elizabethan Way
  LE17 . . . . 244 D7
Elizabeth Ave LE67 . . . . . 95 F2
Elizabeth Cl
  Fleckney LE8 . . . . 222 F6
  Houghton on t H LE7 . . . 157 F4

Elizabeth Cres LE18 . . . . 180 B4
Elizabeth Ct
  Glenfield LE3 . . . . 127 B1
  Wigston LE18 . . . . 180 D2
Elizabeth Dr
  Leicester, Oadby LE2 . . . 181 C4
  Thurmaston LE4 . . . . . 129 E8
Elizabeth Gdns LE8 . . . . 201 F7
Elizabeth Rd
  Fleckney LE8 . . . . 222 F6
  Hinckley LE10 . . . . . . 197 D2
  Stamford PE9 . . . . 143 D4
Elizabeth St LE5 . . . . . . 155 E5
Elizabeth Way LE15 . . . . 189 B5
Elizabeth Woodville Prim
  Sch LE5 . . . . 126 E3
Ellaby Rd LE11 . . . . 51 E6
Elland Rd LE3 . . . . 153 B5
Ellesmere Coll LE3 . . . . . 154 B2
Ellesmere Pl LE3 . . . . . . 154 B2
Ellesmere Rd LE3 . . . . . . 154 B2
Elliot Cl
  Kibworth Beauchamp
    LE8 . . . . 224 A8
  Leicester, Oadby LE2 . . . 181 E4
  Whetstone LE8 . . . . . . 202 A4
Elliots Yd LE8 . . . . 202 F3
Elliott Dr
  Leicester Forest East
    LE3 . . . . 153 B4
  Thurmaston LE4 . . . . . 130 A6
Elliott Rd LE4 . . . . 128 D4
Elliott's La LE67 . . . . 125 A8
Ellis Ave LE4 . . . . 129 A1
Ellis Cl
  Barrow-u-S LE12 . . . . . 76 E8
  Ellistown LE67 . . . . . . 96 E3
  Glenfield LE3 . . . . 153 B8
  Long Eaton NG10 . . . . . 10 C6
  Quorn (Quorndon) LE12 . . 75 F7
Ellis Dr LE9 . . . . 152 F3
Ellis Fields LE2 . . . . 181 E3
Ellison Ave LE4 . . . . 129 A1
Ellison Cl
  Stoney Stanton LE9 . . . 199 D3
  Wigston LE18 . . . . 202 F8
Ellis St LE7 . . . . 127 D6
ELLISTOWN 96 D3
Ellistown Com Prim Sch
  LE67 . . . . 96 E3
Ellistown Terrace Rd
  LE67 . . . . 96 E1
Ellwood Cl LE5 . . . . 156 B4
Elm Ave
  Ashby-de-la-Z LE65 . . . . 69 D7
  Long Eaton NG10 . . . . . 10 C8
  Lutterworth LE17 . . . . 244 B6
Elm Cl
  Groby LE6 . . . . 126 F2
  Ibstock LE67 . . . . 95 E2
  Mountsorrel LE12 . . . . . 76 E1
  Oakham LE15 . . . . 138 B7
Elmcroft Ave LE5 . . . . . . 156 B7
Elmcroft Rd LE17 . . . . . . 246 F3
Elm Ct LE67 . . . . 127 E6
Elmdale Rd LE9 . . . . 198 D6
Elmdale St LE4 . . . . 129 A2
Elm Dr LE16 . . . . 240 C2
ELMESTHORPE 198 F5
Elmesthorpe La LE9 . . . . 198 D6
Elmfield Ave
  Birstall LE4 . . . . 128 F7
  Leicester LE2 . . . . 155 C3
Elmfield Cl LE2 . . . . 179 E8
Elmfield Gdns LE2 . . . . . 155 C3
Elm Gdns LE12 . . . . 76 E1
Elmhirst Rd LE17 . . . . . . 244 B5
Elmhurst Ave LE13 . . . . . 59 A4
Elmhurst Cl LE19 . . . . . . 201 A7
Elm La
  Catthorpe CV23 . . . . . 253 E1
  Eaton NG32 . . . . 22 F6
Elms Cl
  Leicester, Oadby LE2 . . . 181 B5
  Rempstone LE12 . . . . . 32 D5
Elms Ct
  Austrey CV9 . . . . 119 A2
  Leicester LE2 . . . . 180 D8
Elms Dr
  Austrey CV9 . . . . 119 A2
  Peckleton LE9 . . . . . . 176 A7
  Quorn (Quorndon) LE12 . . 75 F7
Elms Farm Ind Est
  LE17 . . . . 233 E2
Elms Gr
  Barrow-u-S LE12 . . . . . 53 D1
  Loughborough LE11 . . . . 52 C3
Elm's La LE8 . . . . 182 F1
Elmsleigh Ave LE2 . . . . . 155 D1
Elmsleigh Cl DE11 . . . . . 44 B6
Elmsleigh Dr DE11 . . . . . 44 B6
Elmsleigh Gr DE11 . . . . . 44 B6
Elmsleigh Inf Sch
  DE11 . . . . 44 B6
Elms Rd
  Leicester LE2 . . . . 180 D8
  Melton Mowbray LE13 . . . 59 D3
Elms Road Hos LE2 . . . . 180 D8
Elm St PE9 . . . . 143 E3
Elms The
  Blaby LE8 . . . . 202 B7
  Countesthorpe LE8 . . . 202 E4
  Leicester, Oadby LE2 . . . 181 B5
  Markfield LE67 . . . . 98 D2
  Whitwick LE67 . . . . 71 D5
Elmsthorpe Rise LE3 . . . 154 A3

Elm Tree Ave LE3 . . . . . . 153 B8
Elmtree Cl LE5 . . . . 130 C2
Elm Tree Dr LE10 . . . . . . 215 F8
Elm Tree Rd LE9 . . . . . . 201 C2
Elm Wlk NN17 . . . . 230 D1
Elmwood Row LE2 . . . . . 180 A4
Elsadene Ave LE4 . . . . . 129 B3
Elsalene Cl LE6 . . . . 126 C5
Elsalene Ct LE6 . . . . 155 D1
Elsalene Dr LE6 . . . . 126 C5
Elsdon Cl LE67 . . . . 71 D5
Elsham Cl LE3 . . . . 153 D5
Elston Fields LE2 . . . . . . 179 F6
Elstop Ave CV23 . . . . . . 252 D5
Elstree Ave LE5 . . . . 156 E8
Elsworthy Wlk LE3 . . . . . 153 D6
Elton Cl PE9 . . . . 143 B4
Elton & Orston Sta
  NG13 . . . . 2 A5
Elton Way LE67 . . . . 96 C2
Elvaston Cl **2** LE65 . . . . 69 C5
Elvaston Dr NG10 . . . . . . 10 A4
Elvaston St DE72 . . . . 9 B7
Elvyn Way LE11 . . . . 51 D2
Elwell Ave LE9 . . . . 175 B1
Elwells Ave LE17 . . . . . . 219 D2
Elwin Ave LE18 . . . . 180 D4
Ely Cl DE11 . . . . 44 D6
Emberton Cl LE18 . . . . . 180 F3
Embleton Cl LE10 . . . . . 197 E3
Emburn Ho LE3 . . . . 153 F8
Emerson Cl LE4 . . . . 128 A3
Emlyns Gdns PE9 . . . . . 143 E4
Emlyns St PE9 . . . . 143 E4
Emmanuel Rd PE9 . . . . . 143 D5
Emperor Way LE8 . . . . . 201 F4
EMPINGHAM 141 A5
Empingham CE Prim Sch
  LE15 . . . . 141 B6
Empingham Rd
  Empingham LE15 . . . . . 140 F2
  Exton LE15 . . . . 113 B2
  Ketton PE9 . . . . 167 E6
  Stamford PE9 . . . . 143 B3
Empire Rd LE3 . . . . 154 D7
Empress Rd LE11 . . . . . . 52 D4
ENDERBY 178 B3
Enderby Rd
  Blaby LE8 . . . . 202 B8
  Thurlaston LE9 . . . . . . 177 B3
  Whetstone LE8, LE19 . . . 178 E1
Enderby Road Ind Est
  LE8 . . . . 178 E1
Enderbys La LE7 . . . . . . 159 B8
Englefield Rd LE5 . . . . . . 156 D5
Englewood Cl LE4 . . . . . 128 D1
English Martyr's RC Prim
  Sch LE15 . . . . 138 B7
English Martyrs RC Sch
  LE4 . . . . 128 B1
Ennerdale Cl LE2 . . . . . . 181 D4
Ennerdale Gdns LE65 . . . 69 D5
Ennerdale Rd
  Barrow-u-S LE12 . . . . . 76 D8
  Corby NN17 . . . . 230 E1
Ensbury Gdns LE5 . . . . . 156 B3
Ensor Cl
  Nuneaton CV11 . . . . . . 214 A6
  Swadlincote DE11 . . . . . 44 D5
Enston St LE9 . . . . 150 B4
Enterprise Ctr The
  LE9 . . . . 198 B6
Epinal Ct LE11 . . . . 51 D5
Epinal Way LE11 . . . . 51 F3
Epping Dr LE13 . . . . 59 C5
Epping Way LE2 . . . . 179 D3
Epsom Rd LE4 . . . . 129 B2
Equity Rd
  Earl Shilton LE9 . . . . . 198 E7
  Enderby LE19 . . . . 178 A2
  Leicester LE3 . . . . 154 D4
Equity Rd E LE9 . . . . . . 198 F7
Erdyngton Rd LE3 . . . . . 153 F4
Erith Rd LE2 . . . . 154 E1
Ermine Cl PE9 . . . . 143 B3
Ermine Rise PE9 . . . . . . 142 D7
Ermine Way PE9 . . . . . . 143 B3
Ernee Cl LE3 . . . . 153 D7
Ernest Hall Way DE11 . . . 44 C4
Erringtons Cl LE2 . . . . . 181 E2
Erskine Cl LE10 . . . . . . 197 A2
Erskine St LE1 . . . . 259 C4
Ervington Ct LE19 . . . . . 178 D6
Ervin's Lock LE18 . . . . . 203 A8
Ervin Way LE7 . . . . 103 E6
Escolme Cl DE11 . . . . . . 44 D4
Eskdale Cl
  Leicester, Oadby LE2 . . . 181 D4
  Long Eaton NG10 . . . . . 10 B5
Eskdale Rd
  Hinckley LE10 . . . . . . 215 A7
  Leicester LE4 . . . . 128 D3
ESSENDINE 117 A6
Essendine Rd PE9 . . . . . 116 F7
Essex Cl
  Desford LE9 . . . . 151 B3
  Melton Mowbray LE13 . . . 82 D8
Essex Gdns LE16 . . . . . 240 D1
Essex Rd
  Leicester LE4 . . . . 129 E2
  Stamford PE9 . . . . 143 D4
  Wigston LE18 . . . . 179 F3
Estelle Ho LE4 . . . . 129 E8
Estima Cl LE2 . . . . 180 C8
Estley Rd LE9 . . . . 218 E2
Estoril Ave LE18 . . . . . . 180 F3
Ethel Rd LE5 . . . . 155 E4

Eton Cl
  Ashby-de-la-Z LE65 . . . . 69 A8
  Leicester LE2 . . . . 180 B8
Eunice Ave LE2 . . . . 200 D7
Eureka Prim Sch DE11 . . . 44 D5
Eureka Rd DE11 . . . . 44 D5
Euro Bsns Pk LE16 . . . . . 241 B4
Europark Ind Est
  CV23 . . . . 253 B2
Euston St LE2 . . . . 154 F1
Evelyn Dr LE3 . . . . 154 D2
Evelyn Rd LE3 . . . . 153 E2
Everard Cl LE4 . . . . 129 E2
Everard Cres CV23 . . . . 257 A5
Everard Way
  Braunstone Town
    LE19 . . . . 178 F5
  Stanton u B LE67 . . . . . 97 F1
Everest Cl LE1 . . . . 155 B7
Everest Dr LE13 . . . . 59 A5
Everett Cl LE4 . . . . 130 A4
Everson Cl LE9 . . . . 218 F5
Every St LE1 . . . . 259 B3
Evesham Rd LE3 . . . . . . 154 C2
EVINGTON 156 A3
Evington Cl LE5 . . . . 156 A3
Evington Ct LE5 . . . . . . 156 A3
Evington Dr LE5 . . . . . . 155 E3
Evington La
  Leicester, Evington
    LE5 . . . . 156 A2
  Leicester LE5 . . . . 155 E3
Evington Mews LE5 . . . . 156 B3
Evington Parks Rd
  LE2 . . . . 155 D3
Evington Pl LE2 . . . . 155 C4
Evington Rd LE2 . . . . . . 155 C3
Evington St LE2 . . . . . . 155 B5
Evington Valley Gdns
  LE5 . . . . 155 D4
Evington Valley Prim Sch
  LE5 . . . . 155 D3
Evington Valley Rd
  LE5 . . . . 155 D4
Ewden Rise LE13 . . . . . . 59 B1
Excalibur Cl LE3 . . . . . . 153 A2
Excelsior Dr DE11 . . . . . . 44 E2
Exchange The LE2 . . . . . 179 E4
Exeter Cl DE11 . . . . 44 E6
Exeter Ct **3** PE9 . . . . . 143 D2
Exeter Gdns PE9 . . . . . . 143 B2
Exeter Rd LE18 . . . . 180 B4
Exmoor Ave LE4 . . . . . . 154 E8
Exmoor Cl
  Ellistown LE67 . . . . . . 96 D4
  Loughborough LE11 . . . . 74 D8
  Wigston LE18 . . . . 180 D1
Exploration Dr LE4 . . . . 128 F2
EXTON 113 B3
Exton CE Prim Sch
  LE15 . . . . 113 B3
Exton Cl PE9 . . . . 143 B3
Exton La LE15 . . . . 112 C2
Exton Rd
  Cottesmore LE15 . . . . . 112 D7
  Empingham LE15 . . . . . 140 F8
  Leicester LE5 . . . . 155 E7
Eyebrook Cl LE5 . . . . . . 130 C3
Eye Brook Cl LE11 . . . . . 51 B2
EYE KETTLEBY 81 F6
Eynsford Cl LE2 . . . . 180 F8
EYRES MONSELL 179 D3
Eyres Monsell Prim Sch
  LE2 . . . . 179 D4

F

Fabis Cl DE11 . . . . 44 A3
Fabius Cl LE10 . . . . 215 C2
Facers La LE7 . . . . 156 F8
Factory La **9** LE16 . . . . 240 E3
Factory Rd LE10 . . . . . . 197 D1
Factory St
  Loughborough LE11 . . . . 52 C3
  Shepshed LE12 . . . . . . 50 B4
Factory The LE2 . . . . . . 179 E8
Fair Acre Rd LE9 . . . . . . 198 A6
Fairbourne Rd LE3 . . . . . 154 A1
Fairburn Ho LE3 . . . . . . 153 F8
Faircharm Trad Est
  LE3 . . . . 154 D2
Fairefield Cres LE3 . . . . . 127 D1
Faire Rd LE3 . . . . 127 D1
Fairestone Ave LE3 . . . . 153 C8
Fairfax Cl
  Ashby-de-la-Z LE65 . . . . 69 D7
  Leicester LE4 . . . . 129 E2
Fairfax Ct LE8 . . . . 205 B8
Fairfax Rd
  Leicester LE4 . . . . 129 E2
  Market Harborough
    LE16 . . . . 240 E1
Fairfield LE67 . . . . 95 F1
Fair Field LE14 . . . . 40 A6
Fairfield Cl
  Langham LE15 . . . . . . 110 C3
  Melton Mowbray LE13 . . . 59 D5
Fairfield Com Prim Sch
  LE18 . . . . 180 A3
Fairfield Cres NG10 . . . . 10 B4
Fairfield Ct
  Coalville LE67 . . . . 96 C6
  Loughborough LE11 . . . . 52 C3

Fairfield Rd
Coalville LE67 . . . . **96** C7
Leicester, Oadby LE2 . . . . **181** B5
Market Harborough
LE16 . . . . **240** D4
Fairfield Sch LE11 . . . . . **52** B3
Fairfield St
Leicester LE5 . . . . **155** C5
Wigston LE18 . . . . **179** F1
Fairfield Terr DE11 . . . . . **44** F3
Fairfield (Uppingham Sch)
LE15 . . . . **188** F4
Fairford Ave LE5 . . . . . . **156** B3
Fairhaven Rd LE7 . . . . . . **127** E8
Fairholme Rd LE2 . . . . . . **180** B6
Fairisle Way LE8 . . . . . . **202** F3
Fair Lea Cl NG10 . . . . **10** D6
Fair Mead LE12 . . . . **101** E8
Fairmeadows Way
LE11 . . . . **75** A7
Fairmount Dr LE11 . . . . . **51** E2
Fairstone Hill LE2 . . . . . **181** B4
Fair View LE8 . . . . **138** B6
Fairview Ave LE8 . . . . . . **201** F7
Fairway
Kibworth Beauchamp
LE8 . . . . **224** B8
Market Harborough
LE16 . . . . **240** D4
Nuneaton CV11 . . . . **214** B1
Fairway Mdws LE17 . . . . **233** B4
Fairway Rd LE2 . . . . **50** D3
Fairway Rd S LE12 . . . . . **50** C1
Fairways Ct LE9 . . . . **198** A3
Fairway The
Blaby LE8 . . . . **202** A7
Hinckley LE10 . . . . **215** F7
Kirby Fields LE9 . . . . **152** F5
Leicester, Aylestone
LE2 . . . . **179** F6
Leicester LE2 . . . . **181** A8
Falcon Bsns Pk LE11 . . . . **52** E2
Falcon Cl
Broughton Astley LE9 . . . **218** E7
Leicester Forest East
LE3 . . . . **152** E2
Falconer Cres LE3 . . . . . **153** E8
Falconers Gn LE10 . . . . . **215** F6
Falcon Rd LE7 . . . . **127** D5
Falcon St LE11 . . . . **52** C5
Falcon Way DE11 . . . . **44** F3
Faldo Cl LE4 . . . . **129** E5
Faldo Dr LE13 . . . . **59** C6
Falkirk Cl PE9 . . . . **143** A4
Falkner Ct LE11 . . . . **51** E2
Fallow Cl
Broughton Astley LE9 . . . **218** F4
Whetstone LE8 . . . . **201** F5
Fallowfield Rd LE5 . . . . . **156** D4
Falmouth Cl CV11 . . . . . . **214** A5
Falmouth Dr
Hinckley LE10 . . . . **197** E4
Wigston LE18 . . . . **180** F1
Falmouth Rd LE5 . . . . . . **156** A4
Falstaff Cl CV11 . . . . **214** A1
Fane Cl PE9 . . . . **143** D5
Faraday Cl LE9 . . . . **218** F4
Faraday Ct LE2 . . . . **259** C3
Faraday Rd LE10 . . . . . . **214** E7
Far Croft DE72 . . . . **9** D8
Faringdon Ave LE17 . . . . **244** D6
Far La LE12 . . . . **30** C4
Far Lash LE10 . . . . **215** F7
Farleigh Ave LE18 . . . . . **180** D3
Farleigh Cl LE9 . . . . **218** E2
Farleigh Gdns LE15 . . . . **189** A5
Farleigh (Uppingham Sch)
LE15 . . . . **189** B5
Farley Rd LE2 . . . . **180** D8
Farley Way
Kirby Muxloe LE9 . . . . . . **152** F6
Quorn (Quorndon) LE12 . . . **75** F7
Farm Cl
Birstall LE4 . . . . **129** B7
Leicester LE2 . . . . **179** F5
Littlethorpe LE19 . . . . . . **201** C7
Long Eaton NG10 . . . . **10** E5
Farmers Cl LE3 . . . . **153** B8
Farmhouse Cl NG13 . . . . . **3** B4
Farm La LE67 . . . . **96** B6
Farm Rd
Barwell LE9 . . . . **198** C8
Hinckley LE10 . . . . **215** E6
FARM TOWN **70** B5
Farmway LE3 . . . . **178** E6
Farndale
Whitwick LE67 . . . . **71** D6
Wigston LE18 . . . . **180** F2
Farndale Cl
Leicester LE2 . . . . **259** A2
Long Eaton NG10 . . . . . . **10** A5
Farndale Dr LE11 . . . . . . **74** F8
Farndale View LE16 . . . . **240** C2
Farndon Ct LE16 . . . . . . **240** D2
Farndon Dr LE9 . . . . **199** D2
Farndon Fields Prim Sch
LE16 . . . . **250** E8
Farndon Rd
Great Oxendon LE16 . . . . **250** D4
Lubenham LE16 . . . . **239** F2
Market Harborough
LE16 . . . . **240** D1
Marston Trussell LE16 . . . **249** D7
Farneway LE10 . . . . **197** B1
Farnham Cl LE7 . . . . **101** E7

Farnham Ct LE12 . . . . . . **76** D3
Farnham Rd LE11 . . . . . . **75** B8
Farnham St
Leicester LE5 . . . . **155** C6
Quorn (Quorndon) LE12 . . . **75** F6
Farnworth Cl LE4 . . . . . . **129** D3
Farrier La LE4 . . . . **128** B4
Farriers Cl
Snarestone DE12 . . . . . . **120** E7
Wymeswold LE12 . . . . **33** B4
Farriers Way
Carlby PE9 . . . . **117** B8
Hinckley LE10 . . . . **215** F6
Stathern LE14 . . . . **13** A3
Farriers' Way LE7 . . . . . **103** D7
Farrington St LE5 . . . . . **155** C7
Farr Wood Cl LE6 . . . . . . **126** E3
Far St LE12 . . . . **33** C4
Farthing Ct NG10 . . . . . . **10** B7
Farthingdale Cl LE9 . . . . **201** E3
Farthings The LE12 . . . . . **30** A1
Fastnet Rd LE5 . . . . **156** E7
Faversham Cl LE3 . . . . . **153** C6
Fayrhurst Rd LE2 . . . . . . **179** E6
Fearn Cl DE72 . . . . **10** A7
Fearon St LE11 . . . . **51** F4
Featherbed La
Ashby-de-la-Z LE65 . . . . . **69** D7
Rugby CV21 . . . . **257** A1
West Langton LE8 . . . . . **224** E7
Featherby Dr LE2 . . . . . . **179** A3
Featherstone Dr LE10 . . . **215** E6
Featherstone Dr LE2 . . . . **179** C2
Feature Rd LE4 . . . . **102** E1
Federation St LE19 . . . . . **178** A3
Feildingway LE17 . . . . . . **244** C7
Feldspar Cl LE19 . . . . . . **178** B5
Fell Cl LE8 . . . . **223** A6
Felley Way LE3 . . . . **154** C8
Felstead Rd LE4 . . . . . . **128** D4
Fencote Rd LE5 . . . . **130** C3
Fen La NG23 . . . . **1** D8
Fennel St LE11 . . . . **52** B4
Fenners Cl LE4 . . . . **128** C7
Fenn Lanes
Dadlington CV13 . . . . . . **173** D2
Fenny Drayton CV13 . . . . **195** D8
FENNY DRAYTON **195** A6
Fenny La LE17 . . . . **222** D2
Fenton Ave DE11 . . . . **45** B1
Fenton Cl
Leicester, Oadby LE2 . . . . **181** A3
Measham DE12 . . . . **93** B3
Fenton Cres DE12 . . . . . . **93** C3
Fenton Dr PE9 . . . . **117** C8
Fenwick Rd LE2 . . . . **181** E4
Fermain Cl LE5 . . . . **156** D5
Fern Cl LE7 . . . . **156** E5
Fern Cres LE6 . . . . **126** D4
Ferndale Cl LE67 . . . . **95** E1
Ferndale Dr LE6 . . . . . . **152** D8
Ferndale Gr LE10 . . . . . . **215** A7
Ferndale Rd
Leicester LE5 . . . . **180** B6
Thurmaston LE4 . . . . . . **129** E6
Ferndene Dr LE3 . . . . . . **153** C6
Ferndown Cl LE3 . . . . . . **153** C6
Ferneley Ave LE10 . . . . . **197** A3
Ferneley Cres LE13 . . . . . **59** E5
Ferneley Rise LE7 . . . . . . **78** F4
Ferness Cl LE10 . . . . . . **197** B2
Ferness Rd LE10 . . . . . . **197** B2
Fernfield Cl LE16 . . . . . . **241** B4
Fernhurst Rd LE3 . . . . . . **178** F8
Fernie Ave LE13 . . . . **59** B3
Fernie Chase LE16 . . . . . **226** A6
Fernie Cl LE2 . . . . **181** C4
Fernie Ct LE17 . . . . **247** E6
Fernie Dene LE8 . . . . . . **182** C1
Fernie Rd
Leicester LE5 . . . . **155** D7
Market Harborough
LE16 . . . . **240** F3
Fernie Sq LE15 . . . . **87** D2
Fernlea LE19 . . . . **177** F1
Fern Ley Cl LE16 . . . . . . **241** B2
Fernleys Cl LE4 . . . . **128** B3
Fern Rise LE5 . . . . **130** C1
Fernvale Prim Sch
LE7 . . . . **156** F6
Ferrars Ct LE3 . . . . **153** D2
Ferrers Cl
Ashby-de-la-Z LE65 . . . . . **68** F5
Castle Donington DE74 . . . **17** A3
Oakham LE15 . . . . **137** D6
Ferrers Croft CV13 . . . . . **149** D7
Ferrers Ctr for Arts &
Crafts ★ LE65 . . . . **46** F7
Ferrers Rd
Lutterworth LE17 . . . . . . **244** B5
Whitwick LE67 . . . . **71** C4
Ferrers Rise LE6 . . . . . . **126** E3
Ferrers St LE2 . . . . **179** F5
Ferrous Cl LE4 . . . . **155** C8
Ferryman Rd LE11 . . . . . . **52** C5
Festival Ave
Breaston DE72 . . . . **9** C7
Thurmaston LE4 . . . . . . **129** E6
Festival Dr LE11 . . . . **52** A6
Fettes Cl LE65 . . . . **69** A8
Field Ave LE12 . . . . **50** C6
Field Cl
Breaston DE72 . . . . **9** F7
Hinckley LE10 . . . . **197** F3
Houghton on t H LE7 . . . **158** A3
Littlethorpe LE19 . . . . . . **201** C7

Field Cl *continued*
Melton Mowbray LE13 . . . . **59** D1
Thringstone LE67 . . . . **71** D7
Field Court Rd LE6 . . . . . **126** F3
Field Crest LE12 . . . . . . **101** D8
Fieldfare Wlk LE5 . . . . . . **155** C7
Fieldgate Cres LE4 . . . . . **128** E8
FIELD HEAD **98** F1
Fieldhead Cl LE16 . . . . . **240** C3
Fieldhouse Rd LE4 . . . . . **129** B3
Fieldhurst Ave LE3 . . . . . **178** E8
Fielding Cl CV9 . . . . **170** D2
Fielding Palmer Hospl
LE17 . . . . **244** D6
Fielding Rd LE4 . . . . **128** F6
Field La
Blackfordby DE11 . . . . . . **45** C2
Tonge DE73 . . . . **27** B3
Fields Farm Cl LE12 . . . . . **34** D7
Fields Farm Rd NG10 . . . . **10** E5
Field St LE12 . . . . **50** B4
Field The LE14 . . . . **108** B2
Field View
Syston LE7 . . . . **102** E3
Thurmaston LE4 . . . . . . **130** A7
Whitwick LE67 . . . . **71** D5
Field Way LE9 . . . . **198** D7
Fieldway Cres LE8 . . . . . **182** B1
Fieldway The LE9 . . . . . . **218** F5
Fieldwork Rd LE14 . . . . . . **36** A5
Fife Cl PE9 . . . . **142** F4
Filbert St E LE2 . . . . **154** F3
Filbert St LE2 . . . . **259** A1
Filbert Village LE2 . . . . . **154** E3
Filbert Way LE2 . . . . **154** E2
Fillingate LE7 . . . . **102** B3
Finch Ave LE15 . . . . **137** D6
Finch Cl
Leicester LE3 . . . . **153** E5
Uppingham LE15 . . . . . . **189** A5
Woodville DE11 . . . . **44** F3
Finches The
Desford LE9 . . . . **151** B2
Market Overton LE15 . . . . **87** A5
Finch-Hatton Dr
NN17 . . . . **213** C1
Finch Way LE19 . . . . **201** A7
Finch Wlk LE14 . . . . **57** E3
Fineshade Ave LE3 . . . . . **154** C8
Finkey St LE15 . . . . **137** F6
Finney Cl DE12 . . . . **67** E1
Finns La NG32 . . . . **14** E3
Finsbury Ave
Loughborough LE11 . . . . . **52** C3
Sileby LE12 . . . . **77** E3
Finsbury Rd LE4 . . . . . . **129** C1
Finson Cl LE18 . . . . **180** D3
Fiona Dr LE7 . . . . **156** F5
Firdale LE14 . . . . **108** C1
Firestone Cl LE3 . . . . . . **153** C6
Firfield Ave
Birstall LE4 . . . . **129** A7
Breaston DE72 . . . . **9** E8
Firfield Prim Sch DE72 . . . . **9** E7
Firfield Villas LE2 . . . . . . **179** E8
Fir Rd PE9 . . . . **142** F5
Firs Ave LE15 . . . . **189** A5
Firs Cl LE7 . . . . **158** A4
Firs Rd LE7 . . . . **158** A4
Firs St NG10 . . . . **10** A4
Firs The
Market Harborough
LE16 . . . . **240** C3
Syston LE7 . . . . **103** A2
Wigston LE18 . . . . **180** E4
Firth Pk LE15 . . . . **189** B4
Firtree Ave LE17 . . . . . . **244** B6
Fir Tree Ave LE8 . . . . . . **202** E4
Firtree Cl LE9 . . . . **198** B8
Fir Tree Cl LE18 . . . . **180** C5
Firtree La LE17 . . . . **254** C3
Fir Tree La LE6 . . . . **126** E4
Firtree Wlk
Groby LE6 . . . . **126** E3
Moira DE12 . . . . **68** B6
Fir Tree Wlk LE16 . . . . . **240** E4
Firwood Rd LE13 . . . . **59** E5
Fisher Cl
Cossington LE7 . . . . **102** D8
Stoney Stanton LE9 . . . . **199** C2
Fishley Cl LE3 . . . . **153** B7
Fishpond La NG13 . . . . **6** C2
Fishponds Cl LE3 . . . . . . **153** B8
Fishpond Way LE11 . . . . . **75** A6
Fishpools LE3 . . . . **178** E7
Fishpool Way LE12 . . . . . **76** D3
Fish Well Cl NG33 . . . . . . **43** B8
Fitzroy St LE3 . . . . **154** D5
Fitzwilliam Cl LE2 . . . . . . **181** D4
Fitzwilliam Rd PE9 . . . . . **143** C5
Fitzwilliam Wlk LE15 . . . . **87** E2
Flagstaff Rd LE14 . . . . . . **36** A5
Flamborough Rd LE5 . . . . **156** D7
Flamingo Dr LE8 . . . . . . **201** F4
Flamville Rd LE10 . . . . . . **216** B5
Flannagan Way LE67 . . . . **97** B7
Flatholme Rd LE5 . . . . . . **156** E8
Flats La CV9 . . . . **119** B1
Flats The
Earl Shilton LE9 . . . . . . **176** A1
Illston on t H LE7 . . . . . **183** F3
Flatten Way LE7 . . . . . . **103** A4
Flatts Cl LE67 . . . . **95** F3
Flavel Ct CV9 . . . . **119** A1
Flaxdown Gdns CV23 . . . . **252** D1
Flaxfield Cl LE6 . . . . **126** F3
Flax La CV9 . . . . **146** D6
Flaxland LE7 . . . . **101** E7

Flaxland Cl LE16 . . . . . . **241** B3
Flaxland Cres LE12 . . . . . **77** C2
Flax Rd LE2 . . . . **129** B2
FLECKNEY **222** E8
Fleckney CE Prim Sch
LE8 . . . . **222** E8
Fleckney Ind Est LE8 . . . **223** A7
Fleckney Rd
Arnesby LE8 . . . . **222** B5
Fleckney LE8 . . . . **223** A6
Kibworth Beauchamp
LE8 . . . . **223** E8
Kilby LE18 . . . . **204** A2
Fleet St LE1 . . . . **259** C4
Fleet The LE9 . . . . **199** E3
Fleetwood Cl LE16 . . . . . **240** D1
Fleetwood Ct
2 Leicester LE2 . . . . . . **155** A1
Stretton LE15 . . . . **89** A7
Fleetwood Gdns LE16 . . . **240** D1
Fleetwood Rd LE2 . . . . . **155** A1
Fleming Ave NG13 . . . . . . **3** C3
Fleming Cl LE11 . . . . **51** D6
Fleming Rd LE10 . . . . . . **214** F7
Flesh Hovel La LE12 . . . . . **76** A8
Fletcher Mall LE4 . . . . . **128** A4
Fletcher Rd
Hinckley LE10 . . . . **215** E7
Stoney Stanton LE9 . . . . **199** E3
Fletchers Cl LE9 . . . . . . **201** B7
Fletcher St NG10 . . . . **10** D8
Fletchers' Way LE7 . . . . . **103** D7
Fletcher's Way LE7 . . . . . **103** D7
Fleury Ct LE7 . . . . **103** D7
Flint Cl
Atherstone CV9 . . . . **170** E2
Ryhall PE9 . . . . **117** A2
Flora St LE3 . . . . **154** D5
Florence Ave LE18 . . . . . **180** A1
Florence Cl CV9 . . . . **170** D1
Florence Rd LE5 . . . . **155** C6
Florence St LE2 . . . . **179** E7
Florence Wragg Way
LE2 . . . . **181** E4
Floret Cl LE67 . . . . **71** A2
Florian Way LE10 . . . . . . **197** A1
Florin Gdns NG10 . . . . . . **10** B7
Floyd Cl LE4 . . . . **129** C5
Fludes Ct LE2 . . . . **181** C5
Foan Hill LE67 . . . . **71** B5
Foley Rd LE8 . . . . **223** E8
Folkington Cl LE4 . . . . . . **129** A5
Folville Jun Sch LE3 . . . . **154** A2
Folville Rise LE3 . . . . . . **154** B2
Folville St LE14 . . . . **105** F4
Fontana Cl LE3 . . . . **153** C7
Fontwell Dr LE2 . . . . **179** B5
Fontwell Gdns PE9 . . . . . **143** D3
Forbes Cl
Glenfield LE3 . . . . **153** C7
Long Eaton NG10 . . . . . . **10** E5
Ford Bank LE16 . . . . **229** D6
Ford Cl LE2 . . . . **179** C3
Ford Rise LE2 . . . . **179** C3
Ford The LE2 . . . . **179** D1
Fordview Cl LE8 . . . . **182** A1
Forest Ave LE4 . . . . **129** E8
Forest Bsns Pk LE67 . . . . **97** C4
Forest Cl
Groby LE6 . . . . **126** D3
Melton Mowbray LE13 . . . . **59** C5
Forest Ct LE11 . . . . **52** A3
Forest Dr
Kirby Fields LE9 . . . . **152** F4
Sileby LE12 . . . . **77** C4
Foresters Cl LE3 . . . . . . **153** B8
Foresters' Row LE7 . . . . . **103** D8
Forest Gate LE7 . . . . . . **127** D6
Forest Gdns PE9 . . . . . . **142** F5
Forest House La LE3 . . . . **152** F2
Forest La LE12 . . . . **49** C4
Forest Lea DE12 . . . . **67** E4
Forest Lodge Prim Sch
LE3 . . . . **153** E8
Forest Rd
Coalville LE67 . . . . **96** D8
Hinckley LE10 . . . . **215** F8
Huncote LE9 . . . . **177** D1
Leicester LE5 . . . . **155** C7
Loughborough LE11 . . . . . **51** E2
Markfield LE67 . . . . **125** C8
Narborough LE19 . . . . . . **177** F3
Quorn (Quorndon) LE12 . . . **75** E5
Woodhouse LE12 . . . . . . **75** C3
Forest Rise
Desford LE9 . . . . **151** C3
Groby LE6 . . . . **126** E3
Leicester Forest East
LE9 . . . . **152** F3
Leicester, Oadby LE2 . . . . **181** C6
Thurnby LE7 . . . . **156** F5
Forest St LE12 . . . . **50** C4
Forest View
Botcheston LE9 . . . . . . **151** C8
Groby LE6 . . . . **126** D4
Overseal DE12 . . . . **67** B4
Forest View Rd LE9 . . . . **198** C7
Forest Way Sch LE67 . . . . **97** A8
Forge Cl
Fleckney LE8 . . . . **222** E8
Glenfield LE3 . . . . **153** A8
Forge Cnr LE8 . . . . **202** B8
Forge Ct LE7 . . . . **103** D8
Forge End LE7 . . . . **101** E5
Forman Cl DE11 . . . . **44** B4
Forman Rd LE12 . . . . **50** C2
Formans Way LE67 . . . . . **71** A2
Forrester Cl
Coleorton LE67 . . . . **70** D4

Forrester Cl *continued*
Cosby LE9 . . . . **201** E3
Forresters Cl LE10 . . . . . **215** F6
Forresters Rd LE10 . . . . **215** F6
Forryan Cl LE9 . . . . **201** D2
Forryan Rd LE10 . . . . . . **215** F7
Forryans Cl LE18 . . . . . . **203** E8
Forsells End LE7 . . . . . . **157** F3
Forsyth Cl LE11 . . . . **51** B6
Forsythia Cl LE17 . . . . . . **244** A6
Forth Cl LE15 . . . . **137** E5
Forties La LE65 . . . . **45** F3
Fort Rd LE12 . . . . **76** D1
Forty Foot La DE73 . . . . . . **26** F7
Fosbrook Dr DE74 . . . . . . **16** F4
Fosbrooke Cl LE67 . . . . . . **95** E8
Fosbrooke Dr NG10 . . . . . **10** D5
Fosse Bldg The LE3 . . . . **154** C6
Fosse Cl
Hinckley LE10 . . . . **216** A5
Narborough LE19 . . . . . . **178** D2
Sharnford LE10 . . . . **217** B4
Fosse La
Leicester LE3 . . . . **154** C7
Thistleton LE15 . . . . **64** C1
Fosse Park Ave LE19 . . . . **178** F5
Fosse Park S LE19 . . . . . **178** F5
Fosse Prim Sch LE3 . . . . **154** D7
Fosse Rd Central LE3 . . . **154** C5
Fosse Rd N LE3 . . . . **154** C6
Fosse Rd S LE3 . . . . **154** C3
Fosse Sh Pk LE19 . . . . . . **178** F5
Fosse Terr LE19 . . . . **201** A7
Fosse Way
Cloudesley Bush
CV23 . . . . **231** F3
Syston LE7 . . . . **102** F3
Fosseway Gdns LE17 . . . . **232** E6
Foster Rd DE11 . . . . **44** F2
FOSTON **203** C2
Foston Gate LE18 . . . . . . **203** E8
Foston La LE8 . . . . **203** C3
Foston Rd
Allington NG32 . . . .**4** F6
Wistow LE8 . . . . **204** D4
Fothergill Cl LE16 . . . . . . **241** B3
Foulds La LE8 . . . . **179** A1
Foundation Ct LE5 . . . . . **155** F5
Foundry Ct 4 PE9 . . . . . **143** C3
Foundry La
1 Leicester LE1 . . . . . **155** A7
Syston LE7 . . . . **102** F3
Foundry Rd
Ryhall PE9 . . . . **116** F3
Stamford PE9 . . . . **143** C3
Foundry Sq 3 LE1 . . . . . **155** A7
Fountains Ave LE2 . . . . . **179** D3
Fountain's Row LE15 . . . . **86** F5
Fount Ct LE16 . . . . **240** F1
Four Lane Ends DE11 . . . . **44** A6
Fowke St LE7 . . . . **101** F6
Fowler Cl LE4 . . . . **128** C4
Fowler St DE72 . . . .**9** B7
Foxbank Ind Est LE9 . . . . **199** D3
Fox Cl
Fleckney LE8 . . . . **223** A6
Long Eaton NG10 . . . . . . **10** D5
Rugby CV21 . . . . **257** B1
Foxcote Dr LE11 . . . . **51** A2
Fox Covert
Loughborough LE11 . . . . . **52** B6
Whetstone LE8 . . . . **201** F5
Fox Covert Cl LE7 . . . . . . **101** C2
Foxcovert La CV13 . . . . . **196** A8
Foxcroft Cl LE3 . . . . **179** C8
Fox Dale PE9 . . . . **143** B4
Fox End LE9 . . . . **177** A3
Foxfield Cl LE17 . . . . **244** D5
Foxfield Way LE15 . . . . . **138** C8
Foxglove Ave
Donisthorpe DE12 . . . . . . **67** E1
Melton Mowbray LE13 . . . . **82** A8
Foxglove Cl
Broughton Astley LE9 . . . **219** A4
East Goscote LE7 . . . . . **103** E8
Mountsorrel LE12 . . . . . . **76** F2
Narborough LE19 . . . . . . **201** A8
Foxglove Dr LE6 . . . . . . **127** A4
Foxglove Rd
Coalville LE67 . . . . **97** A8
Hamilton LE5 . . . . **130** C2
Stamford PE9 . . . . **142** E5
Foxhill LE15 . . . . **85** A1
Foxhill Dr LE2 . . . . **179** A3
Foxhills DE74 . . . . **18** C1
Foxhills Cl CV11 . . . . **214** C1
Foxholes Rd LE3 . . . . . . **153** D4
Fox Hollies LE10 . . . . . . **217** B4
Fox Hollow
Cropston LE7 . . . . **100** F2
East Goscote LE7 . . . . . **103** D8
Leicester, Oadby LE2 . . . . **181** D4
Foxhunter Dr LE2 . . . . . . **180** F6
Foxhunter Rdbt LE19 . . . . **178** D2
Fox La
Kirby Muxloe LE9 . . . . . . **152** D5
Leicester LE1 . . . . **259** B4
Foxon St LE3 . . . . **154** D5
Foxon Way LE3 . . . . **153** D1
Foxpond La LE2 . . . . **181** E2
Fox Rd DE74 . . . . **16** F4
Fox's Covert CV13 . . . . . **194** F6
Fox St LE1 . . . . **259** C3
FOXTON **224** C1
Foxton Canal Mus ★
LE16 . . . . **239** C8
Foxton Ct LE10 . . . . **215** B7
Foxton Lock Cl LE18 . . . . **203** A8

Foxton Locks Ctry Pk★
LE16 . . . . 239 C8
Foxton Prim Sch
LE16 . . . . 239 D8
Foxton Rd
Foxton LE16 . . . . 239 B7
Lubenham LE16 . . . . . . 239 D5
Fox Yd **7** LE16 . . . . . . 240 E3
Frain Gdns DE73 . . . . . 26 F2
Framland Dr LE13 . . . . . 59 C6
Framland Ho **5** LE2 . . 155 B5
Frampton Ave LE4 . . . . 154 B5
Frances Way LE19 . . . . 178 D5
Franche Rd LE3 . . . . . . 154 C6
Francis Ave LE3 . . . . . . 178 F7
Francis Ct
Leicester LE2 . . . . 179 C6
Ryhall PE9 . . . . 116 F2
Francis Dr LE11 . . . . 51 C6
Francis La LE67 . . . . . . 121 D7
Francis St LE2 . . . . 155 D1
Francis Way LE67 . . . . . 96 E3
Frank Bodicote Way
DE11 . . . . 44 D4
Frank Booton Cl LE9 . . 199 B8
Frank King Ho LE67 . . . . 97 B8
Franklin Way LE8 . . . . . 201 F4
Franklyn Rd LE2 . . . . . 179 B6
Frank's La LE17 . . . . . . 245 A6
Frankson Ave LE3 . . . . 154 A1
Franks Rd LE67 . . . . 97 C4
Fraser Cl LE1 . . . . 259 C5
Fearson Rd LE67 . . . . . . 96 B7
Frederick Ave
Hinckley LE10 . . . . 197 B2
Kegworth DE74 . . . . 18 C3
Frederick Cl LE7 . . . . . 103 E6
Frederick Jackson Ho **1**
LE3 . . . . 154 D5
Frederick Rd LE5 . . . . . 155 C6
Frederick St
Long Eaton NG10 . . . . . . 10 F7
Loughborough LE11 . . . . 52 A1
Wigston LE18 . . . . 180 D3
Woodville DE11 . . . . 44 E3
Fredscott Cl LE5 . . . . . 156 E7
Freeboard Rd LE3 . . . . 178 F7
FREEBY 61 B5
Freeby Cl LE13 . . . . 59 E2
Freehold Rd LE4 . . . . . 129 A5
Freehold St
Leicester LE1 . . . . 155 B7
Loughborough LE11 . . . . 52 C4
Quorn (Quorndon) LE12 . . 76 B6
Shepshed LE12 . . . . 50 C4
Free La LE1 . . . . 259 B4
Freeman Rd N LE5 . . . . 155 F7
Freeman's Ct LE6 . . . . 152 D8
Freeman's La LE10 . . . . 216 A5
Freemantle Rd LE2 . . . . 155 E1
Freeman Way LE12 . . . . . 75 F7
Freemen's Common Rd
LE2 . . . . 154 F2
Freemen's Common Trad
Est LE2 . . . . 154 F2
Freemen's Holt LE2 . . . 179 C7
Freer Cl
Blaby LE8 . . . . 202 B8
Houghton on t H LE7 . . . 157 F3
Wigston LE18 . . . . 203 E8
Freeschool La LE1 . . . . 259 A4
Freesia Cl LE11 . . . . 75 A6
French Rd LE5 . . . . 155 E7
Frensham Cl LE2 . . . . . 181 A4
Freshney Cl LE13 . . . . . . 59 B1
Freshwater Cl LE18 . . . 203 D7
Freswick Cl LE10 . . . . . 196 F1
Frewen Dr LE9 . . . . 217 D8
Frewin St LE5 . . . . 155 E7
Friar La LE1 . . . . 259 B3
Friars Cswy LE1 . . . . . . 259 A4
Friar St NG10 . . . . 10 D7
Friary Cl LE10 . . . . 197 E1
Friary Croft DE11 . . . . . 44 A7
Friary Rd CV9 . . . . 170 D1
Friday St LE2 . . . . 259 B5
Friendship Ho LE4 . . . . 155 C8
Frinton Ave LE5 . . . . . . 156 D5
FRISBY 183 E8
Frisby Ave NG10 . . . . . . 10 E6
Frisby CE Prim Sch
LE14 . . . . 80 D7
Frisby La LE15 . . . . 191 C6
FRISBY ON THE WREAKE
. . . . 80 C8
Frisby Rd
Barwell LE9 . . . . 198 B7
Leicester LE5 . . . . 155 D6
Friswell La LE9 . . . . . . 198 A7
Fritchley Cl LE9 . . . . . . 200 E7
Frith Cl LE3 . . . . 153 C8
Frith Way LE10 . . . . . . 197 A3
Froanes Cl LE19 . . . . . . 178 A4
Frobisher Cl LE10 . . . . . 197 D4
FROG ISLAND 154 D7
Frog Island LE3 . . . . . . 259 A5
Frog La NG13 . . . . 12 F8
FROLESWORTH 218 B2
Frolesworth La LE17 . . . 232 F7
Frolesworth Rd
Ashby Parva LE17 . . . . . 233 D7
Broughton Astley LE9 . . . 218 E5
Leicester LE3 . . . . 153 E7
Leire LE17 . . . . 233 E8
Ullesthorpe LE17 . . . . . 233 B6
Frolesworth Way LE3 . . 153 E6
Frome Ave LE2 . . . . 181 D6

Front St
Birstall LE4 . . . . 129 B6
Gaulby LE7 . . . . 183 D7
Frost Fields DE74 . . . . . 17 B4
Fulbeck Ave LE5 . . . . . 156 D5
Fulford Rd LE3 . . . . . . 153 C5
Fullen La NN17 . . . . . . 213 C1
Fuller Cl LE9 . . . . 151 C4
Fullhurst Ave LE3 . . . . 154 B2
Fullhurst Com Coll
LE3 . . . . 154 B3
Fulmar Rd LE7 . . . . . . 127 D6
Fulton Dr LE67 . . . . 71 A2
Fulwell Ave NN17 . . . . 213 C1
Fulwood Dr NG10 . . . . . 10 A7
Furley Cl LE15 . . . . 137 F6
Furlongs Cl LE7 . . . . . . 103 C3
Furlongs The LE16 . . . . 241 B3
Furnace La LE7 . . . . 67 E3
Furnace Lane Ind Est
DE12 . . . . 67 E3
Furnival Cl LE8 . . . . . . 222 E8
Furrow Cl LE7 . . . . 101 E7
Furrows Cl LE19 . . . . . 201 C7
Fydell Row LE15 . . . . . 191 A6
Fyfe Rd NN17 . . . . 230 B1

G

Gables Ct LE17 . . . . . . 218 A2
Gables Lea LE12 . . . . . . 30 B6
Gables The LE65 . . . . . . 69 C4
GADDESBY 105 B7
Gaddesby Ave LE4 . . . . 154 C3
Gaddesby La
Frisby on t W LE14 . . . . 80 E4
Kirby Bellars LE14 . . . . 81 B5
Rearsby LE7 . . . . 104 B8
Rotherby LE14, LE7 . . . . 80 A4
Gaddesby Prim Sch
LE7 . . . . 105 C6
Gaddesby Rd LE7 . . . . . 105 D4
Gainsborough Ave
LE10 . . . . 197 A3
Gainsborough Cl NG10 . . 10 E5
Gainsborough Cres
CV21 . . . . 257 B1
Gainsborough Rd
Kibworth Beauchamp
LE8 . . . . 206 A1
Leicester LE2 . . . . 180 B8
Stamford PE9 . . . . 143 B5
Uppingham LE15 . . . . . 189 B4
Galahad Cl LE3 . . . . . . 153 B6
Galby St LE5 . . . . 155 D8
Gale Cl LE17 . . . . 244 C8
Gallards Hill LE3 . . . . . 153 E4
Galleywood Dr LE4 . . . 128 D2
Gallico Cl LE11 . . . . 51 D6
Gallimore Cl LE3 . . . . . 127 C1
Galloway Cl LE9 . . . . . 197 F7
Gallow Field Rd LE16 . . 239 E7
Gallows La LE12 . . . . . . 93 E4
Gallowtree Gate LE1 . . 259 B4
Gallus Dr LE10 . . . . . . 197 A1
Galsworthy Cres LE13 . . 59 B6
Galsworthy Ct LE3 . . . . 154 A5
Galway Rd LE4 . . . . . . 128 E5
Gamble Cl LE67 . . . . 95 F3
Gamble Way LE12 . . . . . 75 F7
Gamekeepers Ct LE5 . . 130 C3
Gamel Rd LE5 . . . . 156 B5
Gamel Wlk LE5 . . . . . . 156 B5
Ganton Rd LE3 . . . . . . 153 C6
Gaol St LE15 . . . . 137 F6
Garden Cl
Hinckley LE10 . . . . 215 D6
Leicester, Oadby LE2 . . . 181 A5
Stamford PE9 . . . . 142 F3
Garden Cres DE74 . . . . . 17 B3
Gardenfield Rd LE4 . . . 129 F4
Garden La
Ibstock LE67 . . . . 122 F8
Melton Mowbray LE13 . . . 59 A5
Garden Rd
Coalville LE67 . . . . 71 E2
Exton LE15 . . . . 113 B3
Hinckley LE10 . . . . 197 D1
Garden Row DE74 . . . . . 18 D3
Garden St
Leicester LE1 . . . . 259 B5
Thurmaston LE4 . . . . . 129 E7
Wigston LE18 . . . . 179 F1
Gardiner St LE16 . . . . . 240 C3
Gardner Cl LE11 . . . . . . 51 C6
Garendon Ave LE12 . . . . 51 A8
Garendon Cl LE12 . . . . . 50 C3
Garendon Gn LE11 . . . . 51 D4
Garendon High Sch
LE11 . . . . 51 C4
Garendon Rd
Coalville LE67 . . . . 97 C8
Loughborough LE11 . . . . 51 D4
Shepshed LE12 . . . . 50 B3
Garendon St LE2 . . . . . 155 B6
Garendon Way LE6 . . . . 126 E2
Garfield Ave DE72 . . . . . 9 A7
Garfield Pk LE8 . . . . . . 182 B2
Garfield Rd LE67 . . . . . . 96 C7
Garfield St LE4 . . . . . . 155 A8
Garfit Rd LE5 . . . . 152 E5
Garford La PE9 . . . . . . 169 A5
Garganey Cl LE67 . . . . . 97 A8
Garland LE7 . . . . 101 E7
Garland Cres LE3 . . . . . 154 B8
Garland La CV13 . . . . . 124 A2
Garnett Cres LE2 . . . . . 179 C4

Garratt Rd **8** PE9 . . . . 143 D2
Garratt Sq LE18 . . . . . . 201 F7
Garrick Wlk **8** LE1 . . . 259 B4
Garsdale LE18 . . . . 180 F2
Garsington Wlk LE5 . . . 156 A6
Garth Ave LE4 . . . . 128 E4
GARTHORPE 62 B6
Garthorpe Dr LE13 . . . . 59 E2
Garthorpe Rd LE14 . . . . 61 E5
Garth St LE15 . . . . 87 D2
Garton Cl DE12 . . . . . . 119 F8
Garton Rd LE11 . . . . 52 B3
Gartree Cres LE9 . . . . . 198 D8
Gartree Cl LE12 . . . . . . 82 C8
Gartree Dr LE13 . . . . . . 59 D1
Gartree High Sch LE2 . . 181 B3
Gartree Rd
Carlton Curlieu LE8,
LE16 . . . . 206 F8
Great Stretton LE2 . . . . 182 C5
Leicester LE2 . . . . 156 A1
Gascoigne Ave LE7 . . . . 103 E5
Gaskell Wlk LE3 . . . . . 154 A5
Gas La
Stamford PE9 . . . . 143 E3
Wigston LE18 . . . . 180 C1
Gas Mus★ LE2 . . . . . . 154 E1
Gasny Ave DE74 . . . . . . 17 B5
Gas St
Leicester LE1 . . . . 154 F7
Stamford PE9 . . . . 143 E3
Gas Wlk LE14 . . . . 12 B3
Gatcombe Dr LE67 . . . . 97 A8
Gatehouse La
Great Easton LE16 . . . . 229 F6
South Luffenham PE9 . . 166 D1
Gateway St LE2 . . . . . . 259 A2
Gateway The LE2 . . . . . 259 A2
Gateway VI Form Coll
LE2 . . . . 259 A3
GAULBY 183 D7
Gaulby La
Houghton on t H LE7 . . . 158 C2
Leicester LE2 . . . . 156 F1
Little Stretton LE2, LE7 . . 182 C8
Gaulby Nook LE7 . . . . . 183 C8
Gaulby Rd
Billesdon LE7 . . . . 183 E8
Illston on t H LE7 . . . . . 183 E4
Gaul St LE3 . . . . 154 D4
Gavin Cl LE3 . . . . 153 C2
Gavin Dr LE11 . . . . 51 D6
Gawney La LE17 . . . . . . 235 E5
Gayhurst Cl
Braunstone Town LE3 . . 178 F7
Wigston LE18 . . . . 180 E2
Gayton Ave LE4 . . . . . . 129 C1
Gayton Hts LE19 . . . . . 178 A4
Geary Cl
Narborough LE19 . . . . . 201 B7
Ratby LE6 . . . . 152 E8
Whitwick LE67 . . . . 71 D5
Geary's Cl LE67 . . . . . . 124 F3
Gedding Rd LE5 . . . . . . 155 E5
Geddington Cl LE18 . . . 180 E2
Gedge Way LE2 . . . . . . 179 E6
Gee Rd LE67 . . . . 71 E2
Gees Lock Cl LE2 . . . . . 179 B4
GEESTON 168 B4
Geeston Rd PE9 . . . . . . 168 B5
Gelders Hall Ind Est
LE12 . . . . 50 A4
Gelders Hall Rd LE12 . . . 50 A1
Gelert Ave LE5 . . . . . . 156 D6
Gelscoe La LE12, DE73 . . . 27 E1
GELSMOOR 47 F1
Gelsmoor Rd LE67 . . . . 47 F1
George Ave NG10 . . . . . 10 F8
George Foster Cl LE9 . . 176 A1
George Fox La CV13 . . . 195 A6
George Geary Cl LE9 . . 198 C7
Georgeham Cl LE18 . . . 180 D1
George Hill Cl LE9 . . . . 199 D3
George Holmes Bsns Pk
DE11 . . . . 44 A4
George Holmes Way
DE11 . . . . 44 A4
George Hotel Mews The
PE9 . . . . 143 E2
George Hythe Ho LE4 . . 128 C7
George Mariott Cl
LE9 . . . . 199 C1
George St
Anstey LE7 . . . . 127 D6
Barwell LE9 . . . . 198 B6
Enderby LE19 . . . . 178 A3
Hinckley LE10 . . . . 215 D8
Leicester LE1 . . . . 259 C5
Loughborough LE11 . . . . 51 F4
Lutterworth LE17 . . . . . 244 C6
Melbourne DE73 . . . . . . 26 A7
Melton Mowbray LE13 . . . 59 D3
Swadlincote DE11 . . . . . 44 A1
Whitwick LE67 . . . . 71 F4
George Toon Ct LE7 . . . 103 A4
George Ward Ct LE9 . . . 198 B7
George Yd LE11 . . . . . . 52 B4
Georgina Ct DE74 . . . . . 17 B4
Gerrard Cres DE74 . . . . 18 D1
Gerrard Gdns LE16 . . . . 250 D8
Gertrude Rd DE72 . . . . . 9 A7
Gervas Rd LE5 . . . . 156 C7
Geveze Way LE19 . . . . . 219 A4
Gibbet Hill LE17 . . . . . 252 F6
Gibbet La
Bilstone CV13 . . . . 147 B5
Edith Weston LE15 . . . . 166 A4
Shawell LE17 . . . . 253 B6
Gibbons Cl LE4 . . . . . . 155 A8

Gibb St NG10 . . . . 10 E7
Gibson Dr CV21 . . . . . . 257 A1
Gibson Rd LE12 . . . . 77 D4
Gibson's La LE14 . . . . . . 35 C2
Gibson Way LE17 . . . . . 244 A5
Giffard Ct LE16 . . . . . . 240 D3
Gifford Cl LE5 . . . . 156 B3
Gilbert Cl
Leicester LE4 . . . . 129 E4
Market Harborough
LE16 . . . . 241 B2
Gilbert's Dr LE9 . . . . . . 150 B4
Giles Cl LE12 . . . . 76 B5
Gillam Butts LE8 . . . . . 202 E3
Gillamore Dr LE67 . . . . 72 A2
Gillbank Dr LE6 . . . . . . 152 C8
Gilliver St LE2 . . . . 180 B8
Newbold Verdon LE9 . . . 150 B5
Gillman Rd LE4 . . . . . . 154 A8
Gilmore Cl LE15 . . . . . 138 A8
GILMORTON 235 C4
Gilmorton Ave LE2 . . . . 179 B5
Gilmorton Chandler CE
Prim Sch LE17 . . . . . . 235 B5
Gilmorton Cl LE2 . . . . . 179 B4
Gilmorton La LE8 . . . . . 220 D2
Gilmorton Rd
Ashby Magna LE17 . . . . 235 A7
Lutterworth LE17 . . . . . 244 E7
Gilmour Cl LE4 . . . . . . 128 B5
Gilpin Cl LE13 . . . . 59 A1
Gilson Gn LE14 . . . . . . 107 D2
Gilson's Cl LE15 . . . . . 191 A6
Gilstead Cl LE7 . . . . . . 156 F4
Gimson Ave LE9 . . . . . 201 D3
Gimson Cl LE5 . . . . . . 130 A1
Gimson Rd LE3 . . . . . . 154 B5
Gipsy Hollow La LE15 . . 188 F3
Gipsy La
Leicester LE4 . . . . 129 D2
Mountsorrel LE7 . . . . . 101 C8
Stamford PE9 . . . . 143 F5
Gipsy Nook LE14 . . . . . . 40 E2
Gipsy Rd LE4 . . . . 129 B2
Girton Way PE9 . . . . . . 143 C5
Gisborough Way LE11 . . 51 B5
Gisbourne Ct LE5 . . . . 156 A2
Glade The LE2 . . . . 178 F7
Gladstone Ave
Loughborough LE11 . . . . 51 F5
Melton Mowbray LE13 . . . 59 B5
Gladstone Cl LE10 . . . . 197 E4
Gladstone St
Anstey LE7 . . . . 127 E6
Fleckney LE8 . . . . 222 F7
Hathern LE12 . . . . 30 A1
Ibstock LE67 . . . . 95 F1
Kibworth Beauchamp
LE8 . . . . 223 F8
Leicester LE1 . . . . 259 C4
Long Eaton NG10 . . . . . 10 D6
Loughborough LE11 . . . . 52 B5
Lutterworth LE17 . . . . . 244 D6
Market Harborough
LE16 . . . . 240 F2
Wigston LE18 . . . . 180 D3
Gladstone Terr LE15 . . . 215 E8
Glaisdale Cl LE4 . . . . . 128 C3
Glaisdale Rd LE18 . . . . 180 E1
Glamis Cl LE12 . . . . . . 101 D8
Glamorgan Ave LE18 . . 179 F2
GLASTON 190 B6
Glaston Pk LE15 . . . . . 190 B5
Glaston Rd
Bisbrooke LE15 . . . . . . 189 F4
Morcott LE15 . . . . 191 A5
Preston LE15 . . . . 164 C1
Uppingham LE15 . . . . . 189 C5
Wing LE15 . . . . 165 B1
Glazebrook Rd LE3 . . . 154 A8
Glazebrook Sq LE3 . . . 154 A8
Glean Cl LE15 . . . . 218 F4
Glebe Cl
Billesdon LE7 . . . . 159 C1
Empingham LE15 . . . . . 141 A4
Glenfield LE3 . . . . 153 B8
Leicester LE2 . . . . 180 E7
Mountsorrel LE12 . . . . . 76 D2
Wigston LE18 . . . . 180 D3
Glebe Dr LE8 . . . . 202 D3
Glebe Gdns LE2 . . . . . 180 F8
Glebe Ho LE8 . . . . 202 B8
Glebe La CV13 . . . . . . 172 B6
Glebeland Cl LE7 . . . . . 78 F5
Glebelands Prim Sch
LE4 . . . . 128 D8
Glebelands Rd LE4 . . . . 128 D8
Glebelands The LE8 . . . 205 A8
Glebe Rd
Asfordby Hill LE14 . . . . 58 C3
Broughton Astley LE9 . . 218 E6
Groby LE6 . . . . 126 E3
Hinckley LE10 . . . . 215 F8
Leicester, Oadby LE2 . . . 180 F8
Market Harborough
LE16 . . . . 241 A2
North Luffenham LE15 . . 166 C3
Queniborough LE7 . . . . 103 E5
Thringstone LE67 . . . . . 71 C8
Wymondham LE14 . . . . . 62 C2
Glebe Rise CV9 . . . . . . 119 B1
Glebe St
Leicester LE2 . . . . 259 C2
Loughborough LE11 . . . . 52 C5
Swadlincote DE11 . . . . . 44 B3

Fox–Gol **273**

Glebe The CV13 . . . . . . 149 C8
Glebe View LE67 . . . . . . 70 F2
Glebe Way
Oakham LE15 . . . . 137 D5
Syston LE7 . . . . 102 E4
Glenalmond Cl LE65 . . . 69 A8
Glen Ave LE4 . . . . 123 A8
Glen Bank LE10 . . . . . . 197 E1
Glenbarr Ave LE4 . . . . 154 D8
Glenbarr Cl LE10 . . . . . 215 A8
Glenbarr Dr LE10 . . . . . 215 A8
Glenborne Rd LE2 . . . . 180 A4
Glencoe Ave LE4 . . . . . 129 C4
Glen Cres
Essendine PE9 . . . . . . 117 B5
Stamford PE9 . . . . 143 E5
Glencroft LE2 . . . . 179 D1
Glendale Ave LE3 . . . . 127 B3
Glendon Cl LE14 . . . . . . 57 C2
Glendon St LE4 . . . . . . 129 B1
Glendower Cl LE5 . . . . 156 B6
Glen Dr LE15 . . . . 137 F5
Gleneagles Ave LE4 . . . 129 C4
Gleneagles Cl
Hinckley LE10 . . . . 215 D4
Nuneaton CV11 . . . . . . 214 C1
Stamford PE9 . . . . 143 A4
Gleneagles Wlk LE4 . . . 129 C4
GLENFIELD 153 C8
Glenfield Cres LE3 . . . . 153 C8
Glenfield Frith Dr
LE3 . . . . 127 D1
Glenfield Hospl LE3 . . . 127 F2
Glenfield La LE3 . . . . . 152 F7
Glenfield Prim Sch
LE3 . . . . 153 B8
Glenfield Rd
Leicester LE3 . . . . 154 B6
Long Eaton NG10 . . . . . 10 D5
Glenfield Rd E LE3 . . . . 154 D5
Glenfields LE12 . . . . . . 50 B3
Glenfrith Cl
Leicester LE3 . . . . 127 F3
Mountsorrel LE7 . . . . . 76 F1
Glenfrith Gdns LE12 . . . 76 F1
Glenfrith Way LE3 . . . . 127 F2
Glengarry Cl LE3 . . . . . 154 A7
Glengarry Ct LE3 . . . . . 154 A7
Glengarry Way LE3 . . . 153 F8
Glen Gate LE8 . . . . 179 F1
Glen Gorse Rdbt LE2 . . 181 E2
Glenhills Bvd LE2 . . . . 179 D5
Glen Hills Prim Sch
LE2 . . . . 179 A3
Glenhills Way LE2 . . . . 179 D5
Glen Ho PE9 . . . . 117 B6
Glen Ind Est PE9 . . . . . 117 B6
Glenmere Com Prim Sch
LE18 . . . . 180 F3
Glenmore Ave LE12 . . . . 50 B4
Glenmore Rd LE4 . . . . 129 D3
Glen Park Ave LE3 . . . . 127 B3
GLEN PARVA 179 B3
Glen Rd
Leicester, Oadby LE2 . . . 181 C4
Newton Harcourt LE8 . . 204 E7
Glen Rise
Glen Parva LE2 . . . . . . 179 B4
Leicester, Oadby LE2 . . . 181 E2
Glenrothes Cl LE3 . . . . 153 C5
Glen St LE4 . . . . 129 B2
Glenville Ave
Glenfield LE3 . . . . 127 C2
Glen Parva LE2 . . . . . . 179 B2
Glen Way
Coalville LE67 . . . . 96 F7
Leicester, Oadby LE2 . . . 181 C4
Glenwood Cl LE2 . . . . . 155 D1
GLOOSTON 208 B4
Glossop St LE5 . . . . . . 155 C4
Gloucester Ave
Melton Mowbray LE13 . . 82 D8
Syston LE7 . . . . 103 C4
Gloucester Cl
Desford LE9 . . . . 151 B2
Nuneaton CV11 . . . . . . 214 A7
Gloucester Cres
Melton Mowbray LE13 . . 82 D8
Wigston LE18 . . . . 179 F3
Gloucester Rd PE9 . . . . 143 D4
Glover Ct
Cottingham LE16 . . . . . 229 C1
Leicester LE2 . . . . 179 C6
Glover Rd DE74 . . . . . . 17 B4
Glyn Cl LE9 . . . . 198 A7
GOADBY 185 B2
Goadby Rd LE7 . . . . . . 185 B2
GOADBY MARWOOD . . 22 C1
Goadby Rd
Hallaton LE16 . . . . 209 B6
Waltham on t W LE14 . . . 40 A7
Goddard Cl LE7 . . . . . . 157 A5
Goddard Ct **5** LE16 . . 240 E4
Goddards Cl
Kilby LE18 . . . . 204 A3
Leicester LE4 . . . . 128 A2
Leicester, Oadby LE2 . . . 180 F5
Goddards Slang LE2 . . . 180 F5
Godfrey Cl LE4 . . . . . . 128 A6
Godsons Hill CV13 . . . . 148 D3
Godstow Wlk LE5 . . . . 156 A6
Godwin Ave LE18 . . . . 180 C2
Godwin Cl LE18 . . . . . . 180 D2
Godwin Rd NN17 . . . . . 230 F3
Goldcrest LE15 . . . . . . 189 A5

274 Gol–Gwe

Golden Sq LE12 . . . 51 A8
Goldfinch Cl LE11 . . . 51 F3
Goldfinch Rd LE15 . . . 189 A5
Goldhill LE18 . . . 180 A4
Goldhill Gdns LE2 . . . 180 D7
Goldhill Rd LE2 . . . 180 D7
Golding Cl LE11 . . . 51 B6
Goldsmith Rd LE3 . . . 154 A4
Goldspink Cl LE13 . . . 82 C8
Golf Course La LE3 . . . 153 C5
Golf Dr CV11 . . . 214 B1
Goliath Rd LE67 . . . 71 D2
Gonerby La NG32 . . . 4 F5
Goodacre Almshouses
LE17 . . . 233 F5
Goodacre Ct CV23 . . . 257 A5
Goodacre Rd LE17 . . . 233 C4
Goode's Ave LE7 . . . 103 B2
Goode's La LE7 . . . 103 B3
Goodheart Way LE3 . . . 153 C2
Gooding Ave LE3 . . . 154 A3
Gooding Cl LE3 . . . 154 B3
Goodriche Ho LE13 . . . 59 D3
Goodriche St LE13 . . . 59 D3
Goods Yard Cl LE11 . . . 51 F4
Goodwood Cl LE16 . . . 241 B3
Goodwood Cres LE5 . . . 156 B4
Goodwood Rd LE5 . . . 156 B4
Goosehills Rd LE10 . . . 215 E5
Goose La LE9 . . . 198 A5
Gopsall Rd
Congerstone CV13 . . . 147 C8
Hinckley LE10 . . . 197 D2
Gopsall St LE2 . . . 155 B5
Gordon Ave 8 LE2 . . . 155 B4
Gordon Ho 1 LE2 . . . 155 B5
Gordon Rd LE11 . . . 52 B6
Gores La LE16 . . . 241 A3
Gorham Rise LE9 . . . 218 D7
Gorseburn Ho LE3 . . . 153 F8
Gorse Hill
Anstey LE7 . . . 127 E5
Anstey LE7 . . . 127 F5
Gorse Hill City Farm*
LE4 . . . 128 B1
Gorse La
Leicester, Oadby LE2 . . . 181 D3
Moira DE12 . . . 67 E6
Syston LE7 . . . 102 F3
Gorse Rd LE67 . . . 96 C6
Gorsey La DE12 . . . 92 A7
GORSEY LEYS . . . 67 C4
Gorsty Cl LE4 . . . 128 B3
Goscote Dr LE17 . . . 244 C6
Goscote Hall Rd LE4 . . . 128 F6
Goscote Ho 7 LE2 . . . 155 B5
Goseley Ave DE11 . . . 45 A4
Goseley Cres DE11 . . . 45 A4
GOSELEY DALE . . . 45 A5
Gosford Dr LE10 . . . 197 A1
Goshawk Cl LE9 . . . 218 E7
Gosling St LE2 . . . 259 A2
Gotham St LE2 . . . 155 B4
Gough Rd LE5 . . . 155 E6
Goughs La LE15 . . . 187 D7
Goward St LE16 . . . 240 E3
Gower St LE1 . . . 259 C5
Gowrie Cl LE10 . . . 197 B2
Grace Ct LE2 . . . 179 E8
Grace Dieu La LE67,
LE12 . . . 48 F2
Grace Dieu Manor Sch
LE67 . . . 71 F8
Gracedieu Rd LE11 . . . 51 D3
Grace Dieu Rd LE67 . . . 71 E7
Grace Gdns LE2 . . . 179 E7
Gracelands LE16 . . . 240 C2
Grace Rd
Desford LE9 . . . 151 B3
Leicester LE2 . . . 179 E8
Sapcote LE9 . . . 217 E8
Grafton Dr LE18 . . . 180 F2
Grafton Pl LE1 . . . 259 B5
Grafton Rd LE11 . . . 51 E6
Graham Rise LE11 . . . 51 D6
Graham St LE1 . . . 155 B6
Gramer Cotts CV9 . . . 194 A6
Grampian Cl LE2 . . . 179 F7
Grampian Way
Long Eaton NG10 . . . 10 A8
Oakham LE15 . . . 137 D6
Granary Cl
Glenfield LE3 . . . 153 C8
Kibworth Beauchamp
LE8 . . . 224 B7
Market Harborough
LE16 . . . 240 F6
Granary The LE16 . . . 209 E6
GRANBY . . . 5 C5
Granby Ave LE5 . . . 155 D6
Granby Cl LE10 . . . 215 C7
Granby Ct 4 LE5 . . . 130 C3
Granby Dr NG13 . . . 3 A2
Granby Hill NG13 . . . 5 B6
Granby Ho LE13 . . . 59 C3
Granby La
Granby NG13 . . . 5 A7
Plungar NG13 . . . 5 E2
Granby Pl LE1 . . . 259 B3
Granby Prim Sch LE2 . . . 179 D7
Granby Rd
Hinckley LE10 . . . 215 C7
Leicester LE2 . . . 179 D7
Melton Mowbray LE13 . . . 59 D6
Granby St
Leicester LE1 . . . 259 C3
Loughborough LE11 . . . 52 A4
Grange Ave
Breaston DE72 . . . 9 D8
Leicester Forest East
LE3 . . . 153 B3
Rearsby LE7 . . . 103 F8
Grange Bsns Pk LE8 . . . 178 F1
Grange Cl
Ashby-de-la-Z LE65 . . . 69 A5
Glenfield LE3 . . . 153 B8
Great Glen LE8 . . . 182 B1
Langham LE15 . . . 110 D3
Leicester LE2 . . . 179 C3
Melbourne DE73 . . . 26 B8
Newbold Verdon LE9 . . . 150 B4
Ratby LE6 . . . 152 D8
Grange Ct LE9 . . . 151 B4
Grange Dr
Castle Donington DE74 . . . 17 A3
Glen Parva LE2 . . . 179 C3
Hinckley LE10 . . . 215 E5
Long Eaton NG10 . . . 10 F8
Melton Mowbray LE13 . . . 59 E1
Whetstone LE8 . . . 201 F8
Grange Farm Bsns Pk
LE67 . . . 96 E5
Grange Farm Cl DE74 . . . 17 D5
Grangefields Dr LE7 . . . 101 F6
Grange La
Coston LE14 . . . 62 E8
Leicester LE2 . . . 259 B2
Mountsorrel LE12 . . . 101 D8
Nailstone CV13 . . . 123 B5
Seaton LE15 . . . 190 B1
Thorpe Langton LE16 . . . 226 A5
Thurnby LE7 . . . 156 E4
Grange Pk
Leicester LE7 . . . 156 E4
Long Eaton NG10 . . . 10 F8
Grange Prim Sch NG10 . . . 10 F8
Granger Ct LE11 . . . 52 A4
Grange Rd
Broughton Astley LE9 . . . 218 E7
Carlton Curlieu LE8 . . . 206 D7
Coalville LE67 . . . 96 E6
Hartshill Green CV10 . . . 194 C2
Ibstock LE67 . . . 95 F1
Long Eaton NG10 . . . 10 F8
Nailstone CV13 . . . 123 A5
Shepshed LE12 . . . 50 A3
Wigston LE18 . . . 180 D4
Grange St LE11 . . . 52 A5
Grange The
Earl Shilton LE9 . . . 198 E7
Packington LE65 . . . 69 C2
Woodhouse Eaves LE12 . . . 100 B8
Grange Therapeutic Sch
The LE15 . . . 135 F6
Grange View LE67 . . . 123 E8
Grangeway Rd LE18 . . . 180 D4
Granite Cl LE19 . . . 178 A4
Granite Way LE12 . . . 76 C4
Grantham Ave LE9 . . . 218 D8
Grantham Rd
Bottesford NG13 . . . 3 D2
Leicester LE5 . . . 156 C8
Skillington NG33 . . . 43 B8
Grant Way LE2 . . . 179 E4
Grantwood Rd LE13 . . . 59 E5
Granville Ave LE2 . . . 180 F6
Granville Com Sch
DE11 . . . 44 E4
Granville Cres LE18 . . . 180 B5
Granville Ct DE11 . . . 44 C4
Granville Gdns LE10 . . . 215 C8
Granville Rd
Hinckley LE10 . . . 215 C8
Leicester LE1 . . . 155 B4
Melton Mowbray LE13 . . . 59 A5
Wigston LE18 . . . 180 C5
Granville St
Loughborough LE11 . . . 52 A4
Market Harborough
LE16 . . . 240 F2
Woodville DE11 . . . 44 E3
Grapes Garden Cl LE12 . . . 76 E3
Grape St LE1 . . . 259 B4
Grasmere LE67 . . . 72 C2
Grasmere Cl LE12 . . . 76 D8
Grasmere Rd
Loughborough LE11 . . . 74 F7
Wigston LE18 . . . 180 F3
Grasmere St LE2 . . . 259 A2
Grass Acres LE3 . . . 178 E7
Grassholme Dr LE11 . . . 51 A3
Grassington Cl LE4 . . . 128 C4
Grassington Dr
Nuneaton CV11 . . . 214 A2
Wigston LE18 . . . 180 E1
Grassy La LE67 . . . 125 B8
Gravel St LE1 . . . 259 B4
Gravel The LE8 . . . 205 F8
Gray La LE12 . . . 77 D2
Grays Cl DE74 . . . 17 B3
Grays Ct
Barrow-u-S LE12 . . . 76 D8
Narborough LE19 . . . 178 A3
Gray St LE11 . . . 52 B2
Grayswood Dr LE4 . . . 128 A6
Great Arler Rd LE2 . . . 180 A8
GREAT BOWDEN . . . 241 A6
Great Bowden CE Prim
Sch LE16 . . . 241 A6
Great Bowden Hall
LE16 . . . 240 E7
Great Bowden Rd
LE16 . . . 241 A4
GREAT CASTERTON . . . 142 E7
Great Casterton CE Prim
Sch PE9 . . . 142 E7
Great Central Railway
Mus* LE11 . . . 52 C3
Great Central Rd LE11 . . . 52 C3
Great Central Rly*
Birstall LE4 . . . 128 E7
Mountsorrel LE7 . . . 75 E2
Great Central St LE1 . . . 259 A4
Great Central Way
LE3 . . . 154 D2
Great Central Wlk*
CV23 . . . 252 F2
Great Cl NG33 . . . 65 B4
GREAT DALBY . . . 82 B2
Great Dalby Rd LE14 . . . 106 E5
Great Dalby Sch LE14 . . . 82 A1
GREAT EASTON . . . 229 D7
Great Easton Rd
Bringhurst LE16 . . . 229 C6
Caldecott LE16 . . . 230 A7
Drayton LE16 . . . 229 A5
Great Easton LE16 . . . 229 F6
Greatford Rd PE9 . . . 144 E4
GREAT GLEN . . . 205 B8
Great La
Frisby on t W LE14 . . . 80 D8
Greetham LE15 . . . 88 B2
Great Meadow Rd
LE4 . . . 128 B2
Great North Rd
Great Casterton PE9 . . . 114 D4
Stamford PE9 . . . 142 F3
Wothorpe PE9 . . . 169 B8
GREAT OXENDON . . . 250 E3
GREAT STRETTON . . . 182 B6
GREAT WILNE . . . 9 C2
Greaves Ave
Melton Mowbray LE13 . . . 59 B4
Old Dalby LE14 . . . 36 C6
Grebe Cl LE12 . . . 76 E8
Grebe Way LE8 . . . 201 F5
Greedon Rise LE12 . . . 77 C4
Greenacre Dr LE5 . . . 156 B5
Green Acres Cvn Pk
LE16 . . . 240 C6
Greenacres Dr LE17 . . . 244 B6
Green Bank LE13 . . . 59 E3
Greenbank Dr LE2 . . . 181 B5
Greenbank Rd LE5 . . . 130 D1
Greenclose La 1 LE11 . . . 52 A4
Greencoat Ct LE3 . . . 153 E7
Greencoat Rd LE3 . . . 153 E7
Green Croft LE9 . . . 199 E1
Greendale Rd LE2 . . . 179 B3
Green Farm Cl CV23 . . . 258 A6
Greenfield Prim Sch
LE8 . . . 202 E4
Greenfield Rd
Measham DE12 . . . 93 E5
Oakham LE15 . . . 138 A8
Greenfields LE8 . . . 201 F7
Greenfields Dr LE67 . . . 72 A1
Greengate La LE4 . . . 128 E7
Green Gdns LE17 . . . 233 B4
GREENHILL . . . 97 A8
Green Hill LE12 . . . 30 A1
Greenhill Cl
Melton Mowbray LE13 . . . 59 D5
Narborough LE19 . . . 201 A7
Greenhill Dr LE9 . . . 198 B7
Greenhill Rd
Coalville LE67 . . . 72 C1
Leicester LE2 . . . 155 B1
Stoke Golding CV13 . . . 196 D7
Green Hill Rise LE12 . . . 30 A2
Greenhithe Rd LE2 . . . 154 D1
Green La
Ashley LE16 . . . 227 F2
Barton in t B CV13 . . . 122 E3
Braybrooke LE16 . . . 251 F5
Copston Magna LE10 . . . 231 C5
Countesthorpe LE8 . . . 202 F4
Duddington PE9 . . . 193 B6
Earl Shilton LE9 . . . 175 F1
Easthorpe NG13 . . . 3 C1
Goadby Marwood LE14 . . . 22 E3
Granby NG13 . . . 5 C5
Harby LE14 . . . 12 C2
Husbands Bosworth
LE17 . . . 247 E5
Market Harborough
LE16 . . . 240 E1
North Kilworth LE17 . . . 246 F3
Owston LE15 . . . 135 B5
Seagrave LE12 . . . 77 F8
Stamford PE9 . . . 143 D5
Stapleton LE9 . . . 174 E2
Tilton on t H LE7 . . . 159 D6
Upper Broughton LE14 . . . 19 B4
Weston by W LE16 . . . 227 C6
Whitwick LE67 . . . 71 E3
Wibtoft LE17 . . . 232 B3
Wilson DE73 . . . 26 E5
Greenland Ave LE5 . . . 156 A8
Greenland Dr LE5 . . . 156 A8
Green Lands DE11 . . . 44 B7
Green Lane Cl
Leicester LE5 . . . 155 F6
Seagrave LE12 . . . 77 F8
Green Lane Inf Sch
LE5 . . . 155 C7
Green Lane Rd LE5 . . . 155 E6
Greenlawn Wlk LE3 . . . 154 D8
Green Leas DE72 . . . 16 A8
Greenmoor Rd LE10 . . . 215 D5
Green Rd LE9 . . . 218 E7
Greens Cl CV23 . . . 252 C6
Greenside Cl
Donisthorpe DE12 . . . 67 E1
Long Eaton NG10 . . . 10 E7
Nuneaton CV11 . . . 214 C1
Greenside Pl LE2 . . . 179 F5
Greenslade LE13 . . . 59 D3
Greensward LE7 . . . 103 E8
Green The
Allington NG32 . . . 4 F5
Anstey LE7 . . . 127 C6
3 Ashby-de-la-Z LE65 . . . 69 B6
Aston-on-T DE72 . . . 16 B8
Atherstone CV9 . . . 194 A6
Austrey CV9 . . . 119 B1
Barkestone-le-V NG13 . . . 6 B3
Bitteswell LE17 . . . 244 B8
Blaby LE8 . . . 202 C8
Breedon on t H DE73 . . . 26 E2
Caldecott LE16 . . . 230 B8
Castle Donington DE74 . . . 17 A3
Churchover CV23 . . . 252 C6
Coalville LE67 . . . 96 C5
Croft LE9 . . . 200 C5
Dadlington CV13 . . . 196 E8
Diseworth DE74 . . . 28 B5
Draycott DE72 . . . 9 A7
Exton LE15 . . . 113 A3
Great Bowden LE16 . . . 241 B6
Hathern LE12 . . . 30 A1
Hickling LE14 . . . 19 C6
Hose LE14 . . . 20 F7
Huncote LE9 . . . 200 D7
Husbands Bosworth
LE17 . . . 247 E5
Ketton PE9 . . . 167 F5
Leire LE17 . . . 233 E8
Lilbourne CV23 . . . 258 A6
Long Whatton LE12 . . . 29 C3
Lubenham LE16 . . . 239 E3
Lyddington LE15 . . . 212 D7
Lyndon LE15 . . . 165 D5
Markfield LE67 . . . 98 D1
Mountsorrel LE12 . . . 76 E2
Muston NG13 . . . 7 F8
Newton Burgoland
LE67 . . . 121 E6
North Kilworth LE17 . . . 246 F3
Old Dalby LE14 . . . 35 E4
Orton-on-t-H CV9 . . . 145 C4
Seckington B79 . . . 118 A3
Stathern LE14 . . . 13 A3
Stonesby LE14 . . . 40 E6
Syston LE7 . . . 103 B4
Thringstone LE67 . . . 71 D7
Thrussington LE7 . . . 78 F4
Walton on t W LE12 . . . 54 A4
Weston by W LE16 . . . 227 B3
Wigston Parva LE10 . . . 231 E8
Greenway LE8 . . . 224 B8
Greenway Cl LE7 . . . 101 E6
Greenway The LE4 . . . 129 A2
Greenwich Cl
Leicester LE3 . . . 128 B1
Narborough LE19 . . . 201 B8
Green Wlk LE3 . . . 153 E5
Greenwood Rd
Leicester LE5 . . . 155 F6
Stoke Golding CV13 . . . 196 E7
GREETHAM . . . 88 A1
Greetham Rd
Cottesmore LE15 . . . 87 F1
Stretton LE15 . . . 88 F4
Gregory Ave DE72 . . . 9 C8
Gregory Cl
Barlestone CV13 . . . 149 C8
Thurmaston LE4 . . . 130 A7
Gregory Rd CV13 . . . 149 C8
Gregorys Cl LE3 . . . 153 D1
Gregory St LE11 . . . 52 B3
Gregson Cl
Leicester LE4 . . . 129 D5
Swadlincote DE11 . . . 44 B5
Grendon Cl LE18 . . . 180 E3
Grenehams Cl PE9 . . . 167 F5
Grenfell Rd LE2 . . . 180 E8
Grenville Gdns LE16 . . . 240 D1
Gresley Cl
Leicester, Beaumont Leys
LE4 . . . 128 C4
Leicester, Thurnby LE7 . . . 156 F6
Gresley Dr PE9 . . . 143 D2
Gresley Woodlands
DE11 . . . 44 A2
Gresley Wood Rd DE11 . . . 44 A2
Gretna Way LE5 . . . 156 E7
GRETTON . . . 213 C1
Gretton Brook Rd
NN17 . . . 230 E3
Gretton Ct LE13 . . . 59 B3
Gretton Gdns LE14 . . . 62 C2
Gretton Rd
Harringworth NN17 . . . 213 E7
Lyddington LE15 . . . 212 D5
Rockingham LE16 . . . 230 B5
Grewcock Cl LE17 . . . 232 E6
Grey Cl LE6 . . . 126 F3
Grey Cres LE6 . . . 99 D1
Grey Friars LE1 . . . 259 B3
Greylag Way LE8 . . . 201 F4
Greyland Paddock
LE6 . . . 126 F3
Greys Dr LE6 . . . 126 E2
Greystoke Cl LE4 . . . 128 E3
Greystoke Prim Sch
LE19 . . . 201 C8
Greystoke Wlk 1 LE4 . . . 128 E3
Greystone Ave LE5 . . . 156 B6
Griffin Cl
Hamilton LE4 . . . 130 A5
Shepshed LE12 . . . 50 A3
Griffin Rd LE16 . . . 251 E4
Griffith Gdns LE65 . . . 68 F5
Griffiths Cl LE15 . . . 138 A8
GRIFFYDAM . . . 48 B2
Griffydam Prim Sch
LE67 . . . 48 A2
Griggs Rd LE11 . . . 75 B8
Grimes Gate DE74 . . . 28 C6
GRIMSTON . . . 57 B8
Grimston Cl LE4 . . . 130 A4
Grisedale Cl LE2 . . . 259 A1
Grittar Cl LE18 . . . 180 E3
Grizedale Gr LE19 . . . 177 F2
GROBY . . . 126 D3
Groby Com Coll LE6 . . . 126 D2
Groby La LE6 . . . 126 E7
Groby Rd
Anstey LE7 . . . 127 C5
Glenfield LE3 . . . 127 C3
Leicester LE3 . . . 128 A1
Ratby LE6 . . . 126 D1
Grocot Rd LE5 . . . 156 A3
Grosvenor Ave
Breaston DE72 . . . 9 F8
Long Eaton NG10 . . . 10 A4
Grosvenor Cl LE2 . . . 179 D1
Grosvenor Cres
Hinckley LE10 . . . 216 A6
Leicester, Oadby LE2 . . . 180 F7
Grosvenor Ho LE15 . . . 137 F6
Grosvenor St LE1 . . . 259 C5
Grovebury Rd LE4 . . . 128 F3
Grovebury Wlk 4
LE4 . . . 128 F3
Grove Cotts LE14 . . . 108 B2
Grove Ct LE19 . . . 178 D5
Grove Farm Triangle
LE19 . . . 178 E5
Grove La LE12 . . . 76 D7
Grove Pk LE10 . . . 216 A6
Grove Prim Sch The
LE13 . . . 59 B3
Grove Rd
Hinckley LE10 . . . 216 A6
Leicester LE5 . . . 155 C6
Loughborough LE11 . . . 51 E3
Whetstone LE8 . . . 202 A7
Whitwick LE67 . . . 71 E4
Grove St DE11 . . . 44 B4
Grove Stud LE14 . . . 108 A2
Grove The
Asfordby LE14 . . . 57 E3
Breaston DE72 . . . 9 F8
Desford LE9 . . . 151 A3
Hinckley LE10 . . . 215 C8
Syston LE7 . . . 103 A1
Grove Way LE19 . . . 178 F5
Guadaloupe Ave LE13 . . . 59 E1
Guestwick Gn LE5 . . . 130 C2
Guild Cl LE7 . . . 100 F3
Guildford Ave DE11 . . . 44 E6
Guildford Way LE11 . . . 74 C8
Guildhall La LE1 . . . 259 A3
Guilford Dr LE18 . . . 180 B5
Guilford Rd LE2 . . . 155 E1
Guilford St 2 LE2 . . . 155 C4
Guinea Cl NG10 . . . 10 A7
Guinevere Way LE3 . . . 153 A2
Gullet La
Ashley LE16 . . . 227 F2
Kirby Muxloe LE9 . . . 152 C5
Gumbrill Ho LE5 . . . 156 A6
GUMLEY . . . 224 A1
Gumley Rd
Foxton LE16 . . . 239 C7
Laughton LE16, LE17 . . . 238 D8
Smeeton Westerby LE8 . . . 223 F5
Gumley Sq LE19 . . . 178 B3
GUNBY . . . 64 E8
Gunby Hill DE12 . . . 91 F8
Gunby Rd
North Witham NG33 . . . 65 A8
Sewstern NG33 . . . 64 B8
Stainby NG33 . . . 43 E1
Gunnel La LE15 . . . 141 B6
Gunnsbrook Cl LE16 . . . 241 A6
GUNTHORPE . . . 164 B8
Gunthorpe Cl LE15 . . . 138 B7
Gunthorpe Rd LE3 . . . 153 D4
Gurnall Rd LE4 . . . 128 A4
Gurney Cres LE19 . . . 201 C6
Gurney La LE17 . . . 236 A1
Guscott Rd LE67 . . . 71 E1
Guthlaxton Ave
11 Leicester LE2 . . . 155 B5
Lutterworth LE17 . . . 244 C6
Guthlaxton Coll LE18 . . . 180 B2
Guthlaxton Gap LE9,
LE19 . . . 200 F5
Guthlaxton St LE2 . . . 155 B5
Guthlaxton Way LE18 . . . 180 E1
Guthridge Cres LE3 . . . 154 B3
Gutteridge St LE67 . . . 96 C8
Gwash Cl PE9 . . . 116 F2
Gwash Way PE9 . . . 143 F5
Gwash Way Ind Est
PE9 . . . 143 F6
Gwencole Ave LE3 . . . 179 A8
Gwencole Cres LE3 . . . 179 A7
Gwendolen Rd LE5 . . . 155 E4
Gwendolin Ave LE4 . . . 129 B8
Gwendoline Ave LE10 . . . 197 A2
Gwendoline Dr LE8 . . . 202 E4

Gynsill Cl LE7 . . . . 127 E5
Gynsill Ct LE7 . . . . 127 D3
Gynsill La LE7 . . . . 127 D3
Gynsills Hall LE7 . . . . . . 127 D3
Gypsy La CV9 . . . . 170 D2

H

Hackett Cl LE65 . . . . 69 B7
Hackett Rd LE3 . . . . 153 F8
Haddenham Rd LE3 . . . . 154 C2
Haddon Cl LE7 . . . . 102 F3
Haddonian Rd LE3 . . . . . 240 E1
Haddon Rd PE9 . . . . 143 B4
Haddon St LE2 . . . . 155 C6
Haddon Way
  Long Eaton NG10 . . . . 9 F4
  Loughborough LE11 . . . . . 75 A6
Hades La LE12 . . . . 34 D4
Hadfield Cl CV23 . . . . . . 257 A5
Hadfield Dr LE13 . . . . 59 C4
Hadrian Cl
  Hinckley LE10 . . . . 196 F1
  Syston LE7 . . . . 102 E2
Hadrian Rd
  Leicester LE4 . . . . 128 E5
  Thurmaston LE4 . . . . . . 129 E7
Hagley Cl LE16 . . . . 241 B3
Haig Pl LE3 . . . . 154 A2
Hailebury Ave LE65 . . . . . 69 A8
Hailey Ave LE11 . . . . 51 C5
Hainsworth Cl LE15 . . . . 110 C3
Halberd Cl LE15 . . . . 215 D5
Halcroft Rise LE18 . . . . . 180 D1
Half Croft The LE7 . . . . . 103 A4
Half Moon Cres LE2 . . . . 181 C6
Halford Cl
  Great Glen LE8 . . . . 205 B8
  South Witham NG33 . . . . 65 B4
  Whetstone LE8 . . . . 201 F6
Halford Rd LE8 . . . . 223 F8
Halford St
  Leicester LE1 . . . . 259 C3
  Syston LE7 . . . . 103 A3
Halifax Dr LE4 . . . . 128 E4
Halkin St LE4 . . . . 129 B1
Hallam Cl LE3 . . . . 199 A8
Hallam Cres E LE3 . . . . . 154 A2
Hallam Fields LE8 . . . . . . 17 B2
Hallam Fields Rd LE4 . . . 102 A1
Hallamford Rd LE12 . . . . . 50 A6
HALLATON 209 D6
Hallaton CE Prim Sch
  LE16 . . . . 209 D6
Hallaton Rd
  Alleton LE15 . . . . 187 C4
  Horninghold LE16 . . . . . 210 A4
  Leicester LE5 . . . . 155 F8
  Medbourne LE16 . . . . . . 227 F7
  Slawston LE16 . . . . 209 E3
  Tugby LE7 . . . . 185 E5
Hallaton St LE2 . . . . 179 E7
Hallaton Village Mus★
  LE16 . . . . 209 D6
Hallbrook Prim Sch
  LE9 . . . . 218 F4
Hallbrook Rd LE9 . . . . . . 218 F4
Hall Cl
  Blackfordby DE11 . . . . . . 68 C8
  Cossington LE7 . . . . 102 D8
  Cottesmore LE15 . . . . . . 112 C8
  Glen Parva LE2 . . . . 179 B3
  Kibworth Beauchamp
    LE8 . . . . 205 F1
  Weston by W LE16 . . . . . 227 B4
  Whissendine LE15 . . . . . 85 A1
Hall Croft LE12 . . . . 50 B4
Hallcroft Ave
  Countesthorpe LE8 . . . . 202 E3
  Overseal DE12 . . . . 67 B3
Hallcroft Gdns LE8 . . . . . 202 E3
Hall Dr
  Asfordby LE14 . . . . 57 E2
  Burton Lazars LE14 . . . . 82 F6
  Burton o t W LE12 . . . . . 54 A7
  Leicester, Oadby LE2 . . . 181 B6
  'Stoke Golding CV13 . . . 196 E7
Halley Cl LE4 . . . . 128 A6
Hall Farm Cl
  Castle Donington DE74 . . 17 B3
  Queniborough LE7 . . . . . 103 F5
  Swadlincote DE11 . . . . . . 44 C4
Hall Farm Cres LE9 . . . . 219 A5
Hall Farm Ct LE12 . . . . . . 77 F7
Hall Farm Rd
  Swadlincote DE11 . . . . . . 44 C4
  Thurcaston LE7 . . . . 101 B2
Hallfield Cl CV9 . . . . 146 C7
Hallfields CV9 . . . . 146 C7
Hallfields La LE7 . . . . . . 101 F5
Hall Gate
  Coalville LE67 . . . . 97 C8
  Diseworth DE74 . . . . 28 C6
Hallgate Dr LE3 . . . . 127 F3
Hall Gdns
  East Leake LE12 . . . . 31 F8
  Great Glen LE8 . . . . 205 B8
  Hemington DE74 . . . . 17 D4
  Ravenstone LE67 . . . . 95 D8
Hall La
  Ashby Magna LE17 . . . . . 220 A2
  Ashley LE16 . . . . 227 E2
  Bittesdell LE17 . . . . 234 C3
  Coalville LE67 . . . . 72 A2
  Donisthorpe DE12 . . . . . . 92 E8
  Drayton LE16 . . . . 229 A5

Hall La continued
  Eastwell LE14 . . . . 22 B5
  Leicester LE2 . . . . 179 C7
  Odstone CV13 . . . . 122 C4
  Packington LE65 . . . . 69 C2
  South Luffenham LE15 . . 191 E8
  Stainby NG33 . . . . 43 D2
  Ullesthorpe LE17 . . . . . . 233 B4
  Walton LE17 . . . . 236 A2
  Welford NN6 . . . . 256 D6
  Witherley CV9 . . . . 194 B8
Hall Leys LE12 . . . . 76 A5
Hall Orchard CE Prim Sch
  LE12 . . . . 76 D7
Hall Orchard La LE14 . . . . 80 D8
Hall Rd
  Hinckley LE10 . . . . 215 D5
  Scraptoft LE7 . . . . 156 F8
Hall Sch The LE3 . . . . . . 127 E1
Halls Cres LE10 . . . . 217 C5
Hall St
  Ibstock LE67 . . . . 122 E8
  Swadlincote DE11 . . . . . . 44 A2
Hall Wlk LE19 . . . . 178 B4
Hall Wood Cl DE11 . . . . . 44 A2
Hall Yd PE9 . . . . 168 C2
Halsbury St LE2 . . . . 155 D3
HALSTEAD 160 C8
Halstead Rd LE12 . . . . . . 76 D1
Halstead Rise LE7 . . . . . 160 A8
Halstead St LE5 . . . . 155 D6
Halter Slade LE18 . . . . . 180 E1
Halywell Nook LE7 . . . . . 101 F8
Hamble Cl LE9 . . . . 151 B3
Hambledon Cres
  Cottesmore LE15 . . . . . . 87 E2
  Loughborough LE11 . . . . 74 F8
Hambledon Gn LE4 . . . . . 128 D5
Hamble Rd LE2 . . . . 181 D6
Hambleton Cl
  Leicester Forest East
    LE3 . . . . 152 F2
  Oakham LE15 . . . . 138 B6
Hambleton Rd
  Egleton LE15 . . . . 138 C3
  Stamford PE9 . . . . 143 A2
Hamelin Rd LE3 . . . . 153 F4
Hames La B79 . . . . 118 D3
Hamilford Cl LE7 . . . . . . 130 E1
HAMILTON 130 C3
Hamilton Bsns Pk
  LE4 . . . . 130 A4
Hamilton Circ LE5 . . . . . 130 D3
Hamilton Cl LE10 . . . . . . 197 A2
Hamilton Com Coll
  LE5 . . . . 130 E2
Hamilton Ct
  Hamilton LE5 . . . . 130 D3
  Leicester, Oadby LE2 . . . 181 B5
Hamilton Dr
  Melton Mowbray LE13 . . . 59 C1
  Swadlincote DE11 . . . . . . 44 C5
Hamilton Gn DE11 . . . . . . 44 D5
Hamilton La LE7 . . . . 130 E2
Hamilton Pl LE13 . . . . . . 59 C1
Hamilton Rd
  Coalville LE67 . . . . 97 C8
  Long Eaton NG10 . . . . . . 10 D8
Hamilton St LE2 . . . . 155 B4
Hamilton Way LE5 . . . . . 130 B2
Hamlet Cl CV11 . . . . 214 B1
Hammercliffe Rd LE5 . . . 155 C8
Hammond Way LE16 . . . . 240 E4
Hampden Rd LE4 . . . . . . 129 E2
Hampshire Rd LE2 . . . . . 179 D7
Hampstead Cl LE19 . . . . 201 B8
Hampton Cl
  Coalville LE67 . . . . 96 F8
  Glen Parva LE2 . . . . 179 D1
  Wigston LE18 . . . . 180 E2
Hampton Ct LE16 . . . . . . 240 F3
Hanbury Cl LE15 . . . . . . 137 D5
Hanbury Gdns LE15 . . . . 137 A2
Hanbury Rd LE5 . . . . 156 D4
Hand Ave LE3 . . . . 153 D3
Hand Cl LE3 . . . . 153 E4
Handley St LE2 . . . . 179 E7
Hand's Wlk NG13 . . . . 3 A2
Hanford Way LE11 . . . . . . 52 B5
Hanger Bank DE72 . . . . . 16 B8
Hangmans La B79 . . . . . 118 A2
Hannah Clarke Ct LE4 . . . 128 F6
Hannah Par LE4 . . . . 129 A7
Hannah's Field LE15 . . . . 163 E2
Hannam Ct LE1 . . . . 259 B4
Hanover Cl LE5 . . . . 130 B1
Hanover Ct
  Hinckley LE10 . . . . 215 E6
  Loughborough LE11 . . . . . 51 D5
  4 Stamford PE9 . . . . . . 143 E3
Hanover Dr LE12 . . . . 77 D4
Hansen Ct LE18 . . . . 180 B2
Hansom Ct 2 LE10 . . . . . 215 D8
Hansom Rd LE10 . . . . . . 197 F2
Hanworth Cl LE5 . . . . . . 130 C2
Haramead Bsns Ctr
  LE1 . . . . 155 B7
Haramead Rd LE1 . . . . . . 155 B7
Harborough Cl LE15 . . . . . 84 E1
Harborough Hill Rd
  LE15 . . . . 211 B6
Harborough Rd
  Billesdon LE7 . . . . 184 C6
  Braybrooke LE16 . . . . . . 251 D7
  Clipston LE16 . . . . 250 D2
  Dingley LE16 . . . . 241 D5
  Dingley LE16 . . . . 241 E1

Harborough Rd continued
  East Farndon LE16 . . . . . 250 C8
  Glooston LE16 . . . . 208 B3
  Great Oxendon LE16 . . . 250 F4
  Kibworth Beauchamp LE8,
    LE16 . . . . 224 E5
  Leicester, Oadby LE2 . . . 181 B5
  Lubenham LE16 . . . . 240 A3
  Market Harborough
    LE16 . . . . 240 C7
  Theddingworth LE17 . . . 238 F1
HARBY 12 B3
Harby CE Prim Sch
  LE14 . . . . 12 B3
Harby La
  Harby NG13 . . . . 11 B5
  Hose LE14 . . . . 20 F7
  Plungar NG13 . . . . 12 E6
  Stathern LE14 . . . . 12 F3
Harcourt Cl LE7 . . . . 103 A4
Harcourt Est LE8 . . . . . . 206 A1
Harcourt Pl DE74 . . . . 17 B4
Harcourt Rd
  Kibworth Beauchamp
    LE8 . . . . 223 F8
  Wigston LE18 . . . . 180 E1
Harcourt Spinney
  CV13 . . . . 148 E4
Harcourt St LE16 . . . . . . 240 D3
Harcourt Terr 1 PE9 . . . . 143 C3
Harcourt Way LE19 . . . . . 178 D6
Hardacre Cl DE73 . . . . . . 26 A8
Hardie Cres LE3 . . . . 153 D2
Harding St LE1 . . . . 259 A5
Hardwick Cl LE15 . . . . . . 138 B7
Hardwick Cres LE7 . . . . . 102 F3
Hardwick Ct
  Leicester LE3 . . . . 154 C3
  Long Eaton NG10 . . . . 9 F4
Hardwick Dr LE11 . . . . . . 51 C4
Hardwicke Rd LE19 . . . . 200 F3
Hardwick Rd
  Gretton NN17 . . . . 213 B1
  Leicester LE5 . . . . 156 E4
  Stamford PE9 . . . . 143 B4
Hardy Cl
  Hinckley LE10 . . . . 197 D4
  Long Eaton NG10 . . . . . . 10 D6
Hardy's Ave LE4 . . . . 129 C4
Harebell Cl
  Hamilton LE5 . . . . 130 B3
  Swadlincote DE11 . . . . . . 44 E4
Harebell Dr LE13 . . . . 82 A8
Harecroft Cres LE9 . . . . . 217 E8
Harene Cres LE9 . . . . . . 152 E3
Hare Pie View LE16 . . . . 209 C5
Harewood Cl LE15 . . . . . 110 D3
Harewood St LE5 . . . . . . 155 D7
Harker Dr LE67 . . . . 97 A7
Harland Cl
  Asfordby LE14 . . . . 57 F2
  Cosby LE9 . . . . 201 D3
Harlaxton St LE3 . . . . . . 154 C4
Harlech Cl LE11 . . . . 51 E5
Harlech Wlk LE13 . . . . . . 59 C5
Harlequin Rd LE12 . . . . . . 77 C2
Harlequin Way LE8 . . . . . 201 F4
Harles Acres LE14 . . . . . . 19 C6
Harley Cl LE12 . . . . 50 B2
Harley's Ct DE12 . . . . 67 C4
Harolds La LE19 . . . . 178 B5
Harold St LE2 . . . . 179 E8
Harpers La CV9 . . . . 194 A7
Harratts Ct LE67 . . . . 95 F1
Harrier Cl
  Broughton Astley LE9 . . . 218 E7
  Cottesmore LE15 . . . . . . 87 C1
Harrier Parkway
  LE17 . . . . 243 D7
Harriman Cl LE12 . . . . . . 50 B4
Harrimans Dr DE72 . . . . . . 9 F8
Harrington Cl LE12 . . . . . . 76 A6
Harrington Cres LE15 . . . 113 B2
Harrington Rd
  Shepshed LE12 . . . . 50 C3
  South Witham LE15 . . . . 65 B4
  Wigston LE18 . . . . 180 E3
Harrington St
  Draycott DE72 . . . . 9 B7
  Leicester LE4 . . . . 155 C8
  Long Eaton NG10 . . . . . . 10 B5
Harrington Way LE15 . . . 137 E5
HARRINGWORTH 213 F7
Harringworth Rd
  Gretton NN17 . . . . 213 C2
  Leicester LE5 . . . . 156 B5
Harris Cl LE9 . . . . 219 A5
Harris Gn LE3 . . . . 153 C3
Harrison Cl
  2 Earl Shilton LE9 . . . . 198 F8
  Glenfield LE3 . . . . 153 C8
  Market Harborough
    LE16 . . . . 250 D8
  Ratby LE6 . . . . 152 D8
  Whetstone LE8 . . . . 202 A6
  Wigston LE18 . . . . 180 B1
Harrison Ct LE4 . . . . 129 C2
Harrison Pl LE67 . . . . 96 C8
Harrison Rd LE4 . . . . 129 B2
Harrisons Row LE7 . . . . . 103 B4
Harrison St LE4 . . . . 129 E8
Harris Rd
  Corby NN17 . . . . 230 C1
  Leicester LE3 . . . . 128 B3
Harrod Dr LE16 . . . . 241 A4
Harrogate Rd LE4 . . . . . . 129 C1
Harrogate Way LE18 . . . . 180 E2

Harrop Cl LE8 . . . . 202 A8
Harrowbrook Ind Est
  LE10 . . . . 214 E7
Harrowbrook Rd
  LE10 . . . . 214 E7
Harrow Cl
  Ashby-de-la-Z LE65 . . . . . 69 A8
  Leicester Forest East
    LE3 . . . . 152 F1
Harrowden Ct LE5 . . . . . . 156 A6
Harrowden Rise LE5 . . . . 156 A6
Harrowgate Dr LE4 . . . . . 101 F1
Harrow Rd
  Leicester LE5 . . . . 154 C4
  Swadlincote DE11 . . . . . . 44 B7
Harry French Ct LE11 . . . . 51 E4
HARSTON 15 C4
Harston Rd NG32 . . . . 15 F5
Hart Dr DE12 . . . . 93 C5
Hartfield Rd LE5 . . . . 156 D8
Hartington Gn LE10 . . . . 215 E6
Hartington Rd LE2 . . . . . 155 C6
Hartington St LE11 . . . . . 52 C4
Hartland Dr
  Market Harborough
    LE16 . . . . 241 B3
  Melton Mowbray LE13 . . . 82 C8
Hartopp Cl LE7 . . . . 157 A5
Hartopp Rd
  Leicester LE2 . . . . 155 B1
  Melton Mowbray LE13 . . . 82 C8
Hart Rd LE5 . . . . 155 C6
HARTSHILL 194 A1
HARTSHILL GREEN 194 A2
Hartshill Hayes Cty Pk★
  CV10 . . . . 194 A2
Hartshill Rd DE11 . . . . . . 45 A4
Hartshorn Cl LE4 . . . . . . 129 F6
HARTSHORNE 45 A6
Hartshorne CE Prim Sch
  DE11 . . . . 44 F3
Hartshorne Rd DE11 . . . . 44 F3
Hartside Gdns 1 NG10 . . . 10 A8
Harvard Cl LE2 . . . . 181 B6
Harvest Cl
  Leicester LE4 . . . . 128 B3
  Littlethorpe LE19 . . . . . 201 D6
Harvester Cl LE3 . . . . . . 152 F1
Harvesters Cnr LE7 . . . . 103 E7
Harvest Gr DE12 . . . . 68 A5
Harvest Hill DE11 . . . . . . 44 B7
Harvest Way LE9 . . . . . . 218 F4
Harvey Cl
  Barwell LE9 . . . . 198 A8
  Blaby LE8 . . . . 179 B1
Harvey Rd DE74 . . . . 17 B2
Harveys Ct LE9 . . . . 217 D7
Harwin Rd LE5 . . . . 156 B4
Harwood Dr LE10 . . . . . . 197 F4
Haskell Cl LE3 . . . . 153 D2
Haslemere Rd NG10 . . . . . 10 B8
Haslyn Wlk LE67 . . . . 97 B8
Hassal Rd LE3 . . . . 153 E8
Hassell Mews LE7 . . . . . . 78 F1
Hastings Ave LE67 . . . . . . 72 A4
Hastings Cl
  Breedon on t H DE73 . . . 26 E2
  Fleckney NG10 . . . . 223 A6
Hastings Dr LE9 . . . . 198 C2
Hastings High Sch
  LE10 . . . . 215 F7
Hastings Hollow DE12 . . . 93 C4
Hastings Rd
  Kirby Fields LE9 . . . . . . 152 E4
  Leicester LE5 . . . . 155 D8
  Swadlincote DE11 . . . . . . 44 B3
  Woodhouse Eaves LE12 . . 99 F8
Hastings St LE11 . . . . 52 A4
Hasting St DE74 . . . . 17 B2
Hastings The
  Braunstone Town
    LE3 . . . . 153 D1
  Ibstock LE67 . . . . 95 F2
Hastings Way LE65 . . . . . 69 C5
Hastings Wlk LE3 . . . . . . 153 E1
Hathaway Ave LE3 . . . . . 153 F1
Hathaway Dr CV11 . . . . . 214 A1
Hatherleigh Rd LE5 . . . . 155 F3
HATHERN 30 B1
Hathern CE Prim Sch
  LE12 . . . . 30 A1
Hathern Cl NG10 . . . . 10 D5
Hathern Dr LE11, LE12 . . . 50 F6
Hathern Rd
  Long Whatton LE12 . . . . . 29 D3
  Shepshed LE12 . . . . 50 D6
Hathern Turn LE12 . . . . . . 29 F2
Hathernware Ind Est
  LE12 . . . . 30 C5
Hathersage Ave NG10 . . . . 9 F5
Hat Rd LE3 . . . . 178 E7
Hattern Ave LE4 . . . . 128 D4
Hatters Dr CV9 . . . . 170 D2
Hatton Crofts NG10 . . . . . 10 C6
Hatton Dr DE73 . . . . 26 A7
Hatton La NN17 . . . . 213 B1
Haulton Dr DE74 . . . . 17 A4
Havelock St
  Leicester LE2 . . . . 259 A2
  Loughborough LE11 . . . . . 51 F4
Haven Cl
  Belton LE12 . . . . 49 B6
  Leicester Forest East
    LE3 . . . . 152 F2
Havencrest Dr LE5 . . . . . 156 B7
Haven Pk LE11 . . . . 51 E5
Haven Rd CV13 . . . . 148 E2

Haven Wlk LE5 . . . . 156 E6
Hawarden Ave LE5 . . . . . 155 F7
Hawcliffe Rd LE12 . . . . . . 76 C4
Hawk Cl LE9 . . . . 218 E7
Hawker Rd LE2 . . . . 181 D4
Hawkesbury Rd LE2 . . . . 179 E7
Hawkes Hill LE2 . . . . 179 F5
Hawke Way LE17 . . . . . . 243 C7
Hawkins Cl
  Corby NN17 . . . . 230 B1
  Hinckley LE10 . . . . 197 D4
Hawley Cl LE67 . . . . 96 E6
Hawley Rd LE10 . . . . 215 D7
Hawthorn Ave
  Birstall LE4 . . . . 129 B8
  Breaston DE72 . . . . 9 F8
  Netherseal DE12 . . . . . . 91 F7
Hawthorn Cl
  Coalville LE67 . . . . 71 E1
  Leicester Forest East
    LE9 . . . . 152 E2
  Old Dalby LE14 . . . . 35 E4
Hawthorn Cres LE10 . . . . 215 E4
Hawthorn Dr
  Blaby LE8 . . . . 202 B6
  Melton Mowbray LE13 . . . 59 C5
  Uppingham LE15 . . . . . . 189 B5
Hawthorne Ave
  Hathern LE12 . . . . 30 A2
  Long Eaton NG10 . . . . . . 10 C6
Hawthorne Cl
  Leicester, Oadby LE2 . . . 182 A3
  Measham DE12 . . . . 93 C6
Hawthorne Ct LE5 . . . . . . 156 A4
Hawthorne Dr
  Ibstock LE67 . . . . 122 E8
  Leicester LE5 . . . . 156 A3
  Thornton LE67 . . . . 124 E4
Hawthorne Rd LE17 . . . . 246 F3
Hawthorne St LE3 . . . . . . 154 C7
Hawthorne Way LE19 . . . 198 B6
Hawthorne Wlk NN17 . . . 230 E1
Hawthorn Gr LE2 . . . . . . 181 B7
Hawthorn Rd
  Bagworth LE67 . . . . 124 A6
  Castle Donington DE74 . . 17 B5
  Mountsorrel LE12 . . . . . . 76 B2
Hawthorn Rise LE6 . . . . . 126 F3
Hawthorns The
  Countesthorpe LE8 . . . . 202 E4
  Leicester LE5 . . . . 155 D1
  Lutterworth LE17 . . . . . . 244 B6
  Markfield LE67 . . . . 125 E8
Haybarn Cl LE19 . . . . . . 201 D6
Haybrooke Rd LE12 . . . . . 77 D4
Hayden Ave LE2 . . . . 181 D4
Hayden Cl LE4 . . . . 128 E3
Haydon Rd LE11 . . . . 51 E4
Hayes Ave DE72 . . . . 9 B7
Hayes Cl
  Langham LE15 . . . . 110 C3
  Whitwick LE67 . . . . 71 F4
Hayes Cotts LE13 . . . . . . 59 A3
Hayes End LE9 . . . . 151 B3
Hayes Rd LE18 . . . . 180 E3
Hayfield Cl LE3 . . . . 153 B8
Hayhill LE12 . . . . 77 A5
Hayle Cl CV11 . . . . 214 A5
Hayling Cres LE5 . . . . . . 156 A8
Haymarket LE1 . . . . 259 B4
Haymarket Ctr LE1 . . . . . 259 B4
Haymeadow Cl LE11 . . . . . 74 F8
Haynes Rd LE5 . . . . 155 E7
Hays La LE10 . . . . 215 B7
Hayward Ave LE11 . . . . . . 52 C2
Haywood Cl LE5 . . . . 156 B4
Haywoods Rd DE11 . . . . . 44 E1
Hazeland Cl LE17 . . . . . . 244 C6
Hazelbank Cl LE4 . . . . . . 128 D2
Hazelbank Rd LE8 . . . . . 202 F4
Hazel Cl
  Birstall LE4 . . . . 129 B8
  Great Glen LE8 . . . . 205 B8
  Littlethorpe LE19 . . . . . 201 C6
  Measham DE12 . . . . 93 C5
  Swadlincote DE11 . . . . . . 44 A5
  Uppingham LE15 . . . . . . 189 B5
Hazel Ct PE9 . . . . 143 D3
Hazeldene Rd LE5 . . . . . 130 D2
Hazel Dr
  Braunstone Town LE3 . . . 178 F6
  Lutterworth LE17 . . . . . . 244 B6
Hazel Gr
  Hallaton LE16 . . . . 209 C6
  Moira DE12 . . . . 68 B6
  Stamford PE9 . . . . 142 F4
Hazelhead Rd LE7 . . . . . 127 D6
Hazelnut Cl LE5 . . . . 156 B4
Hazel Prim Sch LE2 . . . . 154 F3
Hazel Rd LE11 . . . . 75 A8
Hazelrigg Cl DE74 . . . . . . 16 F4
Hazel St
  Desford LE9 . . . . 151 A3
  Leicester LE2 . . . . 154 F3
Hazel Way LE9 . . . . 198 A7
Hazelwood Rd
  Leicester LE5 . . . . 155 D3
  Wigston LE18 . . . . 180 A1
Hazlemere Cl LE8 . . . . . . 202 B7
Hazlewood Cres LE14 . . . . 57 E3
Heacham Dr LE4 . . . . 128 C2
Headingley Cl
  Coalville LE67 . . . . 97 A7
  Leicester LE4 . . . . 128 C7

Headland Rd LE5 .... 156 A3
Headlands The LE16 .... 240 F4
Headland The LE7 ...... 103 F8
Headley Rd LE3 .... 178 F7
Heafield Dr DE74 .... 18 D2
Healey St LE18 .... 179 F1
Healy Cl LE4 .... 128 D4
Heanor St LE1 .... 259 A5
Heards Cl LE18 .... 203 E8
Hearthcote Rd DE11 .... 44 A3
Hearth St LE16 .... 240 D3
Heath Ave
  Narborough LE19 ..... 178 E2
  Syston LE7 .... 102 F3
Heathbrook Dr LE6 .... 152 D8
Heathcoat St LE11 ..... 52 A4
Heathcote Dr LE12 .... 77 D4
Heathcott Rd LE2 ..... 179 F7
Heath Ct LE9 .... 198 D7
Heath Dr LE15 .... 112 D8
HEATH END 46 D7
HEATHER 95 C2
Heatherbrook Prim Sch
  LE4 .... 127 F6
Heatherbrook Rd LE4 .. 128 A5
Heather Cres
  Breaston DE72 .... 9 F7
  Melton Mowbray LE13 .. 82 A4
Heather Ct CV9 .... 170 D1
Heatherdale LE67 ..... 95 E1
Heather Ho LE67 ...... 95 C2
Heather La
  Normanton Le H LE67 .. 95 A5
  Packington LE65 ..... 69 C1
  Ravenstone LE67 .... 95 D6
Heather Prim Sch
  LE67 .... 95 C2
Heather Rd LE2 .... 180 A8
Heather Way LE8 ..... 202 F3
Heathfield LE67 ...... 71 E8
Heathfield High Sch
  LE9 .... 198 C7
Heathfield Rd LE18 ... 180 D5
Heathgate Cl LE4 .... 128 F8
Heath Gdns DE72 .... 10 A8
Heath La
  Blackfordby DE11 ..... 45 C2
  Earl Shilton LE9 .... 198 D8
  Hartshorne DE11 ..... 45 E4
  Smisby LE65 .... 46 B6
  Wyville NG32 .... 25 F8
Heath La S LE9 ...... 198 D8
Heathley Cl LE3 ..... 152 F2
Heathley Park Dr LE3 . 128 A1
Heath Rd
  Bagworth LE67 ...... 124 C3
  Market Bosworth CV13 . 148 D3
Heawood Way LE3 .... 153 D1
Heays Cl LE3 .... 153 F8
Hebden Cl LE2 .... 179 C2
Hebden Way CV11 .... 214 A2
Hecadeck La LE14 .... 36 C8
Hector Rd LE67 ...... 71 D2
Hectors Way LE15 .... 137 D6
Heddington Cl LE2 ... 180 A5
Heddington Way LE2 .. 180 A5
Hedge Gr DE11 ...... 44 B7
Hedge Rd LE67 ...... 96 C7
Hedgerow La LE9 .... 152 D5
Hedgerow Rd LE3 .... 154 A4
Hefford Gdns LE4 .... 128 D4
Heighton Cres LE19 .. 201 C6
Helena Cres LE4 ..... 128 F4
Helen Roberts Ho
  LE5 .... 155 C7
Helmsdale Cl LE67 ... 97 C8
Helmsley Rd LE2 ..... 179 F6
Helston Cl
  Nuneaton CV11 ...... 214 A5
  Wigston LE18 .... 180 C1
Hemdale CV11 .... 214 A4
Hemdale Bsns Pk
  CV11 .... 214 A4
HEMINGTON 17 D5
Hemington Ct DE74 .. 17 C5
Hemington Hill DE74 . 17 C4
Hemington La DE74 .. 17 E5
Hemington Prim Sch
  DE74 .... 17 D5
Hemington Rd LE5 ... 156 D3
Hemlock Cl LE19 .... 177 F1
Hemplow Dr NN6 .... 256 B2
Hendon Grange LE2 .. 180 E8
Henley Cres LE3 .... 153 F1
Henley Rd LE3 ...... 154 C6
Henray Ave LE2 ..... 179 C2
Henry Cl LE3 .... 152 F2
Henry Dane Way LE67 . 47 E3
Henry St LE10 ...... 197 A2
Henshaw St LE2 ..... 259 B2
Hensman Cl LE8 ..... 223 A6
Henson Cl LE4 ...... 128 F6
Henson's La LE67 .... 71 D8
Henson Way LE10 .... 217 C5
Henton Rd LE3 ...... 154 C5
Hepworth Rd DE11 ... 44 E1
Herald Way LE10 .... 215 D4
Herbert Ave LE4 .... 129 B2
Herbert Cl LE8 ..... 202 A7
Herbert St LE11 .... 52 B5
Herdsmans Cl LE19 .. 201 F2
Hereford Cl LE9 .... 197 F6
Hereford Cres DE11 . 44 D6
Hereford Rd LE2 .... 179 D7
Hereward Dr LE7 .... 156 F5

Herford Way LE10 .... 215 F6
Heritage Cl DE11 .... 44 C3
Heritage Way LE5 .... 130 D3
Herle Ave LE3 ...... 153 F2
Herle Wlk LE3 ...... 153 F2
Hermitage Cl
  Catthorpe CV23 ..... 253 E1
  Leicester, Oadby LE2 . 181 A5
Hermitage Ct
  Leicester, Oadby LE2 . 181 A5
  Whitwick LE67 ...... 71 E3
Hermitage Ind Est The
  LE67 .... 71 C2
Hermitage Park Way **[7]**
  DE11 .... 44 A7
Hermitage Rd
  Birstall LE4 .... 129 A5
  Loughborough LE11 .. 51 C2
  Whitwick LE67 ...... 71 E3
Hermitage The PE9 ... 143 C3
Heron Cl
  Great Glen LE8 ..... 182 B1
  Mountsorrel LE12 ... 76 F2
Heron Dr DE11 ...... 44 F3
Herongate Rd LE5 ... 156 A8
Heron Rd
  Barrow-u-S LE12 .... 76 E8
  Leicester LE5 ...... 155 C7
  Oakham LE15 .... 138 B8
Herons Cl LE10 ..... 215 A7
Heron's Way LE7 .... 103 E8
Heron Way
  Coalville LE67 ..... 97 A8
  Narborough LE19 .... 178 D2
  Syston LE7 .... 102 F4
Herrick Cl
  Enderby LE19 ...... 178 A3
  Sileby LE12 .... 77 B3
Herrick Dr LE7 ..... 156 F5
Herrick Prim Sch LE4 . 129 D4
Herrick Rd
  Leicester LE2 ...... 180 A8
  Loughborough LE11 .. 52 B2
  Woodhouse Eaves LE12 . 74 F2
Herricks Ave LE4 ... 129 F5
Herrick Way LE18 ... 180 E1
Herriot Way LE11 ... 51 D5
Herschell St LE2 ... 155 C3
Herthull Rd LE5 .... 156 C6
Hervey Woods LE67 .. 71 E5
Hesilrige Wlk LE5 .. 156 B8
Hesketh Ave LE4 .... 179 C3
Hesketh Cl LE2 ..... 179 C3
Hesketh Ct LE15 .... 89 A7
Hewes Cl LE2 .... 179 B3
Hewett Cl LE8 ...... 205 A8
Hewitt Dr LE9 ...... 152 F4
Hextall Dr LE67 .... 122 F8
Hextall Rd LE5 ..... 156 A3
Hexter Cl LE8 ...... 201 F4
Heybridge Rd LE5 ... 155 F8
Heybrook Ave LE8 ... 202 A7
Heycock Cl LE8 ..... 223 A6
Heyford Rd LE3 ..... 153 D4
Heygate St LE16 .... 240 E4
Hey St NG10 .... 10 C4
Heythrop Cl LE2 .... 181 D4
Heythrop Rd LE15 ... 87 F3
Heyworth Rd LE3 .... 154 C1
HICKLING 19 C7
Hickling Cl LE7 .... 102 A6
Hickling Ct LE11 ... 51 F4
Hickling Dr LE12 ... 77 D4
Hickling La
  Long Clawson LE14 .. 20 A4
  Upper Broughton LE14 . 19 A2
Hickling Rd LE14 ... 19 B8
Hidcote Rd LE2 ..... 181 A4
Higgs Cl LE5 .... 156 A5
High Acres LE7 ..... 159 C2
Higham Fields Ct
  CV13 .... 196 A6
Higham Fields La
  CV13 .... 196 A6
Higham La
  Hinckley LE10 ...... 196 F3
  Stoke Golding CV13 .. 196 C6
HIGHAM ON THE HILL
  .... 196 A3
Higham on the Hill CE
  Prim Sch CV13 ..... 196 A4
Higham Way LE10 .... 215 E7
Higham Way Ho LE10 . 215 E7
Highbridge LE12 .... 77 C3
Highbrow LE8 ...... 182 C1
Highbury Rd LE4 .... 155 C8
Highcliffe Prim Sch
  LE4 .... 128 F7
Highcliffe Rd LE5 .. 130 A3
High Cres PE9 ...... 142 D7
Highcroft LE17 ..... 247 E6
Highcroft Ave LE2 .. 181 C4
Highcroft Cl NG10 .. 10 E5
Highcroft Rd LE2 ... 181 D3
HIGH CROSS 232 A6
High Cross Rd LE17 . 232 C6
Highcross St
  Leicester LE1 ...... 259 A4
  Market Harborough
  LE16 .... 240 F4
Higher Gn LE8 ..... 205 B8
Highfield PE9 ...... 193 B7
Highfield Ave LE13 . 59 A5
Highfield Cl
  Empingham LE15 .... 140 F6
  Sheepy Magna CV9 .. 171 B8
  Shepshed LE12 ..... 50 C5
Highfield Cotts LE15 . 191 E8

Highfield Cres
  Croxton Kerrial NG32 . 24 B7
  Wigston LE18 .... 180 D4
Highfield Ct LE9 ... 198 E7
Highfield Dr LE8 ... 180 D4
Highfield End LE14 .. 105 F5
Highfield Rd
  Groby LE6 .... 126 E3
  Swadlincote DE11 ... 44 B3
HIGHFIELDS 155 C4
Highfields
  Barrow-u-S LE12 .... 76 D8
  Thornton LE67 ..... 124 F3
Highfields Cl
  Ashby-de-la-Z LE65 .. 68 F6
  Normanton Le H LE67 . 94 F6
Highfields Dr LE11 .. 51 E1
Highfields Prim Sch
  LE2 .... 155 B5
Highfields Rd
  Hinckley LE10 ...... 197 E1
  Mountsorrel LE12 ... 76 D1
Highfield St
  Anstey LE7 .... 127 E6
  Coalville LE67 ..... 96 C7
  Earl Shilton LE9 ... 198 E7
  Fleckney LE8 ...... 222 E8
  Leicester LE2 ...... 155 B4
  Market Harborough
  LE16 .... 240 D3
  Stoney Stanton LE9 . 199 D3
  Swadlincote DE11 ... 44 B3
Highfield (Uppingham
  Sch) LE15 .... 189 B3
Highgate
  Ashby-de-la-Z LE65 .. 69 A8
  Leicester LE2 ...... 180 A4
Highgate Ave LE4 ... 128 E8
Highgate Cl NG13 ... 12 F8
Highgate Com Prim Sch
  LE12 .... 77 D4
Highgate Dr LE2 .... 180 B5
Highgate La NG13 ... 13 A7
Highgate Rd LE12 ... 77 D3
Highgrove Cl LE67 .. 96 F8
Highgrove Cres LE2 . 179 B5
Highgrove Gdns PE9 . 143 A3
Highland Ave LE9 ... 152 E2
Highland Dr LE11 ... 75 B6
Highlands PE9 ...... 116 E2
Highlands Way PE9 .. 143 B3
High Lees LE8 ...... 217 B4
High Mdw LE12 ..... 30 A1
Highmeres Rd LE4 ... 129 F3
High St E LE15 ..... 189 B4
High St W LE15 ..... 189 A4
High St
  Barrow-u-S LE12 .... 76 D7
  Barwell LE9 .... 198 A6
  Bottesford NG32 ..... 3 A2
  Braunston-in-R LE15 . 137 A2
  Carlby PE9 .... 117 B8
  Carlby PE9 .... 117 C8
  Castle Donington DE74 . 17 A2
  Coalville LE67 ..... 71 C1
  Collyweston PE9 .... 168 D2
  Cottingham LE16 .... 229 C1
  Desford LE9 .... 151 B3
  Duddington PE9 .... 193 B6
  Earl Shilton LE9 ... 198 F8
  Easton o t H PE9 ... 169 A5
  Enderby LE19 ...... 178 B3
  Exton LE15 .... 113 A3
  Fleckney LE8 ...... 222 F8
  Great Easton LE16 .. 229 D7
  Great Glen LE8 ..... 205 A8
  Gretton NN17 ...... 213 C1
  Hallaton LE16 ..... 209 D6
  Husbands Bosworth
  LE17 .... 247 E5
  Ibstock LE67 ...... 122 F8
  Kegworth DE74 ..... 18 C2
  Ketton PE9 .... 168 A6
  Kibworth Beauchamp
  LE8 .... 224 A8
  Leicester, Evington LE5 . 156 B2
  Leicester LE1 ...... 259 B4
  Leicester, Oadby LE2 . 181 A5
  Long Eaton NG10 ... 10 E8
  Loughborough LE11 .. 52 B4
  Lutterworth LE17 ... 244 C5
  Market Harborough
  LE16 .... 240 E3
  Measham DE12 ..... 93 C5
  Melbourne DE73 .... 26 A7
  Melton Mowbray LE13 . 59 C3
  Morcott LE15 ...... 191 A6
  North Kilworth LE17 . 246 F4
  Oakham LE15 .... 137 F6
  Packington LE65 .... 69 C2
  Quorn (Quorndon) LE12 . 75 F6
  Sileby LE12 .... 77 C3
  Somerby LE14 ...... 108 B2
  South Witham NG33 .. 65 B3
  Stamford PE9 ...... 143 E3
  Staunton in t V NG13 . 1 B4
  Stoke Golding CV13 .. 196 D7
  Swadlincote, Church Gresley
  DE11 .... 44 C3
  Swadlincote, Newhall
  DE11 .... 44 A6
  Swinford LE17 ...... 254 B3
  Syston LE7 .... 103 A4
  Waltham on t W LE14 . 40 A6
  Walton LE17 .... 236 B3
  Welford NN6 .... 256 E6
  Whetstone LE8 ..... 201 F7
  Woodville DE11 .... 44 F2

High Street St Martin's
  PE9 .... 143 E2
High Tor E LE9 ..... 175 E1
High Tor W LE9 ..... 175 E1
Highway Rd
  Leicester LE5 ...... 155 E2
  Thurmaston LE4 .... 129 F8
Hilary Bevins Cl CV13 . 195 F4
Hilary Cl LE13 ..... 59 E6
Hilary Cres
  Coalville LE67 ..... 72 A3
  Groby LE6 .... 126 D3
Hilcot Gn LE3 ...... 153 C2
Hilders Rd LE3 ..... 154 A6
Hildyard Rd LE4 .... 129 A1
Hillary Cl PE9 ..... 143 F4
Hillary Pl LE4 ..... 154 A2
Hillberry Cl LE19 .. 201 A8
Hill Cl LE9 .... 176 A7
Hillcrest Ave
  Kibworth Beauchamp
  LE8 .... 206 A1
  Market Harborough
  LE16 .... 240 D4
Hillcrest Dr LE11 .. 75 B7
Hillcrest La LE17 .. 247 E5
Hillcrest Rd LE2 ... 180 C6
Hillcroft Cl LE4 ... 129 F8
Hillcroft Rd LE5 ... 155 E5
Hill Ct LE4 .... 156 F4
Hill Dr LE17 .... 244 C5
Hill Farm Ave CV11 . 214 B1
Hill Field LE2 ..... 181 E4
Hill Gdns LE16 ..... 240 C3
Hillier Rd LE5 ..... 130 C3
Hill La
  Countesthorpe LE8 .. 202 B2
  Markfield LE67 ..... 98 C1
Hill Lane Cl LE67 .. 98 D2
Hill Lane Ind Est LE67 . 98 C2
Hillmorton La
  Clifton u D CV23 ... 257 A4
  Lilbourne CV23 .... 257 F5
Hill Rd
  Oakham LE15 .... 137 E7
  Orston NG13 .... 2 A6
Hillrise LE10 ...... 215 F8
Hill Rise
  Birstall LE4 .... 129 A8
  Leicester LE4 ...... 129 F5
  Measham DE12 ..... 93 C6
Hillrise Ave LE3 ... 179 A8
Hillside LE4 .... 129 A8
Hillside
  Appleby Magna DE12 . 119 F8
  Castle Donington DE74 . 17 B4
  Kegworth DE74 ..... 18 D1
  Market Bosworth CV13 . 148 D3
  Markfield LE67 ..... 98 D1
  Uppingham LE15 .... 189 B4
Hillside Ave
  Melton Mowbray LE13 . 59 B5
  Wigston LE18 .... 180 D1
Hillside Cl LE14 ... 56 C4
Hillside Ct DE73 ... 26 F2
Hillside Dr NG10 ... 10 B8
Hillside Rd
  Hinckley LE10 ...... 215 D6
  Market Harborough
  LE16 .... 240 F4
  Woolsthorpe by B NG32 . 8 B1
Hills Rd DE72 ...... 9 C7
Hill St
  Ashby-de-la-Z LE65 .. 69 A6
  Barwell LE9 .... 198 B6
  Croft LE9 .... 200 C5
  Donisthorpe DE12 ... 67 E1
  Hinckley LE10 ...... 215 E8
  Leicester LE1 ...... 259 C4
  Newbold Verdon LE9 . 150 B5
  Swadlincote, Church Gresley
  DE11 .... 44 C3
Hilltop NG13 .... 2 A6
Hill Top
  Castle Donington DE74 . 17 A1
  Earl Shilton LE9 ... 175 F1
Hilltop Ave LE8 .... 182 C1
Hilltop Dr LE15 .... 137 D6
Hilltop Ind Est LE67 . 97 C4
Hilltop Rd LE5 ..... 130 B4
Hill Top Rd LE11 ... 74 F8
Hill View LE19 ..... 178 E3
Hill View Dr LE9 ... 201 D3
Hill View Rd NG33 .. 65 B3
Hill Way LE2 .... 181 C4
Hilton Cl
  Long Eaton NG10 ... 9 F4
  Swadlincote DE11 ... 44 A7
Hilton Gdns DE72 ... 16 A7
HINCKLEY 197 C3
Hinckley Bsns Pk
  LE10 .... 214 F8
Hinckley & District Hospl
  LE10 .... 215 D8
Hinckley & District Mus*
  LE10 .... 197 D1
Hinckley La CV13 ... 196 C5
Hinckley Rd
  Aston Flamville LE10 . 216 E6
  Barwell LE9 .... 197 E5
  Burton Hastings CV11 . 215 A1
  Burton Hastings CV11,
  LE10 .... 215 D1

Hinckley Rd continued
  Burton Hastings LE10 . 215 E1
  Earl Shilton LE9 ... 198 D7
  Hinckley LE10 ...... 216 A6
  Hinkley, Burbage LE9 . 216 D8
  Ibstock LE67 ...... 122 E7
  Kirkby Mallory LE9 . 174 A6
  Leicester Forest East LE3,
  LE9 .... 152 D2
  Leicester LE3 ...... 153 D4
  Leicester, Westcotes
  LE3 .... 154 C5
  Nailstone CV13 .... 123 A2
  Nuneaton CV11 ..... 214 A5
  Sapcote LE9 .... 217 B8
  Stoke Golding CV13 . 196 F7
  Thurlaston LE9 .... 176 E5
Hinckley Sta LE10 .. 215 D7
Hind Ave DE72 ..... 9 C8
Hind Cl LE8 .... 202 A6
Hind Leys Com Coll
  LE12 .... 50 D4
Hind Mews The **[4]**
  LE17 .... 244 C5
Hindoostan Ave LE18 . 179 E2
Hinks Ave LE7 ...... 156 F8
Hipwell Cres LE4 ... 128 E3
HMYOI Glen Parva
  LE2 .... 179 D2
Hoball Cl LE3 ...... 153 E8
Hobart St LE2 ...... 155 B5
Hobbs Wick LE12 ... 77 C3
Hobby Cl LE9 ...... 218 F7
Hobill Cl
  Huncote LE9 .... 200 E8
  Leicester Forest East
  LE3 .... 153 B2
Hobrook Rd LE8 .... 223 A6
Hobson Rd LE4 ..... 128 F3
HOBY 79 D7
Hoby Rd
  Asfordby LE14 ..... 57 C2
  Ragdale LE14 ...... 56 C4
  Thrussington LE7 ... 79 A5
Hoby St LE3 .... 154 D6
Hockey Cl LE11 .... 52 A6
Hockley Farm Rd LE3 . 153 D4
Hockley The LE67 ... 71 F5
Hodgson Cl LE3 .... 128 A1
Hodson Cl LE8 ..... 201 F6
Hodson Cl LE11 .... 52 B2
Hoe La LE10 .... 197 A3
Hogarth Cl LE9 .... 197 A3
Hogarth Dr LE10 ... 197 A3
Hogarth Rd
  Birstall LE4 .... 101 C1
  Whitwick LE67 ...... 71 F5
Hog La
  Foxton LE16 .... 224 E1
  Hallaton LE16 ..... 209 D6
Hoke Ct LE17 ...... 218 E1
Holbeck Dr LE9 .... 219 A6
Holbein Cl LE11 ... 52 C4
Holbourne Cl LE12 . 76 C7
Holbrook LE2 ...... 181 E4
Holbrook Rd LE2 ... 180 E8
Holcombe Cl LE67 .. 71 E6
Holden Ave DE72 ... 16 A8
Holdenby Cl LE16 .. 241 B3
Holden Cl LE8 ..... 202 A5
Holden St LE4 ..... 129 A2
Holderness Rd LE4 . 128 D5
Holdings The DE11 . 44 A1
Holgate Cl LE7 .... 127 E7
Holland Cl LE67 ... 71 E5
Holland Mdw NG10 . 10 D5
Holland Rd
  Leicester LE2 ...... 155 B6
  Stamford PE9 ...... 143 E4
Hollands La LE14 .. 106 C1
Hollands Way DE74 . 18 D2
Holland Way LE19 .. 201 B8
Holliers Walk Prim Sch
  LE10 .... 197 D1
Holliers Way LE9 .. 200 C4
Hollier's Wlk LE10 . 197 D1
Hollies Cl
  Houghton on t H LE7 . 158 A4
  Thurlaston LE9 .... 177 A3
Hollies The CV23 .. 252 F1
Hollies Way LE7 ... 156 F4
Hollington Rd LE5 . 155 D4
Hollins Rd LE3 .... 153 E4
Hollinwell Cl LE3 . 153 C3
Hollow La
  Burton Lazars LE14 . 83 A1
  Frisby on t W LE14 . 80 C8
Hollow Rd
  Anstey LE7 .... 127 D6
  Breedon on t H DE73 . 26 E2
Hollow The
  Castle Donington DE74 . 17 B3
  Earl Shilton LE9 ... 198 F8
  Knossington LE15 .. 136 A6
  Leicester LE5 ...... 156 B2
  Normanton Le H LE67 . 94 F6
  Thornton LE67 ..... 124 D5
Hollowtree Rd LE5 . 130 C2
Holly Ave DE72 .... 9 F8
Holly Bank LE67 ... 96 D6
Hollybank Cl DE11 . 44 A7
Holly Bank Cl LE3 . 130 C2
Hollybank Ct LE2 .. 155 C3
Holly Bank Est CV9 . 119 A2
Hollybrook Cl LE4 . 130 A6
Hollybush Cl
  Leicester LE5 ...... 156 E7
  Syston LE7 .... 102 F4

Holly Bush Cl DE12...... 91 F7
Holly Cl
  Draycott DE72.......... 9 A7
  Hinckley LE10 .... 215 E5
  Market Harborough
    LE16................. 240 E4
  Moira DE12 .... 68 C6
HOLLYCROFT 197 A1
Hollycroft LE10 .... 197 C1
Hollycroft Cres LE10 ... 197 C1
Holly Ct
  Aston-on-T DE72 .... 16 A7
  Leicester, Oadby LE2 .... 181 A7
  Woodville DE11 .... 44 F2
Hollydene Cres LE9 .... 198 D7
Holly Dr LE17 .... 244 B6
Hollygate Cl LE13 ...... 59 E1
Holly Gr LE8 .... 202 B8
Holly Hayes Rd LE67 .. 71 F4
Holly La
  Atherstone CV9 .... 170 D2
  Atherstone, Whittington
    CV9................. 170 C2
  Barwell LE9 .... 198 B7
Holly Lane Ind Est
  CV9................... 170 C2
Holly Rd DE12 .... 93 C5
Holly Tree Ave LE4..... 129 A8
Hollytree Cl
  Hoton LE12 .... 32 D2
  Loughborough LE11 ..... 75 A7
Hollytree La LE14 ...... 20 C3
Holly Tree Wlk LE17.... 232 E6
Holly Wlk CV11 .... 214 A2
Holman Row LE5 .... 156 A6
Holmdale Rd LE7 ...... 103 A3
Holmden Ave LE18 ..... 180 B3
Holme Cl PE9........... 142 F1
Holme Dr LE2 .... 181 B7
Holme Farm Cl LE12 .... 34 E7
Holmes Cl LE6 .... 126 E3
Holmes Ct DE11 .... 44 B5
Holmes Dr PE9 .... 168 B5
Holmes Rd DE72 .... 9 D8
Holmewood Dr LE9 .... 152 F5
Holmfield LE14 .... 79 D7
Holmfield Ave
  Leicester LE2........... 155 D2
  Loughborough LE11 ..... 51 F6
Holmfield Ave E LE3 ... 153 C3
Holmfield Ave W LE3 ... 153 C3
Holmfield Cl LE17...... 244 A6
Holmfield Prim Sch
  LE3.................. 153 B3
Holmfield Rd
  Desford LE9............ 151 B3
  Leicester LE2........... 155 D2
Holmleigh Gdns LE7 ... 156 F4
Holmwood Ct LE3....... 127 E1
Holmwood Dr LE3 ...... 127 E1
Holt Cl LE9 .... 199 D2
Holt Cres LE9 .... 177 A3
Holt Dr
  Kirby Fields LE9......... 152 F4
  Loughborough LE11 ..... 51 F1
Holte Rd CV9 .... 170 D1
Holt La LE17 .... 219 F4
Holt Rd
  Birstall LE4 .... 129 A6
  Hinckley LE10 .... 215 E6
  Medbourne LE16 .... 210 D1
Holt Rise LE12 .... 50 C1
Holts Cl LE2 .... 179 B4
Holt's La LE67 .... 96 B6
Holt The LE11 .... 51 F2
Holt View LE16 .... 229 D7
HOLWELL 37 F4
Holy Bones LE1........ 259 A4
Holy Cross RC Prim Sch
  Leicester LE2........... 179 F4
  Whitwick LE67.......... 71 F5
Holygate Rd LE15 ...... 163 C1
Holyoak Dr LE10 .... 217 B5
Holyoake Cres LE67..... 95 C2
Holyoake Dr
  Heather LE67........... 95 C2
  Long Eaton NG10 .... 10 F7
Holyoake St LE19 ...... 178 B2
Holyrood Cl LE15 ...... 137 F5
Holyrood Dr LE8........ 202 D4
HOLYWELL 90 E5
Holywell Ave LE65 ..... 69 B7
Holywell Cotts LE65 .... 69 A6
Holywell Dr LE11 ...... 51 D1
Holywell Prim Sch
  LE11 .... 74 C8
Holywell Rd
  Castle Bytham NG33 .... 90 D7
  Clipsham LE15 .... 89 F4
  Leicester LE2........... 179 C6
Holywell Way LE11...... 51 D1
Home Ave LE3 .... 153 C1
Home Cl
  Blaby LE8.............. 202 B8
  Kibworth Beauchamp
    LE8................. 224 A8
  South Croxton LE7 ...... 105 C1
Home Close Rd LE7 .... 158 A4
Home Croft Dr LE65..... 69 C2
Home Ct LE15 .... 140 F6
Home Farm Barns
  LE67................. 94 D1
Home Farm Cl
  Burley LE15 .... 111 F2
  East Farndon LE16....... 250 B7
  Gilmorton LE17 .... 235 C5
  Great Casterton PE9 .... 142 E6
  Leicester LE4........... 128 C3

Home Farm Cl continued
  Witherley CV9 .... 194 B8
  Woodhouse LE12 .... 75 B3
Home Farm Ct LE4...... 128 C3
Home Farm Mews
  CV13................. 148 F3
Home Farm Sq LE4 ..... 128 C3
Home Farm Wlk LE4 .... 128 C3
Homefield La LE7....... 101 F7
Homefield Rd LE12...... 77 C4
Home Pastures LE14 .... 20 F7
Home Rd LE67 .... 71 D5
Homer Dr LE7 .... 201 A8
Homestead Cl LE7 ...... 102 D8
Homestead Dr LE8 ..... 180 D1
Homestead Rd LE67 .... 71 D8
Homestead The
  Earl Shilton LE9......... 198 D8
  Mountsorrel LE12 ...... 76 E3
Homestone Gdns LE5 ... 156 E6
Homestone Rise LE5 ... 156 E6
Homeway Cl LE12....... 50 C3
Homeway Rd LE5 .... 155 C5
Homewelland Ho
  LE16................. 240 D4
Honeybourne Cl LE2 ... 181 A4
Honeycomb Cl LE19..... 201 A8
Honeypot La LE17....... 247 E5
Honey Pot La NG33 ..... 65 E8
Honeysuckle Cl
  Coalville LE67.......... 97 A8
  East Goscote LE7 .... 103 F7
  Lutterworth LE17....... 244 A6
  Swadlincote DE11 ...... 44 A6
Honeysuckle Rd LE5 ... 130 C2
Honeysuckle Way
  Loughborough LE11 ..... 75 A6
  Melton Mowbray LE13.... 82 A8
Honeywell Cl LE2 ...... 181 A5
Honiton Cl LE18 .... 180 C1
Hooby La LE15.......... 88 C6
Hood Ct LE65........... 69 B6
Hoods Cl LE4 .... 128 D6
Hooley Cl NG10 .... 10 B6
Hoopers Cl NG13 .... 3 A2
Hopefield Rd LE4 ...... 154 C2
Hope Hamilton CE Prim
  Sch LE5............... 130 C3
Hope St DE73........... 26 A7
Hope's Yd LE15......... 189 B4
Hoppner Cl LE4......... 101 D1
Hopwell Rd DE72 ...... 9 A8
Hopwood Cl LE4........ 128 B3
Hopyard Cl LE2 .... 179 B4
Horeston Grange Sh Ctr
  CV11................. 214 A5
Hornbeam Cl
  Leicester, Oadby LE2 .... 181 A7
  Loughborough LE11 ..... 75 A7
  Narborough LE19........ 201 A8
Hornbeam Rd LE9 ...... 150 B4
Hornby Rd LE5 .... 130 C3
Horn Cl LE13 .... 138 B7
Horndean Ave LE18 .... 180 D3
Hornecroft LE7 .... 101 E6
HORNINGHOLD 210 B7
Horninghold La LE16 ... 210 A5
Horninghold Rd LE16 ... 209 F6
Horn La LE16 .... 209 D6
Horsefair Cl LE16 ...... 240 D4
Horsefair St LE1 .... 259 B3
Horsefair The **8**
  LE10................. 215 D8
Horse Field View LE13 .. 59 A5
Horseguards Way LE13... 59 A6
Horse Hill LE7 .... 185 C1
Horsepool LE10......... 216 A5
Horsepool The CV23 .... 258 A7
Horseshoe Cl
  Cosby LE9 .... 201 D4
  Market Bosworth CV13 ... 148 C3
Horseshoe La **13** PE9 ... 143 D3
Horse Shoe La LE16..... 241 B6
Horse Shoes The DE74.. 17 D4
Horses La DE12 .... 93 D4
Horsewell La LE18 ..... 180 D1
HORSTON HILL 155 F3
Horston Rd LE5......... 155 E3
Horton Cl LE8 .... 202 A8
Horton's Cl LE2 .... 179 B3
Hortons La LE15 .... 85 A1
Horwood Cl LE8........ 180 E4
HOSE 20 F8
Hose CE Prim Sch
  LE14................. 20 F7
Hose La
  Colston Bassett LE14...... 11 B3
  Harby LE14 .... 12 A1
  Hose LE14 .... 21 A8
  Long Clawson LE14 ..... 20 F5
Hoselett Field Rd
  NG10................. 10 E5
Hoskins Cl LE18........ 203 E8
Hospital Cl LE5 .... 156 A4
Hospital La
  Blaby LE8.............. 202 D6
  Ravenstone LE67........ 95 E8
  Swannington LE67 ...... 71 B7
Hospital of Christ The
  LE15................. 189 A4
Hospital Way LE11 ..... 51 E4
Hotel St
  Coalville LE67.......... 71 D1
  Leicester LE1.......... 259 B4
Hothorpe Rd LE17 ..... 248 D8
Hotoft Rd LE5 .... 156 B8

HOTON 32 C1
Hoton Rd LE12......... 33 B3
Hough Hill LE67 .... 71 A3
Houghton La
  Gaulby LE7............183 D7
  Houghton on t H LE2,
    LE7................. 157 B1
HOUGHTON ON THE HILL
  .... 157 E3
Houghton-on-the-Hill CE
  Prim Sch LE7.......... 157 F3
Houghton St LE5........ 155 D7
Houlditch Rd LE2 ...... 180 B8
Housman Wlk LE4 ...... 155 B8
Howard Cl
  Barwell LE9 .... 198 A7
  Loughborough LE11...... 51 C5
Howard Rd
  Glen Parva LE2......... 179 B3
  Leicester LE2........... 155 B2
Howard St LE11........ 52 B5
Howard Way LE16....... 240 D1
Howarth Cl NG10 ...... 10 A7
Howden Cl
  Loughborough LE11 ..... 51 B3
  Swadlincote DE11 ...... 44 A5
Howden Rd LE2........ 179 C4
Howden Rd LE2......... 181 B3
Howe Cl LE9 .... 199 C1
Howe Ct LE5........... 71 D5
Howe La LE7 .... 101 E6
Howe Rd
  Loughborough LE11 ..... 52 B1
  Whitwick LE67.......... 71 D5
Hoylake Cl
  Leicester LE5.......... 155 E2
  Nuneaton CV11 .... 214 B1
Hoy Wlk NN17 .... 230 C1
Hubbard Cl LE8........ 202 A5
Hubbard Rd LE12 ...... 54 A7
Hubbards Cl LE17....... 220 A2
Hubble Rd NN17 .... 230 F1
Hudson Cl
  Leicester LE3.......... 154 A8
  Oakham LE15........... 137 D6
Hudson Rd LE12 .... 77 C4
Hudson St LE11........ 52 C4
Huggett Cl LE4......... 129 E4
HUGGLESCOTE 96 D6
Hugglescote Com Prim
  Sch LE67.............. 96 C6
Hughenden Dr LE2..... 154 E1
Hugh Lupus Ct LE12..... 76 D3
Humber Cl LE5......... 130 B1
Humber Dr LE13........ 59 B1
HUMBERSTONE 156 A8
Humberstone Ct LE5 ... 156 B8
Humberstone Dr LE5.... 156 A8
HUMBERSTONE GARDEN
  .... 130 C1
Humberstone Gate
  LE1.................. 259 B4
Humberstone Inf Sch
  LE5.................. 130 B1
Humberstone Jun Sch
  LE5.................. 130 B1
Humberstone La LE4.... 129 F5
Humberstone Mall **11**
  LE1.................. 259 B4
Humberstone Rd
  Leicester LE5.......... 155 C7
  Leicester LE5.......... 259 C4
Humber Wlk NN17 ..... 230 D2
Humble La LE7 .... 102 E8
Humes Cl LE8 .... 201 F4
Hume St LE11 .... 52 C4
Humphrey Cl LE1 ...... 52 C2
Humphrey Perkins High
  Sch LE12.............. 76 C8
Humphries Cl LE5...... 156 A5
HUNCOTE 200 E8
Huncote Com Prim Sch
  .... 200 D8
Huncote Rd
  Croft LE9 .... 200 B5
  Narborough LE9, LE19.... 200 F7
  Stoney Stanton LE9 ..... 199 E4
HUNGARTON 132 B3
Hungarton Bvd LE5..... 156 C8
Hungarton Dr LE7 ..... 103 C3
Hungarton La LE7...... 131 E4
Hungarton Rd LE7...... 132 F3
Hungary La LE12....... 30 C7
HUNGERTON 25 D8
Hunt Cotts NG32.......8 B2
Hunter Bvd LE17 ...... 243 C7
Hunter Rd LE4......... 129 A1
Hunters Ave LE7 ...... 160 A2
Hunters Cl LE17........ 247 E6
Hunters La CV13 ...... 195 A6
Hunters Rd LE13....... 59 D1
Hunters Rise LE14 ..... 81 B8
Hunters Row LE9 ...... 201 D3
Hunters Way
  Leicester Forest East
    LE3................. 152 F2
  Leicester, Oadby LE2 .... 181 D5
Hunters Wlk CV9 ...... 194 B7
Huntingdon Cl LE12..... 54 A7
Huntingdon Ct
  6 Ashby-de-la-Z LE65 .... 69 B6
  Measham DE12 .... 93 A5
  Melbourne DE73 .... 26 B8
Huntingdon Dr DE74.... 17 A4

Huntingdon Gdns
  LE16................. 240 E1
Huntingdon Rd
  Ashby-de-la-Z LE65 ..... 68 F5
  Leicester LE4........... 129 E2
Huntingdon Way DE12.. 93 A4
Huntings The LE9....... 152 C6
Hunt La CV9 .... 194 B7
Hunts Cl LE9 .... 151 C8
Hunts La
  Desford LE9............ 150 F4
  Netherseal DE12........ 91 E7
Hunt's La
  Hallaton LE16 .... 209 D6
  Ketton PE9............ 167 F6
Huntsmans Cl LE67 .... 125 E8
Huntsman's Cl LE12..... 76 B6
Huntsman's Dale LE7 ... 103 D8
Huntsmans Dr LE15..... 137 E7
Huntsmans Way LE4 ... 129 D3
Hunts Orch LE12........ 51 A8
Hunt St LE15 .... 87 E2
Hunt Way DE11 .... 44 E4
Hurds Cl LE7 .... 127 D6
Hurlingham Rd LE16 ... 240 E1
Hursley Cl LE2......... 181 C5
Hurst Ct DE12 .... 91 F4
Hurst Rd
  Earl Shilton LE9......... 198 E7
  Hinckley LE10 .... 215 D8
Hurst Rise LE5......... 156 A5
Hurstwood Rd LE11..... 51 B3
HUSBANDS BOSWORTH
  .... 247 D5
Husbands Bosworth CE
  Prim Sch LE17......... 247 E5
Huss's La NG10 .... 10 F7
Huston Cl LE12 .... 76 F5
Huston Ct LE11 .... 52 A3
Hutchinson St LE2 ..... 155 B5
Hyacinth Way LE10..... 215 D5
Hyam's La DE74........ 28 D6
Hyde Cl
  Leicester LE3.......... 128 B1
  Leicester, Oadby LE2 .... 181 C3
  Narborough LE19........ 201 B8
Hyde Lodge Rd LE7,
  LE15................. 134 E3
Hydes La LE10 .... 214 E4
Hydra Wlk **4** LE2 ..... 155 B5
Hylion Rd LE2 .... 180 A6

I

Ibbetson Ave LE3 ...... 153 C7
Ibsley Way LE2 ....179 D3
IBSTOCK 95 F2
Ibstock Com Coll LE67 .. 95 F1
Ibstock Jun Sch LE67 ... 95 F1
Ibstock Rd
  Ellistown LE67.......... 96 D3
  Nailstone CV13 .... 123 A4
  Ravenstone LE67........ 95 F8
Ickworth Cl LE5........ 155 E8
Iffley Cl LE5 .... 155 F5
Iffley Ct LE5 .... 156 A5
Iliffe Ave LE2 .... 180 F5
Iliffe Ho
  Hinckley LE10 .... 215 B7
  Leicester, Oadby LE2 .... 180 F5
Iliffe Rd LE4 .... 129 E1
Iliffes Cl LE12......... 76 E8
Illingworth Rd LE5...... 156 B5
Illston Cross Roads
  LE7.................. 184 C2
Illston Gdns LE12 ...... 76 E7
Illston La LE7 .... 183 F4
ILLSTON ON THE HILL
  .... 183 F3
Illston Rd
  Gaulby LE7............ 183 E5
  Illston on t H LE7....... 184 D3
Ilmington Cl LE3 ...... 127 C1
Ilminster Cl LE10 ...... 216 B2
Imperial Ave LE3 ...... 154 B3
Imperial Avenue Inf Sch
  LE3.................. 154 B3
Imperial Rd LE8 .... 223 F8
Impey Cl LE3 .... 153 D1
Industrial Heritage Mus ★
  LE67................. 71 B1
Infirmary Cl LE1 ...... 259 B2
Infirmary Rd LE1, LE2... 259 B2
Infirmary Sq LE1....... 259 B2
Ingarsby Cl LE7........ 158 A4
Ingarsby La LE7 .... 158 A6
Ingarsby Old Hall Cott
  LE7.................. 158 B7
Ingarsby Rd LE7 ...... 131 E2
Ingleberry Rd LE12..... 73 D6
Ingleborough Gdns **6**
  NG10................. 10 A8
Ingleby Cl DE11........ 44 A3
Ingleby Rd
  Long Eaton NG10........9 F4
  Wigston LE18.......... 180 C3
Ingle Dr
  Ashby-de-la-Z LE65 ..... 68 F7
  Ratby LE6............. 152 C8
Ingle Dr LE2 .... 154 D7
Inglehurst Jun & Inf Schs
  LE3.................. 154 B7
Inglenook Mobile Home
  Pk LE4............... 102 F1
Ingles Hill LE65........ 68 F7
Ingle St LE2 .... 154 B7
Ingleton Cl CV11 ...... 214 A2

Ingold Ave LE4 .... 128 D3
Ingrams Way LE18 ..... 203 E8
INGTHORPE 142 C6
Inhams The LE15 ...... 189 E4
Inleys The LE12........ 50 D3
Innage Park Small Ind
  Units CV9 .... 170 C1
Insley's La CV13 .... 121 E2
Interlink Ind Pk LE67.... 97 B3
Invergarry Cl LE4 ...... 129 D4
Iona Cl LE4 .... 128 B3
Iona Rd LE7 .... 102 F4
Iona Way LE8 .... 202 F3
Ipswich Cl LE4......... 128 A6
Irene Pollard Ho LE4.... 129 B3
Ireton Ave LE4......... 129 F2
Ireton Rd
  Leicester LE4.......... 129 E2
  Market Harborough
    LE16................240 D2
Iris Ave
  Birstall LE4 .... 129 B8
  Glen Parva LE2......... 179 B3
Iris Cl
  Hinckley LE10 .... 215 E5
  Mountsorrel LE12 ...... 76 F2
Irlam St LE18 .... 202 F8
Irnham Rd PE9 .... 143 E5
Ironmonger St **6**
  PE9.................. 143 E3
Ironworks Rd LE4....... 155 C8
Irwell Cl
  Melton Mowbray LE13.... 59 B1
  Oakham LE15........... 137 E5
Irwin Ave LE11......... 51 C6
Isabel La LE8 .... 224 A8
Isis Cl LE2 .... 181 D6
Island Cl
  Hinckley LE10 .... 197 E2
  Swadlincote DE11 ...... 67 C8
ISLEY WALTON 27 D7
Islington St LE2 .... 154 F2
Isobella Rd LE3 .... 153 C1
Isobella St LE3 .... 153 C7
Ivanhoe Coll LE65...... 69 B7
Ivanhoe Dr LE65 ...... 68 F7
Ivanhoe Ind Est LE65... 69 A8
Ivanhoe Rd LE18 ...... 179 F2
Ivanhoe St LE3 .... 154 C7
Ivatt Cl LE7 .... 157 A5
Iveagh Cl LE12 .... 93 D5
Ivens Cl LE9 .... 198 A5
Iveshead La LE12 ..... 73 B8
Iveshead Rd LE12 ..... 73 A7
Ivychurch Cres LE5 ... 130 E1
Ivy Cl
  Donisthorpe DE12 ..... 67 C1
  Stoke Golding CV13..... 196 D7
Ivydale Rd LE4 .... 129 F6
Ivydene Cl LE9 .... 198 F8
Ivy House Cl LE12...... 78 A8
Ivy Rd LE3 .... 154 C3

J

Jack Hardy Cl LE7 ..... 103 C4
Jacklin Dr LE4......... 129 D5
Jacknell Rd LE10 ..... 214 D8
Jackson Cl
  Leicester, Oadby LE2 .... 181 D5
  Market Harborough
    LE16................. 250 E8
  Overseal DE12......... 67 B3
Jackson Rd
  Bagworth LE67......... 124 A7
  Rugby CV21........... 257 A1
Jackson St
  Coalville LE67.......... 71 C1
  Leicester LE4.......... 129 B2
Jacks Wlk LE67 .... 96 B7
Jacob Cl LE19 .... 178 A3
Jacqueline Rd LE67 .... 125 F8
Jacquemart LE67....... 72 D1
Jacques Cl LE19 ...... 178 A3
Jacques St LE67 ...... 95 F2
James Ave LE11 ...... 51 C6
James Bond Cvn Pk
  LE17................. 244 B4
James Gavin Way
  LE2.................. 181 E4
James Lambert Dr
  LE13................. 58 F5
James St
  Anstey LE7............ 127 D7
  Blaby LE8............. 202 A8
  Coalville LE67.......... 96 C8
  Earl Shilton LE9......... 198 E7
  Stoney Stanton LE9 ..... 199 D3
  Swadlincote DE11 ...... 44 D5
Jameswgo LE9......... 201 D4
Jamia Islamia (Islamic
  Studies Ctr) CV11...... 196 C3
Janes Way LE67 .... 125 E8
Japonica Cl LE11 ...... 75 A7
Jardine Ct DE72........9 A7
Jarrett Cl LE19........ 178 A3
Jarrom Ct LE2 .... 259 A2
Jarrom St LE2 .... 259 A2
Jarvis Cl LE10 .... 197 D4
Jarvis Dr LE13 .... 59 B4
Jarvis St LE3 .... 259 A4
Jarvis Way LE67 ...... 71 E5
Jasmine Cl
  Hamilton LE5.......... 130 B3

Jasmine Cl continued
Loughborough LE11........ 75 A7
Lutterworth LE17........ 244 A6
Jasmine Ct
Narborough LE19........ 177 F1
Wigston LE18........ 179 F1
Jasper Rd LE15........ 138 B6
Jawbone La DE73........ 26 C8
Jay Cl LE15........ 138 B8
Jay's Cl NG13........ 3 A1
Jean Dr LE4........ 128 D1
Jeffares Cl DE74........ 18 C3
Jeffcoats La LE67........ 71 B7
Jefferies Cl LE10........ 197 E2
Jellicoe Rd LE5........ 155 E6
Jellicoe Way LE10........ 197 D3
Jenkins Rd
Coalville LE67........ 71 C1
Rugby CV21........ 257 A1
Jennett Cl LE5........ 156 C6
Jenny's La LE67........ 95 F8
Jeremy Cl LE4........ 129 B2
Jericho La NG13........ 6 B2
Jermyn St LE4........ 129 B2
Jersey Rd LE4........ 128 E5
Jersey Way LE9........ 198 A6
Jerwood Way LE16........ 240 F2
Jessons Cl LE4........ 129 D3
Jessop Cl LE3........ 154 A8
Jetcott Ave LE5........ 75 A7
Jetties The LE15........ 166 C3
Jetty The LE15........ 165 A3
Jewry Wall Mus & Site★
LE1........ 259 A3
Jewsbury Ave DE12........ 93 D5
Jewsbury Way LE3........ 153 D2
Joe Moore's La LE12........ 99 E6
John Bold Ave LE9........ 199 E3
John Cleveland Coll
LE10........ 197 F1
John Ferneley High Sch
LE13........ 59 C7
John Minto Ho LE4........ 155 B8
John Nichols St LE10........ 215 B7
Johnnie Johnson Dr
LE17........ 244 C8
JOHN O' GAUNT........ 133 F8
John O Gaunt Rural Ind
Est LE14........ 134 A8
John Phillips Cl LE11........ 51 E4
Johns Ave LE12........ 101 E8
Johnscliffe Cl LE6........ 99 D1
John's Cl LE10........ 215 D5
John's Ct LE8........ 202 B8
John's Lee Cl LE11........ 51 F1
Johnson Cl
Barrow-u-S LE12........ 76 D7
Broughton Astley LE9........ 219 A5
Melton Mowbray LE13........ 59 C4
North Luffenham LE15........ 166 D3
Whetstone LE8........ 202 A7
Johnson Rd
Birstall LE4........ 128 F7
Uppingham LE15........ 189 A4
Johnson Rise LE9........ 199 E1
Johnson St LE1........ 259 A5
John St
Enderby LE19........ 178 B3
Hinckley LE10........ 197 E1
Oakham LE15........ 137 F6
Swadlincote DE11........ 44 C2
Swadlincote, Lower Midway
DE11........ 44 C5
Thringstone LE67........ 71 D7
John Taylor Bellfoundry
Mus★ LE11........ 52 C4
John Wesley Cl LE12........ 76 D1
John Wycliffe Prim Sch
LE17........ 244 B5
Jolly Farmers La LE12........ 73 A8
Jonathan Cl LE6........ 127 A3
Jon Baker Ct LE10........ 215 E8
Jordan Ave LE18........ 180 A1
Jordan Cl
Glenfield LE3........ 153 C8
Market Harborough
LE16........ 241 A3
Jordan Ct LE6........ 152 D8
Jordean Ct LE12........ 77 C3
Joseph Cl
Cropston LE7........ 100 E2
Hoton LE12........ 32 C2
Journeyman's Gn LE6........ 152 D8
Jovian Dr LE10........ 197 A2
Jowett Cl LE3........ 128 A1
Joyce Rd LE3........ 154 B8
Jubilee Ave
Asfordby LE14........ 58 A3
Sileby LE12........ 77 D5
Jubilee Cl
Melbourne DE73........ 26 B7
Syston LE7........ 103 B5
Jubilee Cres LE19........ 201 C2
Jubilee Croft LE67........ 94 D2
Jubilee Ct
Newbold Verdon LE9........ 150 B4
Oakham LE15........ 137 F6
Jubilee Dr
Earl Shilton LE9........ 198 E7
Glenfield LE3........ 153 C2
Langham LE15........ 110 C2
Loughborough LE11........ 52 A6
Jubilee Gdns
Leicester LE4........ 155 D8

Jubilee Gdns continued
Market Harborough
LE16........ 240 F4
Jubilee Ho 9 LE10........ 197 D1
Jubilee Pk DE11........ 44 F4
Jubilee Rd
Broughton Astley LE9........ 218 E6
Leicester LE1........ 259 B5
Newbold Verdon LE9........ 150 B4
Jubilee St LE13........ 59 C3
Jubilee Terr DE12........ 67 E1
Judgemeadow Com Coll
LE5........ 156 C3
Judges St LE11........ 52 D3
Judith Dr
Countesthorpe LE8........ 202 F4
Leicester LE5........ 156 B4
Julian Rd LE2........ 179 C2
Juliet Cl CV11........ 214 A1
Junction Rd
7 Leicester LE1........ 155 A7
Long Eaton NG10........ 10 F6
Wigston LE18........ 180 D3
June Ave LE4........ 130 A5
Junior St LE1........ 259 A4
Juniper Cl
Leicester Forest East
LE3........ 152 F2
Lutterworth LE17........ 244 B7
Juniper Way LE11........ 75 A7
Juno Cl LE3........ 153 C7
Jupiter Cl LE2........ 155 B6
Jurist Ho 3 LE10........ 197 D1
Justin Park Cvn Site
LE16........ 250 F7

K

Kamloops Cres LE1........ 259 C5
Kane Cl LE67........ 71 C1
Kapelle Cl LE13........ 59 E6
Kashmir Rd LE1........ 155 B7
Kate St LE3........ 154 D5
Katrine Cl NN17........ 230 B1
Kay Cl LE67........ 97 B8
Kayes Garden Nursery
LE7........ 78 F1
Kay Rd LE3........ 153 F8
Keats Cl
Earl Shilton LE9........ 175 F1
Long Eaton NG10........ 10 B5
Melton Mowbray LE13........ 59 B6
Narborough LE19........ 178 A3
Keats Dr DE11........ 44 C6
Keats Gr PE9........ 143 A3
Keats La LE9........ 175 F1
Keats Wlk LE4........ 155 B8
Keays Way LE7........ 156 F8
Keble Cl PE9........ 143 C5
Keble Dr PE9........ 143 C5
Keble Dr LE7........ 103 C3
Keble Rd LE2........ 155 A1
Kedleston Ave LE4........ 129 A5
Kedleston Cl NG10........ 10 A5
Kedleston Rd LE5........ 155 D4
Keel Dr NG13........ 3 A2
Keenan Cl LE2........ 179 B5
Keepers Cl
Moira DE12........ 68 A4
Swithland LE12........ 100 E6
Keepers' Croft LE7........ 103 E7
Keepers Wlk LE4........ 128 B3
Keep The
East Leake LE12........ 31 F8
Kirby Muxloe LE9........ 152 D5
KEGWORTH........ 18 D3
Kegworth Ave LE5........ 155 F5
Kegworth La LE12,
DE74........ 29 C5
Kegworth Mus★ DE74........ 18 C2
Kegworth Prim Sch
DE74........ 18 D2
Kegworth Rd NG11........ 18 F5
Keightley Rd LE3........ 153 E8
Keightley Wlk LE4........ 129 F6
Kelbrook Cl LE4........ 128 C4
Kelcey Rd LE12........ 75 F7
Kelham Cl LE11........ 75 A6
Kelham Gr LE67........ 95 E8
Kelmarsh Ave LE18........ 180 E2
Kelso Cl
Ashby-de-la-Z LE65........ 69 C6
Measham DE12........ 93 C6
Kelso Gdns LE67........ 71 E8
Kelso Gn LE2........ 179 D3
Kelthorpe Cl PE9........ 168 A4
Kelvon Cl LE3........ 127 D1
Kemble Sq 10 LE1........ 259 B4
Kemp Ho NN17........ 230 F3
Kemp La LE14........ 22 C1
Kemp Rd
Coalville LE67........ 96 C7
Leicester LE3........ 127 F1
Kempson Rd LE2........ 179 E8
Kendall's Ave LE9........ 200 C4
Kendal Pl LE67........ 96 D4
Kendal Rd
Ellistown LE67........ 96 D4
Leicester LE4........ 129 D3
Sileby LE12........ 77 D2
Kendrick Cl LE67........ 71 B2
Kendrick Dr LE2........ 181 B5
Kendricks Cl DE11........ 45 A7
Kenilworth Ave LE11........ 51 C4
Kenilworth Cl
Broughton Astley LE9........ 218 E8

Kenilworth Cl continued
Mountsorrel LE12........ 76 C1
Kenilworth Ct LE18........ 179 F3
Kenilworth Dr
4 Ashby-de-la-Z LE65........ 69 C5
Leicester, Oadby LE2........ 180 F5
Kenilworth Rd LE18........ 179 F2
Ken Mackenzie Cl
LE17........ 244 C8
Kenmore Cres LE67........ 97 D8
Kenmore Dr LE10........ 197 B2
Kennedy Ave NG10........ 10 C5
Kennedy Cl LE15........ 137 E6
Kennedy Way LE3........ 153 B2
Kennel La CV9........ 194 B7
Kenneth Gamble Ct
LE18........ 180 B4
Kennet Way LE13........ 59 A1
Kenny Cl LE8........ 202 A6
Kensington Ave LE11........ 51 C5
Kensington Cl
Glen Parva LE2........ 179 D1
Leicester, Oadby LE2........ 181 C3
Kensington Dr LE18........ 180 D5
Kensington Rd LE67........ 97 A8
Kensington St LE4........ 129 A1
Kent Cres LE18........ 179 F3
Kent Dr
Hinckley LE10........ 197 F4
Leicester, Oadby LE2........ 181 C5
Kenton Ave LE18........ 180 C1
Kent St LE1........ 155 B6
Kent The CV21........ 257 A2
Kentworth Terr 1
LE65........ 69 B6
Kenwood Rd LE2........ 180 C7
Kepston Cl LE2........ 179 D4
Kernan Dr LE11........ 51 F6
Kerrial Gdns LE3........ 153 E7
Kerrial Rd LE3........ 153 E7
Kerry Cl LE9........ 197 F7
Kerrysdale Ave LE4........ 129 D2
Kertley LE18........ 222 F8
Kesteven Rd PE9........ 143 E5
Kestian Cl LE16........ 240 D5
Kestrel Ave DE11........ 44 F3
Kestrel Cl
Broughton Astley LE9........ 218 E7
Fleckney LE8........ 223 A6
Hinckley LE10........ 215 F6
Kestrel Dr
Leicester Forest East
LE3........ 152 E2
Leicester LE5........ 155 C7
Syston LE7........ 102 F4
Kestrel La
Hamilton LE5........ 130 C2
Mountsorrel LE12........ 76 F2
Kestrel Rd
Melton Mowbray LE13........ 82 B8
Oakham LE15........ 138 B8
Kestrels' Field Prim Sch
LE5........ 130 D2
Keswick Ave LE11........ 51 D1
Keswick Cl
Birstall LE4........ 129 B8
Leicester LE2........ 179 C3
Nuneaton CV11........ 214 A6
Keswick Ho LE1........ 259 A3
Keswick Rd LE8........ 202 A7
Ketco Ave PE9........ 168 B7
Kettering Rd
Market Harborough
LE16........ 241 B1
Wothorpe PE9........ 169 C8
KETTON........ 167 F6
Ketton CE Prim Sch
PE9........ 168 A5
Ketton Rd
Collyweston PE9........ 168 C3
Ketton PE9, LE15........ 167 B3
Upper Hambleton LE15........ 139 C4
Kevern Cl LE18........ 180 C1
Kew Dr
Leicester, Oadby LE2........ 181 C3
Wigston LE18........ 180 B5
KEYHAM........ 131 D1
Keyham Cl LE5........ 130 B1
Keyham Ct LE5........ 156 A8
Keyham La
Keyham LE7........ 131 C3
Leicester LE5........ 130 D1
Keyham La E LE7........ 131 C2
Keyham La W LE5........ 130 E1
Keyham Lodge Sch
LE5........ 130 D1
Keythorpe St LE2........ 155 B6
KIBWORTH BEAUCHAMP
.... 206 B1
Kibworth CE Prim Sch
LE8........ 206 A1
KIBWORTH HARCOURT
.... 206 B2
Kibworth High Sch
LE8........ 224 A7
Kibworth High Sch
(Annexe) LE8........ 224 A8
Kibworth Rd
Carlton Curlieu LE8........ 206 E7
Fleckney LE8........ 223 A7
Great Glen LE8........ 205 A3
Saddington LE8........ 223 C6
Tur Langton LE8........ 206 E2
Wistow LE8........ 204 E4
Kidger Cl LE12........ 50 C4
Kielder Cl LE19........ 177 F2
Kilberry Cl LE10........ 197 A1
Kilbourne Cl LE12........ 77 C2
Kilburn Ave LE18........ 180 F6

Kilburn End LE15........ 137 F8
Kilburn Rd LE15........ 137 F7
KILBY........ 204 A3
Kilby Ave LE4........ 129 A5
KILBY BRIDGE........ 203 D6
Kilby Dr LE18........ 180 E1
Kilby Gn LE10........ 215 F6
Kilby Ho NG10........ 10 E7
Kilby Rd
Fleckney LE8, LE18........ 222 F7
Wistow LE8........ 204 C4
Kilby St Mary's CE Prim
Sch LE18........ 203 F3
Kildare St LE1........ 259 B4
Kildare Wlk 12 LE1........ 259 B4
Kilmarie Cl LE4........ 197 A1
Kilmelford Cl LE4........ 129 D4
Kiln Ave LE4........ 129 F6
Kiln Cl LE9........ 219 A5
Kiln Garth LE7........ 76 F1
Kiln Way DE11........ 44 D3
Kilverstone Ave LE5........ 156 D3
Kilwardby St LE65........ 69 A6
Kilworth Dr LE5........ 155 E3
Kilworth Rd
Husbands Bosworth
LE17........ 247 D4
North Kilworth LE17........ 246 C6
Swinford LE17........ 254 C4
Kimball Cl LE11........ 111 B4
Kimberley Rd LE2........ 155 C3
Kimberley St LE8........ 223 F8
KIMCOTE........ 235 E1
Kimcote Rd LE17........ 236 A2
Kincaple Rd LE4........ 129 D4
Kinchley Cl LE3........ 127 F3
Kinchley La LE7........ 76 B1
Kincraig Rd LE4........ 129 D4
Kinder Ave DE11........ 44 A5
Kinder Cl LE8........ 202 A5
Kingcup Cl LE3........ 152 F2
King Edward Ave
LE19........ 201 B8
King Edward Rd
Leicester LE5........ 155 F7
Loughborough LE11........ 52 C3
King Edward's Way
LE15........ 166 B7
King Edward VII Com Coll
LE67........ 72 D2
King Edward VII Sch
LE13........ 82 D8
Kingfisher Ave
Leicester LE5........ 155 C7
Woodville DE11........ 44 F3
Kingfisher Cl
Barrow-u-S LE12........ 76 E8
Coalville LE67........ 72 B2
Desford LE9........ 151 B2
Great Glen LE8........ 182 B1
Leicester Forest East
LE3........ 152 E2
Oakham LE15........ 138 B8
Syston LE7........ 102 F4
Twyford LE14........ 106 D1
Kingfisher Ct
Hinckley LE10........ 214 F6
Loughborough LE11........ 52 A2
Melton Mowbray LE13........ 59 B3
Kingfisher Rd LE12........ 76 F2
Kingfisher Way
Loughborough LE11........ 52 A2
Sheepy Magna CV9........ 171 C7
Kingfisher Wlk LE5........ 155 C7
King George Ave
Ashby-de-la-Z LE65........ 69 B7
Loughborough LE11........ 52 D2
King George Rd LE11........ 52 D2
King George's Way
LE10........ 215 B7
King John's Rd LE67........ 71 F6
King Richard Inf Sch
LE3........ 154 D5
King Richard Rd LE10........ 197 C2
King Richard's Hill
Earl Shilton LE9........ 176 B1
Whitwick LE67........ 71 F5
King Richards Rd LE3........ 154 C5
King Richard Way
LE65........ 69 D7
Kings Ave LE11........ 51 F6
Kingsbridge Cl LE19........ 201 A8
Kingsbridge Cres LE4........ 128 B7
Kings Brook Cl LE12........ 32 D6
Kingsbrook Ct LE12........ 31 E4
Kingsbury Ave LE4........ 156 C4
Kings Cl
Market Overton LE15........ 86 F5
Oakham LE15........ 137 E6
King's Cl LE14........ 38 E5
Kingscliffe Cres LE5........ 156 D4
King's Ct 2 LE16........ 240 E4
Kingsdale Cl NG10........ 10 A5
Kings Dr
Leicester Forest East
LE3........ 153 A3
Wigston LE18........ 180 D3
Kingsfield Rd
Barwell LE9........ 198 B7
Cosby LE9........ 201 C2
Kings Gate DE74........ 17 F4
Kingsgate Ave LE4........ 128 F8
King's Head Pl LE16........ 240 E3
Kings La
Barrowden LE15........ 191 F5
Keyham LE7........ 131 E2
South Croxton LE7........ 105 B1

Burrough on t H LE14........ 107 D2
Newton Regis B79........ 118 D5
Kingsley Cl LE19........ 178 A1
Kingsley Cres NG10........ 10 B4
Kingsley St LE2........ 180 A8
Kings Lock Cl LE2........ 179 B4
Kingsmead Cl LE2........ 180 C6
Kingsmead Rd LE2........ 180 C6
Kings Mill La 4 PE9........ 143 D2
KING'S MILLS........ 16 B4
Kings Newton St LE2........ 155 C4
KING'S NORTON........ 183 B5
Kings Rd
Long Clawson LE14........ 20 C2
North Luffenham LE15........ 166 D3
Stamford PE9........ 143 D4
Swadlincote DE11........ 44 B6
King's Rd
Market Harborough
LE16........ 240 E3
Melton Mowbray LE13........ 59 D4
Oakham LE15........ 137 E6
Shepshed LE12........ 50 B2
Kings Row LE9........ 198 E8
King St
Barkby LE7........ 130 D7
Barwell LE9........ 198 B6
Coalville LE67........ 96 D8
Enderby LE19........ 178 B3
7 Hinckley LE10........ 197 D1
Leicester LE1........ 259 B2
Leicester, Oadby LE2........ 181 B5
Long Eaton NG10........ 10 D8
Loughborough LE11........ 52 C3
Melton Mowbray LE13........ 59 C3
Nether Broughton LE14........ 36 D8
Scalford LE14........ 38 E5
Seagrave LE12........ 77 F8
Sileby LE12........ 77 C3
Twyford LE14........ 133 D8
Whetstone LE8........ 201 F7
Kingsthorpe Cl LE4........ 128 F3
Kingston Ave LE18........ 180 C4
Kingston Dr LE10........ 197 E4
Kingston La LE74, NG11........ 18 F3
KINGSTON ON SOAR........ 18 F4
Kingston Rd LE2........ 155 C3
Kingston Way LE10........ 240 E6
King Street La LE14........ 41 C3
Kingsway
Braunstone Town LE3........ 178 F8
Leicester LE3........ 179 A7
Kings Way LE6........ 126 F2
King's Way LE17........ 244 B5
Kingsway N LE3........ 153 C2
Kingsway Prim Sch
LE3........ 153 E2
Kingsway Rd LE5........ 155 E2
King's Wlk LE9........ 198 E8
Kingswood Ave
Leicester LE3........ 154 B5
Loughborough LE11........ 51 A5
Kingswood Ct LE18........ 180 C2
King Williams Way
LE7........ 127 E7
Kinley Rd LE4........ 128 E4
Kinross Ave LE5........ 156 E6
Kinross Cres LE11........ 51 D5
Kinross Way LE10........ 196 F1
Kinsdale Dr LE5........ 156 F7
Kintyre Cl LE10........ 197 B1
Kintyre Dr LE4........ 129 A5
Kiplin Dr LE19........ 178 A2
Kipling Cl PE9........ 143 A3
Kipling Dr LE13........ 59 B5
Kipling Gr LE4........ 128 A2
KIRBY BELLARS........ 81 B8
Kirby Cl
Mountsorrel LE12........ 101 C3
Sapcote LE9........ 217 D8
Kirby Dr DE74........ 18 C1
KIRBY FIELDS........ 152 F4
KIRBY GRANGE........ 151 D7
Kirby Hall LE11........ 81 B7
Kirby Ho LE16........ 240 F3
Kirby La
Eye Kettleby LE13,
LE14........ 81 E8
Leicester Forest East
LE9........ 152 F3
Melton Mowbray LE13........ 82 D7
KIRBY MUXLOE........ 152 E5
Kirby Muxloe Castle★
LE9........ 152 E6
Kirby Muxloe Prim Sch
LE9........ 152 E5
Kirby Rd
Glenfield LE3........ 153 A8
Gretton NN17........ 213 C1
Leicester LE3........ 154 C5
Kirfield Dr LE10........ 197 F3
Kirk Ave DE74........ 18 D2
Kirkby La
Newbold Verdon LE9........ 150 C3
Peckleton LE9........ 175 E6
KIRKBY MALLORY........ 175 D6
Kirkby Rd
Barwell LE9........ 175 B2
Desford LE9........ 151 A3
Kirkdale Gdns NG10........ 10 B6
Kirkdale Rd
Long Eaton NG10........ 10 B6
Wigston LE18........ 179 F2
Kirkewhite Ave NG10........ 10 C5
Kirkewhite Ho NG10........ 10 D7
Kirke Wlk LE3........ 153 D6

Kirkfield Dr DE72 . . . . 9 D8
Kirkfield Rd LE8 . . . . 202 F4
Kirkhill LE12. . . . . 50 C3
Kirkhill Cl LE67 . . . . 72 D1
Kirk La LE19 . . . . 178 C3
Kirkland Cl
  Ashby-de-la-Z LE65 . . . . . . 69 B6
  Castle Donington DE74 . . . . 17 A3
Kirkland Rd LE3 . . . . 178 F8
Kirkland Way DE11. . . . . . . 44 B1
Kirk Ley Rd LE12 . . . . 31 D8
Kirkman Cl CV13. . . . . 149 C7
Kirk's Cl LE15 . . . . 88 B1
Kirkscroft Wlk 6 LE4 . . . . 128 F3
Kirkstead Wlk 3 LE4 . . . . 128 E3
Kirkstone Cl LE3. . . . . 127 D1
Kirkstone Dr LE11 . . . . 51 D1
Kirkstone Wlk CV11. . . . . 214 A6
Kirkwall NN17. . . . . 230 C1
Kirkwall Cres LE5. . . . . . . 156 E7
Kirloe Ave LE3 . . . . 152 F3
Kirminton Gdns LE5. . . . . 156 C6
Kirtland Cl CV9 . . . . 119 B1
Kirtley Way LE9 . . . . 219 A6
Kirton Ave NG10 . . . . 10 D7
Kirton Dr LE13. . . . . 59 A6
Kirton Rd LE67. . . . . 72 D1
Kitchener Rd
  Anstey LE7. . . . . 127 E7
  Leicester LE5. . . . . 155 E6
Kite Cl LE9 . . . . 218 E8
Klevedon Cl CV11. . . . . . . 214 A1
Klondyke La LE14. . . . . . . 106 F5
Klondyke Way LE14. . . . . . 57 E2
Knapton Cl LE10 . . . . 197 A3
Knight Cl LE4. . . . . 129 F7
KNIGHTON 180 B7
Knighton Church Rd
  LE2. . . . . 180 D7
Knighton Cl LE9 . . . . 219 A4
Knighton Ct LE2 . . . . 155 C2
Knighton Dr LE2 . . . . 155 D1
KNIGHTON FIELDS 180 A8
Knighton Fields Prim Sch
  LE2. . . . . 179 F8
Knighton Fields Rd E
  LE2. . . . . 180 A8
Knighton Fields Rd W
  LE2. . . . . 179 F8
Knighton Grange Rd
  LE2. . . . . 180 E8
Knighton Hayes LE2. . . . . 180 D8
Knighton Junction La
  LE2. . . . . 155 A1
Knighton La LE2 . . . . 179 E8
Knighton La E LE2 . . . . . . 180 A7
Knighton Park Rd
  LE2. . . . . 155 C2
Knighton Rd LE2. . . . . 155 D1
Knighton Rise LE2 . . . . . . 155 E1
Knighton St LE2 . . . . 259 B2
Knighton Yd LE17 . . . . . . 246 F4
Knightsbridge Rd
  LE2. . . . . 179 D1
Knights Cl
  2 Ashby-de-la-Z LE65 . . . 69 A7
  Billesdon LE7. . . . . 159 B2
  Hinckley LE10 . . . . 215 D4
  Stoney Stanton LE9 . . . . . 199 D3
Knight's Cres LE7. . . . . . . 101 E6
Knights Ct LE10 . . . . 214 E8
Knight's End Rd LE16 . . . . 241 B6
Knight's Garth LE67. . . . . . 71 F5
Knights Link LE9. . . . . 176 B1
Knights Rd LE4 . . . . 128 C6
Knightsyard Ct NG10 . . . . . 10 C5
Knightthorpe Ct LE11 . . . . 51 D4
Knightthorpe Lo LE11 . . . . 51 B3
Knightthorpe Rd LE11. . . . 51 F3
KNIPTON 14 F3
Knipton Dr LE11 . . . . 51 C3
Knipton La NG32 . . . . 15 A4
Knipton Rd NG32 . . . . 23 C7
Knob Hill Rd LE15. . . . . . . 210 C8
Knollgate Cl LE4 . . . . 128 E8
Knoll St LE16 . . . . 240 C3
Knoll The DE11 . . . . 44 B6
KNOSSINGTON 136 B6
Knossington Rd
  Braunston-in-R LE15 . . . . 137 A2
  Owston LE15 . . . . 135 D5
  Somerby LE14, LE15 . . . . 135 D8
Knowles Rd LE3 . . . . 153 E7
Knowles View DE11. . . . . . 44 D4
Konfidence Wks The
  LE9 . . . . 198 B7
Koppe Cl DE12. . . . . 68 B6
Krefeld Way LE4 . . . . 128 B4

L

Labrador Cl LE1 . . . . 259 C5
Laburnum Ave
  Lutterworth LE17. . . . . . . 244 B6
  Newbold Verdon LE9 . . . . 150 A3
Laburnum Cl LE12 . . . . 30 A1
Laburnum Dr LE9 . . . . 198 D7
Laburnum Rd
  Leicester LE5. . . . . 130 C1
  Swadlincote DE11. . . . . . . 44 A6
Laburnum Way LE11 . . . . . 75 A6
Lacey Ct LE12 . . . . 50 B3
Ladbroke Gr LE8. . . . . 202 F4
Ladybower Cl DE11 . . . . . . 44 A2
Ladybower Rd LE11 . . . . . . 51 B3
Ladyfields DE11. . . . . 44 D6

Lady Gate DE74. . . . . 28 C5
Lady Hay Rd LE3 . . . . 127 F3
Lady Jane Grey Prim Sch
  LE6 . . . . 126 E2
Lady Jane Mobile Home
  Pk LE6. . . . . 126 E8
Lady Jane Wlk LE7. . . . . . 156 F8
Ladylea Rd NG10. . . . . 10 A4
Lady Leys LE9 . . . . 201 C3
Lady Romayne Cl PE9 . . . 143 E2
Ladysmith Rd
  Kirby Muxloe LE9 . . . . . . 152 D5
  Wigston LE18. . . . . 179 E3
Ladywell LE15 . . . . 138 B7
Ladywood Ct LE17 . . . . . . 244 C7
Lag La LE13, LE14. . . . . . . 60 A4
Lagoona Cvn Pk DE12. . . . 67 C3
Laithwaite Cl LE4 . . . . 128 B6
Lakeside * LE12. . . . . 34 C4
Lakeside Ave NG10. . . . . . . 10 C4
Lakeside Bsns Pk
  LE4 . . . . 129 D6
Lakeside Cres
  Long Eaton NG10. . . . . . . 10 D5
  Whitwick LE67. . . . . 71 E4
Lakeside Ct LE7 . . . . 156 F4
Lakeside Inf Sch NG10 . . . 10 C5
Lakeside View LE67. . . . . . 71 E3
Lake Terr LE13 . . . . 59 A2
Lakeview Chase LE5 . . . . . 130 C3
Lakeview Ct LE5 . . . . 130 C3
Lakeview Rd 1 LE5 . . . . . 130 C3
Lakin Cl LE3 . . . . 153 C2
Lakins The DE12. . . . . 93 D5
Lambert Ave LE12. . . . . 50 B3
Lambert Cl LE13 . . . . 59 C6
Lambert Ct LE5 . . . . 156 A7
Lambert Mews PE9 . . . . . . 143 E2
Lambert Rd
  Allington NG32. . . . . 4 F5
  Leicester LE3. . . . . 154 C2
Lambert's Cl LE15. . . . . . . 191 A6
Lambeth Wlk PE9. . . . . . . 143 C4
Lambley Lodge La
  LE15. . . . . 187 D8
Lamborne Rd LE2. . . . . . . 180 A6
Lambourne Rd LE4. . . . . . 129 B8
Lamen Rd LE3 . . . . 127 E1
Lamford Cl LE10 . . . . 197 B1
Lammas
  Ashby Parva LE17 . . . . . . 233 F5
  Braunston-in-R LE15 . . . . 137 B2
  Husbands Bosworth
    LE17 . . . . 247 C6
Lammas Cotts LE15 . . . . . . 84 F1
Lampad Cl 4 DE73. . . . . . 26 A8
Lamplighters LE8 . . . . 222 F7
Lamport Cl
  Loughborough LE11. . . . . . 51 C4
  Wigston LE18. . . . . 180 F2
Lancashire St LE4. . . . . . . 129 C3
Lancaster Ave CV13. . . . . 148 E2
Lancaster Cl
  Atherstone CV9 . . . . 170 E1
  Coalville LE67 . . . . 72 D1
  2 Desford LE9 . . . . 151 B3
  2 Lutterworth LE17. . . . . 244 C5
Lancaster Ct LE6. . . . . 126 E2
Lancaster Pl LE1 . . . . 259 C1
Lancaster Rd
  Hinckley LE10 . . . . 215 D8
  Leicester LE1. . . . . 259 B2
  Leicester, South Fields
    LE1. . . . . 259 C1
  Stamford PE9. . . . . 143 D4
Lancaster Sch The
  LE2. . . . . 180 A7
Lancaster St LE5. . . . . 155 E6
Lancaster Way LE2. . . . . . 179 E1
Lance Cl LE10 . . . . 215 D5
Lancelot Cl LE3 . . . . 153 A2
Lancers Dr LE13 . . . . 59 A6
Lancing Ave LE3 . . . . 154 A6
Lancut Hill CV23. . . . . 252 D1
Landcroft La LE12. . . . . 30 B8
Landscape Dr LE5 . . . . . . 156 C4
Landsdowne Rd LE2 . . . . . 179 E8
Landseer Cl CV21 . . . . 257 B1
Landseer Dr LE10 . . . . 197 B3
Landseer Rd LE2. . . . . 155 C5
Lands End Way LE15 . . . . 137 F8
Land Society La LE9. . . . . 198 E8
Landyke La LE14. . . . . 38 B7
Lane Cl LE3 . . . . 153 C8
Lanesborough Ct LE11 . . . 52 B2
Lanesborough Dr LE7 . . . 101 B3
Lanesborough Rd
  LE4. . . . . 129 B3
Lanes Cl LE12. . . . . 77 C4
Laneshaw Ave LE11 . . . . . . 51 B2
Lanes Hill Gr LE9 . . . . 199 E1
Laneside Dr LE10 . . . . 197 F3
Lane The
  Barsby LE7. . . . . 105 D3
  Easton o t H PE9 . . . . 169 A5
  Rotherby LE14. . . . . 79 F6
  Weston by W LE16. . . . . . 227 B4
Lanfear Ct LE10. . . . . 215 C7
LANGAR 11 B8
Langar Airfield NG13. . . . . 11 F7
Langar La
  Colston Bassett NG12. . . . 11 A8
  Harby LE14. . . . . 12 A4
Langdale Ave LE11 . . . . 51 D1
Langdale Dr
  Long Eaton NG10. . . . . . . 10 A6
  Nuneaton CV11 . . . . 214 A4

Langdale Rd
  Hinckley LE10. . . . . 215 A8
  Thurmaston LE4. . . . . 129 F7
Langdale Wlk LE16. . . . . . 240 E1
Langen Ct NG10 . . . . 10 E6
LANGHAM 110 D2
Langham CE Prim Sch
  LE15 . . . . 110 C2
Langham Dr LE19 . . . . 201 B8
Langham La LE15. . . . . . . 111 C2
Langham Rd
  Ashwell LE15 . . . . 110 F7
  Leicester LE4. . . . . 129 F3
Langhill The LE5 . . . . 155 F6
Langholm Rd LE5. . . . . . . 156 E6
Langley Ave LE4 . . . . 128 F3
Langley Cl LE9. . . . . 200 E8
Langley Dr LE9 . . . . 18 C2
Langley Wlk 3 LE4 . . . . . 128 F3
Langmoor Prim Sch
  LE2. . . . . 180 F5
Langton Cl LE67 . . . . 71 E6
Langton Ct LE16. . . . . 240 E3
Langton Rd
  Foxton LE16. . . . . 225 A2
  Great Bowden LE16. . . . . 241 A7
  Kibworth Beauchamp
    LE8 . . . . 206 B1
  Slawston LE16. . . . . 209 B4
  Wigston LE18. . . . . 180 D1
Lank's La LE15. . . . . 87 E8
Lansbury Ho 17 PE9 . . . . 143 E3
Lansdowne Ave LE12. . . . . 50 C5
Lansdowne Dr LE11 . . . . . . 52 A1
Lansdowne Gr LE18 . . . . . 180 A1
Lansdowne Rd
  Leicester LE2. . . . . 179 E8
  Shepshed LE12 . . . . 50 B5
  Swadlincote DE11. . . . . . . 44 A3
Lant The LE12 . . . . 50 C4
Lapwing Cl LE4 . . . . 128 B6
Lapwing Ct LE19. . . . . 201 A7
Larch Dr LE17 . . . . 244 B6
Larchfield LE15. . . . . 138 A8
Larch Gr LE3 . . . . 153 C3
Larchmont Rd LE3 . . . . . . 154 D8
Larch Rd NN17. . . . . 230 D1
Larch St LE5 . . . . 155 C7
Larchwood LE8 . . . . 202 E4
Larchwood Ave LE6 . . . . . 126 F2
Larchwood Cl LE2 . . . . . . 180 A7
Larchwood Rise LE15 . . . 136 A6
Larcot Garden Cl
  LE12. . . . . 101 E8
Lark Cl LE3 . . . . 152 F2
Larkin Cl LE11. . . . . 51 D4
Lark Rise LE11. . . . . 75 A6
Larkspur Cl LE5. . . . . 130 B3
Larkswood LE8 . . . . 224 B8
Lastingham Cl LE2 . . . . . . 180 A6
Latham Way LE9 . . . . 152 E4
Lathkilldale Cres NG10. . . 10 A5
Lathkill St LE16 . . . . 240 F1
Latimer Cl
  Blaby LE8. . . . . 202 A6
  Gretton NN17 . . . . 213 C1
Latimer Cres LE16 . . . . . . 240 F2
Latimer Ct LE17 . . . . 127 D5
Latimer Prim Sch The
  LE7 . . . . 127 E5
Latimer Rd LE7 . . . . 100 F3
Latimer St
  Anstey LE7. . . . . 127 E6
  Leicester LE3. . . . . 154 E4
Latymer Cl LE16 . . . . 251 E5
Laud Cl LE67 . . . . 95 E1
LAUGHTON 238 C7
Laughton Ct LE2 . . . . 155 D1
Laughton La LE17 . . . . . . 238 A6
Laughton Rd
  Laughton LE17. . . . . 238 F5
  Lubenham LE16 . . . . 239 C4
Launceston Dr LE67 . . . . . . 96 C7
Launceston Ho LE18 . . . . 203 C8
Launde Cl LE18 . . . . 180 C1
Launde Cross Rds
  LE7. . . . . 161 C6
Launde Gdns PE9 . . . . . . 143 A2
Launde Pk LE16 . . . . 241 A2
Launde Prim Sch LE2 . . . 181 B6
Launde Rd
  Leicester, Oadby LE2 . . . . 181 C6
  Markfield LE67. . . . . 125 C8
  Tilton on t H LE7 . . . . 161 B6
Laundon Cl LE16 . . . . 126 F2
Laundon Way
  Groby LE6. . . . . 126 E2
  Whetstone LE8 . . . . 202 A5
Laundry La LE4 . . . . 129 B3
Launds Gn NG33 . . . . 65 A4
Laura Davies Cl LE13. . . . . 59 C6
Laural Bank Cl LE7. . . . . . 103 C6
Laurel Cl
  Glenfield LE3 . . . . 153 E8
  Mountsorrel LE12 . . . . 76 E2
Laurel Cres NG10 . . . . 10 C6
Laurel Dr
  Aston-on-T DE72 . . . . 16 A7
  Countesthorpe LE8 . . . . . 202 E4
  Leicester, Oadby LE2 . . . . 181 D3
Laurel Fields LE17 . . . . . . 232 E6
Laurel Rd
  Blaby LE8. . . . . 202 B7
  Leicester LE2. . . . . 155 C4
  Loughborough LE11. . . . . . 75 A7
  Narborough LE19. . . . . . . 178 C4
  Swithland LE12 . . . . 100 D5
Laurels The LE67 . . . . 125 E6
Laurel Way NG13 . . . . 2 F3
Laureston Dr LE2 . . . . 155 D2

Lavender Cl
  Blaby LE8. . . . . 202 B8
  Loughborough LE11. . . . . . 75 A6
  Lutterworth LE17. . . . . . . 244 A6
Lavender Ho LE13. . . . . 59 D3
Lavender Rd LE3. . . . . 154 C3
Lavender Way PE9 . . . . . . 142 F5
Lavender Wlk LE67. . . . . . . 70 B7
Laverstock Rd LE18 . . . . . 203 C8
Lawford Rd LE2 . . . . 179 D4
Lawn Ave LE4 . . . . 129 B7
Lawn Cl LE4 . . . . 129 F6
Lawn La LE14 . . . . 35 E2
Lawns Bsns Ctr The 6
  LE10 . . . . 215 E8
Lawns Dr LE11 . . . . 44 A7
Lawns The
  Aston-on-T DE72 . . . . 16 B8
  Hinckley LE10 . . . . 215 E8
Lawnswood LE10 . . . . 215 A8
Lawnwood Rd LE6 . . . . . . 126 D3
Lawrence Ave
  Birstall LE4 . . . . 101 C1
  Ellistown LE67 . . . . 96 C4
  Market Overton LE15. . . . . 86 F5
Lawrence Cl
  Market Bosworth LE9 . . . . 100 C5
Lawrence Ho 12 LE10 . . . 197 D1
Lawrence St LE10 . . . . 10 D8
Lawrence Way LE11. . . . . . 51 C7
Lawson Ave NG10 . . . . 10 E7
Lawson Cl LE4 . . . . 129 F6
Lawson Ct 3 LE12 . . . . . . 77 C3
Law St LE4 . . . . 129 A1
Laxton Cl LE10 . . . . 214 F8
Laxton Cl
  Birstall LE4 . . . . 129 B8
  Wigston LE18. . . . . 180 F2
Laycock Ave LE13 . . . . 59 C4
Layton Ho LE5 . . . . 155 E7
Layton Rd LE5 . . . . 155 E7
Lea Cl
  Broughton Astley LE9 . . . 219 A5
  Thurmaston LE4. . . . . 129 F7
Lea Dr LE11 . . . . 75 B7
Lea La LE67 . . . . 98 F4
Leacrofts The LE67 . . . . . . 95 E8
Lea Dr LE11 . . . . 75 B7
Leake La LE12 . . . . 31 D3
Lealand The LE16 . . . . 250 B8
Leamington Dr LE8 . . . . . 202 B6
Leamington Terr
  LE15. . . . . 189 B4
Leas Cl LE7 . . . . 156 F6
Leas The LE15 . . . . 112 C8
Lea The LE8 . . . . 206 B1
Leatherlands DE74. . . . . . . 18 D3
Leather Mill La CV10 . . . . 194 D4
Lea View LE9 . . . . 116 E2
Leawood Rd DE11. . . . . . . 44 D7
Leckhampton Rd LE11 . . . 51 C4
Leconfield Rd LE11 . . . . . . 74 C8
Ledbury Cl LE2 . . . . 181 D4
Ledbury Gn LE4 . . . . 128 D5
Ledbury Rd LE11 . . . . 74 F7
Ledbury Wlk LE15. . . . . . . 87 E2
Ledwell Dr LE3 . . . . 127 C1
Lee Cl LE9 . . . . 199 E3
Leecrofts The LE9 . . . . . . 198 F8
Lee Rise LE6. . . . . 152 D8
Lees Cres LE67 . . . . 72 A5
Leeside LE9 . . . . 150 F8
Leeson St LE2 . . . . 179 E7
Lee St LE1 . . . . 259 C4
LEESTHORPE 108 D7
Leesthorpe Rd LE14. . . . . 108 D6
Legion Dr LE67 . . . . 122 F8
Legion Way LE19 . . . . 178 D8
LEICESTER 259 C1
Leicester Airport LE2 . . . 182 B8
Leicester Coll (Abbey Park
  Campus) LE1. . . . . 155 A8
Leicester Coll (Bede
  Island Campus) LE3. . . . 154 D3
Leicester Coll (Freeman's
  Park Campus) LE2 . . . . . 154 F3
Leicester Coll (St
  Margarets Campus)
  LE1 . . . . 259 B5
Leicester Commercial Coll
  LE1 . . . . 259 B3
Leicester Cres CV9. . . . . . 170 E1
LEICESTER FOREST EAST
  . . . . 152 D2
LEICESTER FOREST WEST
  . . . . 177 A8
Leicester General Hospl
  LE5 . . . . 156 A4
Leicester Gram Jun Sch
  LE5 . . . . 156 C4
Leicester Gram Sch
  Leicester LE1. . . . . 259 A3
  Leicester LE1. . . . . 259 B3
Leicester High Sch for
  Girls LE2. . . . . 180 E8
Leicester Hospl (BUPA)
  LE2 . . . . 156 A1
Leicester Islamic Acad
  LE2 . . . . 155 C2
Leicester La
  Desford LE9. . . . . 151 D2
  Great Bowden LE16. . . . . 240 D7
  Narborough LE19. . . . . . . 178 C4
  Swithland LE12 . . . . 100 D5
Leicester Mus of Science,
  Ind & Tech * LE4. . . . . . 128 F2

Leicester North Sta *
  LE4 . . . . 128 F5
Leicester Pl LE13 . . . . 59 C3
Leicester Rd
  Anstey LE7. . . . . 127 E5
  Ashby-de-la-Z LE65 . . . . . 69 D5
  Barwell LE9 . . . . 198 C5
  Belton-in-R LE15 . . . . 187 C6
  Billesdon LE7. . . . . 158 E3
  Blaby LE8. . . . . 202 B8
  Broughton Astley LE9 . . . 218 E7
  Countesthorpe LE8 . . . . . 202 F5
  Croft LE9 . . . . 200 D1
  Earl Shilton LE9 . . . . 175 F2
  Fleckney LE8 . . . . 222 F8
  Frisby on t W LE14 . . . . . . 80 D7
  Glenfield LE3 . . . . 127 D2
  Glen Parva LE2, LE8 . . . . 179 B3
  Groby LE6. . . . . 127 A3
  Hinckley LE10, LE9 . . . . . 197 F2
  Husbands Bosworth
    LE17 . . . . 247 D6
  Ibstock LE67 . . . . 96 A3
  Kibworth Beauchamp
    LE8 . . . . 205 D3
  Leicester, Oadby LE2 . . . . 180 F7
  Loughborough LE11,
    LE12. . . . . 52 C2
  Lutterworth LE17. . . . . . . 234 C2
  Market Harborough
    LE16 . . . . 240 D5
  Markfield LE67. . . . . 98 E1
  Markfield LE67. . . . . 125 F8
  Measham DE12 . . . . 93 D5
  Melton Mowbray LE13. . . . 59 B2
  Mountsorrel LE7, LE12 . . . 76 F1
  Mowsley LE17 . . . . 237 E6
  Narborough LE19. . . . . . . 178 D1
  Narborough LE19. . . . . . . 201 C8
  Quorn (Quorndon) LE12. . 76 B5
  Ravenstone LE67. . . . . 96 A7
  Sapcote LE9. . . . . 217 E7
  Sharnford LE10 . . . . 217 C4
  Shepshed LE12 . . . . 50 C2
  South Croxton LE7. . . . . . 133 B7
  Thurcaston LE4, LE7 . . . . 101 B2
  Tilton on t H LE7 . . . . 159 F8
  Uppingham LE15 . . . . 188 F5
  Uppingham, Wardley
    LE15 . . . . 188 C6
  Whitwick LE67. . . . . 72 B4
  Wigston LE18. . . . . 180 C4
Leicester Royal Infmy LE1,
  LE2 . . . . 259 B2
Leicester Royal Infmy
  Mus * LE2 . . . . 259 B2
Leicester St Martins
  Cathedral Church *
  LE1 . . . . 259 B3
Leicestershire Cty Crkt
  Gd * LE2 . . . . 179 E8
Leicestershire Hospice
  The LE3. . . . . 128 A1
Leicester St
  Leicester LE5. . . . . 155 D6
  Long Eaton NG10. . . . . . . 10 E6
  Melton Mowbray LE13. . . . 59 C3
Leicester Sta LE2 . . . . 259 C3
Leicester Tigers (Rugby
  Football Gd) LE2 . . . . . . 259 B1
Leighfield Prim Sch
  LE15. . . . . 189 A3
Leighton Ave LE11 . . . . 51 B3
Leighton Cres LE9 . . . . . . 198 F5
LEIRE 218 F1
Leire La
  Ashby Parva LE17 . . . . . . 233 F7
  Broughton Astley LE9 . . . 218 E4
  Dunton Bassett LE17. . . . 219 C1
Leire Rd LE17. . . . . 218 D1
Leire St LE4 . . . . 129 B2
Leith Cl LE65 . . . . 69 D5
Lema Cl LE4 . . . . 129 E5
Lemon Gr DE11 . . . . 44 A7
Lemontree La LE11 . . . . . . 75 A7
Lemyngton St LE11 . . . . . . 52 B4
Lena Dr LE6 . . . . 126 C5
Len Hollis Ct 6 LE2. . . . . 155 B5
Lenthall Sq LE16. . . . . 240 E1
Leopold Cl LE8 . . . . 202 D4
Leopold Rd LE2. . . . . 155 A1
Leopold St
  Long Eaton NG10. . . . . . . 10 D8
  Loughborough LE11. . . . . . 51 F4
  Wigston LE18. . . . . 179 F1
Leslie Cl LE11 . . . . 51 D7
Leslie Holes Ct LE1 . . . . . 259 B2
Lester Ct LE12 . . . . 29 A4
Letchworth Rd LE3. . . . . . 154 A5
Lethbridge Cl
  Leicester LE1. . . . . 259 C5
  Oakham LE15. . . . . 138 B6
Leven Cl LE10 . . . . 215 B8
Leven Way NN17. . . . . 230 B1
Leveret Dr LE8 . . . . 201 F6
Leveric Rd LE5 . . . . 155 E8
Lever Rd CV21 . . . . 257 A1
Lewett Cl LE4 . . . . 128 D4
Lewis Cl LE4 . . . . 129 F3
Lewis Rd LE11 . . . . 51 D5
Lewis Way LE8 . . . . 202 F3
Lexham St LE4 . . . . 129 B2
Leyburn Cl
  Nuneaton CV11 . . . . 214 A2

Leyburn Cl continued
Swadlincote DE11 . . . . . . 44 B1
Leybury Way LE7 . . . . . . 156 F7
Leycroft Rd LE4 . . . . . . 128 C5
Leyland Rd LE3 . . . . 178 F7
Leys Cl LE2 . . . . 181 C6
Leys Cres LE17 . . . . 246 D1
Leysdale Cl LE4 . . . . 128 B3
Leys Dr LE2 . . . . 181 B4
Leysland Ave LE8 . . . . . . 202 C4
Leysland High Sch
LE8 . . . . 202 C4
Leysmill Cl LE10 . . . . . . 196 F1
Leys The
Countesthorpe LE8 . . . . 202 C3
East Goscote LE7 . . . . . . 103 E8
Hathern LE12 . . . . 51 A8
Hinckley LE10 . . . . 216 A6
Kibworth Beauchamp
LE8 . . . . 206 A1
Leicester LE4 . . . . 128 B3
Newton CV23 . . . . 253 A1
Welford NN6 . . . . 256 B6
Leyton Cl LE17 . . . . 244 D5
Liberty Pk LE2 . . . . 259 A1
Liberty Rd LE3 . . . . 153 D7
Libra Par LE4 . . . . 129 B7
Library Cl LE10 . . . . 216 A5
Lichfield Ave
Broughton Astley LE9 . . . 218 D8
Swadlincote DE11 . . . . . . 44 E5
Lichfield Cl CV11 . . . . . . 214 A7
Lichfield Dr LE8 . . . . . . 202 B6
Lichfield St LE1 . . . . 259 B5
Lidster Cl LE5 . . . . 156 B8
Lightfoot La LE16 . . . . . . 229 B1
Lilac Ave LE5 . . . . 130 C1
Lilac Cl
Hinckley LE10 . . . . 215 E6
Loughborough LE11 . . . . . 75 A4
Lilac Dr LE17 . . . . 244 A6
Lilac Way
East Goscote LE7 . . . . . . 103 F7
Melton Mowbray LE13 . . . . 59 B6
LILBOURNE 258 A6
Lilbourne Rd CV23 . . . . . 257 C5
Lilleshall Way LE11 . . . . . 51 B5
Lillingstone Cl LE67 . . . . . 98 E1
Lily Bank LE67 . . . . 71 C8
Lily Cotts LE67 . . . . 71 A8
Lily Marriott Ho LE2 . . . 179 B4
LILYPOOL 26 B7
Lilypools The DE73 . . . . . 26 B7
Limber Cres LE3 . . . . . . 153 E3
Limby Hall La LE67 . . . . . 71 A6
Lime Ave
Groby LE6 . . . . 126 F1
Loughborough LE11 . . . . . 52 C3
Measham DE12 . . . . 93 C6
Lime Cl LE7 . . . . 103 C3
Lime Dr LE7 . . . . 103 C3
Limefield LE15 . . . . 138 A8
Lime Gr
Bagworth LE67 . . . . 124 B5
Blaby LE8 . . . . 202 B8
Bottesford NG13 . . . . 3 A2
Earl Shilton LE9 . . . . . . 198 E7
Kirby Muxloe LE9 . . . . . 152 D5
Long Eaton NG10 . . . . 10 D8
Lime Grove Cl LE4 . . . . . 128 C4
Limehurst Ave LE11 . . . . . 52 A5
Limehurst High Sch
LE11 . . . . 52 B5
Limehurst Rd LE5 . . . . . 130 D1
Lime Kilns LE18 . . . . . . 203 E8
Limekilns The DE73 . . . . . 26 F2
Lime Kilns The LE12 . . . . 76 D8
Limekiln The★ PE9 . . . . 115 B8
Limes Ave LE13 . . . . 59 D4
Lime St LE14 . . . . 82 F6
Limes The
Market Overton LE15 . . . . 86 F5
Ravenstone LE67 . . . . 71 A2
Thorpe Langton LE16 . . . 226 A5
Limestone Cl DE11 . . . . . 45 A4
Lime Terr NG10 . . . . 10 D8
Limetree Ave DE11 . . . . . 44 B7
Lime Tree Ave
Birstall LE4 . . . . 129 A8
Uppingham LE15 . . . . . . 189 A5
Limetree Gr ◼ LE11 . . . . 52 C5
Lime Tree Rd LE19 . . . . . 178 D2
Linacres Rd LE3 . . . . . . 153 E3
Lincoln Ct LE16 . . . . . . 240 F5
Lincoln Dr
Blaby LE8 . . . . 202 B6
Melton Mowbray LE13 . . . . 82 D8
Syston LE7 . . . . 103 C2
Wigston LE18 . . . . 179 F2
Lincoln Rd
Barwell LE9 . . . . 198 A6
Stamford PE9 . . . . 143 E5
Lincoln St LE2 . . . . 155 B5
Lincoln Way DE11 . . . . . . 44 E5
Linden Ave LE8 . . . . 202 C4
Linden Cl LE67 . . . . 95 E2
Linden Dr
Leicester LE5 . . . . 156 A3
Lutterworth LE17 . . . . . . 244 B6
Linden Farm Dr LE8 . . . . 202 E4
Linden Gr LE12 . . . . 76 E1
Linden La LE9 . . . . 152 F4
Linden Prim Sch LE5 . . . . 156 A3
Linden Rd
Hinckley LE10 . . . . 197 C1

Linden Rd continued
Loughborough LE11 . . . . . 52 A5
Linden St LE5 . . . . 155 E5
Linden Way LE67 . . . . 71 C2
Lindfield Rd LE3 . . . . . . 154 A6
Lindisfarne Dr LE11 . . . . 51 B5
Lindisfarne Rd
Corby NN17 . . . . 230 C1
Syston LE7 . . . . 102 F3
Lindrick Dr LE5 . . . . 155 E2
Lindridge La LE9 . . . . . . 151 A6
Lindsay Ct DE11 . . . . 44 B3
Lindsay Rd LE3 . . . . 154 B1
Lindsey Gdns LE16 . . . . . 250 D8
Lindsey Rd
Stamford PE9 . . . . 143 E4
Uffington PE9 . . . . 144 E4
Lindum Cl LE1 . . . . 102 F2
Lineker Rd LE2 . . . . 154 E1
Linford Cl LE18 . . . . 180 E3
Linford Cres
Coalville LE67 . . . . 72 B1
Markfield LE67 . . . . 125 E8
Linford Rd LE11 . . . . 51 E1
Linford St LE4 . . . . 129 A3
Ling Dale LE7 . . . . 103 E8
Lingdale Cl LE11 . . . . 52 B1
Lingdale Ho LE11 . . . . . . 52 B1
Ling Rd LE11 . . . . 52 B1
Lings LE32 . . . . 22 F7
Linkfield Ave LE12 . . . . . . 76 E1
Linkfield Rd LE12 . . . . . . 76 E1
Link Rd
Anstey LE7 . . . . 127 D7
Leicester LE2 . . . . 180 E7
Queniborough LE7 . . . . . 103 D5
Link Rise LE67 . . . . 125 F8
Links Cl LE67 . . . . 96 D6
Links Rd
Kibworth Beauchamp
LE8 . . . . 224 B8
Kirby Muxloe LE9 . . . . . 152 C5
Linkway Gdns LE3 . . . . . 154 C5
Linley Ave LE12 . . . . 50 C2
Linley Gn LE9 . . . . 201 D3
Linnet Cl
Melton Mowbray LE13 . . . . 82 B8
Rugby CV23 . . . . 252 C1
Linnet Ct LE15 . . . . 189 A5
Linnett Cl LE19 . . . . 201 A7
Linney Rd LE4 . . . . 128 C3
Linthwaite Ct DE74 . . . . . 28 B5
Linthwaite Cl LE4 . . . . . 129 D4
Linton St LE5 . . . . 155 C4
Linwal Ave LE7 . . . . 157 F4
Linwood Ct LE10 . . . . . . 197 B2
Linwood La LE2 . . . . 179 F5
Lionville Cotts LE14 . . . . . 38 D8
Lipton Rd LE4 . . . . 128 B6
Liskeard Cl CV11 . . . . . . 214 A5
Lisle St LE11 . . . . 52 A5
Lismore Dr LE10 . . . . . . 197 C1
Lismore Wlk NN17 . . . . . 230 C1
Lister Cl NN17 . . . . 230 F1
Lister Rd CV9 . . . . 170 E1
Litelmede LE5 . . . . 155 E7
Little Ave LE4 . . . . 129 B3
Little Barley Cl LE4 . . . . 128 B3
LITTLE BOWDEN 241 A2
Little Bowden Manor
LE16 . . . . 240 F3
Little Bowden Sch
LE16 . . . . 240 F2
Little Bytham Rd NG33 . . . 90 C8
LITTLE CASTERTON 143 C8
Little Casterton Rd
PE9 . . . . 143 B6
Little Church La LE12 . . . . 77 C3
Little Cl DE11 . . . . 44 B5
Little Connery Leys
LE4 . . . . 102 A1
LITTLE DALBY 83 A1
Little Dalby Rd
Great Dalby LE14 . . . . . . 82 B1
Little Dalby LE14 . . . . . . 83 A1
Little Dale LE18 . . . . . . 180 C1
Little Dunmow Rd
LE5 . . . . 155 F8
Littlefare The LE3 . . . . . 153 D2
Littlefield La LE9 . . . . . . 151 B3
Little Glen Rd LE2 . . . . . 179 D1
Little Haw La LE12 . . . . . 50 A3
Little Hill Prim Sch
LE18 . . . . 180 C1
Little Holme St LE3 . . . . 154 D5
Littlejohn Rd LE2 . . . . . 179 E4
Little La
Desford LE9 . . . . 151 B4
Greetham LE15 . . . . 88 B1
Leire LE17 . . . . 233 F8
Mountsorrel LE12 . . . . . . 76 E2
Little London La
CV23 . . . . 253 A1
Little Lunnon LE17 . . . . . 219 C1
Little Masons Cl LE3 . . . 153 D1
Littlemeer Cl LE3 . . . . . 153 D1
Little Mill Cl CV13 . . . . . 149 C8
Little Moor La LE11 . . . . . 52 D4
Little Moorside DE72 . . . . 16 B8
Littlemore Cl LE5 . . . . . 155 F6
LITTLE ORTON 145 F6
Little Shaw La LE67 . . . . . 98 A3
LITTLE STRETTON 182 E5
Little Thorn Ind Est
DE11 . . . . 44 F2
LITTLETHORPE 201 C6

Littleton St LE4 . . . . 154 D7
LITTLE TWYCROSS 146 E7
LITTLE WALTON 242 E3
Littleway The LE5 . . . . . 155 F6
Little Wood Cl LE4 . . . . . 128 C4
Littleworth 67 D8
Littleworth La LE15 . . . . 187 D6
Livesey Dr LE9 . . . . 217 C7
Livia Cl LE10 . . . . 196 F1
Livingstone Cl LE15 . . . . 138 A8
Livingstone St LE3 . . . . . 154 C4
Llewellyn Ct LE2 . . . . . . 155 D1
Loake Ct ◼ DE73 . . . . . . 26 A8
Lobbs Wood Cl LE5 . . . . 156 B8
Lobbs Wood Ct LE5 . . . . 156 B8
Lobelia Cl
Hinckley LE10 . . . . 215 E5
Narborough LE19 . . . . . . 200 F8
LOBTHORPE 66 A6
Lochmore Cl LE10 . . . . . 215 A8
Lochmore Dr LE10 . . . . . 215 A8
Lochmore Way LE10 . . . . 215 A8
Locke Ave LE4 . . . . 129 D5
Lockerbie Ave LE4 . . . . . 129 C4
Lockerbie Wlk LE4 . . . . . 129 D4
Lock Gate LE18 . . . . 203 A8
Lockhouse Cl LE2 . . . . . 179 B4
Lockington Rd DE74 . . . . . 17 D5
Lock Keeper Cl LE18 . . . 203 A8
Lock La NG10 . . . . 10 C4
Lockley Cl LE6 . . . . 152 D8
Locksley Cl ◼ LE65 . . . . . 69 A7
Locks The
Loughborough LE11 . . . . . 51 F6
Rugby CV21 . . . . 257 B1
Lockton Cl LE65 . . . . 69 C7
LODDINGTON 161 E1
Loddington La
Belton-in-R LE15 . . . . . . 187 B8
East Norton LE7 . . . . . . 186 D7
Loddington Rd LE7 . . . . . 160 C6
Loddon Cl LE13 . . . . 59 B1
Lodge Cl
Ashby-de-la-Z LE65 . . . . . 69 A5
Atherstone CV9 . . . . 194 A6
Barrow-u-S LE12 . . . . 76 D7
Hinckley LE10 . . . . 216 A5
Huncote LE9 . . . . 200 D8
Kibworth Beauchamp
LE8 . . . . 205 F2
Melton Mowbray LE13 . . . . 59 B2
Syston LE7 . . . . 103 C4
Thurmaston LE4 . . . . . . 129 F6
Lodge Est DE72 . . . . 16 B7
Lodge Farm Rd LE5 . . . . 156 C6
Lodge Gdns LE15 . . . . . . 138 A6
Lodge La LE7 . . . . 100 D3
Lodge Mews
Aston-on-T DE72 . . . . 16 B7
Thurnby LE7 . . . . 156 F2
Lodge Park Tech Coll
NN17 . . . . 230 B1
Lodge Pk LE15 . . . . 110 B2
Lodge Rd
Fleckney LE8 . . . . 222 F6
Long Eaton NG10 . . . . 10 D5
Netherseal DE12 . . . . 91 F8
Lodge St DE72 . . . . 9 A7
Lodge Stables ◼
LE15 . . . . 138 A4
Lodge The LE15 . . . . . . 138 A6
Lodgewood Ave LE4 . . . . 128 F7
Logan Ave LE2 . . . . 179 C6
Logan Cres LE16 . . . . . . 240 C4
Logan Ct LE16 . . . . 240 D4
Logan St LE16 . . . . 240 D3
Loire Cl LE65 . . . . 69 A7
Lombard St NG13 . . . . 2 A6
Lombardy Rise LE5 . . . . 155 C7
Lomond Cl
Corby NN17 . . . . 230 C1
Hinckley LE10 . . . . 215 B8
Lomond Cres LE4 . . . . . 128 C2
London La
Willoughby-on-t-W
LE12 . . . . 34 D7
Wymeswold LE12 . . . . . . 33 B3
London Rd
Castle Donington DE72 . . . 17 B8
Coalville LE67 . . . . 96 E8
Great Glen LE8 . . . . 205 D6
Hinckley LE10 . . . . 215 E8
Kegworth DE74 . . . . 29 C6
Leicester LE2 . . . . 155 B3
Leicester, Oadby LE2 . . . 181 B5
Leicester, Oadby LE2 . . . 181 C2
Leicester, South Knighton
LE2 . . . . 180 E8
Markfield LE65 . . . . 125 E8
Shardlow DE72 . . . . 9 A1
Uppingham LE15 . . . . . . 189 B3
Wothorpe PE9 . . . . 169 F7
London St LE5 . . . . 155 D6
Longate Rd LE13 . . . . 59 C6
Long Brimley Cl LE16 . . . 241 B3
Long Cl
Anstey LE7 . . . . 127 C7
Barrow-u-S LE12 . . . . 76 C8
Quorn (Quorndon) LE12 . . . 75 F7
LONG CLAWSON 20 D3
Long Clawson CE Prim
Sch LE14 . . . . 20 C3
Longcliff Cl LE4 . . . . 35 D4
Longcliffe Gdns LE11 . . . . 74 A7

Longcliffe Rd
Leicester LE5 . . . . 155 C7
Shepshed LE12 . . . . 50 A3
Longcliff Hill LE14 . . . . . . 35 E4
Longcliff Rd LE67 . . . . . . 97 B8
Long Croft DE72 . . . . 16 A8
LONG EATON 10 C7
Long Eaton Sch The
NG10 . . . . 10 C6
Long Eaton Sta NG10 . . . . 10 C6
Long Eaton Trade Ctr
NG10 . . . . 10 F8
Longfellow Rd LE2 . . . . . 180 A8
Long Field High Sch The
LE13 . . . . 59 A2
Longfield Rd LE13 . . . . . . 59 D6
Longford Cl LE18 . . . . . . 203 C8
Long Furlong LE12 . . . . . 101 D8
Long Furrow LE7 . . . . . . 103 E8
Longgrey LE8 . . . . 204 E1
Longhade Furlong
LE7 . . . . 127 F7
Long Hassocks CV23 . . . . 252 E1
Longhedge La
Bottesford NG13 . . . . 2 F3
Orston NG13 . . . . 2 E1
Long Hedge La LE65 . . . . 47 E6
Longhedge Lane Ind Est
NG13 . . . . 2 F3
Long Holden DE74, ... 28 E5
Longhurst Cl LE4 . . . . . . 129 E5
Long La
Billesdon LE7 . . . . 159 B2
Bottesford NG13 . . . . 13 B7
Coalville LE67 . . . . 71 E1
Hickling LE14 . . . . 19 C6
Kegworth DE74 . . . . 18 D5
Leicester LE1 . . . . 259 A4
Owston LE15 . . . . 135 B4
Redmile NG13 . . . . 6 F1
Stathern LE14 . . . . 12 F4
Longlands Rd DE11 . . . . . 44 D7
Longlands The LE16 . . . . 241 B3
Longleat Cl
Leicester LE5 . . . . 155 D8
Market Harborough
LE16 . . . . 241 B3
Long Meadow Dr
LE10 . . . . 214 F7
Long Meadow Way
LE15 . . . . 112 D8
Long Mere La LE12,
DE74 . . . . 28 C3
Long Row
Newton Harcourt LE8 . . . 204 D6
Oakham LE15 . . . . 137 F6
Shardlow DE72 . . . . 9 B2
Sibson CV13 . . . . 172 A6
Long Shoot The CV11 . . . 214 C6
Longslade Com Coll
LE4 . . . . 102 B1
Long St
Belton LE12 . . . . 49 B6
Stoney Stanton LE9 . . . . 199 E2
Wigston LE18 . . . . 180 D2
Longstock Rd CV23 . . . . 252 D1
Longstone Gn LE5 . . . . . 156 E7
LONG WHATTON 29 B3
Long Whatton CE Prim
Sch LE12 . . . . 29 C3
Longwill Ave LE13 . . . . . . 59 D4
Lonsborough Gdns
LE15 . . . . 110 B2
Lonsdale Ct LE4 . . . . . . 129 E6
Lonsdale Rd
Stamford PE9 . . . . 143 A3
Thurmaston LE4 . . . . . . 129 E6
Lonsdale St LE2 . . . . . . 155 C4
Lonsdale Way LE15 . . . . 137 E6
Lord Burghley's Hospl
PE9 . . . . 143 E2
Lord Byron St LE2 . . . . . 180 A8
Lord Cl LE19 . . . . 201 B7
Lord Crewe Cl LE5 . . . . . 150 B4
Lord Morton's Covert
(Nature Reserve)★
LE7 . . . . 159 C7
Lords Ave LE4 . . . . 128 C7
Lords Cl LE67 . . . . 97 A7
Lordship La NG13 . . . . 2 A6
Lord's La NG33 . . . . 43 B8
Lorne Rd LE2 . . . . 155 B1
Lorraine Rd LE2 . . . . . . 179 E7
Lorrimer Rd LE2 . . . . . . 179 E8
Lorrimer Way LE11 . . . . . 51 C5
Loseby La LE1 . . . . 259 B3
Losecoat Cl PE9 . . . . . . 143 F5
Lossiemouth Rd LE10 . . . 196 F1
Lothair Rd LE2 . . . . 154 E1
Lothian Pl DE74 . . . . 17 A3
Loudon Ct ◼ LE65 . . . . . 69 B6
Loudoun Pl DE74 . . . . . . 17 A4
Loudoun Way LE65 . . . . . 68 F5
Loughbon NG13 . . . . 2 A7
LOUGHBOROUGH 52 D1
Loughborough CE Prim
Sch LE11 . . . . 51 F3
Loughborough Coll
LE11 . . . . 51 F3
Loughborough Cotts
LE4 . . . . 129 A2
Loughborough Gram Sch
LE11 . . . . 52 B2
Loughborough High Sch
LE11 . . . . 52 B3

Loughborough Hospl
LE11 . . . . 51 E4
Loughborough Pk
LE11 . . . . 51 B1
Loughborough Rd
Asfordby LE14 . . . . 57 D3
Birstall LE4 . . . . 129 A7
Burton o t W LE12 . . . . . . 53 E7
Cotes LE11 . . . . 52 F6
Cotes LE12 . . . . 53 B6
East Leake LE12 . . . . 31 F7
Hathern LE12 . . . . 51 A8
Hoton LE12 . . . . 53 B8
Loughborough LE12 . . . . . 75 D8
North End LE12 . . . . 76 D3
Peggs Green LE67 . . . . . . 71 A7
Quorn (Quorndon) LE12 . . . 75 E6
Rempstone LE12 . . . . 32 D6
Rothley LE7 . . . . 102 A5
Shepshed LE12 . . . . 50 C4
Thringstone LE67 . . . . . . 71 D8
Walton on t W LE12 . . . . . 53 F4
Whitwick LE67 . . . . 71 F6
Loughborough Sta
LE11 . . . . 52 C5
Loughborough Tech Ctr
LE11 . . . . 51 F3
Loughborough Univ
LE11 . . . . 51 E3
Loughborough Univ Sch of
Art & Design
Loughborough LE11 . . . . . 51 F3
Loughborough LE11 . . . . . 52 A4
Loughland Cl LE8 . . . . . 202 A8
Louise Ave LE6 . . . . 126 F2
Lound Rd LE9 . . . . 217 D8
LOUNT 47 B3
Lount Rd CV13 . . . . 148 F8
Lounts Cres LE16 . . . . . 229 D7
Loveday Cl CV9 . . . . 170 D2
Love La LE10 . . . . 216 A6
Lovelace Cl CV13 . . . . . . 172 A6
Lovelace Cres LE9 . . . . . 198 F5
Lovelace Way LE8 . . . . . 223 A7
Loves La
Dunton Bassett LE17 . . . 219 D1
Empingham LE15 . . . . . . 141 A8
Lovett Ct LE12 . . . . 77 C3
Lovetts Cl LE10 . . . . 214 F8
Loveys Croft DE73 . . . . . . 26 E2
Lowcroft Dr LE2 . . . . . . 181 C4
Lower Bond St LE10 . . . . 197 D1
Lower Brand LE67 . . . . . . 48 A4
Lower Brook St NG10 . . . . 10 E7
Lower Brown St LE1 . . . . 259 B2
Lower Cambridge St
LE11 . . . . 52 B5
Lower Church St
Ashby-de-la-Z LE65 . . . . . 69 B6
Syston LE7 . . . . 103 B4
Lower Farm Cl LE15 . . . . 141 B6
Lower Free La LE1 . . . . . 259 B4
Lower Gladstone St
LE11 . . . . 52 B5
Lower Gn LE11 . . . . 74 D8
Lower Hastings St
LE1 . . . . 259 C2
Lower Hill St LE1 . . . . . . 259 B4
Lower Hilmorton Rd ◼
CV21 . . . . 257 A1
Lower Holme LE12 . . . . . . 30 B3
Lower Keyham La
LE5 . . . . 130 B1
Lower Lee St LE1 . . . . . 259 B4
Lower Leicester Rd
LE17 . . . . 244 D6
LOWER MIDWAY 44 E6
Lower Moor Rd LE67 . . . . 70 E8
Lower Packington Rd
LE65 . . . . 69 B4
Lower St CV21 . . . . 257 B1
Lower Willow St LE1 . . . . 155 A7
LOWESBY 133 D3
Lowesby Cl LE13 . . . . 59 E2
Lowesby La
Tilton on t H LE7 . . . . . . 133 D4
Twyford LE14 . . . . 133 E8
Loweswater Cl
Barrow-u-S LE12 . . . . 53 D1
Nuneaton CV11 . . . . 214 A6
Loweswater Dr LE11 . . . . . 51 D1
Loweswater Gr LE65 . . . . 69 C4
Lowfields La NG32 . . . . . . 4 E6
Lowick Dr LE18 . . . . 180 C2
Lowland Ave LE3 . . . . . . 153 A2
Lowther Cl LE15 . . . . . . 110 C2
Lowther Way LE11 . . . . . . 52 B1
Low Woods La LE12 . . . . . 49 B3
Loxley Dr LE13 . . . . 59 B1
Loxley Rd LE3 . . . . 127 C1
Lubbesthorpe Bridle Rd
Braunstone Town LE3 . . . 153 E1
Enderby LE19, LE3 . . . . . 177 F8
Lubbesthorpe Rd LE3 . . . 178 E6
Lubbesthorpe Way
LE19 . . . . 178 E7
LUBENHAM 239 E3
Lubenham All Saints CE
Prim Sch LE16 . . . . . . 239 F3
Lubenham Hill LE16 . . . . 240 C2
Lubenham Rd
East Farndon LE16 . . . . . 240 B1
Marston Trussell LE16 . . . 239 D1
Lucas Rd LE10 . . . . 215 D6
Lucas Way LE9 . . . . 198 E7
Ludford Cl NG10 . . . . 10 E4
Ludgate Cl LE4 . . . . 128 E8
Ludlam Cl LE8 . . . . 202 C4

Ludlow Cl
 Leicester, Oadby LE2....181 C4
 Loughborough LE11.....74 C8
Ludlow Dr LE13.........59 C5
Ludlow Pl LE12.........50 A2
Luffenham Cl PE9......143 A3
Luffenham Rd
 Barrowden LE15........191 F6
 Ketton PE9............167 E4
 Lyndon LE15...........165 E5
Lullington Mews DE12...67 A3
Lullington Rd DE12.....67 A3
Lulworth Cl
 Leicester LE5.........156 A4
 Wigston LE18..........203 D7
Lumby's Terr PE9......143 E2
Lundy Cl LE10.........197 B1
Lunsford Rd LE5.......155 D8
Lupin Cl LE10.........215 D5
Luther St LE3.........154 C4
LUTTERWORTH...........244 A7
Lutterworth Gram Sch &
 Com Coll LE17.........244 B6
Lutterworth High Sch
 LE17.................244 B5
Lutterworth Mus★......244 D6
Lutterworth Rd
 Arnesby LE8...........221 D4
 Bitteswell LE17.......244 B8
 Blaby LE8.............202 B7
 Churchover CV23, LE17.252 D5
 Dunton Bassett LE17...219 E2
 Gilmorton LE17........235 B2
 Hinckley LE10.........216 C3
 Kimcote LE17..........235 E2
 Leicester LE2.........179 C6
 Lutterworth LE17......244 D4
 Nuneaton CV11.........214 A1
 Pailton CV23, LE17....242 D2
 Shawell LE17..........253 D6
 Swinford LE17.........254 B6
 Ullesthorpe LE17......233 C3
 Walcote LE17..........245 C4
 Whetstone LE8.........202 A3
Lyall Cl LE11.........51 D6
Lychgate Cl
 Cropston LE7..........100 E2
 Hinckley LE10.........216 A5
Lychgate La LE10......216 C5
Lydall Rd LE2.........179 E4
LYDDINGTON............212 C7
Lyddington Rd
 Caldecott LE15, L16...212 D2
 Gretton NN17..........213 A1
Lydford Rd LE4........129 E2
Lyle Cl
 Leicester LE4.........129 E5
 Melton Mowbray LE13...59 C6
Lyme Rd LE2...........155 C3
Lymington Rd LE5......156 D8
Lyn Cl LE3, LE7.......127 F3
Lyncote Rd LE3........179 B8
Lyncroft Leys LE7.....156 F7
Lyndale Cl LE4........129 E6
Lyndale Rd LE3........178 F8
Lynden Ave NG10.......10 D5
Lyndene Cl LE10.......198 F7
Lyndhurst Cl LE10.....216 A7
Lyndhurst Ct LE2......155 C2
Lyndhurst Rd LE2......181 A6
LYNDON................165 D5
Lyndon Dr LE2.........180 F6
Lyndon Hill Nature
 Reserve Visitor Ctr★
 LE15.................165 A8
Lyndon Rd
 Manton LE15...........164 F6
 North Luffenham LE15..166 B4
Lyndon Way PE9........143 A3
Lyndwood Ct LE2.......155 D1
Lyneham Cl LE10.......197 A1
Lyngate Ave LE4.......129 A8
Lynholme Rd LE2.......180 B6
Lynmouth Cl LE3.......153 C7
Lynmouth Dr
 Gilmorton LE17........235 C4
 Wigston LE18..........180 A5
Lynmouth Rd LE5.......156 D8
Lynton Cl
 Gilmorton LE17........235 C4
 Sileby LE12...........77 C1
Lynton Ct LE9.........198 B6
Lynton Rd LE13........59 A6
Lynwood Cl LE9........151 B3
Lyon Cl LE18..........180 A4
Lysander Cl LE10......215 E4
Lytham Rd LE2.........155 A1
Lytton Rd LE2.........155 B1

M

Mablowe Field LE18....203 E8
Macaulay Rd
 Lutterworth LE17......244 C8
 Rothley LE7...........101 E6
Macaulay St LE2.......179 E8
McCarthy Cl LE67......71 E5
McCarthy Rd LE2.......50 A3
Macdonald Rd LE4......129 A1
McDowell Way LE19....201 B7
Machin Dr LE9.........219 A4
Mackaness Cl LE17.....235 C4
McKenzie Way LE1......259 C5
McKenzie Wlk LE5......156 A5
Mackworth Cl DE11....44 B7
Maclean Ave LE11......51 C6

McNeil Gr DE72........9 A7
McVicker Cl LE5.......156 A6
Madeline Cl LE16......241 A5
Madeline Rd LE4.......128 C6
Madras Rd LE1.........155 B6
Magee Cl LE10.........197 C2
Magna Pk LE17.........243 C6
Magna Rd LE18.........180 A1
Magnolia Ave LE11.....75 A7
Magnolia Cl
 Leicester Forest East
 LE3..................152 A2
 Leicester LE2.........179 C5
Magnolia Dr LE17......244 B7
Magnus Rd LE4.........129 C2
Mahatma Gandhi Ho
 LE4..................155 B8
Maidenhair Cl LE11....75 A6
Maidenhead Ave LE5...130 D3
Maiden La PE9.........143 E3
Maiden St LE2.........102 F3
Maidenwell Ave LE5....130 C2
Maidstone Ho 12 LE2..155 B5
Maidstone Rd LE2......155 B5
Maidwell Cl LE18......180 F2
Maino Cres LE17.......244 B5
Main Rd
 Allexton LE15.........187 D5
 Asfordby Valley LE14..58 B3
 Austrey CV9...........119 B1
 Barleythorpe LE15.....137 E8
 Bilstone CV13.........147 C8
 Brentingby LE14.......60 D2
 Claybrooke Magna
 LE17.................232 E5
 Collyweston PE9.......168 D2
 Dingley LE16..........241 F3
 Glaston LE15..........190 B5
 Granby NG13...........5 A4
 Kirby Bellars LE14....81 B8
 Nether Broughton LE14.36 C7
 Newton Regis B79......118 C2
 Old Dalby LE14........35 E4
 Ratcliffe Culey CV9...171 B4
 Redmile NG13..........6 E4
 Sheepy Magna CV9.....171 A6
 Stainby NG33..........43 D2
 Twycross CV9..........146 D7
 Twyford LE14..........106 D1
 Uffington PE9.........144 E3
 Upton CV13............172 C4
 Whitwell LE15.........140 A6
 Wycomb LE14...........39 A6
Main St
 Allington NG32........4 F5
 Asfordby LE14.........57 F3
 Ashby Parva LE17......233 F5
 Ashley LE16...........227 F2
 Bagworth LE67.........124 B5
 Barkby LE7............130 C8
 Barlestone CV13.......149 D8
 Barrowden LE15........191 F5
 Barsby LE7............105 D3
 Barton in t B CV13....122 D1
 Beeby LE7.............131 C5
 Belmesthorpe PE9......117 A1
 Belton-in-R LE15......187 D7
 Bisbrooke LE15........189 E4
 Blackfordby DE11......68 B8
 Botcheston LE9........151 C6
 Branston NG32.........23 C8
 Breaston DE72.........9 D8
 Breedon on t H DE73...26 F2
 Broughton Astley LE9..218 E7
 Bruntingthorpe LE17...221 C1
 Buckminster NG33......42 D2
 Burrough on t H LE14..107 D2
 Burton Overy LE8......182 F1
 Cadeby CV13...........149 C1
 Caldecott LE16........230 B8
 Carlton CV13..........148 D7
 Clifton u D CV23......257 A5
 Clipsham LE15.........89 E5
 Congerstone CV13......147 D7
 Cosby LE9.............201 D2
 Cossington LE7........102 D8
 Cotesbach LE17........244 B1
 Cottesmore LE15.......112 C8
 Countesthorpe LE8.....202 F3
 Croxton Kerrial LE14..24 B7
 Dadlington CV13.......173 E1
 Drayton LE16..........229 A5
 Dunton Bassett LE17...219 D2
 East Farndon LE16.....250 D2
 East Langton LE16.....225 D6
 Eastwell LE14.........22 B6
 Eaton NG32............22 F7
 Egleton LE15..........138 D3
 Empingham LE15........141 A4
 Fleckney LE8..........222 F7
 Foxton LE16...........224 E1
 Frisby on t W LE14....80 D8
 Frolesworth LE17......218 B2
 Gaddesby LE7..........105 B7
 Gaulby LE7............183 D6
 Gilmorton LE17........235 C4
 Glenfield LE3.........127 B1
 Glooston LE16.........208 C4
 Goadby Marwood LE14...22 C1
 Granby NG13...........5 C5
 Great Bowden LE16.....241 A6
 Great Dalby LE14......82 A1
 Great Glen LE8........205 B8
 Great Oxendon LE16....250 E3
 Greetham LE15.........88 B3
 Grimston LE14.........57 B8
 Gumley LE16...........239 A8
 Gunby NG33............64 E8

Main St continued
 Harby LE14............12 A2
 Hartshorne DE11.......45 B6
 Heather LE67..........95 C2
 Hemington DE74........17 D5
 Hickling LE14.........19 C6
 Higham on t H CV13....196 A3
 Hoby LE7..............79 E8
 Holwell LE14..........37 F4
 Houghton on t H LE7...157 F3
 Huncote LE9...........200 D7
 Hungarton LE7.........132 C3
 Illston on t H LE7....183 F3
 Keyham LE7............131 D1
 Kibworth Beauchamp
 LE8..................206 A2
 Kilby LE18............204 A3
 Kirby Bellars LE14....81 B8
 Kirby Muxloe LE9......152 E6
 Kirkby Mallory LE9....175 C6
 Knossington LE15......136 A6
 Laughton LE17.........238 C2
 Leicester, Evington LE5...156 B3
 Leicester, Humberstone
 LE5..................156 B8
 Leicester LE3.........153 F2
 Leire LE17............218 F1
 Lockington DE74.......17 F5
 Loddington LE7........161 D1
 Long Eaton NG10.......10 E7
 Long Whatton LE12.....29 B4
 Lubenham LE16.........239 F3
 Lyddington LE15.......212 C7
 Market Bosworth CV13..148 F3
 Market Overton LE15...98 D1
 Markfield LE67........98 B5
 Medbourne LE16........228 A4
 Moira DE11............44 C1
 Mowsley LE17..........237 F7
 Muston NG13...........3 F1
 Nailstone CV13........123 B3
 Nethersdale LE12......91 F7
 Newbold Verdon LE9....150 B4
 Newton Burgoland
 LE67.................121 E7
 Newton CV23...........253 A1
 Newtown Linford LE6...126 D8
 Normanton le H LE67...94 F6
 Normanton on S LE12...30 D3
 Norton-J-T CV9........120 A2
 Oakthorpe DE12........93 A7
 Old Dalby LE14........36 A5
 Orton-on-t-H CV9......145 D4
 Osgathorpe LE12.......48 D3
 Overseal DE12.........67 B3
 Owston LE15...........135 B4
 Peatling Magna LE8....221 A6
 Peatling Parva LE17...235 F8
 Peckleton LE9.........175 F7
 Pickwell LE14.........108 D3
 Preston LE15..........164 C2
 Queniborough LE7......103 F5
 Ragdale LE14..........56 C4
 Ratby LE6.............152 C8
 Ratcliffe on t W LE7..78 C2
 Ravenstone LE67.......95 B8
 Redmile NG13..........6 F3
 Rempstone LE12........32 D5
 Ridlington LE15.......163 D2
 Rockingham LE16.......230 B4
 Rotherby LE14.........79 F6
 Saddington LE8........223 B4
 Saltby LE14...........24 E1
 Saxelbye LE14.........57 E7
 Scraptoft LE7.........156 F8
 Seaton LE15...........190 C1
 Sewstern NG33.........63 F8
 Shackerstone CV13.....121 E2
 Shangton LE8..........207 B5
 Shawell LE17..........253 D5
 Shearsby LE17.........222 A2
 Shenton CV13..........173 B5
 Skeffington LE7.......160 A2
 Slawston LE16.........209 B1
 Smeeton Westerby LE8..223 F6
 Smisby LE65...........45 F3
 Snarestone DE12.......121 A8
 South Croxton LE7.....105 B1
 Sproxton LE14.........41 F5
 Stanford on S LE12....31 C1
 Stanton u B LE67......97 F1
 Stapleton LE9.........174 F1
 Stathern LE14.........13 A3
 Stoke Dry LE15........211 F6
 Stoke Golding CV13....196 D7
 Stonesby LE14.........40 E6
 Sutton Bassett LE16...227 A1
 Sutton Bonington LE12..30 B7
 Sutton Cheney CV13....174 B6
 Swannington LE67......71 B5
 Swepstone LE67........94 D2
 Swithland LE12........100 E7
 Theddingworth LE17....248 D8
 Thistleton LE15.......87 E8
 Thornton LE67.........124 E4
 Thorpe by Water LE15..213 A5
 Thorpe Satchville LE14.106 E4
 Thringstone LE67......71 B7
 Thurlaston LE9........177 A3
 Thurmaston LE7........103 C1
 Thurnby LE7...........157 A4
 Tilton on t H, Cold Newton
 LE7..................133 B1
 Tilton on t H LE7.....160 A8
 Tugby LE7.............185 E6
 Tur Langton LE16......207 A2
 Twyford LE14..........106 D1
 Ullesthorpe LE17......233 B4

Main St continued
 Wakerley LE15.........192 A4
 Wardley LE15..........188 A5
 Whissendine LE15......84 F1
 Willey CV23...........242 F6
 Willoughby-on-t-W LE12.34 D7
 Willoughby Waterleys
 LE8..................220 C5
 Wilson DE73...........26 E6
 Woodhouse Eaves LE12..75 A2
 Woodthorpe LE12.......75 C7
 Worthington LE65......47 F5
 Wymondham LE14.......62 E2
 Zouch LE12............30 B3
Maitland Ave LE12.....76 E1
Maizefield LE10.......197 C4
Majolica Mews DE11....44 F2
Makey's Cl LE15.......166 A7
Malabar Rd LE1........155 B7
Malcolm Arc 2 LE1....259 B4
Malcolm Sargent Prim
 Sch The PE9..........143 A3
Malham Cl
 Leicester LE4.........128 C3
 Nuneaton CV11.........214 A2
Malham Way LE2........181 D5
Mallard Ave LE6.......126 E3
Mallard Cl
 Essendine PE9.........117 B6
 Measham DE12..........93 B3
Mallard Ct
 Oakham LE15...........137 F7
 Stamford PE9..........143 D2
Mallard Dr
 Hinckley LE10.........215 A4
 Syston LE7............102 F4
Mallard Rd
 Barrow-u-S LE12.......76 E8
 Mountsorrel LE12......76 F2
Mallard Way LE3.......152 E2
Malling Ave LE9.......218 E7
Malling Cl LE4........102 B1
Mallory Cl LE9........150 B3
Mallory Ho LE10.......215 D7
Mallory La 11 PE9....143 D3
Mallory Pl LE5........155 E8
Mallow Ct LE9.........198 C8
Mallow Cl LE5.........130 C3
Malmesbury Ave DE11...44 D6
Malthouse Cl CV13.....123 B3
Maltings LE17.........213 B1
Maltings Rd NN17......213 B1
Maltings The
 Ashley LE16...........227 F3
 Glenfield LE3.........127 B1
 Hamilton LE5..........130 D3
 10 Market Harborough
 LE16.................240 E3
 3 Oakham LE15.........138 A6
 Shardlow DE72.........9 B1
 Sileby LE12...........77 C3
 Stamford PE9..........143 E2
 Wothorpe PE9..........169 E8
Maltings Yd LE15......113 A3
Malting Yd PE9........143 E2
Malt Mill Bank 6
 LE9..................198 A6
Malton Dr LE2.........181 C6
Malvern Ave LE12......50 C2
Malvern Cres
 Ashby-de-la-Z LE65....69 A8
 Cosby LE9.............201 D3
Malvern Gdns 3 NG10..10 A8
Malvern Rd LE2........155 D2
Malvern Wlk LE5.......137 D6
Mammoth St LE67......71 D1
MANCETTER.............194 A6
Mancetter Rd CV9......194 A6
Manchester St NG10....10 D6
Mandarin Cl LE10......215 A6
Mandarin Way LE8......201 F4
Mandervell Rd LE2.....180 F5
Mandora La 6 LE2.....155 B4
Manitoba Rd LE1.......259 C5
Mann Cl LE3...........153 D2
Manners Cl PE9........144 F4
Manners Dr LE13.......59 D6
Manners Rd LE2........179 E2
Mannion Cres NG10....10 B5
Manor Brook Cl
 Coalville LE67........96 C5
 Stoney Stanton LE9....199 D8
Manor Cl
 1 Ashby-de-la-Z LE65..69 C5
 Hinckley LE10.........215 C5
 Leicester, Oadby LE2..181 B8
 Long Whatton LE12.....29 B4
 Melton Mowbray LE13...59 E5
 Ryhall PE9............116 F3
Manor Cres LE9........174 E2
Manor Ct
 Blaby LE8.............179 C1
 Breaston DE72.........9 E8
 Breedon on t H DE73...26 F3
 Cottingham LE16.......229 C1
 Leicester LE3.........128 A1
 Little Stretton LE2...182 D5
 Waltham on t W LE14...40 A6
 Willoughby-on-t-W LE12.33 D4
 Wymeswold LE12........33 A4
Manor Dr
 Leicester LE4.........128 A5
 Loughborough LE11.....75 B8
 Netherseal DE12.......91 F6
 Sileby LE12...........77 C2
 Worthington LE65......47 F5

Manor Farm Animal Ctr★
 LE12.................31 F8
Manor Farm Cl LE9.....218 F6
Manor Farm Ct LE7.....160 A8
Manor Farm La PE9.....117 B6
Manor Farm Mews
 DE72.................16 B8
Manor Farm Rd DE72....16 B8
Manor Farm Way LE3....153 C2
Manor Farm Wlk LE7....160 A8
Manor Farm Yd LE7.....160 A8
Manor Gdns
 Desford LE9...........151 B3
 Glenfield LE3.........153 C8
 Shepshed LE12.........50 B4
Manor Gn PE9..........167 F5
Manor High Sch LE2....181 D7
Manor House Cl LE10...216 E6
Manor House Gdns
 LE5..................156 B8
Manor House Prep Sch
 LE65.................69 C6
Manor House Rd NG10...10 F6
Manor La
 Barleythorpe LE15.....137 D8
 Clifton u D CV23......257 A5
 Glaston LE15..........190 B6
 Granby NG13...........5 A8
 Langham LE15..........110 C3
 Peckleton LE9.........175 F6
 Somerby LE14..........108 B1
Manorleigh DE72.......9 E8
Manor Leigh DE72......9 E8
Manor Paddock NG32....4 F5
Manor Pl 5 LE10......197 D1
Manor Rd
 Barlestone CV13.......149 C8
 Bitteswell LE17.......244 B8
 Carlby PE9............117 C8
 Claybrooke Magna
 LE17.................232 D6
 Coalville LE67........96 C6
 Cosby LE9.............201 D4
 Desford LE9...........151 B3
 Easthorpe NG13........3 C2
 Fleckney LE8..........223 A7
 Great Bowden LE16.....241 A6
 Heather LE67..........95 B2
 Leicester, Oadby LE2..181 A8
 Loughborough LE11.....75 B8
 Medbourne LE16........228 A4
 Sapcote LE9...........217 D8
 Stretton LE15.........88 F4
 Thurmaston LE4........129 D6
 Ullesthorpe LE17......233 A4
Manor Road Extension
 ....181 B7
Manor St
 Hinckley LE10.........197 C1
 Wigston LE18..........180 B2
Manor View
 Hartshorne DE11.......45 B6
 Ketton PE9............168 A6
 Sibson CV13...........172 A6
Manor Way LE9.........215 D5
Manor Wlk LE16........240 E3
Mansfield Ave LE12....76 A6
Mansfield Cl DE11.....44 D4
Mansfield St
 Leicester LE1.........259 B4
 Quorn (Quorndon) LE12.76 A6
Mansion House Gdns
 LE13.................59 C6
Mansion House Hospl
 LE3..................127 F2
Mansion St 1 LE10....215 D8
Mansion The DE72......16 B7
Manston Cl LE4........130 A5
Mantle La LE67........71 C2
Mantle Rd LE3.........154 D6
MANTON................164 E6
Manton Cl LE9.........219 B6
Manton Grange LE15....164 E5
Manton Rd
 Corby NN17............230 F2
 Edith Weston LE15.....166 A7
Maple Ave
 Blaby LE8.............202 B7
 Braunstone Town LE3...153 C3
 Countesthorpe LE8.....202 F4
Maple Cl
 East Leake LE12.......31 D8
 Hinckley LE10.........215 E5
 Leicester LE4.........128 E2
 Melton Mowbray LE13...59 B5
Maple Ct NN17.........230 E1
Maple Dr
 Aston-on-T DE72.......16 A7
 Ibstock LE67..........95 E2
 Lutterworth LE17......244 B6
Maple Gr DE72.........9 F8
Maple Rd
 Castle Donington DE74.17 A5
 Loughborough LE11.....75 B8
 Swadlincote DE11......44 B6
 Thurmaston LE4........129 D6
Maple Rd N LE11.......75 B8
Maple Rd S LE11.......75 B7
Maple St LE2..........155 B5
Mapleton Rd
 Draycott DE72.........9 A8
 Wigston LE18..........180 C3
Maple Tree Wlk LE19...201 C7

Maple Way
Desford LE9 . . . . **151** A3
Earl Shilton LE9 . . . . **198** E6
Maplewell LE67 . . . . **72** B1
Maplewell Dr LE4 . . . . . . **128** A6
Maplewell Hall Sch
LE12 . . . . **99** E7
Maplewell Rd LE12 . . . . **99** F7
Maplin Rd LE5 . . . . **130** E1
Mapperley Ho LE13 . . . . . . **59** D3
Marble St LE1 . . . . **259** B3
Marchant Rd LE10 . . . . . . **215** C8
Marchfont Cl CV11 . . . . . . **214** A1
Marcian Cl LE10 . . . . **196** F1
Marcus Cl LE7 . . . . **102** E2
Mardale Way LE11 . . . . **74** D8
MAREFIELD **134** B5
Marefield Cl LE7 . . . . **157** A5
Marefield La
Burrough on t H LE14 . . . . **134** C8
Lowesby LE7 . . . . **133** E5
Tilton on t H LE7 . . . . **134** B1
Twyford LE14 . . . . **133** F8
Marfitt St LE4 . . . . **129** B2
Margam Cl LE3 . . . . **128** B2
Margaret Anne Rd
LE2 . . . . **181** B4
Margaret Cl LE4 . . . . **129** E8
Margaret Cres LE18 . . . . **180** B3
Margaret Keay Rd
LE11 . . . . **51** E2
Margaret Rd LE5 . . . . **155** E5
Margaret St LE67 . . . . **71** C1
Marie Cl CV9 . . . . **194** A7
Marigold Cl PE9 . . . . **142** E4
Marigold Cres LE13 . . . . . **82** B8
Marigold Dr LE10 . . . . **215** E5
Marigold La LE12 . . . . **76** F2
Marigold Pl DE11 . . . . **44** F4
Marigold Way LE19 . . . . . **200** F8
Marina Dr LE6 . . . . **127** A3
Marina Rd LE5 . . . . **155** D4
Marion Cl LE3 . . . . **127** F2
Marion's Way LE20 . . . . . **200** D4
Marjorie St LE4 . . . . **155** A8
MARKET BOSWORTH
. . . . **148** E3
Market Bosworth Ctry
Pk★ CV13 . . . . **149** A3
Market Bosworth High
Sch & Com Coll
CV13 . . . . **148** E3
Market Bosworth Sta★
CV13 . . . . **148** C3
Market Ct NG33 . . . . **65** B3
MARKET HARBOROUGH
. . . . **240** C2
Market Harborough CE
Prim Sch LE16 . . . . **240** D3
Market Harborough
District Hospl LE16 . . . **240** D3
Market Harborough Mus★
LE16 . . . . **240** E3
Market Harborough Sta
LE16 . . . . **241** A3
Market Mews CV13 . . . . . **148** F3
MARKET OVERTON **86** F6
Market Pl
Belton LE12 . . . . **49** B6
Billesdon LE7 . . . . **159** B2
Hinckley LE10 . . . . **215** D8
Kegworth DE74 . . . . **18** D2
Leicester LE1 . . . . **259** B3
Long Eaton NG10 . . . . **10** E8
Loughborough LE11 . . . . . . **52** B4
Market Bosworth CV13 . . . **148** F3
Melbourne DE73 . . . . **26** B7
Melton Mowbray LE13 . . . . **59** C3
Mountsorrel LE12 . . . . **76** E3
Oakham LE15 . . . . **138** A6
Shepshed LE12 . . . . **50** B4
Uppingham LE15 . . . . **189** B4
Whitwick LE67 . . . . **71** F5
Market Place App
LE1 . . . . **259** B3
Market Pl S LE1 . . . . **259** B3
Market St
Ashby-de-la-Z LE65 . . . . . **69** B6
Bottesford NG13 . . . . **3** B2
Castle Donington DE74 . . . **17** B3
Coalville LE67 . . . . **71** C1
Draycott DE72 . . . . **9** A7
Leicester LE1 . . . . **259** B3
Loughborough LE11 . . . . . . **52** A4
Lutterworth LE17 . . . . **244** C6
Oakham LE15 . . . . **138** A6
Swadlincote DE11 . . . . **44** B4
MARKFIELD **125** E7
Markfield Equestrian Ctr★
LE67 . . . . **98** A3
Markfield La
Botcheston LE9 . . . . **151** C8
Markfield LE67 . . . . **98** F1
Thornton LE67 . . . . **124** F6
Markfield Rd
Groby LE6 . . . . **126** D4
Ratby LE6 . . . . **126** B2
Markham Ret Pk PE9 . . . . **143** F5
Markland LE2 . . . . **179** C4
Marlborough Cl LE10 . . . **216** B7
Marlborough Dr LE8 . . . . **223** A6
Marlborough Ho LE3 . . . . **152** F3
Marlborough Pl LE17 . . . **244** C5
Marlborough Rd
Breaston DE72 . . . . **9** D7

Marlborough Rd *continued*
Long Eaton NG10 . . . . **10** F8
Marlborough Sq LE67 . . . **71** C1
Marlborough St LE1 . . . **259** B3
Marlborough Way
Ashby-de-la-Z LE65 . . . . . **69** A7
Market Harborough
LE16 . . . . **240** E5
Marle Pit Hill LE12 . . . . . . **30** A8
Marl Fields LE7 . . . . **76** F1
Marlow Ct LE16 . . . . **228** A8
Marlow Rd LE3 . . . . **154** D2
Marlsbury Ave LE7 . . . . . **157** A8
Marmion Cl LE4 . . . . **223** A6
Maromme Sq 2 LE18 . . . **180** D3
Marquis Ct DE12 . . . . **67** E5
Marquis Dr DE12 . . . . **67** E5
Marquis Rd LE14 . . . . **36** B6
Marquis St LE1 . . . . **259** B2
Marriott Cl
Asfordby LE14 . . . . **58** A3
Leicester Forest East
LE8 . . . . **153** B3
Marriott Dr LE8 . . . . **224** B8
Marriott Ho LE2 . . . . **181** A5
Marriott Prim Sch
LE2 . . . . **179** E6
Marriott Rd LE2 . . . . **179** E6
Marsden Ave LE7 . . . . **103** D5
Marsden Cl LE67 . . . . **70** F2
Marsden La LE2 . . . . **179** B6
Marshall Ave LE12 . . . . **77** D4
Marshall Cl LE3 . . . . **153** C2
Marshall Ct 2 LE16 . . . . . **240** F2
Marshall Farm Cl NG13 . . . **6** B8
Marshall St LE3 . . . . **154** D7
Marsham Cl LE5 . . . . **130** B2
Marsh Ave LE8 . . . . **206** B1
Marsh Cl LE4 . . . . **129** E5
Marsh Ct NG13 . . . . **3** B3
Marsh Dr LE8 . . . . **206** A1
Marsh Rd LE12 . . . . **76** F1
Marsh's Paddock LE14 . . . **19** C6
Marston Cl
Leicester, Oadby LE2 . . . . **181** A3
Moira DE12 . . . . **68** A5
Marston Cres LE8 . . . . . . **202** E3
Marston Dr LE6 . . . . **126** F3
Marston La
Allington NG32 . . . . **4** F5
East Farndon LE16 . . . . . . **250** A7
Marston Rd
Croft LE9 . . . . **200** B5
Leicester LE4 . . . . **129** E2
Lubenham LE16 . . . . **239** D2
MARSTON TRUSSELL
. . . . **249** C8
Marston Trussell Rd
LE16 . . . . **249** F7
Marston Way LE67 . . . . . . **95** B2
Marstown Ave LE18 . . . . **179** F2
Marteg Cl LE13 . . . . **59** B1
Martin Ave
Barrow-u-S LE12 . . . . **76** D7
Leicester Forest East
LE9 . . . . **152** F3
Leicester, Oadby LE2 . . . . **181** B5
Mountsorrel LE12 . . . . **76** D1
Martin Cl
Leicester LE4 . . . . **155** B8
Oakham LE15 . . . . **138** B8
Stoney Stanton LE9 . . . . . **199** D1
Whitwick LE67 . . . . **71** D6
Martin Ct LE7 . . . . **127** D5
Martindale Cl
Leicester LE2 . . . . **259** B1
Loughborough LE11 . . . . . . **51** D1
Martin Dr LE7 . . . . **102** E4
Martin High Sch LE7 . . . . **127** D7
Martins Dr CV9 . . . . **170** E2
Martinshaw La LE6 . . . . . **126** E3
Martinshaw Prim Sch
LE6 . . . . **126** D4
Martinshaw Wood Nature
Trail★ LE6 . . . . **126** C3
Martin Sq LE6 . . . . **152** D8
Martin St LE4 . . . . **155** C8
Martival LE5 . . . . **155** E7
Marvin Cl LE4 . . . . **154** B7
Marwell Cl LE4 . . . . **128** F4
Marwell Wlk LE4 . . . . **128** F4
Marwood Rd LE4 . . . . **128** D4
Marydene Ct LE5 . . . . **156** C3
Marydene Dr LE5 . . . . **156** C3
Mary Gee Hos LE2 . . . . . **180** D8
Mary La LE14, NG32 . . . . . **40** C8
Maryland Cl LE9 . . . . **197** F6
Maryland DE11 . . . . **44** A7
Marylebone Dr LE17 . . . . **244** D6
Mary Rd LE3 . . . . **154** B8
Mary's Cl LE12 . . . . **33** C3
Marys Ct LE7 . . . . **127** D6
Marys St 3 LE9 . . . . **198** F8
Mary St LE9 . . . . **198** F8
Marywell Cl LE10 . . . . **196** F1
Masefield Ave
Narborough LE19 . . . . **178** A2
Swadlincote DE11 . . . . **44** C6
Masefield Cl
Barwell LE9 . . . . **198** C8
Measham DE12 . . . . **93** B3
Mason Cres DE11 . . . . **44** E4
Mason Cl LE10 . . . . **215** B8
Mason Row LE5 . . . . **130** D3
Masons Cl LE19 . . . . **201** B7
Masterton Cl PE9 . . . . . . **143** F5
Masterton Rd PE9 . . . . . . **143** E5
Matlock Ave LE18 . . . . . . **180** A1

Matlock Ct NG10 . . . . **9** F5
Matlock St LE2 . . . . **155** C6
Matthew Arnold Ct
LE11 . . . . **51** D5
Matthew Clarke Ho 4
LE16 . . . . **240** E4
Matthew Ct LE11 . . . . **52** D4
Matthews Ct LE65 . . . . **68** F7
Matts Cl LE2 . . . . **179** D5
Maughan St LE9 . . . . **175** F1
Maura Cl LE8 . . . . **201** F5
Maurice Dr LE8 . . . . **202** D3
Maurice Rd LE16 . . . . **250** D8
Mavis Ave LE3 . . . . **154** C2
Mawby Cl LE8 . . . . **202** A5
Mawby's La DE12 . . . . **119** F8
Maxfield Ho 3 LE2 . . . . . **155** B5
Maxwell Dr LE11 . . . . **51** C5
Maxwell St DE72 . . . . **9** F8
Maxwell Way LE17 . . . . . **244** C8
May Cl LE3 . . . . **154** A4
Mayfield Dr
Loughborough LE11 . . . . . . **52** B2
Wigston LE18 . . . . **180** D4
Mayfield Rd LE2 . . . . **155** C3
Mayfield St LE13 . . . . **59** B5
Mayfield Way LE9 . . . . . . **198** C7
Mayflower Cl LE67 . . . . . . **125** E8
Mayflower Ct LE67 . . . . . **125** E8
Mayflower Mews
LE15 . . . . **189** B4
Mayflower Prim Sch
LE5 . . . . **155** F4
Mayflower Rd LE5 . . . . . . **155** E3
Mayflower Wlk LE67 . . . . **125** E8
Maylands Ave DE72 . . . . **9** E8
Maylan Rd NN17 . . . . **230** F3
May Meadow CV CV13 . . . **149** D8
Maynard Cl LE67 . . . . **124** A6
Maynard Pk★ LE67 . . . . . **123** F8
Maynard Rd LE2 . . . . **155** B6
Maynard Wlk LE2 . . . . . . **124** A6
Mayns La LE8 . . . . **205** E7
Mayo Cl LE11 . . . . **74** F7
Mayor's Wlk LE1 . . . . **155** A3
Maypole Hill DE11 . . . . **44** A6
Mayre Cl LE9 . . . . **219** B5
Mays Farm Dr LE9 . . . . . **199** D3
Maytree Cl LE9 . . . . **152** E3
Maytree Ct LE9 . . . . **152** E3
Maytree Dr LE9 . . . . **152** E2
May Tree La LE12 . . . . **75** B4
Meadhurst Gdns LE15 . . **189** B4
Meadhurst Rd LE3 . . . . . **154** A5
Meadow Ave LE11 . . . . **52** B6
Meadowbrook Ct
DE12 . . . . **119** F8
Meadowbrook Rd LE8 . . **223** F8
Meadow Cl
Bagworth LE67 . . . . **124** B5
Barrow-u-S LE12 . . . . **76** E8
Draycott DE72 . . . . **9** A7
Market Harborough
LE16 . . . . **240** F4
Ratby LE6 . . . . **152** D8
Sheepy Magna CV9 . . . . . **171** B7
Stoney Stanton LE9 . . . . . **199** D3
Meadow Com Prim Sch
The LE18 . . . . **180** E3
Meadowcourt Rd LE2 . . . **180** F7
Meadow Court Rd
Earl Shilton LE9 . . . . **198** F7
Groby LE6 . . . . **126** F3
Meadow Cres DE74 . . . . . . **17** B2
Meadowcroft Cl LE3 . . . . **153** B7
Meadow Ct LE9 . . . . **178** A1
Meadowdale Prim Sch
LE16 . . . . **241** B4
Meadowdale Rd LE16 . . . **241** B4
Meadow Dr LE10 . . . . **216** A7
Meadow Edge LE19 . . . . **178** A2
Meadowfield LE15 . . . . . . **138** A8
Meadow Furlong
CV23 . . . . **252** D1
Meadow Gdns
Leicester LE2 . . . . **180** A5
Measham DE12 . . . . **93** C3
Meadow Hill LE8 . . . . **182** A1
Meadow La
Birstall LE4 . . . . **129** C8
Coalville LE67 . . . . **72** B2
Long Eaton NG10 . . . . **10** F7
Loughborough LE11,
LE12 . . . . **52** B7
Markfield LE67 . . . . **98** E1
Ryhall PE9 . . . . **116** E1
Stanton u B LE67 . . . . **97** F1
Swadlincote DE11 . . . . **44** A6
Syston LE7 . . . . **102** E4
Thringstone LE67 . . . . **48** D2
Meadow Lane Ind Est
LE11 . . . . **52** B6
Meadow Park Ind Est
PE9 . . . . **117** B5
Meadow Rd
Barlestone CV13 . . . . **149** D7
Barwell LE9 . . . . **198** C7
Mountsorrel LE12 . . . . **101** D8
Woodhouse Eaves LE12 . . . **75** A1
Meadowside CV11 . . . . . . **214** B1
Meadows La LE14 . . . . **11** D1
Meadows Rise LE14 . . . . . **62** D2
Meadow St LE16 . . . . **240** E4
Meadows The
East Goscote LE7 . . . . **103** E8
Hinckley LE10 . . . . **216** A7
Littlethorpe LE19 . . . . **201** D7

Meadows The *continued*
Shepshed LE12 . . . . **50** A3
Meadowsweet PE9 . . . . . . **142** E5
Meadowsweet Cl LE13 . . . **82** A8
Meadowsweet Rd
LE5 . . . . **130** C1
Meadow The LE9 . . . . **219** A5
Meadow View
Botcheston LE9 . . . . **151** C8
Coalville LE67 . . . . **96** C5
East Goscote LE7 . . . . **103** F7
Leicester, Oadby LE2 . . . . **181** B5
Stamford PE9 . . . . **144** A4
Meadow Way
Desford LE9 . . . . **151** C2
Egleton LE15 . . . . **138** D3
Groby LE6 . . . . **126** F3
Melton Mowbray LE13 . . . . **59** D1
Swadlincote DE11 . . . . **44** A6
Wigston LE18 . . . . **180** F2
Meadow Wlk LE67 . . . . **95** F2
Meads The LE3 . . . . **153** E5
Meadvale Rd LE2 . . . . **180** C7
Meadway LE3 . . . . **154** A6
Meadway The
Birstall LE4 . . . . **129** A8
Hinckley LE10 . . . . **215** F7
Syston LE7 . . . . **102** F2
Meadwell Rd LE3 . . . . **153** D3
Mease Cl DE12 . . . . **93** C4
MEASHAM **93** B5
Measham CE Prim Sch
DE12 . . . . **93** D5
Measham Rd
Appleby Magna DE12 . . . . . **92** F1
Ashby-de-la-Z LE65 . . . . . **68** F3
Donisthorpe DE12 . . . . **92** D6
Moira DE12 . . . . **67** F3
Oakthorpe DE12 . . . . **93** A7
Packington LE65 . . . . **69** B1
Snarestone DE12 . . . . **120** E8
MEDBOURNE **227** F6
Medbourne Rd
Ashley LE16 . . . . **227** E4
Drayton LE16 . . . . **228** E4
Hallaton LE16 . . . . **209** E5
Slawston LE16 . . . . **209** C1
Medhurst Cl LE8 . . . . **202** A5
Medina Rd
Corby NN17 . . . . **230** C1
Leicester LE3 . . . . **154** D8
Medway Cl LE16 . . . . **241** A3
Medway Com Prim Sch
LE2 . . . . **155** C4
Medway Dr LE13 . . . . **59** B1
Medway St LE2 . . . . **155** C4
Meer The LE8 . . . . **223** A6
Meeting House Cl LE12 . . . **31** A8
Meeting St LE12 . . . . **75** F5
Melba Way LE4 . . . . **102** B1
Melbourne Brothers
Brewery Mus★ PE9 . . . . **143** D3
MELBOURNE **26** B8
Melbourne Cl LE8 . . . . . . **223** F8
Melbourne Ct NG10 . . . . . . **9** F4
Melbourne Dr LE13 . . . . . . **59** A3
Melbourne Hall & Gdns★
DE73 . . . . **26** C7
Melbourne Ho LE13 . . . . . . **59** D3
Melbourne Inf Sch
DE73 . . . . **26** B8
Melbourne Jun Sch
DE73 . . . . **26** B8
Melbourne La DE73 . . . . . . **26** E2
Melbourne Rd
Ibstock LE67 . . . . **122** E8
Leicester LE2 . . . . **155** C5
Newbold LE67 . . . . **47** D2
Ravenstone LE67 . . . . **95** F5
Stamford PE9 . . . . **143** F4
Melbourne St
Coalville LE67 . . . . **71** D1
Leicester LE2 . . . . **155** B6
Melbray Dr LE13 . . . . **59** C6
Melbreak Ave LE11 . . . . . . **74** E8
Melcombe Wlk 5
LE4 . . . . **128** F3
Melcroft Ave LE3 . . . . . . **154** B5
Melford St LE5 . . . . **155** F7
Melland Pl LE2 . . . . **179** E5
Mellerstain Wlk LE5 . . . **155** E7
Mellier Cl LE19 . . . . **178** A2
Mellor Com Prim Sch
LE4 . . . . **129** B3
Mellor Rd LE3 . . . . **154** A5
Melody Ave LE7 . . . . **127** E6
Melody Dr LE12 . . . . **77** C2
Melrose Cl
Ashby-de-la-Z LE65 . . . . . **69** D6
Hinckley LE10 . . . . **215** B8
Stamford PE9 . . . . **143** A4
Melrose Rd LE67 . . . . **71** E8
Melrose St LE4 . . . . **129** B1
Melton Ave
Leicester LE4 . . . . **129** C5
Melbourne DE73 . . . . **26** A8
Melton Carnegie Mus★
LE13 . . . . **59** D3
Melton Ctry Pk & Visitor
Ctr★ LE13 . . . . **59** D6
Melton & District War
Meml Hospl LE13 . . . . . . **59** C2
Melton Dr LE9 . . . . **218** E8
Melton La LE14 . . . . **107** C6
MELTON MOWBRAY **59** F4
Melton Mowbray Sta
LE13 . . . . **59** C2

Melton Rd
Asfordby Hill LE14 . . . . . . **58** C3
Barrow-u-S LE12 . . . . **76** E8
Burton Lazars LE14 . . . . . **83** B4
Burton o t W LE12 . . . . . . **54** C7
East Goscote LE7 . . . . **103** F8
East Langton LE16 . . . . . . **225** C5
East Leake LE12 . . . . **31** E5
Langham LE15 . . . . **110** C2
Leicester LE4 . . . . **129** C3
Long Clawson LE14 . . . . . . **20** B1
Oakham LE15 . . . . **137** F6
Rearsby LE7 . . . . **79** C2
Scalford LE14 . . . . **38** C3
Shangton LE8 . . . . **207** B6
Syston LE7 . . . . **103** C4
Thurmaston LE4 . . . . **129** D7
Tilton on t H LE7 . . . . **159** E5
Twyford LE7 . . . . **133** D4
Upper Broughton LE14 . . . **19** A1
Waltham on t W LE14 . . . . . **40** A6
Whissendine LE15 . . . . . . **84** C2
Wymondham LE14 . . . . **62** C2
Melton Spinney Rd LE14,
LE13 . . . . **59** F7
Melton St
Earl Shilton LE9 . . . . **198** E8
6 Leicester LE1 . . . . **155** A7
Melville Cl LE11 . . . . **51** B6
Memorial Sq LE67 . . . . . . **71** C1
Memory La 2 LE1 . . . . . . **155** A7
Mendip Ave LE4 . . . . **128** D1
Mendip Cl
Ashby-de-la-Z LE65 . . . . . **69** B5
Shepshed LE12 . . . . **50** C3
Mendip Rd
Edith Weston LE15 . . . . . . **166** C7
Oakham LE15 . . . . **137** D6
Mennecy Cl LE8 . . . . **202** D3
Mensa Cl LE2 . . . . **155** C5
Menzies Rd LE4 . . . . **128** C2
Meon Cl NN17 . . . . **230** C1
Mercenfeld Prim Sch
LE67 . . . . **125** D8
Mercer's Way LE7 . . . . . . **103** E7
Merchant's Comm
LE7 . . . . **103** E7
Mercia Dr LE2 . . . . **180** F6
Mercury Cl 8 LE2 . . . . . . **155** B5
Mere Cl
Leicester LE5 . . . . **155** C6
Mountsorrel LE12 . . . . **101** E8
Meredith Rd LE3 . . . . **154** C1
Mere La
Copston Magna LE10 . . . . **231** C3
Leicester, Oadby LE2 . . . . **181** C2
Queniborough LE7 . . . . . . **103** F5
Mereoak La DE11, DE73 . . . **45** C7
Mere Rd
Great Stretton LE2 . . . . . . **182** C6
Leicester LE5 . . . . **155** C5
Shangton LE8 . . . . **206** F4
Upper Bruntingthorpe
LE17 . . . . **236** C5
Waltham on t W LE14 . . . . . **40** A7
Wigston LE18 . . . . **180** E3
Mere The LE8 . . . . **205** A8
Merevale Ave LE10 . . . . . **215** C7
Merevale Cl LE10 . . . . **215** C7
Merevale La CV9 . . . . **170** B1
Merevale Rd CV9 . . . . **170** C1
Mereworth Cl LE5 . . . . . . **155** D8
Merganster Way LE67 . . . **97** A8
Meridian Bsns Pk
LE19 . . . . **178** D6
Meridian E LE19 . . . . **178** D7
Meridian N LE19 . . . . **178** D7
Meridian S LE19 . . . . **178** D6
Meridian W LE19 . . . . **178** D7
Meridian Way LE3 . . . . . . **153** D2
Meriton Rd LE17 . . . . **244** D6
Merlin Cl
Broughton Astley LE9 . . . . **218** E7
Leicester Forest East
LE3 . . . . **153** A2
Mountsorrel LE7 . . . . **76** F1
Merlin Way DE11 . . . . **44** F3
Merrick Ct LE10 . . . . **215** F5
Merrifield Gdns LE10 . . . **215** E5
Merrin Ct LE11 . . . . **52** B4
Merrydale Inf Sch
LE5 . . . . **155** E8
Merrydale Jun Sch
LE5 . . . . **155** E8
Merry Husrt Pl LE10 . . . . **214** E7
MERRY LEES **151** A8
Merry Lees Ind Est
LE9 . . . . **150** F8
Merrylees Rd
Desford LE9 . . . . **125** A2
Newbold Verdon LE9 . . . . **150** D8
Mersey Gn NN17 . . . . **230** C1
Merton Ave
Leicester LE3 . . . . **154** C5
Syston LE7 . . . . **103** B3
Merton Cl LE9 . . . . **218** D7
Merton Prim Sch The
LE7 . . . . **103** E7
Merton Way LE9 . . . . **205** F1
Merus Ct LE3, LE19 . . . . . **153** D1
Mervyn Rd LE5 . . . . **155** D4
Messenger Cl LE11 . . . . . . **51** E7
Metcalf Cl LE9 . . . . **199** D2
Metcalfe St LE9 . . . . **198** E7
Methuen Ave LE4 . . . . . . **129** C6
Metropolitan Apartments
LE1 . . . . **259** C4

Mews Cotts
Arnesby LE8 221 F5
Great Oxendon LE16 250 E3
Mews The
Great Bowden LE16 240 E7
Melbourne DE73 26 B7
Queniborough LE7 104 A5
4 Rugby CV21 257 A1
Meynell Cl
Leicester, Oadby LE2 181 C4
Melton Mowbray LE13 82 C8
Meynell Rd
Leicester LE5 155 D7
Long Eaton NG10 10 D5
Quorn (Quorndon) LE12 76 A7
Meynells Gorse LE3 153 C4
Meynell St DE11 44 A1
Michael Cl LE7 103 E6
Michael Lewis Ho LE3 154 B6
Michael Ramsey Ct LE2 179 C3
Michael's Wlk LE16 230 B4
Mickleborough Cl LE16 227 B3
Mickleden Gn LE67 72 A2
Mickledon Cl 1 NG10 10 B8
Mickleton Cl DE11 44 B1
Mickleton Dr LE5 156 B3
Middelburg Cl CV11 214 A1
Middle Ave LE11 51 F6
Middlebrook Cl LE6 152 D8
Middlebrook Gn LE16 241 A4
Middle Cl DE11 44 B4
Middledale Rd LE16 241 A3
Middlefield Cl LE10 197 D2
Middlefield Ct LE10 197 D2
Middlefield La LE10 197 D3
Middlefield Pl LE10 197 D3
Middlefield Rd LE7 102 D7
MIDDLE HAMBLETON 139 B3
Middle La LE14 36 D8
Middle Orch LE12 77 C1
Middle Rd LE67 48 A1
Middlesex Rd LE2 179 D7
Middle St
Barkestone-le-V NG13 6 C2
Croxton Kerrial NG32 24 B7
Foxton LE16 224 E1
Hose LE14 20 F7
Owston LE15 135 B4
Skillington NG33 43 B8
Stainby NG33 43 D2
Wing LE15 165 A3
MIDDLETON 229 B1
Middleton Cl
Stoney Stanton LE9 199 E2
Wigston LE18 180 F3
Middleton Pl LE11 52 B2
Middleton Rd
Ashley LE16 228 B3
Bringhurst LE16 229 C4
Middletons Cl LE8 222 F8
Middleton St LE2 179 C6
Midhurst Ave LE3 178 F8
Midland Cotts LE18 180 B2
Midland Ct
Lutterworth LE17 244 D8
Oakham LE15 137 F7
Midland Rd
Ellistown LE67 96 D4
Swadlincote DE11 44 B4
Midland Road Ind Est DE11 44 B4
Midland St
Leicester LE1 259 C4
Long Eaton NG10 10 E8
Midway La LE17 236 B3
Midway Rd
Leicester LE5 155 D2
Swadlincote DE11 44 C5
Mikado Rd NG10 10 C5
Milby Dr CV11 214 A7
Mildenhall Rd LE11 51 C4
Mildmay Cl LE13 59 C6
Milestone Cl LE8 224 C8
Milestone Mews LE16 229 C1
Milfoil Cl LE10 214 F7
Milford Cl LE19 201 A8
Milford Rd LE2 180 B8
Mill DE72 9 A1
Millais Rd LE10 197 A3
Mill Bank LE65 69 B6
Millbrook Cl LE4 128 F3
Millbrook Dr LE9 218 F5
Millbrook Wlk 1 LE4 128 F3
Mill Cl
Birstall LE4 129 B6
Sapcote LE9 217 E8
Shepshed LE12 50 C5
Smeeton Westerby LE8 223 F6
Stapleton LE9 174 E2
Swadlincote DE11 44 C5
Wigston LE18 202 F8
Wing LE15 165 B2
Milldale Rd NG10 10 B6
Mill Dam LE67 96 D6
Mill Dr LE6 152 D7
Millenium Ave DE12 67 E5
Millennium Cl LE17 246 F4
Miller Cl LE4 129 E5
Millers Cl
Glenfield LE3 153 B8
Syston LE7 103 A2
Millersdale Ave LE5 156 D5
Millers Gdns LE16 240 B2
Millers Gn LE10 215 F6
Millers Grange LE9 218 F5
Millers Wlk LE67 95 E7
Miller's Yd 5 LE16 240 E3
Millfield DE72 9 B2
Millfield Ave LE16 229 D1
Millfield Cl
Anstey LE7 127 D5
Ashby-de-la-Z LE65 69 A8
Millfield Com Sch LE3 178 E7
Millfield Cres LE3 178 F6
Millfield Croft 1 DE11 44 B7
Millfield St DE11 45 A2
Mill Furlong CV23 252 D1
Millgate Sch LE2 180 A8
Mill Gdns CV13 196 A3
Mill Gn DE72 9 A1
Mill Gr
Lutterworth LE17 244 D5
Whissendine LE15 84 E1
Mill Hill
Enderby LE19 178 A4
Laughton LE17 238 C4
Leicester LE4 129 A2
Lubenham LE16 239 E3
Stathern LE14 13 B2
Mill Hill Cl LE8 202 A7
Mill Hill Ind Est LE19 178 A4
Mill Hill La
Leicester LE2 155 B4
Markfield LE67 98 D1
Mill Hill Rd
Arnesby LE8 221 F5
Hinckley LE10 197 C1
Market Harborough LE16 240 F3
Mill Ho
1 Hinckley LE10 197 C1
Melton Mowbray LE13 59 D3
Millhouse Ct DE72 9 B7
Millhouse St LE67 71 C8
Milligan Rd LE2 179 E7
Mill La
Asfordby LE14 57 F2
13 Ashby-de-la-Z LE65 69 B6
Atherstone CV9 194 A6
Barrowden LE15 192 A5
Barrow-u-S LE12 76 D6
Belton LE12 49 B7
Bilstone CV13 147 C7
Blaby LE8 202 E8
Caldecott LE16 230 B8
Copston Magna LE10 231 A5
Cottesmore LE15 112 C8
Croxton Kerrial NG32 24 B7
Earl Shilton LE9 199 C8
East Leake LE12 31 F8
Empingham LE15 141 B6
Enderby LE19 178 B2
Frisby on t W LE14 80 D8
Gilmorton LE17 235 D5
Heather LE67 95 C2
Hickling LE14 19 B7
Kegworth DE74 18 D2
Ketton PE9 168 A5
Leicester LE2 259 A2
Long Clawson LE14 20 D3
Long Whatton LE12 29 D4
Loughborough LE11 52 C5
Melton Mowbray LE13 59 D2
Newbold Verdon LE9 150 B4
Orston NG13 2 A8
Peggs Green LE67 71 A7
Sharnford LE10 217 C5
Shearsby LE17 222 A2
Sheepy Magna CV9 171 B7
Shenton CV13 173 B3
Smeeton Westerby LE8 223 F7
Somerby LE14 108 B2
South Witham NG33 64 E2
Thornton LE67 124 E4
Thurmaston LE4 129 D8
Tinwell PE9 142 F1
Waltham on t W LE14 40 A6
Willoughby-on-t-W LE12 34 D8
Witherley CV9 194 A8
Mill Lane Ind Est LE3 127 A1
Mill La The LE3 153 A8
Mill Pond LE67 96 D6
Millpool Cl DE11 45 A7
Mill Race View CV9 170 D2
Mill Rd
Cottingham LE16 229 C2
Gretton LE15, NN17 212 F2
Rearsby LE7 78 F1
Thurcaston LE7 101 B3
Ullesthorpe LE17 233 B4
Woodhouse Eaves LE12 74 F1
Mills Cl DE72 9 A7
Mill St
Barwell LE9 198 A5
Duddington PE9 193 B6
Leicester LE2 259 B2
Melton Mowbray LE13 59 C2
Oakham LE15 138 A6
Packington LE65 69 B2
Ryhall PE9 116 F3
Mills The LE12 76 A5
Millstone La
Leicester LE1 259 B3
Syston LE7 103 C4
Mills Yd LE11 52 B3
Mill View
Hinckley LE10 197 E1
Huncote LE9 200 D7
Millwood Cl LE4 128 E5
Milner Ave DE72 9 A7
Milner Cl LE12 77 C2
Milner Rd NG10 10 D8
Milners Row 16 PE9 143 E3
Milnroy Rd LE5 156 E7
Milton Ave DE11 44 C6
Milton Cl
Hinckley LE10 197 C1
Measham DE12 93 C3
Melton Mowbray LE13 59 B5
Wigston LE18 180 E2
Milton Cres LE4 128 B2
Milton Ct LE11 51 D5
Milton Gdns LE2 181 A5
Milton Ho LE4 128 B3
Milton St
Long Eaton NG10 10 D7
Loughborough LE11 51 E5
Narborough LE19 178 A1
Milton Terr NG10 10 D7
Milverton Ave LE4 128 D1
Milverton Cl LE18 180 C4
Milverton Dr LE18 180 C4
Mimosa Cl LE11 75 A6
Minehead St LE3 154 B5
Minster Cres LE4 128 D1
Minster Ct LE2 259 B2
Minstrel's Wlk LE7 103 D7
Mint Gr NG10 10 A7
Minton Rd DE74 16 F4
Mint Rd LE2 154 D4
Mira Dr CV10 195 D3
MISTERTON 244 F4
Misterton Way LE17 244 D5
Mistletoe Dr DE11 44 F2
Mistral Cl LE10 215 F8
Mitchell Ct CV23 252 C2
Mitchell Dr LE11 51 B6
Mitchell Gr LE7 157 A8
Mitchell Rd LE19 178 A3
Mitchell St NG10 10 E7
Moat Cl LE9 176 F3
Moat Com Coll LE2 155 B5
Moat Ct LE5 156 C8
Moat Gdns LE9 217 D7
Moat Rd
Leicester LE5 155 D5
Loughborough LE11 74 E8
Moat St
Swadlincote DE11 44 B1
Wigston LE18 180 D2
Moat The DE74 17 B4
Moat Way LE9 197 F6
Modbury Ave LE4 128 E4
Model Farm Cl LE11 51 E1
MOIRA 67 E3
Moira Dale DE74 17 C3
Moira Furnace Mus* DE12 67 E3
Moira Inf Sch DE12 68 B6
Moira Rd
Donisthorpe DE12 67 F1
Overseal DE12 67 B3
Shellbrook LE65 68 E6
Swadlincote DE11 67 E8
Woodville DE11 44 E2
Moira St
Leicester LE4 129 B1
Loughborough LE11 52 B3
Melbourne DE73 26 A7
Moir Cl LE12 77 C3
Moles La LE15 190 C1
Molesworth Bglws PE9 168 A6
Molyneux Dr LE12 77 D1
Monal Cl LE8 201 F4
Monarch Cl LE4 129 C8
Monarch Way LE11 52 A6
Monar Cl LE4 129 D4
Mona St LE9 198 E7
Monckton Cl LE1 259 C5
Moneyhill LE65 69 B8
Monica Rd LE3 178 F7
Monks Cres LE4 128 C8
Monks Kirby La CV23 231 F1
Monmouth Dr LE2 179 D2
Monroe Cl LE16 240 D5
Monsaldale Cl NG10 10 B6
Monsarrat Way LE11 51 D6
Monsell Dr LE2 179 C5
Montague Ave LE7 103 B2
Montague Cl LE9 150 B5
Montague Dr LE11 74 C8
Montague Rd
Broughton Astley LE9 218 F7
Leicester LE2 155 B2
Monteith Pl DE74 17 B4
Montford Mews DE74 17 B4
Montgomery Cl LE17 244 A5
Montgomery Rd LE9 199 A8
Montilo La CV23 242 D2
Montreal Rd LE1 155 A7
Montrose Cl
Market Harborough LE16 240 D1
Stamford PE9 143 A4
Montrose Ct LE5 156 A8
Montrose Rd LE2 179 C6
Montrose Rd S LE2 179 D5
Montrose Sch LE2 179 D6
Montsoreau Way LE12 101 D8
Montvale Gdns LE3 154 D8
Moon Cl LE2 155 B5
Moorbarns La LE17 244 B4
Moorcroft Cl CV11 214 B1
Moore Ave DE74 18 D3
Moore Cl DE12 119 F8
Moore Rd
Barwell LE9 198 C7
Moore Rd *continued*
Ellistown LE67 96 E4
Moores Cl LE18 179 E2
Moores La LE19 178 B4
Moores Rd LE4 129 B2
Moorfield Pl LE12 50 B4
Moorfields LE5 156 D8
Moorgate Ave LE4 128 F8
Moorgate St LE4 155 A8
Moorhen Way LE11 51 F3
Moor Hill LE7 186 C2
Moorings The LE12 76 E6
Moor La
Aston-on-T DE72 16 B8
Coleorton LE67 70 F6
East Norton LE7 186 C4
East Norton LE7 186 D5
Loughborough LE11 52 E3
Normanton on S LE12 30 C4
North Luffenham LE15 166 D2
South Witham NG33 64 D4
Stathern LE14 13 A4
Staunton in t V NG23 1 E6
Tonge DE73, DE74 27 B4
Moorland Cl CV13 148 F3
Moorland Rd LE7 102 E3
Moorlands Mobile Home Pk The LE67 70 E3
Moorlands The LE67 70 E4
Moorleas La LE14 39 F5
Moor The LE67 70 E6
Moray Cl
Hinckley LE10 215 A8
Stamford PE9 142 F4
Morban Rd LE2 179 B6
Morcote Rd LE3 153 E3
MORCOTT 191 A5
Morcott Rd
Barrowden LE15 191 D5
Glaston LE15 190 D5
Wing LE15 165 A2
Moreton Ct LE67 96 D7
Moreton Dale LE12 77 D4
Moreton Wlk LE65 68 F5
Morgans Orch LE12 76 D8
Moriston Cl NN17 230 C1
Morkery La NG33 66 C3
Morkery Wood Nature Trail* LE15 66 A3
Morland Ave LE2 180 E8
Morland Dr LE10 197 B3
Morledge St LE1 259 C4
Morley Arc 5 LE1 259 B4
Morley Cl LE13 59 A4
Morley La LE12 50 B1
Morley Rd
Leicester LE5 155 C6
Sapcote LE9 217 E7
Morley St
Loughborough LE11 52 C5
Market Harborough LE16 240 D3
Mornington St LE5 155 D7
Morpeth Ave LE4 128 D5
Morpeth Dr LE2 181 D4
Morris Cam Wlk LE14 57 E3
Morris Cl
Braunstone Town LE3 153 D2
Loughborough LE11 52 C4
Morris Ct LE17 236 C8
Morrison Ct LE8 224 A8
Morris Rd LE2 155 A1
Mortiboys Way LE9 199 D2
Mortimer Pl LE3 154 B1
Mortimer Rd
Melton Mowbray LE13 59 C4
Narborough LE19 201 A7
Mortimer Way
Leicester LE3 154 B1
Loughborough LE11 51 B6
Mortoft Rd LE4 129 B3
Morton Wlk LE5 155 E8
Morwoods The LE2 181 B5
Moscow La
Great Dalby LE14 107 D8
Shepshed LE12 50 A1
Mossdale LE67 71 E6
Mossdale Rd LE3 178 E8
Mosse Way LE2 181 C6
Mossgate LE3 154 A7
Mosswithy LE8 222 F6
Mostyn Ave LE7 103 C4
Mostyn St LE3 154 B5
Mottisford Rd LE4 128 F4
Mottisford Wlk LE4 128 F4
Moulds La LE16 229 D7
Mountain Rd LE4 130 A4
Mount Ave
Barwell LE9 198 C7
Leicester LE5 155 D6
Mountbatten Ave PE9 143 C4
Mountbatten Rd LE15 137 E6
Mountbatten Way LE17 244 B5
Mountcastle Rd LE3 154 C2
Mountfield Rd LE9 198 E8
Mountfields Dr LE11 51 E2
Mountfields Lodge Sch LE11 51 F2
Mount Grace High Sch LE10 197 E1
Mount Grace Rd LE11 51 B5
Mount Pleasant
Castle Donington DE74 17 B3
Kegworth DE74 18 C2
Leicester, Oadby LE2 181 E3
Morcott LE15 191 A6
Mount Pleasant *continued*
Uppingham LE15 189 B4
Mount Pleasant La DE12 92 A8
Mount Pleasant Rd
Morcott LE15 191 A6
Swadlincote DE11 44 A1
Mount Rd
Cosby LE9 201 D3
Hartshorne DE11 45 A4
Hinckley LE10 215 D8
Leicester LE5 155 C6
Leicester, Oadby LE2 181 B5
Mount St Bernard Abbey (Monastery)* LE67 72 D5
MOUNTSORREL 76 D2
Mountsorrel Cotts LE9 199 D2
Mountsorrel La
Rothley LE7 101 E7
Sileby LE12 77 A3
Mount St DE72 9 F7
Mount The
Dunton Bassett LE17 219 D2
Scraptoft LE7 156 F8
Mount View LE8 182 B1
Mowbray Ct LE13 59 B2
Mowbray Dr LE7 103 C4
MOWMACRE HILL 128 D5
Mowmacre Hill LE4 128 E5
Mowmacre Hill Prim Sch LE4 128 D5
MOWSLEY 237 F6
Mowsley Ct LE17 247 E6
Mowsley End LE18 180 D2
Mowsley La LE17 236 D4
Mowsley Rd
Husbands Bosworth LE17 247 E6
Saddington LE8 223 B2
Theddingworth LE17 238 B2
Mowsley St Nicholas CE Prim Sch LE17 237 F7
Muckle Gate La LE12 54 F1
Muirfield Cl LE3 153 C6
Mulberry Ave LE3 153 C6
Mulberry Cl LE17 244 B7
Mulberry Ct LE16 229 A5
Mulberry Gdns DE74 18 D2
Mulberry Way DE72 16 A6
Mull Way LE8 202 F3
Mumford Way LE11 51 D3
Muncaster Cl LE9 219 A4
Mundella St LE2 155 C3
Mundy Cl LE12 53 F7
Munnings Cl LE4 155 B8
Munnings Dr LE10 197 A3
Munnmore Cl DE74 18 C2
Muntjack Rd LE8 201 F5
Murby Way LE3 153 C1
Murdoch Rise LE11 51 D6
Muriel Rd LE3 154 C5
Murphy Dr LE67 124 A6
Murray Cl LE9 218 F4
Murrayfield Rd LE3 153 C5
Murray St LE2 155 B6
Muscovey Rd LE67 97 A8
Museum Sq LE1 259 C2
Musgrove Cl 5 LE3 154 D5
Mushill La LE12 33 D5
Mushroom La DE11 67 D8
Musk Cl LE16 229 D7
Musson Dr LE65 69 A5
Musson Rd LE3 153 E7
MUSTON 7 F8
Muston Gdns LE2 180 B7
Muston La NG13 3 D1
Myrtle Ave
Birstall LE4 102 B1
Long Eaton NG10 10 C6
Myrtle Cl LE9 198 A7
Myrtle Rd LE2 155 C4
Mythe La CV9 194 A8
Mythe View CV9 170 E1

N

Nagle Gr LE4 129 D5
NAILSTONE 123 B3
Nailstone Rd
Barton in t B CV13 122 E1
Carlton CV13 148 E8
Nairn Rd PE9 143 A3
NAMS Tutorial Coll LE1 259 C4
Namur Rd LE18 179 E3
Nanhill Dr LE12 100 A8
NANPANTAN 74 B7
Nanpantan Rd LE11 74 B7
Nansen Rd LE5 155 E4
NARBOROUGH 201 B8
Narborough Rd
Cosby LE9, LE19 201 D4
Huncote LE9 200 D7
Leicester LE3 154 C3
Narborough Rd N LE3 154 D5
Narborough Rd S LE19 178 E4
Narborough Sta LE19 201 C7
Narrow Boat Cl LE18 203 A8
Narrow La
Donisthorpe DE12 92 E8
Hathern LE12 30 A1

Narrow La *continued*
Leicester LE2 . . . . **179** C6
Stathern LE14 . . . . **13** A3
Wymeswold LE12 . . . . **34** B2
Narrows The 1 LE10 . . **215** E8
Naseby Cl
Market Harborough
LE16 . . . . **240** E2
Wigston LE18 . . . . **180** E2
Naseby Dr
Ashby-de-la-Z LE65 . . . . **69** D7
Long Eaton NG10 . . . . **10** E4
Loughborough LE11 . . . . **51** A2
Naseby Rd
Leicester LE4 . . . . **129** E2
Sibbertoft LE16 . . . . **248** F2
Welford NN6 . . . . **256** F6
Naseby Sq LE16 . . . . **240** E2
Naseby Way LE8 . . . . **205** B8
Nathaniel Rd NG10 . . . . **10** F7
National Space Ctr★
LE4 . . . . **128** F2
Navigation Cl LE13 . . . . **59** B2
Navigation Dr LE2 . . . . . . **179** A2
Navigation St
Leicester LE1 . . . . **154** F7
Measham DE12 . . . . **93** C5
Navigation Way LE11 . . . **52** A5
Navins The LE12 . . . . **76** E2
Naylor Ave LE11 . . . . **52** D2
Naylor Rd LE7 . . . . **103** C5
Neal Ave LE3 . . . . **153** E2
Neale St NG10 . . . . **10** E7
Near Mdw NG10 . . . . **10** E5
Near The Church
LE16 . . . . **226** A5
Necton St LE2 . . . . **103** A3
Nedham St LE2 . . . . **155** B6
Ned Ludd Cl LE7 . . . . **127** E6
Needham Ave LE3 . . . . . . **179** A3
Needham Cl
Leicester, Oadby LE2 . . . . . **181** E4
Melton Mowbray LE13 . . . . **59** C4
Needlegate LE1 . . . . **259** A5
Needleworks The
Leicester LE1 . . . . **259** B3
4 Loughborough LE11 . . **52** B4
Needwood Way LE19 . . . **177** F2
Nelot Way LE5 . . . . **156** B5
Nelson Cl LE12 . . . . **50** D4
Nelson Dr LE10 . . . . **197** D4
Nelson Fields LE67 . . . . . **72** A2
Nelson Pl LE65 . . . . **45** F3
Nelson St
Leicester LE1 . . . . **259** C2
Long Eaton NG10 . . . . **10** D6
Market Harborough
LE16 . . . . **240** D3
Swadlincote DE11 . . . . **44** B5
Syston LE7 . . . . **103** B3
Nene Cl LE13 . . . . **59** B1
Nene Cres
Corby NN17 . . . . **230** C1
Oakham LE15 . . . . **137** F5
Nene Ct
Leicester, Oadby LE2 . . . . . **181** C5
3 Stamford PE9 . . . . . . **143** C3
Nene Dr LE2 . . . . **181** C5
Nene Way LE67 . . . . **97** A7
Neptune Cl LE2 . . . . **155** C5
Neston Gdns LE2 . . . . . . **179** F6
Neston Rd LE2 . . . . **179** F6
NETHER BROUGHTON
. . . . **36** C8
Nether Cl LE15 . . . . **112** D8
Nethercote LE67 . . . . **121** D7
Nethercroft Dr LE65 . . . . **69** C2
Nether End
Gaddesby LE7 . . . . **105** B6
Great Dalby LE14 . . . . **82** B2
Nether Farm Cl LE17 . . . **235** C4
Netherfield Cl LE9 . . . . . **219** B6
Netherfield La LE72,
DE74 . . . . **17** F8
Netherfield Rd
Anstey LE7 . . . . **127** E7
Long Eaton NG10 . . . . **10** C4
Nether Field Way
LE3 . . . . **153** D1
NETHER HALL **130** F1
Netherhall La LE4 . . . . . **129** B6
Netherhall Rd LE5 . . . . . **130** D1
Nether Hall Sch LE5 . . . **130** D1
Netherley Ct LE10 . . . . . **197** D3
Netherley Rd LE10 . . . . . **197** D3
NETHERSEAL **91** E7
Netherseal Rd DE12 . . . . . **91** F4
Nether St
Belton-in-R LE15 . . . . . . **187** D7
Harby LE14 . . . . **12** A3
Netherwood Ind Est
CV9 . . . . **170** F1
Netton Cl LE18 . . . . **203** C8
Nevada Pk LE13 . . . . **59** B3
Nevanthon Rd LE3 . . . . . **154** B5
Neville Cl LE12 . . . . **50** B4
Neville Day Cl PE9 . . . . . **168** F5
Neville Dr
Coalville LE67 . . . . **72** A1
Markfield LE67 . . . . **125** D8
Neville Rd LE3 . . . . **154** B5
Neville Smith Cl LE9 . . . **217** D1
NEVILL HOLT **228** D3
Nevill Holt Rd LE16 . . . . **228** F6
Nevis Cl NN17 . . . . **230** C1

Newall Cl LE17 . . . . **244** C7
Newark Cl LE12 . . . . **49** F3
Newarke Cl LE2 . . . . **259** A2
Newarke Houses Mus★
LE1 . . . . **259** A3
Newarke Point LE2 . . . . . **259** A2
Newarke St LE1 . . . . **259** B3
Newarke The LE2 . . . . . . **259** A3
Newark Rd LE4 . . . . **129** E7
New Ashby Ct LE11 . . . . . **51** B2
New Ashby Rd LE11 . . . . **51** B2
New Ave LE7 . . . . **79** A1
Newbery Ave NG10 . . . . . **10** F6
New Bldgs LE10 . . . . **197** D1
NEWBOLD
Ashby-de-la-Zouch **47** E3
Somerby **134** E7
Newbold CE Prim Sch
LE67 . . . . **47** E2
Newbold Cl LE12 . . . . **77** D4
Newbold Ct CV13 . . . . . . **149** D8
Newbold Dr DE74 . . . . **17** B5
NEWBOLD HEATH **150** A4
Newbold La LE65 . . . . **47** E5
Newbold Rd
Barlestone CV13 . . . . **149** E7
Desford LE9 . . . . **151** A4
Kirkby Mallory LE9 . . . . . **175** C7
Owston LE14, LE15 . . . . . **134** F7
NEWBOLD VERDON **150** A5
Newbold Verdon Prim Sch
LE9 . . . . **150** A4
Newbon Cl LE14 . . . . **51** E4
New Bond St LE1 . . . . . . **259** B4
Newborough Cl CV9 . . . . **119** A2
Newboults La PE9 . . . . . **143** C3
New Brickyard La
DE74 . . . . **18** D1
Newbridge High Sch
LE67 . . . . **96** D7
New Bridge Rd LE2 . . . . **179** B2
New Bridge St LE2 . . . . . **154** E3
New Broadway LE67 . . . . **71** C1
Newbury Ave LE13 . . . . . . **59** A5
Newbury Cl LE18 . . . . . . **180** C1
Newby Cl LE8 . . . . **178** F1
Newby Gdns LE2 . . . . **181** D4
New Causeway NG13 . . . . . **6** C2
New Cl
Leicester LE5 . . . . **155** D4
Swannington LE67 . . . . **71** A4
New College Leicester
LE3 . . . . **153** F7
New Coll Stamford
PE9 . . . . **143** E4
Newcomb Ct 2 PE9 . . . **143** D3
Newcombe Rd LE3 . . . . . **154** B2
Newcombe St LE16 . . . . . **240** E2
New Cotts NG32 . . . . **15** D5
Newcroft Prim Sch
LE2 . . . . **50** C2
New Cross Rd PE9 . . . . . **143** D4
New Field Rd LE15 . . . . . **113** B3
Newfields DE12 . . . . **68** A4
New Fields Ave LE3 . . . . **154** A2
New Fields Sq LE3 . . . . . **154** B1
New Forest Cl LE18 . . . . **203** D8
NEW FOUND POOL **154** C7
Newgate End LE18 . . . . . **180** C2
Newgates 2 PE9 . . . . . . **143** E3
Newhall Rd DE11 . . . . **44** C5
Newham Cl LE4 . . . . **130** A5
Newham Rd PE9 . . . . **143** C5
Newhaven Rd LE5 . . . . . **156** D3
New Henry St LE3 . . . . . **259** A5
Newington St LE4 . . . . . **129** B2
Newington Wlk LE4 . . . . **129** B2
NEW INN **184** C5
New Inn Cl LE9 . . . . **219** B5
New Inn La LE7 . . . . **184** C5
New King St LE11 . . . . . . **52** C3
New La LE12 . . . . **54** A4
Newlands Ave LE12 . . . . . **50** C2
Newlands Cl DE11 . . . . . . **44** A2
Newlands Rd
Barwell LE9 . . . . **198** B7
Welford NN6 . . . . **256** E5
Newland St LE16 . . . . . . **251** E5
New Lount (Nature
Trail)★ LE67 . . . . **47** D2
Newlyn Par LE5 . . . . **130** D1
Newmans Cl LE15 . . . . . **166** D3
Newmarket St LE2 . . . . . **180** B8
New Park Rd LE2 . . . . . . **179** E8
NEW PARKS **153** F7
New Parks Bvd LE3 . . . . **153** E7
New Parks Cres LE3 . . . **154** A8
New Park St LE3 . . . . . . **154** D5
New Parks Way LE3 . . . . **153** E7
New Pingle St LE3 . . . . . **259** A5
Newpool Bank LE2 . . . . . **181** E4
Newport Ave LE13 . . . . . . **59** C4
Newport Lo LE13 . . . . **59** C4
Newport Pl LE1 . . . . **259** C3
Newport St LE3 . . . . **154** C7
Newquay Cl LE10 . . . . . . **197** E4
Newquay Dr LE3 . . . . . . **127** C4
New Rd
Appleby Magna DE12 . . . . **119** E7
Belton-in-R LE15 . . . . . . **187** C6
Burton Lazars LE14 . . . . . **82** F6
Clipsham LE15 . . . . **89** D5
Collyweston PE9 . . . . . . **168** C2
Easton o t H PE9 . . . . . . **169** A5
Hinckley LE10 . . . . **216** A6
Illston on t H LE7 . . . . . . **183** E4
Kibworth Beauchamp
LE8 . . . . **224** B8

New Rd *continued*
Leicester LE1 . . . . **259** B4
Peggs Green LE67 . . . . **71** A8
Ryhall PE9 . . . . **116** E2
Staunton in t V NG13 . . . . . **1** D3
Stoney Stanton LE9 . . . . . **199** D2
Stretton LE15 . . . . **88** B7
Woodville DE11 . . . . **44** E2
New Romney Cl LE5 . . . . **156** E8
New Romney Cres
LE5 . . . . **156** E8
New Row
Ibstock LE67 . . . . **122** F8
Moira DE12 . . . . **68** A4
Willoughby-on-t-W LE12 . . . **34** E7
Woolsthorpe by B NG32 . . . **8** B1
Newry The LE2 . . . . **179** F5
NEW SAWLEY **10** B5
New St
Asfordby LE14 . . . . **57** F3
Barlestone CV13 . . . . **149** D8
Barrow-u-S LE12 . . . . **76** D7
Blaby LE8 . . . . **202** B8
Coalville LE67 . . . . **96** D8
Countesthorpe LE8 . . . . . **202** F4
Donisthorpe DE12 . . . . **67** E1
Draycott DE72 . . . . **9** A7
Earl Shilton LE9 . . . . **198** E7
Hinckley LE10 . . . . **197** D1
Kegworth DE74 . . . . **18** E3
Leicester LE1 . . . . **259** B3
Long Eaton NG10 . . . . **10** E8
Loughborough LE11 . . . . . . **52** B3
Lutterworth LE17 . . . . . . **244** C6
Measham DE12 . . . . **93** C6
Melton Mowbray LE13 . . . . **59** C3
Oakham LE15 . . . . **137** F6
Oakthorpe DE12 . . . . **93** A7
Queniborough LE7 . . . . . . **103** E5
Scalford LE14 . . . . **38** E5
Stamford PE9 . . . . **143** E4
Swadlincote DE11 . . . . **44** B2
New Star Rd LE4 . . . . . . **130** A4
NEWSTEAD **144** B4
Newstead Ave
Bushby LE7 . . . . **157** A4
Hinckley LE10 . . . . **215** D4
Leicester LE2 . . . . **128** C1
Wigston LE18 . . . . **180** C4
Newstead Mill PE9 . . . . . **144** B4
Newstead Rd
Belmesthorpe PE9 . . . . . **144** A8
Leicester LE2 . . . . **180** C8
Newstead Way LE11 . . . . **75** A6
NEW SWANNINGTON . . . **71** D4
New Swannington Prim
Sch LE67 . . . . **71** C5
NEWTON **253** A1
NEWTON BURGOLAND
. . . . **121** E7
Newton Burgoland Prim
Sch LE67 . . . . **121** E6
Newton Cl
Barrow-u-S LE12 . . . . **76** E8
Hartshill Green CV10 . . . . **194** B2
Loughborough LE11 . . . . . . **51** D6
Newton Ct CV3 . . . . **257** A8
Newton Dr LE4 . . . . **129** B8
NEWTON HARCOURT
. . . . **204** D7
Newton La
Great Glen LE8 . . . . **205** A7
Newton CV23 . . . . **253** A3
Newton Regis CV9 . . . . . **118** F2
Odstone CV13 . . . . **122** B5
Seckington B79 . . . . **118** B3
Wigston LE18 . . . . **180** E1
Newton Manor La
CV23 . . . . **257** A8
NEWTON-NETHERCOTE
. . . . **121** C7
Newton Park Cl 2
DE11 . . . . **44** A7
Newton Rd
Clifton u D CV23 . . . . . . **257** A7
Heather LE67 . . . . **95** B1
Hinckley LE10 . . . . **214** E7
Odstone CV13 . . . . **122** C4
Swepstone LE67 . . . . **121** D8
NEWTON REGIS **118** D4
Newton Regis CE Prim
Sch B79 . . . . **118** E3
NEWTON UNTHANK . . . **151** D6
Newton Way
Braybrooke LE16 . . . . **251** F6
Broughton Astley LE9 . . . **219** A4
NEWTOWN **143** F2
New Town PE9 . . . . **169** A5
Newtown Cl LE8 . . . . . . **223** F8
Newtown Cres LE15 . . . . **189** A3
Newtown Grange Farm
Bsns Pk LE9 . . . . **151** E5
NEWTOWN LINFORD
. . . . **126** D8
Newtown Linford La
LE6 . . . . **126** E5
Newtown Linford Prim
Sch LE6 . . . . **126** D8
Newtown Rd LE15 . . . . . **188** F3
Newtown St LE1 . . . . . . **259** B2
New Tythe St NG10 . . . . . **10** F7
New Walk Mus & Art
Gall★ LE1 . . . . **259** C2
New Way Rd LE5 . . . . . . **155** D2
New Wharf LE2 . . . . **259** A3
New Wlk
Leicester LE1 . . . . **259** C2

New Wlk *continued*
Sapcote LE9 . . . . **217** D7
Shepshed LE12 . . . . **50** B4
NEW YORK **26** A7
New Zealand La LE7 . . . **103** C6
Nicholas Dr LE6 . . . . **152** D8
Nichols St LE1 . . . . **259** C4
Nicklaus Rd LE4 . . . . . . **129** E5
Nicolson Rd LE4 . . . . . . **129** B8
Nidderdale Rd LE18 . . . . **180** F2
Nightingale Ave LE12 . . . **30** B1
Nightingale Cl LE9 . . . . **170** E1
Nightingale Dr DE11 . . . . **44** F3
Nightingale Gdns
CV23 . . . . **252** C1
Nightingale Way
LE15 . . . . **138** B7
Nine Acres DE74 . . . . **18** C2
Nithsdale Ave LE16 . . . . **240** F2
Nithsdale Cres LE16 . . . **240** F2
Nob Hill CV9 . . . . **120** A2
Noble Cl LE17 . . . . **244** C8
Noble St LE3 . . . . **154** D6
Nock Verges
Earl Shilton LE9 . . . . **176** A1
Stoney Stanton LE9 . . . . . **199** D2
Noel Ave LE15 . . . . **137** E5
Noel St LE3 . . . . **154** D3
NO MANS HEATH **118** F6
No Man's Heath La
CV9 . . . . **119** A3
No Man's Heath Rd
DE12 . . . . **91** F3
Nook Cl
Ratby LE6 . . . . **126** C1
Shepshed LE12 . . . . **50** C2
Nook La LE15 . . . . **140** F5
Nooks Country Park The★
LE8 . . . . **204** D6
Nook St LE3 . . . . **154** B7
Nook The
Anstey LE7 . . . . **127** E6
Bitteswell LE17 . . . . **244** B8
Cosby LE9 . . . . **201** D2
Cottingham LE16 . . . . . . **229** D1
Croxton Kerrial NG32 . . . . **24** A7
Easton o t H PE9 . . . . . . **169** A5
Enderby LE19 . . . . **178** A3
Great Glen LE8 . . . . **205** A8
Markfield LE67 . . . . **98** D1
Sproxton LE14 . . . . **41** F5
Walcote LE17 . . . . **245** B4
Whetstone LE8 . . . . **201** F7
Whissendine LE15 . . . . . . **84** F1
Wymeswold LE12 . . . . **33** C3
Noon Ct LE4 . . . . **129** A2
Norbury Ave LE4 . . . . . . **129** C1
Norbury Cl LE16 . . . . . . **240** D3
Norfolk Cl LE10 . . . . **215** D4
Norfolk Dr LE13 . . . . **82** D8
Norfolk Ho 4 LE3 . . . . . **154** D5
Norfolk Rd
Desford LE9 . . . . **151** B2
Long Eaton NG10 . . . . **10** F8
Wigston LE18 . . . . **179** F3
Norfolk Sq PE9 . . . . **143** D4
Norfolk St LE3 . . . . **154** D5
Norfolk Wlk LE3 . . . . . . **154** D5
Norman Ct
Kegworth DE74 . . . . **18** D1
Leicester, Oadby LE2 . . . . **181** D4
Norman Dagley Cl
LE9 . . . . **198** E7
Normandy Cl LE3 . . . . . . **153** C7
Normandy Way LE10 . . . **197** A3
Norman Rd LE4 . . . . **129** E8
Norman St LE3 . . . . **154** D4
NORMANTON
. . . . **3** C6
. . . . **140** D1
Normanton Church Mus★
LE15 . . . . **140** D1
Normanton Dr
Loughborough LE11 . . . . . . **52** B6
Oakham LE15 . . . . **138** B7
Normanton Gdns★
LE15 . . . . **140** D2
Normanton Gr LE9 . . . . . **177** A3
Normanton La
Bottesford NG13 . . . . **3** B4
Heather LE67 . . . . **95** B3
Stanford on S LE12 . . . . . . **31** B1
NORMANTON LE HEATH
. . . . **94** E6
NORMANTON ON SOAR
. . . . **30** D3
Normanton on Soar Prim
Sch LE12 . . . . **30** D3
Normanton Park Rd
Empingham LE15 . . . . . . **141** A4
Normanton LE15 . . . . **140** E2
Normanton Rd
Edith Weston LE15 . . . . . **166** B8
Leicester LE5 . . . . **155** D4
Packington LE65 . . . . **69** C1
NORMANTON THURVILLE
. . . . **176** D1
Norman Way LE13 . . . . . . **59** C3
Norris Cl LE4 . . . . **128** A3
NORRIS HILL **68** A6
Norris Hill DE12 . . . . **68** B6
Northage Cl LE12 . . . . **76** B4
Northampton Rd
Great Oxendon LE16 . . . . **250** F1
Market Harborough
LE16 . . . . **240** F3
Welford NN6 . . . . **256** E4
Northampton Sq LE1 . . **259** C3

Northampton St LE1 . . . **259** C3
North Ave
Coalville LE67 . . . . **96** D7
Leicester LE2 . . . . **155** C2
Northbank LE16 . . . . **240** E3
North Bridge Pl LE3 . . . **259** A5
North Brook Cl LE15 . . . . **88** A1
North Cl
Blackfordby DE11 . . . . **68** B8
Hinckley LE10 . . . . **215** E6
Northcote Rd LE2 . . . . . **180** B8
Northcote St NG10 . . . . . **10** E7
Northcote Wlk CV9 . . . . **170** D2
North Cres NG13 . . . . **3** A2
Northdene Rd LE2 . . . . . **180** B5
Northdown Dr LE4 . . . . . **129** E6
North Dr LE5 . . . . **156** A8
NORTH END **76** D3
North End LE16 . . . . **209** D6
North End Cl LE2 . . . . . . **179** F6
Northern's Cl NG33 . . . . . **65** B8
NORTH EVINGTON **155** E6
Northfield LE67 . . . . **124** A7
Northfield Ave
Birstall LE4 . . . . **129** B8
Long Eaton NG10 . . . . **10** B4
Wigston LE18 . . . . **180** B4
Northfield Cl LE13 . . . . . **59** C4
Northfield Dr LE67 . . . . . **97** B8
Northfield House Prim
Sch LE4 . . . . **129** E1
Northfield Rd
Blaby LE8 . . . . **179** B1
Hinckley LE10 . . . . **215** C7
Leicester LE4 . . . . **129** E1
Northfields LE65 . . . . **69** B8
NORTHFIELDS **129** E1
Northfields NG10 . . . . **10** B4
NORTHFIELDS **143** E4
Northfields LE15 . . . . . . **103** B4
Northfields Ct PE9 . . . . . **143** E4
Northfold Rd LE2 . . . . . . **180** C6
Northgate LE15 . . . . **137** F6
Northgates LE1 . . . . **259** A4
Northgate St LE3 . . . . . **259** A5
North Hall Dr LE7 . . . . . **105** B7
North Ho LE2 . . . . **155** B2
Northill Cl LE12 . . . . **77** E3
NORTH KILWORTH **246** F3
North La LE16 . . . . **224** D1
North Lea LE16 . . . . **227** B3
Northleigh Gr LE16 . . . . **240** D4
Northleigh Way LE9 . . . **198** D4
NORTH LUFFENHAM
. . . . **166** D4
North Luffenham Rd
North Luffenham
LE15 . . . . **166** B2
South Luffenham LE15 . . . **166** D1
North Meml Homes
LE2 . . . . **181** B6
North Rd
Clifton u D CV23 . . . . . . **257** A6
Long Eaton NG10 . . . . **10** C6
Loughborough LE11 . . . . . . **52** B6
South Kilworth LE17 . . . . **246** D1
North St E LE15 . . . . **189** B4
North St W LE15 . . . . . . **189** A4
North St
Asfordby Valley LE14 . . . . **58** B3
Ashby-de-la-Z LE65 . . . . . **69** B6
Barrow-u-S LE12 . . . . **76** D8
Leicester, Oadby LE2 . . . . **181** A6
Melbourne DE73 . . . . **26** A7
Melton Mowbray LE13 . . . . **59** C4
Rothley LE7 . . . . **101** E6
Stamford PE9 . . . . **143** D3
Swadlincote DE11 . . . . **44** B5
Swinford LE17 . . . . **254** B4
Syston LE7 . . . . **103** A4
Whitwick LE67 . . . . **71** C6
Wigston LE18 . . . . **180** D3
Northumberland Ave
Leicester LE4 . . . . **129** C2
Market Bosworth CV13 . . . **148** E2
Stamford PE9 . . . . **143** C3
Northumberland Rd
LE18 . . . . **179** F3
Northumberland St
LE1 . . . . **259** A5
North View Cl LE14 . . . . . **58** B3
North Warwickshire &
Hinkley Coll LE10 . . . . **215** F8
North Way LE7 . . . . **157** F4
Northwick Rd PE9 . . . . . **167** C5
NORTH WITHAM **65** B8
North Witham Rd
NG33 . . . . **65** B4
North Wlk DE12 . . . . **93** D7
Northwood Dr LE12 . . . . . **50** C6
NORTON-JUXTA-
TWYCROSS **120** B3
Norton La
Austrey CV9 . . . . **119** D1
Gaulby LE7 . . . . **183** C6
Orton-on-t-H CV9 . . . . . . **145** D6
Norton Rd LE9 . . . . **198** C2
Norton St
Leicester LE1 . . . . **259** A2
Uppingham LE15 . . . . **189** B4
Norwich Cl
Nuneaton CV11 . . . . **214** A8
Shepshed LE12 . . . . **50** A2
Norwich Rd LE4 . . . . **128** E3
Norwood Cl LE10 . . . . . . **197** E3
Norwood Rd LE5 . . . . . . **155** E2
NOSELEY **184** F2
Noseley Rd LE7 . . . . **184** A3

Notley Ct LE9 . . . . 198 C8
Notley Manor Dr LE9 . . . . 198 C8
Nottingham East Midlands
Int Airport DE74 . . . . 28 C8
Nottingham La LE14 . . . . . 35 C5
Nottingham Rd
Ab Kettleby LE14 . . . . 37 C4
Ashby-de-la-Z LE65 . . . . . . 69 D7
Ashby-de-la-Z, Lount
LE65 . . . . 46 F1
Barrow-u-S LE12 . . . . 53 E3
Bottesford NG13 . . . . .2 F1
Breedon on t h DE73 . . . . . 26 D1
Kegworth DE74 . . . . 18 D2
Leicester LE5 . . . . 155 D6
Long Eaton NG10 . . . . 10 E8
Loughborough LE11,
LE12 . . . . 52 D6
Melton Mowbray LE13 . . . . 59 B5
Peggs Green LE67 . . . . 71 A8
Worthington LE65 . . . . 47 C5
Nottingham Road Ind Est
LE65 . . . . 69 D8
Nottingham St LE13 . . . . . 59 C3
Nowell Cl LE2 . . . . 179 D1
Nuffield Hospl The
LE5 . . . . 156 B8
Nuffield Rd LE10 . . . . 214 E7
Nugent St LE3 . . . . 154 D6
NUNEATON 214 A4
Nuneaton La CV13 . . . . . . 195 F2
Nuneaton Rd
Atherstone CV9,
CV10 . . . . 194 B4
Hartshill Green CV10 . . . . 194 B2
Nunneley Way LE16 . . . . . 240 F5
Nursery Cl
Empingham LE15 . . . . 141 A6
Queniborough LE7 . . . . . . 103 E5
Shepshed LE12 . . . . 50 C6
Swadlincote DE11 . . . . 44 B6
Thurlaston LE9 . . . . 177 A2
Thurmaston LE4 . . . . 129 D6
Nursery End
Loughborough LE11 . . . . . . 74 D8
Market Harborough
LE16 . . . . 240 C2
Nursery Gdns
Coalville LE67 . . . . 71 E1
Earl Shilton LE9 . . . . 198 D7
Nursery Gr LE2 . . . . 76 E8
Nursery Hollow LE2 . . . . 179 A3
Nursery La
Holwell LE14 . . . . 37 D4
Knipton NG32 . . . . 14 E3
Quorn (Quorndon) LE12 . . . 76 A6
Nursery Rd LE5 . . . . 156 D7
Nurses La LE14 . . . . 62 E2
Nutfield Rd LE3 . . . . 154 C3
Nutkin Cl LE11 . . . . 51 F2
Nutt's La LE10 . . . . 215 A7

O

OADBY 181 C7
Oadby Ct LE2 . . . . 180 F6
Oadby Hill Dr LE2 . . . . . . 180 F6
Oadby Ind Est LE2 . . . . . . 180 F5
Oadby Rd LE18 . . . . 180 E3
Oak Ave LE17 . . . . 218 E1
Oakberry Rd LE17 . . . . . . 244 D8
Oakberry Road Ind Est
LE17 . . . . 244 D8
Oak Bsns Ctr The LE12 . . . 77 D3
Oak Cl
Coalville LE67 . . . . 97 A8
Hinckley LE10 . . . . 215 E6
Loughborough LE11 . . . . . . 75 A6
Market Harborough
LE16 . . . . 240 F4
Measham DE12 . . . . 93 C5
Thurlaston LE9 . . . . 177 A3
Uppingham LE15 . . . . 189 A5
Oak Cres
Braunstone Town LE3 . . . 153 C2
East Leake LE12 . . . . 31 D8
Oakcroft Ave LE9 . . . . 152 E5
Oakdale Cl LE3 . . . . 153 C6
Oakdale Rd LE9 . . . . 198 D7
Oakdene Rd LE2 . . . . 180 A6
Oak Dr
Ibstock LE67 . . . . 95 E1
Syston LE7 . . . . 103 B2
Oakenshaw Cl LE4 . . . . . . 128 E5
Oakfield LE15 . . . . 138 A8
Oakfield Ave
Birstall LE4 . . . . 128 F7
Glenfield LE3 . . . . 127 D2
Lutterworth LE17 . . . . 244 B6
Markfield LE67 . . . . 125 D8
Oakfield Cl LE8 . . . . 182 B1
Oakfield Cres LE8 . . . . . . 202 C6
Oakfield Rd LE2 . . . . 155 C3
Oakfield Way CV9 . . . . . . 171 B8
Oak Gn LE67 . . . . 125 E6
OAKHAM 138 B8
Oakham Castle* ̄
LE15 . . . . 138 A6
Oakham CE Prim Sch
LE15 . . . . 138 A7
Oakham Cl LE11 . . . . 51 E6
Oakham Dr LE67 . . . . 72 C2
Oakham Gr LE65 . . . . 69 A7
Oakham Rd
Ashwell LE15 . . . . 111 B7
Braunston-in-R LE15 . . . . 137 B3

Oakham Rd continued
Exton LE15 . . . . 113 A2
Greetham LE15 . . . . 88 A1
Knossington LE15 . . . . . . 136 A6
Langham LE15 . . . . 110 D2
Leesthorpe LE14 . . . . 83 D2
Oakham LE15 . . . . 138 C8
Owston LE7, LE15 . . . . . . 161 C8
Preston LE15 . . . . 164 C3
Somerby LE14 . . . . 108 D1
Whissendine LE15 . . . . 84 F1
Oakham Sch (Old Sch)
LE15 . . . . 138 A6
Oakham Sta LE15 . . . . . . 137 F7
Oakhurst Ct LE11 . . . . 51 C4
Oak La LE8 . . . . 221 F5
Oakland Ave
Leicester LE4 . . . . 129 C4
Long Eaton NG10 . . . . 10 C5
Oakland Rd LE2 . . . . 155 A1
Oaklands LE11 . . . . 51 F2
Oaklands Pk 4 LE16 . . . . 240 F2
Oaklands Sch LE5 . . . . . . 156 B4
Oaklands Way DE73 . . . . . 26 B8
Oakland Terr LE4 . . . . 10 C5
Oakleigh Ave LE2 . . . . . . 179 E1
Oakley Ave LE12 . . . . 50 B5
Oakley Cl LE12 . . . . 50 B5
Oakley Dr
Long Whatton LE12 . . . . . . 29 D2
Loughborough LE11 . . . . . . 51 F1
Oakley Mews LE16 . . . . . . 240 D3
Oakley Rd
Cottesmore LE15 . . . . 87 E2
Leicester LE5 . . . . 155 C7
Shepshed LE12 . . . . 50 B5
Oakley's Rd LE10 . . . . 10 E7
Oakley's Rd W NG10 . . . . . 10 D6
Oakmeadow LE3 . . . . 153 B7
Oakmeadow Way LE6 . . . . 126 E2
Oakpool Gdns LE2 . . . . . . 179 D3
Oak Rd
Desford LE9 . . . . 151 A3
Littlethorpe LE19 . . . . 201 C6
Melton Mowbray LE13 . . . . 59 C4
Stamford PE9 . . . . 142 F4
Oakridge Cl LE5 . . . . 130 C3
Oakridge Pk DE74 . . . . 17 A5
Oaks Ct LE19 . . . . 201 A8
Oaks Dr
Blaby LE8 . . . . 202 C7
Newbold Verdon LE9 . . . . 150 C4
Oakside Cl LE5 . . . . 156 C4
Oakside Cres LE5 . . . . . . 156 C5
OAKS IN CHARNWOOD
. . . . 73 A4
Oaks Ind Est
Loughborough LE11 . . . . . . 52 A6
Lutterworth LE17 . . . . 244 D7
Ravenstone LE67 . . . . 71 A1
Oaks Ind Est The
LE19 . . . . 201 A7
Oak Spinney Pk LE3 . . . . 153 B4
Oaks Rd
Great Glen LE8 . . . . 205 C8
Whitwick LE67 . . . . 72 C5
Oak St
Leicester LE5 . . . . 155 C7
Swadlincote DE11 . . . . 44 A2
Oaks Way
Earl Shilton LE9 . . . . 198 E8
Leicester, Oadby LE2 . . . . 180 F8
OAKTHORPE 93 B7
Oakthorpe Ave LE3 . . . . . 154 B4
Oakthorpe Prim Sch
DE12 . . . . 93 A7
Oaktree Cl
Groby LE6 . . . . 126 E3
Hamilton LE5 . . . . 130 C2
Kibworth Beauchamp
LE8 . . . . 206 B1
Oak Tree Rd LE67 . . . . 96 B7
Oak Way LE14 . . . . 80 D8
Oakwood Ave LE18 . . . . . 180 D4
Oakwood Cl
Leicester Forest East
LE3 . . . . 152 F2
Thornton LE67 . . . . 124 F3
Oakwood Dr LE11 . . . . 51 B1
Oakwood Rd LE4 . . . . 128 D1
Oasis The LE3 . . . . 153 B8
Oban Cl PE9 . . . . 143 A4
Oban Rd LE10 . . . . 215 A7
Oban St LE3 . . . . 154 C7
Oberon Cl CV11 . . . . 214 A1
Occupation La
Willoughby-on-t-W
LE12 . . . . 34 E5
Woodville DE11 . . . . 44 D1
Occupation Rd
Middleton LE16 . . . . 229 B2
Nailstone CV13 . . . . 123 B3
Swadlincote DE11 . . . . 67 C8
Ocean Cl LE5 . . . . 156 C7
Ocean Rd LE5 . . . . 156 C7
Octopus Bsns Pk
LE15 . . . . 166 F2
Odam Cl LE3 . . . . 153 F2
Oddfellows Row DE12 . . . . 93 C5
Odeon Arc LE1 . . . . 259 B4
ODSTONE 122 D4
Odstone Dr LE10 . . . . 214 F8
Odstone La LE67 . . . . 121 F6
Odstone Rd CV13 . . . . . . 122 D2
Office Village The
LE11 . . . . 52 B6
Offranville Cl LE4 . . . . . . 129 F6
Ogwen Cl LE5 . . . . 156 D6

Okehampton Ave LE5 . . . 155 F3
Old Ashby Rd LE11 . . . . . . 51 B2
Old Barn Pas 7 PE9 . . . . 143 D2
Old Barn Wlk LE4 . . . . . . 128 C3
Old Braunstone The
LE3 . . . . 154 C2
Old Bridewell LE13 . . . . . . 59 D6
Oldbury Rd CV10 . . . . 194 A1
Oldbury View CV10 . . . . . 194 B1
Old Chapel Wlk LE17 . . . . 232 E6
Old Charity Farm LE2 . . . 156 E1
Old Church St LE2 . . . . . . 179 C7
Old City Of Dan LE67 . . . . 71 F4
Old Coach Rd The
LE17 . . . . 219 D2
Old Coffee Mills The 6
LE16 . . . . 240 F2
Old Dairy The LE13 . . . . . . 59 C4
Old Dairy Yd LE15 . . . . . . 113 B3
OLD DALBY 35 E4
Old Dalby CE Prim Sch
LE14 . . . . 35 E4
Old Dalby La LE14 . . . . 36 C6
Old Dalby Trad Est
LE14 . . . . 36 A5
Old End DE12 . . . . 92 F1
Old Engine Yd The
LE12 . . . . 32 E5
Oldershaw Ave DE74 . . . . 18 C2
Oldershaw Rd LE12 . . . . . . 31 F8
Olders Valley DE11 . . . . . . 44 E4
Old Field Cl LE8 . . . . 202 C4
Oldfield Dr DE11 . . . . 44 C5
Old Forge Cl LE7 . . . . 101 F4
Old Forge Cl LE2 . . . . 30 A1
Old Forge La NG13 . . . . .5 C5
Old Forge Rd
Ashby Magna LE17 . . . . . . 220 A2
Fenny Drayton CV13 . . . . 195 A6
Old Garden Cl LE8 . . . . . . 202 B7
Old Gate Rd LE7 . . . . 78 E7
Old Gn LE15 . . . . 227 F6
Old Granary The LE7 . . . . 160 A7
Old Great North Rd
PE9 . . . . 142 E6
Old Hall Cl
Groby LE6 . . . . 126 F3
Thurmaston LE4 . . . . 129 E8
Old Hall Ct B79 . . . . 118 D3
Old Hall Gdns DE11 . . . . . 44 A2
Old Hall La LE16 . . . . 239 F3
Old Hill The NG32 . . . . 14 F3
Old Holly La CV9 . . . . 170 C3
Old Holt Rd LE16 . . . . 228 A7
OLD INGARSBY 158 B7
Old John Twr* ̄ LE6 . . . . . 99 F3
Old La The NG13 . . . . .6 C2
Old Manor Farm LE14 . . . . 20 C3
Old Mill Cl LE9 . . . . 218 F5
Old Mill La LE1 . . . . 259 A5
Old Mill Prim Sch
LE9 . . . . 218 F6
Old Mill Rd LE19 . . . . 218 F5
Old Mill The LE12 . . . . 30 B3
Old Milton St LE1 . . . . . . 259 C4
Old Nurseries The
LE67 . . . . 95 F8
Old Park Cl NG11 . . . . 18 F6
Old Parsonage La
LE15 . . . . 32 C1
Old Post La NG33 . . . . 65 B8
Old Rectory Camping &
Cvn Pk The LE15 . . . . . . 187 C7
Old Rectory Cl
Broughton Astley LE9 . . . 218 F6
Churchover CV23 . . . . 252 C6
Old Rectory Mus* ̄
LE11 . . . . 52 B4
Old School Cl
Ellistown LE67 . . . . 96 E2
North Luffenham LE15 . . . 166 D3
Walton LE17 . . . . 236 A2
Old School Ct 6 LE9 . . . . 198 F8
Old School La LE67 . . . . . 124 B4
Old School Mews
Aston-on-T DE72 . . . . 16 B8
Market Harborough
LE16 . . . . 240 E3
Uppingham LE15 . . . . 189 B3
Old School Wlk LE16 . . . . 225 D7
Old School Yd LE17 . . . . . 217 D7
Old Stableyard The
LE16 . . . . 225 D6
Old Station Cl
Coalville LE67 . . . . 71 D1
Shepshed LE12 . . . . 50 B2
Old Station Dr LE14 . . . . . . 61 C3
Old Station Rd LE67 . . . . . 103 A3
Old Station Yd NG13 . . . . . . .3 C3
Old Surgery The LE67 . . . . 96 D6
Old Tannery Dr 1
LE12 . . . . 77 C3
Old Vicarage Gdns
LE14 . . . . 37 D3
Old Way LE21 . . . . 30 A1
Old Woodyard The
LE12 . . . . 30 A1
Oliver Cl LE7 . . . . 102 F2
Oliver Ct LE2 . . . . 155 D2
Oliver Rd
Leicester LE4 . . . . 129 D2
Loughborough LE11 . . . . . . 52 B2
Oliver St LE2 . . . . 179 E8
Olphin St LE4 . . . . 155 A8
Olympic Cl LE3 . . . . 153 D8
One Barrow La LE12 . . . . . 72 E7
Onslow St 3 LE2 . . . . 155 C4
Ontario Cl LE1 . . . . 259 C5

Orange Hill LE17 . . . . 244 D5
Orange St
Uppingham LE15 . . . . 189 B4
Wigston LE18 . . . . 202 F8
Orchard Ave
Castle Donington DE74 . . . 17 A3
Glen Parva LE2 . . . . 179 B3
Orchard CE Prim Sch
LE9 . . . . 218 D7
Orchard Cl
Austrey CV9 . . . . 119 A2
Barkestone-le-V NG13 . . . . .6 B2
Barlestone CV13 . . . . 149 D8
Breaston DE72 . . . . .9 F8
Cosby LE9 . . . . 201 D3
Diseworth DE74 . . . . 28 C5
East Leake LE12 . . . . 31 D8
Egleton LE15 . . . . 138 C3
Gilmorton LE17 . . . . 235 C4
Glaston LE15 . . . . 190 B5
Hinckley LE10 . . . . 216 A5
Leicester, Oadby LE2 . . . . 181 A4
Melbourne DE73 . . . . 26 A7
Osgathorpe LE12 . . . . 48 C4
Ravenstone LE67 . . . . 70 F2
Shepshed LE12 . . . . 50 B3
1 Stamford PE9 . . . . 143 D3
Sutton Bonington LE12 . . . 30 C5
Uppingham LE15 . . . . 189 B5
Witherley CV9 . . . . 194 B8
Orchard Com Prim Sch
DE74 . . . . 17 A3
Orchard Est LE12 . . . . 75 F6
Orchard Gdns LE4 . . . . . . 129 F6
Orchard Ho LE1 . . . . 259 B5
Orchard La
Countesthorpe LE8 . . . . . 202 F3
Great Glen LE8 . . . . 205 B7
Gretton NN17 . . . . 213 C1
Orchard Pk Mobile Home
Pk LE7 . . . . 103 B4
Orchard Rd
Birstall LE4 . . . . 129 B7
Broughton Astley LE9 . . . 218 E7
Langham LE15 . . . . 110 C3
Lutterworth LE17 . . . . 244 B5
Stamford PE9 . . . . 143 D3
Willoughby Waterleys
LE8 . . . . 220 C5
Orchards Dr LE18 . . . . . . 180 B2
Orchardson Ave LE4 . . . . 155 B8
Orchard St
Fleckney LE8 . . . . 222 F7
Hinckley LE10 . . . . 215 E8
Ibstock LE67 . . . . 95 F1
Leicester LE1 . . . . 259 B5
Long Eaton NG10 . . . . 10 E7
2 Loughborough LE11 . . . 52 A4
Market Harborough
LE16 . . . . 240 E4
Orchards The
Newton CV23 . . . . 252 F1
Thornton LE67 . . . . 124 F4
Orchard Terr NN6 . . . . . . 256 E6
Orchard Way
Groby LE6 . . . . 126 E3
Lyndon LE15 . . . . 165 D5
Seagrave LE12 . . . . 77 F8
Sibbertoft LE16 . . . . 249 A2
Stoney Stanton LE9 . . . . . 199 E2
Orchard View LE12 . . . . . 101 E8
Orchard Wlk LE17 . . . . . . 233 D7
Orchid Cl
Hamilton LE5 . . . . 130 C2
Melton Mowbray LE13 . . . . 82 A8
Mountsorrel LE12 . . . . 76 F2
Narborough LE19 . . . . 178 A1
Orchid Pl LE9 . . . . 219 B4
Oriel Dr LE7 . . . . 103 C3
Orkney Cl LE10 . . . . 197 C1
Orkney Way LE8 . . . . 202 F3
Orlando Rd LE2 . . . . 155 B2
Orly Ave DE74 . . . . 17 A2
Orme Cl LE4 . . . . 128 A3
Ormen Gn LE3 . . . . 153 D6
Ormes La LE7 . . . . 171 B4
Ormond Cl LE9 . . . . 198 A7
Oronsay Rd LE4 . . . . 128 B3
Oronsay Rd LE4 . . . . 128 B3
Orpine Rd LE5 . . . . 130 B3
Orsett Cl LE5 . . . . 156 A8
Orson Dr LE18 . . . . 180 B3
Orson St LE5 . . . . 155 D5
ORSTON 2 A6
Orston La NG13 . . . . .2 E5
Orston Prim Sch NG13 . . . .2 A7
Orton Cl LE7 . . . . 78 F1
Orton Hill CV9 . . . . 145 E8
Orton La
Austrey CV9 . . . . 145 B8
Norton-J-T CV9 . . . . 120 A2
Orton-on-t-H CV9 . . . . . . 145 D5
Orton-on-t-H CV9 . . . . . . 145 F2
Sheepy Magna CV9 . . . . . 146 A3
Twycross CV9 . . . . 146 B3
ORTON-ON-THE-HILL
. . . . 145 D4
Orton Rd
Earl Shilton LE9 . . . . 198 A8
Leicester LE4 . . . . 128 F3
Ortons Ind Est LE67 . . . . . 71 D1

Not–Oxe **285**

Orwell Cl
Clifton u D CV23 . . . . 257 A5
Loughborough LE11 . . . . . . 51 D6
Orwell Dr LE4 . . . . 128 A4
OSBASTON 149 D5
Osbaston Cl LE10 . . . . . . 197 F3
Osbaston La CV13 . . . . . . 149 D5
Osborne Rd
Leicester LE5 . . . . 155 D5
Loughborough LE11 . . . . . . 51 C6
Osbourne Ct LE8 . . . . 201 F8
OSGATHORPE 48 D4
Osiers Business Pk The
LE19 . . . . 178 E6
Osiers The
Braunstone Town LE3 . . . 178 F7
Kegworth DE74 . . . . 18 E2
Loughborough LE11 . . . . . . 75 A7
Mountsorrel LE12 . . . . 76 C1
Osmaston Cl NG10 . . . . .9 F5
Osmaston Rd LE5 . . . . . . 155 D4
Osprey Cl LE9 . . . . 218 F7
Osprey Rd LE4 . . . . 128 A6
Osterley Cl LE11 . . . . 51 C4
Ostler La LE14 . . . . 57 D7
Oswin Rd LE3 . . . . 153 E5
Ottawa Rd LE1 . . . . 259 C4
Otter La LE12 . . . . 76 F2
Otter Way LE8 . . . . 201 F5
Oundle Cl LE65 . . . . 69 A8
Our Lady's Convent Sch
LE11 . . . . 52 B2
Outfields Dr LE7 . . . . 100 F2
Outlands Dr LE10 . . . . . . 197 A2
Outram Dr DE11 . . . . 44 D4
Outwood Cl LE3 . . . . 153 D5
OUTWOODS 47 E1
Outwoods Ave LE11 . . . . . 51 F1
Outwoods Dr LE11 . . . . . . 51 F1
Outwoods Edge Prim Sch
LE11 . . . . 75 A7
Outwoods La LE6 . . . . 70 E8
Out Woods Nature
Reserve* ̄ LE11 . . . . 74 C5
Outwoods Nature Trail
The* ̄ LE11 . . . . 74 C5
Outwoods Rd LE11 . . . . . . 74 F8
Outwoods The LE10 . . . . 215 F8
Oval Cl LE15 . . . . 166 D4
Oval The
Coalville LE67 . . . . 97 A7
Leicester LE1 . . . . 259 C2
Leicester, Oadby LE2 . . . . 180 F4
Market Harborough
LE16 . . . . 240 E4
Nailstone CV13 . . . . 123 B3
Stoney Stanton LE9 . . . . . 199 E2
Woodhouse LE12 . . . . 75 A3
Overbrook Grange
CV11 . . . . 196 A1
Overdale Ave LE3 . . . . . . 127 B3
Overdale Cl
Anstey LE7 . . . . 127 B2
Long Eaton NG10 . . . . 10 A6
Market Harborough
LE16 . . . . 241 A3
Overdale Inf Sch LE2 . . . . 180 C6
Overdale Jun Sch
LE2 . . . . 180 C7
Overdale Rd
Leicester LE2 . . . . 180 C7
Thurmaston LE4 . . . . 129 F6
Overfield Ave LE16 . . . . . 240 F5
Overfield Cl
Narborough LE19 . . . . 201 A7
Ratby LE6 . . . . 152 B8
Overfield Wlk LE6 . . . . . . 126 D1
Overing Cl LE4 . . . . 129 A3
Overpark Ave LE3 . . . . . . 154 A3
OVERSEAL 67 A3
Overseal Prim Sch
DE12 . . . . 67 B4
Overseal Rd LE3 . . . . 153 E8
Overton Cl LE67 . . . . 70 E7
Overton Rd
Ibstock LE67 . . . . 122 F7
Leicester LE5 . . . . 155 D7
Owen Ave NG10 . . . . 10 F6
Owen Cl
Braunstone Town
LE3 . . . . 153 D1
Leicester LE4 . . . . 129 E5
Owen Cres LE13 . . . . 59 D4
Owen Dr LE13 . . . . 59 D4
Owen St LE67 . . . . 71 C1
OWSTON 135 B4
Owston Dr LE18 . . . . 180 B3
Owston Rd
Knossington LE15 . . . . . . 135 F5
Somerby LE14 . . . . 108 C1
Owston Wood Rd
LE15 . . . . 135 E3
Oxbow Cl LE13 . . . . 59 A2
Oxburgh Cl LE11 . . . . 51 C5
Oxendon Hall LE16 . . . . . 250 E3
Oxendon Rd
Braybrooke LE16 . . . . 251 D5
Clipston LE16 . . . . 250 B1
East Farndon LE16 . . . . . 250 B5
Great Oxendon LE16 . . . . 251 A1
Oxendon St LE2 . . . . 155 B5
Oxendon Wlk 9 LE2 . . . . 155 B5
Oxey Cross Rds LE7 . . . . 161 B3

Oxford Ave LE2 155 B3
Oxford Ct
Leicester LE1 259 B2
Syston LE7 103 C4
Oxford Dr
Melton Mowbray LE13 82 D8
Wigston LE18 179 F2
Oxford Rd
Desford LE9 151 A3
Leicester LE2 155 B2
Stamford PE9 143 C5
Oxford St
Barwell LE9 198 B7
Coalville LE67 71 E1
Earl Shilton LE9 198 F8
Leicester LE1 259 B2
Long Eaton NG10 10 D8
Loughborough LE11 51 F4
Shepshed LE12 50 B2
Swadlincote DE11 44 A1
Syston LE7 103 C3
Oxley Cl LE12 50 A3
Oxley Prim Sch LE12 50 A3
Oxon Way LE5 156 A6
Oxted Rise LE2 181 A3
Ozier Holt NG10 10 C6

P

Packer Ave LE3 153 B4
Packe St LE11 52 A4
Packe Terr LE8 205 B8
Packhorse Dr LE19 178 D2
Packhorse Gn LE2 179 D3
Pack Horse La LE11 52 B3
Packhorse Rd LE2 179 D3
Pack Horse Rd DE73 26 B8
PACKINGTON 69 C2
Packington CE Prim Sch LE65 69 B2
Packington Hill DE74 18 C2
Packington Nook La LE65 69 A4
Packman Gn LE8 202 F3
Packwood Rd LE4 128 E3
Paddock Cl
Castle Donington DE74 16 F3
Countesthorpe LE8 202 E4
Leicester, Oadby LE2 180 F6
Melton Mowbray LE13 59 D1
Quorn (Quorndon) LE12 76 B5
Rothley LE7 101 E5
Whissendine LE15 85 A1
Paddock Ct LE16 240 E3
Paddock La LE16 228 D8
Paddock St LE18 180 D2
Paddocks The
Bottesford NG13 3 A2
Carlby PE9 117 C8
Littlethorpe LE19 201 D7
Queniborough LE7 104 A5
Sedgebrook NG32 8 F8
Sutton Bonington LE12 30 B6
Tinwell PE9 142 F1
Waltham on t W LE14 40 A7
Willoughby Waterleys LE8 220 C5
Paddocks View NG10 10 B8
Paddock The
Allington NG32 4 F5
Claybrooke Magna LE17 232 E6
Kibworth Beauchamp LE8 224 A8
Markfield LE67 98 E1
Newbold Verdon LE9 150 A4
Newton CV23 253 A1
Shepshed LE12 50 B4
Stamford PE9 143 C3
Paddock View
Skillington NG33 43 B8
Syston LE7 102 F3
Paddock Way LE10 214 F6
Paddy's La LE14 35 A1
Padgate Cl LE7 156 F6
Padstow Rd LE4 129 E3
Padwell La LE7 157 A4
Page Cl LE17 244 C8
Page La DE74 28 C5
Paget Ave LE4 129 B7
Paget Ct LE8 224 A8
Paget Rd
Heather LE67 95 F3
Leicester LE3 154 D6
Lubenham LE16 239 E3
Paget's End LE14 20 D4
Paget St
Kibworth Beauchamp LE8 224 A8
Leicester LE2 179 C6
Loughborough LE11 51 F4
Paigle Rd LE2 179 C6
PAILTON 242 A1
Painter St LE1 155 A8
Palace Hill LE7 158 C4
Palfreyman La LE2 181 E4
Palissy Cl DE11 44 D4
Pall Mall LE13 59 E5
Palmer Ave LE11 51 F5
Palmer Dr LE17 244 C5
Palmer Rd LE10 197 B2
Palmers La LE7 185 C3
Palmer St LE4 129 A3
Palmerston Bvd LE2 180 C6
Palmerston Cl LE8 223 F8
Palmerston Ct DE73 26 B7
Palmerston Rd LE13 59 A6
Palmerston Way LE2 180 D6
Palms Pk LE11 51 D5
Pamela Pl LE4 128 E4
Pankhurst Rd LE4 128 B6
Pantain Rd LE11 51 F1
Paper Mill Cl LE7 127 D6
Parade The
Glen Parva LE2 179 A2
6 Hinckley LE10 215 D8
Leicester, Oadby LE2 181 A6
Shepshed LE12 50 A2
Paradise Cl DE12 68 A4
Paradise La LE14 35 F4
Paramore Cl LE8 202 A5
Pares Cl LE67 71 E5
Parham Cl LE3 128 B1
Paris Cl LE65 69 A7
Park Ave
Allington NG32 4 F5
Castle Donington DE74 16 F3
Leicester LE2 179 E8
Loughborough LE11 52 B1
Markfield LE67 98 E1
Melton Mowbray LE13 59 B3
Shepshed LE12 50 C2
Park Cl
Ashby-de-la-Z LE65 69 A5
Cosby LE9 201 D2
Earl Shilton LE9 175 E1
Foxton LE16 224 E1
Shepshed LE12 50 B4
Park Cotts LE15 190 A5
Park Cres LE2 181 C4
Park Ct
Loughborough LE11 52 B2
Swadlincote DE11 44 C5
Parkdale LE67 95 E1
Parkdale Rd LE4 129 E6
Park Dr
Braunstone Town LE3 153 C3
Glenfield LE3 153 C8
Market Harborough LE16 240 E4
Parker Dr LE4 128 E2
Parkers Cl
Blackfordby DE11 45 B1
Ellistown LE67 96 D3
Parkers Fields LE12 76 A7
Park Farm LE65 93 F8
Park Farm Bsns Units LE7 159 E2
Parkfield Cl LE6 152 D8
Parkfield Cres DE12 92 F1
Parkfield Rd
Oakham LE15 137 E7
Ryhall PE9 116 F1
Parkhill LE2 179 D8
Park Hill LE7 105 B7
Park Hill Ave LE2 179 D7
Park Hill Dr LE2 179 D8
Park Hill La LE12 78 B6
Park Ho LE16 240 E4
Park House Cl LE4 129 A5
Park House Ct
Blaby LE8 202 B8
Sapcote LE9 217 D7
Parkinson Dr CV9 170 E2
Park La
Bagworth LE67 124 A7
Castle Donington DE74 16 E3
Leicester LE2 155 D2
Melton Mowbray LE13 59 C3
Oakham LE15 137 F6
Skillington NG33 43 B8
Stamford PE9 143 E2
Sutton Bonington LE12 30 C5
Walton LE17 236 B3
Parkland Dr LE2 181 A6
Parkland Mews NG10 10 D8
Parkland Prim Sch The LE18 179 F1
Parklands Ave LE6 126 D3
Parklands Dr LE11 75 A8
Park Mews
Market Harborough LE16 240 E4
Wigston LE18 202 F8
Park Rd
Allington NG32 4 F5
Anstey LE7 127 D5
Ashby-de-la-Z LE65 69 B7
Birstall LE4 128 F6
Blaby LE8 202 B8
Coalville LE67 71 D1
Cosby LE9 201 D3
Donisthorpe DE12 67 E2
Earl Shilton LE9 198 E8
Hinckley LE10 215 E8
Ketton PE9 167 F5
Loughborough LE11 52 B2
Loughborough, Shelthorpe LE11 75 A8
Melton Mowbray LE13 59 C3
Narborough LE19 201 B7
Overseal DE12 67 A6
Ratby LE6 152 D7
Sapcote LE9 217 D7
Sileby LE12 77 C4
Swadlincote, Church Gresley DE11 44 C2
Tilton on t H LE7 133 B4
Wigston LE18 202 F8
Park Rise
Leicester LE3 153 E5
Shepshed LE12 50 B4
Parkside LE6 126 F4
Parkside Ave NG10 10 B8
Parkside Cl LE4 128 A6
Parkside Ct LE10 215 E8
Parkside Dr NG10 10 B8
Parkside The NG33 65 B4
Parks Prim Sch LE3 154 A8
Parks Specl Sch The LE15 137 F7
Park St
Breaston DE72 9 F8
Fleckney LE8 222 F8
Leicester LE1 259 B3
Loughborough LE11 52 B3
Market Bosworth CV13 148 F3
Swadlincote DE11 44 A6
Parkstone Cl LE18 203 C8
Parkstone Rd
Desford LE9 151 B2
Leicester LE5 156 D8
Syston LE7 103 B5
Park The
Langham LE15 110 B2
Leicester LE2 155 B3
Market Bosworth CV13 149 A3
Park Vale Rd LE5 155 C5
Park View
Aston-on-T DE72 16 B7
Leicester LE3 153 E5
Sharnford LE10 217 B4
Sheepy Magna CV9 171 B7
Stamford PE9 143 F2
Park View Cl LE9 218 F6
Park View Riding Sch* LE7 101 A1
Parkway The LE5 156 B7
Park Wlk PE9 169 A6
Parlour Cl LE18 180 C2
Parnell Cl LE19 201 C6
Parnham's Cl LE14 36 C8
Parry St LE5 155 C7
Parsons Cl
Swadlincote DE11 44 A1
Willey CV23 242 F6
Parsons Dr
Glen Parva LE2 179 A3
Sileby LE12 77 E4
Parsons La LE10 217 C4
Parson's La LE10 215 F8
Parsonwood Hill LE67 71 E5
Partridge Cl
Mountsorrel LE12 76 F2
Syston LE7 102 F4
Upper Bruntingthorpe LE17 236 D5
Partridge Dr DE11 44 F3
Partridge Rd LE4 129 F6
Partridge Way LE15 138 B8
Parvian Rd LE2 180 A4
Paske Ave LE7 105 C7
Pasley Cl LE2 179 D4
Pasley Rd LE2 179 D4
Pass Ctyd 5 LE65 69 B6
Pasture La
Barleythorpe LE15 137 D8
Gaddesby LE7 105 B8
Hathern LE12 30 B2
Hose LE14 21 A4
Knipton NG32 14 F4
Leicester LE1 259 A5
Newbold Verdon LE9 150 B4
Stathern LE14 12 F1
Sutton Bonington LE12 30 A6
Thorpe Satchville LE14 106 B7
Pasture La N LE14, LE7 80 E1
Pastures La DE12 93 C7
Pastures Prim Sch The LE19 177 F2
Pastures The
Barrow-u-S LE12 76 E6
Broughton Astley LE9 218 F5
Cottesmore LE15 112 D8
Leicester, Oadby LE2 181 E4
Market Harborough LE16 240 C3
Narborough LE19 178 A1
Shepshed LE12 73 A8
Syston LE7 102 E3
Pate Rd LE13 81 F8
Paterson Cl LE4 128 B6
Paterson Dr LE12 74 F1
Paterson Pl LE12 50 B5
Paton St LE3 154 D4
Patrick St LE16 240 F2
Patterdale Dr LE11 51 C1
Patterdale Rd LE4 129 E6
Paudy Cross Roads LE12 54 D2
Paudy La LE7, LE12 55 C5
Paul Dr LE4 129 F4
Pauline Ave LE4 129 B4
Paulyn Way LE65 68 F5
Pavilion Way LE11 52 A6
Pawley Cl LE8 202 A6
Pawley Gdns LE2 179 D4
Pawley Gn LE2 179 D4
Payne's La LE16 227 F7
Payne St LE4 129 B3
Peace Hill LE7 185 C2
Peach La NG32 4 F4
Peacock Dr LE8 201 F5
Peacock La LE1 259 A3
Peakdale LE18 180 F1
Peakdale Cl NG10 10 A6
Peake Rd LE4 129 D1
Peartree Ave LE12 50 D3
Peartree Cl
Anstey LE7 127 D5
Peartree Cl *continued*
Castle Donington DE74 17 A3
Glenfield LE3 153 B7
Pear Tree Cl
Barwell LE9 198 B8
Hartshorne DE11 45 A7
Lutterworth LE17 244 A6
Peartree Ct LE65 47 F5
Pear Tree Gdns LE16 240 D2
Pear Tree La LE11 51 A6
Pear Tree Way LE11 51 B6
Peashill Cl LE12 77 E3
Peatling Grainger LE17 220 A2
PEATLING MAGNA 221 B6
PEATLING PARVA 235 F8
Peatling Rd
Ashby Magna LE17 220 B1
Countesthorpe LE8 202 F2
Pebble Cotts LE17 248 D8
PECKLETON 176 A7
Peckleton Comm LE9 176 B7
Peckleton Gn LE9 198 B8
Peckleton La
Desford LE9 151 B2
Peckleton LE9 176 E8
Peckleton Lane Bsns Pk LE9 176 C7
Peckleton Rd LE9 175 D6
Peckleton View LE9 151 B2
Pedlars Cl LE4 128 B3
Peebles Way LE4 129 D3
Peeble Yd LE14 82 A1
Peel Cl LE8 223 F8
Peel Dr LE11 52 C4
Peel St NG10 10 E8
Peewit Cl LE2 179 A3
Pegasus Cl LE2 155 B5
Peggs Cl
Earl Shilton LE9 198 F8
Measham DE12 93 D5
Peggs Grange LE67 96 D6
PEGGS GREEN 71 A8
Peggs La LE7 103 F5
Peldar Pl LE67 97 B8
Peldon Cl LE4 128 D2
Pelham St
Leicester LE1 259 B2
Leicester, Oadby LE2 181 A6
Pelham Way LE1 259 B2
Pell Cl LE12 76 E8
Pells Cl LE8 222 F8
Pembroke Ave
Syston LE7 103 C2
Wigston LE18 179 F2
Pembroke Rd PE9 143 C5
Pembroke St LE5 155 C7
Pembury Cl LE8 182 B1
Pen Cl LE2 179 E4
Penclose Rd LE8 222 E8
Pendene Rd LE2 155 C1
Pendlebury Dr LE2 180 A7
Pendleton Cl NG33 65 B3
Pendragon Way LE3 153 A2
Penfold Cl
Hathern LE12 30 A2
Sapcote LE9 217 D8
Penfold Dr LE8 202 D4
Penhale Rd LE3 178 F8
Penistone St LE67 95 F2
Peniston Rise DE73 26 A7
Penkridge Rd DE11 44 B1
Penkridge Wlk LE4 128 E4
Penman Way LE19 178 E5
Pennant Cl LE3 153 D7
Pennant Rd LE10 215 D5
Penney Cl LE18 180 C3
Pennie Cl NG10 10 D4
Pennine Cl
Leicester, Oadby LE2 181 D5
Shepshed LE12 50 C2
Pennine Dr LE15 166 C7
Pennine Way
Ashby-de-la-Z LE65 69 B5
Swadlincote DE11 44 A3
Pennine Way Jun Sch DE11 44 A2
Penn La
Melbourne DE73 26 B7
Stathern LE14 12 F4
Wibtoft LE17 232 C2
Penn Moor Cl NG10 10 A6
Penn St LE15 138 A6
Pennyfields Bvd NG10 10 B7
Penny La LE9 198 A6
Penny Long La LE3 152 F3
Penrith Ave LE12 49 F2
Penrith Rd LE4 129 C2
Penryn Cl CV11 214 A4
Penryn Dr LE18 180 C1
Pensilva Cl LE18 180 C1
Pentland Ave LE12 50 D3
Pentland Cl LE10 197 B1
Pentland Ct LE15 137 D6
Pentland Rd LE65 69 D6
Pentridge Cl LE18 203 C8
Penzance Ave LE18 180 D1
Penzance Cl LE10 197 E4
Penzance Way CV11 214 A5
Peppercorn Cl LE4 128 D3
Pepper Dr LE12 75 F7
Pepper's Cl LE12 76 D4
Peppers Dr DE74 18 B2
Pepper's La LE14 82 F7
Pera Tech Pk LE13 59 B4
Percival St LE5 155 D7
Percy Rd
Cottesmore LE15 87 E2
Percy Rd *continued*
Leicester LE2 179 E7
Percy St LE3 179 A8
Peregrine Cl DE12 93 C4
Peregrine Rd LE9 218 E7
Peregrine Rise LE4 128 A6
Perkins Cl LE16 240 F4
Perkin's La LE14 36 A1
Perkyn Rd LE5 156 D6
Perran Ave LE67 72 A2
Perry Cl LE12 74 F2
Perry Gr LE11 52 C1
Perseverance Rd LE4 129 A5
Perth Ave LE3 154 A7
Perth Rd PE9 143 A4
Peterborough Ave LE15 138 B6
Peterborough Rd LE15 191 D6
Peterfield Rd LE67 72 A3
Petergate 1 PE9 143 D2
Peterhouse Cl PE9 143 D5
Peterlees The DE12 67 E1
Peters Ave LE9 150 C4
Peters Cl DE73 27 B3
Peter's Cl LE9 199 C2
Peters Dr LE5 156 B7
Petersfield LE9 200 D4
Petersfield Rd LE13 59 B4
Petersham Rd NG10 10 B8
Peters Way LE15 189 F3
Pettiver Cres 2 CV21 257 A1
Petunia Cl LE3 152 F2
Petworth Dr
Leicester LE3 154 B6
Loughborough LE11 51 C5
Market Harborough LE16 241 B2
Pevensey Ave LE5 156 D3
Pevensey Rd LE11 51 E5
Peverel Ct LE3 153 E1
Peverel Rd LE3 154 A2
Peveril Cres NG10 9 F5
Peveril Rd LE17 220 A2
Phillip Dr LE2 179 E1
Phillips Cres LE4 128 B6
Phillips Ct PE9 143 E2
Phipps Cl LE8 202 A6
Phoenix Bsns Pk LE10 214 E8
Phoenix Cl LE3 154 B7
Phoenix Dr LE12 77 D2
Phoenix Pk LE67 71 B3
Phyllis Gr NG10 10 F7
Piccaver Rise LE3 153 D6
Pickards La LE14 39 A6
Pick Bldg The LE1 259 B3
Pickering Cl
Leicester LE4 129 D1
Stoney Stanton LE9 199 D2
Pickering Dr LE67 96 C4
Pickering Rd LE9 218 F4
Pickford Cl CV11 214 A1
Pickhill Rd LE5 130 D3
Picks Cl LE16 241 B3
Pick St LE12 50 B4
PICKWELL 108 C3
Pickwell Cl LE3 153 E8
Pickwell Rd
Leesthorpe LE14 108 E8
Somerby LE14 108 C2
PICKWORTH 115 C8
Pickworth Cl LE15 138 B7
Pickworth Rd PE9 115 D3
Pied Bull Cl PE9 168 A6
Piers Rd LE3 127 C1
Pike Cl LE10 215 D5
Pilgrim Gdns LE5 156 A3
Pilgrims Gate LE10 216 A6
Pilgrims La CV23 252 F1
Pilkington Rd LE3 153 E3
Pillings Rd LE15 137 F8
PILTON 165 F2
Pilton Cl LE15 138 B6
Pilton Rd LE15 166 B2
Pimpernel Cl LE19 177 F1
Pincet La
Husbands Bosworth LE17 237 B2
North Kilworth LE17 247 A6
Pindar Rd LE3 154 A7
Pine Cl
Ashby-de-la-Z LE65 69 D7
East Leake LE12 31 D8
Loughborough LE11 75 A7
Lutterworth LE17 244 A7
Stamford PE9 142 F4
Stoke Golding CV13 196 E7
Pine Ct DE12 68 B6
Pine Dr LE7 103 B2
Pine Gr CV21 257 A1
Pinehurst Cl LE3 153 C6
Pinel Cl LE9 219 A4
Pine Rd LE3 153 C8
Pines The
Bushby LE7 157 B4
Draycott DE72 9 B7
Great Bowden LE16 241 A6
Pine Tree Ave
Groby LE6 126 F2
Leicester LE5 156 A8
Pine Tree Cl
Leicester, Oadby LE2 181 B4
Newbold Verdon LE9 150 C4
Pine Tree Gdn LE2 181 B4
Pine Tree Gr LE9 152 E2
Pine View LE3 153 B4
Pine Wlk NN17 230 E1

Pinewood Ave LE4 . . . . . . 129 E6
Pinewood Cl
  Countesthorpe LE8 . . . . . 202 E4
  Leicester LE4 . . . . 128 A5
Pinewood Ct LE67 . . . . . . 125 E6
Pinewood Dr LE67 . . . . . . 125 E6
Pinfold LE3 . . . . 178 F7
Pinfold Cl
  Bottesford NG13 . . . . 3 A3
  Hinckley LE10 . . . . 214 F7
  North Luffenham LE15 . . . 166 C4
  South Luffenham LE15 . . . 191 E8
Pinfold Ct LE14 . . . . 106 E4
Pinfold Gate
  Ketton PE9 . . . . 167 F5
  Loughborough LE11 . . . . 52 B4
Pinfold Gdns LE11 . . . . 52 B4
Pinfold Jetty **6** LE11 . . . . 52 B4
Pinfold La
  Bottesford NG13 . . . . 3 A3
  Harby LE14 . . . . 12 C3
  Market Overton LE15 . . . . . 87 A6
  North Luffenham LE15 . . . 166 E1
  South Luffenham LE15 . . . 166 E1
  Stamford PE9 . . . . 143 E2
  Stamford PE9 . . . . 143 F3
Pinfold Pl LE14 . . . . 12 C3
Pinfold Rd LE4 . . . . 129 D6
Pinfold The
  Markfield LE67 . . . . 125 E8
  Newton Burgoland
  LE67 . . . . 121 D7
  Ratby LE6 . . . . 152 C8
Pingle La
  Morcott LE15 . . . . 191 B6
  Potters Marston LE9 . . . . . 199 E6
Pingle Sch The DE11 . . . . . 44 A5
Pingle St LE3 . . . . 259 A5
Pingle The
  Barlestone CV13 . . . . 149 D8
  Long Eaton NG10 . . . . 10 D8
  Melbourne DE73 . . . . 26 A7
  Quorn (Quorndon) LE12 . . . 75 E5
Pintail Cl LE8 . . . . 201 F4
Pintail Ct DE12 . . . . 93 B4
PINWALL 170 D5
Pinwall La CV9 . . . . 170 E4
Pipe La CV9 . . . . 145 C4
Piper Cl
  Leicester LE3 . . . . 154 A7
  Long Whatton LE12 . . . . . . 29 D3
  Loughborough LE11 . . . . . . 51 F1
  Shepshed LE12 . . . . 50 C6
Piper Dr LE12 . . . . 29 C2
Piper La LE67 . . . . 95 F8
Piper Way LE3 . . . . 154 A7
Pipewell Wlk **2** LE4 . . . . 128 E5
Pipistrelle Dr CV13 . . . . . 148 C3
Pipistrelle Way LE2 . . . . . 181 E4
Pipit Cl DE12 . . . . 93 C4
Pipit Wlk CV23 . . . . 252 C1
Pisca La LE67 . . . . 95 D2
Pitchens Cl LE4 . . . . 127 F5
Pitchers La LE16 . . . . 229 D7
Pit Hill LE8 . . . . 223 F6
Pithiviers Cl LE65 . . . . 69 A5
Pit La PE9 . . . . 168 A7
Pits Ave LE3 . . . . 178 E7
Pitsford Dr LE11 . . . . 51 A2
Pitt La LE67 . . . . 70 E5
Pitton Cl LE18 . . . . 203 C8
Plackett Cl DE72 . . . . 9 D8
Plain Gate LE7 . . . . 101 C8
Plantagenet Way LE65 . . . . 69 D7
Plantation Ave LE2 . . . . . 179 C6
Plantations The **7**
  NG10 . . . . 10 A8
Plantation The LE8 . . . . . 202 E4
Plant La NG10 . . . . 10 A4
Platts La LE7 . . . . 102 C4
Player Cl LE4 . . . . 129 D5
Pleasant Cl
  Leicester Forest East
  LE3 . . . . 152 F2
  Loughborough LE11 . . . . . . 52 A4
Pleasant Pl LE2 . . . . 18 D2
Pleasant Terr LE15 . . . . . . 189 B4
Plough Cl
  Broughton Astley LE9 . . . . 219 A4
  Leicester Forest East
  LE3 . . . . 152 F1
  Mountsorrel LE12 . . . . 101 D8
Ploughmans Cl LE12 . . . . . 50 C5
Ploughman's Lea LE7 . . . 103 D7
Ploughmans Yd **11**
  LE16 . . . . 240 E3
Plover Ave DE11 . . . . 44 F3
Plover Cl LE15 . . . . 138 B8
Plover Cres LE4 . . . . 128 B6
Plover Rd DE7 . . . . 117 A6
Plowman Cl LE3 . . . . 127 C1
Plummer La DE74 . . . . 18 C2
Plummer Rd DE11 . . . . 44 A5
Plumtree Cl LE11 . . . . 51 F6
Plumtree Way LE7 . . . . . . 103 B3
PLUNGAR 12 F8
Plungar La NG13 . . . . 6 A1
Plungar Rd NG13 . . . . 5 C4
Pluto Cl LE2 . . . . 155 B5
Plymouth Dr LE5 . . . . 155 F4
Plymstock Cl LE3 . . . . 154 B4
Poachers Cl LE3 . . . . 153 B8
Poachers Cnr LE67 . . . . 72 B8
Poachers Pl LE2 . . . . 181 D4
Pochin Dr LE16 . . . . 240 F5
Pochin's Bridge Rd
  LE18 . . . . 203 A8
Pochin Sch The LE7 . . . . . 130 D8

Pochins Cl LE18 . . . . 180 C1
Pochin St LE7 . . . . 200 C4
Pochin Way LE12 . . . . 77 D4
Pocket End LE11 . . . . 74 E8
Pocklingtons Wlk
  LE1 . . . . 259 B3
Polaris Cl LE2 . . . . 155 B5
Polden Cl LE12 . . . . 50 C2
Polebrook Cl LE3 . . . . 127 E3
Polebrook Mews LE9 . . . . 151 D8
Police Hos LE15 . . . . 138 A7
Pollard Cl LE13 . . . . 59 E5
Pollard Ct LE2 . . . . 155 D2
Pollard Rd LE3 . . . . 153 E3
Pollards Cl LE15 . . . . 191 F5
Pollard Way LE67 . . . . 71 A2
Polly Bott's Lane Or Lea La
  LE67 . . . . 98 F4
Pomeroy Dr LE2 . . . . 180 F5
Pond End DE74 . . . . 17 B6
Pond La LE15 . . . . 88 B1
Pond St LE12 . . . . 77 F7
Pool Rd
  Leicester LE3 . . . . 154 C6
  Melbourne DE73 . . . . 26 D6
Pool St DE11 . . . . 44 D2
Pope Cres LE19 . . . . 178 A3
Pope St LE2 . . . . 180 A8
Poplar Ave
  Birstall LE4 . . . . 129 A7
  Countesthorpe LE8 . . . . . . 202 E4
  East Leake LE12 . . . . 31 D8
  Lutterworth LE17 . . . . 244 B6
  Markfield LE67 . . . . 125 D8
  Moira DE12 . . . . 67 E2
  Swadlincote DE11 . . . . 44 B6
Poplar Cl LE15 . . . . 189 B5
Poplar Dr DE12 . . . . 93 C6
Poplar Hill LE12 . . . . 54 A4
Poplar Rd
  Breaston DE72 . . . . 9 F8
  Corby NN17 . . . . 230 D1
  Littlethorpe LE19 . . . . 201 B6
  Loughborough LE11 . . . . . . 75 B7
Poplars Cl LE6 . . . . 126 E3
Poplars Ct LE16 . . . . 240 D4
Poplars The
  Billesdon LE7 . . . . 159 C2
  Earl Shilton LE9 . . . . 176 A1
  Hartshill Green CV10 . . . . 194 B2
  Leicester LE3 . . . . 179 A7
  Ratby LE6 . . . . 126 B1
Poplar Terr CV13 . . . . 147 E8
Poppins The LE4 . . . . 128 B6
Popple Cl LE9 . . . . 219 A5
Poppy Cl
  Coalville LE67 . . . . 97 A8
  Groby LE6 . . . . 127 A3
  Leicester LE2 . . . . 179 F4
  Loughborough LE11 . . . . . . 75 A6
Porlock Cl
  2 Long Eaton NG10 . . . . 10 A8
  Shepshed LE12 . . . . 50 C2
Porlock Dr LE17 . . . . 235 C4
Porlock St LE3 . . . . 154 B5
Portcullis Rd LE5 . . . . 130 E1
Porter's La PE9 . . . . 169 A5
Portgate LE18 . . . . 180 E1
Portia Cl CV11 . . . . 214 A5
Portland Dr LE10 . . . . 197 E4
Portland Rd
  Kirby Fields LE9 . . . . 152 E4
  Leicester LE2 . . . . 155 C1
  Long Eaton NG10 . . . . 10 B4
Portland St LE9 . . . . 201 D4
Portland Twrs LE2 . . . . . . 180 E8
Portland Wlk LE2 . . . . 181 C3
Portloc Dr LE18 . . . . 203 D8
Portman St LE4 . . . . 129 B2
Portmore Cl LE4 . . . . 128 C2
Portreath Dr CV11 . . . . . . 214 A5
Portsdown Rd LE2 . . . . . . 180 D6
Portslade Ho LE3 . . . . 153 C6
Portsmouth Rd LE4 . . . . . 129 B1
Portwey The LE5 . . . . 155 F8
Portwood Ind Est DE11 . . . 44 A1
Post Office La
  Lyndon LE15 . . . . 165 D5
  Newton Harcourt LE8 . . . . 204 D6
  Plungar NG13 . . . . 5 F1
  Redmile NG13 . . . . 6 F4
  Ryhall PE9 . . . . 116 F2
  Twyford LE14 . . . . 106 E1
  Witherley CV9 . . . . 194 B7
Post Office Row NG13 . . . . 7 F8
Post Rd LE4 . . . . 102 E1
Posy La DE72 . . . . 16 A7
Pott Acre LE7 . . . . 76 F1
Potters Croft DE11 . . . . 44 A5
Potters La LE12 . . . . 31 F8
POTTERS MARSTON 199 F5
Potter St
  Leicester LE1 . . . . 259 C4
  Melbourne DE73 . . . . 26 B7
Potters Yd DE73 . . . . 26 B7
Potterton Rd LE4 . . . . 128 D3
Pougher Cl LE9 . . . . 217 E7
Poulteney Dr LE12 . . . . 75 F6
Poultney La LE17 . . . . 235 F1
Powell Row LE17 . . . . 244 B8
Powers Rd LE9 . . . . 197 F5
Powys Ave LE2 . . . . 155 E1
Powys Gdns LE2 . . . . 155 E1
Poynings Ave LE3 . . . . . . 154 A6
Praetor Ho **2** LE10 . . . . 197 D1
Prebend St LE2 . . . . 155 B4

Preceptory The NG33 . . . . 43 D2
Precinct The LE17 . . . . 244 B1
Premier Drum Works
  LE18 . . . . 202 F8
Prentice Cl LE12 . . . . 68 A4
Presents La LE12 . . . . 49 B6
Prestbury Rd LE11 . . . . 51 B4
PRESTON 164 B2
Preston Cl
  Ratby LE6 . . . . 152 E8
  Sileby LE12 . . . . 77 C2
  Stanton u B LE67 . . . . 97 F1
Preston Ct LE15 . . . . 164 F1
Preston Dr LE9 . . . . 150 B5
Preston Rd
  Hinckley LE10 . . . . 197 B2
  Wing LE15 . . . . 164 E2
Preston Rise LE5 . . . . 130 C1
Preston's La LE67 . . . . 70 E6
Prestop Dr LE65 . . . . 68 F6
PRESTWOLD 53 D8
Prestwold La LE12 . . . . 53 D7
Prestwold Rd LE5 . . . . . . 155 D8
Prestwood Park Dr
  DE11 . . . . 44 D5
Pretoria Cl LE4 . . . . 128 C7
Pretoria Rd
  Ibstock LE67 . . . . 96 B2
  Kirby Muxloe LE9 . . . . 152 D5
Prevost Gdns LE12 . . . . 76 A6
Price Way LE4 . . . . 130 A7
Pride Pl LE16 . . . . 240 D2
Priesthills Rd LE10 . . . . . . 215 D8
Priestley Rd LE3 . . . . 154 A4
Priestman Rd LE3 . . . . 153 C1
Priest Mdw LE8 . . . . 222 F7
Primethorpe Wlk LE9 . . . . 218 E7
Primrose Cl
  Groby LE6 . . . . 127 A3
  Narborough LE19 . . . . 201 A8
Primrose Dr LE10 . . . . 215 E5
Primrose Hill LE2 . . . . 180 F6
Primrose Mdw DE11 . . . . . 44 B7
Primrose Way
  Kirby Muxloe LE9 . . . . 152 B5
  Queniborough LE7 . . . . . . 103 E6
  Stamford PE9 . . . . 142 E5
Prince Albert Dr LE3 . . . . 153 C7
Prince Charles St LE14 . . . 57 F3
Prince Dr LE2 . . . . 181 C5
Princes Cl LE7 . . . . 127 E6
Princes Rd
  Old Dalby LE14 . . . . 36 C6
  Stamford PE9 . . . . 143 E4
Princess Anne Sq LE14 . . . 57 F3
Princess Ave
  Leicester, Oadby LE2 . . . . 181 C4
  Oakham LE15 . . . . 137 E6
Princess Cl DE11 . . . . 44 F2
Princess Ct LE11 . . . . 52 A6
Princess Dr
  Kirby Muxloe LE9 . . . . 152 D4
  Melton Mowbray LE13 . . . . 82 C7
Princess Rd
  Atherstone CV9 . . . . 170 E1
  Hinckley LE10 . . . . 215 E4
Princess Rd E LE1 . . . . . . 259 C2
Princess Rd W LE1 . . . . . . 259 C2
Princess Road Backways
  LE1 . . . . 259 B2
Princess St
  Long Eaton NG10 . . . . 10 D8
  Loughborough LE11 . . . . . . 52 B3
  Narborough LE19 . . . . 201 C8
  Swadlincote DE11 . . . . 67 A8
Prince St
  Coalville LE67 . . . . 96 D8
  Long Eaton NG10 . . . . 10 D8
Prince William Rd
  LE11 . . . . 52 A6
Prince William Way
  LE11 . . . . 52 A6
Princewood Rd NN17 . . . 230 E3
Printers Yd LE15 . . . . 189 B4
Print Room The LE1 . . . . . 259 B3
Priorfields LE65 . . . . 69 C5
Prior Park Flats **6**
  LE65 . . . . 69 C5
Prior Park Ho **7** LE65 . . 69 C5
Prior Park Rd LE65 . . . . . . 69 B5
Priory Bsns Pk LE8 . . . . . 205 E2
Priory Cl
  Swadlincote DE11 . . . . 44 A6
  Syston LE7 . . . . 102 F3
  Thringstone LE67 . . . . 71 C8
Priory Cres LE3 . . . . 153 E5
Priory Ct NG33 . . . . 65 B3
Priory Gdns PE9 . . . . 143 F3
Priory La LE67 . . . . 98 E4
Priory Rd
  Loughborough LE11 . . . . . . 74 E8
  Manton LE15 . . . . 164 E6
  Market Bosworth CV13 . . . 148 D2
  Stamford PE9 . . . . 143 F3
Priory View LE14 . . . . 81 B8
Priory Wlk
  4 Hinckley LE10 . . . . . 197 E1
  Leicester Forest East
  LE3 . . . . 153 A3
Private Rd LE67 . . . . 96 B7
Proctor's Park Rd LE12 . . . 76 C7
Progress Way LE4 . . . . . . 130 A3
Prospect Hill LE5 . . . . 155 C6
Prospect Rd
  Kibworth Beauchamp
  LE8 . . . . 223 F8
  Leicester LE5 . . . . 155 D6
Prospect Way LE9 . . . . . . 198 E8

Providence Ct DE11 . . . . . 44 F2
Pryor Rd LE12 . . . . 77 D4
Pudding Bag La
  Exton LE15 . . . . 113 A3
  Shepshed LE12 . . . . 72 F8
Pudding La LE14 . . . . 19 C5
Pughe's Cl LE10 . . . . 216 A6
Pulford Dr LE7 . . . . 157 A6
Pullman Rd LE18 . . . . 180 B2
Pullman Trad Est
  LE15 . . . . 189 C3
Pulteney Ave LE11 . . . . 75 B8
Pulteney Rd LE11 . . . . 75 B8
Pumping Station Cott
  LE16 . . . . 230 A7
Pump La
  Asfordby LE14 . . . . 57 F2
  Shenton CV13 . . . . 173 B5
Purbeck Ave LE12 . . . . 50 D3
Purbeck Cl
  Long Eaton NG10 . . . . 10 A8
  Wigston LE18 . . . . 203 D8
Purcell Rd LE4 . . . . 155 A8
Purdy Ct LE15 . . . . 137 F6
Purdy Mdw NG10 . . . . 9 F5
Purley Rd LE4 . . . . 129 C1
Purley Rise LE12 . . . . 50 C2
Putney Rd LE2 . . . . 155 A2
Putney Rd W LE2 . . . . 154 F2
Pyeharps Rd LE10 . . . . . . 215 E5
Pyke The LE7 . . . . 76 F1
Pym Leys NG10 . . . . 9 F5
Pymm Ley Cl LE6 . . . . 126 F3
Pymm Ley Gdns LE6 . . . . 126 F3
Pymm Ley La LE6 . . . . 126 F3
Pytchley Cl
  Cottesmore LE15 . . . . 87 F4
  Leicester LE4 . . . . 128 E5
Pytchley Dr LE11 . . . . 74 F8

Q

Quadrant The
  Leicester LE4 . . . . 128 F2
  Uppingham LE15 . . . . 189 B4
Quaker Cl
  Fenny Drayton CV13 . . . . . 195 A6
  Melbourne DE73 . . . . 26 A8
Quaker Rd LE12 . . . . 77 C1
Quantock Rise LE12 . . . . . 50 C2
Quarry Berry La
  Chilcote DE12 . . . . 91 F1
  Newton Regis DE12 . . . . . 118 E8
Quarry La
  Atherstone CV9 . . . . 194 A6
  Enderby LE19 . . . . 178 A4
  Snarestone DE12 . . . . 93 F1
Quarrymans Ct LE67 . . . . 98 D1
Quarry Mobile Home Pk
  LE67 . . . . 125 D8
Quay The LE12 . . . . 76 D3
Quebec Rd LE1 . . . . 259 C4
Queen Eleanor Tech Coll
  PE9 . . . . 143 D5
Queen's Cl LE14 . . . . 38 E5
Queens Ct DE72 . . . . 9 A7
Queens Dr
  Leicester Forest East
  LE3 . . . . 153 A3
  Narborough LE19 . . . . 178 D2
  Wigston LE18 . . . . 180 B2
Queen's Dr DE11 . . . . 44 B6
Queensferry Par LE2 . . . . 179 C3
Queensgate Dr LE4 . . . . . 128 E8
Queensmead Cl LE6 . . . . 126 E2
Queensmead Com Prim
  Sch LE3 . . . . 153 F4
Queen's Park Ct **3**
  LE10 . . . . 215 E8
Queen's Park Flats **2**
  LE10 . . . . 215 E8
Queen's Park Terr **4**
  LE10 . . . . 215 E8
Queens Park Way
  LE2 . . . . 179 D2
Queens Rd
  Kegworth DE74 . . . . 18 D2
  Leicester LE2 . . . . 155 B1
Queen's Rd
  Blaby LE8 . . . . 202 B7
  Hinckley LE10 . . . . 215 E4
  Loughborough LE11 . . . . . . 52 C4
  Oakham LE15 . . . . 138 A7
  Uppingham LE15 . . . . 189 A4
Queens St LE9 . . . . 143 D4
Queen's St DE12 . . . . 93 C5
Queen St
  Barkby LE7 . . . . 130 C7
  Barwell LE9 . . . . 198 B6
  Bottesford NG13 . . . . 3 B2
  Coalville LE67 . . . . 96 D8
  Leicester LE1 . . . . 259 C3
  Leicester, Oadby LE2 . . . . 181 B5
  Long Eaton NG10 . . . . 10 E7
  2 Loughborough LE11 . . 52 C3
  Market Harborough
  LE16 . . . . 241 A2
  Markfield LE67 . . . . 125 D8
  Shepshed LE12 . . . . 50 B4
  Swadlincote DE11 . . . . 44 A1
  Uppingham LE15 . . . . 189 B4
Queensway
  Barwell LE9 . . . . 198 C2
  Castle Donington DE74 . . . 16 F4
  Melbourne DE73 . . . . 26 B8
  Melton Mowbray LE13 . . . . 82 C8
  Old Dalby LE14 . . . . 36 C6

Queensway Ho DE12 . . . . . 93 C5
Queen's Wlk PE9 . . . . 143 C3
Queen Victoria Ct **10**
  LE10 . . . . 197 D1
Queen Victoria Dr
  DE11 . . . . 44 B5
Quelch Cl LE67 . . . . 96 D6
Quemby Cl LE4 . . . . 129 A2
Quenby Cres LE7 . . . . 103 C3
Quenby Hall LE7 . . . . 132 E2
Quenby St LE5 . . . . 155 D7
QUENIBOROUGH 103 F5
Queniborough CE Prim
  Sch LE7 . . . . 103 F5
Queniborough Hall
  LE7 . . . . 104 A5
Queniborough Ind Est
  LE7 . . . . 103 D5
Queniborough Rd
  Leicester LE4 . . . . 129 C1
  Queniborough LE7 . . . . . . 103 E5
  Syston LE7 . . . . 103 D2
Quick Cl DE73 . . . . 26 A7
Quickthorns LE2 . . . . 181 B7
Quiney Way LE2 . . . . 181 C6
Quinton Rise LE2 . . . . 181 A4
Quorn Ave
  Ab Kettleby LE14 . . . . 37 C2
  Leicester, Oadby LE2 . . . . 181 D4
  Melton Mowbray LE13 . . . . 59 B3
Quorn Cl LE11 . . . . 52 C2
Quorn Cres
  Coalville LE67 . . . . 97 B8
  Cottesmore LE15 . . . . 87 F3
Quorndon Cres NG10 . . . . 10 D5
Quorndon Rise LE6 . . . . . 126 E2
Quorndon Terr LE12 . . . . . 75 F6
Quorndon Waters Ct
  LE12 . . . . 75 F6
Quorn Flats LE12 . . . . 76 A5
Quorn Hunt Kennels The
  LE14 . . . . 81 B4
Quorn Mill LE12 . . . . 76 A5
Quorn Pk LE12 . . . . 54 B1
QUORN (QUORNDON)
  . . . . 76 B4
Quorn Rd LE5 . . . . 155 D7
Quorn & Woodhouse Sta
  LE12 . . . . 75 D5

R

Racecourse La LE14 . . . . . 83 A6
Racecourse Rd PE9 . . . . . 169 D5
Racemeadow Prim Sch
  CV9 . . . . 170 E1
Racemeadow Rd CV9 . . . 170 E1
Radar Rd LE3 . . . . 153 D5
Radcliffe Cl PE9 . . . . 143 D3
Radcliffe Rd PE9 . . . . 143 D3
Radcot Lawns LE2 . . . . . . 179 D3
Radford Cl CV9 . . . . 170 E2
Radford Dr LE3 . . . . 153 C3
Radford Ho LE3 . . . . 153 C3
Radford Mdw DE74 . . . . . 16 F3
Radiant Rd LE5 . . . . 156 C7
Radleigh Grange DE11 . . . 45 A2
Radley Cl LE65 . . . . 69 A8
Rad Mdws NG10 . . . . 10 C6
Radmoor Rd LE11 . . . . 51 F3
Radmore Rd LE10 . . . . . . 197 D3
Radnor Ct LE19 . . . . 177 F2
Radnor Dr LE2 . . . . 50 B5
Radnor Rd LE18 . . . . 180 A3
Radstone Wlk LE5 . . . . . . 156 A6
Raeburn Rd LE2 . . . . 155 B1
RAGDALE 56 D4
Ragdale Rd
  Leicester LE4 . . . . 129 D1
  Ragdale LE14 . . . . 56 D1
Railway Cl NG33 . . . . 65 B3
Railway Side DE11 . . . . . . 44 B1
Railway St LE18 . . . . 202 F8
Railway Terr LE11 . . . . 52 C5
Raine Way LE2 . . . . 181 B3
Rainsborough Gdns
  LE16 . . . . 250 D8
Rainsbrook Dr CV11 . . . . . 214 A1
Rainsford Cres LE4 . . . . . 128 E3
Raleigh Cl LE10 . . . . 197 D4
Ralph Cl LE11 . . . . 74 D8
Ralph's Cl LE17 . . . . 219 D2
Ralph Toon Ct LE14 . . . . . . 57 F3
Rambler Cl DE11 . . . . 44 A5
Ramsbury Rd LE2 . . . . . . 180 B5
Ramscliff Ave LE12 . . . . . . 92 F8
Ramsdean Ave LE18 . . . . . 180 C3
Ramsden Rd CV9 . . . . 194 A7
Ramsey Cl
  Hinckley LE10 . . . . 197 B1
  Lutterworth LE17 . . . . 244 D6
Ramsey Gdns LE5 . . . . . . 130 E1
Ramsey Way LE5 . . . . 130 E1
Ramson Cl LE5 . . . . 130 C2
Rancliffe Cres LE3 . . . . . . 154 A4
Randall Cl LE7 . . . . 105 D3
Randle Dr LE7 . . . . 157 A4
Randles Ct LE7 . . . . 157 A4
Range Rd LE65 . . . . 69 C6
Range The LE5 . . . . 110 B3
Ranksborough Dr
  LE15 . . . . 110 B3
*Ranksborough Hall***
  LE15 . . . . 110 B2

Rannoch Cl
Hinckley LE10 ... 215 B8
Leicester LE4 ... 128 C2
Rannoch Way NN17 ... 230 C1
Ranton Way LE3 ... 154 C8
Ranworth Wlk LE4 ... 128 E4
RATBY ... 152 B8
Ratby La
Braunstone Town LE3 ... 153 A5
Kirby Muxloe LE9 ... 152 E7
Markfield LE67 ... 125 E7
Ratby Meadow La
LE19 ... 178 E3
Ratby Prim Sch LE6 ... 152 C8
Ratby Rd LE6 ... 126 E3
Ratcliffe Cl LE65 ... 69 A6
Ratcliffe Coll LE7 ... 78 A3
Ratcliffe Ct LE2 ... 180 D8
RATCLIFFE CULEY ... 171 B3
Ratcliffe Dr LE9 ... 200 D7
Ratcliffe House La
CV9 ... 171 C4
Ratcliffe La
Atherstone CV9 ... 170 F4
Lockington DE74 ... 18 C7
Sheepy Magna CV9 ... 171 A5
RATCLIFFE ON SOAR ... 18 F6
RATCLIFFE ON T WREAKE
... 78 C2
Ratcliffe Rd
Atherstone CV9 ... 170 E1
Hinckley LE10 ... 215 F6
Leicester LE2 ... 180 D8
Loughborough LE11 ... 52 C5
Sileby LE12 ... 77 E3
Thrussington LE7 ... 78 E3
Ratcliffe St LE4 ... 129 B2
Ratts La LE15 ... 137 A2
Ravel Cl PE9 ... 143 B4
Raven Cl DE12 ... 93 B4
Ravenhurst Prim Sch
LE3 ... 178 F8
Ravenhurst Rd LE3 ... 178 F8
Raven Rd LE3 ... 153 E3
Ravensbridge Dr LE4 ... 154 E8
Ravenslea LE67 ... 95 E8
Ravensthorpe Dr LE11 ... 51 B3
Ravensthorpe Rd
LE18 ... 180 E2
RAVENSTONE ... 95 F8
Ravenstone Ct LE67 ... 95 E8
Ravenstone Rd
Heather LE67 ... 95 C4
Ibstock LE67 ... 95 E3
Ravenstone LE67 ... 71 A2
Ravenwood DE11 ... 44 C3
Rawdon Cl DE74 ... 17 A4
Rawdon Rd DE12 ... 67 E5
Rawdon Side DE11 ... 44 D4
Rawdon Terr 11 LE65 ... 69 B6
Raw Dykes Rd LE2 ... 154 E2
Rawlings Ct LE2 ... 181 E4
Rawlins Cl LE12 ... 75 A1
Rawlins Com Coll LE12 ... 76 A6
Rawlinson Ct LE3 ... 128 A1
Rawson St
Enderby LE19 ... 178 B3
Leicester LE1 ... 259 C2
Rawsthorne Wlk LE4 ... 155 A8
Rayleigh Gn LE5 ... 130 E1
Rayleigh Way LE5 ... 130 E1
Raymond Ave LE11 ... 51 D6
Raymond Rd LE3 ... 154 C3
Rayner Rd LE4 ... 129 F3
Raynes Wlk LE13 ... 59 D4
Raynham Dr LE11 ... 51 C5
REARSBY ... 79 A1
Rearsby La LE7 ... 104 E7
Rearsby Rd
Leicester LE4 ... 129 C1
Queniborough LE7 ... 103 E6
Thrussington LE7 ... 79 A3
Recreation Ground Rd
PE9 ... 143 E3
Recreation St NG10 ... 10 F7
Rectory Cl
Breedon on t H DE73 ... 26 E2
Swinford LE17 ... 254 C4
Wigston LE18 ... 180 D1
Rectory Ct
Bottesford NG13 ... 3 B3
East Farndon LE16 ... 250 B6
Rectory Dr LE14 ... 19 A1
Rectory Gdns
Aston-on-T DE72 ... 16 A7
Leicester LE2 ... 156 B2
Rectory La
Appleby Magna DE12 ... 92 E1
Bottesford NG13 ... 3 B3
Burrough on t H LE14 ... 107 D2
Cadeby CV13 ... 149 D1
Edith Weston LE15 ... 166 B7
Kibworth Beauchamp
LE8 ... 206 A1
Market Bosworth CV13 ... 148 F3
Market Harborough
LE16 ... 241 A2
Medbourne LE16 ... 228 A7
Nailstone CV13 ... 123 B3
North Witham NG33 ... 65 B8
Thurcaston LE7 ... 101 B2
Woolsthorpe by B NG32 ... 15 B8
Rectory Pl
Loughborough LE11 ... 52 B4
Wymeswold LE12 ... 33 C3
Rectory Rd
Breaston DE72 ... 9 E8
Loughborough LE11 ... 52 B5
Markfield LE67 ... 98 E1
Wanlip LE7 ... 102 B2
Redbrook Cres LE13 ... 59 A1
Redburrow La LE65,
LE67 ... 94 C7
Redcar Rd LE4 ... 129 C1
Redcliffe Cl LE3 ... 127 F3
Redcot Gdns PE9 ... 143 D4
Redcot Mews PE9 ... 143 D3
Red Cswy The LE14 ... 12 B2
Redens The NG10 ... 10 B4
REDGATE ... 189 B3
Red Hall Dr LE9 ... 198 B7
Red Hall Rd LE9 ... 198 C7
RED HILL ... 200 F8
Red Hill
Leicester LE4 ... 128 F5
Uppingham LE15 ... 189 B3
Red Hill Ave LE19 ... 201 A8
Redhill Circ LE4 ... 128 F4
Red Hill Cl LE4 ... 129 E8
Red Hill Field Prim Sch
LE19 ... 201 A8
Redhill La LE67 ... 71 C6
Red Hill La LE4 ... 129 F8
Redhill Lodge Rd 6
DE11 ... 44 A7
Red Hill Way LE4 ... 128 D4
Red House Cl LE2 ... 179 C4
Red House Gdns
Allington NG32 ... 4 F5
Leicester LE2 ... 179 C4
Red House Rd LE2 ... 179 C4
Red House Rise LE2 ... 179 C4
Redland Cl LE15 ... 191 F5
Redland Rd LE15 ... 137 D7
Redlands Com Prim Sch
LE12 ... 77 C3
Redlands Est LE67 ... 96 A3
Redliech Cl LE16 ... 241 B3
Red Lion La LE9 ... 150 C4
Red Lion Sq 12 PE9 ... 143 D3
Red Lion St
8 Stamford PE9 ... 143 D3
Stathern LE14 ... 13 A3
Red Lodge Rd LE7,
LE15 ... 134 B2
Redmarle Rd LE3 ... 154 A3
REDMILE ... 6 F3
Redmile CE Prim Sch
NG13 ... 6 F3
Redmile La NG13 ... 6 D3
Redmile's La PE9 ... 168 A5
Redmires Cl LE11 ... 51 B3
Redmoor Cl CV13 ... 148 D2
Redmoor High Sch
LE10 ... 197 B3
Redpath Cl LE4 ... 155 B7
Redruth Ave LE18 ... 180 C1
Redruth Cl CV11 ... 214 A4
Redruth Ct LE18 ... 203 C8
Redway Croft 3 DE73 ... 26 A8
Redwing Cl LE15 ... 138 B7
Redwing Wlk LE5 ... 155 C7
Redwood Ave LE13 ... 59 D5
Redwood Rd LE11 ... 75 A7
Redwood Wlk LE5 ... 155 C7
Reedman Rd NG10 ... 10 B4
Reedpool Cl LE8 ... 202 F4
Rees Cl LE15 ... 189 A5
Rees Gr LE4 ... 129 D5
Reeth Cl LE4 ... 128 C3
Reeves Cl LE8 ... 201 F5
Reeves La LE15 ... 165 A3
Reeves Rd LE10 ... 215 F6
Reeve's Yd LE15 ... 189 B4
Reform St PE9 ... 143 B3
Regal Ct LE19 ... 178 D2
Regal Gdns NG33 ... 90 C8
Regan Rd DE12 ... 68 A4
Regency Cl LE2 ... 179 D1
Regency Ct
Hinckley LE10 ... 216 A7
Leicester LE3 ... 154 C5
Regency Rd LE14 ... 57 F3
Regent Cl LE18 ... 180 B2
Regent Coll LE1 ... 259 C1
Regent Ct
5 Hinckley LE10 ... 215 D8
Loughborough LE11 ... 52 A5
6 Lutterworth LE17 ... 244 C5
Swadlincote DE11 ... 44 B2
Regent Pl LE13 ... 59 D2
Regent Pl Ret Pk LE11 ... 52 A4
Regent Rd
Countesthorpe LE8 ... 202 F4
Hoby LE14 ... 79 D7
Leicester LE1 ... 259 C2
Regent St
Barwell LE9 ... 198 B7
Hinckley LE10 ... 215 D8
Leicester LE1 ... 259 C2
Leicester, Oadby LE2 ... 181 A6
Long Eaton NG10 ... 10 D8
Loughborough LE11 ... 52 A4
Lutterworth LE17 ... 244 C5
Melton Mowbray LE13 ... 59 D2
Narborough LE19 ... 201 C8
Swadlincote DE11 ... 44 B2
Thrussington LE7 ... 78 F5
Regent Street Ind Est
LE19 ... 201 C7
Regents Wlk LE3 ... 153 A3
Reg's Way LE67 ... 97 B4
Reliant Cl DE11 ... 44 E1
REMPSTONE ... 32 D6
Rempstone Rd
Belton LE12 ... 49 D7
East Leake LE12 ... 31 E7
Griffydam LE67 ... 47 F2
Hoton LE12 ... 32 C2
Wymeswold LE12 ... 33 B4
Zouch LE12 ... 31 B6
Rendell Prim Sch LE11 ... 52 B5
Rendell Rd LE4 ... 129 B1
Rendell St LE11 ... 52 B5
Renfrew Rd LE5 ... 156 E8
Renishaw Dr LE5 ... 155 E2
Rennes Cl LE65 ... 69 A6
Renning End LE12 ... 101 E8
Repington Ave CV9 ... 170 D2
Repington Row LE2 ... 179 F5
Repton Cl LE65 ... 69 A8
Repton Rd
Hartshorne DE11 ... 44 F8
Long Eaton NG10 ... 9 F4
Oakthorpe DE12 ... 93 A5
Wigston LE18 ... 180 B4
Repton St LE3 ... 154 D7
Rescue Way LE65 ... 69 B5
Reservoir Hill DE12 ... 67 D6
Reservoir Rd
Cropston LE7 ... 100 E3
Thornton LE67 ... 125 A3
Reservoir View LE8 ... 223 B4
Reservoir Way DE11 ... 44 E1
Resolution Rd LE65 ... 69 D7
Resthaven DE11 ... 44 B5
Retreat The
Barrow-u-S LE12 ... 76 D8
Easton o t H PE9 ... 168 F5
Leicester LE5 ... 155 F5
Revell Cl LE12 ... 76 B6
Reynolds Chase LE18 ... 180 E3
Reynolds Cl
Hinckley LE10 ... 197 A3
Rugby CV21 ... 257 B1
Reynolds Pl LE3 ... 154 A2
Rhodes Cl LE16 ... 240 C2
Ribble Ave LE2 ... 181 D6
Ribble Dr LE12 ... 76 D6
Ribblesdale Ave LE10 ... 197 E3
Ribblesdale Rd NG10 ... 10 A5
Ribble Way LE13 ... 59 B1
Ribble Wlk LE15 ... 137 E5
Riber Cl NG10 ... 10 D5
Richard Cl
Braunstone Town LE3 ... 153 C3
Melton Mowbray LE13 ... 59 D3
Richard Hill CE Prim Sch
LE7 ... 101 B2
Richard III Rd LE3 ... 259 A3
Richardson Cl LE9 ... 199 D1
Richardsons Cl LE9 ... 219 A5
Richil Ct LE15 ... 189 B4
Richil Ho LE15 ... 189 B4
Richmond Ave
Leicester LE2 ... 179 E8
Long Eaton DE72 ... 10 A8
Richmond Cl
Cosby LE9 ... 201 C2
Desford LE9 ... 151 B2
Fleckney LE8 ... 222 F7
Leicester LE2 ... 179 E8
Richmond Dr
Glen Parva LE2 ... 179 E1
Melton Mowbray LE13 ... 82 D8
Richmond Gate LE10 ... 197 C3
Richmond Ho LE10 ... 197 C3
Richmond Prim Sch
LE10 ... 197 C3
Richmond Rd
Coalville LE67 ... 96 B4
Hinckley LE10 ... 197 C3
Leicester LE2 ... 179 E8
Richmond St LE2 ... 259 A2
Richmond Way LE2 ... 181 C3
Richmore Rd LE5 ... 130 C3
Rickmans Cnr Cvn Site
DE12 ... 67 A6
Riddington Rd
Braunstone Town LE3 ... 178 F7
Littlethorpe LE19 ... 201 C6
Riddon Dr LE10 ... 215 B8
Ridgemere Cl LE7 ... 103 D4
Ridgemere La LE7 ... 104 B2
Ridge View LE16 ... 240 E5
Ridgeway LE19 ... 201 C6
Ridge Way LE2 ... 181 B3
Ridgeway Dr LE4 ... 129 F6
Ridgeway Prim Sch
LE16 ... 240 F5
Ridgeway The
Hinckley LE10 ... 215 D6
Leicester LE3 ... 154 A7
Market Harborough
LE16 ... 240 F5
Rothley LE7 ... 101 C6
Ridgeway W LE16 ... 240 E5
Ridgway Rd
Ashby-de-la-Z LE65 ... 68 F5
Leicester LE2 ... 180 D8
Ridings Cl LE14 ... 58 A3
Ridings The
Mountsorrel LE7 ... 101 C7
Queniborough LE7 ... 103 E5
Riding The LE4 ... 128 B6
Ridley Cl
Blaby LE8 ... 202 A6
Cropston LE7 ... 100 E2
Ridley St LE3 ... 154 D4
RIDLINGTON ... 163 D2
Ridlington Rd LE15 ... 164 B1
Rigsty The LE12 ... 75 E6
Riley Cl
Market Harborough
LE16 ... 240 B2
Stoney Stanton LE9 ... 199 D1
Rills The LE10 ... 197 E2
Ringers Cl LE2 ... 181 A8
Ringer's Spinney LE2 ... 181 A8
Ring Fence LE12 ... 50 B2
Ring Rd LE2 ... 180 E7
Ringway The LE7 ... 103 F6
Ringwood Cl
Desford LE9 ... 151 B3
Wigston LE18 ... 180 C1
Ringwood Rd
Leicester LE5 ... 130 E1
Shepshed LE12 ... 50 C5
Rink Dr DE11 ... 44 B3
Ripley Cl LE16 ... 241 B3
Ripley Rd LE16 ... 229 D1
Ripon Dr LE8 ... 202 B6
Ripon St LE2 ... 155 C3
Riseholme Cl 4 LE3 ... 178 F7
Rise The
Houghton on t H LE7 ... 157 F4
Narborough LE19 ... 178 A2
Rothley LE7 ... 102 A6
Risley La DE72 ... 9 E8
Riston Cl LE2 ... 181 B3
Ritchie Pk LE16 ... 250 E8
River Bldg The 2
LE3 ... 154 D4
River Ct PE9 ... 143 B8
Riverdale Cl LE7 ... 103 A4
River Dr CV9 ... 170 D2
Riversdale Cl LE4 ... 129 B6
Riversdale Rd CV9 ... 194 A8
River Sence Way LE67 ... 96 D6
Riverside
Market Harborough
LE16 ... 241 A4
Witherley CV9 ... 194 B7
Riverside Cl
Bottesford NG13 ... 3 A3
Great Glen LE8 ... 182 B1
Sheepy Magna CV9 ... 171 B8
Riverside Com Coll
LE3 ... 179 B8
Riverside Com Prim Sch
LE4 ... 129 B7
Riverside Ct
Littlethorpe LE19 ... 201 C7
Market Harborough
LE16 ... 240 D2
Measham DE12 ... 93 A4
Riverside Dr LE2 ... 179 C7
Riverside Ind Est
LE16 ... 241 A4
Riverside Mews LE7 ... 102 C2
Riverside Pl PE9 ... 143 E2
Riverside Rd
Lutterworth LE17 ... 244 D5
Melton Mowbray LE13 ... 59 A3
Riverside Way LE19 ... 201 C7
Riverside Wlk
Asfordby LE14 ... 57 F2
Bottesford NG13 ... 3 A3
River Soar Living 3
LE3 ... 154 D4
Rivers St LE3 ... 154 D6
River View
Barrow-u-S LE12 ... 76 F6
Long Eaton NG10 ... 10 A3
Riverview Ct LE2 ... 154 E1
Rivets Meadow Cl
LE3 ... 153 D1
Rivington Dr LE11 ... 51 B2
RNIB Vocational Coll
LE11 ... 51 F3
Robert Bakewell Prim Sch
LE11 ... 51 D6
Robert Hall Rd LE8 ... 221 F5
Robert Hall St LE4 ... 128 F3
Robert Hardy Wharf
LE11 ... 52 D4
Robert Hill Cl CV21 ... 257 A1
Robertsbridge Ave
LE4 ... 128 E3
Robertsbridge Wlk 8
LE4 ... 128 E3
Roberts Cl DE74 ... 18 D1
Roberts Dr NG13 ... 2 F3
Robert Smyth Sch The
LE16 ... 240 E5
Robertson Cl
Clifton u D CV23 ... 257 A5
Stoney Stanton LE9 ... 199 D2
Roberts Rd LE4 ... 129 A1
Robian Way DE11 ... 44 A4
Robin Cl
Leicester LE2 ... 179 E7
Oakham LE15 ... 138 B8
Robin Cres LE13 ... 82 B8
Robin Hood Pl DE11 ... 44 C2
Robinia Cl LE17 ... 244 A5
Robin Mews LE11 ... 52 A3
Robin Rd LE67 ... 96 F8
Robins Field LE6 ... 152 D8
Robinson Rd
Leicester LE5 ... 155 E7
Swadlincote DE11 ... 44 A6
Whitwick LE67 ... 71 D5
Robinson Way
Hinckley LE10 ... 215 F4
Markfield LE67 ... 125 F8
Roborough Gn LE5 ... 156 E6
Robotham Cl
Huncote LE9 ... 200 E7
Robotham Cl *continued*
Narborough LE19 ... 201 B7
Roby Lea DE74 ... 16 F4
Rochdale Cres LE67 ... 72 D1
Roche Cl LE2 ... 179 C4
Rochester Cl
Kibworth Beauchamp
LE8 ... 205 F2
Long Eaton NG10 ... 10 A7
Mountsorrel LE12 ... 101 C8
Rochester Gdns LE16 ... 240 D1
Rockbridge Rd LE2 ... 181 D4
Rockcliffe Cl DE11 ... 44 B1
Rockery Cl LE5 ... 156 A7
Rockhill Dr LE12 ... 76 E1
ROCKINGHAM ... 230 B4
Rockingham Castle &
Gdns* LE16 ... 230 B3
Rockingham Cl
3 Ashby-de-la-Z LE65 ... 69 C5
Blaby LE8 ... 202 B6
Leicester LE5 ... 156 B6
Shepshed LE12 ... 50 A2
Rockingham Dr LE13 ... 59 A4
Rockingham Ind Est
LE16 ... 241 B3
Rockingham Rd
Caldecott LE16 ... 230 B6
Corby NN17 ... 230 E2
Cottingham LE16 ... 229 E2
Gretton LE16, NN17 ... 230 E7
Gretton NN17 ... 213 A1
Loughborough LE11 ... 51 E6
Market Harborough
LE16 ... 241 B4
Mountsorrel LE12 ... 101 C8
Stamford PE9 ... 143 A4
Rockland Rise LE67 ... 71 F6
Rockleigh Gdns LE65 ... 69 A6
Rockley Rd LE4 ... 128 C1
Rock Rd PE9 ... 143 C3
Rock Terr PE9 ... 143 D3
Rock The NG32 ... 23 C7
Rodney Cl LE10 ... 197 D4
Roebuck Cl LE8 ... 201 F5
Roecliff Cl LE67 ... 98 E1
Roecliffe Rd LE7 ... 100 B4
Roedean Cl LE65 ... 69 A7
Roehampton Dr LE18 ... 180 B5
Roe House La CV9,
DE12 ... 119 D4
Roesta Cl LE12 ... 49 B6
Rogerstone Rd LE5 ... 156 D4
Rogue's La
Cottesmore LE15 ... 87 D1
Hinckley LE10 ... 197 C6
ROLLESTON ... 184 E6
Rolleston Cl LE16 ... 241 A3
Rolleston Prim Sch
LE2 ... 179 D2
Rolleston Rd
Billesdon LE7 ... 184 C8
Wigston LE18 ... 180 B3
Rolleston St LE5 ... 155 D6
Roman Bank PE9 ... 143 B3
Roman Cl
Claybrooke Magna
LE17 ... 232 E6
Desford LE9 ... 151 C3
Earl Shilton LE9 ... 176 A1
Roman Hill LE18 ... 203 E8
Roman Rd LE4 ... 129 A5
Romans Cres LE67 ... 72 D1
Roman St LE3 ... 154 D4
Romans The LE12 ... 76 E1
Roman Way
Market Harborough
LE16 ... 240 E4
Syston LE7 ... 102 E2
Romney Cl LE10 ... 197 A3
Romorantin Pl NG10 ... 10 E7
Romulus Ct LE19 ... 178 D8
Romway Ave LE5 ... 155 E2
Romway Cl LE12 ... 50 C3
Romway Rd LE5 ... 155 E2
Rona Gdns LE5 ... 156 E7
Ronald Ct LE2 ... 155 C1
Ronald Toon Rd LE9 ... 199 A8
Ronald West Ct LE11 ... 51 D1
Roods The LE7 ... 101 E6
Rookery LE6 ... 126 F3
Rookery Cl
Fenny Drayton CV13 ... 195 A7
Kibworth Beauchamp
LE8 ... 224 B8
Rookery La
Groby LE6 ... 126 F3
Stretton LE15 ... 88 F4
Thurmaston LE4 ... 129 D6
Wymondham LE14 ... 62 D2
Rookery The
Barrow-u-S LE12 ... 76 C8
Heather LE67 ... 95 B2
Langham LE15 ... 110 C3
Woodville DE11 ... 44 F2
Rookwell Dr LE16 ... 240 F1
Roosevelt Ave NG10 ... 10 C5
Ropewalk DE74 ... 18 C2
Rosamund Ave LE3 ... 179 A8
Rose Acre Cl LE7 ... 156 F7
Rosebank Rd LE8 ... 202 F4
Rosebank View DE12 ... 93 C5
Rosebarn Way LE5 ... 130 D1
Roseberry Ave LE14 ... 58 B3
Rosebery Ave
Kibworth Beauchamp
LE8 ... 223 F8
Melton Mowbray LE13 ... 59 D3

Rosebery Rd LE7........ 127 E7
Rosebery St
  Leicester LE5...........155 D6
  Loughborough LE11...... 51 F4
Rose Cl LE15..........166 D3
Rose Cres LE3 ....152 F2
Rosecroft Gdns DE11.... 44 C3
Rosedale LE67 ....71 E7
Rose Dale LE17 ......247 A4
Rosedale Ave LE4......129 D2
Rosedale Cl NG10...... 10 B6
Rosedale Rd LE18......180 F2
Rosedene Ave LE4......129 E6
Rosedene Cl LE9.......152 F4
Rosedene View DE12.... 67 C4
Rose Farm Cl LE3......153 F4
Rosehill LE11...........51 C4
Rose Hill DE11..........44 E3
Rosemary Cres LE67 .... 72 A4
Rosemary Way LE10 ....215 B7
Rosemead Dr LE2.......181 A4
Rosemoor Cl LE16.......241 B3
Roseneath Ave LE4......129 E3
Rose St LE4 ....128 F2
Rose Tree Ave LE4......129 A8
Rose Valley DE11........44 A5
Roseway
  Leicester LE4.........129 D3
  Stoke Golding CV13....196 D7
Rosewood Cl LE10 .....215 F6
Rosewood Way LE11.... 75 A6
Roslyn St LE2..........155 C4
Rosminian Way LE7.... 78 A2
Rossal Dr LE65..........69 A7
Ross Cl LE13............59 E5
Rossendale Rd LE9......198 E7
Rossett Dr LE4..........128 D2
Rossetti Rd LE19........178 A3
Rosshill Cres LE5.......156 E7
Rosslyn Ave LE12 ......76 C1
Rosslyn Rd LE67 ....71 F4
Ross Wlk LE4..........129 A1
Ross' Wlk LE4..........155 A8
Roston Dr LE10.........215 A8
ROTHERBY 79 F6
Rotherby Ave LE4......129 D1
Rotherby La LE14.......80 B7
Rotherby Rd LE7........80 B1
Rotherwood Dr LE65.... 69 B7
ROTHLEY..........101 E6
Rothley CE Prim Sch
  LE7 ....101 E7
ROTHLEY PLAIN 101 B8
Rothley Rd LE12 ......76 E1
Rothley St LE4.........129 A1
Rothley Sta★ LE7.......101 B5
Rouen Way LE65........69 A6
Roughton St LE4........129 B2
Roundhay Rd LE3......154 C2
Roundhill LE9..........152 E5
Roundhill Cl
  Market Harborough
    LE16.............241 B2
  Syston LE7...........102 F2
Roundhill Com Coll
  LE4 ....102 E1
Roundhill Rd LE5.......155 E3
Roundhills The LE9 ....198 F5
Roundhill Way LE11.... 51 B3
Roundway The LE4 ....129 F5
Routh Ave DE74.........17 B2
Rowan Ave
  Coalville LE67 ....97 B8
  Hathern LE12..........30 A2
  Market Harborough
    LE16.............240 E1
Rowanberry Ave LE3...153 C6
Rowan Cl
  Measham DE12 ....93 C5
  Moira DE12...........68 B6
Rowan Ct NN17.........230 E1
Rowan Dr
  Ibstock LE67 ....95 E1
  Lutterworth LE17......244 B6
Rowan The LE3.........154 C7
Rowans The LE8........202 E4
Rowan Way LE9 ....151 B3
Rowbank Way LE11..... 51 B3
Rowe Leyes Furlong
  LE7................76 F1
Rowena Ct LE12 ......101 E8
Rowena Dr LE65........69 B7
Rowlandson Cl LE4 ....101 D1
Rowlands The LE67 .... 70 F6
Rowlands Way LE2.....179 B2
Rowland Way CV9 .....170 C2
Rowlatts Hill Prim Sch
  LE5................156 A6
Rowlatts Hill Rd LE5...156 A6
Rowlett Rd NN17 ......230 E1
Rowley Cl
  Fleckney LE8 ....223 A6
  Swadlincote DE11...... 44 D5
Rowley Ct DE11.........44 B4
ROWLEY FIELDS 154 B1
Rowley Fields Ave
  LE3................179 B8
Rowsley Ave
  Leicester LE5..........155 D4
  Long Eaton NG10...... 10 A5
Rowsley St LE5.........155 D4
Row The
  Garthorpe LE14........62 A6
  Rotherby LE14.........79 F5
  Slawston LE16........209 B1
Roxburgh Rd PE9......143 B4
Royal Arc ▮ LE1......259 B4
Royal Ct LE10.........215 D7

Royal East St LE1......259 B5
Royal Kent St LE1......259 A5
Royal La LE12 ....67 B4
Royal Meadow Dr
  CV9................170 E2
Royal Oak Cl LE67......122 E8
Royal Rd LE4 ....129 B2
Royal Way LE11........52 A6
Royce Cl
  Braunstone Town LE3 ..153 C2
  Corby NN17..........230 F1
Roy Cl LE19...........201 C8
Roydale Cl LE11........51 E6
Roydene Cres LE4 .....128 C2
Royland Rd LE11........52 B3
Royston Cl LE2.........179 D2
Rubicon Cl LE12 ....76 F1
Ruby St LE3...........154 C7
Rudbeck Ave LE15......59 A4
Ruddington Wlk LE4 ...128 E4
Ruddle Way LE15......110 D3
Ruding Rd LE3.........154 D4
Ruding St LE3.........259 A4
Rudyard Cl LE11........51 B2
Rufford Cl
  Hinckley LE10 ....215 D3
  Loughborough LE11..... 51 B5
Rufford Rd NG10........10 B4
Rufford St LE5.........155 E6
RUGBY..............257 B2
Rugby Cl
  Ashby-de-la-Z LE65 .....69 A8
  Market Harborough
    LE16.............240 D2
Rugby Rd
  Cotesbach LE17........244 B3
  Hinckley LE10 ....215 D5
  Lilbourne CV23 ....257 F6
  South Kilworth LE17 ...254 E6
  Swinford LE17 ....254 B3
Rugby St LE3..........154 C7
Rugeley Ave NG10 .....10 F7
Rumsey Cl
  Quorn (Quorndon) LE12.. 75 E6
  Thringstone LE67.......71 C8
Rumsey Dr LE8 ....202 A8
Runcorn Cl LE2.........179 D3
Runcorn Rd LE2.........179 D3
Runnymede Gdns
  LE3................153 D7
Rupert Brooke Rd
  LE11................51 D4
Rupert Cres LE7.......103 E6
Rupert Ho LE2.........179 C2
Rupert Law Cl LE12 .....75 F7
Rupert Rd LE16........240 E1
Rupert St LE1.........259 B5
Ruperts Way LE8 .....205 B8
Rushby Rd LE67........96 E3
Rush Cl LE9...........150 B3
Rushden Ho LE3.......153 C6
Rushes La LE16........239 F3
Rushes The LE11.......54 A4
Rushes The LE11.......54 A4
Rushes The LE67.......98 C4
Rushey Cl
  Barlestone CV13 ......149 D7
  Leicester LE4.........129 C4
Rushey La LE7..........76 B2
RUSHEY MEAD 129 E4
Rushey Mead Prim Sch
  LE4................129 C2
Rushey Mead Sec Sch
  LE4................129 E4
Rushford Cl LE4 ....129 D1
Rushford Dr LE4 ....129 D1
Rush Leys NG10........10 D5
Rushmere Wlk LE3.....153 A2
Rushton Dr LE2........179 B4
Rushton Yd ▮▮ LE65 ....69 B6
Ruskin Ave
  Long Eaton NG10.......10 B5
  Syston LE7...........103 C2
Ruskin Field LE7.......127 C7
Ruskington Dr LE18....180 D5
Russ Cl LE17...........75 F7
Russell Ct LE2.........179 C6
Russell Sq ▮ LE1.......155 A7
Russell St
  Loughborough LE11..... 52 C4
  Swadlincote DE11...... 44 C3
Russett Cl
  Barwell LE9 ....198 A7
  Market Harborough
    LE16.............240 F5
Russet Way LE4........102 C1
Ruston Cl DE11.........44 B4
Rutherford Rd LE4 .....128 A4
Rutland Ave
  Hinckley LE10 ....215 C7
  Leicester LE2.........154 E1
  Wigston LE18.........180 B3
Rutland Belle Cruise★
  LE15...............140 B4
Rutland Butterfly &
  Aquatic Ctr★ LE15....140 D5
Rutland Cl
  Leicester Forest East
    LE3..............153 A3
  South Witham NG33 .....65 B3
  Uppingham LE15 ......189 A5
Rutland Coll The
  LE15...............137 F7
Rutland Ctr LE1........259 C4
Rutland Cty Mus★
  LE15...............138 A6
Rutland Dr LE4 ....129 E7

Rutland Falconry & Owl
  Ctr★ LE15...........112 C1
Rutland Farm Pk★
  LE15...............138 A5
Rutland Ho LE13.......59 D3
Rutland La NG13.........3 B2
Rutland Meml Hospl
  LE15...............137 E6
Rutland Open Air
  Theatre★ PE9........116 C2
Rutland Railway Line★
  LE15...............111 F8
Rutland Railway Mus★
  LE15...............111 F8
Rutland Rd PE9........143 F5
Rutland Sq NG13........6 C2
Rutland St
  Leicester LE1.........259 C3
  Loughborough LE11..... 52 C3
  Melton Mowbray LE13...59 D3
Rutland Terr PE9.......143 C2
Rutland Water★ LE15...139 E1
Rutland Water Nature
  Reserve★ LE15.......138 F6
Rutland Water
  Watersports Ctr★
  LE15...............140 B5
Rutland Way
  Loughborough LE11..... 51 E1
  Ryhall PE9...........116 F1
Rutland Wlk LE16......240 F5
Rycroft Rd DE74.......17 D6
Rydal Ave
  Loughborough LE11..... 51 D1
  Nuneaton CV11 ....214 A6
Rydal Cl LE10.........214 F7
Rydal Gdns LE65.......69 C4
Rydal St LE2..........259 A2
Ryde Ave LE2.........180 C3
Ryder Rd LE3..........153 C6
Ryderway LE17.........244 B5
Rye Cl LE2............179 E4
Ryefield LE15.........138 A8
Ryegate Cres LE4......128 F8
Rye Hill Ave LE17......244 D5
RYHALL..............116 F1
Ryhall CE Prim Sch
  PE9................116 F2
Ryhall Rd
  Great Casterton PE9....115 F1
  Stamford PE9.........143 F5
Ryhall Rd Ind Est PE9...143 F5
Rylands Cl LE16........241 B3

S

Sabaramati Ho LE1 .....155 B7
Sacheverell Way LE6....126 E1
Sacheverel Rd LE3.....153 D6
Sackville Gdns LE2.....180 C8
Sacred Heart RC Prim Sch
  Leicester LE5.........155 C6
  Loughborough LE11..... 52 A1
SADDINGTON 223 C4
Saddington Rd
  Fleckney LE8 ....223 A7
  Mowsley LE17.........237 F7
  Shearsby LE8, LE17....222 C3
  Smeeton Westerby LE8 ..223 E6
Saddle Cl LE13.........59 A5
Saddler Rd LE5........130 C3
Saddlers Cl
  Glenfield LE3.........153 B8
  Hinckley LE10 ....215 F6
  Loughborough LE11..... 51 F6
Saddlers' Cl LE7.......103 D7
Sadlers Wells LE12.....49 B6
Saffron Cl LE9........198 C8
Saffron Ct
  ▮ Barwell LE9 ......198 A6
  Leicester LE2.........179 F5
Saffron Hill Rd LE2.....179 E8
Saffron Rd LE18........179 E2
Saffron Way LE2.......179 E6
Sage Cross St LE13 .....59 C3
Sage Dr DE11..........44 F4
Sage Rd LE2..........154 D4
St Aidan's Ave LE7......102 F3
St Albans Cl
  Long Eaton NG10.......10 E5
  Oakham LE15.........138 B6
St Albans Rd ▮ LE2....155 B4
St Andrew's CE Prim Sch
  LE17...............246 E3
St Andrews Cl
  Burton o t W LE12.....54 A7
  Great Easton LE16.....229 D7
  Whissendine LE15......84 F1
St Andrew's Cl LE67.....71 D8
St Andrews Ct LE5.....156 A2
St Andrew's Dr CV11....214 B1
St Andrew's Dr LE2.....155 F1
St Andrew's Rise DE74..18 C1
St Annes Cl
  Oakham LE15.........137 F6
  Syston LE7...........103 C2
St Annes Dr LE2.......179 D7
St Anne's La
  Castle Donington DE74 ..17 B3
  Sutton Bonington LE12 ..30 B6
St Augustine Rd LE3....154 D5
St Augustine's RC Prim
  Sch The PE9.........143 E5
St Austell Cl CV11......214 A5
St Austell Rd LE5......156 E7

St Barnabas CE Prim Sch
  LE5................155 E7
St Barnard's Rd LE67....72 A4
St Bartholomew CE Prim
  Sch LE12...........75 E5
St Bartholomews Way LE13,
  LE14...............58 F6
St Bernards Ave LE4....129 B3
St Bernard's Cl LE12 ....50 A3
St Bernard St LE4.....129 B2
St Botolph Rd LE12.....50 B3
St Botolph's CE Prim Sch
  LE12...............50 C4
St Buryan St CV11 .....214 A5
Saintbury Rd LE3 ......127 D2
St Catharines Terr
  LE7................157 F4
St Catharines Way
  LE7................157 F4
St Catherines Ave
  CV13...............148 E3
St Catherine's Cl LE10...215 F7
St Chad's Cl DE72......9 A7
St Charles's RC Prim Sch
  DE12...............93 D5
St Christophers Pk Cvn
  Site LE67...........96 F3
St Christopher's Rd
  LE67...............96 E2
St Clares Ct LE67......96 E8
St Clare's RC Prim Sch
  LE67...............96 D8
St Clement's Rd LE3....143 C3
St Clements Ct LE3 ....154 B7
St Columba Way LE2....102 F4
St Crispin's Sch LE2....155 B3
St Crispin's Way LE4....102 E1
St Cuthbert's Ave LE8...205 B8
St Cuthbert's CE Prim Sch
  LE8................182 C1
St Davids Cl LE3 ......152 F3
St David's Cl LE2......155 E1
St David's Cres LE67....72 C1
St Davids Ct LE67......72 C1
St Davids Rd LE3......153 C6
St Denys CE Inf Sch
  LE67...............95 E1
St Denys' Cres LE67....95 E1
St Denys Rd LE5......156 B3
St Dunstan Rd LE3.....154 C6
St Edwards CE Prim Sch
  DE74...............17 B3
St Edward's RC Prim Sch
  DE11...............44 B5
St Edward's Rd DE74....17 B2
St Faiths Dr LE67......96 C8
St Francis Cl LE10 .....197 C3
St Francis RC Prim Sch
  LE3................59 B2
St Georges Ave PE9....143 F4
St George's Ave LE10...197 C1
St George's CE Prim Sch
  Stamford PE9.........143 E5
  Swadlincote DE11...... 44 B1
St Georges Cl LE9......150 B5
St George's Hill LE67....71 A7
St George's Rd CV9 ....170 E1
St George's Ret Pk
  LE1................155 B6
St George's Sq ▮
  PE9................143 E3
St George's St PE9......143 E3
St George St LE1.......259 C3
St Georges Way LE1....259 C3
St Giles Cl CV13 ......149 D8
St Gregory's Dr LE12....77 D3
St Helens Cl LE4......128 C1
St Helen's Cl LE10......217 C4
St Helens Dr LE4......128 D1
St Hildas Cl LE67......103 C2
St Ives Cl LE67........97 B8
St Ives Rd
  Leicester LE4.........129 E2
  Wigston LE18.........180 D1
St James Cl
  Huncote LE9 ....200 D7
  Leicester, Oadby LE2 ...181 C3
  Shepshed LE12 ....50 B2
  Twycross CV9 ....146 D6
St James Ct LE2.......155 C3
St James Rd
  Leicester LE2.........155 C3
  Shepshed LE12 ....50 B3
St James's Cl LE10.....215 D5
St James St LE1.......259 C4
St James Terr LE2.....155 C3
St John Fisher RC Prim
  Sch LE18...........180 E4
St Johns
  Hinckley LE10 ....197 E1
  Narborough LE19......178 E3
St John's Ave LE2......103 C3
St John's Bsns Pk
  LE17...............244 D4
St John's Cl
  Coalville LE67 ....96 D6
  Heather LE67.........95 B2
  Lutterworth LE17......244 B5
  Ryhall PE9...........116 F2
St Johns Cl LE13.......59 D3
St John's Dr LE13......59 D3
St Johns Rd
  Asfordby Hill LE14......58 D3
  Leicester LE2.........155 C3
St John's St
  Long Eaton NG10.......10 D7
  Stamford PE9.........143 D3

St John St LE1.........259 B5
St John's Terr ▮ PE9....143 C3
St John the Baptist CE
  Prim Sch LE2........155 C2
St Joseph's RC Prim Sch
  Leicester LE5.........156 D8
  Market Harborough
    LE16.............240 E3
St Laurence CE Prim Sch
  NG10...............10 E6
St Laurence Cl NG10 ....10 E6
St Leonards Cl LE2......54 A7
St Leonards Ct LE2.....155 B2
St Leonards Rd
  Leicester LE2.........155 B1
  Leicester LE2.........155 B2
St Leonard's St PE9.....143 E3
St Luke's CE Prim Sch
  LE7................156 F4
St Luke's Cl LE7.......156 F4
St Luke's Hospl LE10....240 D5
St Margaret Rd CV13...196 E7
St Margaret's CE Prim Sch
  CV13...............196 D7
St Margarets Dr LE67...233 E8
St Margaret's St LE1....259 B5
St Margaret's Way LE4,
  LE1................154 E8
St Marks Sh ▮ LE1.....155 A7
St Martins
  Leicester LE1.........259 B3
  Stapleton LE9........174 E2
St Martin's LE10.......215 E6
St Martin's Cl PE9.....143 E2
St Martin's Dr LE9.....151 A3
St Martins E LE1.......259 B3
St Martin's RC Sch
  CV13...............196 F4
St Martins Sq LE1.....259 B3
St Martins Wlk LE1.....259 B3
St Martins Yd ▮ LE16...240 F3
St Mary & St John CE
  Prim Sch LE16.......166 C3
St Marys Ave LE5.......156 C8
St Mary's Ave
  Barwell LE9 ....197 F5
  Braunstone Town LE3 ..153 C3
  Coalville LE67 ....96 B6
  Draycott DE72 ....9 A7
St Mary's CE Prim Sch
  Bitteswell LE17.......244 B8
  Hinckley LE10 ....215 D8
  Melton Mowbray LE13...59 A6
St Marys Cl
  Broughton Astley LE9 ..218 E6
  Burton o t W LE12.....54 A7
  Congerstone CV13.....147 D7
  Osgathorpe LE12......48 E4
St Mary's Cl
  Bottesford NG13 ......3 B3
  Edith Weston LE15.....166 B7
  Loughborough LE11..... 51 F4
St Marys Ct
  Coalville LE67 ....96 B6
  Leicester LE5.........156 C8
St Mary's Ct
  Barwell LE9 ....198 A5
  Braunstone Town LE3 ..153 C3
  Market Harborough
    LE16.............241 A4
St Mary's Fields Inf Sch
  LE3................154 C2
St Marys Gr B79 ....118 D3
St Mary's Hill PE9.....143 E2
St Mary's Ho LE17 .....244 C6
St Mary's Hospl LE13...59 D3
St Mary's La
  Bottesford NG13 ......3 B2
  Ravenstone LE67......96 A4
St Mary's Mews LE9....198 A5
St Mary's Pl
  Market Harborough
    LE16.............240 F3
  Stamford PE9.........143 E3
St Mary's RC Prim Sch
  LE11...............52 A4
St Marys Rd LE2.......155 B2
St Mary's Rd
  Hinckley LE10 ....215 D8
  Lutterworth LE17......244 B5
  Manton LE15 ....164 D6
  Market Harborough
    LE16.............240 F3
  Sileby LE12 ....77 C4
St Mary's St PE9.......143 D3
St Mary's Way LE13....59 C3
St Matthew's Ave LE65...47 F6
St Matthews Bsns Ctr
  LE1................259 C5
St Matthews Way LE1...259 C4
St Maxime Ho LE2.....155 C1
St Mellion Cl LE4......128 B7
St Michael & All Angels
  CE Prim Sch LE7......79 A1
St Michaels Ave LE4....129 C3
St Michaels Cl CV9.....170 F1
St Michael's Cl
  Ashby-de-la-Z LE65 ....69 C5
  Markfield LE67........98 D1
St Michael's St LE4....129 E7
St Michael's Cl LE67....95 E8
St Michael's Dr DE12...119 F8
St Michaels Ho LE12....30 B8
St Michaels Wlk LE7 ...183 F3

St Nicholas CE Prim Sch
LE15 . . . . 112 C8
St Nicholas Circ LE1 . . 259 A3
St Nicholas Cl
Austrey CV9 . . . . 119 B2
Market Harborough
LE16 . . . . 240 F2
St Nicholas Ct LE15 . . 112 C8
St Nicholas Pl LE1 . . . . 259 A3
St Nicholas Way LE16 . 240 F2
ST NICOLAS PARK 214 A7
St Nicolas Park Dr
CV11 . . . . 214 A6
St Olaves Cl LE11 . . . . . 51 B5
St Oswalds Rd LE3 . . . 153 C4
St Patrick's RC Prim Sch
LE4 . . . . 129 B2
St Paul's CE Prim Sch
LE12 . . . . 75 A1
St Pauls Cl LE2 . . . . . . 181 D6
St Pauls Cl LE7 . . . . . . 103 B4
St Paul's Dr LE7 . . . . . 103 A3
St Pauls Gdns LE10 . . 197 E1
St Pauls RC Sch LE5 . . 156 C4
St Pauls Rd LE3 . . . . . . 154 C6
St Paul's St PE9 . . . . . . 143 E3
St Peter & St Paul CE
Prim Sch LE7 . . . . . . 103 B5
St Peters Ave LE12 . . . . 30 A1
St Peter's Ave CV9 . . . 194 B7
St Peter's CE Prim Sch
Market Bosworth
CV13 . . . . 148 D3
Netherseal DE12 . . . . 91 F6
Whetstone LE8 . . . . 201 F7
Wymondham LE14 . . . . . 62 D2
St Peter's Cl
Glenfield LE3 . . . . 153 B8
Leire LE17 . . . . 218 F1
Market Bosworth CV13 . 148 D3
Oakham LE15 . . . . 138 A6
Witherley CV9 . . . . 194 B7
St Peters Ct
2 Hinckley LE10 . . . . . 197 E1
Leicester LE2 . . . . 155 B4
Market Bosworth CV13 . 148 F3
Mountsorrel LE12 . . . . . . 76 E3
St Peter's Ct
2 Stamford PE9 . . . . . 143 D2
Syston LE7 . . . . 103 B4
St Peter's Dr LE8 . . . . 201 F8
St Peter's Hill **15** PE9 . 143 D3
St Peters La LE1 . . . . . 259 B4
St Peter's Path LE2 . . . 181 A5
St Peters Pl CV13 . . . . 121 E2
St Peter's RC Prim Sch
LE9 . . . . 176 A1
St Peter's RC Sch
LE10 . . . . 197 E1
St Peters Rd
Atherstone CV9 . . . . 194 A7
Leicester LE2 . . . . 155 C4
St Peter's Rd LE8 . . . . 221 F5
St Peter's St
Stamford PE9 . . . . 143 D3
Syston LE7 . . . . 103 A3
St Peters Terr LE7 . . . . 160 A8
St Peter's Vale PE9 . . . 143 D2
St Philip's Ct LE5 . . . . 155 D3
St Philips Rd
Burton o t W LE12 . . . . . . 54 A7
Leicester LE5 . . . . 155 D3
St Saviour's Hill LE5 . . 155 C6
St Saviours Rd
Coalville LE67 . . . . 96 C8
Leicester LE5 . . . . 155 C6
St Saviour's Rd LE5 . . 155 E5
St Stephen's Ct DE11 . . 44 E3
St Stephens Rd LE2 . . 155 C4
St Swithin's Rd LE5 . . 156 D5
St Thomas More RC Prim
Sch LE2 . . . . 180 C8
St Thomas Rd LE2,
LE18 . . . . 179 E1
St Thomas's Rd LE8 . . 182 C1
St Tibba Way PE9 . . . . 116 E1
St Vincent Cl NG10 . . . . 10 E6
St Vincents Cl LE67 . . . 96 C7
St Wilfrid's Cl LE8 . . . 206 A1
St Winefride Rd LE2 . . . 50 B3
St Winefride's RC Prim
Sch LE2 . . . . 50 B4
St Winifreds Ct NG11 . . . 18 F4
St Wolstan's Cl LE18 . . 180 E3
Salcombe Cl LE18 . . . . 180 C1
Salcombe Dr LE3 . . . . 153 C8
Salem Rd LE10 . . . . . . 215 F5
Salford Cl NN6 . . . . . . 256 E6
Salisbury Ave
Croft LE9 . . . . 200 C4
5 Leicester LE2 . . . . . 155 B4
Melton Mowbray LE13 . . 59 D4
Salisbury Cl
Blaby LE8 . . . . 202 B6
Desford LE9 . . . . 151 A2
Salisbury Ct **10** LE2 . . 155 B4
Salisbury Dr DE11 . . . . 44 E5
Salisbury Ho LE10 . . . . 197 C4
Salisbury La DE73 . . . . . 26 B7
Salisbury Rd
Hinckley LE10 . . . . 216 B7
Leicester LE1 . . . . 155 B4
Salisbury St
Long Eaton NG10 . . . . . . 10 E7

Salisbury St continued
Loughborough LE11 . . . . 52 C4
Salkeld Rd LE2 . . . . . . 179 C2
Salmon Mews LE12 . . . . 50 B4
Saltash Cl LE18 . . . . . . 180 C1
SALTBY 24 E1
Saltby Rd
Croxton Kerrial NG32 . . . 24 B7
Sproxton LE14 . . . . 41 F6
Saltcoates Ave LE4 . . . 129 C4
Salter Cl DE74 . . . . 16 F4
Saltersford Rd LE5 . . . 155 F7
Saltersgate Dr LE4 . . . 129 A8
Salter's Hill Dr LE14 . . 106 E4
Salt's Cl LE19 . . . . 178 B2
Salt St B79, CV9 . . . . . . 119 B5
Sam Brown Ind Est
LE8 . . . . 201 F5
Samphire Cl LE5 . . . . . 130 D2
Samson Rd
Coalville LE67 . . . . 71 D3
Leicester LE4 . . . . 154 B7
Samual Ct LE15 . . . . . . 189 A5
Samuel St LE1 . . . . 155 B6
Sanara Cl LE4 . . . . 129 B3
Sandacre St LE1 . . . . . 259 B4
Sandalwood Rd LE11 . . . 51 E1
Sandcliffe Pk DE11 . . . . 44 D7
Sandcliffe Rd DE11 . . . . 44 D6
Sandcroft Cl DE11 . . . . . 44 D5
Sanderman Ho DE11 . . . 44 E3
Sanders Cl CV9 . . . . . . 170 E1
Sanderson Cl LE18 . . . 202 A6
Sanders Rd LE12 . . . . . . 75 F5
Sandfield Cl LE4 . . . . . 129 E5
Sandfield Close Prim Sch
LE4 . . . . 129 E5
Sandford Ave NG10 . . . . 10 E7
Sandford Cl
Hinckley LE10 . . . . 197 F1
Leicester LE5 . . . . 156 A6
Sandford Ct LE5 . . . . . 156 A6
Sandford Rd LE7 . . . . . 103 A3
Sand Furrows PE9 . . . . 167 F5
Sandgate Ave LE4 . . . . 128 F8
Sandham Bridge Rd
LE7 . . . . 100 F3
Sandhill Dr LE19 . . . . . 178 D1
Sandhills Ave LE5 . . . . 130 C3
Sandhills Cl
Belton LE12 . . . . 49 B6
Measham DE12 . . . . 93 C4
Sandhills The LE12 . . . . 75 E6
Sandhole La LE12 . . . . . 49 D1
Sandhurst Cl LE3 . . . . 154 B6
Sandhurst Gdns LE3 . . 154 B6
Sandhurst Rd LE3 . . . . 154 B6
Sandhurst St LE2 . . . . 181 A6
Sandiacre Dr LE4 . . . . 129 F8
Sandlands The DE11 . . . 44 D6
Sandown Rd
Glenfield LE3 . . . . 127 C1
Leicester LE2 . . . . 155 D1
Wigston LE18 . . . . 180 D4
Sandpiper Cl
Leicester LE5 . . . . 155 C1
Rugby CV23 . . . . 252 C1
Sand Pit La LE14 . . . . . . 20 C2
Sandringham Ave
Earl Shilton LE9 . . . . . . 198 D7
Leicester LE4 . . . . 129 B3
Sandringham Cl
Oakham LE15 . . . . 137 E5
Stamford PE9 . . . . 143 D5
Swadlincote DE11 . . . . . 44 B3
Sandringham Dr LE11 . . 51 D5
Sandringham Rd
Coalville LE67 . . . . 96 F8
Glen Parva LE2 . . . . 179 E1
Sandringham Rise
LE12 . . . . 49 F2
Sandringham Way
LE16 . . . . 241 B3
Sands The LE14 . . . . 20 D3
Sandtop Cl DE11 . . . . . . 68 B8
Sandtop La DE11 . . . . . . 68 C8
Sandwell Cl NG10 . . . . . 10 A6
Sandy Cres LE10 . . . . . 197 C1
Sandyhurst LE3 . . . . . . 153 E4
Sandy La
Melton Mowbray LE13,
LE14 . . . . 82 D5
Newton Regis B79 . . . . . 118 D6
Scalford LE14 . . . . 38 E5
Sandy Rise LE18 . . . . . 180 F4
Sankey Dr DE11 . . . . 44 C1
Sanvey Cl LE2 . . . . 179 C6
Sanvey Gate LE1 . . . . . 259 A5
Sanvey La LE2 . . . . 179 C6
Sanvey Mill LE1 . . . . . 259 A5
SAPCOTE 217 D7
Sapcote Dr LE13 . . . . . . 59 E1
Sapcote Rd
Hinckley LE10 . . . . 216 B7
Stoney Stanton LE9 . . . 199 E1
Sargent's Ct PE9 . . . . . 143 C4
Sarson Cl LE14 . . . . 58 A2
Sarson St LE12 . . . . 75 F6
Saunderson Rd LE4 . . . 128 D4
Savernake Rd LE4 . . . . 128 C1
Saville Cl LE10 . . . . 197 E2
Saville Dr LE12 . . . . 77 C2
Saville Rd LE8 . . . . 202 C6
Saville St LE5 . . . . 155 E6
Sawbridge Cl LE67 . . . . 96 E3
Sawday St LE2 . . . . 154 E3
Sawgate Rd LE14 . . . . . 83 D7

SAWLEY 10 A4
Sawley Inf Sch NG10 . . . 10 A5
Sawley Jun Sch NG10 . . 10 A5
Sawley Rd
Breaston DE72 . . . . 9 E6
Draycott DE72 . . . . 9 B7
Sawley St LE5 . . . . 155 D3
Sawmand Cl NG10 . . . . . 10 C6
SAXBY 61 E4
Saxby Rd LE13 . . . . 59 E3
Saxby Road Ind Est
LE13 . . . . 59 E3
Saxby St LE2 . . . . 155 B4
SAXELBYE 57 E7
Saxelbye La LE14 . . . . . 57 B8
Saxelby Rd LE14 . . . . . . 57 E4
Saxon Cl
Breedon on t H DE73 . . . 26 F2
Market Harborough
LE16 . . . . 240 F4
Saxon Ct PE9 . . . . 143 E2
Saxon Dale LE2 . . . . . . 179 C2
Saxondale Rd LE18 . . . 203 E8
Saxons Lea LE14 . . . . . 108 D3
Saxons Rise LE6 . . . . . 126 C1
Saxon St LE3 . . . . 154 D4
Saxon Way LE65 . . . . . . 69 A7
Saxthorpe Rd LE5 . . . . 130 B2
Scalborough Cl LE8 . . 202 C4
SCALFORD 38 E5
Scalford CE Prim Sch
LE14 . . . . 38 E5
Scalford Rd
Eastwell LE14 . . . . 22 A5
Melton Mowbray LE13 . . 59 C6
Scalpay Cl LE4 . . . . 128 B3
Scarborough Ct LE5 . . 155 D4
Scarborough Rd LE4 . . 129 C2
Schofield Rd
Loughborough LE11 . . . . 51 C3
Oakham LE15 . . . . 138 A8
Scholars Wlk LE2 . . . . 155 C2
School Cl
Croft LE9 . . . . 200 C3
Hinckley LE10 . . . . 216 A6
Moira DE11 . . . . 44 C1
School Cotts LE14 . . . . 108 B2
School Cres LE9 . . . . . 218 F7
School Farm Yd LE16 . . 227 B3
Schoolgate LE2 . . . . . . 179 F5
School Gdns CV21 . . . . 257 A1
School Hill
Sproxton LE14 . . . . 41 F5
Walton on t W LE12 . . . . 54 A4
School House Cl LE7 . . 127 D5
School La
Barkby LE7 . . . . 130 D8
Barrowden LE15 . . . . . . 191 F5
Belton LE12 . . . . 49 B6
Birstall LE4 . . . . 129 A6
Braybrooke LE16 . . . . . 251 F5
Castle Donington DE74 . . 17 A4
Cottingham LE16 . . . . . 229 C1
Cranoe LE16 . . . . 208 E3
Croxton Kerrial NG32 . . . 24 A7
Empingham LE15 . . . . . 141 B6
Gaulby LE7 . . . . 183 D6
Harby LE14 . . . . 12 B3
Houghton on t H LE7 . . . 157 F3
Huncote LE9 . . . . 200 D7
Husbands Bosworth
LE17 . . . . 247 E5
Leicester LE5 . . . . 156 B2
Long Clawson LE14 . . . . 20 C3
Lubenham LE16 . . . . . . 239 F3
Market Harborough
LE16 . . . . 240 E3
Morcott LE15 . . . . 191 A6
Narborough LE19 . . . . . 201 B7
Newbold LE67 . . . . 47 E2
Newton Burgoland
LE67 . . . . 121 E6
Normanton Le H LE67 . . 94 F6
Peatling Magna LE8 . . . 221 B6
Peggs Green LE67 . . . . . 48 A1
Quenideborough LE7 . . 103 F5
Quorn (Quorndon) LE12 . 76 A4
Rempstone LE12 . . . . . . 32 D5
Scalford LE14 . . . . 38 E5
Sedgebrook NG32 . . . . . . 8 E8
Sewstern NG33 . . . . 42 E1
Sharnford LE10 . . . . . . 217 C4
South Croxton LE7 . . . . 105 B1
Stapleton LE9 . . . . 174 E2
Stathern LE14 . . . . 13 A2
Swinford LE17 . . . . 254 B4
Thistleton LE15 . . . . 64 E1
Uffington PE9 . . . . 144 E4
Uppingham LE15 . . . . . 189 B4
Whitwick LE67 . . . . 71 D6
Woodhouse LE12 . . . . . . 75 B3
School Rd
Gretton NN17 . . . . 213 B1
Kibworth Beauchamp
LE8 . . . . 224 A8
Oakham LE15 . . . . 138 A7
School St
Churchover CV23 . . . . . 252 C6
Fleckney LE8 . . . . 222 F7
Loughborough LE11 . . . . 52 B4
Moira DE12 . . . . 67 F2
Oakthorpe DE12 . . . . 93 A7
Rothley LE7 . . . . 101 F6
Rugby CV21 . . . . 257 A1
Swadlincote DE11 . . . . . 44 B2
Syston LE7 . . . . 103 B4
School View NG13 . . . . . 3 A2
School Wlk LE8 . . . . . . 224 A8

Scoborough Rd LE16,
LE17 . . . . 239 A1
Scotgate
Harringworth NN17 . . . . 213 F7
Stamford PE9 . . . . 143 D3
SCOTLAND 182 F1
Scotland End LE16 . . . . 240 F1
Scotland La
Burton Overy LE8 . . . . . 182 F1
Houghton on t H LE7 . . . 157 F4
Scotland Rd LE16 . . . . 241 A2
Scotlands Dr LE67 . . . . . 96 C8
Scotlands Ind Est LE67 . 96 E8
Scotlands Rd LE67 . . . . 96 C8
Scotland Way LE8 . . . . 202 F3
Scotswood Cres LE2 . . 179 D3
Scott Cl
Market Harborough
LE16 . . . . 240 E5
Uppingham LE15 . . . . . 189 B4
Scott Ct LE7 . . . . 180 A8
Scotts Cl LE65 . . . . 69 B7
Scott St LE2 . . . . 180 A8
SCRAPTOFT 156 F8
Scraptoft La
Beeby LE7 . . . . 131 C4
Leicester LE7 . . . . 156 C7
Scraptoft Mews LE5 . . 156 A7
Scraptoft Rise LE7 . . . 156 F8
Scraptoft Valley Prim Sch
LE7 . . . . 156 E8
Scrivener Cl LE7 . . . . . 157 B5
Scudamore Rd LE3 . . . 153 C5
Sculthorpe Cl LE15 . . . 138 B6
Seacole Cl LE3 . . . . . . 153 D2
Seaford Rd LE2 . . . . . . 179 C5
Seaforth Dr LE10 . . . . 197 A1
SEAGRAVE 77 F8
Seagrave Cl LE67 . . . . . 72 D1
Seagrave Dr LE2 . . . . . 180 F6
Seagrave Rd
Sileby LE12 . . . . 77 D5
Thrussington LE7 . . . . . . 78 E5
Seagrave Village Prim Sch
LE12 . . . . 77 F8
SEAGRAVE WOLDS 55 C4
Seals Cl LE12 . . . . 54 A7
Seals Rd DE12 . . . . 67 E1
SEATON 190 C1
Seaton Cl LE10 . . . . . . 216 B7
Seaton Dr LE15 . . . . . . 189 C4
Seaton Rd
Barrowden LE15 . . . . . . 191 C4
Braunstone Town LE3 . . 153 C1
Glaston LE15 . . . . 190 B4
Harringworth NN17 . . . . 213 E8
Stamford PE9 . . . . 143 D3
Uppingham LE15 . . . . . 189 E2
Wigston LE18 . . . . 180 C1
Seaton Rise LE5 . . . . . 130 E1
SECKINGTON 118 A3
Seckington La B79 . . . . 118 C3
Second Drift PE9 . . . . . 169 D8
Seddons Cl LE4 . . . . . . 128 D4
SEDGEBROOK 8 E8
Sedgebrook Cl LE5 . . . 156 E4
Sedgebrook Rd
Allington NG32 . . . . 4 F4
Leicester LE5 . . . . 156 E4
Woolsthorpe by B NG32 . . 8 B3
Sedgefield Dr
Leicester LE7 . . . . 156 F6
Syston LE7 . . . . 102 E3
Sedgemoor Rd NG10 . . . 10 E5
Segrave Rd LE3 . . . . . . 154 B2
Seine La LE19 . . . . 177 F4
Selbourne Ct LE11 . . . . 52 C4
Selbourne St LE11 . . . . 52 C4
Selbury Dr LE2 . . . . . . 180 F5
Selby Ave LE5 . . . . 130 D1
Selby Cl LE16 . . . . 250 E8
Selina Cl DE74 . . . . 17 A4
Selina St DE73 . . . . 26 A7
Selkirk Rd LE4 . . . . 129 D4
Selvester Dr LE12 . . . . . 76 B5
Selwyn Rd PE9 . . . . . . 143 C5
Senator Ct LE7 . . . . . . 102 F2
Sence Cres LE8 . . . . . . 205 A8

Sence Valley Forest Pk*
LE67 . . . . 95 E3
Sennen Cl CV11 . . . . . . 214 A5
Seton Cl LE11 . . . . 51 C7
Severn Ave LE10 . . . . . 215 A8
Severn Cl
Cosby LE9 . . . . 201 D3
Oakham LE15 . . . . 137 E5
Severn Cres LE15 . . . . 166 D2
Severn Hill LE13 . . . . . . 59 B1
Severn Rd LE2 . . . . 181 D6
Severn St LE2 . . . . 155 B4
Severn Wlk NN17 . . . . 230 C1
Seward St LE1 . . . . 52 A3
SEWSTERN 63 F8
Sewstern La
Allington NG23 . . . . 4 B8
Harston NG32 . . . . 15 D3
Muston NG32 . . . . 8 B8
Sewstern Rd NG33 . . . . 64 D8
Sextant Rd LE5 . . . . . . 156 C7
Seymour Cl LE11 . . . . . . 51 B5
Seymour Rd
Burton o t W LE12 . . . . . 53 F7
Leicester LE2 . . . . 155 B1
Seymour St LE2 . . . . . . 155 B4
Seymour Way LE3 . . . . 152 F3
Shackelton Way LE17 . . 243 D5
Shackerdale Rd LE2,
LE18 . . . . 180 B5

SHACKERSTONE 121 E2
Shackerstone Rd
CV13 . . . . 147 D8
Shackerstone Sta*
CV13 . . . . 121 F2
Shackerstone Wlk
CV13 . . . . 148 C6
Shackland Dr LE12 . . . . 93 D5
Shackleton Dr LE10 . . . 215 E4
Shackleton St **4** LE1 . . 155 A7
Shades Cl LE3 . . . . 200 C4
Shadows La CV13 . . . . . 147 D7
Shadrack Cl LE2 . . . . . 199 D1
Shady La LE2 . . . . 156 B1
Shaeffer Ct LE4 . . . . . . 128 B2
Shaftesbury Ave
Leicester LE4 . . . . 129 B2
Long Eaton NG10 . . . . . . 10 B4
Shaftesbury Jun Sch
LE3 . . . . 154 D4
Shaftesbury Rd LE3 . . . 154 D4
Shakespear Cl DE74 . . . 28 C5
Shakespeare Cl
Braunstone Town LE3 . . 153 E1
Swadlincote DE11 . . . . . 44 C6
Shakespeare Dr
Diseworth DE74 . . . . 28 C5
Hinckley LE10 . . . . 197 C1
Leicester LE3 . . . . 153 F1
Nuneaton CV11 . . . . . . 214 A1
Shakespeare St
Leicester LE2 . . . . 179 F8
Loughborough LE11 . . . . 52 B4
Shakespeare Way
NN17 . . . . 230 D1
Shambles Ct LE17 . . . . 244 D6
SHANGTON 207 A5
Shangton Rd LE8 . . . . . 207 B3
Shanklin Ave LE2 . . . . 180 D7
Shanklin Dr LE2 . . . . . 180 D7
Shanklin Gdns
Leicester Forest East
LE3 . . . . 153 B3
Leicester LE2 . . . . 180 D7
Shannon Way LE15 . . . 137 E5
Shanti Margh LE4 . . . . 129 C2
SHARDLOW 9 B1
Shardlow Rd
Aston-on-T DE72 . . . . . . 16 B7
Wigston LE18 . . . . 180 C3
Sharmon Cres LE3 . . . . 153 C4
Sharnbrook Gdns
LE10 . . . . 217 C4
SHARNFORD 217 C4
Sharnford CE Prim Sch
LE10 . . . . 217 C4
Sharnford Rd
Aston Flamville LE10 . . . 216 F6
Sapcote LE9 . . . . 217 E6
Sharp Cl NG10 . . . . 10 C6
Sharpe's Plain PE9 . . . 167 F5
Sharpe Way LE19 . . . . 201 B7
Sharpland LE2 . . . . 179 C5
Sharpless Rd LE10 . . . 215 F7
Sharpley Ave LE67 . . . . 72 A2
Sharpley Dr LE4 . . . . . 128 A6
Sharpley Rd LE11 . . . . . 51 C2
Sharply Hill LE6 . . . . . . 99 E3
Sharp's Cl LE67 . . . . . . 124 F4
Sharpswood Manor
DE11 . . . . 44 E4
Sharrads Way LE15 . . . 110 D3
Shaw Cl LE8 . . . . 201 F6
SHAWELL 253 D5
Shawell Rd
Cotesbach LE17 . . . . . . 244 D1
Swinford LE17 . . . . 254 A4
Shaw La LE67 . . . . 97 C4
Shaw Wood Cl LE6 . . . 126 E3
Shearer Cl LE4 . . . . . . 129 E4
Shearers Ct LE11 . . . . . 52 C5
SHEARSBY 222 A2
Shearsby Cl LE18 . . . . 180 D2
Shearsby Rd LE8 . . . . . 222 E4
Shearwater Dr CV23 . . 252 C1
Sheene Rd LE4 . . . . . . 128 A4
Sheepcote LE7 . . . . . . 101 E7
Sheepdyke LE15 . . . . . 112 C8
Sheep Market **14** PE9 . 143 D3
Sheepy Cl LE10 . . . . . . 197 F1
Sheepy La CV9 . . . . . . 145 E3
SHEEPY MAGNA 171 A7
Sheepy Magna CE Prim
Sch CV9 . . . . 171 B8
SHEEPY PARVA 171 C7
Sheepy Rd
Atherstone CV9 . . . . . . 170 D2
Atherstone, Pinwall
CV9 . . . . 170 E6
Sibson CV13 . . . . 172 A6
Twycross CV9 . . . . 146 C5
Sheet Hedges Wood CPry
Pk* LE6 . . . . 126 F6
Sheets Stores Ind Est
NG10 . . . . 10 D5
Sheffield St LE3 . . . . . 154 D3
Shelbourne St LE5 . . . 155 C6
Sheldon Cl LE11 . . . . . . 51 B6
Sheldon St LE1 . . . . . . 155 B6
Shelford La CV9 . . . . . 120 C3
Shelford Wlk **7** LE4 . . 128 E3
Shelland Cl LE16 . . . . . 241 C2
SHELLBROOK 68 E6
Shellbrook Cl LE65 . . . . 68 E6
Shellduck Cl LE8 . . . . . 201 F4
Shelley Ave LE13 . . . . . 59 B5
Shelley Cl
Measham DE12 . . . . 93 C3

Shelley Cl continued
Stamford PE9 . . . . 143 A4
Shelley Dr
Corby NN17 . . . . 230 D1
Lutterworth LE17 . . . . 244 C7
Shelley Gdns LE10 . . . . . 197 E3
Shelley Rd
Narborough LE19 . . . . . . 178 A2
Swadlincote DE11 . . . . 44 C5
Shelley St
Leicester LE2 . . . . 180 A8
Loughborough LE11 . . . . . . 51 D5
SHELTHORPE 75 C8
Shelthorpe Ave LE11 . . . . 52 B1
Shelthorpe Com Sch
LE11 . . . . 52 C1
Shelthorpe Rd LE11 . . . . . 52 B1
Shenley Rd LE18 . . . . . . 180 E4
SHENTON 173 B5
Shenton Cl
Stoke Golding CV13 . . . . . 196 E7
Thurmaston LE4 . . . . 130 A6
Whetstone LE8 . . . . 201 F7
Wigston LE18 . . . . 180 C3
Shenton La
Market Bosworth
CV13 . . . . 148 E2
Shenton CV13 . . . . 173 C4
Sibson CV13 . . . . 172 C5
Upton CV13 . . . . 172 E4
Shenton Prim Sch
LE5 . . . . 155 C7
Shenton Rd LE9 . . . . 198 B7
Shenton Sta★ CV13 . . . . 173 D5
Shepheard Cl LE5 . . . . . . 130 C3
Shepherd Cl LE9 . . . . . . 152 E3
Shepherds Cl
Loughborough LE11 . . . . . . 51 D1
Shepshed LE12 . . . . 50 C5
Shepherd's Cl LE12 . . . . . 30 C5
Shepherds Croft LE13 . . . 59 B5
Shepherds La LE15 . . . . . 88 B2
Shepherd's Way LE15 . . . 188 F5
Shepherd's Wlk PE9 . . . . 117 A1
Shepherd's Wlk LE7 . . . . 103 D7
Shepherd Wlk DE74 . . . . 18 C1
Sheppards Cl NG13 . . . . . . 3 A2
Sheppards Orch LE12 . . . 33 C4
SHEPSHED 50 A4
Shepshed High Sch
LE12 . . . . 50 C5
Shepshed Rd LE12 . . . . . 50 E8
Sherard Prim Sch
LE13 . . . . 59 E1
Sherborne Ave LE18 . . . . 203 D8
Sherborne Rd LE10 . . . . 216 B7
Sherbourne Dr LE65 . . . . . 69 A7
Sherford Cl LE18 . . . . . . 180 C2
Sheridan Cl LE19 . . . . . . 178 A2
Sheridan St LE2 . . . . . . 179 F8
Sheringham Rd LE4 . . . . 128 D2
Sherloyd Cl LE4 . . . . . . 129 F4
Sherrard Cl LE15 . . . . . . 84 F2
Sherrard Dr LE12 . . . . . . 77 C1
Sherrard Rd
Leicester LE5 . . . . 155 C6
Market Harborough
LE16 . . . . 240 E5
Sherrard St LE13 . . . . . . 59 C3
Sherrard Way LE3 . . . . . 153 D1
Sherrier CE Prim Sch
LE17 . . . . 244 C7
Sherrier Way LE17 . . . . . 244 A5
Sherwood Cl
Ellistown LE67 . . . . 96 D4
Stamford PE9 . . . . 143 B3
Sherwood Dr LE3 . . . . . . 59 A4
Sherwood Rd CV13 . . . . 196 C4
Sherwood St LE5 . . . . . . 155 C6
Shetland Rd LE4 . . . . . . 129 C1
Shetland Way
Corby NN17 . . . . 230 C1
Countesthorpe LE8 . . . . . 202 F4
Shield Cres LE12 . . . . . . 179 C2
Shields Cl LE15 . . . . 189 E4
Shields Cres DE74 . . . . . . 16 F3
Shilling Way NG10 . . . . . 10 A7
Shilton Rd
Barwell LE9 . . . . 198 B6
Kirkby Mallory LE9 . . . . . 175 E4
Shipley Rd LE5 . . . . 155 D4
Shipman Rd LE3 . . . . . . 178 F7
Shipston Hill LE2 . . . . . . 181 A4
Shipton Cl LE18 . . . . . . 180 F2
Shipton Rd LE5 . . . . 130 C3
Shire Cl LE3 . . . . 153 E5
Shire Rd NN17 . . . . 230 C1
Shires La LE1 . . . . 259 A4
Shires Orch NG32 . . . . . . 24 B7
Shires The LE1 . . . . 259 B4
Shirley Ave LE2 . . . . 180 D8
Shirley Cl LE4 . . . . 17 A4
Shirley Cres DE72 . . . . . . 9 D8
Shirley Dr LE7 . . . . 103 B5
Shirley Pk DE72 . . . . . . 16 B7
Shirley Rd LE2 . . . . 180 D8
Shirley St
Leicester LE4 . . . . 129 A2
Long Eaton NG10 . . . . 10 A4
Shirreffs Cl LE12 . . . . . . 76 E8
SHOBY 57 A5
Shoby La LE14 . . . . 57 A8
Shoe Makers The
LE5 . . . . 127 D6
Shoesmith Cl LE9 . . . . . . 198 A6
Shooting Close La
LE12 . . . . 76 D7
Short Cl LE8 . . . . 222 F7

Shortheath DE12 . . . . . . 67 C3
SHORT HEATH 67 D2
Shortheath Rd DE12 . . . . 67 E3
Short Hill DE73 . . . . 26 E6
Short La DE74 . . . . 16 F4
Shortridge La LE19 . . . . 178 B2
Short Row LE8 . . . . 204 D6
Short St LE1 . . . . 259 B4
Shortwheat Hill CV23 . . . 252 D1
Shottens Cl LE4 . . . . 128 B2
Shottery Ave LE3 . . . . . . 153 F1
Shoulbard LE8 . . . . 222 E8
Shrewsbury Ave
Leicester LE2 . . . . 180 A6
Market Harborough
LE16 . . . . 241 B2
Shrewsbury Cl LE9 . . . . 198 A7
Shrewsbury Wlk LE67 . . . 71 D8
Shropshire Cl LE16 . . . . 240 E4
Shropshire Pl LE16 . . . . 240 E4
Shropshire Rd LE2 . . . . . 179 D7
Shrubbery The DE11 . . . . 45 A4
Shuttleworth La LE9 . . . 219 D7
SIBBERTOFT 248 F2
Sibbertoft Rd
Clipston LE16 . . . . 249 E1
Husbands Bosworth
LE17 . . . . 247 F2
Marston Trussell LE16 . . . 249 B6
SIBSON 172 A7
Sibson Dr DE74 . . . . 18 B2
Sibson La CV13 . . . . 172 E6
Sibson Rd
Birstall LE4 . . . . 129 A7
Ratcliffe Culey CV9 . . . . . 171 E4
Sheepy Magna CV9 . . . . . 171 D7
Sibton La LE2 . . . . 181 A4
Sickleholm Dr LE5 . . . . . 155 E2
Side Ley DE74 . . . . 18 C3
Side St NG32 . . . . 4 F5
Sidings The
Bottesford NG13 . . . . 2 F3
Oakham LE15 . . . . 137 F6
Swannington LE67 . . . . . . 71 B7
Sidmouth Ave LE5 . . . . . 156 A4
Sidney Ho LE13 . . . . 59 D3
Sidney Rd LE2 . . . . 180 D7
Sidney St LE2 . . . . 180 D7
Sidwell St LE5 . . . . 155 E5
Signal Rd LE14 . . . . 36 A5
Silbury Rd LE4 . . . . 128 C1
SILEBY 77 C4
Sileby Rd
Barrow-u-S LE12 . . . . 76 E6
Mountsorrel LE12 . . . . . . 76 E3
Sileby Sta LE12 . . . . 77 C3
Silkstone Cl DE11 . . . . . . 44 B1
Silsden Rise LE2 . . . . . . 179 D3
Silver Arc 3 LE1 . . . . . . 259 B4
Silver Birches LE2 . . . . . 75 F6
Silverbirch Way LE11 . . . 75 A6
Silver Birch Way LE7 . . . 103 E8
Silverdale Dr LE4 . . . . . 129 F6
Silver La 10 PE9 . . . . . . 143 D3
Silver St
Leicester LE1 . . . . 259 B4
Newton CV23 . . . . 253 A1
Oakthorpe DE12 . . . . 93 A6
Whitwick LE67 . . . . 71 F4
Silverstone Dr LE4 . . . . . 129 D5
Silverton Rd
Leicester, Oadby LE2 . . . . 181 C6
Loughborough LE11 . . . . . 74 F8
Silver Wlk LE1 . . . . 259 B4
Silverwood Cl LE5 . . . . . 156 C6
Silverwood Rd NG13 . . . . 3 A2
Simborough Way
LE16 . . . . 241 B3
Simmins Cl LE2 . . . . 179 D4
Simmins Cres LE2 . . . . . 179 D4
Simmonds Way CV9 . . . . 170 D2
Simons Cl LE18 . . . . 203 E8
Simon's Orch LE17 . . . . 233 F5
Simons Wlk 2 LE12 . . . . 77 C3
Simpson Cl
Blaby LE8 . . . . 202 A6
Syston LE7 . . . . 102 E2
Sir Henry's La DE73 . . . . 26 A4
Sir Herbert Wragg Way
DE11 . . . . 44 C3
Sir John Moore CE Prim
Sch DE12 . . . . 119 E7
Sir Jonathan North Com
Coll LE2 . . . . 180 A7
Sir Robert Martin Ct
LE11 . . . . 51 D5
Siskin Cl DE12 . . . . 93 B4
Siskin Hill LE2 . . . . 181 A4
Siskin Rd LE15 . . . . 189 A5
Sisley Way LE10 . . . . . . 197 A3
Sitch Cl LE9 . . . . 219 A5
Sitwell Wlk LE5 . . . . . . 155 F2
Snibston Dr LE67 . . . . . . 71 A1
Snipe Cl LE67 . . . . 96 B7
Snowdens End LE18 . . . . 180 E1
Snowdon Ave LE15 . . . . 137 E6
Snowdon Cl LE12 . . . . . . 50 C2
Snowdrop Cl LE19 . . . . . 200 F8
Snow Hill
Leicester LE4 . . . . 128 C1
Melton Mowbray LE13 . . . 59 D4
Snows La LE7 . . . . 131 D1
Soarbank Way LE11 . . . . 51 E7
Soar Cl LE13 . . . . 59 B1
Soar Gn NN17 . . . . 230 C1
Soar La
Leicester LE3 . . . . 259 A4
Normanton on S LE12 . . . 30 D3

Skeg Hill Rd LE7 . . . . . . 133 B2
Skelton Dr LE2 . . . . 180 A6
Skelwith Rise CV11 . . . . 214 A6
Skerry La NG13 . . . . 4 A2
SKETCHLEY 215 C6
Sketchley Cl LE5 . . . . . . 156 D6
Sketchley Hall Gdns
LE10 . . . . 215 C5
SKETCHLEY HILL 215 E7
Sketchley Hill Prim Sch
LE10 . . . . 215 E5
Sketchley La
Hinckley LE10 . . . . 215 C5
Ratcliffe Culey CV9 . . . . . 171 E4
Sketchley La Ind Est
LE10 . . . . 215 B5
Sketchley Manor La
LE10 . . . . 215 D5
Sketchley Mdws LE10 . . . 215 C5
Sketchley Meadows Bsns
Pk LE10 . . . . 215 C4
Sketchley Old Village
LE10 . . . . 215 C5
Sketchley Rd LE10 . . . . . 215 E5
Skevington Ave LE11 . . . 51 E4
SKILLINGTON 43 B8
Skillington Rd NG33 . . . . 43 D3
Skinner's La LE67 . . . . . . 71 F5
Skinners Way DE11 . . . . . 44 D5
Skippon Cl LE16 . . . . . . 240 D2
Skipworth St LE2 . . . . . . 155 C4
Skye Rd NN17 . . . . 230 B1
Skye Way LE8 . . . . 202 F3
Skylark Ave LE12 . . . . . . 76 F1
Skylark Cl DE12 . . . . 93 B4
Slackey La DE12 . . . . . . 67 C4
Slack La DE11 . . . . 45 B6
Slade Cl LE3 . . . . 153 C2
Slade Gns The LE2 . . . . . 179 C4
Slade La DE73, DE74 . . . . 26 F6
Slade Pl LE2 . . . . 179 C4
Slash La LE12 . . . . 76 F4
Slate Brook Cl LE6 . . . . . 126 F3
Slate Cl LE3 . . . . 153 B8
Slate Drift PE9 . . . . 168 E3
Slate Pit La LE6 . . . . 126 B4
Slater Prim Sch LE3 . . . . 259 A5
Slater St LE4 . . . . 154 E7
Slate St LE2 . . . . 259 C3
SLAWSTON 209 B1
Slawston Rd
Medbourne LE16 . . . . . . 227 E7
Slawston LE16 . . . . 209 A2
Welham LE16 . . . . 226 F6
Slaybarns Way LE67 . . . . 95 F2
Sloane Cl LE19 . . . . 178 A3
Sludge Hall Hill LE7 . . . . 159 C7
Small Thorn Pl DE11 . . . . 44 E1
Smart Cl LE3 . . . . 153 D2
Smedley Cl LE65 . . . . 68 F5
Smedmore Rd LE5 . . . . . 155 D8
Smeeton Rd LE8 . . . . . . 224 A7
SMEETON WESTERBY
. . . . 223 F6
SMISBY 45 F3
Smisby Rd LE65 . . . . 69 B8
Smith Ave
Melbourne DE73 . . . . 26 B8
Thurmaston LE4 . . . . 129 F6
Smith Cres LE67 . . . . 97 C8
Smith Ct LE67 . . . . 71 D5
Smith Dorrien Rd LE5 . . . 155 E7
Smith Way LE19 . . . . . . 178 E4
Smithy Cl CV13 . . . . 149 D8
Smithy Farm Dr LE9 . . . . 199 D2
Smithy La
Burbage LE9, LE10 . . . . . 198 C1
Long Whatton LE12 . . . . . 29 A2
Odstone CV13 . . . . 122 C4
Sapcote LE9 . . . . 216 D8
Smithy Rd LE65 . . . . 69 C7
Smithy Way LE12 . . . . . . 50 C4
SMOCKINGTON 231 D8
Smockington La LE10 . . . 231 B7
Smore Slade Hills
LE2 . . . . 181 E4
Smyth Cl LE16 . . . . 240 E5
SNARESTONE 120 F7
Snarestone CE Prim Sch
DE12 . . . . 120 E7
Snarestone Rd
Appleby Magna DE12 . . . . 120 B8
Newton Burgoland
LE67 . . . . 121 C7
Snarrow's Rd LE67 . . . . . 48 E2
Snell's Nook La LE11 . . . 74 A8
Snelston Cl LE15 . . . . . . 138 B7
SNIBSTON 96 A7
Snibston Ct LE67 . . . . . . 71 B2
Snibston Discovery Pk★
LE67 . . . . 71 B1

Soar La continued
Sutton Bonington LE12,
DE74 . . . . 30 A8
Soar Mill La LE9 . . . . . . 218 D8
Soar Rd
Quorn (Quorndon) LE12 . . 76 B6
Thurmaston LE4 . . . . 102 E1
Soar Valley Coll LE4 . . . . 129 D3
Soar Valley Way LE2,
LE19 . . . . 179 A5
Soar Way LE10 . . . . 215 A8
Soho St LE13 . . . . 59 C3
Solway Cl LE13 . . . . 59 B1
SOMERBY 108 B1
Somerby Cl PE9 . . . . 143 D5
Somerby Dr LE2 . . . . . . 181 C5
Somerby Prim Sch
LE14 . . . . 108 B2
Somerby Rd
Burrough on t H LE14 . . . 107 E3
Cold Overton LE14,
LE16 . . . . 136 A8
Knossington LE15 . . . . . . 135 C6
Leicester LE7 . . . . 156 F6
Owston LE15 . . . . 135 F7
Pickwell LE14 . . . . 108 C2
Somerfield Way LE3 . . . . 152 F2
Somerfield Wlk LE4 . . . . 128 B2
Somerscales Wlk LE4 . . . 155 B7
Somerset Ave LE4 . . . . . 128 D2
Somerset Cl
Burton o t W LE12 . . . . . 53 F7
Melton Mowbray LE13 . . . 82 D8
Somerset Dr LE3 . . . . . . 153 C7
Somerset Rd LE15 . . . . . 87 E2
Somers Rd LE5 . . . . 156 C6
Somerville Rd
Leicester LE3 . . . . 154 C1
Stamford PE9 . . . . 143 C4
Somes Cl PE9 . . . . 144 E4
Sonning Way LE2 . . . . . 179 C2
Sopers Rd LE9 . . . . 200 C3
Sorrel Cl LE2 . . . . 76 E2
Sorrel Ct PE9 . . . . 142 F4
Sorrel Dr DE11 . . . . 44 E4
Sorrel Rd LE5 . . . . 130 C2
Sorrel Way LE19 . . . . . . 177 F1
South Albion St LE1 . . . . 259 C3
Southampton St LE1 . . . . 259 C4
South Ave
Leicester Forest East
LE3 . . . . 153 B3
Ullesthorpe LE17 . . . . . . 233 B4
Wigston LE18 . . . . 180 C2
South Charnwood High
Sch LE67 . . . . 125 A7
South Church Gate
LE1 . . . . 259 A5
South Cl
Arnesby LE8 . . . . 221 F5
Blackfordby DE11 . . . . . . 68 B8
Scalford LE14 . . . . 38 E5
South Cres NG33 . . . . 3 A2
SOUTH CROXTON 105 C1
South Croxton Rd
Queniborough LE7 . . . . . 104 E4
South Croxton LE7 . . . . . 132 F8
Southdown Dr LE4 . . . . . 129 E5
Southdown Rd
Leicester LE5 . . . . 155 D6
Loughborough LE11 . . . . . 75 A8
Southdown Wlk LE15 . . . 87 E2
South Dr
Leicester LE5 . . . . 156 A8
Stoney Stanton LE9 . . . . . 199 E2
SOUTH END 76 E2
Southernhay Ave LE2 . . . 155 C1
Southernhay Cl LE2 . . . . 155 C1
Southernhay Rd LE2 . . . . 155 C1
Southey Cl
Enderby LE19 . . . . 178 A2
Leicester LE4 . . . . 155 B8
Southfield Ave LE7 . . . . 103 B3
Southfield Cl
Glen Parva LE2 . . . . 179 A3
Scraptoft LE7 . . . . 156 F7
Southfield Prim Sch
LE15 . . . . 137 E5
Southfield Rd
Gretton NN17 . . . . 213 C1
Hinckley LE10 . . . . 215 E7
Loughborough LE11 . . . . . 52 B3
Southfields NG10 . . . . . . 10 E7
SOUTH FIELDS 259 C2
Southfields Ave LE2 . . . . 180 F6
Southfields Dr LE2 . . . . . 179 F5
Southfield Way CV13 . . . 148 E2
Southgates LE1 . . . . 259 A3
Southgates Underpass
LE1 . . . . 259 A3
SOUTH KILWORTH 255 D8
South Kilworth CE Prim
Sch LE17 . . . . 255 C8
South Kilworth Rd
North Kilworth LE17 . . . . 246 E2
Walcote LE17 . . . . 245 D3
Welford NN6 . . . . 256 B5
South Kingsmead Rd
LE2 . . . . 180 C6
SOUTH KNIGHTON 180 D7
South Knighton Rd
LE2 . . . . 180 D7
South La LE67 . . . . 97 D4
Southland Rd LE3 . . . . . 180 D6
South Leicester Ind Est
LE67 . . . . 96 E4
South Leicestershire Coll
LE18 . . . . 180 B2

Southleigh Gr LE16 . . . . 240 D4
SOUTH LUFFENHAM
. . . . 191 D8
Southmeade LE2 . . . . . . 180 F8
Southmeads Cl LE2 . . . . 181 A7
Southmeads Rd LE2 . . . . 181 A7
South Par LE13 . . . . 59 C3
South Rd
Clifton u D CV23 . . . . . . 257 A5
Ibstock LE67 . . . . 122 F8
Southside Rd LE3 . . . . . 178 F6
South St
Asfordby Hill LE14 . . . . . 58 D3
Ashby-de-la-Z LE65 . . . . . 69 B6
Barrow-u-S LE12 . . . . . . 76 D7
Draycott DE72 . . . . 9 A7
Ellistown LE67 . . . . 96 D4
Leicester, Oadby LE2 . . . . 181 A6
Long Eaton NG10 . . . . . . 10 E7
Loughborough LE11 . . . . . 52 B3
Melbourne DE73 . . . . 26 A7
Oakham LE15 . . . . 137 F6
Oakham LE15 . . . . 138 A6
Scalford LE14 . . . . 38 E4
Swadlincote DE11 . . . . . . 45 A1
South View
Asfordby LE14 . . . . 57 E2
Burrough on t H LE14 . . . 107 D2
Preston LE15 . . . . 164 C1
Uppingham LE15 . . . . . . 189 B7
South View Bsns Pk
PE9 . . . . 143 B1
South View Cl LE15 . . . . 164 E5
Southview Cl LE9 . . . . . . 152 F3
Southview Dr LE5 . . . . . 155 F2
Southway LE8 . . . . 202 B6
South Way LE8 . . . . 206 B1
Southwell Cl LE13 . . . . . 59 A7
South Wigston High Sch
LE2, LE18 . . . . 179 E1
South Wigston Sta
LE18 . . . . 179 F2
SOUTH WITHAM 65 C4
South Witham Com Prim
Sch NG33 . . . . 65 B3
South Witham Nature
Res★ NG33 . . . . 65 E3
South Wlk LE6 . . . . 126 C1
SOUTHWOOD 46 B7
Southworth Rd DE73 . . . 26 E2
Sovereign Ct LE11 . . . . . 52 B3
Sovereign Gr NG10 . . . . 10 B7
Sovereign Pk LE16 . . . . 240 F1
Sowters La LE12 . . . . . . 54 B6
Spa Cl LE10 . . . . 197 E1
Spa Dr LE9 . . . . 217 D8
Spa La
Hinckley LE10 . . . . 197 E1
Orston NG13 . . . . 2 B7
Wigston LE18 . . . . 180 D2
Spalding St LE5 . . . . 155 E6
Sparkenhoe
Croft LE9 . . . . 200 C3
Newbold Verdon LE9 . . . . 150 C4
Sparkenhoe Com Prim
Sch LE2 . . . . 155 B4
Sparkenhoe Com Prim
Sch (Gopsall Annexe)
LE2 . . . . 155 B5
Sparkenhoe Est LE67 . . . 95 B2
Sparkenhoe St LE2 . . . . 155 B5
Sparrow Hill LE11 . . . . . 52 B4
Sparsis Gdns LE19 . . . . 178 D1
Speeds Pingle LE11 . . . . 52 A4
Speedwell Cl
Coalville LE67 . . . . 71 E1
Narborough LE19 . . . . . . 177 F1
Woodville DE11 . . . . 44 F4
Speedwell Dr
Broughton Astley LE9 . . . 219 A4
Hamilton LE5 . . . . 130 B3
Speedwell Rd LE12 . . . . 76 F2
Speers Rd LE3 . . . . 153 E8
Spellow Cl CV23 . . . . . . 252 D1
Spencefield Dr LE5 . . . . 156 B3
Spencefield La LE5 . . . . 156 C4
Spencer Ave LE4 . . . . . . 129 E7
Spencer Rd LE17 . . . . . . 244 C6
Spencers Rd PE9 . . . . . . 167 F5
Spencer St
Hinckley LE10 . . . . 197 D1
Leicester, Oadby LE2 . . . . 181 A6
Market Harborough
LE16 . . . . 240 D3
Spencer View LE67 . . . . . 96 E3
Spence St LE5 . . . . 155 D7
Spendlove Dr NN17 . . . . 213 C1
Spendlow Gdns LE2 . . . . 179 E4
Spendlow Gn LE2 . . . . . 179 E4
Sperry Ct LE67 . . . . 95 F1
Spey Dr LE15 . . . . 137 E4
Spiers Cl LE19 . . . . 201 B7
Spindle Rd LE11 . . . . . . 75 A6
Spindles The LE10 . . . . . 215 F5
Spinner Cl LE9 . . . . 219 B6
Spinners Way LE12 . . . . 50 B3
Spinney Ave LE8 . . . . . . 202 F4
Spinney Cl
Ashby-de-la-Z LE65 . . . . . 69 B5
Braunstone Town LE3 . . . 153 C2
Gilmorton LE17 . . . . 235 C4
Glen Parva LE2 . . . . 179 A3
Groby LE6 . . . . 126 E2
Market Harborough
LE16 . . . . 240 C3

Spinney Cl *continued*
Melton Mowbray LE13.... **59** E5
Ryhall PE9............ **116** E2
Syston LE7............ **102** E3
Spinney Ct LE9...... **200** C4
Spinney Dr
Barlestone CV13...... **149** D7
Botcheston LE9........ **151** C8
Kibworth Beauchamp
LE8.............. **206** A1
Quorn (Quorndon) LE12.... **75** F5
Spinney Farm Cotts
LE14.............. **79** F4
Spinney Halt LE8..... **201** F7
Spinney Hill
Market Bosworth
CV13............. **148** D3
Melbourne DE73...... **26** A7
Spinney Hill Dr LE11... **51** D2
Spinney Hill Prim Sch
LE5............... **155** D5
Spinney Hill Rd LE5.... **155** C7
SPINNEY HILLS........ **155** C5
Spinney La
Ryhall PE9.......... **116** E2
Stretton LE15........ **88** F4
Spinney Mdw LE7..... **159** C1
Spinney Mobile Home Pk
The LE67........... **70** E3
Spinney Nook LE7..... **185** E6
Spinney Rd
Hinckley LE10........ **215** C6
Ketton PE9.......... **167** F5
Spinney Rise LE4...... **129** A7
Spinneyside LE6...... **126** E2
Spinney The
Atherstone CV9....... **194** A7
Castle Donington DE74.. **17** A4
Coalville LE67........ **96** C6
Cottesmore LE15...... **112** B7
Leicester, Oadby LE2.... **182** A4
Thurnby LE7.......... **156** E4
Spinney View LE18..... **182** C1
Spion Kopje LE2....... **181** E1
Spires The LE17....... **235** C4
Spire View NG13....... **3** B3
Spittal DE74.......... **17** A4
Spittal Hill DE74...... **17** A4
Sponne Rise LE2....... **179** E4
Sports Field La LE9.... **200** D8
Sports Rd LE3........ **153** D8
Spring Back Way
LE15.............. **189** A4
Spring Bank LE16...... **227** F7
Springbrook Dr LE7.... **156** F6
Spring Cl
Breaston DE72........ **9** C8
Leicester LE2........ **179** D5
Lutterworth LE17...... **244** C5
Market Overton LE15.... **86** F5
Ratby LE6........... **152** D8
Shepshed LE12........ **50** C2
Swadlincote DE11..... **44** A1
SPRING COTTAGE...... **67** D5
Spring Cottage Rd
DE12.............. **67** D5
Springdale Rd LE4..... **129** E6
Springfield
Kegworth DE74....... **18** B2
Thringstone LE67..... **71** E8
Springfield Ave
Long Eaton NG10....... **10** F8
Market Bosworth CV13... **148** D3
Springfield Cl
Broughton Astley LE9... **218** F5
Burton o t W LE12...... **53** F7
Ibstock LE67........ **95** F1
Kibworth Beauchamp
LE8.............. **224** B7
Loughborough LE11.... **74** E8
Rothley LE7.......... **101** E7
Swadlincote DE11..... **44** B6
Spring Field Cl LE3.... **153** B7
Springfield Cres LE8... **224** B8
Springfield Ct 1
LE16.............. **240** F2
Springfield Jun Sch
DE11.............. **44** C5
Springfield La LE8..... **224** A6
Springfield Pk LE10.... **197** A3
Springfield Rd
Hinckley LE10........ **215** D7
Leicester LE2........ **155** C2
Shepshed LE12........ **50** B3
Sileby LE12.......... **77** D4
Swadlincote DE11..... **44** B6
Springfield St
Market Harborough
LE16.............. **240** F2
Melton Mowbray LE13... **59** B5
Springfield Way LE15... **138** A8
Spring Gdns
Littlethorpe LE19...... **201** C6
Sapcote LE9......... **217** E8
Springhill DE11....... **45** A8
Springhill Gdns LE16... **240** C2
Spring La
Ab Kettleby LE14...... **37** A3
Glaston LE15......... **190** B5
Long Whatton LE12..... **29** D2
Packington LE65...... **69** E4
Shepshed LE12....... **50** B2
Swannington LE67..... **71** B4
3 Wigston LE18....... **180** D3
Wymondham LE14...... **62** D2

Spring Rd LE67....... **96** A2
Spring St DE11....... **67** A8
Springs The
Broughton Astley LE9... **218** E6
Swinford LE17........ **254** C4
Spring Terr LE16...... **228** A6
Springway NG10....... **10** D5
Springway Cl LE5...... **156** E5
Springwell Cl LE8..... **202** E4
Springwell Dr LE8..... **202** D4
Springwell La LE8..... **201** F4
Springwood Farm Rd
DE11.............. **44** B7
SPROXTON........... **41** E5
Sproxton Rd
Buckminster NG33..... **42** D2
Skillington NG33...... **43** A8
Spruce Ave LE11....... **75** A7
Spruce Way LE17...... **244** B7
Square Ct LE4........ **129** B7
Square The
Bagworth LE67....... **124** B5
Bottesford NG13....... **3** A3
Countesthorpe LE8..... **202** F3
Earl Shilton LE9...... **198** E8
Frolesworth LE17..... **218** B1
Glenfield LE3........ **127** B1
Littlethorpe LE19..... **201** C6
Long Whatton LE12..... **29** B4
Market Harborough
LE16.............. **240** E3
Newton Harcourt LE8... **204** D6
Oakthorpe DE12....... **93** A7
Ryhall PE9.......... **116** F2
Shearsby LE17........ **222** A2
Skillington NG33...... **43** B8
South Luffenham LE15... **191** D8
Sutton Cheney CV13.... **174** B6
Welford NN6......... **256** E6
Squires Cl LE15....... **110** C3
Squires Gn LE10...... **215** F6
Squire's Ride LE7..... **103** D8
Squirrel Cl LE19...... **201** A7
Squirrel La DE73...... **26** E3
Squirrel's Cnr LE7.... **103** E8
Squirrel Way LE11..... **51** F2
Squirrel Wlk DE12..... **67** B3
Stable Cl LE19........ **201** C7
Stablegate Way LE16... **241** A3
Stable Mews LE11..... **44** F2
Stables Ct LE15....... **137** F6
Stables The
Burley LE15.......... **111** E1
Hinckley LE10........ **215** D5
Stable Yd The
Coleorton LE67....... **70** C7
Stoke Golding CV13.... **196** D7
Stablford Cl LE12..... **50** B4
Stackley Rd LE8...... **182** B1
Stackyard The NG32... **24** A7
Stadium Cl LE67...... **96** C8
Stadium Ind Pk NG10... **10** F8
Stadium Pl LE4....... **128** E2
Stadon Rd LE7........ **127** D6
Stafford Ave LE13..... **59** D4
Stafford Dr LE18...... **179** F2
Stafford Leys LE3..... **152** F3
Stafford Leys Com Prim
Sch LE3........... **152** F2
Staffords Acre DE74... **18** C2
Stafford St
Barwell LE9......... **198** A6
Leicester LE4........ **129** C3
Long Eaton NG10...... **10** F8
STAINBY............ **43** E3
Stainby Rd
Buckminster NG33..... **42** E2
Gunby NG33.......... **64** B8
Staindale LE18....... **180** F2
Stainforth Cl CV11.... **214** A2
Stainmore Ave LE19... **178** A2
Stainsdale Gn LE67.... **72** A2
Staley Ave LE65...... **68** F5
STAMFORD.......... **143** E1
Stamford Bsns Pk
PE9............... **143** F4
Stamford Cl
Glenfield LE3........ **153** C8
Long Eaton NG10...... **10** E4
Market Harborough
LE16.............. **240** E2
Ratby LE6........... **126** C1
Stamford Dr
Coalville LE67....... **72** D1
Cropston LE7........ **100** F2
Groby LE6........... **126** F2
Stamford End LE15.... **113** B3
Stamford Hall LE2.... **180** F8
Stamford High Sch
PE9............... **143** E2
Stamford Jun Sch
PE9............... **143** D2
Stamford Mus★ PE9.... **143** E3
Stamford Rd
Carlby PE9.......... **117** C8
Duddington PE9...... **193** C7
Easton o t H PE9...... **169** B5
Empingham LE15, PE9... **141** C4
Essendine PE9....... **117** A5
Exton LE15.......... **113** B3
Ketton PE9.......... **168** C8
Kirby Fields LE9...... **152** E4
Oakham LE15......... **138** B5
Sewstern NG33....... **63** D6
South Luffenham LE15... **191** D7
Stamford Ret Pk PE9... **143** F4
Stamford Rise LE6..... **126** E8

Stamford & Rutland Hospl
PE9............... **143** F4
Stamford St Gilbert CE
Prim Sch PE9....... **143** C3
Stamford Sch PE9..... **143** E3
Stamford Sch (Welland
Ho) PE9........... **143** E2
Stamford St
Glenfield LE3........ **153** B8
Leicester LE1........ **259** B3
Ratby LE6........... **126** C1
Stamford Sta PE9..... **143** D2
Stamford Wlk 7 PE9... **143** E3
Stanage Rd LE12...... **77** E4
Stanbrig LE18........ **203** E8
Stancliff Rd LE4...... **129** F5
Standard Hill LE67..... **96** B7
Stanfell Rd LE2....... **180** B8
Stanford Hall★ LE17.... **254** F3
Stanford Hill LE11..... **52** B6
STANFORD HILLS..... **31** D4
Stanford La LE12..... **52** D7
STANFORD ON AVON............ **254** F2
STANFORD ON SOAR... **31** C1
Stanford Rd
Normanton on S LE12... **30** D2
Swinford LE17........ **254** D3
Stanhope Glade DE15... **44** A8
Stanhope Rd
Swadlincote DE11..... **44** B3
Wigston LE18........ **180** E1
Stanhope St
Leicester LE5........ **155** D5
Long Eaton NG10...... **10** D8
Stanier Dr LE4....... **130** A4
Stanier Rd
Broughton Astley LE9... **219** A6
Corby NN17.......... **230** F1
Staniforth Ct 8 LE9... **198** A6
Stanilands LE15...... **84** E1
Stanleigh Gdns DE12... **92** E8
Stanleigh Ho DE12.... **92** E8
Stanleigh Rd DE12.... **67** B4
Stanley Burroughs
Almshouses LE9..... **217** D7
Stanley Cl
Netherseal DE12...... **91** F7
Woodville DE11....... **44** F3
Stanley Ct LE2....... **155** C3
Stanley Dr LE5....... **156** A8
Stanley Rd
Hinckley LE10........ **197** C2
Leicester LE2........ **155** C3
Market Bosworth CV13.. **148** E2
Stanleys La LE14..... **22** A6
Stanley St
4 Barwell LE9....... **198** A6
Long Eaton NG10...... **10** E7
Loughborough LE11.... **52** B2
Melton Mowbray LE13... **59** D3
Stamford PE9........ **143** E3
Swadlincote DE11..... **44** C4
Stanton La
Croft LE9........... **200** A5
Sapcote LE9......... **217** B8
Stanton u B LE67...... **97** F3
Thornton LE67....... **124** E6
Stanton Rd
Asfordby Hill LE14.... **58** D3
Elmesthorpe LE9...... **199** B3
Sapcote LE9......... **217** D8
Stanton Row LE2..... **179** F6
STANTON UNDER
BARDON........... **97** E2
Stanton under Bardon
Prim Sch LE67...... **97** F1
Stanton Vale Sch
NG10.............. **10** C7
Stanway Cl LE16...... **241** A3
Stanyon Cl LE8....... **202** F4
STAPLEFORD......... **61** B1
Stapleford Rd
Leicester LE4........ **128** D4
Whissendine LE15..... **84** E3
Staplehurst Ave LE3... **178** E8
Staples Dr LE67...... **97** B7
STAPLETON......... **174** F2
Stapleton La
Barwell LE9......... **197** F8
Dadlington CV13...... **174** A1
Kirkby Mallory LE9.... **175** B5
Starkie Ave DE74..... **16** F3
Star La 3 PE9....... **143** E3
Star Lane Mews 18
PE9............... **143** E3
Starmer Cl LE9....... **201** E3
Statham St LE9....... **150** B5
STATHERN.......... **13** A3
Stathern Prim Sch
LE14.............. **13** A2
Stathern Rd
Eastwell LE14........ **22** B6
Harby LE14.......... **12** C3
Station App LE15..... **137** F7
Station App The LE7... **133** F3
Station Ave
Loughborough LE11.... **51** F5
South Witham NG33.... **65** B3
Station Cl LE9....... **152** E4
Station Cotts LE14.... **21** B2
Station Dr
Kirby Fields LE9...... **152** E4
Moira DE12.......... **67** F4
Station Hill
Swannington LE67..... **71** A4
Twyford LE14........ **133** F8
Station Hollow LE8.... **224** A8

Station La
Asfordby LE14....... **57** F2
Leire LE17.......... **218** E1
Scraptoft LE7........ **156** F7
Station Mews LE65.... **69** B5
Station Rd
Ashby-de-la-Z LE65.... **69** B5
Bagworth LE67....... **124** A6
Birstall LE4......... **128** F5
Bottesford NG13....... **3** B3
Broughton Astley LE9... **219** A5
Castle Bytham NG33... **90** C8
Castle Donington DE74.. **17** B5
Coalville LE67....... **96** D6
Countesthorpe LE8..... **202** E3
Croft LE9........... **200** C4
Cropston LE7........ **101** A4
Desford LE9......... **151** C3
Draycott DE72........ **9** B7
Dunton Bassett LE17... **219** E2
Earl Shilton LE9...... **198** E7
Ellistown LE67....... **96** F1
Elmesthorpe LE9..... **198** F5
Essendine PE9....... **117** B6
Glenfield LE3........ **127** C1
Great Bowden LE16.... **241** A6
Great Glen LE8...... **205** A6
Gretton NN17........ **213** B1
Hemington DE74...... **17** C5
Higham on t H CV13... **195** F4
Hinckley LE10........ **215** D8
Husbands Bosworth
LE17.............. **247** D3
Ibstock LE67........ **95** D1
Kegworth DE74, LE12... **18** E3
Ketton PE9.......... **168** A5
Kirby Fields LE9...... **152** E4
Leicester LE5, LE7.... **156** F6
Lilbourne CV23...... **258** A7
Littlethorpe LE19..... **201** C7
Long Eaton NG10...... **10** F8
Lutterworth LE17..... **244** D5
Market Bosworth CV13.. **148** D3
Melbourne DE73...... **26** C8
Morcott LE15........ **191** B6
North Kilworth LE17... **247** A4
Oakham LE15........ **137** F7
Old Dalby LE14...... **35** F5
Quorn (Quorndon) LE12.. **76** A6
Ratby LE6........... **152** D7
Rearsby LE7......... **79** A2
Shackerstone CV13.... **121** E2
South Luffenham LE15.. **166** E2
Stamford PE9........ **143** D2
Stamford PE9........ **143** E2
Stoke Golding CV13.... **196** C7
Stoney Stanton LE9.... **199** C3
Theddingworth LE17... **248** D8
Ullesthorpe LE17..... **233** B4
Upper Broughton LE14.. **35** C8
Uppingham LE15...... **189** B4
Waltham on t W LE14... **22** F3
Whissendine LE15.... **85** A4
Wigston LE18........ **180** B2
Wing LE15........... **164** E3
Woodville DE11...... **44** F2
Station Road Ind Est
CV13.............. **148** C3
Station St
Kibworth Beauchamp
LE8.............. **224** A8
Leicester LE1........ **259** C3
Long Eaton NG10...... **10** E7
Loughborough LE11.... **51** F5
Swadlincote DE11..... **67** A8
Whetstone LE8....... **201** F8
Wigston LE18........ **180** A1
Station Terr
Bagworth LE67....... **124** A4
Heather LE67........ **95** D2
Station Yd DE73...... **26** C8
Staunton Cl DE74..... **17** A4
STAUNTON IN THE VALE..............**1** B4
Staveley Cl
Sileby LE12.......... **77** D2
Wigston LE18........ **180** E2
Staveley Ct LE11..... **52** B5
Staveley Rd
Leicester LE5........ **155** D4
Melton Mowbray LE13... **59** A4
Staythorpe Rd LE4.... **130** A5
Steadfold La PE9..... **168** C8
Steadman Ave LE9.... **201** E3
Stebbings Rd LE2..... **179** D5
Steele Cl LE15....... **156** A5
Steeple Cl LE18...... **180** E4
Steeple Ct LE11...... **52** B4
Steeple Row LE11..... **52** B4
Steins La LE5........ **156** B8
Stelle Way LE7....... **127** D3
Stemborough La
LE17.............. **219** A2
Stenor Cl LE8........ **222** E8
Stenson Rd
Coalville LE67....... **71** E2
Leicester LE3........ **128** A1
Stephens Ct LE7...... **102** F3
Stephenson Cl
Broughton Astley LE9... **219** A5
Groby LE6........... **126** E3
Stephenson Coll
Ashby-de-la-Z LE65.... **69** C6
Coalville LE67....... **71** C3
Stephenson Ct
Glenfield LE3........ **127** C2
Ravenstone LE67...... **71** A3
Stephenson Dr LE3.... **154** C7

Stephenson Ind Est
LE67.............. **71** B2
Stephenson Pl LE67.... **96** D8
Stephenson Rd LE10... **214** E7
Stephenson Way
Coalville LE67....... **71** D3
Groby LE6........... **126** E3
Sterling Pk LE10..... **214** D8
Sterndale Rd NG10.... **10** B4
Stevens Cl
Stoney Stanton LE9.... **199** E2
Ullesthorpe LE17..... **233** B4
Stevens La DE72...... **9** D8
Stevenson Ave DE72... **9** B8
Stevenson Gdns LE9... **201** D4
Stevens St LE16...... **240** D3
Stevenstone Cl LE2.... **181** D5
Stewards Ct LE9...... **151** B3
Stewart Ave LE19..... **178** A2
Stewart Dr LE11...... **51** C6
Steyning Cres LE3.... **127** D1
Stiles Cl LE9........ **218** F5
Stiles The LE7....... **103** B4
Stimpson Rd LE67.... **71** E1
Stinford Leys LE16.... **241** B3
Stinson Way LE67.... **71** E5
Stirling Ave
Hinckley LE10........ **197** A1
Loughborough LE11.... **51** D5
Stirling Cl
Mountsorrel LE12..... **101** C8
Quorn (Quorndon) LE12.. **75** F7
Stirling Dr LE7....... **156** F6
Stirling Rd
Melton Mowbray LE13... **59** B4
Stamford PE9........ **143** B3
Stocken Hall Farm Cotts
LE15.............. **66** B1
Stocken Hall Mews
LE15.............. **66** B1
STOCKERSTON....... **211** B8
Stockerston Cres
LE15.............. **188** F3
Stockerston Cross Rds
LE16.............. **210** F5
Stockerston La LE16... **211** B3
Stockerston Rd
Allexton LE15........ **187** E4
Uppingham LE15...... **188** D2
Stockingers Ct LE11... **52** C5
STOCKING FARM..... **128** E3
Stocking La DE73..... **48** B8
Stocking Leys LE10... **216** A7
Stockland Rd LE2..... **179** E4
Stocks Hill LE15..... **164** E6
Stock's Hill PE9...... **168** A5
Stocks Rd LE7........ **156** F8
Stockton Ho LE3...... **153** C6
Stockton Rd LE4...... **129** E1
Stockwell Cl LE16.... **241** B3
Stockwell Head LE10... **197** D1
Stockwell Rd LE2..... **180** D7
Stockwell The LE2.... **33** C3
Stockwood Dr NN17... **230** F1
Stoke Albany Rd LE16.. **227** E1
STOKE DRY......... **211** E6
STOKE GOLDING..... **196** E4
Stoke La
Higham on t H CV13.... **196** A4
Stoke Golding CV13.... **196** B6
Stoke Rd
Hinckley LE10, CV13... **197** A4
Lyddington LE15...... **212** C7
Upton CV13.......... **172** D2
Stokes Cl LE8........ **202** A8
Stokes Dr LE3....... **154** B8
Stokes Paddock LE14... **20** B3
Stokes Wood Prim Sch
LE3............... **154** B8
Stonebow Cl LE11..... **51** B8
Stonebow Prim Sch
LE11.............. **51** B6
Stonebridge St LE5.... **155** D6
Stonechat Rd CV23.... **252** D1
Stonechat Wlk LE5.... **155** C6
Stone Cl LE4......... **128** A6
Stonecroft LE8....... **202** C3
Stonecrop Rd LE5..... **130** C2
Stone Dr NG33, LE15... **66** A2
Stonehaven Cl LE67... **72** D1
Stonehaven Rd LE4.... **129** D4
Stonehill DE74....... **17** B2
Stonehill Ave LE4.... **129** A8
Stonehill Ct LE8..... **182** C1
Stonehill Dr LE8..... **182** C1
Stonehill High Sch The
LE4............... **102** B3
Stonehills DE74...... **18** C2
Stonehouse Ct CV23... **258** A6
Stonehurst Family Farm &
Mus★ LE12......... **76** D3
Stonehurst La LE12.... **30** D3
Stonehurst Rd LE3.... **178** F8
Stoneleigh LE2....... **155** B2
Stoneleigh Cl CV10.... **194** B2
Stoneleigh Manor 1
LE2............... **155** D2
Stoneleigh Way LE3... **154** C8
Stoneley Rd CV13..... **196** D6
Stone Mdws NG10.... **10** E5
Stonepit Dr LE16..... **229** D1
Stonepit La NG33..... **43** B8
Stonepit Terr LE14.... **108** D3
Stone Row LE67...... **71** D1
STONESBY.......... **40** E6
Stonesby Ave LE2..... **179** F4
Stonesby Rd
Saltby LE14......... **24** D1

Stonesby Rd continued
Sproxton LE14 . . . . 41 E5
Waltham on t W LE14 . . . . 40 B6
Stonestyle Gdns LE14 . . . . 38 E5
Stoney Cl LE17 . . . . 246 F3
Stoney Cove Diving Ctr★
LE9 . . . . 199 E1
Stoneycroft 2 LE2 . . . . . . 155 C2
Stoneycroft Rd LE9 . . . . . 198 E7
STONEYGATE 155 D2
Stoneygate Ave LE2 . . . . . 155 C1
Stoneygate Coll LE2 . . . . . 155 C2
Stoneygate Ct LE2 . . . . . . 155 C2
Stoneygate Dr LE2 . . . . . . 197 F3
Stoneygate Rd LE2 . . . . . . 155 C2
Stoneygate Sch LE8 . . . . . 205 C6
Stoney Hollow LE17 . . . . 244 C5
Stoney La
Appleby Magna DE12 . . . . . 92 F1
Coleorton LE67 . . . . 70 F8
Stanton u B LE67 . . . . 98 B1
STONEY STANTON 199 D3
Stoneywell Rd LE4 . . . . . . 127 F5
Stonton Rd LE16 . . . . 225 D8
STONTON WYVILLE 207 F3
Stoop La LE12 . . . . 76 A6
Stordon La LE67 . . . . 48 B2
Storer Cl LE12 . . . . 77 D3
Storer Rd LE11 . . . . 51 F4
Stores La LE8 . . . . 222 F7
Storey St LE3 . . . . 154 D7
Stornaway Rd LE5 . . . . . . 156 D6
Stornoway Rd NN17 . . . . . 230 C1
STOUGHTON 156 D1
Stoughton Ave LE2 . . . . . 155 D1
Stoughton Cl LE2 . . . . 181 B6
Stoughton Dr LE5 . . . . 155 F2
Stoughton Dr N LE5 . . . . . 155 D3
Stoughton Dr S LE2 . . . . . 180 F8
Stoughton Farm Pk★
LE2 . . . . 156 C1
Stoughton La LE2 . . . . 156 C2
Stoughton Rd
Gaulby LE7 . . . . 183 C6
Leicester LE2 . . . . 155 D1
Leicester, Oadby LE2 . . . . 181 B7
Thurnby LE5, LE7 . . . . 156 F3
Stoughton St S LE2 . . . . . 155 B5
Stoughton St LE2 . . . . 155 B5
Stour Cl LE2 . . . . 181 D6
Stourdale Cl NG10 . . . . . . 10 A6
Stour Rd NN17 . . . . 230 D1
Stove Ct LE15 . . . . 89 A7
Stowe Cl
Ashby-de-la-Z LE65 . . . . . 69 A7
Leicester LE3 . . . . 128 A1
Stow Hill LE14 . . . . 41 F5
Strachan Cl LE12 . . . . 76 F1
Strancliffe La LE12 . . . . . 53 C1
Strand The 1 LE2 . . . . . . 155 A1
Strasbourg Dr LE4 . . . . . . 128 C3
Stratford Rd LE3 . . . . 153 F1
Strathaven Rd LE4 . . . . . . 129 D4
Strathay Wlk NN17 . . . . . . 230 C1
Strathern Rd LE3, LE7 . . . 127 F3
Strathmore Ave LE4 . . . . . 129 D3
Strathmore Cl LE67 . . . . . 97 C8
Strathmore Rd LE10 . . . . . 215 A4
Stratton Cl LE16 . . . . 240 D1
Strawberry Ct LE14 . . . . . 108 D3
Strawberry Gdns
LE19 . . . . 177 F4
Strawberry La DE11 . . . . . 45 B1
Streamside Cl LE9 . . . . . . 218 F5
Street The
Goadby LE7 . . . . 185 B2
South Luffenham LE15 . . . 191 B8
Strensall Rd LE2 . . . . 179 D3
STRETTON 88 F4
Stretton Cl LE10 . . . . 215 D6
Stretton Ct
Great Glen LE8 . . . . 205 B8
Hinckley LE10 . . . . 215 D3
Stretton Dr LE8 . . . . 72 C1
STRETTON EN LE FIELD
. . . . 92 D4
Stretton Hall Dr LE2 . . . . 181 E4
Stretton La LE7 . . . . 157 E2
Stretton Rd
Clipsham LE15 . . . . 89 C4
Great Glen LE8 . . . . 182 C3
Greetham LE15 . . . . 88 D2
Leicester LE3 . . . . 154 C5
Stretton View DE12 . . . . . 93 A6
Stroller's Way LE7 . . . . . . 103 E7
Stroma Way LE8 . . . . 202 F3
Stroud Ct NG13 . . . . 3 B3
Stroud Rd LE5 . . . . 155 D7
Stroud's Cl LE14 . . . . 20 F8
Strudwick Way LE8 . . . . . 179 A1
Strutt Rd LE10 . . . . 216 A5
Stuart Cres LE16 . . . . 239 F7
Stuart Ct LE8 . . . . 224 A8
Stuart Rd
Glen Parva LE2 . . . . 179 C3
Market Harborough
LE16 . . . . 240 E2
Stuart St
Kibworth Beauchamp
LE8 . . . . 224 A8
Leicester LE3 . . . . 154 D4
Stuart Way LE65 . . . . 69 B5
Stubbs Rd LE4 . . . . 155 B8
Studbrook Cl DE74 . . . . . . 16 F3
Studfall Ave NN17 . . . . . . 230 F1
Studfarm Cl DE73 . . . . . . 26 E2
Sturdee Cl LE2 . . . . 179 D4
Sturdee Gn LE2 . . . . 179 C4

Sturdee Rd LE2 . . . . 179 D4
Sturrock Cl LE7 . . . . 156 F6
Stygate La LE14 . . . . 108 E5
Styon Rd LE3 . . . . 127 E1
Sudbury Ct NG10 . . . . 9 F4
Sudeley Ave LE4 . . . . 128 E2
Suffolk Cl
Melton Mowbray LE13 . . . . 82 E8
Wigston LE18 . . . . 180 A3
Suffolk St LE5 . . . . 155 E5
Suffolk Way LE9 . . . . 151 B2
Sulby Hall Old Dr
NN6 . . . . 248 B1
Sulby Rd
Welford NN6 . . . . 248 B1
Welham LE16 . . . . 256 F7
Sulgrave Rd LE5 . . . . 155 D7
Sullington Rd LE12 . . . . . 50 C3
Sullivan Way LE11 . . . . . . 51 F6
Sulthorpe Rd PE9 . . . . 167 F5
Summerlea Rd LE5 . . . . . . 156 C6
Summerpool Rd LE11 . . . . 51 F7
Summers Cl LE9 . . . . 175 D6
Summers Way LE16 . . . . . 240 D2
Sunbury Gn LE5 . . . . 156 E7
Sunbury Rise LE8 . . . . 202 C4
Sundew Rd LE5 . . . . 130 C2
Sundial Rd LE5 . . . . 130 C3
Sunningdale Cl CV11 . . . . 214 A1
Sunningdale Ind Pk
LE3 . . . . 153 B4
Sunningdale Rd
Coalville LE67 . . . . 96 F8
Leicester LE3 . . . . 153 B4
Sunnybank PE9 . . . . 143 E3
Sunnycroft Rd LE5 . . . . . . 154 A5
Sunnydale Cres LE10 . . . . 215 A7
Sunnydale Rd LE10 . . . . . 214 F7
Sunnyfield LE5 . . . . 138 A8
Sunnyfield Cl LE5 . . . . . . 156 C5
Sunnyhill LE10 . . . . 215 F7
Sunnyhill Rd LE11 . . . . . . 51 F1
Sunnyhill S LE10 . . . . 215 F6
Sunnyside
Hinckley LE10 . . . . 197 D3
Ibstock LE67 . . . . 122 E8
Sunny Side LE8 . . . . 181 C4
Sunnyside LE8 . . . . 178 F1
Sunnyside Hospl
LE10 . . . . 197 D5
Sunnyside Ind Est
LE10 . . . . 197 D4
Sun St DE11 . . . . 44 F2
Sun Way LE3 . . . . 153 D3
Surrey Cl LE10 . . . . 215 E4
Surrey St LE4 . . . . 155 B8
Susan Ave LE5 . . . . 156 B4
Sussex Ave LE13 . . . . 82 D8
Sussex Rd
Stamford PE9 . . . . 143 D4
Wigston LE18 . . . . 179 F3
Sussex St LE1 . . . . 155 B6
Sutherington Way
. . . . 127 E7
Sutherland St 1 LE2 . . . . 155 C4
Sutherland Way PE9 . . . . 143 B3
Suthern Cl LE15 . . . . 138 A8
Suthers Rd DE74 . . . . 18 C2
Sutton Ave LE4 . . . . 129 C2
SUTTON BASSETT 227 A1
SUTTON BONINGTON 30 B8
Sutton Bonington Prim
Sch LE12 . . . . 30 B6
SUTTON CHENEY 174 B6
Sutton Cl
Hinckley LE10 . . . . 197 F3
Leicester, Oadby LE2 . . . . 181 B3
Quorn (Quorndon) LE12 . . 75 F5
Sutton Bonington LE12 . . . 30 C5
Sutton Ct LE9 . . . . 218 E8
Sutton Ct LE16 . . . . 240 E1
SUTTON IN THE ELMS
. . . . 218 E8
Sutton La
Dadlington CV13 . . . . 173 F1
Granby NG13 . . . . 5 D6
Market Bosworth CV13 . . . 148 F1
Sutton Cheney CV13 . . . . 174 D8
Sutton Pl
Leicester LE4 . . . . 129 C2
Swadlincote DE11 . . . . . . 44 F4
Sutton Rd
Great Bowden LE16 . . . . . 241 B6
Kegworth DE74 . . . . 18 C1
Leicester LE2 . . . . 180 A8
Sutton Bassett LE16 . . . . 241 E7
Weston by W LE16 . . . . . . 227 B3
Suttons Ave DE11 . . . . 44 E1
Suttons Bsns Pk DE11 . . . 44 E1
SWADLINCOTE 44 D4
Swadlincote Rd DE11 . . . . 44 E3
Swadlincote Ski Ctr
DE11 . . . . 44 C3
Swains Gn LE10 . . . . 215 F6
Swainson Rd LE4 . . . . 155 E8
SWAINSPARK 67 B7
Swainspark Ind Est
DE12 . . . . 67 B6
Swain St LE1 . . . . 259 C4
Swale Cl
Corby NN17 . . . . 230 D1
Leicester, Oadby LE2 . . . . 181 D6
Melton Mowbray LE13 . . . 59 B1
Swallow Cl LE12 . . . . 76 F2
Swallow Ct LE10 . . . . 214 F7
Swallow Dale LE67 . . . . . . 71 D7
Swallowdale Dr LE4 . . . . . 128 B6

Swallowdale Prim Sch
LE13 . . . . 82 B8
Swallowdale Rd LE13 . . . . 82 B8
Swallow Dr LE7 . . . . 102 F4
Swallow Rd DE11 . . . . 44 F3
Swallows Cl LE3 . . . . 152 E1
Swallow's Dale LE7 . . . . . 103 E8
Swallows Dr LE14 . . . . 12 F3
Swallow Wlk LE12 . . . . . . 30 A1
Swan Cl
Barrow-u-S LE12 . . . . 76 E8
Glen Parva LE2 . . . . 179 A2
Melton Mowbray LE13 . . . 82 B8
Mountsorrel LE12 . . . . . . 76 F2
Swan Ct LE12 . . . . 30 B6
Swann Cl LE15 . . . . 166 D3
SWANNINGTON 71 A5
Swannington CE Prim Sch
LE67 . . . . 71 A5
SWANNINGTON COMMON
. . . . 71 B7
Swannington Rd
Broughton Astley LE9 . . . 219 A6
Leicester LE3 . . . . 154 C7
Ravenstone LE67 . . . . 70 F2
Swannymote Rd LE67,
LE12 . . . . 72 B7
Swanscombe Rd LE2 . . . . 154 D1
Swanson Ho PE9 . . . . 143 F4
Swan St
Leicester LE3 . . . . 259 A4
Loughborough LE11 . . . . . 52 B4
Seagrave LE12 . . . . 77 F8
Sileby LE12 . . . . 77 C3
Swan Way
Coalville LE67 . . . . 96 F8
Syston LE7 . . . . 102 E4
Swedish Cl LE16 . . . . 224 E1
Sweetbriar PE9 . . . . 142 E5
Sweetbriar Rd LE3 . . . . . 154 C3
Sweethill DE12 . . . . 68 A5
SWEPSTONE 94 D2
Swepstone Rd
Heather LE67 . . . . 95 A2
Measham DE12 . . . . 94 B4
Snarestone DE12, LE67 . . 94 C1
Swift Cl
Melton Mowbray LE13 . . . 82 B8
Syston LE7 . . . . 102 F4
Woodville DE11 . . . . 44 F3
Swifts Cl LE67 . . . . 95 F2
Swift's Cl LE12 . . . . 33 C3
Swift Valley Ind Est
CV21 . . . . 252 A1
Swift Way LE17 . . . . 244 C7
Swinburne Rd LE10 . . . . . 197 C1
Swindale Cl LE2 . . . . 259 A2
Swinfen Cl LE67 . . . . 96 C3
Swinfield Rd LE12 . . . . 76 A6
SWINFORD 254 C3
Swinford Ave LE2 . . . . . . 179 D2
Swinford CE Prim Sch
LE17 . . . . 254 B4
Swinford Cnr LE17 . . . . . . 254 A8
Swinford Ct LE2 . . . . 179 D2
Swinford Rd
Cotesbach LE17 . . . . 244 E2
Shawell LE17 . . . . 253 D5
Walcote LE17 . . . . 245 B2
Swingbridge Rd LE11 . . . . 51 F7
Swingbridge St LE16 . . . . 239 E8
Swinstead Rd LE5 . . . . . . 156 D4
SWITHLAND 100 D7
Swithland Ave LE4 . . . . . 128 F1
Swithland Cl
Loughborough LE11 . . . . . 51 C5
Markfield LE67 . . . . 125 E8
Swithland Ct
3 Braunstone Town
LE3 . . . . 178 F7
Swithland LE12 . . . . 100 A8
Swithland La LE7 . . . . 101 B7
Swithland Rd
Coalville LE67 . . . . 97 C8
Swithland LE12 . . . . 100 E4
Swithland Resr Nature
Reserve★
Mountsorrel LE7 . . . . 75 D1
Swithland LE12 . . . . 100 F8
Swithland St Leonard's CE
Prim Sch LE12 . . . . 100 E7
Swithland Woods Nature
Reserve★ LE12 . . . . . . 100 B5
Sword Cl LE3 . . . . 153 C7
Sword Dr LE10 . . . . 197 B3
Sybil Rd LE3 . . . . 154 B1
Sycamore Ave DE11 . . . . . 44 A7
Sycamore Cl
Barton in t B CV13 . . . . . 122 D1
Corby NN17 . . . . 230 E1
Hinckley LE10 . . . . 215 E5
Ibstock LE67 . . . . 95 E1
Leicester LE5 . . . . 155 F1
Leicester, Oadby LE2 . . . . 182 A3
Melton Mowbray LE13 . . . 59 B5
Newbold Verdon LE9 . . . . 150 A4
Syston LE7 . . . . 103 B2
Sycamore Dr
Ashby-de-la-Z LE65 . . . . . 69 D7
Groby LE6 . . . . 126 F2
Lutterworth LE17 . . . . 244 A6
Moira DE12 . . . . 68 B6
Sycamore Gr LE6 . . . . 126 F3
Sycamore La LE14 . . . . . . 62 D2
Sycamore Rd
Birstall LE4 . . . . 129 A6
Castle Donington DE74 . . 17 B5
Coalville LE67 . . . . 97 A8

Sycamore Rd continued
East Leake LE12 . . . . 31 D8
Long Eaton NG10 . . . . . . 10 C5
North Luffenham LE15 . . . 166 D3
Sycamores The LE8 . . . . . 202 B8
Sycamores The
South Kilworth LE17 . . . . 255 D8
Swadlincote DE11 . . . . . . 44 E4
Sycamore Way
Littlethorpe LE19 . . . . . . 201 B6
Loughborough LE11 . . . . . 75 A7
Market Bosworth CV13 . . . 148 F2
Sydney Rd DE72 . . . . 9 A7
Sykefield Ave LE3 . . . . . . 154 C4
Sykes La LE15 . . . . 140 E5
Sylvan Ave LE5 . . . . 155 D6
Sylvan St LE3 . . . . 154 C7
Sylvan Way LE3 . . . . 153 B4
Symington Way LE16 . . . . 240 E3
SYSONBY 58 F3
Sysonby Grange La
LE13 . . . . 58 F2
Sysonby St LE13 . . . . 59 A4
SYSTON 103 D3
Syston Rd
Cossington LE7 . . . . 102 C7
Queniborough LE7 . . . . . . 103 E6
South Croxton LE7 . . . . . . 104 F1
Syston St E LE1 . . . . 155 B7
Syston St W LE1 . . . . 155 A8
Syston Sta LE7 . . . . 103 A3
Sywell Ave LE11 . . . . 51 C3
Sywell Dr LE18 . . . . 180 F2

T

Tabberer Cl LE15 . . . . 138 A8
Tadcaster Ave LE2 . . . . . . 179 D3
Tadcaster Gn LE2 . . . . . . 179 D3
Tailby Ave LE5 . . . . 155 E8
Tailor's Link LE7 . . . . 103 D7
Talbot La
Leicester LE1 . . . . 259 A3
Whitwick LE67 . . . . 71 C7
Talbot Pl DE12 . . . . 92 E8
Talbot St
Leicester LE4 . . . . 129 A3
Swadlincote DE11 . . . . . . 44 A1
Whitwick LE67 . . . . 71 D6
Talbott Cl LE9 . . . . 219 A4
Talbot Yd LE16 . . . . 240 E3
Tamar Gn NN17 . . . . 230 D1
Tamar Rd
Leicester LE4 . . . . 129 E2
Leicester, Oadby LE2 . . . . 181 D5
Melton Mowbray LE13 . . . 59 B1
Tamerton Rd LE2 . . . . 179 E5
Tame Way LE10 . . . . 215 A8
Tamworth Cl LE12 . . . . . . 49 F2
Tamworth Rd
Appleby Magna DE12 . . . . 92 E2
Ashby-de-la-Z LE65 . . . . . 69 A5
Castle Donington DE72,
NG10 . . . . 9 E1
Long Eaton NG10 . . . . . . 10 C5
Measham DE12 . . . . 93 B4
Tandy Ave DE12 . . . . 68 B5
Tanner's La LE12 . . . . 30 A1
Tannery The LE15 . . . . . . 192 A5
Tanni Gray Ho 6 LE2 . . . 52 A4
Tanser Cott LE17 . . . . 255 C8
Tansey Cres LE9 . . . . 199 C2
Tansley Ave LE18 . . . . 180 A1
Tanyard LE7 . . . . 71 B5
Tan Yd LE67 . . . . 71 B5
Tara St LE67 . . . . 97 B4
Tarbat Rd LE5 . . . . 156 D7
Tarragon Rd LE2 . . . . 154 D4
Tatlow Ho LE3 . . . . 153 D6
Tatlow Rd LE3 . . . . 153 C6
Tatmarsh LE11 . . . . 52 B5
Tatton Cl LE3 . . . . 128 A1
Tatwin Ct DE73 . . . . 26 F2
Taunton Cl LE18 . . . . 180 C1
Taunton Rd LE3 . . . . 154 B5
Taurus Cl LE2 . . . . 155 B5
Taverner Dr LE6 . . . . 152 D7
Taverners Rd LE4 . . . . . . 128 C7
Tavistock Cl LE67 . . . . 96 C6
Tavistock Dr LE5 . . . . 155 F3
Tay Cl
Corby NN17 . . . . 230 D1
Oakham LE15 . . . . 137 E4
Tayleur Cl LE67 . . . . 96 E8
Taylor Cl
Moira DE12 . . . . 68 A4
Syston LE7 . . . . 103 A3
Taylor Ho
Loughborough LE11 . . . . . 52 C4
Uppingham LE15 . . . . 189 A4
Taylor Rd LE1 . . . . 155 A7
Taylor Road Prim Sch
LE1 . . . . 155 B7
Taylor's Bridge Rd
LE18 . . . . 180 A1
Taylors Cl LE9 . . . . 199 D2
Teal Bsns Ctr LE10 . . . . . 214 D7
Tealby Cl LE17 . . . . 235 C4
Teal Cl
Coalville LE67 . . . . 96 F8
Leicester Forest East
LE3 . . . . 152 F2
Teal Dr LE10 . . . . 215 A6
Teal Way LE7 . . . . 102 E4
Teasel Cl LE19 . . . . 201 A8
Teasel Dr
Melton Mowbray LE13 . . . 82 A8

Sto–Tho 293

Teasel Dr continued
Woodville DE11 . . . . 44 F4
Tebbs Cl LE8 . . . . 202 C4
Tedder Cl LE17 . . . . 244 A5
Tedworth Gn LE4 . . . . 128 D5
Tees Cl LE15 . . . . 137 F5
Teesdale Rd NG10 . . . . . . 10 A6
TEIGH 86 A5
Teigh Rd
Ashwell LE15 . . . . 86 A1
Market Overton LE15 . . . . 86 D5
Teign Bank Cl LE10 . . . . . 197 D2
Teign Bank Rd LE10 . . . . . 197 D2
Teignmouth Cl LE5 . . . . . 155 F3
Telford Way
Coalville LE67 . . . . 71 B2
Leicester LE5 . . . . 156 E5
Tellis Pl LE3 . . . . 93 D5
Tempest Rd LE4 . . . . 128 F6
Templars Way
South Witham NG33 . . . . . 65 A4
Whitwick LE67 . . . . 71 F5
Templar Way LE7 . . . . 101 E6
Temple Bldgs LE5 . . . . . . 155 E5
Temple Cl LE12 . . . . 50 C1
Temple Hill LE67 . . . . 71 F6
Temple Rd LE5 . . . . 155 E5
Tendring Dr LE18 . . . . 180 F3
Tennis Ave LE13 . . . . 59 C1
Tennis Court Dr LE5 . . . . 156 A8
Tennyson Ave DE11 . . . . . 44 C6
Tennyson Cl DE12 . . . . . . 93 B4
Tennyson Rd
Hinckley LE10 . . . . 197 C1
Loughborough LE11 . . . . . 51 D4
Lutterworth LE17 . . . . 244 C7
Tennyson St
Leicester LE2 . . . . 155 C3
Narborough LE19 . . . . . . 178 A1
Tennyson Way
Melton Mowbray LE13 . . . 59 B6
Stamford PE9 . . . . 143 A4
Tentas The LE67 . . . . 48 A2
Tenter Cl NG10 . . . . 10 D5
Tentercroft Ave LE7 . . . . 103 C4
Tenter Ct PE9 . . . . 143 E2
Tenterfield DE74 . . . . 28 B5
Tenter La 13 PE9 . . . . . . 143 E3
Tern Ave LE67 . . . . 44 F3
Terrace Cotts LE9 . . . . . . 200 C4
Terrace The
Copt Oak LE67 . . . . 98 C8
7 Lutterworth LE17 . . . . 244 C5
Test Gn NN17 . . . . 230 D1
Tetbury Dr LE12 . . . . 49 F2
Tetuan Rd LE3 . . . . 154 C6
Teviot Cl NN17 . . . . 230 D1
Tewkesbury Rd NG10 . . . . 10 C4
Tewkesbury St LE3 . . . . . 154 D6
Thackeray St LE2 . . . . . . 179 F8
Thames Dr LE13 . . . . 59 B1
Thames St LE1 . . . . 259 B5
Thames Wlk NN17 . . . . . . 230 D1
Thatcher Cl LE4 . . . . 128 B4
Thatchers' Cnr LE7 . . . . . 103 D7
Thatch Meadow Dr
LE16 . . . . 241 B3
Theatre Mall 9 LE1 . . . . 259 B4
THEDDINGWORTH 248 C8
Theddingworth Rd
Husbands Bosworth
LE17 . . . . 248 A6
Lubenham LE16 . . . . 239 C2
Marston Trussell LE16 . . . 249 B8
Mowsley LE17 . . . . 237 F5
THE FORTIES 45 F3
Thimble Hall Rd LE7,
LE14 . . . . 133 C8
Thirlmere LE67 . . . . 72 C1
Thirlmere Ct LE12 . . . . . . 76 D8
Thirlmere Dr LE11 . . . . . . 74 D8
Thirlmere Gdns LE65 . . . . 69 C4
Thirlmere Rd
Barrow-u-S LE12 . . . . 76 D8
Hinckley LE10 . . . . 215 A7
Wigston LE18 . . . . 180 E3
Thirlmere St LE2 . . . . 259 A1
Thistle Cl
Cropston LE7 . . . . 100 F2
Narborough LE19 . . . . . . 201 A8
Woodville DE11 . . . . 44 F4
THISTLETON 87 F8
Thistleton La NG33 . . . . . 65 A2
Thistleton Rd LE15 . . . . . 87 A6
Thistley Cl LE3 . . . . 153 C2
Thistly Meadow Prim Sch
LE8 . . . . 202 C7
Thomas Cl
Houghton on t H LE7 . . . . 157 F4
Leicester LE3 . . . . 179 A8
Thomas Cook Cl DE73 . . . 26 A7
Thomas Estley Com Coll
LE9 . . . . 218 F6
Thomas Firr Cl LE12 . . . . 76 A7
Thomas Fryer's
Almshouses LE15 . . . . 164 E6
Thomas Rd
Kegworth DE74 . . . . 18 C1
Whitwick LE67 . . . . 71 D5
Thomasson Rd LE5 . . . . . 156 B6
Thomas St
Ibstock LE67 . . . . 122 F8
Loughborough LE11 . . . . . 52 D3
Thompson Ave LE12 . . . . . 49 B6

Thompson Cl
Quorn (Quorndon) LE12.... **75** F6
Swadlincote DE11 .... **44** E4
Thompsons La LE15.......**190** C1
Thomson Cl LE4 ....**129** D6
Thomson Ct LE67 ....**125** F8
Thoresby Rd NG10....... **10** C6
Thoresby St LE5 ....**155** E6
THORNBOROUGH **71** D3
Thornborough Cl
Market Harborough
LE16...................**241** A2
Narborough LE19........**200** F7
Thornborough Rd
LE67.....................**71** C3
Thornby Gdns LE18 .....**180** E2
Thorndale Rd LE4........**129** F7
Thorndale LE67 .... **95** E1
Thorneycroft Cl LE9......**219** B4
Thorneywood Rd NG10.... **10** F8
Thornfield Ave CV13 .....**196** E7
Thornfield Sq NG10...... **10** F8
Thornfield Way LE10.....**215** E8
Thornhills LE19...........**178** A2
Thornhills Gr LE19 ....**178** A2
Thornholme Cl LE4 ......**128** C4
Thorn St LE11 .... **44** F2
Thorn Street Mews
DE11.................... **44** F2
THORNTON **124** E4
Thornton Cl
Braunstone Town
LE3...................**153** D3
Broughton Astley LE9 ...**219** A4
Coalville LE67 .... **72** C1
Thornton Com Prim Sch
LE67 ....**124** E4
Thornton Cres LE16.....**225** D7
Thornton Dr LE19 ....**201** C8
Thornton La
Bagworth LE67 ....**124** C4
Markfield LE67..........**125** C5
Stanton u B LE67........**124** E7
Thorntop Cl DE11........ **68** B8
Thorntree Cl
Leicester LE4...........**127** F2
Ravenstone LE67........ **70** F2
Thornville Cl LE4 ....**129** E1
Thorny Cl LE11........... **51** D6
Thornycroft Rd LE10 .....**215** E8
THORPE ACRE **51** C4
Thorpe Acre Inf Sch
LE11 .... **51** D4
Thorpe Acre Jun Sch
LE11 .... **51** D4
Thorpe Acre Rd LE11..... **51** D5
THORPE ARNOLD **60** A5
THORPE ASTLEY **153** C1
Thorpe Downs Rd
DE11.................... **44** B1
Thorpe Dr LE18..........**180** D4
Thorpe End LE13.......... **59** D3
Thorpe Field Dr LE4 .....**129** F8
Thorpe Gdns LE15 .... **84** E1
Thorpe Hill LE11......... **51** C4
THORPE IN THE GLEBE
.... **33** D8
Thorpe La LE7............**130** D8
THORPE LANGTON **226** A5
Thorpe Langton Rd
East Langton LE16.......**225** D6
Welham LE16............**226** D6
Thorpe Leys NG10 ...... **10** D5
Thorpe Rd
Lyddington LE15 ....**212** D6
Melton Mowbray LE13.... **59** E4
Shepshed LE12 .... **50** A3
THORPE SATCHVILLE
.........................**106** F4
Thorpe Satchville Rd
Great Dalby LE14........ **82** A1
Kirby Bellars LE14....... **81** C5
Thorpe Satchville LE14 ..**106** F7
Twyford LE14............**106** E2
Thorpe Side LE14........ **38** F4
Thorpes La NG32 .... **24** B7
Thorpe St LE3 ....**154** D5
Thorpe's Terr LE15 ......**189** A4
Thorpe Way LE19 ....**178** D4
Thorpewell LE5...........**155** F6
Threadcutters Way
LE12.................... **50** B3
Threadgold Cl LE4.......**128** B6
Three Gates Rd LE7.....**184** C2
Three Pots Rd LE10 .....**215** E4
Three Turns La LE7......**105** C2
Threshers Wlk LE7.......**103** E7
THRINGSTONE **71** D8
Thringstone Prim Sch
LE67 .... **71** D8
Thrumpton Ave NG10 .... **10** F7
Thrush Cl LE13........... **82** B8
THRUSSINGTON **78** F4
Thrussington CE Prim Sch
LE7 .... **78** F5
Thrussington Rd
Hoby LE14 .... **79** C6
Thrussington LE7........ **78** D3
THURCASTON **101** C2
Thurcaston La LE7.......**101** B4
Thurcaston Rd
Leicester, Mowmacre Hill
LE4...................**128** D6

Thurcaston Rd continued
Leicester, Stocking Farm
LE4...................**128** F4
Thurcroft Cl LE2 ....**179** D3
THURLASTON **177** B3
Thurlaston CE Prim Sch
LE9 ....**177** A3
Thurlaston La
Croft LE9 ....**200** B7
Enderby LE9, LE19......**177** D4
Thurlaston LE9..........**176** B1
Thurlby Rd LE5 ....**155** D7
Thurlington Rd LE3 ......**154** A3
Thurlow Cl
Atherstone CV9 ....**170** D2
Leicester, Oadby LE2....**181** D4
Thurlow Rd LE2..........**155** A1
THURMASTON **129** E7
Thurmaston Bvd LE4 ....**129** F3
Thurmaston Footpath
LE4.....................**129** F4
Thurmaston La LE4......**130** A3
THURNBY **156** F5
Thurnby Hill LE5, LE7....**156** E5
Thurnby La LE2, LE5.....**156** E2
THURNBY LODGE **156** E7
Thurnby Lodge Prim Sch
LE5 ....**156** D6
Thurncourt Cl LE5 ....**156** C7
Thurncourt Gdns LE5 ...**156** F6
Thurncourt Rd LE5......**156** D6
Thurnview Rd LE5.......**156** C3
Thurso Wlk NN17.......**230** D1
Thyme Cl LE2............**259** A2
Thythorn Field Com Prim
Sch LE18..............**203** D7
Tiber Way LE19..........**178** D8
Tichborne Ct ◪ LE2......**155** B4
Tichborne St LE2 ....**155** B4
TICKENCOTE **142** B8
Ticknall Rd DE11......... **45** B7
Tickow La LE12........... **49** E3
Tiffany Ct LE2 ....**155** D2
Tigers Cl LE18 ....**179** E2
Tigers Rd LE18 ....**179** E2
Tigers Way LE1, LE2.....**259** C1
Tilbury Cres LE4.........**130** A5
Tilford Cres LE2 ....**179** D2
Tillett Rd LE3............**153** D2
Tillingham Rd LE5 ....**155** F8
Tilling Rd LE4...........**128** C4
Tilton Cutting Nature
Reserve★ LE7 ....**160** E7
Tilton Dr LE2 ....**181** A3
Tilton La LE7 ....**159** C7
TILTON ON THE HILL
.........................**160** B8
Tilton Rd
Hinckley LE10 ....**215** E6
Twyford LE14...........**106** C1
Timbergate Rd PE9 .....**167** E5
Timber Hill NG33 .... **64** A8
Timber St LE18 ....**179** F1
Timberwood Dr LE6.....**126** E2
Timson Ct LE16 ....**240** D5
Tindall Sq LE15 .... **87** D2
Tinker's Dell LE7 ....**103** D4
Tinsel La CV13 ....**172** D8
Tintagel Way CV11......**214** A5
TINWELL **142** E1
Tinwell Rd PE9 ....**143** B2
Tinwell Road La PE9 .....**143** B3
Tipnall Rd DE74......... **17** A3
Tippings La LE15.........**191** F5
Tiptree Cl LE4 ....**128** D2
Tithe Barn Row LE15.... **88** B2
Tithe Cl
Stoke Golding CV13......**196** D6
Thringstone LE67........ **71** C8
Tithe St LE5 ....**155** E6
Tithings The LE8.........**206** A1
Tiverton Ave
Coalville LE67 .... **72** A2
Leicester LE4...........**129** C2
Tiverton Cl
Leicester, Oadby LE2....**181** C5
Narborough LE19........**200** F8
Tiverton Mews LE4 .....**129** C2
Tiverton Rd
Cottesmore LE15....... **87** E2
Loughborough LE11..... **74** F7
TIXOVER **192** E5
Tixover Grange PE9......**192** F8
Tobias Gr PE9 ....**142** E5
Todd's Hill PE9 ....**193** B6
Tod's Terr LE15 ....**189** B4
Toft's Hill LE14 .... **13** A3
Tofts The LE18..........**180** D1
Toft The LE12........... **49** B6
Tokye's Cl LE15..........**187** D7
Tolcarne Rd LE5 ....**156** C8
Tolchard Cl LE5..........**156** A5
Tolethorpe Cl LE15......**138** B6
Tolethorpe Sq PE9......**143** D4
TOLL BAR **142** F6
Toll Bar LE15 ....**112** D8
Toll Bar Ave NG13 .... **3** A3
Tollemache Ave LE4 ....**128** E2
Tollemache Fields
NG33 .... **65** B3
Toller Rd
Leicester LE2...........**155** C1
Quorn (Quorndon) LE12.... **75** E5
Tolton Rd LE4 ....**128** D4
Tolwell Rd LE4 ....**128** C5
Tom Eatough Ct LE9 ....**199** A8
Tomlin Rd LE4...........**129** E1

Tomlinson Ct LE2 ....**181** A6
Tom Paine LE3 ....**153** D2
Toms Cl LE17 ....**248** D8
Toms Ct DE74........... **18** D2
TONGE **27** B3
Tonge La
Breedon on t H DE73.... **26** F3
Tonge DE73............. **27** A3
Toon Cl LE12 .... **50** A1
Toothill Rd LE11 .... **52** B5
Tooth St DE11 .... **44** E1
Top Cl LE3 ....**153** D1
Top End LE14............ **82** A1
Top Gn LE14............. **19** A1
Tophall Dr LE8 ....**202** E3
Top La LE15 ....**189** E4
Top Lo NN17............**193** A1
Top Mdw DE11 .... **44** B7
Top Rd
Croxton Kerrial NG32 .... **24** B7
Griffydam LE67......... **48** A2
Ridlington LE15 ....**163** E2
Top St
Appleby Magna DE12....**119** F7
Exton LE15..............**113** B3
Wing LE15 ....**165** A2
Top Yard Farm LE16 ....**240** F6
Torch Cl LE16............**209** E6
Torch Way LE16 ....**250** F8
Torcross Cl LE3..........**153** E8
Torkington Gdns ◪
PE9 ....**143** D3
Torkington St PE9 ......**143** C3
Toronto Cl LE1 ....**259** C5
Torrance Dr LE13........ **59** C6
Torridon Cl
Corby NN17.............**230** C1
Leicester LE4...........**128** D3
Torridon Way LE10 .....**197** B1
Torridon Ave LE67 ...... **72** A2
Torridon Gr LE12, LE18...**203** D8
Totland Rd LE3 ....**154** C8
Totnes Cl LE67.......... **96** C7
Toulmin Dr DE11 .... **44** B4
Toulouse Pl LE65 .... **69** A7
Tournament Rd LE3.....**153** D7
Tovey Cres LE3 ....**179** D4
Tower Ct LE16 ....**239** F3
Tower Furlong CV23 ....**252** D1
Tower Gdns LE65 .... **69** A6
Tower Rd
Earl Shilton LE9 ....**198** F8
Hartshorne DE11........ **45** A6
Towers Cl LE9 ....**152** E4
Towers Dr LE9 ....**152** E4
Towers Hospl The
LE5 ....**129** F1
Tower St LE1 ....**259** B2
Towers The LE11 .... **51** E3
Towers Way LE11....... **51** E3
Towle Rd LE3............**153** E8
Towles Fields LE12 ..... **53** F6
Towles Mill LE11........ **52** C5
Towles Pastures DE74... **17** A3
Towle St NG10.......... **10** A4
TOWN END **28** C5
Town End
Barkestone-le-V NG13.... **6** C2
Hungarton LE7..........**132** B3
Somerby LE14..........**108** C1
Townend Cl LE14 .... **57** E2
Townend Rd LE9........**198** A7
Town End Rd DE72......**9** B7
TOWN GREEN **101** E5
Town Green St LE7 .....**101** E5
Town Hall Mews ◪
LE65...................**69** B6
Townlands CE Prim Sch
LE9 ....**198** F7
Townsend Cl
Broughton Astley LE9 ...**219** B5
Leicester LE4...........**129** D5
Newton Regis B79......**118** D4
Townsend La LE67 ...... **96** B5
Townsend Rd
Enderby LE19...........**178** B3
Stoney Stanton LE9 .....**199** D1
Townsends Cl CV11.....**215** A1
Townside Cl NG10 ...... **10** B4
Towns La LE14.......... **22** C1
Town Sq LE7 ....**103** B4
Town St LE8 ....**205** F8
Towpath Cl LE11........ **52** C5
Towpath Link LE18......**203** A8
Trackside Cl LE11....... **51** D4
Trafalgar Cl LE7 ....**103** A3
Trafalgar Rd NG10 ...... **10** D6
Trafalgar Sq NG10 ...... **10** E7
Trafalgar Terr
Long Eaton NG10 .... **10** F7
Stamford PE9...........**143** E4
Trafalgar Way LE2 ......**179** D1
Trafford Cl CV9.........**170** D2
Trafford Rd
Hinckley LE10 ....**197** F2
Leicester LE5...........**155** F7
Tranter Pl LE4...........**129** D2
Travell's Hill LE12........ **31** A7
Treasure Cl LE3..........**153** C7
Treaty Rd LE3 ....**153** D7
Tredington Rd LE3.......**127** D1
Treetops Cl LE5..........**156** B7
Trefoil Cl
Broughton Astley LE9 ...**219** B4
Hamilton LE5 ....**130** C2
Melton Mowbray LE13... **82** B8
Trelissick Cl LE11........ **51** B5

Tremaine Dr LE18........**180** C1
Trenant Rd LE18 ....**179** F4
Trent Ave LE4 ....**128** D7
Trent Bank LE13 .... **59** A1
Trent Bridge Rd PE9 .... **97** A7
Trent Cl
Broughton Astley LE9 ...**219** A6
Leicester, Oadby LE2....**181** D5
Trent Coll NG10......... **10** C8
Trent Cotts NG10....... **10** F6
Trentham Rd CV10 .....**194** B2
Trent Ho NG10.......... **10** A4
Trent La
Castle Donington DE74... **17** A5
Long Eaton NG10....... **10** F5
Trent Lane Ind Est
DE74................... **17** B5
TRENTLOCK **10** E3
Trent Rd
Corby NN17.............**230** D1
Hinckley LE10 ....**215** A8
Oakham LE15...........**137** E4
Trent St NG10 .... **10** E8
Trescoe Rise LE3 ....**153** E5
Tressall Rd LE67 .... **72** A3
Tressell Way LE3 ....**153** D2
Trevanth Rd LE4.........**129** F3
Trevino Dr LE4 ....**129** E5
Trevor Rd LE10 ....**197** F1
Trevose Gdns LE5.......**156** F7
Tribune Ho ◪ LE10......**197** D1
Trigo Cl LE4 ....**128** A4
Trillium Cl LE5 ....**130** C3
Trinity Cl
Allington NG32..........**4** F5
Ashby-de-la-Z LE65 ..... **69** A5
Syston LE7 ....**103** B3
Trinity Cres LE12 .... **33** B3
Trinity Ct
Ashby-de-la-Z LE65 ..... **69** B6
Hinckley LE10 ....**215** C8
Trinity Gr LE11 .... **44** B3
Trinity Hospl LE2 ....**259** A3
Trinity La
Hinckley LE10 ....**215** C8
Leicester LE1 ....**259** B2
Trinity Rd
Narborough LE19........**178** E2
Stamford PE9...........**143** C4
Whetstone LE8 ....**201** F8
Trinity St LE1 .... **52** C3
Trinity Vicarage Rd
LE10...................**215** C8
Trinity View NG10....... **10** E8
Tripontium Bsns Ctr
CV23..................**253** A4
Tristram Cl LE3..........**153** A2
Triumph Rd LE3 ....**153** D7
Trojan Way LE7..........**102** E2
Troon Cl PE9 ....**143** A4
Troon Ind Area LE4 .....**130** A4
Troon Ind Est LE4 ......**129** F4
Troon Way
Hinckley LE10 ....**215** D4
Leicester LE4...........**129** E4
Troon Way Bsns Ctr
LE4 ....**129** F4
Troughton Wlk NG33.... **65** A4
Trowell La LE12......... **30** E7
Truesdale's ◪ PE9.......**143** D3
Trueway Dr LE12........ **50** C2
Trueway Dr S LE12...... **50** C2
Trueway Rd LE5 ....**155** E2
Truro Cl
Hinckley LE10 ....**197** E4
Swadlincote DE11 ...... **44** E5
Truro Dr LE18 ....**180** D1
Trusteel Hos CV23 .....**252** C5
Tuckers Cl LE11 .... **52** C2
Tuckers Rd LE11........ **52** D2
Tuckett Rd LE12 .... **74** F2
Tuckey Cl LE9 ....**217** E7
Tudor Cl
Ashby-de-la-Z LE65 ..... **69** B5
Leicester LE3...........**154** C8
Market Bosworth CV13 ..**148** E2
Tudor Cres CV9..........**170** D2
Tudor Dr
Cosby LE9 ....**201** D2
Leicester, Oadby LE2....**181** B6
Tudor Gr LE65 ....**126** F1
Tudor Hill LE13 .... **82** C8
Tudor House Cl DE11 ... **44** A7
Tudor Rd
Hinckley LE10 ....**197** C3
Leicester LE3...........**154** D6
Tudor Way DE11 .... **44** A6
Tuffleys Way LE3 ....**153** C1
TUGBY **185** E7
Tugby CE Prim Sch
LE7 ....**185** E6
Tugby Rd
Goadby LE7.............**185** C3
Tilton on t H LE7........**160** F6
Tugwell La LE67 ....**209** D6
Tumbledown Farm Pk★
LE14 .... **60** A7
Tungstone Way LE16....**240** E1
Tunicliffe Ct DE11 ...... **44** D4
Tunstall Cres LE4 ....**155** E8
TUR LANGTON **207** A2
Turnbull Cl LE7 ....**159** B2
Turnbull Dr LE3.........**178** E6
Turnbury Way LE5 ......**155** E1
Turner Ave LE11 .... **52** A2
Turner Cl LE12.......... **75** F7
Turner Dr LE10 ....**197** A3

Turner Rd
Leicester LE5...........**155** F5
Long Eaton NG10....... **10** C4
Turner Rise LE2 ....**181** B4
Turner St LE1 ....**259** B2
Turnpike Cl
Lutterworth LE17.......**244** D8
Market Harborough
LE16...................**240** D5
Turnpike Rd PE9........**116** C3
Turnpike Way LE67 .....**125** E8
Turnpole Cl PE9 ....**143** F5
Turn St LE1 ....**103** A4
Turnstone Wlk LE5......**155** C7
Turolough Rd LE67...... **71** C7
Turvey La LE12 .... **29** D2
Turville Cl
Hinckley LE10 ....**215** F5
Wigston LE18...........**203** E8
Turville Rd
Gilmorton LE17 ....**235** C5
Leicester LE3...........**154** B3
Tuskar Rd LE5 ....**156** D7
Tutbury Cl ◪ LE65 ...... **69** C5
Tuthill Furlong CV23 ....**252** D1
Tuxford Rd LE4 ....**130** A3
Tweed Dr LE13 .... **59** B1
Tweedside Cl LE10......**197** F3
Tweentown LE67 .... **96** C5
Twells Rd LE14 .... **40** B6
Twenty Acre La CV13....**174** B5
Twickenham Rd LE2 ....**179** C2
Twin Lakes Pk★ LE14 ... **60** A7
Twitchbed La LE15......**189** B5
Twitchell La CV9.........**171** B7
TWYCROSS **146** D7
Twycross House Prep Sch
CV9...................**146** D6
Twycross La
Bilstone CV9, CV13 .....**147** A7
Orton-on-t-H CV9........**145** F6
Twycross Rd
Bilstone CV13...........**147** C7
Hinckley LE10 ....**215** F6
Sheepy Magna CV9 .....**146** C2
Sibson CV13............**172** B7
Twycross St LE2 ....**155** C5
Twycross Zoo★ CV9......**119** F1
Twycross Zoo Staff
Apartments CV9........**120** B1
TWYFORD **106** E1
Twyford Cl LE67 .... **72** C1
Twyford Ct LE9 ....**198** B7
Twyford Rd
Burrough on t H LE14 ...**107** C1
Long Eaton NG10.........**9** F4
South Croxton LE7......**105** E1
Thorpe Satchville LE14 ..**106** E3
Twyford LE7............**133** F5
Tyburn Cl LE3, LE7......**127** F3
Tyers Cl LE9 ....**177** A3
Tyes End LE4 ....**128** A3
Tyler Ave LE11.......... **51** F5
Tyler Cl LE15 ....**166** B7
Tyler Ct LE12 .... **50** C6
Tyler Rd LE6............**152** D8
Tylers Rd LE12.......... **49** B6
Tymecrosse Gdns
LE16...................**240** D5
Tyndale St LE3 ....**154** D4
Tyndale Cl
Leicester, Oadby LE2....**181** D5
Long Eaton NG10....... **10** A6
Tyndale Rd LE11........ **74** C8
Tyne Rd
Corby NN17.............**230** D1
Oakham LE15...........**137** F5
Tyringham Rd LE18 .....**180** E2
Tyrrell St LE3 ....**154** D6
Tysoe Hill LE3 ....**127** D1
Tythe The DE11......... **44** B7
Tythorn Dr LE18 ....**180** A5

U

UFFINGTON **144** F4
Uffington CE Prim Sch
The PE9................**144** E4
Uffington Rd PE9 ....**144** A4
Uist Wlk NN17 ....**230** C1
Uldale Gr DE11 .... **44** C1
ULLESTHORPE **233** C4
Ullesthorpe CE Prim Sch
LE17 ....**233** B4
Ullesthorpe Ho LE17 ...**233** A4
Ullesthorpe Rd
Ashby Parva LE17 ....**233** E5
Bitteswell LE17 ....**233** E2
Gilmorton LE17 ....**234** E4
Ulleswater Cres LE65 ... **69** C4
Ullswater Ave
Barrow-u-S LE12........ **53** D1
Edith Weston LE15......**165** F7
Nuneaton CV11.........**214** A6
Ullswater Cl LE9 ....**198** F7
Ullswater Dr LE2........**181** C5
Ullswater Rd LE13 ...... **59** A2
Ullswater St LE2 ....**259** A2
Ullswater Wlk LE2 ......**181** C5
Ulverscroft Dr LE6......**126** F2
Ulverscroft La LE6...... **99** B3
Ulverscroft Rd
Leicester LE4...........**155** C8
Loughborough LE11..... **74** E8
Ulvers Croft Way LE67 .. **98** E1
Una Ave LE3............**179** A8
Underwood Cres LE9....**217** E8

Underwood Ct LE3 153 B8
Underwood Dr LE9 199 D1
Unicorn St LE4 129 E8
Union Pas 14 LE65 69 B6
Union Rd DE11 44 B5
Union St
Long Eaton NG10 10 E8
Loughborough LE11 52 A4
Melbourne DE73 26 A7
Union Way LE11 51 E3
Unitt Rd LE12 76 B4
Unity Cl DE11 44 A1
Unity Rd LE3 153 C8
University Cl LE7 103 B3
University Rd
Leicester LE1 259 C1
Loughborough LE11 51 D2
Univ of Leicester
Leicester LE1 155 A3
Leicester LE1 155 B4
Univ of Leicester Botanic Gdn★ LE2 180 F7
Univ of Nottingham Dept of Ag Economics LE12 30 B8
Univ of Nottingham Sutton Bonington Campus LE12 30 B8
Unwin Gn NG33 65 A4
Upex Cl LE8 201 F4
Upland Cl LE67 98 D1
Upland Dr LE67 98 D1
Uplands Farm The LE12 29 A4
Uplands Inf & Jun Sch LE2 155 C5
Uplands Pl LE12 29 A4
Uplands Rd
Leicester LE2 179 F5
Leicester, Oadby LE2 181 C6
Measham DE12 93 C4
Uplands The LE13 59 B2
Upper Bond St LE10 197 D1
UPPER BROUGHTON 19 B1
Upper Brown St LE1 259 B3
UPPER BRUNTINGTHORPE 236 D5
Upper Charnwood St LE2 155 B6
Upper Church St
Ashby-de-la-Z LE65 69 C6
Syston LE7 103 B4
Upper George St LE1 259 C5
Upper Gn LE11 74 D8
Upper Green Pl LE16 241 A6
Upper Hall Cl LE5 156 C8
Upper Hall Gn LE5 156 C8
UPPER HAMBLETON 139 C4
Upper Holme LE12 30 B3
Upper King St LE1 259 B2
UPPER MIDWAY 44 C7
Upper Nelson St LE1 259 C2
Upper New Wlk LE1 155 B4
Upper Packington Rd LE65 69 C5
Upper Temple Wlk LE4 128 A3
Upper Tichborne St LE2 155 B4
Upperton Rd LE2 259 A1
Upperton Rise LE3 154 C4
UPPINGHAM 189 A3
Uppingham CE Prim Sch LE15 189 A5
Uppingham Cl LE5 156 C5
Uppingham Com Coll LE15 189 B2
Uppingham Dr
Ashby-de-la-Z LE65 69 A7
Broughton Astley LE9 218 D8
Uppingham Rd
Billesdon LE7 159 C2
Bisbrooke LE15 189 F5
Blaston LE16 210 D3
Caldecott LE16 212 B2
Corby NN17 230 B1
East Norton LE7 186 C5
Houghton on t H LE7 157 E5
Houghton on t H LE7 158 D3
Leicester LE5 156 C6
Oakham LE15 138 A5
Preston LE15 189 B8
Stockerston LE15 211 B8
Thurnby LE7 157 A5
Uppingham Sch
Uppingham LE15 189 A4
Uppingham LE15 189 B4
UPTON 172 C4
Upton Cl DE74 17 B4
Upton Dr LE18 180 F2
Upton La
Shenton CV13 173 A5
Sibson CV13 172 C5
Stoke Golding CV13 196 B7
Upton CV13 172 B2
Utah Cl LE3 153 C7
Uttoxeter Cl LE4 129 D5
Uxbridge Rd LE4 129 C4

V

Valebrook Rd LE14 12 F3
Vale Cl
Leicester LE5 156 C7
Loughborough LE11 75 B7
Vale End LE7 156 F5
Valence Rd LE3 154 B4
Valentine Dr LE2 180 F6
Valentine Rd LE5 156 D5
Vale of Catmose Coll LE15 137 E7
Vale Rd
Hartshorne DE11 45 A3
Swadlincote DE11 44 B6
Valerie Rd DE72 16 A7
Vale The LE15 138 A5
Valiant Cl
Glenfield LE3 153 D7
Hinckley LE10 215 E4
Valjean Cres LE9 152 E3
Valley Ct LE15 189 B4
Valley Dr
Braunstone Town LE3 153 C2
Rugby CV21 252 A1
Valley House Mews LE8 205 B7
Valley La
Bitteswell LE17 244 B8
Staunton in t V NG23 1 D8
Valley Rd
Ibstock LE67 95 E1
Leicester LE5 130 B4
Loughborough LE11 74 E8
Markfield LE67 125 E8
Melton Mowbray LE13 82 B8
Overseal DE12 67 A3
Weston by W LE16 227 B3
Valley Rise DE11 44 B5
Valley View LE67 47 E3
Valley Way
Market Harborough LE16 241 B4
Whitwick LE67 71 D5
Val Wilson Ct LE11 51 B2
Vancouver Rd LE1 155 A7
Vandyke Rd LE2 181 B4
Vanguard Rd
Diseworth DE74 28 A8
Long Eaton NG10 10 D5
Vann Wlk LE4 129 A2
Vaughan Ave NG13 3 C2
Vaughan Cl LE16 250 E8
Vaughan Coll LE1 259 A3
Vaughan Rd LE2 179 E7
Vaughan St
Coalville LE67 96 C8
Leicester LE3 154 D6
Vaughan Way LE1 259 A3
Velbert Ho NN17 230 E1
Vence Cl PE9 143 C3
Ventnor Rd LE2 180 D7
Ventnor Rd S LE2 180 D6
Ventnor St LE5 155 D5
Venture Ct LE10 214 E8
Vercor Cl LE67 72 D1
Verdale Ave LE4 130 A5
Verdon Cres LE67 72 B1
Vernon Rd LE2 179 E7
Vernon Row NG13 6 F3
Vernon St LE3 154 D6
Verona Cl CV11 214 A1
Vero's La CV13 123 B3
Vestry St LE1 259 C4
Vetch Cl LE19 200 F8
Viadevana DE12 67 E3
Vicarage Cl
Billesdon LE7 159 C1
Blackfordby DE11 68 C8
Kirby Muxloe LE9 152 E7
Newbold LE67 47 E3
Syston LE7 103 B4
Vicarage Ct LE9 198 F8
Vicarage Dr LE16 224 E1
Vicarage Gdns DE11 44 C4
Vicarage La
Barkby LE7 130 D8
Belton LE12 49 B6
Eaton NG32 22 F7
Leicester, Humberstone LE5 156 B8
Leicester LE4 129 A3
Whetstone LE8 178 F1
Vicarage Rd
Oakham LE15 138 A6
Swadlincote DE11 44 C4
Woodville DE11 44 E2
Vicarage St
5 Earl Shilton LE9 198 F8
Whitwick LE67 71 F5
Vicars Cl LE15 113 B2
Vicary La LE12 75 C3
Victoria Ave
Draycott DE72 9 A7
Leicester LE2 155 B4
Market Harborough LE16 240 D5
Victoria Cl LE67 71 D5
Victoria Ct
Leicester LE2 155 C2
Leicester, Oadby LE2 180 F7
Long Eaton NG10 10 D7
Victoria Dr
Groby LE6 126 F2
Woodville DE11 44 E1
Victoria Gdns LE2 155 C3
Victoria Mews LE1 259 C2
Victoria Par 6 LE1 259 B4
Victoria Park Rd LE2 155 B2
Victoria Pl LE11 52 B3
Victoria Rd
Coalville LE67 71 D1
Draycott DE72 9 A7
Heather LE67 95 F3
Hinckley LE10 215 F5
Victoria Rd *continued*
Ibstock LE67 97 A1
Stamford PE9 143 D4
Whetstone LE8 201 F8
Woodhouse Eaves LE12 99 F8
Victoria Rd E LE5 129 E1
Victoria Rd N LE4 129 B3
Victoria St
Castle Donington DE74 17 B5
Fleckney LE8 222 F7
Hinckley LE10 197 D1
Long Eaton NG10 10 B5
Loughborough LE11 52 B3
Melbourne DE73 26 A7
Melton Mowbray LE13 59 C1
Narborough LE19 201 C8
Quorn (Quorndon) LE12 76 B6
Syston LE7 103 B3
Thurmaston LE4 129 E8
Wigston LE18 180 D3
Victoria Terr LE2 155 B3
Victor Rd LE3 153 D8
Victors Cl LE2 179 C4
Victory Cl NG10 10 E5
Viking Bsns Ctr DE11 44 F3
Viking Rd LE18 180 A4
Vilia Cl LE10 215 F4
Village Rd LE12 30 D2
Village St
Sedgebrook NG32 8 F8
Woolsthorpe by B NG32 15 B8
Villa St DE72 9 B7
Villas The LE8 206 A1
Villers Ct LE8 202 B8
Vincent Cl LE3 154 B6
Vine Cl NG13 3 A1
Vinehouse Cl LE7 101 B3
Vineries The LE8 202 D3
Vine St
Leicester LE1 259 A4
Stamford PE9 143 E3
Vine Tree Terr LE12 32 C1
Vineyard The LE17 232 E6
Violet Cl DE12 67 E1
Viscount Beaumont's CE Prim Sch LE67 70 D6
Viscount Rd DE74 28 C7
Vislok Cl LE16 240 E1
Vitruvius Way LE19 178 C8
Vostock Cl LE2 155 B5
Vulcan Ct LE67 71 D2
Vulcan Ho LE5 155 C6
Vulcan Rd LE5 155 C6
Vulcan Way
Coalville LE67 71 D2
Willey LE17 243 C7
Vyner Cl LE3 153 C2
Vyse Dr NG10 10 C6

W

Waddesdon Wlk LE4 155 D8
Wade St LE4 128 F3
Wade's Terr LE15 189 B4
Wadkins Way LE7 157 B5
Wagtail Cl LE8 223 A6
Wain Dr LE11 51 C6
Waingroves Wlk 2 LE4 128 F3
Wainwright Ave LE5 130 C3
Wainwright Rd LE67 96 D6
Waistrell Dr LE11 51 B6
Wakefield Ct DE74 17 C4
Wakefield Dr
Welford NN6 256 D5
Whitwick LE67 71 E5
Wakefield Pl LE4 129 C2
Wakeley Cl LE19 201 A7
Wakeling Cl LE8 201 F5
WAKERLEY 192 A3
Wakerley Ct LE5 155 D6
Wakerley Great Wood Forest Trail★ LE15 192 C2
Wakerley Great Wood Orienteering Course★ LE15 192 B2
Wakerley Rd
Barrowden LE15 192 A4
Harringworth NN17 213 F7
Leicester LE5 155 F3
Wakes Cl LE17 219 D2
Wakes Rd LE18 180 D3
WALCOTE 245 C4
Walcote Cl LE10 214 F8
Walcote Rd
Leicester LE4 129 E2
South Kilworth LE17 246 B2
Walcot Rd LE16 240 E2
Walcot Way PE9 143 A4
Waldale Dr LE2 155 D2
Waldron Ct LE11 52 A6
Waldron Dr LE2 181 C5
Wale Rd LE8 201 F7
Wales Orch LE17 218 E1
Walford Cl NG13 3 A2
Walk Cl DE72 9 A7
Walker Cl LE9 219 A4
Walker Manor Ct LE17 244 D6
Walker Rd
Bardon LE67 97 C4
Birstall LE4 128 F6
Thurmaston LE4 129 F6
Walkers Cl NG13 3 D2
Walkers La LE7 101 E5
Walkers Stad (Leicester City FC) LE2 154 E2
Walkers Way LE7 103 B4
Walks The PE9 168 D2
Wallace Dr
Groby LE6 126 D5
Sileby LE12 77 C1
Wallace Rd LE11 52 A2
Walled Gdn The
Hallaton LE16 209 E6
West Langton LE16 225 A7
Wallingford Ave CV11 214 A7
Wallingford Rd LE4 128 F2
Wallis Cl
Draycott DE72 9 A7
Thurcaston LE7 101 B3
Wallis Ho DE11 44 E3
Walney Cl LE10 197 B1
Walnut Ave LE4 128 F7
Walnut Cl
Aston-on-T DE72 16 B8
Bisbrooke LE15 189 E3
Broughton Astley LE9 219 A6
Empingham LE15 141 A6
Leicester, Oadby LE2 181 A5
Markfield LE67 125 D8
Stathern LE14 13 A2
Stretton LE15 88 F4
Swadlincote DE11 44 A5
Walnut Gr LE2 179 B4
Walnut Leys LE9 201 D2
Walnut Paddock LE14 12 B3
Walnut Rd
Bottesford NG13 3 A2
Loughborough LE11 75 A8
Walnut St LE2 259 A1
Walnut Way
Blaby LE8 202 B6
Countesthorpe LE8 202 E4
Walpole Ct LE3 153 F5
Walsgrave Ave LE5 156 D5
Walshe Rd LE5 156 B6
Walsingham Cres LE3 153 B3
Walter Hull Ct LE11 52 C2
Waltham Ave LE3 154 A2
Waltham Cl NN17 230 D1
Waltham Ho LE15 137 F5
Waltham La
Eaton NG32 22 F5
Harby LE14 12 B1
Long Clawson LE14 20 E2
WALTHAM ON THE WOLDS 40 B7
Waltham on the Wolds CE Prim Sch LE14 40 A6
Waltham Rd
Branston NG32 23 C7
Eastwell LE14 22 B4
Stonesby LE14 40 D6
Waltham Rise LE13 59 E2
WALTON 236 B3
Walton Cl
Kirby Fields LE9 152 F4
Swadlincote DE11 44 A3
Whissendine LE15 84 E1
Walton Ct DE74 18 C2
Walton Hill
Castle Donington DE74 17 A4
Isley Walton DE74 27 D7
Walton La LE12 53 C4
Walton New Road Ind Est LE17 236 C5
WALTON ON T W 54 B4
Walton Rd LE17 235 F2
Walton St
Leicester LE3 154 D3
Long Eaton NG10 10 D8
Walton Way LE12 101 D8
Wand St LE4 129 A1
WANLIP 102 C2
Wanlip Ave LE4 129 B7
Wanlip La LE4 129 B8
Wanlip Rd LE7 102 E3
Wanlip St LE1 155 A7
Wansbeck Gdns LE5 156 C8
Wanstead Ind Pk LE3 153 A5
Wanstead Rd LE3 153 A5
Ward Cl LE2 179 C7
Wardens Wlk LE3 153 C3
WARDLEY 188 A5
Wards Closes LE18 203 E8
Ward's Cres LE12 77 D3
Ward's End LE11 52 A3
Ward's La DE72 9 D8
Wareham Rd LE8 202 B6
Warehouse The LE16 240 D4
Waring Cl LE3 127 E1
Warke Flatt DE74 17 B6
War Meml Homes LE7 156 E8
Warmsley Ave LE18 180 C4
Warn Cres LE15 137 D5
Warner Cl
Markfield LE67 98 D1
Whetstone LE8 202 A5
Warner Pl LE11 52 C4
Warner's La 1 LE11 52 B4
Warner St LE12 76 D7
Warren Ave LE4 130 A5
Warren Cl
Leicester LE5 156 A8
Markfield LE67 125 E8
Warren Ct LE19 178 B5
Warren Dr LE4 130 A5
Warren Hill LE6 99 F5
Warren Hills Com Prim Sch LE67 72 D2
Warren Hills Rd LE67 72 D2
Warren La
Castle Donington DE74, NG10 10 B2
Leicester Forest East LE3 152 E2
Whitwick LE67 71 F7
Warrenne Keep PE9 143 D2
Warren Park Way LE19 178 A5
Warren Rd
Narborough LE19 178 D1
Wothorpe PE9 169 E7
Warren St LE3 154 D6
Warren The LE7 103 C7
Warren View LE4 130 A5
Warrington Dr LE6 126 E2
WARTNABY 37 A3
Wartnaby Rd LE14 37 C3
Wartnaby St LE16 240 D3
Warton La
Austrey CV9 119 A1
Orton-on-t-H CV9 145 C4
Warwick Ave LE12 75 E6
Warwick Cl
Bagworth LE67 124 B6
Desford LE9 151 A2
Market Bosworth CV13 148 F3
Market Harborough LE16 240 F5
Swadlincote DE11 44 E5
Thornton LE67 124 F3
Warwick Ct LE11 51 D5
Warwick Dr CV9 170 D2
Warwick Flats NG13 3 A2
Warwick Gdns LE10 197 E3
Warwick La CV13 148 E3
Warwick Rd
Broughton Astley LE9 218 E8
Kibworth Beauchamp LE8 205 E1
Littlethorpe LE8, LE19 201 E6
Long Eaton NG10 10 F7
Melton Mowbray LE13 59 C1
Wigston LE18 180 B3
Warwick St LE3 154 D6
Warwick Way
Ashby-de-la-Z LE65 69 C5
Loughborough LE11 51 E6
Washbrook La
Burton Overy LE8 182 E1
Wigston LE2 180 F4
Washdyke La LE14 58 B1
Washdyke Rd LE15 134 F4
Washington Cl
Barwell LE9 198 A6
Melbourne DE73 26 A7
Wash La LE67 70 F1
Washpit La CV13 149 D8
Wash Pit La LE17 246 F4
Washstones La LE14 80 B8
Waste La CV9 170 A1
Watchcrete Ave LE7 103 D5
Watchorn Cl DE11 44 D5
Watchorn Ct LE15 137 F7
Waterfall Way
Barwell LE9 198 A5
Medbourne LE16 227 F6
Waterfield Cl LE5 156 B5
Waterfield Pl LE16 240 E5
Waterfield Rd LE7 100 F2
Waterfield Way LE10 215 C5
Waterfront The LE3 259 A3
Waterfurlong PE9 143 C2
Watergate
East Goscote LE7 103 E7
12 Stamford PE9 143 E3
Watergate 1 LE3 178 F6
Watergate La LE3, LE19 178 E7
Water La
Ashwell LE15 111 B8
Eastwell LE14 22 B6
Frisby on t W LE14 80 C8
Long Clawson LE14 20 E4
Seagrave LE12 77 F8
South Witham NG33 65 B3
Stainby NG33 43 D2
Stathern LE14 13 A2
Water Leys Prim Sch LE18 180 B4
Waterloo Cres
Countesthorpe LE8 202 D3
Wigston LE18 180 E4
Waterloo Pl DE11 44 B4
Waterloo Rd LE10 215 D8
Waterloo Spinney La LE12 75 B4
Waterloo Way LE2 259 C2
Watermead Ctry Pk★ LE4 129 D8
Watermead Ctry Pk (North)★ LE7 102 D3
Watermead La LE11 74 D8
Watermeadows The NG10 10 B8
Water Meadow Way LE67 122 F8
Watermead Way LE4 129 B5
Waters End LE9 198 A5
Waterside PE9 116 F2
Waterside Cl
Loughborough LE11 52 B5
Melton Mowbray LE13 59 D6
Waterside Ct LE10 214 F7
Waterside Rd LE5 130 A4

Waterside The LE12...... 76 D3
Water St PE9............ 143 E2
Waterville Cl LE3....... 153 C6
Waterworks Rd LE67.... 97 A7
Waterworks Way
LE17............... 247 F5
Watery Gate La LE9..... 199 B3
Watkin Rd LE2......... 154 D3
Watling Cl LE10........ 215 C4
Watling Cres CV23..... 253 C1
Watling Dr LE10....... 215 C4
Watling St
Atherstone CV9....... 170 A1
Leicester LE2........ 259 B5
Mountsorrel LE12..... 76 E2
Nuneaton CV11, LE10 .. 214 C8
Watson Ave LE16....... 250 D8
Watson Cl NN17........ 230 E2
Watson Rd LE4......... 129 C2
Watson's La LE14...... 12 B2
Watt La LE8........... 221 A6
Watts Cl LE4.......... 128 A3
Waudby Cl LE9........ 201 C6
Waughs Dr LE12....... 101 D8
Waveney Cl LE10....... 215 A8
Waveney Rise LE2...... 181 D6
Waverley Cl LE11....... 51 B5
Waverley Ct LE13....... 59 D1
Waverley Gdns PE9..... 143 B4
Waverley Pl PE9....... 143 B4
Waverley Rd
Blaby LE8............ 202 C6
Rugby CV21........... 257 A1
Wigston LE18......... 179 F2
Waverley St NG10...... 10 E8
Wavertree Cl LE9...... 201 D4
Wavertree Dr LE4..... 129 B3
Wayfarer Dr LE7....... 103 E8
Wayne Way The
Birstall LE4.......... 129 A7
Leicester LE5........ 155 F6
Wayside Dr
Leicester, Oadby LE2.. 181 C5
Thurmaston LE4...... 129 E6
Weare Cl LE7.......... 159 C1
Weares Cl LE15....... 191 B5
Weaver Cl
Loughborough LE11.... 52 C1
Whitwick LE67........ 71 C1
Weaver Gn LE13........ 59 B4
Weaver Rd
Earl Shilton LE9...... 199 A8
Leicester LE5........ 156 F2
Weavers Ave LE12...... 50 B3
Weavers Cl LE12....... 76 A5
Weavers Close CE Prim
Sch LE9............. 198 F8
Weavers Ct
8 Hinckley LE10....... 197 D1
Narborough LE19...... 201 B7
Weaver's Wynd LE7..... 103 E2
Webb Cl LE3........... 153 B2
Webbs Way LE9........ 199 D2
Webster Rd LE3........ 153 E4
Websters Cl LE1....... 50 A1
Weddington Country
Wlk★ CV10.......... 195 C1
Weddington La CV10.... 195 A3
Weddington Rd CV10 ... 195 B1
Weir Cl LE18.......... 203 B8
Weir La LE7........... 158 A3
Weir Rd
Kibworth Beauchamp
LE8.............. 224 A7
Saddington LE8....... 223 B4
Welbeck Ave
Hinckley LE10........ 215 D4
Leicester LE4........ 128 E2
Welbeck Cl LE8....... 202 C6
Welbeck The Defence
Sixth Form Coll LE12.. 75 B3
Welby La LE13......... 58 E6
Welby Rd LE14......... 58 D4
Welcombe Ave LE3..... 153 F1
Weldon Ave LE12...... 77 D4
Weldon Rd
Loughborough LE11.... 51 E7
Wigston LE18......... 180 A4
WELFORD.............. 256 E5
Welford Cl LE2........ 180 B7
Welford Pl LE1........ 259 B3
Welford Rd
Blaby LE8............ 202 B8
Husbands Bosworth
LE17............. 247 E3
Kilby LE8, LE18...... 203 E5
Leicester, Knighton LE2.. 180 B7
Leicester LE1, LE2.... 259 B2
Shearsby LE8, LE17.... 222 A2
Sibbertoft LE16...... 248 D2
South Kilworth LE17... 255 D7
Welford NN6......... 256 E7
Welford Sibbertoft &
Sulby Endowed Sch
NN6............... 256 E5
WELHAM.............. 226 E5
Welham La
Cranoe LE16.......... 208 D2
Great Bowden LE16.... 241 C8
Welham Rd
Great Bowden LE16.... 241 A8
Slawston LE16........ 209 B1
Thorpe Langton LE16.. 226 B5
Weston by W LE16..... 227 A4
Welham Wlk LE4....... 129 F4

Welland Ave LE16...... 239 E7
Welland Bsns Pk
LE16............... 241 B4
Welland Cl
Caldecott LE16........ 230 C8
Coalville LE67........ 97 A8
Welland Ct
3 Market Harborough
LE16............. 240 F2
Market Harborough, Little
Bowden LE16........ 241 A4
Welland Mdws PE9..... 192 F8
Welland Mews PE9..... 143 F2
Welland Park Com Coll
LE16............... 240 E2
Welland Park Rd
LE16............... 240 E2
Welland Rd
Barrow-u-S LE12...... 76 D6
Edith Weston LE15.... 166 D7
Welland Rise
Melton Mowbray LE13.. 59 C1
Sibbertoft LE16...... 248 F2
Welland St LE2........ 155 B4
Welland Vale Rd
Corby NN17.......... 230 E1
Leicester LE5........ 156 D4
Welland View PE9...... 142 F1
Welland View Rd
LE16............... 229 D1
Welland Way LE15...... 137 E5
Wellbrook Ave LE12.... 77 D3
Well Cross LE15....... 166 B7
Well Ct LE15.......... 140 F6
Wellesbourne Dr LE3 .. 127 D1
Welles St LE1......... 259 A4
Wellfield Cl
South Witham NG33.... 65 B4
Tugby LE7........... 185 E6
Well Field La LE14..... 80 C8
Wellgate Ave LE4..... 129 A8
Wellhouse Cl LE18..... 203 C8
Wellingar Cl LE3...... 153 C2
Wellinger Way LE3..... 153 E4
Wellington Cl LE10.... 215 E4
Wellington La **9** PE9 .. 143 D3
Wellington Parkway
LE17............... 243 D6
Wellington St
Leicester LE1........ 259 B3
Loughborough LE11.... 52 C1
Syston LE7.......... 103 B3
Wellington Way LE13 .. 59 A5
Well La
Ab Kettleby LE14..... 37 D2
Blackfordby DE11..... 45 B1
4 Hinckley LE10....... 197 D1
Upper Broughton LE14 .. 19 A1
Wells Ave LE18........ 203 F3
WELLSBOROUGH........ 147 C1
Wellsborough Rd
Sheepy Parva CV9,
CV13............. 146 E1
Wellsborough CV13.... 147 D2
Wells Cl LE17......... 247 E5
Wellsic La LE7........ 101 E6
Well Spring Hill LE18.. 203 E8
Wells Rd LE65........ 68 F4
Well St LE15.......... 110 C3
Wellwood Rd DE11..... 44 A6
Well Yard LE12........ 50 C3
Welton Cl LE18........ 223 F8
Welwyn Rd LE10....... 197 F1
Wembley Rd LE3...... 153 B5
Wembrook Coppice
CV9............... 171 B8
Wembury Gdns LE4.... 128 A4
Wendover Dr LE10..... 197 E4
Wendys Cl LE5........ 156 D7
Wenlock Way LE4..... 130 A3
Wensleydale Ave LE9 .. 198 A5
Wensleydale Ave LE9 .. 198 A5
Wensleydale Rd
Long Eaton NG10..... 10 B6
Wigston LE18........ 180 F1
Wensley Rise LE2..... 179 C2
Wensum Cl
Hinckley LE10........ 215 B8
Oakham LE15........ 138 B7
Wentbridge Rd LE4.... 129 D3
Wenton Cl LE15....... 112 B7
Went Rd LE4.......... 129 A6
Wentworth Cl
Hinckley LE10........ 197 E3
Kibworth Beauchamp
LE8............. 224 B7
Wentworth Ct LE5..... 156 A2
Wentworth Dr CV11.... 214 A1
Wentworth Gn LE9..... 152 D4
Wentworth Rd
Coalville LE67........ 96 C8
Fleckney LE8........ 223 A7
Leicester LE3........ 154 C6
Wesley Cl
Hathern LE12......... 30 A1
Loughborough LE11.... 51 B6
Ratby LE6........... 152 C8
Sapcote LE9......... 217 E7
Wesley Hillman Ct
DE12.............. 93 C5
Wesley St LE4......... 128 F3
Wesley Way LE67..... 125 F8
Wessex Dr LE3........ 153 E5
West Ave
Leicester LE2........ 155 B2
Melton Mowbray LE13.. 59 A4
Wigston LE18........ 180 B3
West Bank Mews DE74.. 18 C2

Westbourne Ho LE13... 59 B3
Westbourne St LE4.... 155 A8
Westbridge Cl LE3..... 259 A3
Westbridge Ind Est
LE3............... 259 A3
Westbury Rd LE2...... 155 A1
West Cl LE10......... 215 D7
WESTCOTES........... 154 C4
Westcotes Dr LE3..... 154 C4
West Cross La LE12.... 101 C7
West Ct LE1.......... 259 C2
Westdale Ave LE2..... 179 A2
Westdale Cl NG10..... 10 A5
Westdown Dr LE4..... 129 E6
West Dr LE5.......... 156 A8
WEST END............ 48 C4
West End
Barlestone CV13...... 149 D8
Barton in t B CV13.... 122 C1
Exton LE15.......... 113 A3
Long Clawson LE14.... 20 C3
Long Whatton LE12.... 29 A4
Welford NN6......... 256 D4
Wymondham LE14..... 62 D2
West End Cl NG13..... 3 A3
West End Cotts LE14... 108 C3
West End Villas **5**
PE9............... 143 C3
Westerby Cl LE18..... 180 D4
Westerby Ct LE17..... 244 B5
Westerby La LE8...... 223 F6
Westerdale Rd LE18... 180 F2
Western Ave
Easton o t H PE9..... 168 F5
Fleckney LE8........ 222 F6
Market Harborough
LE16............. 240 D1
Ravenstone LE67..... 71 A2
Western Bvd LE2...... 259 A2
Western Cl LE65...... 69 B4
Western Cotts LE17... 246 F4
Western Dr
Blaby LE8........... 202 B7
Claybrooke Parva LE17.. 232 E5
Westernhay Rd LE2.... 155 C1
WESTERN PARK........ 154 A6
Western Park Rd LE3 .. 154 A5
Western Rd
Asfordby LE14........ 57 F3
Leicester LE3........ 154 D4
Old Dalby LE14...... 36 A5
West Farm Dr LE15.... 191 E5
Westfield Ave
Countesthorpe LE8.... 202 D4
Oakham LE15........ 137 E6
Wigston LE18........ 180 B4
Westfield Cl
Market Harborough
LE16............. 240 C3
Rearsby LE7......... 103 F8
Westfield Cres NN6.... 256 E6
Westfield Ct LE10..... 215 C7
Westfield Dr LE11..... 51 F4
Westfield Inf Sch
LE10.............. 215 B7
Westfield Jun Sch
LE10.............. 215 B7
Westfield La LE7...... 101 D5
Westfield Rd
Hinckley LE10........ 215 B7
Leicester LE3........ 154 A6
Swadlincote DE11.... 44 B6
Westfields CV13...... 149 D8
West Fields PE9...... 168 F5
Westfields Ave LE65... 68 F6
Westfields Terr LE65... 68 F7
Westgate LE67........ 122 E8
West Gate NG10...... 10 E7
Westgate Ave LE4..... 128 E8
Westgate La LE16..... 239 E3
Westgate Rd LE2..... 180 B6
West Gate Sch LE3.... 153 F6
Westgate St LE15..... 137 F6
Westhaven PE9....... 169 A5
Westhaven Ct CV13.... 148 E3
Westhill Rd LE3...... 154 A6
West Holme St LE3.... 154 D5
Westhorpe
Ashley LE16......... 227 E2
Sibbertoft LE16...... 248 F2
Westhorpe Cl LE15.... 165 A3
Westhorpe Dr NG10... 10 C8
West Hyde LE10...... 214 F7
WEST KNIGHTON...... 180 B6
West La
Bardon LE67......... 97 C3
Billesdon LE7........ 159 B2
Ridlington LE15...... 163 D2
Westland Cl LE16..... 239 E3
Westland Rd LE15..... 112 D8
WEST LANGTON........ 225 B6
West Langton Rd LE8,
LE16............. 224 E7
Westleigh Ave LE3.... 154 C3
Westleigh Bsns Pk
LE8.............. 179 B1
Westleigh Rd
Glen Parva LE2...... 179 E1
Leicester LE3........ 154 C3
Westley Grange LE18 .. 180 B3
West Mdws NG32..... 4 E5
Westmeadow La LE12 .. 28 F3
West Meadow Rise
DE74.............. 16 E5
Westmeath Ave LE5... 156 B6
West Mill PE9........ 168 F4
Westminster Cl LE13... 59 A6

Westminster Dr
Glen Parva LE2...... 179 D1
Hinckley LE10........ 215 F4
Westminster Ind Est
DE12.............. 93 B4
Westminster Rd LE2... 155 E1
Westminster Way LE65.. 69 A8
Westmorland Ave
Leicester LE4........ 129 C2
Loughborough LE11.... 51 D1
Wigston LE18........ 179 F2
WESTON BY WELLAND
.... 227 A3
Weston Cl
Hinckley LE10........ 197 A1
Leicester, Oadby LE2... 181 E4
Rearsby LE7......... 78 F1
Weston Cres LE10..... 9 F4
Weston Dr CV13...... 148 E2
Weston Rd
Ashley LE16......... 227 D3
Aston-on-T DE72..... 16 A7
Edith Weston LE15.... 166 A7
Sutton Bassett LE16... 227 A2
Welham LE16........ 226 F5
Westons La LE15..... 110 C3
Westonville PE9...... 168 D2
West Orch LE4....... 77 C1
Westover Rd LE3..... 153 C1
Westray Dr LE10..... 197 C1
West Park Ct NG10.... 10 D7
West Rd LE15........ 137 F6
West St Open **1** LE3 .. 154 D4
West Side LE14....... 58 D3
Westside Ct **4** LE9.... 198 F8
West St
Blaby LE8........... 179 A1
Clipsham LE15....... 89 D5
Earl Shilton LE9...... 175 F1
Easton o t H PE9..... 169 A5
Enderby LE19....... 178 B2
Glenfield LE3........ 127 C1
Leicester LE1........ 259 C2
Stamford PE9........ 143 D3
Swadlincote DE11.... 44 B4
Syston LE7.......... 103 A4
Welford NN6........ 256 E6
West Street Gdns
PE9............... 143 C2
West Thorpe LE12.... 34 C7
West View
Somerby LE14........ 108 B1
Stamford PE9........ 142 D7
West View Ave LE2.... 179 B3
West Way NG32...... 4 F4
West Wlk
Ibstock LE67........ 95 F1
Leicester LE1........ 259 C2
Wetherby Cl LE7..... 103 E6
Wetherby Rd LE4..... 129 D3
Wexford Cl LE2...... 181 D4
Weymouth Cl LE18.... 203 D8
Weymouth St LE4..... 155 B8
Whaddon Chase LE15 .. 87 E2
Whaddon Dr LE11.... 52 C1
Whall Cl LE12........ 76 A5
Wharfedale Rd
Corby NN17......... 230 E1
Long Eaton NG10..... 10 A6
Wharf La CV13....... 174 A4
Wharf Rd PE9........ 143 E3
Wharf St N LE1...... 259 C5
Wharf St S LE1...... 259 C4
Wharf St LE4........ 129 E8
Wharf The DE72..... 9 A2
Wharf View DE12.... 93 C5
Wharf Way LE2...... 179 B2
Wharf Yd LE10....... 215 A7
Wharncliffe Rd LE11... 52 C4
Whatborough Rd LE7,
LE15.............. 135 B2
Whatoff Lodge Farm★
.... 75 D5
Whatton Oaks LE7.... 101 E8
Whatton Rd
Hathern LE12........ 29 E2
Kegworth DE74, LE12.. 29 C7
Whatton's Cl NG32.... 4 F1
Wheat Cl LE12....... 76 D3
Wheatfield Cl LE3..... 153 C7
Wheatfield Way LE10 .. 197 C4
Wheatland Cl LE2.... 181 D5
Wheatland Dr LE11.... 52 C2
Wheatland Rd LE4.... 128 D5
Wheatlands DE11..... 44 B7
Wheatlands Cl PE9.... 167 F5
Wheatlands Dr LE8.... 202 D4
Wheatley Ave LE15... 189 B5
Wheatley Cl LE2..... 76 E7
Wheatley Rd LE4.... 128 D4
Wheatley's Rd LE4.... 129 D7
Wheatsheaf Ctyd
CV13.............. 148 F3
Wheatsheaf La LE15... 88 B1
Wheat St LE1........ 259 C4
Wheeldale LE18...... 180 F2
Wheeldale Cl LE4..... 128 D3
Wheeler Cl LE17..... 244 C5
Wheel La LE15....... 191 F5
Wheel Tappers Way
LE11.............. 51 F4
Wheelwright Cl LE17... 246 F4
WHETSTONE.......... 201 E7
Whetstone Ct LE8.... 201 F7
Whetstone Dr LE67... 71 E1

Whetstone Gorse La
LE8............... 202 A1
Whiles La LE4........ 129 B7
Whinchat Ct DE12.... 93 B4
Whinchat Rd LE5..... 155 C6
Whincups Yd PE9..... 143 E2
Whinham Ave LE9.... 218 D7
WHISSENDINE......... 84 E1
Whissendine CE Prim Sch
LE15.............. 84 F1
Whissendine Rd
Ashwell LE15........ 110 E8
Leesthorpe LE14..... 83 E3
Whissendine Windmill★
.... 84 E1
Whiston Cl LE5...... 156 D7
Whitby Cl
Broughton Astley LE9 .. 218 E8
Loughborough LE11.... 51 B5
Whitcroft Cl LE67.... 125 E8
Whitcroft's La LE67... 98 D6
Whiteacres LE8...... 201 E5
White Barn Dr LE9.... 201 D3
Whitebeam Cl LE19... 201 A8
Whitebeam Rd LE2... 181 A7
White Cl LE9........ 219 A6
Whitefield Rd LE4.... 128 F3
Whitegate LE11...... 52 C5
Whitegates Field
LE8.............. 180 E1
Whitehall Cl CV10.... 194 A2
Whitehall Prim Sch
LE5.............. 156 B4
Whitehall Rd LE5.... 156 B4
White Hart Cl LE9.... 159 B2
Whitehead Cres LE18.. 180 B3
Whitehill Rd LE67.... 96 E3
White Horse Ct LE12.. 33 C4
White Horse La LE4... 129 B6
White Hos CV13..... 172 A7
Whitehouse Ave LE11.. 52 C2
White House Cl
Bagworth LE67....... 124 B5
Groby LE6.......... 126 E3
Leire LE17.......... 218 E1
Whitehouse Way DE12.. 93 C6
Whitelake Cl LE13.... 59 A1
White Leys Ct LE67... 71 C1
White Lion Gdns LE15.. 137 F6
Whitemoors Cl CV13... 196 E7
Whitemoors Rd CV13.. 196 E7
Whiteoaks Rd LE2.... 181 C3
White Post Ct NN17... 230 E7
Whitesand Cl LE3.... 127 D1
White St
Kibworth Beauchamp
LE8.............. 223 F8
Quorn (Quorndon) LE12.. 75 F6
Whitethorns Cl LE17... 254 B3
Whitley Cl LE3...... 154 B8
Whitlock Way LE14... 57 F3
Whitman Cl LE3...... 153 D6
Whitteney Dr LE2.... 179 D4
Whittier Rd LE2..... 179 F7
WHITTINGTON........ 170 B3
Whittington Ct LE6... 126 C1
Whittington Dr LE6... 126 C6
Whittington La CV9... 170 B2
Whittington Rd LE3... 127 F3
Whittle Cl LE8...... 201 F6
Whittle Rd
Hinckley LE10........ 214 E7
Lutterworth LE17.... 244 B5
WHITWELL........... 140 B6
Whitwell Nature Trail★
.... 140 A5
Whitwell Rd LE15.... 140 D5
Whitwell Row LE2.... 179 E5
WHITWICK........... 71 F5
Whitwick Bsns Pk
LE67.............. 71 B7
Whitwick Moor LE67... 71 D7
Whitwick Rd
Coalville LE67....... 71 D2
Copt Oak LE67...... 98 C4
Whitwick St John the
Baptist CE Prim Sch
LE67.............. 71 E6
Whitwick Way LE67... 154 C8
Whitworth Ave LE10... 214 F7
Whitworth Cl DE12.... 67 E4
Whysall Rd NG10.... 10 B7
WIBTOFT............ 232 B4
Wicken Rise LE18.... 180 E4
Wickham Rd LE2..... 181 B4
Wicklow Ave LE13.... 59 D1
Wicklow Dr LE5...... 156 A6
Wicklow Dr LE5...... 156 A6
Wicklow Lo LE13.... 59 D1
Wiclif Way LE17..... 244 C7
Widdowson Rd NG10.. 10 B5
Wide La
Hathern LE12........ 30 A1
Wymeswold LE12..... 34 C3
Wideshaft DE11...... 44 C4
Wide St LE12........ 51 B8
Widford Cl LE3...... 156 A8
Widmerpool La LE12... 34 D8
Widon The LE11..... 74 D8
Wigeon Dr DE12..... 93 B4
Wightman Cl
Shepshed LE12....... 50 B3
Stoney Stanton LE9... 199 B3
Wightman Rd LE4.... 129 F4
Wigley Rd LE5....... 156 C8
WIGSTON............ 179 E2
Wigston Framework
Knitters Mus★ LE18... 180 C2

WIGSTON HARCOURT 203 F8
Wigston La LE2 ...... 179 D6
WIGSTON MAGNA 180 D2
WIGSTON PARVA 231 F8
Wigston Rd
  Blaby LE8 ...... 202 C8
  Leicester, Oadby LE2 ...... 180 F4
  3 Rugby CV21 ...... 257 A1
Wigston St
  Countesthorpe LE8 ...... 202 F4
  Leicester LE1 ...... 259 C3
Wilberforce Rd LE3 ...... 154 D3
Wildgoose Cl LE67 ...... 95 F2
Wild Rose Wlk LE7 ...... 103 E8
Wileman's Cl LE9 ...... 198 E6
Wilf Brown Cl LE9 ...... 176 B1
Wilford Ho LE8 ...... 202 A8
Wilfred Gdns LE65 ...... 69 A5
Wilfred Pl LE65 ...... 69 B5
Wilkes Ave DE12 ...... 93 C4
Wilkes Gdns LE15 ...... 189 B4
Wilkes Way LE7 ...... 102 F2
Willars Way LE67 ...... 95 F8
Willcox Dr LE13 ...... 59 E1
Willday Dr CV9 ...... 170 D2
Willersley Ho NG10 ...... 10 A5
WILLESLEY 68 E2
Willesley Cl LE65 ...... 68 F4
Willesley Gdns LE65 ...... 68 F4
Willesley La
  Moira DE12 ...... 68 B4
  Willesley LE65 ...... 68 D3
Willesley Prim Sch
  LE65 ...... 69 A4
Willesley Woodside
  ...... 68 D2
Willet Cl 4 LE12 ...... 77 C3
WILLEY 242 E6
William Bradford Com
  Coll LE9 ...... 198 C8
William Cl LE7 ...... 103 E6
William Ct
  Enderby LE19 ...... 178 A3
  Stamford PE9 ...... 143 C5
William Dalby Ho
  LE15 ...... 138 A5
William Dalby Wlk
  LE15 ...... 137 F6
William Iliffe St LE10 ...... 215 B7
William Lyon Ct LE11 ...... 52 B5
William Peardon Ct
  LE18 ...... 180 C3
Williams Cl LE19 ...... 201 B6
William St
  Leicester LE1 ...... 259 C4
  Loughborough LE11 ...... 52 A4
  Narborough LE19 ...... 201 B7
Willn Cl LE67 ...... 97 B8
Willoughby Cl
  Breaston DE72 ...... 9 F8
  Melton Mowbray LE13 ...... 59 E2
Willoughby Ct LE15 ...... 189 A4
Willoughby Dr LE15 ...... 141 A6
Willoughby Gdns
  Leicester Forest East
    LE3 ...... 153 A3
  Oakham LE15 ...... 137 F6
Willoughby Ho DE11 ...... 44 C4
WILLOUGHBY-ON-THE-
  WOLDS 34 C8
Willoughby Prim Sch
  LE12 ...... 34 C7
Willoughby Rd
  Ashby Magna LE17 ...... 220 B4
  Countesthorpe LE8 ...... 202 C2
  Morcott LE15 ...... 191 A6
  Stamford PE9 ...... 143 E5
WILLOUGHBY WATERLEYS
  ...... 220 D6
Willowbank Rd LE10 ...... 215 C7
Willowbrook Cl
  Ashby-de-la-Z LE65 ...... 69 B8
  Broughton Astley LE9 ...... 218 F7
  Queniborough LE7 ...... 103 E6
  Sharnford LE10 ...... 217 C4
Willow Brook Cl LE3 ...... 127 C2
Willowbrook Pk LE11 ...... 51 E6
Willowbrook Prim Sch
  LE5 ...... 156 E6
Willow Brook Rd
  Corby NN17 ...... 230 D1
  Leicester LE5 ...... 155 D7
Willowbrook View
  LE5 ...... 156 E6
Willowbrook Way
  LE7 ...... 103 E7
Willow Cl
  Aston-on-T DE72 ...... 16 B7
  East Leake LE12 ...... 31 D8
  Hinckley LE10 ...... 215 E5
  Littlethorpe LE19 ...... 201 C6
  Measham DE12 ...... 93 C6
  Moira DE12 ...... 68 B6
  Newbold Verdon LE9 ...... 150 B3
  Uppingham LE15 ...... 189 B5
  Whissendine LE15 ...... 84 F2
Willow Cres
  Market Harborough
    LE16 ...... 240 C2
  Oakham LE15 ...... 138 B7
Willowcroft LE12 ...... 75 E5
Willow Ct
  1 Braunstone Town
    LE3 ...... 178 C4
  10 Leicester LE2 ...... 155 B5
  Swadlincote DE11 ...... 44 C4
Willowdale LE10 ...... 215 A7

Willowdene Way LE9 ...... 198 B6
Willow Dr
  Countesthorpe LE8 ...... 202 E4
  Groby LE6 ...... 126 E1
  Melton Mowbray LE13 ...... 59 D4
Willow Farm Bsns Pk
  DE74 ...... 17 B6
Willowfields Rd CV11 ...... 214 A1
Willow Gn LE67 ...... 72 C2
Willow Gr LE12 ...... 76 C1
Willow Herb Cl LE2 ...... 181 E4
Willow Park Dr LE8 ...... 180 C3
Willow Park Ind Est
  CV13 ...... 196 C7
Willow Park Way DE72 ...... 16 A7
Willow Pl LE18 ...... 180 D2
Willow Poole La LE12 ...... 30 C5
Willow Rd
  Barrow-u-S LE12 ...... 53 D1
  Blaby LE8 ...... 202 B7
  Castle Donington DE74 ...... 17 B5
  Loughborough LE11 ...... 75 A8
  Stamford PE9 ...... 142 F5
Willow St
  Desford LE9 ...... 151 A3
  Leicester LE1 ...... 155 A7
Willows The
  Atherstone CV9 ...... 170 E2
  Burton o t W LE12 ...... 53 F6
Willowtree Cl LE9 ...... 130 C2
Willow Tree Cl LE9 ...... 198 B8
Willow Tree Cres
  LE17 ...... 244 A6
Willow Way LE67 ...... 95 E1
Willow Wlk LE7 ...... 102 F3
Willsmer Cl LE9 ...... 219 A5
Willson Cl LE16 ...... 241 A3
Wilmington Ct
  Leicester, Oadby LE2 ...... 180 F8
  Loughborough LE11 ...... 52 C2
Wilmington Rd LE4 ...... 154 C3
Wilmore Cres LE13 ...... 153 D3
Wilmot Rd DE11 ...... 44 B3
Wilne Ave NG10 ...... 10 A5
Wilne Cl NG10 ...... 9 F4
Wilne La
  Breaston DE72 ...... 9 D4
  Shardlow DE72 ...... 9 B2
Wilne Rd
  Draycott DE72 ...... 9 B5
  Long Eaton NG10 ...... 9 F4
Wilne St LE2 ...... 155 C4
Wilnicott Rd LE3 ...... 153 F1
Wilsford Cl LE18 ...... 203 C8
Wilshere Cl LE9 ...... 152 D5
WILSON 26 F6
Wilson Cl LE3 ...... 153 D2
Wilson Ct LE15 ...... 89 A7
Wilson Rd LE18 ...... 179 E1
Wilson Rise DE73 ...... 26 E6
Wilson St LE2 ...... 155 C6
WILSTHORPE 10 B7
Wilsthorpe Rd
  Breaston DE72 ...... 9 F8
  Long Eaton, New Sawley
    NG10 ...... 10 B7
Wilstone Cl LE11 ...... 51 C3
Wilton Ave LE11 ...... 52 C2
Wilton Cl LE2 ...... 181 C5
Wilton Ct LE13 ...... 59 B2
Wilton Pl LE13 ...... 59 C3
Wilton Rd LE13 ...... 59 C3
Wilton St LE1 ...... 259 B5
Wilton Terr LE13 ...... 59 C3
Wiltshire Ho LE4 ...... 128 D2
Wiltshire Rd
  Leicester LE4 ...... 128 D2
  Wigston LE18 ...... 180 B3
Wimberley Way NG33 ...... 65 A4
Wimbishthorpe Cl NG13 ...... 3 A3
Wimbledon St LE1 ...... 259 C4
Wimborne Cl LE18 ...... 180 C1
Wimborne Rd LE2 ...... 180 D6
Winchendon Cl LE5 ...... 155 E8
Winchester Ave
  Blaby LE8 ...... 179 A1
  Leicester LE3 ...... 154 C3
Winchester Ct LE67 ...... 95 F2
Winchester Dr
  Hinckley LE10 ...... 216 B7
  Melton Mowbray LE13 ...... 59 A6
  Swadlincote DE11 ...... 44 D6
Winchester Rd LE8 ...... 202 C6
Winchester Way LE65 ...... 69 A7
Winchilsea Dr NN17 ...... 213 B1
Winckley Cl LE7 ...... 157 F4
Windermere Ave
  Ashby-de-la-Z LE65 ...... 69 C5
  Nuneaton CV11 ...... 214 A6
Windermere Cl LE9 ...... 198 F8
Windermere Dr LE9 ...... 200 D4
Windermere Rd
  Barrow-u-S LE12 ...... 76 D8
  Edith Weston LE15 ...... 166 A7
  Wigston LE18 ...... 180 F3
Windermere St LE2 ...... 259 A1
Winders Ct LE2 ...... 179 D5
Winder's Way LE2 ...... 179 D5
Windleden Rd LE11 ...... 51 B3
Windley Rd LE2 ...... 180 A5
Windmill Ave LE4 ...... 129 B8
Windmill Bank LE18 ...... 180 E1
Windmill Cl
  Ashby-de-la-Z LE65 ...... 69 C5
  Castle Donington DE74 ...... 17 B2
  Cottingham LE16 ...... 229 D1
  Mountsorrel LE12 ...... 76 D3

Windmill Cl continued
  Ratby LE6 ...... 152 D8
  Ravenstone LE67 ...... 95 F1
  Thurmaston LE4 ...... 129 F8
Windmill End LE7 ...... 101 E7
Windmill Gdns LE8 ...... 206 A1
Windmill La CV9 ...... 119 C3
Windmill Rd
  Atherstone CV9 ...... 170 D1
  Loughborough LE11 ...... 52 D3
Windmill Rd Ind Est
  LE11 ...... 52 D3
Windmill Rise
  Cottingham LE16 ...... 229 D1
  Groby LE6 ...... 126 E3
  Woodhouse Eaves LE12 ...... 74 F2
Windmill St DE11 ...... 44 A1
Windmill View LE67 ...... 71 A6
Windmill Way
  Kegworth DE74 ...... 18 B2
  Lyddington LE15 ...... 212 D6
Windrush Dr
  Hinckley LE10 ...... 215 A8
  Leicester, Oadby LE2 ...... 181 D6
Windsor Ave
  Glen Parva LE2 ...... 179 E1
  Groby LE6 ...... 126 F2
  Leicester LE4 ...... 129 B2
  Melbourne DE73 ...... 26 A8
Windsor Cl
  Coalville LE67 ...... 72 B1
  Leicester, Oadby LE2 ...... 181 C3
  Mountsorrel LE12 ...... 101 D8
  Quorn (Quorndon) LE12 ...... 76 B6
  Stamford PE9 ...... 143 D5
  Swadlincote DE11 ...... 44 A6
Windsor Ct
  Hinckley LE10 ...... 216 A5
  Long Eaton NG10 ...... 10 E7
  Market Harborough
    LE16 ...... 240 D4
  Stoney Stanton LE9 ...... 199 D2
Windsor Dr
  Oakham LE15 ...... 137 E5
  Shepshed LE12 ...... 50 A2
Windsor Rd
  Ashby-de-la-Z LE65 ...... 69 B5
  Loughborough LE11 ...... 51 D5
  Waltham on t W LE14 ...... 40 B7
Windsor St
  Hinckley LE10 ...... 216 A5
  Melton Mowbray LE13 ...... 59 C3
Windyridge PE9 ...... 142 D7
Winforde Cres LE3 ...... 153 D4
WING 165 A2
Wingfield St LE4 ...... 129 B2
Wing Hall LE15 ...... 165 A2
Wing Maze ★ LE15 ...... 165 B2
Wing Rd
  Glaston LE15 ...... 190 B6
  Manton LE15 ...... 164 E5
  Morcott LE15 ...... 190 F7
Winifred St LE2 ...... 259 A2
Winkadale Hill LE7 ...... 157 C4
Winser Ct DE74 ...... 18 D2
Winslow Dr LE18 ...... 180 E4
Winslow Gn LE5 ...... 156 C8
Winstanley Com Coll
  LE3 ...... 153 E1
Winstanley Dr LE3 ...... 154 A4
Winster Cres LE13 ...... 59 B1
Winster Dr LE4 ...... 129 E8
Winster Way NG10 ...... 9 F5
Winston Ave LE9 ...... 200 D4
Winston Cl PE9 ...... 167 F5
Winterbeck Cl NG13 ...... 3 A3
Winterbeck Ind Est
  NG13 ...... 2 F3
Winterburn Gdns LE8 ...... 201 F7
Winterburn Way LE11 ...... 51 B3
Winterfield Cl LE3 ...... 153 B7
Wintergreen Cl LE5 ...... 130 C3
Wintersdale Rd LE5 ...... 156 D5
Winterton Cl LE4 ...... 129 F8
Winton Ave LE3 ...... 154 C2
Wire La LE16 ...... 228 D2
Wisp The LE15 ...... 136 D1
WISTOW 204 E4
Wistow Cl LE18 ...... 204 A3
Wistow Rd
  Kibworth Beauchamp
    LE8 ...... 205 D2
  Kilby LE18 ...... 204 B3
  Newton Harcourt LE8 ...... 204 D6
  Wigston LE18 ...... 180 E1
Witchley Cl LE15 ...... 138 B6
Witham Ave LE15 ...... 137 E5
Witham Cl
  Melton Mowbray LE13 ...... 59 B1
  Stamford PE9 ...... 143 E4
Witham Rd
  Gunby NG33 ...... 64 F8
  Thistleton LE15 ...... 65 A1
Withcote Ave LE5 ...... 156 C6
Withens Cl LE3 ...... 154 A7
Witherdell LE4 ...... 128 A3
WITHERLEY 194 B7
Witherley CE Prim Sch
  CV9 ...... 194 B7
Witherley Rd CV9 ...... 194 B6
Withers Cl LE15 ...... 138 A8
Withers Way LE9, LE3 ...... 153 D1
Withington Cl LE3 ...... 153 D2
Wittering Cl NG10 ...... 10 E1
Woburn Cl
  Hinckley LE10 ...... 197 E3
  Leicester LE2 ...... 179 C4
  Loughborough LE11 ...... 51 C4

Woburn Cl continued
  Market Harborough
    LE16 ...... 241 A3
  Wigston LE18 ...... 180 A3
Wodehouse Rd LE3 ...... 154 A4
Wokingham Ave LE2 ...... 179 D2
Wolds Cl LE12 ...... 32 E5
Wolds La LE10 ...... 231 B3
Wolds The LE7 ...... 103 E8
Wollaton Ave LE11 ...... 51 C4
Wollaton Cl LE3 ...... 153 B8
Wolsey Cl
  Fleckney LE8 ...... 222 F8
  Groby LE6 ...... 126 E2
  Leicester Forest East
    LE3 ...... 152 F2
Wolsey Dr LE8 ...... 126 B1
Wolsey House Prim Sch
  LE4 ...... 128 E3
Wolsey La LE8 ...... 222 F8
Wolsey Rd LE67 ...... 71 C2
Wolsey St LE4 ...... 154 E8
Wolsey Way
  Loughborough LE11 ...... 52 C4
  Syston LE7 ...... 102 F3
Wolverton Rd LE3 ...... 154 C2
Wolvey Rd LE10 ...... 215 E4
Woodbank
  Glen Parva LE2 ...... 179 B2
  Hinckley LE10 ...... 216 A7
Woodbank Rd
  Groby LE6 ...... 126 D3
  Leicester LE2 ...... 180 C6
Woodbine Ave 7 LE2 ...... 155 B4
Woodbine Cres LE17 ...... 244 C5
Woodborough Rd
  LE5 ...... 156 B4
Woodboy St LE1 ...... 155 A7
Woodbreach Dr LE16 ...... 241 B3
Woodbridge Rd LE4 ...... 129 B3
Woodbrook Rd LE11 ...... 51 E1
Woodbrook Vale High Sch
  LE11 ...... 74 F7
Woodbury Rise LE8 ...... 182 C1
Woodby La LE17 ...... 243 E8
Wood Cl LE12 ...... 50 D3
Woodcock Cl LE17 ...... 235 C4
Woodcock Dr LE13 ...... 82 B8
Woodcock Way LE65 ...... 69 C7
Woodcote LE65 ...... 69 B8
Woodcote Prim Sch
  LE65 ...... 69 B7
Woodcote Rd LE3 ...... 178 E7
Woodcroft Ave LE2 ...... 180 A6
Woodcroft The DE74 ...... 28 C5
Wood End LE3 ...... 154 A7
Wood Farm La DE11 ...... 44 E4
Woodfield Rd LE9 ...... 168 D1
Woodfield Cl LE19 ...... 201 B8
Woodfield Cotts DE12 ...... 93 D5
Woodfield Dr DE11 ...... 44 C5
Woodfield Rd
  Hinckley LE10 ...... 215 C6
  Leicester, Oadby LE2 ...... 181 B7
  Rothley LE7 ...... 101 E6
Woodfold La LE14 ...... 60 D5
Woodford Cl LE18 ...... 203 C8
Woodford Glebe NN6 ...... 256 E5
Woodford La CV10 ...... 194 C4
Woodford Rd LE2 ...... 154 D3
Woodgate
  Foxton LE16 ...... 239 E8
  Leicester LE3 ...... 154 D7
  Rothley LE7 ...... 101 E6
Wood Gate LE11 ...... 52 B3
Woodgate Cl LE16 ...... 241 B2
Woodgate Dr LE4 ...... 128 F8
Woodgate Hill LE14 ...... 82 B1
Woodgate Rd
  East Leake LE12 ...... 31 C8
  Hinckley LE10 ...... 216 A8
Woodgon Rd LE7 ...... 127 D6
Woodgreen Rd LE4 ...... 129 D1
Woodgreen Wlk LE4 ...... 129 D1
Woodhall Cl
  Leicester LE3 ...... 153 D5
  Nuneaton CV11 ...... 214 A2
Woodhead Cl
  Market Overton LE15 ...... 86 F5
  Stamford PE9 ...... 143 F5
Wood Hill
  Leicester LE5 ...... 155 D6
  Old Dalby LE14 ...... 35 E3
Woodhill Ind Est LE14 ...... 35 E4
WOODHOUSE 75 C3
Woodhouse Cl LE67 ...... 98 E1
WOODHOUSE EAVES 75 A1
Woodhouse La LE11 ...... 74 C5
Woodhouse Rd
  Asfordby LE14 ...... 57 F3
  Coalville LE67 ...... 97 B8
  Narborough LE19 ...... 201 A8
  Quorn (Quorndon) LE12 ...... 75 E6
WOODHOUSES 26 A5
Woodhouse St DE11 ...... 44 D3
Wood La
  Barkestone-le-V NG13,
    LE14 ...... 13 E6
  Braunston-in-R LE15 ...... 137 A1
  Cadeby CV13 ...... 149 C1
  Higham on t H CV13 ...... 195 E3
  Norton-J-T CV9 ...... 120 C2
  Quorn (Quorndon) LE12 ...... 76 B4
  Stathern LE14 ...... 13 B4
  Swadlincote DE11 ...... 44 A7
  Tugby LE7 ...... 185 D2
Woodland Ave
  Breaston DE72 ...... 9 F8

Woodland Ave continued
  Claybrooke Magna
    LE17 ...... 232 E6
  Hinckley LE10 ...... 216 A7
  Leicester LE2 ...... 155 C1
  Melton Mowbray LE13 ...... 59 D1
  Narborough LE19 ...... 178 B1
Woodland Cl LE67 ...... 125 E8
Woodland Dr LE3 ...... 153 D3
Woodland Grange Prim
  Sch LE2 ...... 181 D4
Woodland Rd
  Cottesmore LE15 ...... 87 E2
  Hinckley LE10 ...... 197 F1
  Leicester LE5 ...... 155 D7
Woodlands Ave
  Breaston DE72 ...... 9 F8
  Corby NN17 ...... 230 F1
Woodlands Cl
  Leicester, Oadby LE2 ...... 182 A4
  Melbourne DE73 ...... 26 A8
  Wymeswold LE12 ...... 33 C3
Woodlands Cres DE12 ...... 67 B4
Woodlands Ct LE2 ...... 181 E4
Woodlands Dr
  Groby LE6 ...... 126 D3
  Loughborough LE11 ...... 52 A2
  Shepshed LE12 ...... 50 C5
Woodlands La LE9 ...... 152 E6
Woodlands Rd DE12 ...... 67 B4
Woodlands The
  Countesthorpe LE8 ...... 202 D4
  Hartshill CV10 ...... 194 A1
  Leicester LE2 ...... 155 C1
  Market Harborough
    LE16 ...... 240 C4
  Melbourne DE73 ...... 26 B8
  Wigston LE18 ...... 180 F4
Woodlands Way
  Melbourne DE73 ...... 26 B8
  Moira DE12 ...... 68 B6
Woodland View
  Chilcote DE12 ...... 91 F3
  Oakham LE15 ...... 138 B7
Woodlawn LE2 ...... 180 D8
Woodlea Ave LE17 ...... 244 A6
Woodley Rd LE6 ...... 152 C8
Woodman's Chase
  LE7 ...... 103 D7
Woodmans Way LE12 ...... 50 C5
Woodmarket LE17 ...... 244 C5
Woodnewton Dr LE5 ...... 156 D4
Woodpecker Cl LE3 ...... 152 E2
Wood Rd LE67 ...... 123 E6
Woods Cl
  Coalville LE67 ...... 96 C6
  Leicester, Oadby LE2 ...... 181 C7
Woodshawe Rise LE3 ...... 153 E2
Woodside
  Ashby-de-la-Z LE65 ...... 68 F5
  Barrow-u-S LE12 ...... 76 C8
Woodside Cl
  Leicester LE4 ...... 129 D1
  Narborough LE19 ...... 200 F8
Woodside Cres NG10 ...... 10 B8
Woodside Rd LE2 ...... 181 D3
Woods Mews LE12 ...... 30 B4
Wood St
  Ashby-de-la-Z LE65 ...... 69 C6
  Earl Shilton LE9 ...... 198 E8
  Hinckley LE10 ...... 197 D1
  Leicester LE1 ...... 259 B5
  Swadlincote DE11 ...... 44 B2
Woodstock Cl
  Hinckley LE10 ...... 216 A5
  Leicester LE4 ...... 128 E4
Woodstock Prim Sch
  LE4 ...... 128 E4
Woodstock Rd LE4 ...... 128 E4
Woodstone Com Prim Sch
  LE67 ...... 95 E7
Wood Street Cl LE10 ...... 197 E1
WOODTHORPE 75 C7
Woodthorpe Ave LE11 ...... 52 B1
Woodthorpe Rd LE11 ...... 52 B1
WOODVILLE 44 E3
Woodville CE Jun Sch
  DE11 ...... 44 F2
Woodville Gdns LE18 ...... 180 C5
Woodville Inf Sch
  DE11 ...... 44 F2
Woodville Rd
  Hartshorne DE11 ...... 45 A5
  Leicester LE3 ...... 154 B5
  Overseal DE12 ...... 67 B4
Woodward Ave LE12 ...... 75 E6
Woodward's Pl DE11 ...... 44 C3
Woodward Way DE11 ...... 44 D4
Woodway La LE17 ...... 232 D4
Woodway Rd LE17 ...... 244 B5
Woodwell Head La 86 A8
Woodyard La LE8 ...... 178 F1
Wooldale Cl LE7 ...... 127 E7
Woollen Hill Com Prim
  Sch LE7 ...... 127 E7
Woolley's La NG33 ...... 66 B7
Woolrooms The LE67 ...... 70 F8
WOOLSTHORPE BY
  BELVOIR 8 B1
Woolsthorpe La
  Harston NG32 ...... 15 B5
  Muston NG32 ...... 8 C5
Woolsthorpe Rd NG33 ...... 43 F5
Woolstitch Pk DE12 ...... 91 E7
Woolston Ct NN17 ...... 213 C1

Wootton Cl LE8 . . . . 201 F6
Wootton Rise LE2 . . . . 179 D5
Worcester Ave LE4 . . . . . . 129 C8
Worcester Cl LE9 . . . . 198 A7
Worcester Cres PE9 . . . . . 143 D4
Worcester Dr
  Market Harborough
    LE16 . . . . 240 E5
  Melton Mowbray LE13 . . . . . 82 D8
  Wigston LE18 . . . . 179 F2
Worcester Rd LE2 . . . . . . 179 D7
Wordsworth Ave
  Corby NN17 . . . . 230 D1
  Swadlincote DE11 . . . . 44 C6
Wordsworth Cres
  LE19 . . . . 178 A1
Wordsworth Rd
  Leicester LE2 . . . . 180 A8
  Loughborough LE11 . . . . 51 D4
Wordsworth Way DE12 . . . . 93 C3
Workhouse La LE10 . . . . . 216 A4
Workspace 17 LE67 . . . . . . 96 C7
Worrall Cl LE3 . . . . 153 D4
Worrall Rd LE3 . . . . 153 D4
Worsh Cl LE8 . . . . 201 F5
Worsley Way LE8 . . . . 202 A6
WORTHINGTON 47 F5
Worthington La
  Breedon on t H DE73 . . . . . . 26 F1
  Newbold LE65, LE67 . . . . 47 E4
  Woolsthorpe by B NG32 . . . 8 B1
Worthington Sch LE65 . . . 47 F6
Worthington St LE2 . . . . . 155 C5
Wortley Cl
  Coalville LE67 . . . . 71 E1
  Shepshed LE12 . . . . 50 C6
Wortley Cotts LE9 . . . . . . 198 F5
Wortley Ct LE11 . . . . 52 B4
WOTHORPE 169 D8
Wothorpe Hill PE9 . . . . . . 169 C7
Wothorpe Mews PE9 . . . . . 143 D2
Wothorpe Rd PE9 . . . . . . 143 E2
Wothorpe Villas PE9 . . . . 169 D8

Woulds Ct DE12 . . . . 68 B6
Wranglands The LE8 . . . . 223 A7
Wreake Ave LE7 . . . . 103 B4
Wreake Cres LE14 . . . . 57 E2
Wreake Dr LE7 . . . . 79 A3
Wreake Rd LE4 . . . . 129 E8
Wreake Valley Com Coll
  LE7 . . . . 103 C5
Wreake Wlk LE15 . . . . 137 E5
Wreford Cres LE5 . . . . 156 E7
Wrekin Cl LE65 . . . . 69 C4
Wren Cl
  Appleby Magna DE12 . . . . . 119 E8
  Leicester LE2 . . . . 179 E7
  Loughborough LE11 . . . . 51 F3
  Melton Mowbray LE13 . . . . . 82 B8
  Oakham LE15 . . . . 138 A8
  Syston LE7 . . . . 102 E4
  Woodville DE11 . . . . 44 F3
Wren Ct NG10 . . . . 10 A3
Wrendyke Cl LE15 . . . . . . 191 A6
Wright Cl LE8 . . . . 202 A4
Wright La LE2 . . . . 181 E4
Wrights Acre LE12 . . . . 77 B4
Wrights Cl LE12 . . . . 75 F5
Wrights La LE14 . . . . 62 E2
Wroxall Way LE3 . . . . 154 C8
Wyatt Cl LE3 . . . . 153 C4
Wyatt Rd LE67 . . . . 71 E2
Wych Elm Cl LE8 . . . . 182 B1
Wych Elm Rd LE2 . . . . 181 A7
Wychwood Rd LE8 . . . . . . 202 A5
Wycliffe Ave
  Barrow-u-S LE12 . . . . 76 D8
  Melton Mowbray LE13 . . . . . 59 C4
Wycliffe Ind Est LE17 . . . 244 D7
Wycliffe St LE1 . . . . 259 B3
Wycliffe Terr LE17 . . . . . . 244 D6
WYCOMB 39 A6
Wycombe Gr LE13 . . . . 59 E2
Wycombe Rd LE5 . . . . 155 F8
Wycomb La LE14 . . . . 22 B1
Wye Cl LE10 . . . . 215 A8
Wye Dean Dr LE18 . . . . . . 180 D2
WYFORDBY 60 E3
Wyfordby Cl LE13 . . . . 59 E1
Wyggeston Ave NG13 . . . . . 3 B2

Wyggeston & Queen
  Elizabeth I Coll LE1 . . . . 155 A2
Wyggeston Rd
  Bottesford NG13 . . . . 3 B3
  Coalville LE67 . . . . 96 D8
Wyggeston's Hospl
  LE3 . . . . 154 C4
Wyggeston Terr NG13 . . . . . 3 B2
Wygston's House Mus★
  LE1 . . . . 259 A3
Wykeham Cl LE8 . . . . 202 B6
WYKIN 196 F4
Wykin La CV13, LE10 . . . . . 196 E5
Wylam Cl LE3 . . . . 154 A8
Wymar Cl LE4 . . . . 128 C3
WYMESWOLD 33 C4
Wymeswold CE Prim Sch
  LE12 . . . . 33 C3
Wymeswold Ind Est
  LE12 . . . . 33 A1
Wymeswold La LE12 . . . . . . 54 A8
Wymeswold Rd
  Hoton LE12 . . . . 32 F2
  Rempstone LE12 . . . . 32 F5
  Thorpe in t G NG12 . . . . . . 33 C8
WYMONDHAM 62 D1
Wymondham Drift
  LE14 . . . . 62 F2
Wymondham Rd LE14 . . . . . 62 A6
Wymondham Way
  LE13 . . . . 59 C6
Wymondham Windmill &
  Craft Ctr★ LE14 . . . . 62 D3
Wyndale Dr LE7 . . . . 103 B5
Wyndale Rd LE2 . . . . 180 B7
Wyndham Ave LE13 . . . . . . 59 C1
Wyndham Cl LE2 . . . . 181 C7
Wyndham Rd LE11 . . . . 51 B6
Wynfield Rd LE3 . . . . 154 B5
Wyngate Dr LE3 . . . . 154 B4
Wynthorpe Rise LE3 . . . . . 154 A4
Wynton Cl LE8 . . . . 202 C6
Wysall La
  Rempstone LE12 . . . . 32 F6
  Wymeswold LE12 . . . . 33 D5
Wytchley Rd PE9 . . . . 167 E5
Wythburn Cl LE11 . . . . 51 D1

Wyvelle Cres DE74 . . . . . . 18 C3
Wyvenhoe Dr LE12 . . . . . . 75 E5
Wyvern Ave
  Leicester LE4 . . . . 129 D2
  Long Eaton NG10 . . . . 10 D5
Wyvern Cl
  Broughton Astley LE9 . . . . 219 A5
  Hinckley LE10 . . . . 215 E4
Wyvern Prim Sch LE4 . . . 129 D2
Wyvern Terr LE13 . . . . 59 D3
WYVILLE 25 E7
Wyville Row LE3 . . . . 154 A1

Y

Yard Cl DE11 . . . . 44 B4
Yardley Cl NN17 . . . . 230 D1
Yardley Dr LE2 . . . . 180 B5
Yarmouth St LE1 . . . . 259 B5
Yarrow Cl LE5 . . . . 130 C1
Yarwell Dr LE18 . . . . 180 E2
Yates Ave DE72 . . . . 16 A7
Yates Cl DE12 . . . . 68 A5
Yaxley Cl LE7 . . . . 157 A5
Yeats Cl LE3 . . . . 153 D2
Yelvertoft Rd CV23 . . . . . 258 D6
Yelverton Ave LE5 . . . . . . 156 C3
Yeoman La LE1 . . . . 259 C4
Yeomanry Ct LE16 . . . . . . 240 E3
Yeoman's Dale LE7 . . . . . 103 D8
Yeoman's Keep LE17 . . . . 244 B8
Yeoman St LE1 . . . . 259 C4
Yew Cl
  Corby NN17 . . . . 230 E1
  East Leake LE12 . . . . 31 D8
  Leicester Forest East
    LE3 . . . . 152 F1
Yews The
  Great Dalby LE14 . . . . 82 B2
  Leicester, Oadby LE2 . . . . . 181 B6
Yew Tree Cl
  Barwell LE9 . . . . 198 C8
  Lutterworth LE17 . . . . 244 A6
  Willoughby Waterleys
    LE8 . . . . 220 D6
Yew Tree Cres LE13 . . . . . . 59 C5

Yew Tree Ct CV9 . . . . 119 A2
Yew Tree Dr LE3 . . . . 153 C6
York Ave CV9 . . . . 170 E1
York Cl
  Glen Parva LE2 . . . . 179 E1
  Market Bosworth CV13 . . . 148 E2
  Measham DE12 . . . . 93 C5
  Mountsorrel LE12 . . . . 101 D8
  Swadlincote DE11 . . . . 44 D6
York Pl
  Coalville LE67 . . . . 72 D1
  Leicester LE1 . . . . 259 C3
York Rd
  Hinckley LE10 . . . . 197 D3
  Leicester LE1 . . . . 259 B3
  Loughborough LE11 . . . . 52 A4
  Stamford PE9 . . . . 143 D4
  Swadlincote DE11 . . . . 44 B2
Yorkshire Rd LE4 . . . . 129 C2
York St
  Leicester LE1 . . . . 259 C3
  Market Harborough
    LE16 . . . . 240 F3
Yukon Way LE1 . . . . 259 C5

Z

Zara Ct PE9 . . . . 143 D4
Zealand Cl LE10 . . . . 197 F3
Zebra Cotts PE9 . . . . 143 B4
Zenith Bldg LE1 . . . . 259 C3
Zetland Cl LE67 . . . . 96 C8
Zetland Sq LE15 . . . . 87 F4
Zetland Wlk LE4 . . . . 128 C5
Zion Hill LE67 . . . . 71 A8
Zion Ho DE11 . . . . 44 C1
ZOUCH 30 B3
Zouch Rd LE12 . . . . 30 A3

Addresses

Name and Address	Telephone	Page	Grid reference

NG NH NJ NK
NM NN NO NP
NR NS NT NU
NX NY NZ
SC SD SE TA
SH SJ SK TF TG
SM SN SO SP TL TM
SR SS ST SU TQ TR
SW SX SY SZ TV

Any feature in this atlas can be given a unique reference to help you find the same feature on other Ordnance Survey maps of the area, or to help someone else locate you if they do not have a Street Atlas.

The grid squares in this atlas match the Ordnance Survey National Grid and are at 500 metre intervals. The small figures at the bottom and sides of every other grid line are the National Grid kilometre values (**00** to **99** km) and are repeated across the country every 100 km (see left).

To give a unique National Grid reference you need to locate where in the country you are. The country is divided into 100 km squares with each square given a unique two-letter reference. Use the administrative map to determine in which 100 km square a particular page of this atlas falls.

The bold letters and numbers between each grid line (**A** to **F**, **1** to **8**) are for use within a specific Street Atlas only, and when used with the page number, are a convenient way of referencing these grid squares.

Example   *The railway bridge over DARLEY GREEN RD in grid square B1*

Step 1: Identify the two-letter reference, in this example the page is in **SP**

Step 2: Identify the 1 km square in which the railway bridge falls. Use the figures in the southwest corner of this square: Eastings **17**, Northings **74**. This gives a unique reference: **SP 17 74**, accurate to 1 km.

Step 3: To give a more precise reference accurate to 100 m you need to estimate how many tenths along and how many tenths up this 1 km square the feature is (to help with this the 1 km square is divided into four 500 m squares). This makes the bridge about **8** tenths along and about **1** tenth up from the southwest corner.

This gives a unique reference: **SP 178 741**, accurate to 100 m.

Eastings (read from left to right along the bottom) come before Northings (read from bottom to top). If you have trouble remembering say to yourself Along the hall, THEN up the stairs !

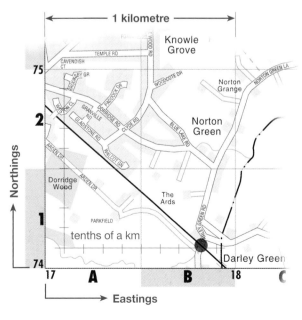

PHILIP'S MAPS

the Gold Standard for drivers

◆ **Philip's street atlases cover every county in England, Wales, Northern Ireland and much of Scotland**

◆ Every named street is shown, including alleys, lanes and walkways

◆ Thousands of additional features marked: stations, public buildings, car parks, places of interest

◆ Route-planning maps to get you close to your destination

◆ Postcodes on the maps and in the index

◆ Widely used by the emergency services, transport companies and local authorities

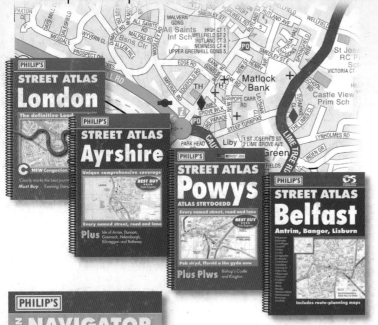

Street atlases currently available

England

Bedfordshire and Luton	Surrey
Berkshire	East Sussex
Birmingham and West Midlands	West Sussex
	Tyne and Wear
Bristol and Bath	Warwickshire and Coventry
Buckinghamshire and Milton Keynes	Wiltshire and Swindon
Cambridgeshire and Peterborough	Worcestershire
	East Yorkshire Northern Lincolnshire
Cheshire	North Yorkshire
Cornwall	South Yorkshire
Cumbria	West Yorkshire
Derbyshire	
Devon	**Wales**
Dorset	Anglesey, Conwy and Gwynedd
County Durham and Teesside	Cardiff, Swansea and The Valleys
Essex	Carmarthenshire, Pembrokeshire and Swansea
North Essex	
South Essex	
Gloucestershire and Bristol	Ceredigion and South Gwynedd
Hampshire	
North Hampshire	Denbighshire, Flintshire, Wrexham
South Hampshire	
Herefordshire Monmouthshire	Herefordshire Monmouthshire
Hertfordshire	Powys
Isle of Wight	
Kent	**Scotland**
East Kent	Aberdeenshire
West Kent	Ayrshire
Lancashire	Dumfries and Galloway
Leicestershire and Rutland	Edinburgh and East Central Scotland
Lincolnshire	Fife and Tayside
Liverpool and Merseyside	Glasgow and West Central Scotland
London	Inverness and Moray
Greater Manchester	Lanarkshire
Norfolk	Scottish Borders
Northamptonshire	
Northumberland	**Northern Ireland**
Nottinghamshire	County Antrim and County Londonderry
Oxfordshire	County Armagh and County Down
Shropshire	
Somerset	Belfast
Staffordshire	County Tyrone and County Fermanagh
Suffolk	

For national mapping, choose
Philip's Navigator Britain
the most detailed road atlas available of England, Wales and Scotland. Hailed by Auto Express as 'the ultimate road atlas', the atlas shows every road and lane in Britain.

How to order

Philip's maps and atlases are available from bookshops, motorway services and petrol stations. You can order direct from the publisher by phoning **0207 531 8473** or online at **www.philips-maps.co.uk**
For bulk orders only, e-mail philips@philips-maps.co.uk